RICHARD NIXON

Richard Nixon

California's Native Son

PAUL CARTER

Foreword by

TRICIA NIXON COX

Potomac Books

An imprint of the University of Nebraska Press

Library of Congress Cataloging-in-Publication Data
Names: Carter, Paul (Paul Jeffrey), author. | Cox, Patricia
Nixon, 1946– writer of foreword.
Title: Richard Nixon: California's native son / Paul Carter;
foreword by Tricia Nixon Cox.
Other titles: Richard Nixon, California's native son
Description: Lincoln: Potomac Books, an imprint
of the University of Nebraska Press, 2023. | Includes
bibliographical references and index.
Identifiers: LCCN 2022051311
ISBN 9781640125605 (hardback)
ISBN 9781640125971 (epub)
ISBN 9781640125988 (pdf)
Subjects: LCSH: Nixon, Richard M. (Richard Milhous),
1913–1994. | Presidents—United States—Biography. |
Politicians—California—Biography. | Nixon, Richard
M. (Richard Milhous), 1913–1994—Homes and haunts—
California, Southern. | Nixon, Richard M. (Richard
Milhous), 1913–1994—Travel—California. | Nixon,
Richard M. (Richard Milhous), 1913–1994—Last years. |
United States—Politics and government—20th century. |
California, Southern—Biography. | BISAC: BIOGRAPHY
& AUTOBIOGRAPHY / Presidents & Heads of State
Classification: LCC E856 .C337 2023 | DDC 973.924092
[B]—dc23/eng/20221028
LC record available at https://lccn.loc.gov/2022051311

Set in Minion Pro by A. Shahan.

For my mom, who taught me to pursue my dreams
And for my sweet
Bailey, Marissa, Willie, and Chris—
Always pursue your dreams!

Contents

Illustrations

Foreword

TRICIA NIXON COX

"I was born in a house my father built." My father began his one-thousand-page memoirs with that short sentence. As simple as that opening is, it carries a great deal of meaning. With those nine words, Richard Nixon—the thirty-seventh president of the United States—set the stage for telling his story of an extraordinary journey from a small, loving home in then-rural Orange County, California, to the most renowned house in America, the White House.

In *Richard Nixon: California's Native Son*, Paul Carter brings to life my father's formative years, from the time he took his first breath on a record-cold January morning in 1913 on a small lemon ranch in Yorba Linda, California, to his first steps on the national stage, as a young, newly elected congressman from the Golden State's Twelfth Congressional District, and beyond—and, if I may add a personal note, as a new father.

Paul Carter provides special insight, as only a fellow native Californian can, into how my father's character, beliefs, aspirations, and accomplishments were influenced and nourished by his Quaker roots and his upbringing in a state that in 1913 was just beginning to make its mark on the nation and the world.

Much has been written about Richard Nixon's life and career. Yet despite the hundreds of volumes and countless profiles that have been penned, no author has ever taken such a richly detailed and deeply researched look into my father's formative years as Paul Carter has. I was pleasantly surprised that although I knew my father very well, even I learned things about those early years that I had not known before.

Through this vivid and engaging book, Paul Carter tells the story of the growth of a future world leader as seen through the eyes of his acquaintances, friends, teachers, mentors, and colleagues, living in and through a profoundly formative time in California's and America's history.

The person who emerges from these pages is the man my family and I knew, loved, and admired through all seasons. His lifelong commitment to peace in the world and justice at home took root in the fertile religious, social, educational, cultural, and political environment in which my father was raised. The people he knew—and who knew him—helped create the man he was and the world leader he would become.

The words my father spoke at his first inaugural address—"The greatest honor history can bestow is the title of peacemaker"—were both a prayer and a goal that had been born and nurtured in his youth and early adulthood in Southern California. The fulfillment of that hope, realized through the policy achievements of his entire public life, inaugurated a generation of peace for America that began with his presidency and reached its apex, twenty years later, with the end of the Cold War.

On a sweltering July day in 1990, before an enthusiastic crowd of fifty thousand, my father spoke at the opening of the Richard Nixon Library and Birthplace, just steps away from the little house his father had built some eighty years before. He observed, "It's a long way from Yorba Linda to the White House." As he and my mother stood there on the dais, alongside three of their successors as president and first lady, everyone in attendance could sense how long and extraordinary that journey, from a humble small town to the world stage, had been.

Not quite four years later we laid my father to rest next to my mother, just a few feet from the bedroom in the house in which he had been born. Today you can visit that site in a peaceful garden on the grounds of the Richard Nixon Presidential Library and Museum.

If, thanks to Paul Carter's book, you go there to pay your respects, you will do so with a greater understanding of Richard Nixon and of the place and the time in which he came of age. But even if you don't have that opportunity, through the pages you are about to read you will come to more fully appreciate why my father's headstone contains just one simple sentence. Captured in only eleven words is the dream that first captured his youthful imagination as the only native Californian yet to serve as president of the United States: "The greatest honor history can bestow is the title of peacemaker."

Since the days of the gold rush, California has long been a place from which people can pursue and achieve their fondest hopes and dreams. In the first half of the twentieth century it was that place for my father, as Paul Carter has so beautifully written about. I feel certain that you will find this book every bit as worthwhile a read as I have and that you will come away with a fuller appreciation of my father and of the time and place in which he grew from a young boy into the man he was.

Preface

I didn't set out to write this book. I never imagined I would write any book, let alone a biography of Richard Nixon. I am a trained trial attorney. While I have been interested in Nixon as a political figure, my thoughts on him were originally no different from the commonly held perception that he was a flawed man, humorless, probably a bit insecure, and maybe even a little evil.

My earliest memory of Nixon was his resignation when I was nine years old. My father came home early from work one hot August afternoon and told me to come in and watch the president resign. I am the product of public schools, and what I learned (and believed) of Nixon while growing up was not favorable. At my mother's urging, while earning my bachelor's degree in political science at California State University, Fullerton, I volunteered as a docent at the Richard Nixon Library and Museum. It never occurred to me that I might meet the former president, but I did.

To my shock and utter surprise, the Richard Nixon that I met on November 4, 1991, could not have been more friendly and engaging. He brought Hollywood legends Bob Hope, Arnold Schwarzenegger, Buddy Ebsen, and others with him to entertain his docent volunteers. I was struck by the dichotomy between Nixon's public image and what he was actually like as a human being. I received my degree in May 1992, then was off to Drake University Law School, after which I married and began building a family while I was building a successful law practice.

Adm. Michael Shatynski (USNR) and his brother Stephan, a reserve commander, arranged for me to participate in the navy's Leaders to Sea program, spending the day off the coast of California on the warship USS *Princeton* on May 26, 2009. Our group included the mayor of Whittier. I knew that Nixon was raised in Whittier, although I had never visited the town. In making small talk with the mayor, I was dismayed when he told me that most of the Nixon landmarks in his hometown had basically slipped into history without any designation.

My strong suit is cross-examining witnesses in trial; I am not a mapmaker or an artist, but virtually on the spot I decided to make a map of Nixon's life in Whittier. My expectation was that it would take no more than six months. I compiled a list of locations to photograph to build into the map. I bought a camera and a special wide-angle lens that would enable me to photograph entire properties from relatively close, as many of the locations were on narrow streets. I picked up a copy of Stephen Ambrose's *Nixon: The Education of a Politician* as a reference. When I read that Ambrose had been researching Nixon for seven years, I thought, "Well, he's crazy!"

I first went to photograph the stately former Nixon residence in College Hills, a home that was now occupied by Austin McCormack and his family. It was a beautiful Sunday morning. There I was, a stranger standing in the front yard about to take pictures of his house. I decided I should knock on the door, introduce myself, and explain what I was doing so he knew I was not up to no good. I didn't want to freak people out as I stood in their front yard, clicking away with my camera. So I knocked. The truth is, I was on the fence about my map project. All I needed was to be met with a strange look, and this project would have collapsed on the spot.

Austin answered the door and listened intently as I described my project; then his face lit up in excitement and he invited me in. As I entered, I realized that Austin was hosting a morning brunch party, with several guests joining his family, and they were ready to sit down to eat. Nevertheless, Austin provided me a tour of his beautiful home, recounting stories passed down from when the Nixons resided there. His enthusiastic encouragement was all it took to persuade me to continue my mapmaking effort.

To locate places and events that were part of the Nixon universe in Whittier, I accessed the Richard Nixon collection in the Oral History Program at Cal State Fullerton, digesting the 207 oral histories of Nixon intimates, friends, and associates who grew up with and knew Nixon, which amounted to 4,052 pages. I immediately realized that there was much more than a map to be made, and the idea of writing *Richard Nixon: California's Native Son* based on these oral histories was conceived.

Following the philosophy that whatever is worth doing is worth overdoing, I continued my chase down the rabbit hole, consuming the Whittier College oral history collection on Nixon, made up of over 360 interviews of Nixon intimates and filling 6,241 pages. The Richard M. Nixon in the Warren Era collection at the UC Berkeley Bancroft Library held additional oral histories of Nixon intimates, as did the Paul Bullock Papers at the UCLA Charles E. Young Research Library. The Bela Kornitzer Papers at Drew University provided me with another 40 oral histories consisting of 654 pages.

Then there were the collections at the Whittier Public Library, Whittier Historical Society, Whittier College, Fullerton Public Library, University of Southern California, Yorba Linda Public Library, and Orange County Archives, as well as the National Archives at the Nixon Library and the Nixon Foundation. All told, I reviewed well over a hundred boxes of materials containing more than 125,000 pages of documents. There were also 10,906 pages of the president's Daily Diary and tens of thousands of photographs. Finally, I conducted more than sixty personal interviews. Laid end to end, the combined materials would be over fifty-six linear feet. That is quite a trek down a rabbit hole!

What really struck me was that the bulk of the research I conducted had never been done before, although the information has been readily available. More often than not, when working with documents at the National Archives, I had to ask the archivists to remove staples and paper clips that had rusted through the pages before I could separate and handle them. The documents from the various periods of Nixon's life had not been touched since the day they were stapled, clipped, or bound together with rubber bands and stored.

Just as *Wicked* redefined *The Wizard of Oz*, likewise, *Richard Nixon: California's Native Son* boldly challenges common conceptions of America's thirty-seventh president. What emerges is the story of Richard Milhous Nixon. It is not political. It is nothing more than a straightforward biography that reveals an incredible life. Richard Nixon was not flawed, humorless, insecure, or evil. He was a human being who, like everyone else, made some mistakes on his journey through life. He is typically all-American.

Joseph Dmohowski at Whitter College and I have been trading Nixon stories for years, and Joe has been a kind friend and honest critic in reviewing this manuscript. Joseph Sierra, a retired professor at Pasadena City College, generously gave his time to review this project and make insightful recommendations, as did Joseph Valenzano. Maureen Nunn reviewed an early draft and has never wavered in her willingness to respond to all my inane requests for assistance. Likewise, Roberta Dorn and Frank Gannon provided their insights, and I am immensely grateful for all their efforts. In the years before he passed, Ed Nixon reviewed the manuscript and called me periodically to see how soon *California's Native Son* would be published; I regret that he did not see this day.

Susan Kim and my sister Angela provided tremendous assistance in helping me break down, analyze, and digest the more than 10,000 pages of oral histories I consumed in my research. My assistant Liz Amozoc spent countless hours helping me track down documents and reference materials. Brooke Selling, Courtney Eldridge, and in particular Laura Hurwitz guided me as I slowly developed as a writer. Trust me, this process took some time, and they were patient.

Fellow CSU Fullerton Titan Dorissa Martinez, along with Greg Cumming and his team consisting of Ryan Pettigrew, Carla Braswell, Pam Eisenberg, Jonathan Fletcher, Olivia Anastasiadis, and Meghan Lee-Parker at the National Archives, assisted me in every step. In particular, Dorissa responded to all my inquiries, morning, noon, and night, and I look forward to cheering on our beloved Titans with her in the years to come. Ron Walker, Sandy Quinn, Jim Byron, Jonathan Movroydis (Hoover Institute), Shane Westbrook, Joe Lopez (a fellow Titan), Jason Schwartz, and Ann Brown from the Nixon Foundation assisted with arranging interviews and access to materials.

Gavin Herbert graciously provided a tour of La Casa Pacifica. Tim Tessalone, sports information officer for USC, provided a pass so I could share Nixon's experience of seeing a game from the sideline in the Coliseum.

I regret that Ruth Lynch, a kind soul at the Whittier Public Library, did not live to see this book in print. Ruth was instrumental in her research assistance. Fortunately, Rachel Fiore has stepped in to fill the void created with Ruth's passing, but Ruth will forever be a part of this work. The staff at the Whittier Historical Society provided wonderful collections to review, and I encourage everyone to visit the museum when in Whittier.

You would not be reading these pages if it were not for Jacqueline Flynn at Joelle Delbourgo Associates. Jacqueline read my proposal, then we talked for a couple of hours and she agreed to take a chance; Tom Swanson at Potomac Books has been a pleasure to work with in bringing this book to fruition. Fortunately for me, Potomac then brought in Joyce Bond as copyeditor. I will always be indebted to Jacquie, Tom, and Joyce.

Irv Gellman is the preeminent Nixon historian and author. I cannot adequately describe how gratifying it is to persevere at something for over ten thousand hours, researching, crafting a narrative, assembling and organizing the evidence, writing, rewriting, then writing and rewriting some more, all the while feeling trepidation about how it will be received, and then to have it warmly embraced and recognized as scholarship on Nixon's life that has never been done before. Simply put, Irv is amazing in his kindness, and he has a delicious sarcastic wit.

I want to thank my brother, David; my mother, Susan, and her husband, Bill (the greatest father figure ever!); my beautiful children, Bailey, Marissa, Willie, and Chris; and the always lovely Candy Archila. Both Candy and my mom provided endless commonsense editorial advice, and I am so thankful for all the support from my friends and family.

I started my research in 2009, so I guess Ambrose has the last laugh! But researching and writing this book has been quite a bit of fun. In time I came to know Ed Nixon somewhat well and was pleased to arrange to meet him at Austin McCormack's residence so Ed could regale us with stories from when the Nixons called the place home. Seeing the excitement on Austin's face as his listened to President Nixon's brother give firsthand accounts of their life in his home was priceless. I hope you too will have an Austin McCormack to encourage you at just the right moment so that you too will pursue your passion and follow your dreams.

I am a trial attorney. I am quite aware that actions speak louder than words, and I know the thoroughness required to assemble evidence, presenting it layer by layer until the full story emerges. That is what I have done with *Richard Nixon: California's Native Son*, and now it is time for you to be the judge.

ONE

New Beginnings

1908–22

Richard Milhous Nixon, born in Orange County and raised in Los Angeles County, is the only native son of the Golden State to become president. Nixon's connection to Southern California predates his birth, when his mother, Hannah Milhous, moved there in 1897 from Indiana. Born on March 7, 1885, Hannah was thirteen when she arrived in the small town of Whittier, California, along with her parents, siblings, and grandmother. Hannah's father, Franklin Milhous, built the family's first home on the south side of Whittier Boulevard, a mile down the hill from Whittier College and the First Friends Church. In 1952 the home was moved five hundred feet to its current location on Starbuck Street.[1]

The Milhouses were a close-knit family of devout Quakers who set down roots in Whittier, becoming members of the First Friends Church, and Franklin quickly became a popular man in the community.[2] His mother, Elizabeth, was a preacher and performed a great deal of missionary work, giving sermons and starting Sunday schools.[3] His wife, Almira, was the anchor of the family and one of the spiritual leaders of their new community. Instilled with their religious commitment, daughter Hannah was devoted to her family, church, and school. An excellent student, she earned her high school diploma from the fledgling Whittier Academy.[4] Friends described Hannah as a wonderful young woman, "very intelligent," "down-to-earth," and, in her minister's words, "one of the finest Christian ladies you could ever know."[5]

In early 1907 Frank Nixon worked his way from Columbus, Ohio. His favorite Bible verse was "In the sweat of thy face shalt thou eat bread," and he was willing to do any type of work, including jobs as a sheep shearer, barber, glassblower, ox team driver, bricklayer, carpenter, house painter, steeplejack, tractor driver, potato farmer, oilfield roustabout, potter, hand-crank telephone installer, electrical linesman, and streetcar motorman.[6] Years later Frank entertained his son Richard with memorable tales of his "saga of onward, if not upward, job mobility."[7] Though he was not a birthright Quaker, Frank was a deeply spiritual person who regularly read the Bible and attended church services in various towns as he made his way west.[8]

By 1903 the Pacific Electric Railway "Red Line" streetcar served Whittier with a station near the center of town. Within a few years Frank Nixon found a job as a motorman on the line.[9] And so it was that Hannah Milhous and Frank Nixon came to reside in Whittier, California, their lives intersecting at the First Friends Church on Valentine's Day 1908.[10] Exhibiting her characteristic restraint, Hannah's first impression of Frank was that "he was very polite," whereas Frank was immediately smitten. The two saw each other every day thereafter, with Frank often riding in his horse-drawn buggy from the Judson Ranch, where he worked a second job, to the Milhous home.[11] To some it may have appeared an unexpected relationship. Hannah was demure, while Frank was often loud and opinionated. Hannah was insulated by her family and her community, obedient to religion, while Frank was a man about town, independent and freethinking.

When Hannah met Frank, he was rooming near the Whittier Station at Charles and Louama Semans's boardinghouse, which Hannah referred to as "a taffy pull," meaning a place where residents sat around, endlessly debating topics of the day.[12] This was a perfect setting for Frank, recognized as intelligent and very articulate. "He'd debate you on any subject and let you choose any side you wanted. Nobody could dominate Frank Nixon. Nobody."[13] People knew that when Frank got an idea, he stuck to it. "Two sledge hammers and a crowbar—you couldn't move him," and yet "he had a wild sense of humor" and was well liked.[14]

Frank and Hannah courted for four months before they wed on June 25, 1908, followed by a dinner reception at the Women's Improvement Club of East Whittier.[15] Frank's employer at the Judson Ranch thought highly enough of him to host a wedding shower in his honor.[16] Yet some believed Hannah had married "below her station," a sentiment delicately explained by her cousin Jessamyn West: "The Milhouses were reticent. But Frank was a different creature. He said what he thought."[17] Since she had already completed two years at Whittier College, other members of Hannah's family hoped she would finish her degree.[18] Then there was her younger sister Rose, who "didn't think anyone ought to get married ever," and indignantly carved "Hannah is a bad girl" into a tree on the family property.[19] All that aside, Franklin Milhous approved of the union, and more importantly, the two were in love, and Frank often closed his letters to Hannah with "sealed with a kiss."[20] By June 1909 they welcomed Harold, their first of five sons (followed by Richard in 1913, Francis Donald in 1914, Arthur in 1918, and Edward in 1930).

The same year Frank and Hannah met and married, the Janss Investment Company acquired 3,500 acres in Orange County and platted the town site of Yorba Linda, thirty miles east of the city of Los Angeles. Yorba Linda was generally characterized by "rural roads," according to the earliest mention in the *Orange County Directory*.[21] It was so remote that one resident compared Yorba Linda to a "filling station in the desert," and another commented, "You went through it and you didn't know you went through it."[22] The land was home to squirrels, jackrabbits, rattlesnakes, horned toads, trapdoor spiders, and coyotes, along with turkey mullein, cactus, and tumbleweed, and was planted with avocado and citrus groves, as well as crops like barley, alfalfa, and beans.[23]

The climate was semiarid, and the topography featured rolling hills with few trees. There were no windbreaks, just "a complete flow of air, from the hills clear out to the ocean, with nothing to stop it," only sagebrush sweeping through the canyons.[24] The town's buildings were protectively sided with one-by-twelve-inch boards and had floors made of two-by-twelve-inch boards, with cracks a half inch wide.[25] But still the winds were so forceful that they would "shake the bedsteads and rattle the crockery," and since the houses weren't constructed to withstand bad weather, the winds would often "blow the roof off the barn or off the house."[26] Longtime Yorba Lindan Ralph Navarro lamented, "The Santa Ana winds, oh, Jesus!"[27]

Land was generally sold in five-acre parcels at $250 per acre, selling out within eighteen months from when it was platted in mid-1908.[28] The area "was very popular," as many Whittier Quakers moved to Yorba Linda to plant orchards.[29] In 1910 Frank and Hannah Nixon made a down payment of $25 to purchase nine acres.[30]

The town had no modern conveniences to speak of—no gas, no electricity, no paved roads—and what roads did exist were "exceedingly crooked," not to mention extremely dusty, as they were never oiled.[31] At one end of his acreage, Frank built a nine-hundred-square-foot, two-story mail-order frame house and a barn.[32] The first floor of the home contained a kitchen, living room, and bedroom for Frank and Hannah. A narrow flight of stairs led to a second bedroom that was so tiny, with a ceiling so low, that an average-size adult could not stand upright.[33]

Although oranges were the most successful groves in Yorba Linda, Frank planted lemon trees because they grew in abundance in Whittier, where he had previously lived. To prepare the land, he employed teams of horses and mules to haul barrels of water by wagon from the Anaheim Union Canal, adjacent to his orchard.[34] When he needed help, Frank hired labor at the going rate of 20 cents an hour.[35]

The Anaheim Union Canal, better known as the "Anaheim ditch," was ten feet wide and three feet deep.[36] The canal ran just north of the Nixon's east-facing home and had a bridge leading to the closest road, which went into town.[37] Quite isolated, Yorba Linda had no sewer or municipal water systems.[38] Like the other residents, the Nixons had no running water, refrigeration, telephone, radio, or motorcar. Oil lamps provided light, and Hannah cooked on a wood-burning stove that also provided heat.

Richard Nixon made his arrival into the world in dramatic fashion as one of the first children born in Yorba Linda.[39] On the evening of January 9, 1913, Hannah Nixon lay in labor in the front room of their home, while the doctor, H. P. Wilson, and his nurse, Henrietta Shockley, traveled the sixteen miles from Whittier by horse-drawn carriage on roads that were not much more than a "cow path."[40] Further complicating matters, Yorba Linda was in the midst of a record-breaking cold snap, the coldest weather ever in the history of Southern California agriculture.[41]

Now thirty-six degrees, the night was growing dark, and the doctor was late. The nearest neighbors were the Truebloods, who lived "just across the country block." Panicking, Frank Nixon ran to their house for help.[42] Ella Furnas, who lived with the Truebloods, recalled, "He was just awfully nervous. He wanted me to hurry up and get there, and we went. Hannah didn't seem to be worried or concerned at all. It was all right with her. She was getting along."[43] The doctor arrived in the nick of time, and Richard Milhous Nixon was born at 9:35 p.m., weighing in at a substantial eleven pounds, with "a powerful set of lungs and abundant black hair."[44] The event was so overwhelming for young Ella that she fell into the Anaheim ditch on her way home and had to be rescued by Frank.[45] Nevertheless, the following morning, fully recovered from the night's events, an excited Frank exclaimed to his workers, "I've got another boy! I've got another boy!"[46]

Like most of the families in Yorba Linda, the Nixons were mostly self-sufficient.[47] They grew their own green beans, corn, lettuce, cabbage, little green onions, carrots, and turnips, and as Gerald Shaw explained, they "ate a lot of vegetables in those days because it was cheap."[48] The Nixons also had chickens for eggs and a cow for milk, and it was a common practice to eat the local rabbits as well.[49]

The Nixon boys relied on each other and their imagination for entertainment.[50] Hannah recalled that in those early years, Harold and Dick "played a great deal before the fireplace in the evening, and they played train; one was the engineer, one the conductor. Dick was the engineer."[51] The centerpiece of the home, and Frank's pride and joy, was that fireplace, even though the county building inspector had ordered the fireplace rebuilt so that bricks would not fall inside the house during an earthquake.[52] Frank steadfastly ignored the man's edict, but the inspector insisted until Frank finally told him, "All right. I'll tear my fireplace down and build it the way you want. But as soon as you're gone and I get my approval, I'll tear it down again and build it back the way I want." Ultimately, the inspector relented, and the original fireplace stands to this day.[53]

Richard's earliest memory was of a scalp injury when he was three years old.[54] One Sunday afternoon Hannah, Richard, his brother Donald, and a babysitter were returning home from dropping off Richard's great-aunt at the Placentia train station. As they rounded a curve along the bank of the irrigation ditch leading to their house, Richard fell out of the horse-drawn carriage, slicing his scalp from the top of his forehead to the back of his neck, his skin separated from his skull bone for several inches. "I must have been in shock," he later explained, "but I managed to get up and run after the buggy while my mother tried to make the horse stop."[55]

Frantic, Hannah called Austin Marshburn, who had served as head usher at her wedding and lived just west of the Nixons. Austin cranked up his Ford Model T, the fastest car in town, and raced Hannah and Richard across gravel and oiled roads to the Fullerton Hospital at speeds up to twenty-five miles per hour.[56] Hannah cradled Richard as Austin tried to comfort her: "Hannah, the baby is not hurt seriously. No small baby could have a brain injury and flap his arms like he's doing and yell. It's just a scalp wound." Be that as it may, Hannah was inconsolable at seeing her child covered in blood, until the doctor reassured her by sewing up the wound with eighteen wide stitches.[57] Richard was fortunate on that count, because at the time scalp lacerations were typically "brought together by picking up strands of hair from each side and tying them together over the wound."[58] Hannah spent the next four days by her son's side, until finally, much to her relief, Richard was discharged from the hospital.[59]

Another day, after the family bought a Ford Model T, Hannah parked on a slope and left Richard and Donald to play in the car while she visited a nearby friend. Before long, the boys abandoned the car to play in the dirt down the slope. Hannah hadn't set the brake tightly enough, and the Model T began rolling down the hill toward the boys, but neighbor Harry Barton was able to jump in and set the brake just in time to prevent the boys from being run over.[60] In yet another incident, the boys were taking baths one Saturday evening during winter, relying on a kerosene stove for heat, when one of them accidentally knocked over the stove, immediately setting fire to the bathroom. Frank threw the stove outside and extinguished the fire before anyone was seriously injured, though he suffered burns to his hands and face.[61]

The Nixon boys had no bicycles, wagons, or tricycles; the family didn't even have a phonograph to listen to music. Instead, their toys were primitive, like stick horses made from broom handles. After the youngest, Arthur, outgrew his baby buggy, they played with that.[62] One of their favorite games was catching a local cat, dressing it up, putting it in the buggy, and rolling the buggy down the street until the cat jumped out. Asked how often they did this, family friend Gerald Shaw boasted, "Every time we could catch the cat."[63]

The Shaw and West families lived across the Anaheim Union Canal, just north of the Nixons, and a red bridge separated their homes.[64] Local resident Ralph Navarro was employed as a zanjero (person in charge of water distribution) to patrol the canal, maintaining its water supply to the orchards by keeping it clear of obstructions, as well as preventing local kids from playing in the water.[65] The bridge in front of the Nixon home was the perfect spot for kids to gather and swim because they could keep a lookout for the zanjero and hide under the bridge as he passed.[66] Whenever Navarro caught them, he would chase Richard and the other children from the canal, telling them "more better you go now," but invariably they returned.[67] Richard later reminisced, "Sometimes the boss would catch us. He said that he would put us in jail the next time he caught us, but we haven't been there yet!"[68]

The Nixon boys' lives revolved around the canal, where they'd have rock fights across the ditch or build make-believe cars, boats, or airplanes with blocks of wood from orange crates and packing boxes. As Gerald Shaw remembered, "We used to make paddles out of boards and think we were paddling with Tom Sawyer up and down the river. It was quite a lot of fun."[69] Other times they would pour buckets of water from the canal onto the bank and slide down the hillside. They also enjoyed swimming, catching tadpoles, and fishing in the canal and nearby local reservoir.

As the Nixon boys grew, so did Yorba Linda. By 1920 the population "swelled" to 350.[70] The center of town was directly north of and in between what is now Imperial Highway and Main and Olinda Streets, each one block in length. The blacksmith shop, Stein & Fassel general store, post office, and Buckmaster Hardware were on these two streets.[71] Stein & Fassel was in the middle of the west side of Main Street. The blacksmith shop sat across Main Street; Buckmaster Hardware was around the corner on Olinda Street, along with a dry goods store and post office, along with the San Pedro Lumber Yard. At the northwest corner of Imperial Highway and Olinda stood a large concrete "horse fountain."[72]

Stein & Fassel sold virtually everything imaginable. "You could buy a cow or you could buy a plow horse. You could buy a sewing machine or you could buy a mowing machine," said one early resident.[73] The store also made deliveries, and in 1916, when Richard was three years old, Jack Gauldin was its deliveryman, driving a Model T single-seat flatbed truck.[74] Automobiles were scarce in those days, and Gauldin knew the Nixon boys "got a kick out of riding on the truck," so whenever the boys were in town, he let them ride along.[75] Since the town blacksmith shop was the social meeting place for men, Frank and his sons walked the five blocks into town so that the Nixon boys could ride deliveries while their father debated his favorite subjects, religion and politics, at the Spit and Argue Club.[76] Frank was well read, and although he raised his voice quite a bit, according to family friend Mary Elizabeth Rez, "he was a very genuine person and if he found out he was wrong, he was quick to admit it."[77]

In 1918 the Masons organized in Yorba Linda and moved into a hall on Main Street.[78] The area had no theaters, so movies were a rarity; those shown were at the Masonic Hall, and everyone in town attended.[79] A more typical treat was the monthly venture to buy a quart of ice cream, but the only problem was, according to one resident, "There was no way to keep it on hand afterwards so everybody always ate it. You ate 'til you couldn't stand it."[80]

Above all, Yorba Linda was a religious community, and the activities of everyday life were deeply and specifically rooted in the Quaker faith.[81] The Quaker movement, known as the Religious Society of Friends, was originally organized in 1652 by George Fox in England, the basic doctrine of the church being that "there is a spark of good—a divine light—in every human being."[82] The first Quaker church in Yorba Linda was the sixty-seven-member First Friends Church, established across from the schoolhouse on School Street in 1913, the same year Richard was born.[83] Frank was one of the carpenters who volunteered to construct the church building, and in addition to the Nixons, early members included their relatives, the Marshburn, Harrison, and West families.[84]

Dedicated, the Nixon family was prompt at church.[85] Although raised a Methodist, Frank led a Sunday school class of twenty young people and was known as "a wonderful teacher."[86] He taught with "force and vigor," making a connection between living life as a Christian and participating in civic institutions, explaining that governing should be done "in a Christian way."[87] Cousin Jessamyn West was one of Frank's pupils, and she "felt that Frank was the greatest teacher" she ever had.[88]

The Nixon family of six was tight-knit, literally and figuratively, with four boys sharing two tiny beds on the second floor of the nine-hundred-square-foot home. At bedtime they loved to be read James Whitcomb Riley's poems, including Richard's favorites, "Our Hired Girl" and "Raggedy Man."[89] Hannah's father, Franklin Milhous, who was "full of love, faith and optimism," often read to his grandsons, and his favorite tale was Riley's "Bear Story."[90] After reading, the boys each recited this prayer: "Jesus Holy Savior, hear me while I pray, look upon thy little child, bless me all the day. Forgive me when I'm naughty, take all my sins away. Help me to love Thee better, dear Jesus every day."[91] For his part, every night, Richard would "clasp his little hands and close his eyes, and you could just feel it. He was really praying instead of just saying his prayers."[92]

In 1919 Frank's brother-in-law died, leaving his sister Carrie Wildermuth to care for her two young boys in Ohio. Richard desperately wanted to accompany his parents back to Ohio for the funeral because they were traveling by train. The boy was fascinated by trains; during the day he could see smoke from the coal-powered steam engines as the trains roared down the tracks about a mile from his home, and at night he was sometimes awakened by the train whistle and would lie awake dreaming of faraway places he wanted to visit one day.[93] While in Ohio, Frank insisted Carrie and her sons, Floyd and Merrill, move to California and live with his family until she was able to establish herself, so Carrie, Floyd, and Merrill moved into the Nixons' tiny house and stayed for a year.[94]

As small as their home was, the Nixons owned nine acres of land, with a barn in which Frank kept cows and horses.[95] The barn also had a hayloft, from which feed was thrown down to livestock. The Nixon boys played and enjoyed spending nights in that haymow.[96] They often entertained themselves the lemon grove as well, where older brother Harold and cousin Floyd played games that fueled Richard's competitive spirit. Floyd recounted:

> Harold and I used to get down in one end of the grove when we wanted something from the house and Dick was around, Harold could always say, "Well, Dick, I'll bet you can't get up to the house and bring us back a bag of cookies before we can count to one hundred." We'd start out with one, two, and Dick would take off. We would

wait until just before Dick would be coming back, then we'd pick up around ninety. We'd count about ninety-eight just as he'd get there. He always would win. He always played as hard as he could play.[97]

The year 1919 was also when Richard first attended Yorba Linda Elementary School. Hannah taught Richard to read before enrolling him in first grade, fostering a seemingly endless thirst for knowledge and skill for analytical problem-solving. The main school was built on the northwest corner of School Street and Lemon Drive. Behind the school, across Valencia Street, the school trustees rented a small, one-room building equipped with a potbellied stove; this became Nixon's first-grade classroom.[98] The school playground consisted of a single swing set and one maypole.[99] Although Hannah told the first-grade teacher, "Please call my son Richard and never Dick. I named him Richard," he was known as Dick to friends and classmates.[100]

Like most children at that time, Dick and his brothers frequently walked to school barefoot.[101] Their route passed through the Trueblood property, where the boys often enjoyed picking grapes. Although Mrs. Trueblood didn't mind, it angered Hannah, who forbade the children to take grapes unless they were given express permission to do so.[102] Despite his playfulness on the way, once he got to school, Dick was entirely focused. Mary Skidmore, his teacher, described the young student as "one of those rare individuals born with knowledge," and astoundingly, he read thirty to forty books in his first-grade year.[103]

At the end of the year, Dick, who never caused trouble and got along well with all his classmates, was advanced from first to third grade.[104] It was clear that he "understood what he was in school for. He was there to learn" and "had more depth" than most youngsters.[105] His peers variously described him as shy, quiet, serious, introspective, studious, and neat.[106] Strong-willed like his father, and always competing academically with classmate Yoneko Dobashi, one of the few Asian students in the community, in the three years that he attended Yorba Linda Elementary School, Dick was consistently at the top of his class.[107]

His first-grade classroom eventually became the first Yorba Linda Library. Dick and Gerald Shaw often ran the five blocks from home to the library for books, sometimes reading two a day.[108] Young Dick was such a voracious reader that Frank was known to complain that it was hard to get his son "to do his chores because he would be down on the floor reading a book."[109] Dick's studiousness was not merely the way he approached schoolwork, but the way he approached life. To his third-grade teacher, he "was almost retiring," and Hannah even described her young son this way: "From the time he was first able to understand the world around him, he has reacted the same way to the same situations. . . . He was very mature even when he was five or six years old. He was thoughtful and serious. 'He always carried such a weight.' That's an expression we Quakers used for a person who doesn't take his responsibilities lightly."[110]

Nixon also possessed an understanding of politics that was quite unusual for his age. He later recounted, "I got an interest in politics very early because I can even remember my father berating my mother for having voted for Wilson in 1916."[111] Incumbent Woodrow Wilson, who had pledged to keep America out of war, narrowly defeated challenger Charles Hughes. That same year marked the first time Dick's picture appeared in the local paper. A news photographer saw them shopping with their mother to buy school clothes on a trip to Los Angeles, when Hannah saw that a collection was being taken to benefit war orphans in Europe. The family didn't have much, yet Hannah had taught her boys that they should still be generous with what they had. Hannah gave each child a nickel to donate for the collection, and a news photographer witnessing the event took the family's picture.[112]

America was soon pulled into World War 1, and though he was only five years old when the war ended, Nixon later reflected on how his community had responded on November 11, 1918: "The church bell rang, the big whistle at the packing house came on full blast, everyone was enormously excited. We went from Yorba Linda to Placentia where the American Legion had a parade, and I remember they had an effigy of the Kaiser hanging on one of the floats and I thought it was the real Kaiser they had hanging there!"[113]

He also saw the effects of war firsthand when his grandmother Almira Milhous took him to visit bedridden wounded soldiers at the Sawtelle Veterans Hospital in West Los Angeles.[114] In 1920 Dick surprised even his friends with the depth of his political knowledge at the age of seven. One day while he and his cousin Merle West were walking back to school after lunch, Dick stopped in front of the Yorba Linda National Bank to discuss politics and explain to the first, second, and third graders why Warren Harding should be elected.[115]

As a couple, Frank and Hannah were well liked in Yorba Linda. Hannah was committed to her community and served meals to the men who were building Yorba Linda Boulevard.[116] She was active in the PTA and was a charter member of the Yorba Linda Federation of Women and chair of its Education Committee.[117] As a whole, the Nixon family "was considered to be among the stable people in the community," regarded as "a mighty fine class of people."[118] In 1922, when Frank, Hannah, and the boys left to pursue new economic opportunities in Whittier, it was a real loss to the town. Life in Yorba Linda had been simple "old-time country living," a life that was hard but happy.[119] People settled there hoping to find peace and prosperity, but although the Nixons certainly found peace, prosperity eluded them, as Frank's lemon grove never produced and could not support the family. Years later, during a visit to his birthplace, Nixon commented, "The land in Yorba Linda was better for raising kids than lemons."[120]

Apart from their house and nine acres of orchard, the universe into which Richard Nixon was born consisted of a four-block area of Yorba Linda, but the simplicity and insularity of his surroundings never stopped the young Nixon from dreaming big. In fact, when he was no more than three years old, Richard told his cousin Emily Burdg that "when he got big, he was going to kill wild animals and elephants and lions and tigers."[121] His small-town upbringing in combination with a voracious appetite for reading nurtured a vivid imagination and sparked a deep desire to see the world. Life in Yorba Linda, a strong and loving community, provided the foundation for the man Richard Nixon would become.

TWO

Early Success

1922–26

Whittier was the epicenter of the Quaker community, "a first-name basis kind of town" with a reputation as a "very clean place" that "stood for the good things."[1] Hannah's sister and brother-in-law Olive and Oscar, along with their kids, lived with Almira, whose husband, Franklin, had died in 1919 in the Spanish flu epidemic. The Nixons moved in, staying while Frank built a house nearby on South Painter Avenue.[2] Shortly after the home was completed, a promising business opportunity arose in East Whittier, just inside the Los Angeles County line, adjacent to Orange County.[3]

East Whittier grew up along the seven-mile stretch of Whittier Boulevard, a narrow, unpaved road full of chuckholes and rocks, between Whittier and La Habra.[4] It was sparsely populated, consisting mostly of barley and hay fields, as well as endless rows of walnut, lemon, and orange orchards.[5] Since most lots were at least ten acres, families could live a mile or two apart and still be neighbors.[6] East Whittier was a separate community from the town of Whittier, "out in the country" where life was "carefree and uncomplicated."[7]

Frank and Hannah foresaw the automobile as the wave of the future and persuaded the owner of a ten-acre lot to sell them an acre at the southeast corner of Whittier Boulevard and Santa Gertrudes, where Frank built East Whittier's first gas station.[8] The property was surrounded by two huge citrus ranch operations: the five-hundred-acre Leffingwell Ranch and the much larger five-thousand-acre Murphy Ranch. The Leffingwell Ranch had hundreds of laborers, including 200 Mexican and 125 Japanese workers. On its grounds were a packing house, fire station, laboratory, and a boardinghouse and cook shack for the single men. There were also twelve houses for the married families, as everyone working on the ranch lived there.[9]

Although East Whittier had few families, they each had many children, all of whom were friends with the Nixon boys.[10] Not only did everyone know each other, but many were related, as the Milhous family was particularly large.[11] Franklin Milhous had four siblings, nine children, and twenty-seven grandchildren. In addition, three of Frank Nixon's four siblings lived nearby with all their children. Neighbor Agnes Brannon reflected, "I think about half of the community there was related in some way to the Milhous and the Nixon families. They were all interrelated."[12]

Closeness was one positive aspect of the move to Whittier; economic opportunity was another. After Frank opened the gas station, behind it he built a two-car garage with living quarters above.[13] He added a gray wooden house, facing Santa Gertrudes, with a yard out front.[14] The main house was "quite small," having one bedroom and a bath, a fair-sized living-dining room, a kitchen with wood counters, and a dinette area with a great big table covered with oilcloth.[15] According to cousin Martha Cato, "The furnishings were very simple, made of wood. There were rugs and antimacassars on the chair arms, the little doilies over the chair arms and the backs of the chairs."[16] The boys' bedrooms were situated over the detached garage, and to reach them, one had to go outside, off the kitchen, and up a covered wooden stairway.[17]

Nine packing houses serviced the orchards surrounding the Nixon gas station, with thousands of sheep grazing the acreage not used for growing fruit.[18] It was commonplace for local children to work long hours for minimal wages, and the Nixon boys were no exception, as Frank taught his boys to believe in "the dignity of labor."[19] His gas station was open from 6:00 a.m. until 8:00 p.m., seven days a week.[20] Staffing the gas station was a family affair, and in their younger years Harold and Dick helped pump gas.[21]

There were no conveniences between Whittier and La Habra, so customers began to request that goods be stocked at the station to avoid the long drive into town.[22] Frank began offering thread, socks, bread, and canned items for sale in the back room, which he added to the east side of the gas station. He also had a good cow and began selling milk.[23] A business area began to develop when "Slim" Craddick opened a fruit stand next door, and neighbor Samuel Horney, a barber, cut the Nixon boys' hair for 25 cents each.[24]

The town of Whittier was four miles to the west, with a population of nine thousand and a police force of fewer than ten officers.[25] Since his family was so isolated and several robberies had occurred in the area, Frank placed a .32 caliber revolver under the cash drawer, announcing, "No one robs this store when I'm within reach of that gun."[26] Yet Hannah warned the boys, "Don't any of you use that revolver. It's all right to use it to scare people with, but don't shoot them."[27] Thankfully, the gun didn't prove necessary. In 1924, when a customer was caught shoplifting, Frank wanted to prosecute her, and even the sheriff urged him to press charges.[28] But eleven-year-old Dick diplomatically suggested a compassionate compromise of having the shoplifter pay back the value of the goods she admitted to stealing in weekly installments of $5.[29]

Frank and Hannah both instilled traditional values in their own way.[30] Frank demanded the best from his boys, while Hannah offered them safe haven for their feelings, talking through issues whenever they needed advice and emotional support.[31] Childhood best friend Herman Brannon, who often stayed with the Nixons during periods when his family suffered economic hardship, witnessed their different parenting styles: "Mrs. Nixon looked after me just like my own mother would. She used to call me her other boy. To her I was just like one of her own, and Frank used to holler at me just like he did at Don and Dick."[32] That said, Frank would not holler about anything in particular: "It was just Frank's way. I mean, he just couldn't say something, he hollered it."[33] Even when he joked, Frank hollered, as Brannon explained that Frank would "yell at Don and just look over and wink."[34]

The East Whittier Friends Church was the only church between Whittier and La Habra until the 1950s, and regardless of any previous church affiliation, many East Whittier families attended services there.[35] Herman Brannon's brother Doug noted that after his Baptist family moved to East Whittier, "the Nixon boys invited us to Sunday school, and we started going to East Whittier Friends Church."[36] The Nixons lived across the street from the church, and like all the other families, they generally spent Sundays there and were seen as "devout in their religion and regular in their attendance."[37] The day began with Sunday school at 10:00 a.m., followed by regular morning worship service an hour later, Christian Endeavor for the youths in the afternoon, and finally an evening service. On Wednesday evenings there was a prayer meeting group as well.[38] As Hannah's sister Olive observed, "Church was the social life" for Dick's generation.[39]

Harley Moore was a popular minister who helped the East Whittier Friends Church develop its "evangelical sense."[40] He had a terrific sense of humor and genuinely loved his young congregants, forming strong connections with the children during his thirteen years as pastor.[41] Church activities began with Sunday school, which was structured and emphasized punctuality. When the church bell rang, all the children met in the main sanctuary, each class taking roll and announcing how many of its pupils had arrived on time before the bell stopped ringing.[42] This was followed an opening song, which Dick often played on the piano, before the students disbanded into Sunday school classes.[43]

Dick's classmates likely would have agreed with Raymond Burbank, who went on to become a Quaker minister, that Dick "was consistently thoughtful. He didn't come up with an answer without first thinking it through," and when he did speak up in class, he made definitive statements, "always on the side of the Bible."[44] Whenever class discussions led to politics or current events of the day, Dick was abreast of the issues.[45]

Following Sunday school, the Nixon family attended church. They tithed regularly and had a bench on the left side of the back row.[46] The morning service was simple and plain.[47] Some were even "quiet services," which cousin Lucille Parsons described: "You just go in and sit for an hour, and no one says a word, and you get up and leave."[48] Many preferred these "unprogrammed" services, where congregants "open themselves to the Holy Spirit which moves through them."[49] In the afternoon the youths participated in Christian Endeavor, a combination of social activities and religious teaching, which had a leadership-training component where each participant took turns bringing and serving refreshments, then selecting a topic and leading the discussion.[50] Although the boys and girls had separate Sunday school classes, they often participated together in Christian Endeavor, which included potlucks in the church basement, hayrides, and excursions to the beach or Saturday night shows in Whittier.[51] As Martha Cato explained, "Out in East Whittier, you could just head off in any direction and be out in the wilds! There were ever so many places to go, to ride horseback, or to hayride. Everybody had barns, so we always had our Halloween parties in the barns."[52]

Sunday worship concluded with a less formal, "fundamentally Protestant" service, which included a sermon and singing.[53] After the evening service, the family sat down for Sunday dinner at the kitchen table, where Hannah kept a little box of Bible verses. Their meals began with everyone bowing heads in individual silent prayer, after which each person around the table recited a verse from the Bible.[54]

The Nixon home was a common meeting place.[55] The boys' bedrooms over the detached garage became a clubhouse of sorts for their friends to meet for "bull sessions."[56] The kids enjoyed playing baseball and football on Whittier Boulevard, and Dick, who credited his father with instilling his "competitive feeling," was an active participant who played hard and tried to win but also possessed a strong sense of fair play.[57] According to childhood friend Ray Burbank, "If a situation or judgment between individuals or groups seemed unfair to him, it disturbed him."[58] For Dick, the question of how a game was played was more important than who won.[59]

As the kids grew, they typically became more active in the church, and that was particularly true of Dick.[60] The East Whittier Friends Church was progressive, meaning it allowed music, so Dick often played the piano at the services and sang in the choir.[61] In time he also led "extensive prayers" at church, often emphasizing his favorite Bible verse, "If God is for us, who can be against us."[62] Although he was roughly the same age as the others in attendance, he even led a Sunday school class.[63] For Herman Brannon, young Dick "was a leader, and everybody looked to him as a leader. He was always serious, and he took care of anything that had to be done. He was responsible, and you always looked to Dick for the answers."[64] Perhaps more important, Brannon found that when Dick led Sunday school, it "was always a very fun class, and we would laugh and discuss things. We didn't just sit there and listen to him read or talk, we entered into it and had discussions."[65]

Early on, Reverend Moore recognized young Dick's talent and was known to comment, "He'll be President someday."[66] His uncle Eldo West, who was also his favorite Sunday school teacher, felt the same way, telling his son Merle, "You know, if I ever met a boy that I would say might someday be President of the United States, it would have to be Dick Nixon." "Why?" asked Merle. "Well, his thinking is clear, his mind is sharp," replied his father.[67] For Raymond Burbank, Dick "would be one who could stand up for the position of the Church, and know why. He would take the part of the Church and interpret it to the young fellows who might have a divergent opinion, and he could explain logically so that they could grasp why we believed."[68] At the same time, Dick was well balanced and did not take his religion too seriously; as Brannon commented, "He lived it, but he didn't live just his religion alone. He lived his life, too."[69]

The church frowned on movies and forbade dancing or playing cards.[70] Still, Frank and Hannah took their sons to see Cecil B. DeMille's classic film *The Ten Commandments* with a live prologue at Grauman's Chinese Theatre.[71] While Dick did not care much for dancing, he liked to have a good time, and Raymond Burbank recalled that "he was clever, he was witty and . . . people enjoyed having him around because he added a lot of life to the party."[72] Nixon was pragmatic in his views; he didn't see anything wrong with cards or going to the show, and his favorite game was Pit by Parker Brothers, in which players trade cards in an effort to corner the market on commodities.[73] He loved going over to cousins' homes to play carrom, a sort of billiard game, with Merle West and Russell Harrison Jr.[74] Lucille Parsons summed him up by saying, "He likes music; he likes a good time; he likes all the sports there are; and he likes people."[75]

Dick enrolled at East Whittier Elementary, where the student population comprised a cross section of the community, including Hispanic and Japanese students.[76] The small, isolated community fostered Nixon's academics, since apart from church and working with family, there was nothing to do in East Whittier "but just plain study, study, study."[77]

Dick, always well groomed, rode his bike to school.[78] Never late, he frequently received perfect attendance certificates and was described as "rather quiet, a little shy, but very pleasant, very courteous, and helpful."[79] He was attentive, liked to read, and especially enjoyed history.[80] To his benefit, he had a tremendous power of concentration and a good memory.[81] Dick's fifth-grade teacher said of her young pupil: "The thing that's really outstanding is that he made good use of his time. Industrious. He just didn't waste time at all. And very cooperative. He was always ready to help."[82]

Dick began participating in debate at East Whittier Elementary, where the girls debated against the boys.[83] Assigned his first debate topic, "whether it was better to own or rent a home," he was determined to argue in favor of renting, although he had been taught it was far better to own.[84] Nixon later explained how his father helped: "My father advised me to concentrate on the financial aspects of owning and renting. He pointed out that it might make you feel better to own a home, but it cost less to rent one because you left the burdens of repairs and utilities to the landlord. He helped me add up the numbers in a sample case."[85] Using that line of argument, Dick helped the boys' team defeat the girls'.[86] Over the course of the year, inspired by teacher Lewis Cox, Dick continued to debate various topics, such as "resolved: that insects are more beneficial than harmful" and "whether a cow or a horse was more beneficial to the human race."[87]

Nixon, with encouragement from his father, worked to hone his research and analytical skills. When he tackled the issue of insects, he traveled out to Riverside to interview Frank's brother Ernest, an entomologist, who explained that without bees and other insects to carry pollen from tree to tree and bush to bush, all foliage would die.[88] With that compelling argument, Nixon's team prevailed.[89] Through these experiences, Nixon came to realize that relating arguments to real-life situations was "more important than a lot of flamboyant oratory in determining the outcome of the debate."[90]

Combining his mother's calmness and his father's passion, Dick excelled at public speaking.[91] He learned to state his position just as boldly as his father, yet was sensitive and sincere like his mother.[92] His brother Edward once reminisced, "From our earliest years, Dick, Don and I listened to discussions on current events, political philosophy, and business. At the dinner table, in the store, or in the car—wherever Dad was—he would instigate lively conversations, which often ended in arguments."[93] At the same time, their cousin Sheldon Beeson noted that Hannah "had a tolerant quality about her that Dick has. It's a side of him that is seldom portrayed in anything that you hear or read about him. Actually, he is a most tolerant person, tolerant of your ideas and your viewpoint."[94] Being naturally friendly and "easy to talk to," as well as competitive, Dick made lasting impressions on classmates.[95]

Even though Dick loved school, his neighbors saw him as "all boy." On the playground, he played baseball, basketball, and soccer, and he got along well with the other children.[96] At the same time, he possessed a sensitive side and had musical ability, having been taught to play the violin and piano by his aunt Jane Beeson and uncle Griffith Milhous.[97] When he wasn't out playing or reading, Dick spent hours practicing piano in his living room and quickly progressed.[98] Aunt Jane, with whom he stayed for several months to learn piano, claimed that Nixon learned as much in a year's time as an average student would in three years.[99] His favorite songs were "Rustle of Spring" and "Country Garden," and he was said to make the piano "talk" at Sunday services.[100]

Possessing a mischievous side, playing the violin in the school orchestra, he would stand behind a classmate and try to read from her music sheet because he never brought his own. Whenever the conductor looked away, Dick liked to take his bow and poke the girl in the back, causing her to miss a little of the music.[101] When he performed in recitals, he was known to leapfrog over the piano stool.[102]

There is no doubt that Dick was a well-rounded, all-American boy. In eighth grade he wrote, "My plans for the future if I could carry them out are to finish Whittier High School and College and then I would like to study law and enter politics for an occupation so that I may be of some good to the people."[103] Portentous words, indeed, and ones displaying remarkable vision and dedication to high ideals. Dick was elected class president and graduated from East Whittier Elementary School on June 2, 1926, at the top of his class, speaking at the graduation ceremony.[104]

After Franklin died, Almira, who was considered "one of the jewels of the community," maintained her house and six acres on Whittier Boulevard.[105] Her house had a parlor, living room, dining room, kitchen, and five bedrooms, and Almira hosted the family events.[106] Dick had fifty-two first cousins, whom he referred to as the "Milhous tribe." They would all gather at the Milhous home, where Almira enjoyed presiding over the family get-togethers at the holidays or midsummer picnics where the kids all played ballgames in the yard or slid down the banister inside the home.[107] Known for her hospitality, Almira made her home "a place of peace, love and good cheer," where Aunt Olive always baked Dick's favorite loquat pie.[108] After dinner, the family gathered in the living room and parlor, where Dick played the piano while the family sang along.[109] On other occasions, he entertained everyone with readings of Henry Wadsworth Longfellow poems "The Village Blacksmith" and "The Midnight Ride of Paul Revere."[110]

Cousin Sheldon Beeson noted Almira's impact on Dick: "She was such a good listener, and this is a quality that he has. Whenever you're with him, you never get the impression that he's trying to promote Dick Nixon. He never wants to tell about himself. Even as a boy, when you talked to Dick he always looked you right in the eye. He just beams right in on you when he is talking to you."[111] Almira Milhous had thirty-two grandchildren but singled out Dick: "That boy will one day be a leader."[112]

In July 1925 the Nixons' quiet family life was shaken when seven-year-old Arthur became gravely ill with tubercular meningitis.[113] "The doctors are afraid that the little darling is going to die," sobbed Frank as his son's condition worsened. In early August Dick was home with Hannah as she prepared one of Arthur's favorite dishes, tomato gravy on toast. "I remember going upstairs with my mother, and how much Arthur seemed to enjoy it. But then, while it was still in the middle of the day, he said he was very sleepy, and he thought he should say his prayers, and he recited, 'If I should die before I wake, I pray the Lord my soul to take,' and then he went into a coma."[114]

As Arthur's condition worsened, Frank and Hannah sent their other sons to stay with their aunt Carrie Wildermuth in Fullerton. Arthur died three days later, on August 10; services at the East Whittier Friends Church were officiated by White Emerson, and Arthur was buried in the Milhous plot at nearby Rose Hills Cemetery.[115] Dick was devastated, and within a few years he wrote of his younger brother's death, noting a lovely picture of Arthur: "When I am tired and worry, and am almost ready to quit trying to live as I should, I look up and see the picture of a little boy with sparkling eyes and curly hair; I remember the childlike prayer; I pray that it may prove true for me as it did for my brother Arthur."[116] Throughout the rest of his life, Nixon found it impossible to talk about those days of bereavement, even to those closest to him, and over fifty years later he wrote, "For weeks after Arthur's funeral there was not a day that I did not think about him and cry."[117]

He was not alone in his grief. Believing that Arthur's death was punishment for selling gas and groceries on Sundays, Frank vowed never to open his business on a Sunday again.[118] Known to proclaim, "What we need is a revival. We've got to get these people more cognizant of the value of religion," Frank began taking his sons to revival crusades and rallies, where they regularly saw Sister Aimee at the Angelus Temple or "Fighting Bob" Shuler at Trinity Methodist Church in Los Angeles.[119] Dick's religious "conversion experience" occurred while watching Paul Rader, head of the World Wide Gospel movement, preach at the Angelus Temple.[120] The boy was so inspired that when Rader commanded those in attendance to "come forward for Christ!" Dick rose up from his seat and dedicated his life anew to God.[121] Hannah believed that "it was Arthur's passing that first stirred within Richard a determination to help make up for our loss by making us very proud of him. Now his need to succeed became even stronger."[122]

....

THREE

Nixonville

1926–30

Matriculating at Fullerton High School in Orange County on September 4, 1926, Dick began his high school career in the thick of the Roaring Twenties. Eight miles from the Nixon home, Fullerton High was twice as far as Whittier High School, but Fullerton offered bus service and Whittier did not.[1] Dick walked to the county line to catch the bus every day and rode the first bus home to work at the store.[2] He had an uncomfortable hour-long ride in a bus that had a single bench lining each side, so that students faced each other, and traveled no faster than seventeen miles per hour.[3]

Fullerton High shared its campus with Fullerton Junior College, and teachers taught classes at both.[4] As part of the dress code, girls wore color-coordinated scarves so teachers knew their grade.[5] Boys were simply required to be neatly dressed and typically wore corduroy trousers.[6] The fad was to go without washing their cords to see how dirty they could get. Although Dick tended to be more conservative in his attire, wearing a clean white shirt and often a tie, classmate C. Robert McCormick remembered, "He wore those balloon-type cords, almost to the ground, and dirty, just like the rest of us."[7] Dick enjoyed attending Fullerton, where he was well liked and remembered as "easy to talk to" and "quite friendly."[8] At the same time, he had a sense of purpose, as Dean Burney reflected: "I still see him coming down the street that divided the campus, a serious, content person. He was going somewhere. You could just sense it."[9]

Dick felt at home in Fullerton, where his aunt Carrie Wildermuth lived on Jacaranda Street with his cousins Merle and Floyd.[10] The Nixons and Wildermuths enjoyed Sunday afternoon picnics, after which all the boys gathered outside for football games.[11] Former Yorba Lindans Virginia and Gerald Shaw lived across the street from the Wildermuths, as did Dick's cousin Loren Nixon.[12] These familiar faces provided Dick a sense of comfort and support in Fullerton, and he often stayed with the Wildermuths during the school week.[13]

Dick was a dedicated student. When his geometry teacher, Miss Ernsberger, promised an automatic A to anyone arriving at the answer to an advanced problem before the next class period, Nixon seized the opportunity. Refusing to go to bed on that bitterly cold night, Nixon kept warm by lighting the gas oven and leaving the door open. By the time his mother awoke at 4:00 a.m., he had finally solved the problem, the only student to do so. Surprised, Miss Ernsberger awarded Dick the promised A, and Nixon later reflected, "After that, I never thought there was a problem I couldn't solve if I worked hard and long enough."[14]

In addition to his studies, Dick relaxed by playing the piano at home and also played the violin in the school orchestra.[15] The students wore formal uniforms and were led by Harold Wahlburg. Nixon sat in the front row, next to classmate Richard Heffern, and played second violin.[16] When Heffern wore a bowtie one day instead of the standard red necktie, Dick told him, "Wait until old Wahlburg sees you in that necktie!" Sure enough, when Mr. Wahlburg came in, he looked at Heffern and said, "You stick out like a sore thumb!" For his part, Heffern delighted in getting payback by raking his violin bow through Nixon's curly hair as they played, pushing the hair down over Dick's face; all Dick could do was to sit there and continue playing. Heffern reminisced how they played the entire piece "with Walburg looking at my spotted tie and at Dick's mussed-up hair."[17]

Nixon continued to develop his debate skills at Fullerton High. He explained the importance of his teacher H. Lynn Sheller's advice: "Sheller used to say to me over and over again, 'Remember, speaking is conversation. If you have an audience, you may raise the level of your voice, but don't shout at people. Talk to them. Converse with them.' I have used, to the greatest extent possible, the conversation tone ever since."[18] Sheller recognized that Dick was competitive and had a talent not merely for debating but for winning. On March 30, 1928, in a competition held at Brea Olinda Union High School, sophomore Dick Nixon became the constitutional oratorical champion of the Fifth National Oratorical Contest.[19] The topic was the

U.S. Constitution, and Dick titled his speech "The Ever-Increasing Strength of the Constitution," an assignment through which he came to revere the document and the Founding Fathers.[20] He deemed the Constitution "the most perfect instrument struck off the hand of men," and his sophomore yearbook lauded his "excellent work as the representative of the West Coast High Schools in the National Oratorical Contest."[21]

Dick also was a successful athlete, participating on the high school football team, the Fullerton Indians. What most distinguished him as a player was his dedication.[22] Despite his small build (125 to 130 pounds), he went out for football, suiting up as tackle.[23] Football players had to maintain a B average, which was the easiest requirement for Nixon. According to teammate James Grieves, Dick didn't "know the meaning of give up or defeat," always playing with every ounce of energy.[24] It paid off when his freshman football team, coached by Art Nunn, won the California Interscholastic Federation Championship at Wrigley Field in Los Angeles.[25]

In 1926 Fullerton was a small town with few paved roads, surrounded by acres of farmland.[26] Orange groves were everywhere, and the sweet aroma was "just simply overwhelming."[27] For entertainment, the Rialto Theater featured vaudeville acts every Thursday night; on Friday or Saturday night the Fox Fullerton showed movies and the Moose Hall and Masonic Lodge hosted dances.[28] On Saturday afternoon games were held at Amerige Park, followed by band concerts in the evening.[29]

Young people often ventured to Los Angeles, the Santa Monica Pier, Long Beach Pike, and the Rendezvous Ballroom at Balboa Island via streetcar. Frank Nixon enjoyed taking the boys and their friends to Anaheim Landing or Newport Beach in his 1922 Nash touring car.[30] Dick and his friends were always well mannered on these excursions. One night Dick went to the Long Beach Pike with a group of friends including neighbor Harriett Palmer, whose mother had made her promise not to ride on the Jack Rabbit Racer roller coaster because there had been an accident just the week before. When the group decided to go on the roller coaster, Harriett declined, keeping her promise to her mother. So Dick stayed with her as their friends rode the roller coaster, not wanting her to be alone at the pike, and then he went on the ride by himself after the others returned. Harriett was touched by Nixon's kindness: "I thought that was real thoughtful of him."[31]

Throughout high school Nixon maintained his focus, as cousin Merle West pointed out: "He didn't goof off or mess around. He had too many things on his own that he was doing. He was studying and working hard."[32] Outside of school, Dick worked at the family business, which continued to grow as Frank gradually offered more merchandise for sale at the gas station.[33] In 1927, when the East Whittier Friends dedicated a new church, Frank acquired the original forty-by-seventy-five-foot building and moved it across the street using trucks with rollers. He removed the front and replaced it with steel net accordion doors to make it an open storefront, adding the F. A. Nixon General Merchandise store to his property.[34] What had been the belfry became Frank's office overlooking the store.[35]

The Nixon market was a "well kept" general store, set up with cracker barrels containing flour and other products and glass cases filled with candy. Customers could buy a loaf of bread or a quart of milk for 10 cents.[36] The floors, walls, and ceiling were built of wood, and toward the back of the store, a long glass case displayed butchered meat. The store also had a thick meat-cutting block with large wooden legs, surrounded by sawdust on the floor.[37] East Whittier's economy included bartering, and it was common to "trade rabbits for chickens and milk for pigs."[38] Bartering was so normal that most people said they "traded at the store." The Nixon market was the only store between Whittier and La Habra, so everyone in the area traded there.[39] Some residents even referred to the area as "Nixonville," as the Nixons' store was the center of community life in East Whittier.[40]

Operating the market was a family affair. Every day at 4:30 a.m. Dick went with his father to purchase vegetables on Market Street in Los Angeles. They would load their truck with fresh produce, which Dick would wash and display in the store before heading to school.[41] Frank ordered, priced, and stocked the canned goods.[42] Since they didn't have an adding machine, Hannah totaled up the groceries by pencil, while Frank stood by the register and handled the cash. Dick's brother Don grew up behind the meat counter.[43] After working all day in the store, Hannah took home any fruit that might spoil to make pies, cakes, jelly, and jam to sell the following day.[44] Her baking secret was to stand outside and whip the cold morning air into her egg whites, and Wilma Funk remembered Hannah as "a marvelous baker! Marvelous!"[45]

Every morning their home came alive when Dick and his parents woke at 4:00 a.m. so Hannah could finish baking pies and Dick could make the journey with Frank to Los Angeles to pick up fruits and vegetables and be back in time to wash them before school.[46] Making the trip in the family's delivery truck (an old Model A touring car from which Frank had removed the back seat, replacing it with a truck bed) wasn't easy, since some of the roads through the Belvedere Gardens portion of East Los Angeles were not paved.[47] Dick and his father selected the produce at the Los Angeles market with careful scrutiny, and the Nixon store was known to have "the best vegetables that anybody could get."[48]

Because the Nixon home was in constant motion, a pot of stew was always on the stove, ready to feed anyone who was coming or going.[49] Cousin Wilma Funk remembered, "They had a great big table in the kitchen, and there was food and meals going on there all the time because those boys would get hungry and come in."[50] Since the Nixon boys were working in the store, they were not expected to do many chores around the house; instead, Hannah hired her young nieces at the rate of 10 cents a day to sweep floors, make beds, and wash dishes.[51] Although she liked to work, Hannah never enjoyed doing dishes. Cousin Martha Cato reminisced, "That sink would be piled. Hannah would be baking pies during the night, and they'd had their dinner and all, then they had their breakfast, then the canning. Oh, there were dishes!"[52]

In time Frank offered delivery service for customers who made telephone orders.[53] After school, Dick made the rounds fulfilling orders throughout East Whittier.[54] Once Dick ran out of gasoline. After he walked back to the store, retrieved a can of gasoline, and returned to the truck, he couldn't get it started. In those days vehicles had a vacuum tank instead of a gas pump; it created a vacuum that sucked the gasoline into the carburetor to run the engine. If the vehicle ran out of gasoline and the vacuum ran dry, there wasn't any suction and the engine would not start. Nixon tried in vain to start the car until he ran the battery down, then walked back to the store, again complaining of his predicament. Don took a can of gas and went to the truck with Dick, primed the vacuum tank, started up the truck, and drove it back to the store.[55] When he returned, Nixon's cousin Merle Wildermuth asked, "Dick, in your studies you have, I am sure, studied the workings of a vacuum tank." Nixon replied, "Yeah." Merle asked, "Well, what does it do?" Dick gave him the complete rundown of the vacuum tank and its components, construction, and operation. Unfortunately, even though he had a fine theoretical grasp, he did not have a pragmatic understanding of the engine, a great lesson young Nixon took to heart.[56]

One of the most important principles Frank and Hannah taught their sons was to treat all people equally.[57] A community of about two hundred Mexican families lived and worked on the adjacent Leffingwell Ranch. Like everyone else, they traded at the Nixon market, as did the local Japanese families, and the Nixons treated all customers with respect, regardless of race or socioeconomic background.[58] Dick related how his father, who believed in working for everything he had, treated any down-and-out individuals stopping at the store for a handout: "He never turned them down, but he always insisted that they do some work for what he gave them. The work did not amount to much, but he said that no one should get something for nothing."[59] Hannah and Frank used those instances to teach their sons how to stand against racial prejudice. Nixon reflected, "Those who came to work on occasion in the store—an Indian girl, a black man, a Mexican boy—always had dinner and supper with the family. There was never a second table in our home."[60]

Despite the hard work their store required, the Nixons liked to have fun, occasionally playing practical jokes on visiting salesmen. When neighbor Mattie Wood, who was "stone deaf," was shopping in the store, a salesman was making a pitch to Frank. As Frank listened, he watched Mattie picking up and inspecting various items. Finally, Frank yelled over at her, "Take your dirty hands off the canned goods. Quit shuffling items around!" The mortified salesman about "fell over dead," while Frank laughed, knowing that Mattie had not heard a word.[61]

Another day the Nixon boys rigged up a radio in the house to act as a microphone, with the speaker in the store. As Dick played the piano, the music was piped to the store. When a deliveryman from the Luer Packing Company arrived, Dick played the Luer jingle, as his brothers announced over the speaker that "the Nixon store was handling Luer's bacon and meats." Floyd Wildermuth remembered how the deliveryman "stood there and his mouth just fell open," unable to understand how the "radio" announcers knew he was there.[62]

Frank was "a likable fellow" with a "heart of gold," who had no trouble expressing his opinions.[63] According to George Irving, "If he wanted to call you a nut, he'd call you a nut."[64] Some of the neighborhood women took to lightheartedly teasing him, calling him "Brother Nixon."[65] When they came in the store they would ask, "Brother Nixon, how are you this morning?" to which Frank would reply, "I'm just as pretty as I was yesterday."[66] Hannah, on the other hand, was a "gentle, soft-spoken person" who was "never going to say anything against anybody."[67]

Through everything, the Nixons worked together to make their business and their home life a productive and supportive atmosphere.[68] Unfortunately, only a few years after Arthur died, Dick's oldest brother, Harold, who had gone back east to study, contracted tuberculosis. He returned to Southern California from Mount Hermon, a prep school in Massachusetts, because the dense winter fogs were compounding his illness, and Dick picked him up at the Pasadena Santa Fe train station.[69]

In 1928, believing the arid climate would be best for her ailing son, Hannah moved with Harold to Prescott, Arizona, rented a small place, and took in three other people with tuberculosis to help offset the costs.[70] Dick remembered them as "Leslie from a town in the Midwest; Larry from the East; and a third man, 'the Major,' a Canadian."[71] Though it was obviously a difficult situation for his family, Dick was proud of Hannah: "It was my mother's finest hour. She loved and cared for each of those three patients as if they were her own sons. . . . My mother, alone, with no help whatever, took care of them all. She did the cooking, the cleaning, took care of their laundry, gave them their bed baths, carried their bedpans, gave them their alcohol rubs—everything that in those days a nurse would do for a patient, she did by herself." Unfortunately, her three patients all died.[72]

Frank, Dick, and Don remained in Whittier, and the experience brought the three closer than ever.[73] Although they were "disorganized housekeepers," they took turns preparing a limited menu of canned chili, spaghetti, pork and beans, soup, hamburgers, or fried eggs.[74] Dick later reflected, "Odd as it may seem, I still like all those things." On the other hand, he also had a sweet tooth. "There were many mornings when I had nothing for breakfast but a candy bar."[75]

Frank and the boys made the sixteen-hour drive almost every weekend to see Hannah and Harold. With no paved road connecting Whittier to Prescott, the ride across the desert was often treacherous on tires and the radiator, but Frank and Hannah demonstrated their commitment to each other and their boys through these trips, which allowed the family to be together for a full Saturday.[76] Throughout the summers of 1928 and 1929, Dick enjoyed long visits in Prescott and worked the summer rodeo festival, Frontier Days. Only a teenager, he was a fairground barker at a stall he named Dick's Wheel of Fortune, which became the best moneymaking concession at the fairground.[77]

The old adage "absence makes the heart grow fonder" must have been true for Hannah and Frank: in 1930, at the age of forty-five, Hannah gave birth to their fifth son, Edward. By this time Harold had recovered, and they all returned to East Whittier. Edith Brannon, a close family friend who dated Harold Nixon after he returned from Arizona, described him as "different in his appearance" from his brothers, "because he was blond and blue-eyed; the others were more dark and they were brown-eyed."[78] The adventurer of the family, Harold liked to have a good time; he was very sociable, fun-loving, and in contrast to Dick, interested primarily in social activities. Still, Harold recognized his younger brother's talents and encouraged him, as Edith recalled: "I remember when Dick graduated from grammar school in East Whittier, Harold was very proud of the fact that Richard was at the top of his class."[79]

After his first two years at Fullerton High, Whittier finally began bus service, so Dick transferred to Whittier High School.[80] There was only one bus, which made an hour-long circular route through South and East Whittier, carrying Dick and thirty classmates.[81] Transferring high schools was undoubtedly difficult for Nixon. Although the school was only four miles away, Whittier was a small town and East Whittier was all countryside, so the bused students were considered outsiders from out in the country.[82] Most of the East Whittier parents were ranchers, whereas most of the Whittier parents worked in the more urbanized sectors or held white-collar jobs.[83] Moreover, the new school was cliquish, as Nixon's classmate Arthur

Remly explained: "The rest of us had gone up through all the grade schools together, and so we knew each other pretty well. By this time we had kind of formed our little groups, and these people coming in from East Whittier were kind of outsiders."[84]

Meanwhile, because Harold had been so ill, Frank and Hannah took Dick and Don to the doctor to have their lungs checked. Both showed signs of scar tissue, although Dick's was from a bout with pneumonia when he was four. Still, the doctor forbade him to play football. For Dick that proved one of the saddest days of his life, being forced to return his football equipment and tell the coach he could not play on the team.[85]

Nixon soon overcame his disappointment. Despite the rigid social hierarchy at his new school, he succeeded in his new environment and was well liked and considered "very affable."[86] He kept busy; in addition to academics, he still worked in the family store and was active in church. He also participated in Hi-Y, the youth organization of the YMCA.[87] He was on the debate team, belonged to the Latin Club and the Scholarship Society, participated in theater, and spoke at school assemblies.[88] In class Nixon typically sat in the back and continued to hone his reputation as a capable and serious student who enjoyed being challenged by his teachers.[89] Harold Stone, who took advanced algebra and trigonometry with Nixon, was impressed with his classmate's diligence when their teacher, Miss Heise, presented the class with a series of problems, along with the promise that any student solving all the problems correctly did not have to come to class anymore. Dick was the first one to complete the challenge. "When he finished first, we all realized and remembered who he was."[90]

Six months after transferring to Whittier High, at sixteen, Dick Nixon ran for student body president in a three-way race against Roy Newsom and Bob Logue, a decision that reflected considerable confidence.[91] For Jack Mele, who eventually became the school principal, it was "quite unusual" for a new student to come in and "run an extremely close race." Although Dick lost the campaign to classmate Bob Logue, he was not discouraged despite suffering his first political defeat.[92] The faculty acknowledged Nixon's honesty and leadership ability, selecting him to be student body general manager for his senior year.[93] It was quite a responsibility and highly unusual for a transfer student to be granted the position, which placed him in charge of ticket sales for football, basketball, and theater productions, plus advertisements in the yearbook, including accounting for all moneys received.[94]

Nixon joined the Constitutional Orators Society to compete in debates on the Constitution, which he was able to relate to his family's life experiences, enjoying freedom of religion and the ability to move freely from Yorba Linda to start a new business and then pursue opportunities in East Whittier.[95] Their coach was Jennie McGregor, a Scottish lady considered "just marvelous" for her warm personality, though she was also exacting in her criticisms and able to help her students excel in their debate preparation.[96]

Fellow teammates included Albert Flory, the son of the local judge, and Merton Wray, whose father had been narrowly defeated in the Nebraska governor's race before moving to Southern California.[97] Wray was Nixon's main competition and was expected to win all the school debates, but Dick quickly defeated him.[98] Merton Wray recalled, "Nixon was a tremendous orator then, and had a tremendous empathy to communicate with his audience. He had a way of reaching out and getting a hold of them. It is something you are born with and, in all justice, you develop."[99] In his presentation, Nixon told the audience, "For as long as the Constitution is respected, its laws obeyed, and its principles enforced, America will continue to progress. But if the time should ever come when America will consider this document too obsolete to cope with changed ideals of government, then the time will have arrived when the American people as an undivided nation must come back to normal and change their ideals to conform with those mighty principles set forth in our incomparable Constitution."[100]

Dressed in the only suit he ever wore, a brown one, Dick was "perfectly at ease" speaking before crowds as he beat more than sixty students to become the Whittier area champion in the *Los Angeles Times* Constitutional Oratorical Contests for 1929 and 1930.[101] The debates were held in the high school auditorium so everyone in Whittier could attend, and classmate Wayne Long, a fellow participant, said of Nixon, "He won first place right down the line from the beginning through area debates into the finals, and came out on top."[102] Another observer reflected, "You would think he was a man of 40 or 45 and had been a lecturer all his life."[103] Of course, Frank Nixon loved watching his boy debate and provided encouragement and advice, which Dick credited as the primary factors inspiring him to develop his talents.[104]

As at Fullerton, Dick received enthusiastic support from his fellow students and teachers.[105] To his credit, while his classmates liked to say "Dick Nixon's a brain," he was modest about his talent and had fun with his debate skills, demonstrating his wit as he challenged classmates to argue whether a giraffe with a sore throat suffered more than a centipede with corns.[106]

Nixon was active in the Latin Club, and in his senior year the group put on a play, where Dick met his first girlfriend, Ola Welch, "a pretty blue-eyed brunette."[107] Ola was the daughter of the Whittier police chief and knew Nixon from watching his debates.[108] Dick and Ola were the leads in a May 1930 performance of the Greek tragedy *The Aeneid*, commemorating the two thousandth anniversary of Virgil's birth.[109] According to Ola, Dick "was a marvelous actor, quick, perceptive, responsive, industrious."[110] The play reached its climax when Aeneas (Dick) declared his love for Dido (Ola) and embraced her, and then the couple threw themselves onto a funeral pyre.[111] However, wearing silver boots three sizes too small, Nixon had to tiptoe around the stage throughout the performance, and Ola later reflected, "I was never so embarrassed in my whole life." For his part, Nixon remembered it as "sheer torture" (literally and figuratively, one assumes), leaving him with a lifelong aversion to wearing boots.[112] Yet the play afforded him the opportunity to introduce Ola to his parents.[113]

Dating for Dick and Ola consisted of going into town on Saturday nights; for $1, they'd get a sandwich and a glass of orange juice and see a show.[114] They attended Christian Endeavor and Hi-Y meetings together, with fun getaways including the Long Beach Pike and Balboa Island, as well as Laguna Beach, where one of Dick's aunts had a house.[115] Sometimes they went on "adventurous" double dates with Nixon's cousin Merle West to Los Angeles, where they enjoyed performances at the Pantages Theater. One time, intending to go to the Pantages, they saw the marquee of the Burbank Burlesque Theater on Main Street, which looked inviting, so they decided to go there instead. Once they got over the shock of the atmosphere, they were entertained by Mickey Rooney's father, Joe Yule, a vaudeville comedian.[116] Ola later reflected on their relationship: "You have no idea how tremendously interesting and engrossing he was to me, the daughter of a small town police chief. I considered myself provincial and him worldly."[117]

However worldly he may have appeared to some, during his years at Whittier Nixon was often seen sitting on the school steps, either reading a book or staring into space, daydreaming.[118] His aunt Olive reminisced, "I can still see him lying on the lawn, sky viewing and dreaming."[119] He sought solitude a few blocks from home in the hills of Whittier off Santa Gertrudes Avenue and West Road. He enjoyed hiking in the hills and daydreaming, once saying, "I just love to go up there and think."[120] From their heights, he could see the coastal towns of Seal Beach and Long Beach, with Catalina off in the distance and ships crossing the channel.[121]

Nixon succeeded because of his incredible ability to concentrate. He could be so focused on a thought that sometimes he did not see friends as he passed them by on the street.[122] Whittier High School teacher Frances King relayed an incident at school when she and a coworker were walking past the student body office. Just as they approached the door, it flew open and out walked Dick with two other students in the middle of a discussion. Nixon didn't see the teachers and bumped into King's coworker, knocking off her glasses. He stopped long enough to pick them up and return them to her with an apology, then went on down the hall, continuing his banter. King summed up the episode: "I don't believe that he really realized that he had bumped into anybody."[123]

Whatever his future held, the fundamental belief in hard work and discipline that Frank and Hannah had instilled in him paid off when, in his last year, Richard Nixon was selected as the outstanding male student of his senior class, graduating from Whittier Union High School on June 19, 1930.[124] Looking back on those years, he acknowledged, "It was not an easy life, but it was a good one, centered around a loving family and a small, tight-knit, Quaker community. For those who were willing to work hard, California in the 1920s seemed a place and time of almost unlimited opportunity."[125]

FOUR

Depression-Era Education

1930–37

Nixon was selected as best all-around student by the Harvard Club of California and received scholarship offers from both Harvard and Yale.[1] Choosing Whittier College instead, he explained his decision: "My folks needed me. They needed me in the store. There was no way I could go. After all, Harold was still sick and this was the time when the medical expenses were enormous. So I decided to stay home and I have no regrets. I was not disappointed because the idea of college was so exciting that nothing could have dimmed it for me."[2]

Comprising an area of three square miles, Whittier had at its heart the six-story Bank of America Building at Greenleaf Avenue and Philadelphia Street, the tallest building for miles.[3] Whittier was essentially a crime-free town. A red light hung between the four corners of the buildings at Philadelphia and Greenleaf to serve as a signal: when the light was turned on, it meant the police officer on duty had to call the station and report in.[4] Whittier College was just a couple of blocks to the east.

The students took great pride in their campus and would sing, "We invite you down to Quaker town, for you the light streams out."[5] A quiet tree-shaded haven, the campus mirrored the community. At its entrance was a large granite boulder known simply as the Rock, a landmark since 1912, when it was carted from the local mountains on a horse-drawn wagon and installed as a prank by Nixon cousin Austin Marshburn.[6] Each fall the campus came alive as the freshman and sophomore classes battled for the right to paint their class year on the Rock.[7] Battles included turning fire hoses on each other and even spilled over into the campus lemon orchard, where students armed themselves with citrus and charged after each other.[8] Nixon enjoyed the "anything goes" competition, joining in with steely determination to help his freshman class win the right to paint the Rock.[9]

Small and distinctly charming, Whittier College had fewer than five hundred students, who knew each other well, were given individual attention, and learned that each person was uniquely important.[10] Bruce Burchell, a member of the class of 1935, remembered, "Everybody in the college stressed friendliness and the importance of each individual. We all felt that we all belonged."[11] Nixon immersed himself in every aspect of college life and was seen as "out front right from the beginning."[12] And though he was only seventeen, he "put some fire into" everything he did.[13]

The center of campus was Founders Hall, a three-story structure dating to 1893.[14] Founded by Quakers, Whittier College promoted religious pursuits, including compulsory chapel three times a week in Founders Hall, where students had assigned seats and the faculty "counted noses."[15] The tone was inspirational, emphasizing that the faculty and students were united in spirit, and included lectures, religious services, and rallies.[16]

The year Nixon enrolled at Whittier, the Athletics Department underwent two significant changes: Verne Landreth was hired as coach of the varsity basketball team and athletic director, and Wallace "Chief" Newman joined the faculty as a coach.[17] Dick had a healthy interest in athletics, and disregarding his doctor's admonition against playing sports, he went out for football and basketball his first year.[18] Nixon's freshman basketball team lost every game, but the student body still packed Wardman Gym to cheer on what was best described as "scrambleball."[19] For his efforts, Nixon's only trophy was a gold-rimmed cap from breaking his front tooth.[20]

As a member of the freshman football team, Dick played every game. He weighed just under 150 pounds, about 50 pounds underweight for a tackle.[21] His teammates were amazed at his tenacity, as Herman Fink reflected: "His lack of ability and size was compensated by his courage and inspiration."[22] Because there were not enough players for substitutions, the team called themselves the "Iron Men," with Nixon always the last to give up.[23]

Coach Newman was a brawny, intelligent man whom Dick admired, and he learned more from his coach than any other man in his life except for his father.[24] The Chief asked only that his player do their best, and they would do anything for him.[25] After the University of Southern California football team won back-to-back national championships in 1931 and 1932, Whittier opened the season on September 23, 1933, against the ferocious Trojans at the Los Angeles Memorial Coliseum. It was the first of a doubleheader, with Occidental taking on USC afterward.[26] Whittier lost 51–0, and Occidental fared only slightly better, losing 39–0, before thirty-five thousand fans. At twenty years old, standing five-foot-eleven and weighing 176 pounds, Nixon wore number 23 and played tackle. He related how Chief Newman inspired him: "You know in those days they used to say . . . it isn't whether you win or lose but how you play the game that counts. And the Chief said, 'That's all fatuous nonsense. Of course how you play the game counts. You must always play fair. But it also counts whether you win or lose. You play to win.'"[27]

Lacking in speed, coordination, and mobility, Nixon played all through college, and it was clear to his teammates that he "just loved the game."[28] After his freshman year, Dick played only a few minutes in each game, but still, according to Hubert Perry, a student team manager, if any person emerged as a team leader, it was Nixon: "He gave the team its spark. He would give a speech in the half time, and often his pep talk was the difference between winning and losing."[29]

Football was a different game in 1930; headgear was not required, and those using it did so only to keep their "hair on and ears in."[30] Team captain Keith Wood reminisced, "I can still see his helmet flying off" as Nixon was knocked on his back, but he always got up, "ready for more."[31] "Why he went out for four years is beyond me," 220-pound teammate Clint Harris said. "I'd play opposite him in scrimmages and we couldn't let up or the coach would be on us. So I'd have to knock the little guy for a loop. Oh my gosh, he did take it. The harder you hit him the more he came back at you."[32] Teammate Joe Gaudio recognized Nixon's dedication: "He felt himself a good enough student of the game. He really believed in himself, and he couldn't see himself quitting, and therefore he stayed it through."[33] Frank often attended his son's practices, and he insisted that the family attend all of Dick's games.[34]

Whittier's chief rival was Occidental College, and every year before the big game, the students had a rally and bonfire on Fire

Hill, the highest point of the campus, behind Wardman Hall.[35] The students spent days collecting anything that would burn, and in the words of teammate Nathanial George, "Everything that wasn't tied down or nailed down ended up in the bonfire."[36] As a junior, Nixon was elected rally chairman, and his enthusiasm was contagious.[37] Normally, the bonfire was topped with a "one-holer" outhouse, which was the "symbol of all bonfires," but Nixon and his friends were able to locate a "four-holer" eight miles away in Downey.[38] In the dead of night, Dick and his crew disconnected the outhouse and removed it, then built a woodpile thirty feet high and topped it with the four-holer—a record that stands to this day.[39]

As is typical of collegiate rivalries, many antics took place between Whittier and Occidental.[40] On the eve of homecoming in November 1931, after some Oxy students painted over the Whittier Rock, several Whittier student athletes went to Occidental. Finding themselves lost on campus, they painted "To Hell with Oxy!" on the front steps and columns of the Occidental Chapel, raising quite a ruckus.[41] In the ensuing uproar, Whittier College came close to having to leave the athletic conference, and naturally, Whittier's Quakers were very upset, demanding that the students involved be expelled.[42] So the Joint Council of Control, run by students and faculty, worked to address student and community issues. Dick, a member since his freshman year, appreciated the predicament, knowing that his friends were wrong but not believing that they should be expelled or the college should be thrown out of the conference.[43] With Nixon "at the forefront of trying to mediate" the uproar, ultimately the students were allowed to stay, Whittier remained in the conference, and the revelry continued.[44]

During Nixon's senior year, not all his teammates could participate in pranks at Occidental, since many were in jail.[45] Traditionally, following the annual bonfire rally on Fire Hill, the students wound their way in a "serpentine parade" across the campus and into town to the Scenic Theater, where they crashed the gate to watch a movie.[46] Nixon, who had a way of exciting his classmates, led the way, but the Scenic's new night manager did not appreciate the prank. Teammate Halliday described the events: "The lights came on, and the police came and took us to jail for crashing the gate."[47] A quick-thinking Nixon called well-known Whittier alumnus Judge Swain, a friend of the Nixon family for over twenty-five years, who saw to it the team was released.[48]

On the opposite end of the spectrum from football was the Glee Club, in which Nixon was a basso and master of ceremonies.[49] While football consumed his afternoons, the Glee Club practices were at 7:00 a.m., and Nixon described the tough initiation ceremony: "The process was to require us to strip down, bend over and be slapped hard with a paddle on the rear end, in order to heat us up. Then, we were required to sit on a cake of ice to cool off. We would stand up and take another crack at the paddle and sit down again. By the time we had been through this about twenty times, most of us had lost whatever voice we had."[50] If any member was late to practice, he faced "sockery," which meant each member "took a crack" at the tardy member with a large paddle.[51] Decked out in tuxedos, the Glee Club toured as the "Ambassadors of Song," performing at the Whittier Women's Club, churches, and high schools. Halfway through their high school performances, the singers took a break so that Dick could talk to the students about attending Whittier.[52]

Nixon's greatest legacy at Whittier College was the formation of the Orthogonian Society only six weeks into his freshman year.[53] Whittier College did not permit fraternities or sororities, although in the 1890s there had been literary societies, one of which was the Atheneum.[54] In time the literary societies waned and disappeared.[55] In March 1922 the Atheneum Society was resurrected as an all-male organization and renamed the Franklin Society.[56] Less than two months later Dick's cousin Jessamyn West helped form the all-female Palmer Literary Society.[57] In April 1929 the all-female Thalian Society was formed, followed by the Athenian Society, then the Metaphonian Society.[58] By Nixon's freshman year in 1930 these societies filled the gap of national fraternities and sororities.[59]

Four factors led to the formation of the Orthogonian Society: Whittier's Athletics Department hired Verne Landreth and Chief Newman; Dean Triggs, a friend of Dick's from Whittier High School, transferred from Colorado College, where he belonged to a fraternity; a men's society that was representative of the student athletes was needed; and Dick Nixon was available to lead the group.[60] Coach Landreth, who came from Huntington Park, and Chief Newman, who was hired from Covina High School, each recruited several of their high school athletes to attend Whittier.[61] The athletes all immediately bonded on the football field, and encouraged by Triggs, who knew of fraternity life, they formed an organization to "meet the needs of the athletes a little better."[62]

It was time. According to classmate Hubert Perry, a member of the Franklin Society, the Orthogonians "came about at a time when the college needed it."[63] The challenge was that the charter members, all on the football team, wanted a leader "that would keep the organization from becoming just another athletic association."[64] William Krueger described the first Orthogonian meeting in the back of Wardman Gym: Nixon "had been talked about as a real sharp person and I was just a little leery, me a big sophomore and he a freshman," but Dick, who enjoyed the camaraderie, was able to communicate "eye to eye, shoulder to shoulder" with the athletes, and they admired his grit and determination both on and off the field.[65] That night the group elected Nixon president.[66]

Highly effective as president, Dick created the Orthogonian name and wrote the group's constitution.[67] He also created its mascot, a wild boar; wrote the lyrics for its song; created the initiation ritual; and dreamed up its symbol, the four b's. Nixon explained: "The four b's stood for beans, brains, brawn and bowels. The bowels were for the guts of the football players; brains, we were all students; the brawn, we were going to be strong; the beans were the bean feeds we had every week. In those Depression years we didn't have meat, so we had beans."[68]

Orthogonians could be loosely translated as "straight shooters," and Nixon saw the group's purpose as providing fellowship and service to the school.[69] Fellow Orthogonians considered him an idealist who emphasized Orthogonian rituals to develop moral behavior among the members.[70] Members also provided tutoring for one another: if one member excelled in a class, he was appointed to assist his Orthogonian brothers in that class to keep their grade averages up so they could stay eligible to play sports.[71]

The Franklins opposed the formation of the Orthogonians because they wanted the charter members to join their group, but the establishment of the Orthogonian Society ushered in a new era at Whittier College, spurring the formation of several other men's societies, including the Lancers, William Penn Society, and

Elithonter Society.[72] Charter member John Chapin pointed out how the Orthogonians were initially perceived: "We were considered a bunch of dumb athletes," so the faculty "kept their eye on us."[73] For good reason: the Orthogonians enjoyed pranks, like the time they disassembled a Model T and reassembled it in the belfry of Founders Hall, or when they constructed a fountain in front of Founders Hall and regularly stocked it with goldfish liberated from nearby Central Park.[74]

In contrast, the Franklins were a staid bunch who sponsored afternoon teas and had their annual pictures taken in tuxedos borrowed from Glee Club members.[75] To distinguish themselves from the Franklins, whom they called "kite flyers," the Orthogonians, who were known on campus as "a no-neck and merry crew," took a far more informal approach. For their annual pictures, they wore short-sleeved white shirts with open collars, their muscles bulging.[76] Choosing not to wear a suit and tie for an annual picture was considered new and independent, and the Orthogonians, outgoing men who viewed themselves as "rugged individualists" and "cowboys of the western region," were considered "revolutionaries" by their fellow students.[77] During this period of transition for Whittier, there was intense competition for pledges, with the Orthogonians, who were immediately popular and seen as "the big shots on the campus," attracting "the cream of the crop."[78]

The Depression years were a difficult time to attend Whittier College, and most of Nixon's high school classmates went to the more affordable Fullerton Junior College.[79] As one former classmate recalled, "Everybody was having a hard time making it."[80] Even Nixon's girlfriend Ola Welch had to borrow money to stay in school.[81] Students lived where they could—in garages, on a cot in a closet behind the men's locker room, and in the attic space in Founders Hall.[82] The faculty at Whittier College had their salaries cut voluntarily, lived on credit from local stores, and were sometimes paid in land.[83] Willing to do anything to make a dollar, students prayed for cold winters so they could get smudging jobs, lighting oil heaters in the orchards to protect the citrus trees from freezing.[84] The work was dirty, lasted throughout the night, and took place in freezing weather.[85] Money was tight. Often a student would make a meal out of a 10-cent tamale or go into the college orchard to pick fresh avocados.[86] Knowing the difficulty many of his classmates faced, Nixon often brought pies and sandwiches from his family store.[87]

The Nixons were not wealthy but comfortable. Many of Dick's relatives, including his mother, had attended Whittier College, and his grandfather Franklin had created the Milhous Family Scholarship.[88] To provide Dick with spending money, his parents gave him the produce portion of the market so he could use the profits to cover his expenses.[89] While at Whittier, Dick bought his first car, a 1930 Model A Ford Cabriolet, for $300 at the local William F. Lester Chevrolet.[90]

Initially, there was concern whether the Orthogonians would just be another athletic club, but Nixon "welded them into an organization that has endured through the years."[91] Taking a modern and open-minded approach, Dean Triggs explained that Nixon "felt very strongly that we should have representation from minority groups in our organization."[92] Bill Brock, one of the only Black students on the football team, credited Nixon with bringing him into the group.[93] When their team traveled to Arizona for a game and their hotel refused to serve Brock in the dining room, Nixon took him out for a steak dinner.[94]

Several Orthogonians eventually moved into what was known as the Barn, a garage with one big second-story room and a sleeping porch, not much more than "a lean-to covered with flooring with wire fencing around it." It was a few blocks off campus, and rent was $2 per month.[95] The Barn became the Orthogonian house, and all Orthogonians were welcome.[96] Looking back at the time spent at the Barn, Nixon reflected, "The good fellowship and fun I shall always treasure."[97]

The Orthogonian Society was a challenge to the Franklin Society, but the prevailing environment at Whittier was that everyone knew each other and there was no rift or distinction between the students.[98] There was, however, competition over school elections.[99] The Franklins historically ran college politics, but once the Orthogonians were established, they quickly became the campus leaders. Within two years Herschel Daugherty was the first Orthogonian elected student body president, beating the Franklin candidate by a margin of two to one.[100] Over the next nine years, through 1939, two-thirds of the student body presidents were Orthogonians, and the Orthogonian membership included most of the varsity team captains. Throughout the 1930s the Orthogonian Society was the dominant campus organization.[101]

Nixon pursued competitive debate at Whittier, teaming with Kenneth Ball, a Franklin, in his freshman year to win the interclass debate trophy.[102] With his deep speaking voice, Dick was at ease speaking in front of a crowd, confident the audience was following his every word.[103] He once told classmate Louis Valla, "To be a good debater, you've got to be able to get mad on your feet without losing your head."[104] Impressively, Nixon joined the varsity debate team as a freshman. The following year the team of Dick, Joe Sweeney, Ed Miller, and Joe Bosio went on a 3,500-mile tour of the Pacific Northwest, through California, Oregon, and Washington, in the Nixon family's seven-passenger Packard. They met twenty-seven opponents and won every match before returning home to win the conference championship.[105] In Dick's junior year the squad of Sweeney, Nixon, and Emmett Ingrum toured Nevada, Colorado, and Arizona on their way to a second conference championship, and in his senior year, he won the Southern California Intercollege Extemporaneous Speaking Championship.[106] Football teammate Robert Farnham was frank: "He wasn't the king of the mountain on the football field, but he was king of the mountain at the debating scene."[107]

Comfortable on stage, Nixon went out for theater.[108] Whittier College had a strong theater program that was well supported by the town.[109] The college chapel at the top of a "rickety stairway" in Founders Hall served as the Ye Poet Theatre, with two hundred balcony seats and four hundred floor seats.[110] Professor Albert Upton, the theater coach, was close to Nixon, also serving as a faculty advisor for the Orthogonian Society.[111] Dr. Upton remembered him as "one of our first successful actors."[112] When not acting, Nixon served as stage or prop manager.[113] According to classmate Robert Farnham, "He just liked to be involved, and he didn't care if it was in the backstage or the front of the stage or the middle of the stage or the top of the stage."[114] Theater helped a reserved Nixon "learn to project his feelings to an impersonal audience" and even provided his first stage kiss.[115]

Dick's roles included Mr. Inglesby in *The Trysting Place*, a Scottish miner in *The Price of Coal*, Thomas Greenleaf (the lead) in *Bird in Hand*, Mr. Eldridge in *Philip Goes Forth*, and a comic vagabond in *The Tavern*.[116] In *Bird in Hand*, he played the "heavy role" of old Thomas Greenleaf, "a middle class English inn keeper" who ultimately broke down crying, garnering praise from the *Quaker Campus* as "the finest dramatic performance yet witnessed at Whittier College," where Nixon "carried his part with exceptional skill. His interpretation of a difficult character was accompanied with finesse seldom displayed by amateurs."[117]

There was a piano in the chapel, which Dick frequently played for his fellow students.[118] In fact, after Nixon received instruction from Margaretha Lohmann, an established concert pianist at Whittier, he gave a student concert performance of Brahms Rhapsody in G Minor.[119] Lohmann, who often shared Los Angeles Philharmonic performances with Nixon, knew that Dick favored composers Frederic Chopin and Johannes Brahms, leading her to conclude, "He is a romanticist at heart, but he doesn't like to let this show."[120]

Nixon was a student leader and active in student politics since the first week of his freshman year, when he was elected president of his freshman class; he was reelected the second semester.[121] As a freshman, Nixon also advised upperclassman Tolbert Moorehead, a Franklin, on his campaign for student body president, even writing a spirited endorsement of Tolbert in the school paper. Dick visited Moorehead at his house to coach him, advising the candidate, "Get up and sock it to them. You've got to get up there and stand on your feet. You've got to tell 'em what you believe."[122]

For his sophomore year, Dick was elected to an at-large seat on the Student Executive Committee, receiving 231 votes—more than either of the candidates for student body president.[123] In his junior year, he was elected student body vice president with a vote of 267–73, and in his senior year, he was elected student body president, defeating Dick Thomson, a yell leader and member of the Franklin Society.[124] When Nixon ran for student body president, athletes, Orthogonians, and their girlfriends "banded together to vote for Nixon."[125] Many Franklin members actually supported Nixon's candidacy, and Thomson, who was one of Nixon's best friends, felt that the Franklins had picked him to run against Nixon because no one else would do it.[126]

According to classmate Joe Gaudio, Nixon "had a genius for organization that manifested itself all over the campus."[127] Causes included raising money for a student exchange program with the University of Hawaii, fighting for the return of baseball, and helping his fellow students secure jobs, because Nixon knew that if a student could get a job or join a team, he would likely remain in school.[128] Nixon was honored to be selected for the Whittier College Knights, which consisted of student leaders who were also honor students and served as a sort of "police force" in charge of conduct.[129] The purpose of the group was to assist in student activities, supervise the induction of freshmen into the complexities of college life, set examples for social relations and conduct, and raise the standards of character and fellowship on campus.[130]

The largest issue Nixon challenged was the prohibition against dancing by the Whittier College Board of Trustees, as it was frowned upon by several of the school's large donors.[131] And they were serious. Twenty-five years before, when a local bank teller tried to organize a dance at the nearby Women's Clubhouse, the president of Whittier College protested, which led to the teller being fired and forced from the Friends Church.[132] While Nixon was not known for dancing, he had demonstrably good rhythm through his skill at playing the piano. He did not believe dancing was immoral and felt that the rule was archaic and should be changed, so he fought for dancing and didn't care whether the trustees liked him.[133] Raymond Burbank summed up Nixon by saying, "He's tough, he's always been that way. He was not soft-spoken; he was outspoken."[134]

At the same time, he was pragmatic. When he appeared before the board of trustees at the age of twenty, he advanced the argument that dances were going to take place at a variety of off-campus venues, such as "clubs, restaurants and juke joints," and that the college was far better off providing a proper environment for its students to hold dances.[135] With an allocation of $200 from the board, Nixon arranged eight dances at the Whittier Women's Club during his senior year.[136] The school yearbook raved, "After one of the most successful years the college has ever witnessed, we stop to reminisce and come to the realization that much of the success was due to the efforts of this very gentleman. Always progressive and with a liberal attitude, he has led us through the year with flying colors."[137]

While Dick enjoyed a successful college career, he and his family suffered tragedy. His brother Harold had never recovered from his bout with tuberculosis, and although he had been a well-built, husky young man full of life, over time the illness ravaged his body.[138] On March 6, 1933, Harold and Dick drove to Whittier Hardware to buy a new electric cake mixer for their mother's birthday the following day. The boys selected a $10 model, had it wrapped, and brought it home.[139]

The next morning, Dick was in the bathroom getting ready for school when Harold asked if Dick could hurry, as he didn't feel well and wanted to rest. Before Dick left, Harold reminded him to give the present to their mother that night when he returned from school. Three hours later Dick was studying in the Redwood Library when an assistant librarian came over and told him he should go home. Immediately, Dick knew what had happened. He arrived home to find a hearse in front of the house and his parents crying inconsolably as the undertaker removed Harold's body.[140]

Just as Dick was leaving for the library that morning, Harold had said, "Ask Mother to come in." That evening Dick asked his mother what had happened after he left. As Nixon described later, "She said he had asked her to put her arms around him and hold him very close. Harold was not a particularly religious boy but he said to my mother, 'This is the last time I shall see you until we meet in heaven,' and then he died."[141] Harold's services were held on March 9 at the White Emerson Chapel in Whittier, attended by Nixon's Orthogonian brothers.[142]

The following day Dick was home with his youngest brother, Edward, when an earthquake struck at 5:54 p.m. Dick grabbed three-year-old Eddie and stood in the front doorway, looking outside and watching as the power lines and power poles danced and wobbled back and forth. The devastating quake, centered in Long Beach and estimated at 6.4 on the Richter scale, significantly damaged the Nixon store and home, even knocking down Frank's handcrafted fireplace.[143]

Throughout college Dick remained dedicated to his studies, student projects, football, and the Nixon store and was described as "a brute for discipline."[144] One early job was picking string beans, working twelve hours to earn a single dollar. Nixon considered this one of the hardest jobs he'd ever had, later admitting, "I still can't stand the sight of string beans."[145] He pumped gasoline, picked fruit, lit smudge pots, culled rotten potatoes and apples, delivered groceries, and managed the produce at the Nixon store.[146] During his four years at Whittier College, he continued to wake up every day at 4:00 a.m. and drive to the Seventh Street Market in Los Angeles to select the best fruits and vegetables, returning to Whittier to wash, sort, and arrange the produce in the store before going to school by 8:00.[147] On days when the Glee Club practiced, he had to be on campus by 7:00 or face the paddle.

The store was popular, as Whittier Boulevard was Los Angeles County's busiest thoroughfare in the 1930s.[148] As the store's business grew and the Nixons' pies and baked goods became more popular, they hired more family members and neighborhood kids. The youngsters considered it an honor to be asked to work at the Nixon store.[149] Hannah was well known for her apple, pumpkin, berry, peach, raisin, and especially cherry pies.[150]

The Nixons, who were solvent and paid all their bills on time, often extended credit to customers who were struggling.[151] According to Dick's cousin Russell Harrison Jr., who stayed with the family after his mother, Elizabeth (Hannah's sister), passed away and his father remarried, the Nixons "kept a good three-fourths of East Whittier in groceries, carrying them month after month before they were paid."[152] Many of the accounts were significantly overdue, yet Frank and Hannah worked with their customers to make sure they had food and supplies, even if it meant giving the food away.[153] When heavy rains flooded the area, Frank waded through the water to the Leffingwell Ranch, carrying bags of food to make sure the Hispanic workers were cared for.[154] Despite Depression financial difficulties, in the mid-1930s Frank expanded his business to include a couple of rental houses and a small store across from East Whittier Elementary that he staffed with relatives.[155] While the Nixons' means were modest, many in the East Whittier community believed the family was wealthy, since they had a house, a service station, two stores, a rental property, two cars, and a son in college.[156]

Nixon was one of four history majors in his class, with an emphasis on constitutional history and government.[157] While Nixon developed close relationships with all his professors, his favorite was

Dr. Paul Smith, in charge of the department.[158] As was common at the time, Nixon and his fellow history majors often met at Smith's home.[159] The man was a dynamic, albeit somewhat absent-minded professor with an excellent sense of humor. He was known to wear a felt hat, which he placed on the seat in front of him in class. He sometimes got so carried away with his lecture that he would put his foot on the chair and crush the hat.[160] Smith, a liberal professor in a conservative town, inspired Nixon to analyze the Constitution and encouraged his studies, including reading John Hay and John Nicolay's ten-volume biography *Abraham Lincoln*.[161] Nixon later acknowledged that there was "no question about the influence of Paul Smith" on his thinking, and he too was liberal in college, with the caveat that he was "not a flaming liberal."[162]

Dick was analytical rather than philosophical, a pragmatist who got to the heart of an issue, and his professors rated him an exceptional student.[163] Yet he was modest about his academic success and considerate of fellow students. Classmate Channing Perdue Mason related an instance in which she embarrassed herself: "Once in Dr. Smith's class I asked a stupid question about the Wars of the Roses. Before an answer could be given, the whole class was in laughter. It was one of those things everyone else knew. Dr. Smith turned to Dick and asked him to answer me, which he did. Dr. Smith picked him because he obviously felt that he was the only one in the class who was capable of handling delicate questions with tact and diplomacy."[164]

In front of the Redwood Library, where Nixon often studied, were a patio and grass quad for students to socialize.[165] Classmate Robert Halliday, who was quarterback of the football team, explained that Nixon "didn't have the time to sit on the lawn and do nothing like some of the rest of us," yet he was known to join in bull sessions and play horseshoes.[166] Dean Triggs described the scene: "He would be just laying down the line, just talking his head off to two or three people."[167]

Throughout most of his college years, Dick continued to date Ola Welch, a vivacious young lady who was "a lot of fun," but there were periods when they broke up and dated others.[168] Nixon often double dated with classmates Hubert Perry or Clint Harris, riding around town in the rumble seat of Clint's car.[169] Frequent dates were college formals and dances at the Cocoanut Grove at the Ambassador, the Biltmore in Los Angeles, the Huntington Hotel in Pasadena, and the Villa Riviera and Pacific Coast Club in Long Beach.[170] One year Athenian Helen Hampson brought Nixon to a beach party at Ocean Park in Santa Monica, and struck by his sense of humor, she reminisced how they ran along the beach, laughing, and even went on the roller coaster, saying, "He really was a fun date."[171]

His friends knew Nixon to be generous. Classmate Richard Spaulding was invited to a formal party that Nixon was also attending. Spaulding knew Nixon had just bought a new tuxedo, so he asked to borrow Dick's old one. Nixon agreed but then tried to lend Spaulding the new tux, which Spaulding would not accept.[172] During his senior year, Nixon wanted his brothers to have "a real good meal" and arranged a dinner at the Milhous family home for his fellow Orthogonians. The Nixon family cooked chicken and Hannah baked pies. They filled two rooms with tables. After dinner, Nixon pounded out tunes on the piano while his Orthogonian brothers sang along.[173] He had a special relationship with his younger cousin Edith Gibbons, picking her up each day and driving her to college with him. As protective as any older brother, he'd admonish her for wearing too much lipstick and counsel her as to whom she should date and which clubs she should join.[174] Edith fondly recalled those rides: "He'd drive with his chin on his hand, fifteen miles per hour."[175] Another day the Nixons arranged a dinner at their home for cousin Edith and her closest girlfriends from her class. Dick, who was student body president, served them all, and Edith remembered that "the girls were so thrilled."[176]

As Nixon prepared to graduate, he was popular and was known on campus as an honest young man with unquestionable integrity.[177] Believing he got out of college only as much as he put into it, Nixon put everything into his college experience, enthusiastically participating in all aspects of college life, and earned a solid reputation for giving all he had.[178] Still, he was modest, as Professor Smith observed: "He was never a one man show trying to get ahead. Rather, he was always the representative of a loyal group."[179]

Classmate Joe Gaudio, who played sports with Nixon, sang with him in Glee Club, and was an Orthogonian brother, saw Nixon as someone who "embodied a personality and character that Whittier

College was all about; the enterprising young fellow being given an opportunity for an education, an opportunity to express the entire spectrum of his individual personality."[180] For cousin Edith, Dick was so popular and well liked that in a way she was glad to see him graduate, because she was known only as "Dick Nixon's cousin" while he was on campus.[181]

In May 1934 Nixon learned that he had been awarded a full scholarship to Duke University Law School, and he and his girlfriend, Ola, drove around town celebrating.[182] Ola recalled fondly, "He was as happy as I had ever seen him."[183] Whittier College president Walter Dexter wrote in his recommendation for Nixon to Duke, "I believe Nixon will become one of America's important, if not great leaders."[184] His classmates felt the same way, voting Nixon best man on campus.[185] Upon graduation, a group of Nixon's classmates wrote a letter to him, saying, "Out of every graduating class, there is at least one person who becomes an outstanding person and we all feel that you are destined to be that person."[186] On June 9, 1934, at 5:30 p.m., with First Lady Lou Henry Hoover serving as honored guest, Richard Nixon walked through the commencement exercises in the Whittier College Amphitheater, graduating second in his class.[187] Professor Albert Upton summed up Nixon's years at Whittier College: "He came to us as a boy, and four years later he left as a man."[188]

At the end of the summer Frank loaded up the family car and drove Dick to Duke in Durham, North Carolina.[189] Nixon remained committed to his studies and lived a Spartan existence but found time to support the Duke football team.[190] One classmate reminisced, "He was unquestionably the most enthusiastic rooter at school. I know that some students used to sit near him at the games simply because of the kick that they got out of his uninhibited manifestations of enjoyment. Sometimes after a football game, he'd be too hoarse to talk until the next day."[191] Far more significant in Duke's extremely competitive environment, Nixon was sensitive and compassionate, "a thoroughly decent guy" known for his "inner warmth."[192] Classmate Fred Cady was left disabled by polio and required crutches, so Nixon met him at the law school entrance and carried him up the steep steps and into the lecture hall every day.[193] When classmate Charles Rhyne was hospitalized for several months with a "poisoned arm," Nixon read over his notes on the day's lectures at his classmate's bedside each night so that Rhyne would not fall behind in class.[194]

Nixon attended Quaker, Presbyterian, and Methodist services while at law school, often held in the Duke University Chapel.[195] Having come from a family that taught racial equality, he was disappointed that the preachers never addressed the subject of race relations in the South.[196] The Nixon family's tolerance can be traced back to his Milhous ancestors, who were abolitionists.[197] In 1854, when Hannah's father, Franklin, was a young boy, the Milhous family farm in Jennings County, Indiana, was a safe haven for runaway slaves on the Underground Railroad.[198]

Douglas Maggs, a tough professor who taught torts and constitutional law, was known to challenge students to recite cases, leaving them flustered in front of the class.[199] When he called on Nixon, the first-year student rose from his chair and stood flat-footed, his feet spread apart, like a football tackle "hunkering down on the field."[200] Nixon was the first in his class to fight back, engaging Professor Maggs as he recited his cases. When Nixon finished, everyone, including Maggs, believed it had been a great performance.[201] Nixon was named to *Duke Law Review*, where he had two items published, and he even received a commendation from U.S. Supreme Court justice Robert Jackson.[202] Well liked by his classmates, he was elected president of the Duke Law School Student Bar Association over Hale McCown, who was the most popular student in his class.[203]

Dick missed the family Christmas celebration for the first time in his life now that he was living in North Carolina. He wrote to his beloved grandmother Almira, "At this Christmas season I should like to be sending you a gift which would really express my love for you—but it will probably be several years before I reach such a high financial level—if ever." The note went on to say that instead of a present, he was sending her "this Christmas note."[204] Homesickness made the holidays difficult for Nixon, but fortunately, Professor William Roalfe and his wife invited Nixon and some classmates into their home for Christmas.[205] Having recently received a shipment of avocados, Dick prepared one of Almira's specialties, avocado on toast, which, after some hesitation, his dinner mates found to be delicious.[206]

Nixon returned to Whittier for the summers, and though he and Ola tried to maintain a long-distance relationship while he was away at law school, it proved too difficult. In the summer of 1935 he enjoyed several dates with Marie Actis.[207] Marie and, even more significantly, her mother found Dick to be "a perfect gentleman all the time."[208] One memorable evening was spent on a gambling ship off the coast of Long Beach, where Nixon promptly hit the jackpot on a quarter slot machine, enabling the couple to celebrate with a nice dinner.[209]

Nixon graduated second in his class in June 1937. Duke Law School dean H. Claude Horack saw Nixon as "one of the finest young men, both in character and ability."[210] Believing that the best route to politics was through one's hometown, Horack advised Nixon, "If you want to go into politics, you had better go back to Whittier and go into a local law firm."[211] Classmate Sigrid Pedersen understood that Nixon planned to practice law in California: "He was always very much a Californian and did quietly cant the glories of his home state."[212] For Frank Nixon, who had quit school when he was thirteen, this moment was one of the high points of his life, and he drove Hannah, Don, Edward, and Almira Milhous across the country to attend Dick's graduation.[213] Kenneth Ball, a Whittier College classmate who knew the entire family, summed up Frank's joy: "Mr. Nixon came here to California, uneducated and had to work at whatever work he could. It was a dream to see his kids educated and able to have a better place in life than he had."[214]

....

FIVE

Service to Community and Country

1937–45

O n returning to Whittier, Nixon celebrated his law school graduation with dinner at the famed Paris Inn in downtown Los Angeles. The setting resembled a Parisian street scene, right down to the Eiffel Tower, where patrons were entertained by Bert Rovere's singing waiters, and Nixon enjoyed seeing iconic comedians Stan Laurel and Oliver Hardy.[1] After the homecoming celebration, Nixon's first order of business was to secure a position at Wingert & Bewley, Whittier's oldest and best law firm, on the sixth floor of the Bank of America Building at the center of town.[2]

Partner Tom Bewley, who belonged to the Franklin Society at Whittier College, had a lifelong association with the Milhous family. He first met Franklin Milhous as a child in Butlerville, Indiana, where Tom's and Dick's grandfathers were old friends.[3] When Bewley's family moved to California, young Tom was ill with pneumonia, and Franklin insisted the Bewley family live at a property he owned, where they stayed for two years.[4] Bewley had known Frank and Hannah for years, as even when Bewley could barely afford one secretary during the Depression, he still rushed out every Saturday morning to buy a Nixon cherry pie for 35 cents.[5] He had to be at the store by 10:00 a.m. or Hannah's pies would be sold out, but it was well worth it to him. He recalled, "They were the most delicious pies I've ever had."[6]

In the spring of 1937 Hannah approached Bewley about hiring Dick.[7] Knowing of Nixon since his days at Whittier High School, Bewley asked Professor Paul Smith and others if they thought he should hire Nixon.[8] Smith later admitted that his reply—it "would not be a mistake" to hire Nixon—was the "most colossal understatement" he ever made in his life.[9] After returning from Duke, Dick met with Bewley, who was impressed by Nixon's "mature looks, actions, and thinking." He recalled that Dick "was decisive; he knew what he wanted; he was direct and to the point."[10] Likewise, Bewley's secretary Evlyn Dorn remembered Nixon as "very punctual, very correct, and neatly dressed in a blue serge suit. He looked the part."[11] At that first interview, Bewley and Nixon discussed the practice of law and Nixon's desire to participate in community affairs.[12] Immediately deciding to hire Nixon, Bewley didn't even inquire about Nixon's scholastic record before offering him a position: "I talked to him for ten minutes. I was satisfied he knew more law than I did and I knew he was top-flight."[13]

Wingert & Bewley arranged for Nixon to take the bar exam, providing him office space in which to study and a six-week Burby law review course.[14] Nixon usually prepared for the bar in the comfortable solitude of his grandmother's house for up to sixteen hours a day, taking breaks when Almira prepared his favorite dish, finely chipped beef on toast.[15] On warm summer days, he often did his studying at the shore in Long Beach, from which he returned with a tan.[16] He also gained practical experience by researching cases, drawing up contracts, and preparing briefs for Bewley, who even brought Nixon along to court. In reviewing Nixon's work, Bewley was "immediately impressed" with his succinct writing style.[17]

After taking the three-day bar exam on September 7–9, 1937, Nixon told Bewley, "I felt like I really answered the questions and knocked them over."[18] Sure enough, Nixon passed, and on November 9, with a backlog of work waiting for him, he went to the supreme court in San Francisco to be sworn into the California bar at the earliest possible moment.[19]

Nixon was essentially a country lawyer handling a multitude of legal matters. Bewley, as city attorney, named him assistant city attorney, with Nixon taking over the misdemeanor criminal case trials, drafting ordinances, and keeping the council happy.[20] Whenever the city clerk had a legal question, Bewley told him, "Go see Dick Nixon."[21] Nixon demonstrated his problem-solving abilities when it was discovered that the Boston Café, a "greasy spoon" in the center of town, was selling alcohol within city limits, and Whittier Quakers could not tolerate such "hoodlumism."[22] Bewley relayed how Nixon handled the situation:

The city fathers called me on the carpet one day and said, "You know the police department thinks there is liquor being sold in this café." It was illegal to serve liquor there. So I said, "Dick, we've got to do something about that, and I wish you'd take on the project." Dick contacted the chief of police, who was a very understanding man, and the first thing I knew they had an officer down there in front of that café. Every time someone came out of the café staggering or reeling and had alcohol on his breath, the police picked him up and Dick would prosecute the drunkenness charge. Those prosecutions were so successful that the café closed in a short while and we had the problem solved. The city fathers were very pleased with the Assistant City Attorney's work. This was a practical approach that he applied to the elimination of the nuisance.[23]

So that Nixon could gain experience as a trial lawyer, Bewley brought him along whenever he had a trial in the superior court. The firm represented Victor York, a local oilman, as a defendant in a fraud case involving oil and gas, and Nixon prepared the trial brief. Bewley's partner Henry Knoop tried the case before Judge Ruben Schmidt, and the opposing counsel was a member of the Los Angeles City Council. The case against York was weak; the defense rested after the plaintiff rested, and Judge Schmidt immediately issued a judgment for defendant York. At one point during the trial, Bewley saw Nixon with a legal pad and stopwatch and asked what he was doing. To his surprise, Nixon had been timing how long the attorneys spoke, how long the witnesses testified, and how long it took the judge to make rulings and decide the case.[24] Bewley was amazed, recalling, "He made constant notes during the trial and learned more about the case, just by sitting there, than did I, who represented the defendant."[25]

Nixon made one of his first court appearances after Bewley woke up ill and asked him to stand in on short notice. This was one of Bewley's more complicated cases involving judgment creditor rights at a court-ordered execution sale.[26] Bewley's client, Marie Schee, had a judgment of $2,160.75 against her uncle, Otto Steuer, and was forcing the sale of his home to satisfy the debt. Nixon appeared at the sale and acquired the real property to satisfy the outstanding judgment. The property was worth $6,500 and outstanding liens totaled $3,000 against the property, so when the senior lien holder started foreclosure proceedings, Bewley recommended that Schee's stepmother buy out the senior lien holder and, for unknown reasons, that she continue with the foreclosure, which she did. At the foreclosure sale, a third party bought the property for the value of senior liens, and the client ended up with no property and no money to collect on her judgment, so she claimed legal malpractice against Nixon and the firm.[27] While the mistake, if any, was Bewley's, the claim haunted Nixon, and from then on, he carried annual date books filled with copious notes regarding his conduct as an attorney, including any mistakes he made, so that he might reflect on his practice and continue to grow as a lawyer.[28]

Nixon often worked through lunch, dining on hamburgers and pineapple malts that Evlyn Dorn bought for him next door at McNair's Drugstore.[29] When the office closed at day's end, Dick and Bewley enjoyed sitting in the law library for bull sessions about their cases and legal issues of the day.[30] Though a dyed-in-the-wool Quaker, Nixon sometimes used off-color expressions, such as describing a cantankerous witness as "a bitch on wheels" or referring to a difficult situation as "strong and formidable as a brick shit house."[31]

Nixon routinely handled family law cases but found divorces particularly unsettling. He was initially surprised by some of the intimate matters involved, as well as by the fact that people could calmly sit down and tell a relative stranger about them. He believed it was his duty to talk his clients into reconciling, though he seldom succeeded.[32] He even ruminated over a case to a friend one evening: "I did everything I could to persuade them to stay together, but they were as adamant as mules. I can't understand why they didn't even try to make an effort at reconciliation."[33] He described another aspect of his distaste for divorce work: "I had a divorce to handle and this good-looking girl, beautiful, really, began talking to me about her intimate marriage problems. . . . I turned fifteen colors of the rainbow. I suppose I came from a family too un-modern, really. Any kind of personal confession is embarrassing to me personally."[34] Not surprisingly, Nixon was relieved to expand his practice to other areas and soon became Wingert & Bewley's chief trial lawyer.[35] In his first eighteen months Nixon handled nine civil trials, most of which were in superior courts of Orange and Los Angeles Counties, including the granite-and-red-stone Orange County Courthouse in Santa Ana, and in courtrooms at the Los Angeles City Hall.[36]

With his experience in theater and public speaking, Nixon had a dramatic flair in court. According to Bewley, when Nixon was in trial, "he had the right stance, he used the right voice, his voice was low, he built it up. He dressed for the part."[37] His talents served him well, and soon Nixon developed a reputation as an aggressive courtroom attorney: "He could talk so that butter wouldn't melt in his mouth, or he could take hold of a cantankerous witness and shake him like a dog."[38]

Skilled at research, Nixon reduced arguments to the essentials and had an uncanny ability to pick out the principle of law involved, then cite relevant case authority where the court had previously ruled in his favor on the issue.[39] Nixon liked to pace behind his desk as he dictated correspondence and legal briefs, which led the partners to joke that he'd "wear out that carpet before he wears out any of the rest of the office."[40] He was a tireless worker; many nights, as patrons of the nearby Wardman Theatre walked to their cars, they would see Nixon up in his sixth-floor office working as late as 10:30 or 11:00 p.m.[41] Yet he was far from a taskmaster. Evlyn Dorn, who by 1939 was Dick's legal secretary, described him as a very considerate person, "the kind of man you wanted to do your best for."[42] As Bewley put it, "Dick is a natural leader, and in times of stress or times of inquiry, he is the type of person that people naturally turn to. He's strong. He's forthright. He's lucid in his thinking, acting and talking."[43]

While Nixon was driving with a client, local accountant Raymond Black, to an emergency meeting called on short notice, his car ran out of gas not far from their destination. A hill lay between them and their meeting place. Nixon surveyed the situation, took off his coat, and told Black, "If we push the car to the top of the hill, we'll get there in time yet."[44] At the meeting, which Black described as a "touchy situation that had to be handled right," Nixon, unflustered, "did a perfect job."[45]

Many of the firm's clients congratulated Wingert & Bewley on having such a bright young attorney in the office and only wanted Nixon to handle their cases.[46] Often seen driving around town in his Model A Cabriolet, Nixon enjoyed a good rapport with clients, including Dema Harshbarger, Heda Hopper's secretary, who hired Nixon to prepare her will.[47] Bewley recalled, "Up to the day she passed away, she kept telling me how great Dick had been in handling her affairs."[48] Wingert & Bewley concluded that hiring Nixon was one of the best decisions the firm had ever made.[49]

Nixon's practice included drafting wills, handling estates, and dealing with various other matters, including federal income taxes and at least one adoption.[50] Initially earning $50 per month for the first two months, he eventually was paid a salary of $250 per month. Ultimately, Nixon made $1,480 in 1938, $2,970 in 1939, and $3,971 in 1940.[51] He charged as little as $1 for general legal advice and as much as $40 for divorces, but handling estates brought in the largest fees, ranging from $15 to $400.[52]

Nixon's reputation for excellence soon became known in the community. One Whittier attorney reflected to his wife, Annabelle Tupper, "All my life I've associated with young men, and I've never seen anyone Richard's age with such a good judicial mind."[53] He was "driven, popular and highly successful" and enjoyed an active social calendar.[54] For relaxation, he enjoyed playing handball, bridge, poker, swimming, movies, dancing, and reading, with Sundays reserved as a family day. After church, Hannah, Frank, and their boys took trips to the beach or to a cousin's cabin in the local mountains.[55] They spent Sunday evenings at home, sitting around the fireplace and making popcorn, content in each other's company.[56]

Wallace Black was another young Whittier attorney.[57] He and Nixon were members of the 20-30 Club, a service organization, and also belonged to the Young Republican Club. Black reflected, "We all knew that he had political ambitions. He was . . . the fair-haired boy among the Quakers here."[58] One day Black ran into Nixon in the office elevator and suggested he audition for the Whittier Community Players, a local theater group.[59] Black then called theater director Louise Baldwin, suggesting she call Nixon to persuade him to join, which she did.[60]

Dick Nixon appeared in three productions: *First Lady*, *Dark Tower*, and *Night of January 16th*, where he played a lawyer.[61] In *Night of January 16th*, a courtroom drama by Ayn Rand, Nixon played the lead opposite longtime friend Hortense Behrens.[62] Billed as a "baffling thriller with a unique plot," the story was a murder trial, with the audience issuing verdicts each night.[63] Nixon was a success, projecting a delightful warmth on stage.[64] But it was the audition for *Dark Tower*, a mystery drama, that would prove life-changing for young Dick Nixon.[65]

Pat Ryan taught evening classes in shorthand at Whittier Union High School, and her supervisor suggested she try out for the *Dark Tower*, as did student Elizabeth Cloes, telling Pat that there was "a perfectly charming young man" she wanted her friend to meet.[66] Elizabeth then told Nixon that a "glamorous" new schoolteacher was going to try out for the play.[67] On the evening of the audition, Elizabeth met Pat for dinner at the Hoover Hotel before they walked to the Saint Matthias Church together.[68]

When Dick arrived at the church, his friend Grant Garman helped introduce him to Pat.[69] According to Garman, Pat was "a very striking and beautiful girl, pleasant and animated. Dick just took one look at her and that was it."[70] Nixon himself admitted, "I found I could not take my eyes away from her. For me it was a case of love at first sight."[71]

That first evening and frequently thereafter, Nixon drove Pat home in his Model A.[72] Normally shy and reserved, Dick told Pat, "You may not believe this, but I am going to marry you some day."[73] Though she later acknowledged admiring Dick "from the very beginning," Pat also admitted, "I thought he was nuts or something. I couldn't imagine anyone ever saying something like that so suddenly. Now that I know Dick much better, I can't imagine that he would ever say that, because he is very much the opposite, he's more reserved."[74] On February 17, the evening of the first performance of *Dark Tower*, Dick brought Pat home to meet his parents.[75]

Pat Ryan was born Thelma Catherine Ryan on the day before St. Patrick's Day, March 16, 1912, in Ely, Nevada. Dubbed Pat by her father, she was the youngest by two years, with brothers Bill born in 1910 and Tom in 1911. She also had two older half-siblings, Neva Bender, born in 1909, and Matt Bender, born 1907, from her mother's first husband, who had died in a flash flood.[76] Pat's father suffered from silicosis, a disease miners contracted from breathing dust, so his wife persuaded him to move the family to California when Pat was a year old, and they settled in Artesia, a tiny hamlet twenty miles southeast of Los Angeles best known for its beet dumps.[77] Pat was raised in a white ranch house on ten acres on South Street near Pioneer Boulevard about a mile east of town.[78] Like the Nixons during their early days in Yorba Linda, the Ryans didn't have gas or electricity and relied on coal lamps.[79] There was no interior bathroom, and Pat's "bedroom" was really just the back area of the front room.[80]

Pat's mother, Katherine Halberstadt Bender Ryan, was a German Lutheran with a thick accent who loved to bake bread, pies, and cinnamon rolls.[81] Her father, William M. Ryan Sr., was a tall, kind man of Irish descent, with a wonderful sense of humor, who enjoyed amusing the children with jokes while never cracking a smile.[82] The Ryans farmed their land, growing corn, potatoes, tomatoes, peppers, and cauliflower.[83]

Possessing an independent streak, a temper, and her father's sense of humor, Pat rode her family's work horses bareback for fun.[84] She was athletic and insisted on wearing overalls to school rather than dresses.[85] She and her brothers walked to Artesia Grammar School, an old red-brick building on Pioneer Boulevard, and their classmates were a diverse group, among them Mexican and Japanese children.[86]

In 1926, during Pat's freshman year at Excelsior High School, her mother died of cancer.[87] Following the services at the Bellflower Undertaking Company, Pat's half sister, Neva, moved in with her paternal grandparents in Los Angeles, so it fell to Pat to cook, wash, and iron for her father and her two brothers, though Neva returned on weekends to help.[88] Though she was barely a teenager, Pat managed to keep a "very neat and clean" home.[89]

Pat joined the debate team, dramatic club, and Spanish club, and she was involved in student government and the scholarship society.[90] Nicknamed "Buddy" by her friends, she was seen as one who "could do anything well when she put her mind to it," a "very friendly, rather vivacious" classmate, yet "quiet and hard-working."[91] Among the top students in her class, Pat was advanced two grades and eventually graduated the same year as her brother Tom and the eldest, Bill, who had been held back a year.[92]

Pat loved the ocean, and her favorite beach was at the foot of Bixby Park in Long Beach, where she sometimes brought along a hand-crank record player.[93] Pat and the Raine sisters, Louise and

Myrtle, her closest friends and neighbors, enjoyed the ocean so much that they rode their bicycles more than ten miles from their homes to get there, though they usually borrowed a car.[94] Pat, who had a license since age fourteen, was the designated driver.[95] Pat, Louise, and Myrtle were lured by the new sport of surfing and took to the waves next to Rainbow Pier at the Pike in Long Beach.[96] When not in the water, Pat and her friends frequented the Pike's dance auditoriums, skating rinks, and chop suey parlors, where they could enjoy five rides for 50 cents and have a complete Chinese dinner for another 50 cents.[97]

While in high school, Pat worked as a teller at Artesia First National Bank and Trust.[98] Howard Frampton, who ran the bank, saw Pat as "a hard worker and a mighty fine girl . . . a first-class citizen even in her early years."[99] Following high school, Pat took shorthand at Woodbury College in Los Angeles while continuing to live at home, caring for her father as his silicosis worsened.[100] After a brief stay at the Dore Sanitarium in Monrovia, he died on May 7, 1930.[101]

She officially changed her name to Pat to honor her father after his death.[102] She enrolled at Fullerton Junior College and joined the drama club, playing the lead in *Broken Dishes*.[103] Pat and her brother Tom lived at the family home, and she continued to work at the local bank. One eventful day, she was robbed at gunpoint and forced to hand over $2,000 from her teller cage.[104] When culprit was apprehended, Pat had to appear in court and testify at his trial.[105]

In 1934 she entered the University of Southern California on a research fellowship, where she met Virginia Shugart.[106] They often worked as extras in movies, with Pat earning $25 for an uncredited dancing scene in *Becky Sharp*, as well as $7 per day for *The Great Ziegfeld* and *Small Town Girl*.[107] Pat also waited on customers at the glamorous Bullocks Wilshire.[108]

After graduating cum laude from USC in 1937, Pat immediately accepted a teaching job at Whittier Union High School, making $1,800 a year. She later said the only reason she took the position was that she was destined to meet Richard Nixon in his hometown.[109] Pat moved to Whittier, renting a room from Raymond Collins and his wife. She treated herself to dinner at Whittier's Green Arbor Restaurant once a week.[110] At Whittier High, Pat impressed students and teachers alike.[111] She taught shorthand, stenography, general business, and typing in the Business Education Department.[112]

Despite initial progress, Dick's budding relationship with Pat did not proceed as rapidly as he'd hoped, but he was persistent, even showing up unannounced in hopes of spending time with her.[113] Some of Pat's male high school students were so taken with her that they would go by her apartment at night. They'd occasionally find Pat and Dick sitting in his car, where they would then shine lights on them.[114] While Pat was not as immediately smitten as Dick, she was sufficiently impressed that she told her friends that Nixon was "going to be president someday."[115]

Pat and Dick had a great deal in common: they were the same age, were raised in rural settings, succeeded in school, and had skipped the second grade. The two had also suffered immediate family members' tragic deaths while still young. In terms of personality, both were very private and described as reserved, yet acted in theater, participated in debate, and served in student government.[116] Emotionally, they were "orderly in their thinking, meticulously organized, slow to anger, and even-tempered."[117] They also shared a love for the outdoors, especially the beach and the Pacific Ocean, and were dedicated sports fans.[118]

On New Year's Day 1939, when Duke played USC in the Rose Bowl, a very excited Nixon landed tickets for the "Grandaddy of them all."[119] With Duke leading 3–0 as the clock wound down to the final minute, USC came roaring back to score a touchdown, winning the game and handing Duke its only loss of the season.[120] Pat's brother Bill, a USC fan who liked to kid Dick about the loss, described Nixon's reaction: "He always took it very gracious, saying 'Well, some are won and some are lost, but we always try hard.'"[121]

Since Pat enjoyed ice-skating, each week she, Dick, and their friends skated at the Iceland rink in Paramount.[122] Kenneth Ball, Nixon's debate partner at Whittier College, who had grown up ice-skating in Iowa, was surprised when Nixon turned up to practice at the Iceland rink: "After about three afternoons of practice, he wasn't getting any better, in fact, he was getting worse. I remember him flying out of control and hitting his face on the ice so hard that he was all covered in blood. I picked him up and asked him, 'Dick, why do you keep doing this?' His answer was, 'I've got a great date to go ice-skating with on Saturday night and I *must* be able to keep up with her.'"[123]

As their relationship progressed, their range of activities expanded to include skiing in the mountains and golf lessons at a club in La Habra Heights.[124] They frequented the Cocoanut Grove, Biltmore, Hollywood Bowl, and the famed Philippe's in Los Angeles for French dip sandwiches.[125] Pat's brother Tom coached football at Glendale Junior College, and she introduced Dick to her brothers when Tom's team played Compton Community College in 1939.[126] When she and Dick weren't cheering on USC or Whittier, they often attended Tom's games.[127]

Pat and Dick frequently double-dated with Virginia Shugart and her fiancé, J. Curtis Counts.[128] Curtis described a memorable evening at Topsy's nightclub in nearby South Gate: "We thought it was a wild place because they had striptease dancers there. Dick made us dress up in way-out clothes for the occasion. He put on his mother's raccoon coat, which made him look extraordinary."[129]

The couple's happiest times were at their favorite courting places at the ocean in Seal Beach, Laguna Beach, and San Clemente, often taking Dick's Irish setter, King, to the beach to run on the sand or enjoy a picnics and sunset.[130] Pat later reminisced, "When I first knew him, right after the Depression, we didn't have a dime, but we had fun."[131]

By 1938, already a successful attorney and treasurer of the Whittier Bar Association, Nixon decided to venture into private enterprise with Ralph Ober and Don Brings, who were developing a frozen orange juice business.[132] They had a unique formula for preserving juice by freezing it in plastic bags, and many believed it was the finest orange juice they had ever tasted.[133] Nixon was enthusiastic, serving as president and drafting the articles of incorporation to form the Citri-Frost Company, which issued 125 shares of stock with a par value of $125 per share.[134]

By March 1939 they commenced construction of a fifty-by-fifty-foot plant, which Frank Nixon helped build in nearby Pico, and began purchasing equipment.[135] By August Citri-Frost had contracts in place to sell its orange juice at 85 cents a gallon.[136] Over 21,000 gallons of orange, lemon, and grapefruit juice were squeezed from seven thousand boxes of fruit, and nearly two-thirds of the inventory quickly sold.[137] Citri-Frost was producing 425 gallons of juice per eight-hour period.[138] Clients included Streamland Park, an amusement park west of Whittier; the Owl Drug Company, with stores throughout Los Angeles; and Matson Navigation, with a fleet of ocean liners. Anticipated contracts were as large as $150,000.[139] After practicing law all day, Nixon rushed to the plant to cut and squeeze oranges late into the night, where, according to Bewley, he "worked like a dog."[140] Money was tight at the fledgling business, but Dick was dedicated to its success, even enlisting his father to work long hours to save on labor costs.[141]

A tireless worker, Nixon was described as "the type of person that . . . no matter what was going on, he was always in the middle of it."[142] He joined civic-minded organizations and soon became a leader in his community.[143] He lived by this philosophy: "You must live your life for something more important than your life alone. One who has never lost himself in a cause bigger than himself has missed one of life's mountaintop experiences. Only by losing yourself in this way can you really find yourself."[144]

The local 20-30 Club limited its membership to men between twenty and thirty years of age.[145] This was a highly dedicated group of young men, and as Donald Fantz described it, "The 20-30 Club, back in those days was more than just a club, actually it was kind of a way of life."[146] Club members furnished the manpower to help build the swimming pool for the local YMCA, worked to convert an old cemetery to Founders Park, and sponsored a Boy Scout troop and YMCA club for Latino kids in an area known as "Jim Town."[147] Fantz reminisced, "We had a tremendous amount of good times and fun and Dick entered into that very spiritedly."[148]

On June 6, 1939, "well-known Whittier attorney" Richard Nixon was elected president of the Whittier 20-30 Club.[149] He held board meetings in his law office and weekly Tuesday evening dinner meetings at the William Penn Hotel on Philadelphia Street.[150] He ensured that the program chairman had guest speakers lined up, assessed fines of a nickel or dime, and even played the piano as his fellow members sang along.[151] Nixon impressed member Doug Ferguson as friendly and gracious, with "a very nice ability to work with people." His success was evident as he concluded his term as club president at a January 1940 dinner dance he'd organized, where a record number of ten new members were initiated into the club.[152]

The 20-30 Club was just one part of Nixon's civic involvement. On Tuesday, October 25, 1938, the community held a preelection meeting at the Jonathan Bailey School Auditorium, where Nixon led a lively discussion on a ballot proposition regarding veteran benefits.[153] He was the general chairman of the Inter-Service Club Banquet, with more than three hundred members of the 20-30 Club, Rotary, Kiwanis, Lions, Progress, and Junior Chamber of Commerce in attendance at the Women's Club House.[154] He was president of the Duke Alumni Association, program chairman for the Junior Chamber of Commerce, taught a course in practical law at Whittier College, and was elected the first president of the newly formed Orange County Association of Cities.[155] At the 1938 Whittier College Homecoming, Nixon was honored to be elected president of the Whittier College Alumni Association.[156] He even found time to oversee the Orthogonians' initiation rituals at his friend Judge Frank Swain's home in East Whittier.[157]

In 1939 Nixon was the youngest person ever invited to join the prestigious Whittier College Board of Trustees, a distinguished group that included former First Lady Lou Henry Hoover, whom Nixon found to be "vivacious, thoughtful and a stimulating conversationalist."[158] At the same time, he became more active with the East Whittier Friends Church, singing bass in the choir and even persuading his brother Don to join.[159] He also taught a popular Quaker young people's class there, leading religious discussions, coaching the students on public speaking, and taking them on outings to the beach.[160]

Apart from his law practice, Citri-Frost, civic groups, and church, Dick continued courting Pat, and she grew closer to the Nixon family.[161] She helped Hannah bake pies in the mornings and worked at the store on Saturdays and during the summer.[162] Dick usually stopped by the store to pick her up in the afternoon, but she also had a room at the Nixon home in case she wanted to spend the night.[163] Dick's brother Eddie, seventeen years younger, also was immediately taken with Pat, and one of the first times they met, she took him to Huntington Beach, where they spent the afternoon having foot races in the sand.[164] Dick took his younger brother under his wing, and in 1939, when he decided to buy a new coupe through his Whittier College classmate Clint Harris, Dick and nine-year-old Eddie took a train to Lansing, Michigan, and then spent spring break driving home together across the country.[165] Eddie enjoyed time with his brother because Dick "had a way of intriguing kids."[166]

In late summer 1939 Frank and Hannah purchased the Stoody estate on Worsham Drive. Overlooking Whittier College, the estate had a view of Los Angeles, and Frank landscaped the terraced hillside with an incredible flowing fountain and ponds.[167] Frank was very proud of their large and elegant new home, which had a main floor with a living room, dining room, kitchen, breakfast room, and garage, as well as bedrooms for each son on the floor below.[168] The house had a circular turret observatory with a rotating, retractable roof, but Frank cautioned the family, "No, I don't want to open that turret. It might start leaking," so the observatory became Dick's study.[169]

Though he now lived just blocks from his law office, in August, the twenty-six-year-old Nixon established a branch office for Wingert & Bewley in La Habra, across the county line from East Whittier.[170] The Nixons were well known in this small, lawyerless crossroads community, surrounded by walnut, avocado, and citrus groves, and Dick's arrival made front-page news in the *La Habra Star*.[171] Initially, Nixon intended to occupy a room at his dentist's office, but he decided that crying children would not be good for business.[172] Instead, he set up his office in the rear of the Ben Roberts Realty office.[173]

In La Habra, Nixon and several local businessmen typically met for morning coffee at Epperly's pharmacy.[174] J. W. Burch, who owned a Ford dealership, was president of the chamber of commerce and appointed Nixon as one of the chamber's directors.[175] Nixon also joined—and incorporated—the La Habra Kiwanis, serving as program chairman.[176] His legal clients included the Hacienda Country Club, the La Habra Valley Riding Club, and the local water company.[177]

Burch arranged for Nixon to speak at a joint meeting of the La Habra and Whittier Kiwanis Clubs at the William Penn, where Nixon gave a speech titled "The Nine Old Men of the Supreme Court." He told the groups, "So long as we have the procedural guarantees which the Constitution gives us, such as free speech, free assembly, freedom of worship and religion, no dictator can reign in this country. These guarantees are the greatest guardianship against a dictatorship. We citizens of the United States accept the privileges the Constitution has bestowed on us and we should accept the responsibilities which go with those privileges."[178] Following this "tremendously interesting" speech, Nixon was booked for speaking engagements at Lions, Kiwanis, Elks, and Rotary Clubs across Southern California, where he'd even play all the different clubs' songs on the piano.[179]

Ever since his freshman year in college, when he lost a front tooth playing basketball, Nixon had a gold bridge.[180] According to Nixon, Pat had an obsession about good dentistry and insisted that he have it replaced with a porcelain bridge.[181] Nixon was not necessarily the best dental patient, even one time biting the dental assistant's finger, but ultimately saw the dentist so much that he even had him over for dinner.[182] The dental work apparently paid off; in March 1940 Dick and Pat drove down Golden Lantern Street to the cliffs of Dana Point, overlooking San Clemente beach, and as they sat in his Oldsmobile, Dick proposed and Pat immediately accepted.[183]

Nixon, believing "a man only buys a ring once in his lifetime, and that should be a ring that his wife would always be proud to wear," bought an engagement ring for $324 at the jewelry exchange on Spring Street in Los Angeles and had it wrapped in flowers at Malins Flower Shop in Whittier.[184] His cousin Tom Seulke delivered the flowers to Pat in her classroom at Whittier High, but neither Pat nor Tom knew there was a ring in the flower wrapping, which Pat threw out as she put the flowers in a vase. Nixon had to rush to the school, arriving after the janitor had dumped the trash, and comb through rubbish to find the ring.[185] Luckily, he did, and Pat and Dick announced their engagement at a dinner party at Tom Bewley's home.[186] Frank and Hannah were ecstatic, celebrating with a preengagement party at their Worsham home on May 1.[187] Hannah also hosted a wedding shower at the Green Arbor Restaurant, where she said, beaming, "We're so fond of Pat, and we're going to help her feel at home with us."[188]

On the afternoon of June 21, 1940, Dick and Pat, attended by a small group of family members and friends, drove to Riverside and were married by W. O. Mendenhall, president of Whittier College, in the Presidential Suite of the Mission Inn.[189] Ed Nixon described the scene: "Medieval Spanish artwork and stained-glass windows created a warm, colorful atmosphere. Heavy drapery in Mediterranean hues decorated the ceiling of the small chapel where Dick and Pat said their Quaker vows."[190] Following the service, there was a small reception in the Spanish art gallery of the inn, where guests enjoyed a wedding cake that Frank had baked and Hannah carried on her lap in the car to ensure its safe arrival.[191] A large wedding reception was held at Hannah and Frank's Worsham home, and the following day the *Whittier News* reported, "A wedding of interest to many local people took place yesterday afternoon."[192]

The newlyweds' first apartment was in Long Beach, where they discovered their favorite Chinese restaurant, a tiny family establishment that served the best fried shrimp they'd ever had. There was also Vivian Laird's steakhouse, where they enjoyed dinner and an evening of dancing for $5.[193] When summer was over they moved to a tiny apartment with a living room, bedroom, kitchen, and bath over a garage in La Habra Heights, near Whittier.[194] From there they moved to a small, newly constructed bungalow with a kitchenette at the rear of a fourplex in Whittier, which they rented for $35 a month.[195] Nixon described each apartment as "a step upwards," and they eventually moved into one of Frank's three rental houses on Whittier Boulevard, across from East Whittier Elementary.[196]

Shortly after their wedding, the Nixons began their lifelong friendship with Jack and Helene Drown.[197] Helene taught at Whittier High with Pat, who was chairman of the school's Pep Committee.[198] Pat asked Helene to assist her, and they immediately hit it off, with Dick and Jack becoming fast friends as well.[199] To Helene, Pat "had gaiety and a love for life, and a sparkle in her eye that just was very radiant and very contagious," and Dick was an "immensely interesting, fun-loving, creative and great man."[200]

Dick and Pat were very active. They bowled and attended Whittier College plays, alumni activities, and local dances.[201] Nixon's cousin Wilma Funk was a waitress at Hillman Café on Whittier Boulevard, where Pat and Dick's favorites were the signature dishes of liver and onions and banana cream pie.[202] They took in baseball games at Hollywood Park and enjoyed dancing the conga at Earl Carroll's outlandish Hollywood nightclub on Sunset Boulevard.[203] At Earl Carroll's, male patrons participated in a garter toss contest, where showgirls lay on the dance floor with one leg extended into the air, and the men tossed garter "hoops" to see who could land the most around the women's legs—a contest Nixon won.[204]

Pat and Dick's growing social group included Virginia and Curtis Counts, Evlyn and Laurence Dorn, Jack and Helene Drown, Alyce and Eugene Koch, and Don Nixon, and they often met for dinner parties where they played charades and sang along as Dick played the piano.[205] As ambitious as he was, Nixon had a personable and humorous side, which he indulged among friends. Virginia Counts said of Dick, "I was impressed by his wit. He was fun to be with."[206] To Eugene Koch, Nixon "was interested in everyone he met," a man "full of passion" for life. He especially enjoyed situation humor, pointing out incongruities rather than joke-telling, relating funny stories to cases he was handling.[207] Nixon later reflected on those first years of marriage: "We had many good times going out with old friends. . . . It was a period when we really enjoyed life to the full."[208] When members of their social circle were married, they stood up for each other's weddings, as Dick did in the weddings of Virginia and Curtis Counts, Lincoln Dietrick, and Dean Triggs.[209]

Unfortunately, during this time of tremendous personal and professional success, Citri-Frost was proving to be a difficult challenge. In December 1940 the company contracted for a train boxcar of over six thousand gallons of product to be shipped to New York City. The refrigeration failed and the orange juice warmed, which caused the bags to burst, resulting in a total loss and a sticky mess when the train arrived in New York.[210] Then by mid-1941 the plastic bags Citri-Frost had purchased turned out to be defective and did not seal properly, so there were complaints about the taste, and many shareholders wanted out.[211] By December 1941 the business failed.[212] Feeling that he had not met his moral obligation, Dick sat in his car in the parking lot of Whittier First Friends Church one afternoon, pouring his heart out to Evlyn Dorn, then personally repaid the shareholders' losses from his own funds.[213] Later he commented, "I experienced my first, and I trust my last, failure in business."[214]

In November 1941 Nixon received a telegram from the Office of Price Administration for an interview at the Biltmore Hotel in Los Angeles, as David Cavers, son of the Duke Law School dean, had recommended him.[215] Nixon sat for the interview and was offered a position, which he accepted, believing that it would give him an opportunity to participate in events that would "shape the life of America and the world for years to come."[216] Just a few weeks later

Pat and Dick emerged from a Hollywood theater after a matinee on Sunday, December 7, and learned of the attack on Pearl Harbor when a newspaper boy told Nixon, "We're at war, mister."[217] Pat and Dick immediately went to Frank and Hannah's home to listen to reports on the radio.[218]

Less than a month later, on January 2, 1942, the *Whittier News* reported in a front-page article, "Nixon to Washington."[219] Pat and Dick immediately left for the capital, where Nixon was well received at the Office of Price Administration.[220] In time, however, he became impatient with bureaucratic red tape and incompetence, witnessing the effect of the war and its threat to the American way of life.[221] Wanting to do more for his country, he joined the U.S. Navy, a decision that could not have been easy for Nixon, having been raised a Quaker, historically a religion of pacifists who were conscientious objectors during wartime.

While a student at Whittier College, Nixon had frequently walked through the foyer of the administration building, noting two service flags hanging in that hall. One flag had stars on it, each for a soldier who had served in World War I. Alongside was another flag with the names of conscientious objectors, each name marked by a peace symbol.[222] The two sets of flags, one supporting servicemen, the other supporting pacifists, reflected how differently the Whittier and East Whittier Friends viewed military service.[223] Edwin Bronner, the son of a minister who preached in both churches, said he knew of at least twenty conscientious objectors from the Whittier First Friends Church, but he did not know a single pacifist from the East Whittier Friends Church.[224]

More important than a blanket pacifist policy was the Quaker belief that military service was a matter of individual conscience.[225] Kathryn Bewley explained, "It doesn't really matter whether one is a conscientious objector or not to a Quaker. A real Quaker feels that everyone must make his decision for himself, and your decision should be dignified by your attitude toward it, that if it's right for him, you accept that."[226] Nixon was not the only East Whittier Quaker to serve, as many of his friends and family members, and even his role models, were not conscientious objectors, including Professors Paul Smith and Albert Upton.[227] The common feeling among many young men was that so long as the country was at war, it was their duty to serve.[228] After Pearl Harbor, even Nixon's classmate Merton Wray, who was a conscientious objector, realized that "the days of talking were over" and it was time to fight.[229] Tom Bewley explained Nixon's decision to join the navy: "In his mind and influenced by his religion, he felt that that was the only right and proper thing that he could do."[230]

Nixon followed fellow Whittier attorney Wallace Black in the next officer training class at Quonset.[231] At basic training Nixon befriended Desales Harrison, who at over forty was the oldest man in the class. Harrison was unable to make his bunk with the required hospital corners, and each morning his superiors reprimanded him for his incompetence, so Nixon "came to his rescue" and made his bed for him every day.[232]

Initially assigned to a base in Ottumwa, Iowa, Nixon requested orders to the South Pacific, and he and Pat returned home to Whittier for a brief stay with family and friends before he went off to war.[233] On May 29, 1943, his grandmother Almira, Frank and Hannah, Don and his wife, Clara Jane, Ed Nixon, and various aunts and uncles, as well as Evlyn Dorn and Tom and Kathryn Bewley, gathered at Union Station in Los Angeles to see Dick and Pat off to San Francisco, where Dick was to board a ship for the South Pacific. They met at Union Station's Fred Harvey House for breakfast, knowing it might be the last time they would see him.[234] At breakfast, everyone tried to keep the conversation upbeat, but there was no denying the undercurrent of sadness, as Nixon remembered, "It was a painful meal."[235]

As Dick and Pat boarded the train, everyone waved goodbye, and true to her stoic nature, Hannah held her emotions in check, but not Frank. Evlyn Dorn later described the scene: "Frank Nixon started to sob and really everyone got upset, although Mrs. Nixon just stood up straight and strong. The last thing that happened was that Dick pointed to Eddie, who was only thirteen at the time, and said in a very powerful voice, 'Eddie, *you* take care of your mother!'"[236] Two days later, on May 31, Nixon sailed from San Francisco on ss *President Monroe*, a luxury liner built to accommodate 250 but now ferrying 3,000 servicemen to war in the South Pacific.[237] For her part, Pat remained in San Francisco throughout the war.

After seventeen days at sea, they landed at Nouméa, New Caledonia, and Nixon was transferred to nearby Espiritu Santo Island, where he was assigned to the South Pacific Combat Air Transport Command (SCAT), operating airfields and moving men and supplies to and from the front lines.[238] The U.S. forces battled from island to island, and in time, Espiritu Santo was in the rear area of the South Pacific theater.[239] Nixon, not content to be so far from the action, asked his commanding officer, Maj. Carl Fleps, to send him "up the line" with the invasion force to the next island.[240] Until that time, a marine officer had always been in charge of the SCAT detachment for each invasion force, but Fleps was impressed with Nixon and agreed.[241]

From Espiritu, Nixon was first transferred to Vella Lavella, then Bougainville, as the war advanced through the Solomon Island chain.[242] On Bougainville, two airstrips were built, one near sea level close to the beach and another at a higher elevation inland.[243] Nixon and Ens. Hollis Dole initially shared a tent in the mosquito-infested jungle, but finding sleeping under mosquito nets burdensome, Nixon used his negotiation skills to obtain a pint of medical alcohol, which he then traded to the Navy Seabees (Construction Battalion) for a newly built mosquito- and vermin-proof tent at the end of the inland runway.[244] Unfortunately, the new quarters did not stand up to the tropical elements, and on their first night an inch-and-a-half-wide, eight-inch-long lobster-red centipede crawled onto Nixon's hand, startling him awake as he flipped it onto Dole, sleeping in the bunk below. The agitated centipede promptly bit Dole, causing his arm to swell to twice its normal size.[245]

When the Japanese counterattacked the island, the Americans were forced to retreat from the inland runway.[246] For weeks the Japanese bombed the American troops at night, forcing Nixon and Dole to abandon their custom tent for a foxhole, where they spent twelve consecutive nights.[247] On March 15, 1944, a prolonged Japanese offensive left thirty-five artillery-shelled holes within a hundred feet of their foxhole and completely destroyed the tent.[248] Another day a Japanese bomber came in under radar, dropping bombs right down the airfield. Nixon dove into his foxhole just in time to miss the impact, but casualties were heavy in the battle.[249] Once the main Japanese attacks were repelled, Nixon took Jonathan Dyer, a young marine officer, with him several miles into the jungle to inspect the area from which the Americans had been forced to retreat. After surveying the area for fifteen minutes, they were beginning to drive away when Japanese mortars started raining down. Dyer was amazed at how Nixon kept calm, reflecting that the attack "didn't mean anything to him, but it did to me, because I hadn't been under that kind of attack."[250]

Within a few months Nixon transferred to Green Island, where he was the officer in charge as the U.S. forces advanced through the Solomon Islands.[251] Lt. James Stewart and Nixon were tentmates on Green Island, where they were bombed continually for the first three weeks.[252] When Stewart arrived, the island was under attack and everyone was "running around like mad."[253] But Nixon "was a sort of calm island in a storm, and had picked a place to operate from and directed everybody to set about doing what he decided should be done without any fanfare. It all took place rather calmly."[254]

With little to do in the South Pacific when not bringing in aircraft and supplies, the men played poker during their free time. Stewart, who tutored Dick in poker, explained that Nixon once asked, "Is there any sure way to win?" Stewart replied that he had "a theory for playing draw poker; you had to have the guts never to go unless you thought you had everyone at the table beaten at the time of the draw, and if so you wouldn't lose."[255] Nixon became legendary for his strategy of never going in for a pot unless he was convinced he had the best hand.[256]

Stewart and Nixon spent their off-duty hours sitting on a veranda overlooking the cliffs, facing toward California, and talking about "anything and everything under the sun." Dick confided to Stewart that the only woman he had ever slept with was Pat.[257] Nixon also spent a good deal of time reading his Quaker Bible and wrote letters to Pat every day, numbering each so that she would know if she missed one.[258] In one, Nixon copied this poem under the title "Materialist—Eva Byron":

Oh I can hear your voice my love
Though wide the sea between us lies
And I can sit alone and look
Deep in your eyes.

I feel your touch upon my hand
Across the half of all creation
Because, my darling, I possess
Imagination.

In dreams I have you with me, love
Quite charming and ethereal
But, oh, I must prefer you more
Material.[259]

Through letters, Nixon also kept up with family and friends from Whittier.[260] Childhood friend Raymond Burbank from East Whittier went on to become a pastor, with his first pastorate at the Yorba Linda Friends Church, but shortly after his first assignment in 1942, he had to resign due to illness. Burbank was touched by his old friend's loyalty: "I remember when I was ill . . . Dick was out in the Pacific somewhere in World War II as an officer. . . . And he heard that I was ill, and he sent me a . . . money gift when I was in the hospital."[261] When Don and Clara Jane's first daughter, Lawrene, was born in the summer of 1943, Nixon wrote to his new niece, "I thought you might like to hear a little V-mail scuttlebutt about your new relations," as he lovingly described Don, Clara Jane, Hannah, and Frank, before concluding, "So you see, you've come into the world with everything on your side. My hope for you is that when you have boyfriends they won't have to send V-mail to write to you. Love Dick."[262]

Eventually, Nixon was assigned to Headquarters Company at Guadalcanal, where he worked to have his enlisted men promoted "from at least one grade to as much as three grades" and was able to have the officers reassigned back to the United States.[263] Returning from South Pacific on August 3, 1944, Nixon's c-54 military transport flight stopped at Wake Island for refueling, and as he gazed at the National Cemetery, he "was overcome with the ultimate futility of war and the terrible reality of the loss that lies behind it."[264] Just one year before, on July 23, 1943, Richard's beloved grandmother Almira Milhous had died; the news reached him on Nouméa, where he was devastated by the loss, even writing to a cousin that he could not bear to return to her home and find her no longer there.[265] Almira, a dedicated Quaker and loving grandmother, never questioned his decision to serve in the navy.[266]

Nixon impressed others as someone who did not throw his weight around; rather, Nixon "conducted himself at all times in the traditions of the Navy. He was a gentleman and a good officer."[267] Lieutenant

Stewart explained, "The night before Dick left Green Island the enlisted men in our outfit went and borrowed all the liquor they could find and they gave him a party, and the next morning when he left most of them were in tears. I say this because I had never seen this before or since."[268]

All told, Richard Nixon served in Nouméa, New Caledonia, Espiritu Santo, Vanuatu, Munda, Bougainville, and Green Islands, earning a commendation and three battle stars.[269] He took pride in his service, and when he returned from the South Pacific, Pat met him on the tarmac in San Diego. Together they headed to Whittier, where more than thirty friends and relatives attended his welcome home luncheon.[270] Seeing his brother, Ed noticed many changes in his mood and demeanor, as did Whittier College professor Albert Upton, who recognized that Nixon's "ingenuous adolescence was replaced by sophisticated manhood."[271]

SIX

Congressional Race

1945–46

I t was 1945. Jerry Voorhis, first elected to Congress in 1936, had served five terms as the representative from California's Twelfth Congressional District, which included 205,000 voters within a four-hundred-square-mile area of Los Angeles County, including South Pasadena, San Marino, Alhambra, Whittier, El Monte, and Pomona.[1] Voorhis was a liberal Democrat, and any grassroots Republican attempts to defeat him promised to be an uphill battle, as Voorhis was voted the best congressman west of the Mississippi by Washington correspondents and rated as holding one of the top three safest Democratic House seats of 1946.[2]

That summer Republican activists formed the Committee of 100, tasked with recruiting a candidate capable of defeating Voorhis.[3] The core of this group included attorney Earl Adams; Roy Crocker, the president of Crocker National Bank; Frank Jorgenson, a vice president of Metropolitan Life Insurance; Boyd Gibbons, a Ford dealer from Pasadena; insurance salesman Rockwood Nelson; Roy Day, a printer from Pomona; Sam Gist, a furniture dealer from Pomona; and Herman Perry, the Whittier Bank of America branch manager.[4] Perry, Whittier's own "Mr. Republican," had been Frank and Hannah's banker since 1917. He knew Dick well, both as his son Hubert's classmate and from when Nixon practiced law for over four years in the Bank of America Building.[5] The two had much in common, as both were reserved, deeply religious, and warm in their friendships.[6] "Dick grew up under his wing," said Whittier attorney Wallace Black, and Hubert Perry knew his father looked at Nixon "as a son."[7]

In the fall the Committee of 100 ran newspaper advertisements seeking potential candidates.[8] Meetings were held at Eaton's restaurant in Santa Anita, the William Penn in Whittier, and the Monrovia

Women's Club House.[9] At the time, Roy Day of Pomona advised the committee that it should avoid prospective candidates from the "silk stocking" area of San Marino but instead recruit from the district's more rural areas, and Herman Perry thought of Nixon, who had returned from the South Pacific and was stationed on the East Coast, negotiating the termination of war contracts.[10]

Floating his idea among Whittierites, Perry recognized a potential groundswell of support for Nixon.[11] Walter Dexter, who was president of Whittier College during Nixon's tenure there and had since become the California superintendent of education, and who knew Nixon from when both were speakers at Dick's eighth-grade graduation, reflected the local sentiment: "This man will go to the top. He's that caliber of person. He's a born leader."[12]

Buoyed by the favorable response, Perry sent a wire to Dick to gauge his interest.[13] Nixon immediately embraced the idea, promising to campaign as a progressive Republican seeking "solutions to post-war problems."[14] After confirming Nixon was still a registered Republican, Perry recommended him to Frank Jorgensen.[15] In turn, Jorgensen and fellow committee members Boyd Gibbons and Rockwood Nelson met Frank and Hannah at their store, thereby completing their due diligence in reviewing Dick as a potential candidate.[16]

On October 3 Perry recommended Nixon to the Committee of 100 at the Ebell Club House in Pomona, bringing along Nixon's friend Donald Fantz from the Whittier 20-30 Club to speak to Nixon's qualities.[17] At age thirty-two Nixon believed a good candidate required five qualities: brains, heart, judgment, guts, and experience. He felt he possessed these very qualities, though he was not convinced running for office was the best decision, as "Voorhis looked impossible to defeat."[18]

Nixon discussed the opportunity with several colleagues, including James Stewart, with whom he had served in the South Pacific, telling Stewart he had doubts as to whether he could win the election. Nixon told Stewart that if he did not run for Congress, he intended to return to his Whittier law firm, and if he ran and lost, he would still return to the law firm. Stewart facetiously remarked that since Nixon had the law firm in Whittier to return to no matter what happened, "It was almost a heads I win, tails I win proposition."[19]

Another concern was the cost. Pat and Dick had saved $10,000 during the war, mainly from Nixon's poker winnings. James Udall, another veteran who had served with Nixon in the South Pacific, remembered that Nixon "was as good a poker player as, if not better than, any one we had ever seen."[20] But the couple didn't own a house, a car, or even a civilian suit for Dick.[21] For her part, Pat was dubious about spending their savings on "what at best was a risky campaign," but she was ambitious and had confidence in her husband, so she told Dick the decision was his.[22] In the words of Helene Drown, "Pat often said she never cared what Dick did. She felt he was a very smart, brilliant man who had a lot to offer to the world, but that as far as she was concerned, whatever he did that he felt was fulfilling and what he wanted to do, would be all right with her."[23] Pat had two ground rules: first, she would not make any political speeches, and second, their home must remain a quiet refuge in which to raise their children.[24] Pat and Dick then committed half their savings to the congressional campaign.[25]

With the decision made, Nixon had yet to appear before the Committee of 100 to win its endorsement. In 1945 securing air travel was difficult, but since committee member Boyd Gibbons was a friend of the president of American Airlines, he arranged for Pat and Dick to fly to California on November 1.[26] The couple stayed with Frank and Hannah while Dick composed his presentation in Eddie's bedroom in the quiet corner of the house.[27] Hannah cautioned Eddie, "Richard is studying. Don't bother him right now. He's back in your bedroom just reading up a storm and making notes."[28]

Nixon's return home made the *Whittier News*, as Rex Kennedy announced in his Heard in the Barbershop column that he would "break bread" with guest of honor Lt. Cdr. Dick Nixon at the Dinner Bell Ranch on November 1.[29] The welcome home party was a dollar-a-plate testimonial dinner for Nixon, with forty people in attendance.[30] Organized by Herman Perry, the event was presided over by longtime Nixon neighbor Harry Schuler, who introduced both Dick and Frank Nixon.[31] The next day Nixon attended a special noon luncheon at the University Club of Los Angeles with several members of the Committee of 100, including Roy Day, Earl Adams, Frank Jorgenson, McIntyre Faries, and Harrison McCall, so they could assess Nixon as a potential candidate. Tom Bewley and Gerald

Kepple, a former state assemblyman from Whittier and now vice president and general counsel for Consolidated Telephone Company, served as his escorts.[32] Nixon, wearing his navy uniform, "made a tremendous impression," according to committee member Faries. "Here's a man who's really on the ball. He had a lot of brains, and a lot of fight in him. We could see he was a comer."[33]

That evening the full Committee of 100 held a forum for prospective candidates at the William Penn.[34] Nixon stated his case in a ten-minute presentation, telling the committee, "I believe the returning veterans want a respectable job in private industry where they will be recognized for what they produce, or they want an opportunity to start their own business. If the choice of this committee comes to me I will be prepared to put on an aggressive campaign on a platform of practical liberalism" rather than the New Deal, which he characterized as "government control in regulating our lives."[35] He then stole the show by promising a "fighting, rocking, socking campaign."[36] Roy Day was immediately impressed and kept circling the room, repeating, "This man is salable merchandise."[37]

The committee, which included many prominent Whittierites, such as Adela Rogers St. Johns, met at the Alhambra YMCA on November 28 and selected Nixon as its candidate.[38] Highly motivated on receiving the good news, Nixon wrote to Roy Day in December, "We are going to build a fire in this district that won't die until Voorhis's goose is cooked."[39]

In January 1946 Dick and Pat, who was eight months pregnant with their first child, returned to Whittier and moved in with Frank, Hannah, and Eddie, sharing their three-bedroom home across the street from the East Whittier Friends Church.[40] Getting straight to work to reestablish himself in the local community, Nixon's first stop was at the John P. Evans clothing store, the "style headquarters" in Pomona, where Roy Day helped him select two new suits.[41] Although Nixon preferred flashy ties, Day suggested more subdued ones so people would "concentrate on his words, not his neckwear."[42] Dressed suitably for his new role, Nixon resumed his law partnership at the renamed firm of Bewley, Knoop & Nixon, joined the Whittier American Legion Post 51, and made the rounds, visiting old friends like Wallace Black, who had also returned from the navy to practice law.[43]

Nixon developed several speeches for his congressional run, including "The Challenge to Democracy," "America's New Frontiers," "Here Is Your Serviceman," "The Veteran in Peacetime," and "The Bougainville." In his speeches, he combined his personal experiences with policy ideas and goals.[44] Still in uniform, he made his first appearance on January 14 before the Whittier Rotary, where, delivering "The Bougainville," he told of how he and nine men had worked together one day on Bougainville Island, unloading heavy equipment from transport planes while tending to wounded troops from a Japanese air raid.[45] The group included an Irishman, a Pole, an Italian, a Texan, and an American Indian, with varying degrees of formal education. The men were given six hours to accomplish what one officer estimated would take thirty hours. But Nixon knew how to manage men. He assigned each a specific job and gave his men the latitude to use their own ingenuity to complete the task at hand. Nixon reflected that the group did the work of a hundred men, giving him "a deep appreciation of the average American and what he could do when he had a real challenge."[46]

Nixon gave his first political speech on February 5 before the Alhambra–San Gabriel Women's Republican Study Club, after which he and his supporters held an informal campaign kick-off dinner event at Eaton's in Santa Anita.[47] The following day his "down-to-earth message" was received as the best presentation the South Pasadena Kiwanis had heard "in quite some time."[48] Nixon made his formal announcement on February 12, addressing 425 guests at a $2-a-plate Lincoln Day Dinner at the Pomona Ebell Club House.[49]

The Committee of 100 formed a subcommittee to oversee Nixon's campaign and provide structure. Roy Crocker served as chairman, Samuel Gist as vice chairman, Roy Day as the primary election campaign manager, and Arthur Kruse, president of the First Federal Savings & Loan Association of Alhambra, as campaign treasurer.[50] They met every Saturday for lunch and strategy sessions at the Old Orchard Inn in Alhambra.[51] Crocker explained that when Nixon "first ran for Congress, his name was so little known and he'd had such little exposure that we thought we ought to meet every Saturday at noon."[52]

Nixon's candidacy was strictly an amateur operation, and since Voorhis had been reelected in both 1942 and 1944 by wide margins, the fledgling campaign faced a real battle, with little support from the Republican Party.[53] In fact, Nixon's group was "just a rump, inexperienced organization," and donors were told by the party that they would do much better to send their money to the Republican headquarters so it could be spent elsewhere.[54] Even some of Nixon's relatives weren't sure he had much of a chance.[55] Ultimately, the local Republican leadership agreed to let Nixon and his supporters try their hand at winning the primary, with assistance from Murray Chotiner, an attorney and veteran political strategist.[56]

Late on the morning of February 21 Pat went into labor, arriving at the Murphy Memorial Hospital in Whittier with Helene and Jack Drown.[57] Since Pat was thirty-four, the doctor anticipated a long labor, so Dick kept a commitment to give a speech at the Los Angeles Athletic Club. Immediately after lunch, he rushed to the hospital, where his first child, Patricia "Tricia" Nixon, was born at 1:26 p.m.[58]

Nixon was well suited for fatherhood. He loved children and they loved him. Whenever Pat and Dick visited Jack and Helene Drown at their Long Beach home, the Drowns' daughter Maureen joyfully ran up and down the halls as Dick playfully knelt down and enthusiastically called out to her to go get her stuffed rabbit. Other times Nixon would sit on the floor and read to her.[59] Nixon was a frequent guest at Roy Day's Pomona home, and Day's daughter Linda reflected, "I can remember Nixon sitting in the rocking chair, sitting on his lap. He had such a deep comforting voice. . . . I remember a very strong presence, but it was a soft presence."[60]

Sharing the house with Frank, Hannah, and Eddie was cramped, so a move became necessary after Tricia was born.[61] However, a postwar housing shortage complicated matters for the young family. One day, while driving through Whittier, Nixon saw his longtime barber, Waymeth Garrett, standing on the sidewalk. Nixon hollered over to him, "Hello Waymeth, do you know where I can rent a house?" Fortuitously, Garrett happened to have a vacant rental, which Nixon rented on the spot, sight unseen.[62]

A few weeks after Tricia's birth, the new family moved into Garrett's "atrociously furnished" one-bedroom bungalow on Walnut Street, for which they paid $35 a month.[63] The bungalow proved to be a good work space; Nixon and Roy Day spent many hours at the house poring over issues, analyzing opponents' positions, and devising campaign strategy.[64] However, as a home, it was "less than ideal," since Garrett used the vacant lot next door for a smelly mink farm, keeping three hundred of the creatures just fifty feet from Nixon's new residence.[65] Over forty-five years later Nixon described the problem: "Minks make beautiful coats, but as animals they are repulsive because they eat their young. I can still remember working on speeches late at night and hearing the screaming of baby minks next door."[66]

An even more distressing event occurred with fellow rookie Republican candidate Donald Jackson, running in the neighboring Sixteenth Congressional District. Both men were in need of campaign contributions, and one day Jackson called Dick and invited him to meet with a wealthy donor. When they arrived at the large, gated Beverly Hills estate, which reminded Nixon of the home in the film *Sunset Boulevard*, a butler greeted them and led them to an impressive library, with a fire roaring in the fireplace, where they met the man of the house. They immediately realized the gentleman, wearing a "handsome smoking jacket," was speaking nonsense. As Dick rolled his eyes at Jackson, the butler returned, armed with a pistol, and began accusing his employer of killing his first two wives before pointing the gun at Nixon and Jackson, who began to sweat. When the butler turned his attention back to his boss, the two candidates backed out of the room and fled the house. Nixon described their reaction: "We got out of the door and we were both perspiring on a very cool evening and Jackson said, 'I think we need a drink.' And I said, 'Fine, let's go to your place.' He says, 'Oh, no. Let's go to a bar.' I said, 'To a bar? I wouldn't think of going to a bar during the campaign, not in the 12th District.' He said, 'Well, in the 16th District we campaign in bars.' So we went to the closest bar and we both had double scotch."[67]

Despite this unsettling experience, Nixon understood that it was important to meet as many people as possible. Roy Day devised a strategy of "coffee hours" and "house meetings," the first of which was at his own home in Pomona.[68] Relaxed in these intimate settings, voters had an opportunity to really meet with Nixon, who was known to have "a nice, good sense of humor."[69]

Dick and Pat kept a full campaign schedule, and they worked in tandem.[70] At each event, Pat listened as Dick made his remarks and answered questions. When he departed for the next appearance,

Pat remained to socialize and thank the female volunteers for their efforts before joining Dick at the next home.[71] Roy Day recognized that Pat "was a hell of an asset" who "won a lot of Brownie points for Dick with those appearances."[72] Nixon held informal get-togethers throughout the district, and more often than not, his hosts were people of modest means.[73] While Nixon was reserved rather than a "back slapper," he was warm and personable and genuinely enjoyed the coffee hours.[74] According to Harold Stone, "Dick was not the type that's the life of the party, but he was the type of fellow that you loved to be around. His conversation was always good."[75] These private gatherings were a great start to Nixon's campaign, allowing him to meet people individually and affirming his belief that when you look at each person, "if you give them thirty seconds, you are theirs alone."[76]

Between February and the end of May Nixon spoke to every service club and organization he could fit into his schedule, from the Masonic Blue Lodge in Pasadena to the Pomona Rotary and everything in between, including the El Monte Lions Den.[77] Marion Hodge, a classmate from Whittier College, reflected, "He was young and so enthusiastic and committed toward a cause that one could not help but be interested in following his progress."[78] Former Whittier assemblyman Gerald Kepple described the infectious spirit Nixon generated: "I have never seen such enthusiastic support of people getting out and working as there was in that campaign."[79]

Nixon enlisted the help of Evlyn Dorn, his trusted legal secretary. Nixon was close to Evlyn, visiting her and her husband, Laurence, during his short trip home to meet with the Committee of 100 the previous November.[80] Now as a candidate, Dick frequently spent time at Evlyn's home, where he would sit at the table or pace the floor as he thought out and dictated speeches.[81] An important asset to his campaign, Evlyn took down all his speeches and debates in shorthand so that Nixon had the ability to review and improve his campaign style.[82] Dick understood that her contributions to his campaign placed a burden on her home life, as she was a mother of three. So when visiting the Dorn home, Dick frequently took Evlyn's youngest daughter, Roberta, out in the yard to play ball, and over the course of the campaign, he developed a strong relationship with the entire family.[83]

In the spring of 1946 Nixon made his first official visit to the *Los Angeles Times*, seeking the endorsement of its political editor, Kyle Palmer.[84] "My first impression of Nixon," Palmer reflected, "was that here was a serious, determined, somewhat gawky young fellow who was out on a sort of a giant killer operation" in challenging the incumbent Democrat. Palmer and most Republicans "generally felt that it was a forlorn effort, particularly when it was being made by a youngster who seemed to have none of the attributes of a rabble-rouser who can go out and project himself before a crowd." That said, Palmer soon realized, "We had an extraordinary man on our hands" and that Nixon had "just a tremendous fund of common sense and a wonderful sense of loyalty."[85]

Palmer arranged a meeting for Nixon with *Times* publisher Norman Chandler. "My first impression was simply one of awe," Nixon said. "After all, I was nothing at the time, a smalltime lawyer just out of the Navy. Being received in the publisher's office made a great impression on me."[86] Following their first meeting, Chandler concluded, "This young fellow makes sense to me, he looks like a comer, he has a lot of fight and fire."[87] What impressed him was Nixon's outlook and commitment to "just plain hard work." He was amazed how "that fellow works night and day, he can go fourteen and eighteen hours a day and never gives up."[88] With that, Chandler directed Palmer to support Nixon's candidacy, and Palmer in turn nurtured Nixon's political ambitions.[89]

As the campaign proceeded, Nixon continued to hone his speaking style. Sometimes he wrote out his speeches and read them; other times he relied on extensive notes. One evening he threw away his prepared text and spoke without notes, and after seeing the audience's enthusiastic response to this speech, he consistently began speaking without notes.[90] His primary concern with sounding new and fresh was put to rest one evening when he had the privilege of sitting with Dr. Robert Millikan, the Nobel Prize–winning chairman of the executive council at Cal Tech, at a black-tie dinner in Los Angeles. It was a prestigious audience, and Nixon told Millikan that he was worried that some in the audience might have previously heard remarks he intended to give. Nixon was reassured when Millikan told him, "Don't worry about it. The ten percent or so that have heard you before are probably your friends. Only friends really bother to come hear a speaker a second time. Direct your remarks to the ninety percent who have not heard you. Your friends won't mind, and the rest of the audience will probably like what you say."[91] Nixon incorporated this advice into his speaking style.

Working tirelessly to inspire and motivate voters paid off, and on June 4, 1946, Dick won the Republican primary. After the victory, Harrison McCall was hired as chairman of the general campaign.[92] Nixon moved his campaign headquarters from downtown Pomona to room 26 of the St. Johns Building in Whittier, on the southeast corner of Philadelphia Street and Bright Avenue.[93] The building was one of the oldest structures in Whittier and was owned by writer Adela Rogers St. Johns, who was a Nixon store customer and Committee of 100 member.[94] The new campaign office was an unoccupied storeroom that Nixon furnished with two chairs and a sofa donated by Hannah, a typewriter borrowed from his law partnership, and a throw rug from his brother Don.[95] Each day McCall went to Waymeth Garrett's barbershop for a shave and to gauge the sentiments of local voters.[96] For the general election campaign, Nixon adopted the Republican themes, asking voters whether they "Had Enough?" of Democratic rule and promoting the message "Time for Change."[97]

Naturally, the race was a family affair. Each day Pat dropped Tricia off with Hannah before heading to the campaign headquarters, where she worked as the single full-time office staff member, with Evlyn Dorn and others assisting when they had time.[98] With Pat at the office, Dick stopped by his brother Don's house most afternoons to rest up, shower, and work on speeches.[99] Don's wife, Clara Jane, frequently made dinner for Nixon at four in the afternoon so that he did not have to eat when making dinner appearances, with Dick's favorite dish being her enchiladas.[100] While Hannah took care of Tricia, Frank showed his support, maybe even clairvoyance, by telling his customers, "Watch my son, someday he'll be president."[101]

The house parties continued throughout the district, but when held in the tony area of San Marino, there was a new twist: $25-a-plate dinners. Earl Adams, who considered Nixon "a man of talent and ability," hosted one such dinner in his home, as did his neighbor Kenneth Norris.[102] While Nixon continued meeting personally with every group possible, Whittierites consisting of extended family, friends, and supporters got involved as well, walking the streets, knocking on doors, and passing out campaign literature.[103]

Roy Day frequently attended Voorhis campaign appearances and observed that Nixon's opponent "was always twitching his glasses and just naturally was nervous."[104] Early in the campaign, Voorhis sent Nixon a note stating that he hoped the candidates could meet and discuss issues of concern to the Twelfth District. Unbeknownst to Voorhis, Nixon was known as "a pretty hard guy to beat in a debate," so Nixon's campaign announced its agreement to debate the congressman.[105] Nixon then began touring the district, visiting every local newspaper, speaking to editors, publishers, and reporters. This strategy paid off. Nixon discussed a full range of issues in preparation for the debates with Voorhis, and twenty-six of the thirty newspapers in the district endorsed Nixon, including the *Los Angeles Times*.[106]

Nixon and Voorhis held five Lincoln-Douglas debates, which were by far the most exciting part of the campaign.[107] The first debate, held on September 13, was a town meeting at the South Pasadena Middle School Auditorium, hosted by the Independent Voters of South Pasadena.[108] Former assemblyman Kepple recollected, "As far back as I can remember, a political meeting was usually made up of inarticulate speakers who just threw mud around, and you could hardly get a baker's dozen to come to a political meeting; but these debates were organized very effectively."[109] A crowd of one thousand packed the auditorium on the hot late-summer evening, even spilling into the aisles, to listen to the presentations.[110] During these debates, Nixon developed the knack of repeating verbatim questions asked of him from the floor, which gave him time to think through and develop the answer.[111] The technique allowed him to frame the question for those in attendance before providing a response.

At the first debate, after Voorhis spoke, Nixon "proceeded to take Voorhis apart piece by piece and toss him around the audience," as Lyle Otterman described it. "He was definitely in the minority when he started his speech because most of the people from the area were Democratic and they fully expected to see Voorhis get this young boy and throw him to the wolves. But I could pick up around me the feeling that 'This guy's not so bad after all, is he? He seems to have something on the ball.'"[112] Roy Day's calculation regarding Voorhis's nervousness paid off, as Hubert Perry pointed out: "I sat right down in front. You could see the sweat on Voorhis's face."[113] After the debate, Jerry Voorhis asked his friend, Congressman Chester Holifield, "How did it go?" to which Holifield replied, "Jerry, he cut you to pieces."[114]

Whittier's Ex-Servicemen Association sponsored the second meeting, held at the Whittier Patriotic Hall on September 20.[115] Now on his home turf, Nixon won the second debate.[116] Two days later the *Los Angeles Times* predicted that the election would be close, saying that the primary issue for voters was whether to send a new and able man to Congress or return "one who must be regarded as . . . fumbling, stumbling and . . . crumbling."[117]

The third debate was on October 11, at the Big Bridges Auditorium at Claremont College, sponsored by the League of Women Voters and the Claremont Kiwanis Club, and held before a capacity audience of 1,850.[118] The fourth debate was held on October 23 at Monrovia High School, a campus Nixon knew from his days performing with the Glee Club in college.[119] That night a capacity crowd of 1,200 heard Nixon point out that Voorhis's only legislation was a law concerning jurisdiction of rabbit farming. Nixon mock-complained, "One has to be a rabbit to get effective representation in this Congressional District."[120] According to Roy Day, "The house almost came apart at the seams. . . . This was the point at which we broke Voorhis in two, and he was never the same" in the campaign.[121]

The fifth and final debate was held on October 28 at the San Gabriel Mission Playhouse. The debates had gained in popularity as Nixon's campaign built momentum, attracting a standing-room-only crowd of two thousand, with seven hundred more outside listening over loudspeakers.[122] Afterward, Voorhis said of Nixon, "This fellow has a silver tongue," and the general consensus was that the congressman had made a mistake in agreeing to debate Nixon.[123] Whittier city clerk Guy Dixon summed up Voorhis's performances: "I didn't even want to read about them because Voorhis was not a debater. He was just absolutely the worst."[124] According to Earl Adams, the debates "were tremendously decisive" to the outcome of the campaign; Harold Lutz, assistant vice president of the Whittier

Bank of America, who held a high opinion of Jerry Voorhis, pointed out that Nixon "made Jerry Voorhis look pretty weak."[125]

Throughout the debates, Nixon pushed forward with his packed campaign schedule. From rallies with as many as 150 volunteers at the Garfield School in Alhambra to a Halloween night celebration before a packed Covina City Park, Nixon barnstormed the district.[126] An election eve party was held at the Whittier Women's Club, and festivities started with a thirty-five-car torchlight parade through Whittier, led by a live elephant.[127] The event was organized and emceed by Wallace Black and included movie stars Randolph Scott and Lee Bowman, who both spoke on Nixon's behalf.[128]

On election night, November 5, 1946, Pat and Dick spent the evening watching the returns come in at the *Los Angeles Times* executive suite.[129] Ultimately, he won by 65,586 to 49,994, a decisive margin of 15,592 votes out of 117,069 cast, capturing 56 percent to Voorhis's 43 percent.[130] Nixon even won Voorhis's hometown of San Dimas by 491 to 401.[131] According to Roy Day and campaign manager Harrison McCall, both of whom attended all the events, the debates "were what won the election."[132] In celebration, the Committee of 100 organized a stag party at the Huntington Hotel in Pasadena. Nixon recalled, "As the evening wore on and we all got boisterous, I repaired to the piano in the room and began pounding out songs for group singing. Unexpectedly, a couple of the fellows decided to relieve Frank Jorgensen of his pants, a project in which everyone joined. I flinch now even as I recount the story of how we tossed Frank's pants on a high chandelier and of the hoots and guffaws of all of us there as Frank leapt up again and again to rescue his trousers. Victory celebrations in later years were more contained."[133]

Wallace Black and Tom Bewley drove Pat, Dick, and Tricia to Fullerton and put them on the train for Washington, Nixon's first trip east as a congressman-elect. As soon as he arrived in the capital, the first person Nixon visited was Voorhis, who recounted, "One day, when I came back from lunch, he was standing there in the outer office. He smiled and so did I. We shook hands and went into the inner office, which by that time was pretty bleak and bare. We talked for more than an hour and parted, I hope and believe, as personal friends. Mr. Nixon will be a Republican congressman. He will, I imagine, be a conservative one. But I believe he will be a conscientious one. And I know I appreciated his coming to see me very sincerely indeed."[134]

Years later Nixon reminisced, "The first race was the best. Campaigning was new, politics was new, and the feeling of stepping on Capitol Hill for the first time beat any other feeling in politics."[135]

··

SEVEN

National Prominence

1947–49

B y 1947 Don had taken over the Nixon market and set about expanding the business.[1] Where the gas station once stood, he added a coffee shop, and he also built the first drive-in restaurant on the West Coast, serving milkshakes and Nixonburgers.[2] Frank once joked, "Don's got the salesman's personality. He can be president of a corporation. Dick's got the brains. He can be president of the United States." Though Don possessed a different temperament and was not as articulate as Dick, he was certainly successful in his own right.[3] Cousin William Alan Milhous described Don as an easygoing "dynamo" with whom nobody could keep up, "almost impossible to dislike."[4]

Meanwhile, Dick and Pat were welcomed to Washington DC by Roger Johnson, who had practiced law with Nixon at the Bank of America Building in Whittier. Johnson was now working in DC, and the Nixons and Johnsons spent a great deal of time together. While his family was finding its social niche, Nixon settled into his congressional office.[5] Robert Finch, who first met Nixon in 1947, was struck that he "had that great faculty for making the person he was talking to feel he was the most important person in the world, and that his advice was the most important advice he had ever received."[6] Nixon's friend Donald Jackson was elected in California's neighboring Fourteenth District, and the two organized fifteen of their fellow Republican freshmen congressmen, including Gerald Ford of Michigan, to form the Chowder and Marching Club, which met each Wednesday afternoon.[7]

The Republican Party took control of the House of Representatives in 1946, electing Joe Martin as Speaker. Martin appointed Nixon to the Herter Committee, which was formed to conduct a fact-finding mission through England, Germany, France, Greece, and Italy to evaluate the need for U.S. assistance in the reconstruction of war-torn Europe.[8] Nixon considered his work on the Herter Committee to be the most important of his congressional career.[9]

The Herter Committee set sail on the famed cruise ship RMS *Queen Mary*, departing from New York City on August 27, 1947, and arriving in Southampton on September 1.[10] After a month spent evaluating the destruction throughout Europe, Nixon and his fellow committee members reboarded the *Queen Mary* on October 4 and departed for New York.[11] On the voyage home, Dick wrote to Pat just as he had done throughout the trip, beginning each letter with "Dearest" and closing with an endearment. While in Italy, he bought linen placemats, gloves, silk scarves, and ties for Pat, daughter Tricia, and family friends. When he learned that the delegation would have an audience with the pope, he wrote that the Holy Father had blessed "everything you carry on your person," saying, "I am going to buy a few crucifixes and have them with me."[12]

The Herter Committee's findings provided a compelling basis for the establishment of the Marshall Plan, funding reconstruction of Europe.[13] Nixon returned to the United States convinced that only a massive infusion of American aid could prevent Western Europe from falling prey to Soviet-dominated Eastern Europe.[14] However, when he took a poll in his district, he found that 75 percent of his constituents did not support sending American dollars to rebuild Europe.[15] Regardless, Nixon knew firsthand that Europe had been devastated by the war. He saw that its people were hungry and desperate, the leaders virtually powerless to begin the task of rebuilding their shattered economies. He could see that "Communist parties and movements were filling the breach with their empty but insidiously appealing promises of a better world."[16] Rather than risk his congressional seat by going against the will of his constituents, "strong willed and determined," Nixon booked more than fifty speeches to share what he had learned from the committee's trip to Europe.[17]

Events ranged from the Whittier Rotary at the William Penn to a crowd of five hundred at the Pomona Chamber of Commerce to a capacity crowd at a joint meeting of local service clubs at the Alhambra YMCA.[18] At each event Nixon described people near starvation, eating one meal a day, and his belief that there was "no question" that Communists would take over if the United States stopped sending aid.[19] Acknowledging his dismay at Europeans' tendency to "go to the left" politically, Nixon strongly urged continued aid to the war-torn continent.[20] Advocating "bread and freedom, free enterprise and free labor," he responded to isolationists that the United States "must take a realistic approach for our best interest."[21] He argued that "only the generosity of the American people could save our allies from starvation and Communism."[22]

Nixon succeeded in persuading voters to aid Europe.[23] Bob DiGiorgio, who first met Nixon in 1947, was "impressed with the sincerity of his approach and of his outspokenness and his wholehearted devotion to what he thinks is best."[24] On December 15, when President Truman called a special session of Congress to address sending American dollars to rebuild Europe, Nixon and the majority of the House voted overwhelmingly in favor of the Marshall Plan.[25] Nixon later reflected, "For the first time, I understood the vital importance of strong leadership to a people and a nation, and I saw the sad consequences when such leadership is lacking or when it fails. From just this brief exposure, I could see that the only thing the Communists would respect—and deal with seriously—was power at least equal to theirs and backed by a willingness to use it."[26]

Another important outcome of the Herter Committee was that Nixon met Rose Mary Woods. On returning from Europe, Nixon and the other congressmen turned in their vouchers for their European expense accounts, and Rose Mary remembered, "Many of them were scribbled on small pieces of paper, very hard to decipher, or some just gave us an amount and said, 'Work it out.' However, when Mr. Nixon sent in his expense account, it was neatly typed on the correct voucher form, and while he had traveled to one more country than most of the committee members, his expense account was the smallest one turned in."[27] Woods later took a position on Nixon's staff, in 1951, as she was "proud to be associated with a man of his character and ability."[28]

Up for reelection in 1948, Nixon had opened a district office at the Alhambra Post Office on Monday, September 29, 1947.[29] Nixon's strategy of crisscrossing his district to generate support for the Marshall Plan was so successful that his popularity increased to the extent that the Democrats offered no significant challenger to oppose his reelection.[30] Once the Marshall Plan passed, Pat and Dick returned to spend the New Year holiday in Southern California. At the Rose Bowl on New Year's Day, seated in the official box of Tournament of Roses Committee, they watched their beloved USC Trojans suffer a 49–0 defeat at the hands of the Michigan Wolverines.[31] Always mixing business with pleasure and sport with politics, Nixon held a campaign strategy meeting after the game at Frank Jorgensen's nearby San Marino home. Later his reelection headquarters were opened out of Harrison McCall's South Pasadena home.[32]

In 1948 a candidate for office could cross-file in both the Republican and Democratic primaries. Nixon did so, and though he had no viable opponent, the primary race was not without at least some tense moments. Nixon made a campaign trip to Southern California, departing from Washington DC on an American Airlines DC-6 at 4:30 p.m. on Friday, May 21.[33] The plane was forced to land in Oklahoma City because of trouble in the cockpit, and the passengers switched planes. Then over Amarillo, Texas, a fire alarm required the second plane to make an emergency landing, so Nixon didn't arrive in Los Angeles until 1:30 p.m. on Saturday.[34] There he immediately boarded yet another plane, flying to an El Monte airfield, where he was met by a police motorcade that escorted him south to Whittier for a luncheon with several hundred supporters at the William Penn. After lunch, he returned to El Monte to join Rev. Dan Cleveland of the Church in the Barn for a barbecue in Nixon's honor.[35]

Reverend Cleveland, a Democrat, was an influential local minister with a popular radio program, broadcast from his church, literally a church in a barn. Cleveland was concerned about the construction of the Whittier Narrows Dam, designed to provide flood control to Whittier, downstream from El Monte. His concern was appropriate, considering that the proposed dam would have flooded the reverend's church property, along with hundreds of homes and community facilities in El Monte, which was a Democratic stronghold.[36] In response, Nixon worked out a compromise, and the proposed dam site was moved downstream, sparing Cleveland's church and the surrounding community.

Nixon received strong support from Democrats. The night before the election, Reverend Cleveland took to the airwaves, declaring, "I'm a Southern Democrat . . . and I urge every other Democrat to join me in voting for Richard Nixon."[37] Leland Poage, a Democratic farmer from nearby Azusa, organized Democrats for Nixon.[38] Nixon of course garnered support from prominent Republicans, including Harold Stassen, the popular former governor of Minnesota.[39] Stassen's support was secured in part through the efforts of Kyle Palmer of the *Los Angeles Times*, who had come to believe Nixon was the "best young politician he had ever seen."[40]

Nixon's congressional district was balkanized among various municipalities, from South Pasadena to Pomona to Whittier, with citrus orchards and even smaller towns in between.[41] William Price explained the effect: "The people in South Pasadena, for example, didn't know or care much about what was going on in Whittier or Pomona. So you had to get a bunch of town committees." Thus local endorsements were very important, and Nixon's campaign structure needed a strong chairman in each of these towns, which was what he had in Frank Jorgensen from San Marino, Harrison McCall from South Pasadena, Roy Day from Pomona, and Harold Lutz from Whittier.[42]

Nixon was effectively reelected when he won both the Republican and Democratic June primaries.[43] Following his victory, he traveled to the Republican National Convention in Philadelphia, where his roommate was Roy Day, his first campaign manager.[44] After the convention, he returned to Washington DC feeling even more "on top of the world" when his second daughter, Julie, was born on July 5, 1948.[45]

Winning the Democratic primary created a unique opportunity. Nixon served on the House Un-American Activities Committee (HUAC). When he was appointed to the committee, he was apprehensive, confiding to Donald Jackson, "Politically, it can be the kiss of death." Nixon's concern was whether, if the liberal criticisms of the committee were well founded, HUAC could still "do a sound job." Ultimately, he felt it was his moral obligation to serve and accepted his assignment to HUAC.[46]

On August 3 Whittaker Chambers appeared and testified before the committee regarding Alger Hiss, a career diplomat. Hiss had been president of the student council at Johns Hopkins University in Baltimore and editor of the *Harvard Law Review* at Harvard Law School, from which he graduated summa cum laude. He clerked for Supreme Court justice Oliver Wendell Holmes, served as temporary secretary general of the San Francisco conference at which the Charter of the United Nations was drafted, and by 1948 was serving as president of the Carnegie Foundation under John Foster Dulles.[47]

Chambers testified that he had been close to Hiss and that Hiss and three of his associates—Nathan Witt, former secretary of the National Labor Relations Board; John Abt, a former Labor Department attorney; and Lee Pressman, former assistant general counsel for the Agricultural Adjustment Bureau—were active Communists who had infiltrated the U.S. government.[48] Hiss vehemently denied the charge, volunteering to appear before the committee under oath, and in his August 5 testimony again denied the charge by claiming he never knew Chambers.[49] Hiss's performance before HUAC was brilliant, and most of those present, including the media, were convinced that Hiss had been wrongly accused.[50] Nixon summed up HUAC's problem: "Hiss was popular, the committee was unpopular, and the Administration and media were lined up against us."[51]

Nixon's fellow committee members believed they'd been "had" and were "ruined."[52] President Truman termed the incident a "red herring" and wanted HUAC terminated.[53] But Nixon's Whittier friends knew that Dick was not afraid to speak his mind and had the "courage of his convictions."[54] His core belief, "that individual freedom and human rights are grounded in religious faith and because they come from God cannot be taken away by men," derived from his Quaker roots.[55] What's more, Nixon knew from his Herter Committee experience in Europe that the battle against Communism was not merely theoretical. He had fought against imperialism in the South Pacific and saw firsthand the ravages of war on Europe.

William Rogers, who first met Nixon in officer training at Quonset in August 1942 and was now working as counsel to the U.S. Senate Special Committee to Investigate the National Defense Program, recognized a trait that Bewley and others had observed years earlier: "[Nixon has] complete control of himself and his mental faculties under great pressure. The minute he faces a problem, he is most certain calm and he is most controlled and has complete confidence. It is just the opposite of the average person."[56] Nixon was the sole member of the committee to fight for an investigation into Hiss, insisting they had a responsibility to pursue the case.[57] Nixon argued, "If Chambers is lying, he should be exposed, and if Hiss is lying, he should be exposed."[58] Most of all, he believed it was the committee's moral responsibility to "find out who was telling the truth."[59]

Since Nixon was assured reelection, he was able to pursue the congressional inquiry. His considerable experience in observing witnesses on the stand as chief trial attorney for Wingert & Bewley led him to suspect that Hiss was not being forthright: "I had learned that those who were lying or trying to cover up something generally make a common mistake—they tend to overact, to overstate their case."[60] During the investigation, Nixon's religious upbringing became his greatest asset when Chambers told him that Hiss's wife, Priscilla, used Quaker "plain speech" when at home. Plain speech used *thou, thee,* and *thy* in addressing a person. Nixon knew his mother, Hannah, used plain speech only in private at home and that only someone who had been in the Hiss home would know such information.[61] To further prove that he had been close to Hiss, Chambers also told the committee that Hiss had given him a car and that Hiss, a bird-watcher, had once bragged of spotting a rare songbird, a prothonotary warbler.

HUAC recalled Hiss to testify, and Nixon used his cross-examination skills, honed in the Los Angeles and Orange County Superior Courts, to uncover inconsistencies in Hiss's story.[62] Hiss acknowledged that he actually had known Chambers, although under a different name; his wife used Quaker plain speech at home; he had given away his car to a known Communist; and he had spotted a prothonotary warbler. Ultimately, Hiss was proven to have lied under oath regarding his relationship with Chambers. Nixon and his fellow committee members believed they "had succeeded in preventing injustice being done to a truthful man and were now on the way to bringing an untruthful man to justice."[63]

Rather than assist Hiss, Abt and Pressman invoked their right against self-incrimination.[64] Elizabeth Bentley, who had dated a Russian spy throughout World War II, appeared before the committee, admitting to engaging in pro-Soviet activities during the war and naming Hiss as one of her boyfriend's "contacts."[65] By the end of August, with 80 percent of Americans believing HUAC should continue its investigation, Nixon had become a national celebrity as he persevered in uncovering the truth about Hiss's perjury and passing state secrets to the Russians.[66] Ultimately, the media also recognized the case against Hiss, and the *St. Louis Post-Dispatch* editorialized, "Whatever else President Truman may say in the future about spy investigations, he cannot again call it a 'red herring.' It is no longer a 'red herring' after the release of more than two hundred documents which are out of their places in the confidential files of the State Department."[67]

Nixon knew that HUAC succeeded in the Hiss case for three reasons: First, HUAC was on the right side in determining which man—Chambers or Hiss—had perjured himself. Second, the case was thorough. Third, the committee, guided by Nixon, followed judicious investigative methods of issuing subpoenas and examining witnesses. For Nixon, "this is not the easy way to conduct a congressional investigation and certainly not the best way to make sensational headlines. But it is the way which produces results."[68] There was a cost, however, noted by historian Kevin Starr: "Nixon's role in helping to bring down such an establishment figure . . . earned him the lifetime enmity of the liberal wing of the eastern establishment, embarrassed by Hiss's conviction but equally affronted by the unintimidated doggedness of the suburban Californian congressman."[69]

In early September Nixon flew to home to California for an extended stay.[70] Since Frank and Hannah Nixon had relocated to Pennsylvania to be closer to Dick, Pat, and Tricia in Washington DC, Don and Clara Jane Nixon had moved into Frank and Hannah's Whittier Boulevard home, a three-bedroom, one-bathroom house across from East Whittier Friends Church.[71] Dick, Pat, and their daughters lived in one bedroom; Don, Clara Jane, and their children shared another bedroom; and Pat's sister Neva came to lend a hand and stayed in the third bedroom.[72] Pat and Dick often stopped in at the Nixon store to visit with customers and attended services at the East Whittier Friends Church.[73] Nixon also relied on continued support from Bewley, Knoop & Nixon, which provided Nixon access to its offices and financial remuneration for his prior clients.[74] More important, perhaps, the firm "loaned" longtime secretary Evlyn Dorn to Dick to assist with coordinating his schedule.[75]

Nixon was in demand as a speaker.[76] His first stop was the barbecue dinner of the Sons of the Golden West, at the Whittier Riding Club, where he gave an account of the Hiss investigation.[77] Audiences loved hearing him recount the story of Alger Hiss and Elizabeth Bentley as he traveled throughout Southern California, speaking to as many different groups as his schedule allowed, making three appearances a day.[78]

His "frank, clear-cut and thorough" presentations, which ranged from the Hiss case and his thoughts on Cold War treason to local issues such as the Whittier Narrows Dam project, were well received, though audiences took particular interest in his behind-the-scenes analysis of Hiss and Bentley.[79] Nixon correlated the Hiss case with the deeper issue of Communist infiltration in the United States, explaining that Communist activities must be brought into the open because Communism "is dangerous only when underground."[80] He then reassured his audiences, "A real and successful effort is being made to rout Communists and their friends from positions in the government where they serve the interests of a possible enemy."[81]

In the years following World War II the nation began to realize the nature and depth of the spread of Communist support in the United States and viewed domestic Communism as a threat to national security. Nixon discussed these issues as he explained the Hiss case and argued for diligent screening of federal workers in sensitive employment positions.[82] Law student William Price first saw Nixon speak at a packed USC Law School forum titled "Congressional Investigating Committees: What Limitations Are Desirable on Their Powers?" According to Price, "Nixon gave his usual well-organized discourse," charming the audience with his candor and forthrightness.[83] Afterward, Price and another law student, Patrick Hillings, spoke with Nixon, who surprised the young students by telling them, "It looks like you're interested in politics," adding, "I'm staying with my brother and sister-in-law out in Whittier. Why don't you come out there Friday night, bring some of your friends, and we'll just sit around and talk politics." Price and Hillings took Nixon up on his offer, staying from 6:30 p.m. until 2:00 a.m.[84] Price found Nixon to be "a very cordial individual" who had "a good sense of humor." That night, as he and Hillings drove home, Price told his friend, "You know, I think maybe we were just sitting and talking to a future president of the United States."[85]

Nixon appeared before the joint session of the California and Washington State Committees on Un-American Activities at the

California State Building in Los Angeles, telling these organizations that the work of HUAC had exploded the "myth" that all Communists were poor.[86] He noted that "of the thirty people under investigation, all earned more than five thousand dollars a year in government jobs, and most were in the top brackets."[87] Further demonstrating his anti-Communist chops, Nixon coauthored the Mundt-Nixon Bill, which required the registration of Communists, and in his public appearances he argued for nonpartisan support against the Communist threat, believing "anti-communism is not a policy. It is a faith—faith in freedom."[88]

At the same time, he cautioned that "we must not be so blinded by the threat of Communism that we can no longer see the principles of freedom."[89] At the William Penn, he cautioned his friends and supporters against burning schoolbooks to oppose Communism.[90] Nixon was confident that capitalism would prevail over Communism, believing "capitalism does not, and government should not, guarantee equality in economic outcomes. People are created equal in terms of their inalienable natural rights but not in terms of their innate capabilities."[91]

On November 2, 1948, Election Day, Nixon watched returns come in at his El Monte Election Headquarters before bringing the celebration to the *Los Angeles Examiner* at Broadway and Eleventh Streets.[92] As the evening progressed and victory was assured, Pat and Dick continued the celebration with Jack and Helene Drown at the Cocoanut Grove.[93] With Truman defeating Dewey and the Democrats regaining control of the House, there were more Democrats celebrating than Republicans.[94] The evening's entertainment was Hildegarde, the famous vaudeville singer whom *Time* magazine called a "luscious, hazel-eyed Milwaukee blonde who sings the way Garbo looks."[95]

Unbeknownst to Nixon, Drown arranged for Hildegarde to introduce him to the audience as a congressman and great statesman.[96] Nixon stood up, thanked Hildegarde, and said with a deadpan expression, "I realize there are mostly Democrats here having fun, and I almost wish I were one of you! But don't jump to conclusions, I'm not going to switch parties. But it just happens that I love Democrats, I even married one. I would like to introduce my beautiful wife who was a Democrat when I married her. Patricia Ryan was born on St.

Patrick's Day—and if they come any more Irish or more Democrat than that, I don't know what it could be." Nixon's line "brought the house down." Drown reflected, "Those who say Dick has no sense of humor should have been at the Grove that night."[97]

Before departing for the East Coast at the end of his extended visit, Dick asked Evlyn Dorn to arrange a meeting with his old 20-30 Club friend Donald Fantz. Nixon told Fantz, "Pat and I are staying out at Don's. You know, he hasn't got any heat in that place. It's cold, boy, it's real cold. I wonder if you'd do me a favor. Will you go out there and look it over and see what it needs, see what you could put in there in the way of some floor furnaces or some heat, or something, to make it warm and comfortable for them. They've done so much for Pat and me, and we're staying there, and we can't do anything for them. This is one way that I can kind of pay them back a little bit for what they've done for us." Dick arranged to pay for the installation of a new heater, telling Fantz, "That's the only way I know of I can do something for Don."[98] Not surprisingly, Clara Jane loved the new heater, even using the floor vent to dry clothes on rainy days.[99]

Although the Democratic Party had captured the White House and House of Representatives, Nixon was immensely popular, using his speaking engagements in Southern California to lay out his agenda for the Republican Party to succeed. At the Biltmore Bowl, Nixon enumerated a six-point plan, proposing to cut the size of government bureaucracy, fight abuses by both management and labor, take positive action on the plight of civil rights, resist socialization of American institutions, fight Communist infiltration, and place national security above partisan politics.[100]

In April 1949 the Nixons closed escrow on their first home in South Whittier, a property built by William T. Hughes, developer of the Hugheston Meadows, the site of many Nixon campaign events.[101] The house was across a dirt road from the Hugheston Meadows restaurant and the ninth hole at Candlewood Country Club. The area was rural at the time, and only four homes had been built. The Nixons shared their telephone service on a party line with ten to thirteen others, including a market, a dentist, a musician, a convalescent home, and a woman bookie who kept her receiver off the hook.[102]

Returning to Southern California again in May and August 1949,

Nixon evaluated the state's political landscape to determine whether he should run for reelection or seek a different office. Having been in Congress for four years, Richard Nixon was seen as a "scholarly— but unstuffy—man of assiduous work habits, with a reputation for thoroughness and integrity."[103] The Herter Committee exposed Nixon to the Communist influence in Europe and provided him a platform from which to advocate the Marshall Plan at home. His pragmatism in dealing with the Whittier Narrows Dam ensured his reelection, which then afforded him the time and focus to conduct the Alger Hiss investigation. Exposing Hiss elevated Nixon to national prominence and prepared him for even greater challenges that lay ahead.

EIGHT

Senator

1949–51

Nixon's House seat was up for reelection again in 1950. Despite his popularity, Nixon felt he was "a 'comer' with no place to go," since the Republicans no longer held majority control of the House of Representatives.[1] Consequently, he began to assess the feasibility of challenging incumbent Democratic senator Sheridan Downey for the U.S. Senate.

In early 1949 core Committee of 100 members—Roy Day, Frank Jorgenson, Herman Perry, Charlie Cooper, and Frank Lutz—met at Jorgenson's San Marino home and agreed to raise funds for what they believed was Nixon's impending Senate race.[2] By August Nixon confided in Jorgensen, "I do not see any great gain in remaining a member of the House . . . if it means that we would be simply a vocal but ineffective minority."[3] With that in mind, the Nixons drove cross-country from Washington DC to Whittier so that Dick could explore his Senate race options.

Many, including some Nixon relatives, were against the idea of a Senate run.[4] Nevertheless, those in favor began to develop momentum, and in October the Arcadia Young Republicans announced they were joining the movement to draft Dick as a candidate.[5] Visiting Whittier High School, Dick promised to "wage an aggressive, hard-hitting campaign" if he entered the contest.[6] On October 7 Nixon expressed his desire to run for the Senate to Herman Perry, who was opposed and called a meeting at Tom Bewley's law office, summoning Nixon's closest advisors.[7] On the way to the meeting, Nixon met Roy Day for dinner in Pico, where they strategized how to persuade the group in their favor.[8]

All indications were that Sheridan Downey planned to run for reelection. Nixon knew Downey to be "a popular, non-controversial, establishment Democrat," so the overall consensus was that a Senate run would be political suicide.[9] Perry did not want Nixon to risk a safe House seat on such a long shot.[10] However, Roy Day countered that Nixon was so popular and talented that "he could whip Abraham Lincoln if necessary in the Senate fight."[11] Having been named the "most outstanding member of the present Congress" by *Newsweek* a few months earlier, Nixon was ready for the challenge.[12]

To evaluate whether he would have major media support, Nixon met journalist Kyle Palmer for lunch at the Biltmore. Palmer told him, "I think you would be a damn fool to run against Downey, but if you decide to run, I am authorized to tell you that the *Times* will support you and that the *Chronicle* and *Tribune* will probably follow suit."[13]

Pat Nixon, "the strongest supporter of Nixon's own urge to advance," was in favor of a Senate run and was intrigued by the long odds most had given her husband's chances of success.[14] Knowing Dick best, she understood that with her husband, "the tougher the going the better he gets."[15] In the end Nixon's decision to enter the Senate race was his alone, as he preferred to make decisions through "an individual process and individual thinking."[16] He later compared his decision to run for Senate to his first congressional race: "Two of my biggest decisions, the one to run for Congress and the one to run for the Senate, were made over the objections of most political experts, and most of my friends."[17] Nevertheless, Pat supported the bid, and when asked how she felt about her husband's decision to run, she replied, "Prouder than anything in the world."[18]

Nixon turned his focus to shoring support in Northern California. John Dinkelspiel, an influential Republican from San Francisco, arranged a meeting at his office. Dinkelspiel, the son of a former California State Assembly member, graduated from Harvard Law School and passed the California bar exam before he was twenty years old. He was a founding member of the Jewish Community Relations Council of San Francisco. Dinkelspiel and his associates were so impressed with Nixon that they established a Northern California campaign committee on the spot.[19] Joe Moore Jr., the nephew of former California governor James Rolph, who was also San Francisco's longest-serving mayor, observed that Nixon had "wisdom, personality, and it seemed to me that this was a man who was going to be a winner and a fine man."[20]

As word of Nixon's Senate decision spread, he was summoned downtown to the Merchants and Manufacturers Association Building to meet with Los Angeles County supervisor Raymond Darby, who strongly discouraged him from running. Nixon, who had brought Frank Jorgenson along to the meeting, sat and listened as Darby took staged calls from supporters making large contributions. He told Nixon, "Dick, you're a nice fellow but you can't win. I'll just smother you." Laughing off the charade, Jorgenson chided Darby, "Thank you very much. We're still running for the United States Senate."[21]

With Nixon making a bid for the Senate, a candidate had to be selected to run for his congressional seat. The original Committee of 100 from 1946 remained loyal to Nixon, and he was equally loyal to the committee, which evolved into the California Committee of Nixon supporters as he developed national prominence. When Nixon convened his California Committee in Arcadia, the group endorsed twenty-six-year-old Pat Hillings, who had worked for Nixon since they met in 1948.[22] Hillings was chairman of the Los Angeles County Young Republicans, which had formed a Nixon for Senate Committee early in 1949.[23]

Murray Chotiner took on the role of Nixon's campaign manager. The two worked well together; Nixon insisted on perfection and considered Chotiner one of the "ablest campaign technicians in the country."[24] Earl Adams recognized that Chotiner gave Nixon "the best, most solid advice" of any man around.[25] Bernard Brennan, an influential Republican who had backed Gov. Earl Warren for vice president in 1948, supported Nixon's decision to run for the Senate early on and became campaign chairman.[26]

A great believer in luck, on November 3 Nixon returned to the Ebell Club House in Pomona, the site of his 1946 congressional announcement. He spoke to an enthusiastic capacity crowd, with his speech carried live over the Don Lee mutual radio network. Nixon, using a favorite phrase since his college days, predicted a tough race: "There is only one way we can win. We must put on a fighting, rocking, socking campaign and carry that campaign directly into every county, city, town, precinct and home in the state of California."[27]

Nixon's Senate campaign initially occupied space in Frank Jorgenson's ninth-floor Metropolitan Life Insurance office in the Garland

Building in Los Angeles. When clients came to see Jorgensen, he had to ask Dick to go to a back office so he could conduct insurance business. The building's owner, Jack Garland, brother-in-law of *Los Angeles Times* publisher Norman Chandler, had been a Nixon friend and supporter since 1946.[28] By November 1949 Garland, who had entertained Dick in his San Marino home over the years, arranged for Nixon to occupy suite 201. His campaign eventually took up the entire second floor.[29] Since his weekly meetings at the Old Orchard Inn in Alhambra had been so successful, Dick and his core campaign team held weekly breakfast meetings in the coffee shop at the Biltmore.[30]

Nixon embarked on a tireless campaign, speaking as often as fourteen times a day.[31] Henry Kearns, an Alhambra auto dealer, provided Nixon with a secondhand 1949 Mercury Woody station wagon, which he used to tour the state.[32] Nixon for U.S. Senate signs were attached to the wood-paneled sides and the roof, and a turntable with external speakers was installed.[33] Ace Anderson, "a veteran campaign worker whose major qualification was that he was a good driver," served as chauffeur and sound system technician.[34] Typically, Nixon and Ace would drive into a town, park at a busy intersection, and pass out leaflets to passersby as the candidate said, "My name is Richard Nixon and I'm running for Senate. Would you stand still a minute while I tell you why?" He'd then climb onto the station wagon's tailgate and give a short speech using plain language to explain his platform.[35] Whenever Ace was not available, Pat joined Dick on the road trips. Nixon volunteer Pat Hitt recalled that the couple "always were full of enthusiasm" and would "get a few dollars in at a rally and run out and print up something, load it in the station wagon," and be off campaigning together.[36]

Congresswoman Helen Gahagan Douglas of California's Fourteenth District, also an actress and wife of fellow actor and liberal Democrat Melvyn Douglas, challenged incumbent Downey in the Democratic primary.[37] The two attacked each other for several months, until Downey announced his withdrawal from the campaign on March 28, 1950, citing an ulcer, which left him unfit for "waging a personal and military campaign against the vicious and unethical propaganda" of Douglas.[38] The hostility between the Democrats was so bitter, in fact, that Douglas retorted that Downey's claim of ill health was "a cheap gimmick."[39] The day after Downey withdrew, Manchester Boddy, publisher of the *Los Angeles Daily News*, entered the race against Douglas, and Downey endorsed Boddy's candidacy.[40]

Since the issue of the day was Communism, targeting her extreme left-wing positions, Downey, Boddy, and other leading Democrats dubbed Douglas "the Pink Lady."[41] Boddy even charged that Douglas and her supporters "constituted 'a statewide conspiracy on the part of a small subversive clique of red-hots to capture through stealth and cunning the nerve centers of our Democratic Party.'"[42] Unrestrained, Boddy and his supporters tagged Douglas a "Russia Firstie" and "playmate in the mire of Communism," and newspaper reports followed suit, describing her as "the darling of the Hollywood Parlor Pinks" and "the Red Queen."[43]

While Boddy and Douglas attacked each other, Nixon unified Republican support and began courting Democrats.[44] California Democrats for Nixon was headed up by George Creel, a real coup for Nixon, as Creel had originally supported Helen Douglas. Creel was the publicity man in Woodrow Wilson's administration, and as a progressive, he had run for California's governorship in the primary against Upton Sinclair in 1934.[45]

Forging ahead, on April 25 Nixon appeared at the Spit and Argue Club, put on by the University by the Sea, an outdoor debating society dating to 1904, which consisted of a battered podium on Rainbow Pier at the Long Beach Pike. It was open twenty-four hours a day, and each day a new chairman was selected; speakers were limited to five minutes but were allowed an additional ten minutes "if the audience desires it," and profanity was forbidden.[46] Nixon, the first actual politician to ever appear at the university, told the assembled crowd, "I used to come to Long Beach often as a youngster and I always enjoyed attending the University by the Sea."[47]

Afterward, Nixon went a block down Ocean Boulevard to deliver a one-hour-and-forty-five-minute address at the Municipal Auditorium. Along the way, the candidate and his supporters had fun with the Woody's record turntable, playing "If I Knew You Were Comin' I'd've Baked a Cake" for picketers at the auditorium trying to obstruct his appearance. Nixon took the protesters lightly, explaining, "Well, I sort of expected something like this. You know, I think it might be well if we played a special record for them."[48]

In his speech, Nixon argued that the Truman administration did not understand the depth of the Communist threat and that Communism was not merely a "political scandal." Calling for a strong front against Communism at home and abroad, he defended the Mundt-Nixon Act, which required Communists to register with the government and prevented them from holding office in tax-supported institutions. Having spent much of his youth at the beaches of Long Beach, Nixon discussed state concerns regarding California's right to water from the Colorado River and other local issues, warning that the Truman administration's attempt to control the tidelands could adversely affect the nearby Belmont Shore–Naples shoreline.[49]

At the Biltmore Bowl, Nixon reiterated the need to contain Communism and to rein in "wild government spending" on the domestic front. He staunchly argued that the major provisions of the Taft-Hartley Act were "to get the government out of industrial relations to the greatest extent possible" and promote new energy resources to create new businesses and jobs in California.[50] All told, he gave over six hundred speeches during the primary campaign, culminating in a hometown rally in Whittier, where five thousand supporters joined the Nixons in a torchlight parade.[51] On June 6 Nixon won the Republican primary, as Douglas defeated Boddy and other opponents in the Democratic primary. However, Boddy, Nixon, and Douglas ran in both primaries, and there was one telltale sign in the voting: although the Democrats had a 900,000 registered voter advantage over Republicans, and 400,000 more Democrats voted than Republicans, Nixon won over 150,000 more votes in total than Douglas in the two primaries.[52]

Nixon immediately focused on fostering Democratic support. Ed Pauley, a prominent Los Angeles Democrat and a good friend of Harry Truman's, had served as treasurer of the Democratic National Committee, among other prominent positions in the Truman administration. Early the morning following the primary, Nixon was the first caller at Pauley's office, seeking his advice as to how to defeat Douglas. Pauley told Nixon that, being a staunch Democrat, it would be unbecoming for him to openly support a Republican, though he was not for Douglas and did not believe she had the background and qualifications to be U.S. Senator representing the great state of California. He felt that his lack of support, along with failing to encourage other people to support her, would be about as much help as Nixon could expect. And this is exactly how Pauley helped Nixon: by doing absolutely nothing to help Douglas.[53] Others soon followed Pauley's lead, including Johnny Johnson, a prominent Long Beach Democrat, who announced, "Although a lifelong Democrat, I will do all I can to elect Richard Nixon in the November election."[54]

The Senate race between Nixon, a champion of the Hiss case, and Douglas, a liberal Democrat, attracted national attention, with *Newsweek* declaring the contest a referendum on the Truman administration.[55] Senator Downey despised Douglas so much that when President Truman implored him to support Douglas, he not only refused but recommended that his friend Janet Goeske volunteer on behalf of Nixon, which she did.[56] Goeske was impressed that candidate Nixon made a special effort to frequently stop by the campaign headquarters and see how everyone was doing. She saw that the Nixons were a close-knit family and was equally struck by the man himself, describing Nixon as "just like what I think almost every mother would want her son to be."[57]

As summer progressed, the campaign heated up, and Nixon's friends and supporters marveled at his energy.[58] A typical campaign day began with a breakfast meeting with the Elks Club of Alhambra, a noon luncheon at the Civic Auditorium in El Monte, an afternoon meeting with the Baldwin Park Chamber of Commerce, and an evening community dinner at the Ebell Club House in Pomona.[59] The official kickoff was even more extravagant. On September 18 rallies were held statewide. A fellow World War II serviceman of Nixon's, James Udall, flew Dick and Pat from a morning rally in San Diego to Los Angeles for an event at the Biltmore Bowl, then to Fresno for another rally before taking off again for San Francisco to complete the day with an evening party. This was the first time a statewide candidate had traveled so extensively in a campaign.[60]

Udall first met Nixon in April 1943, when they were on the steamship *President Monroe*, bound for the South Pacific.[61] He knew Nixon as a quiet, studious young man but also recognized that there was "more than actually met the eye."[62] Udall and his fellow servicemen had "made the prophecy that whatever he did when he returned, he would be a success."[63] However, Udall initially advised Nixon to keep his safe congressional seat and not to run for Senate. Nixon responded that "he felt that if he lost the fight" by failing to win the election, but "he had pulled a good campaign, had told people the truth, and he had tried to sell them on what the country really needed in Washington in the way of a senator, and how he would represent them," that defeat would be acceptable, since he would have done his best.[64] Campaigning with Nixon, Udall observed people's shifting perceptions of Nixon before and after meeting him. Udall recalled hearing this sentiment from many people: "I didn't like Dick Nixon until I met him, but after I met him, I began to see the power, the sincerity and the goodness of the man, and I completely changed my views."[65]

Nixon's campaign addressed this by publishing a *Manual of Information*, which said, "Above all, Dick Nixon is human. He came from the people, and he is still of the people, a regular guy. He is not infallible, and may make a mistake, but he will always stand on principle, and act with sincerity and forthrightness."[66] This genuineness resonated with voters like Alphonzo Bell, who remembered meeting Nixon for the first time: "The exact spot was in Beverly Hills. I was very much impressed." He went on to become a California Committee member.[67] Bell compared Nixon to Presidents Abraham Lincoln for "his humility, kindness, and friendliness," Andrew Jackson for "his tremendous courage," and Teddy Roosevelt for being "youthful and vigorous."[68]

At a campaign stop at Whittier High, Nixon was introduced by Hortense Behrens, an old friend and fellow thespian from his Whittier Community Players days. Backstage, Behrens implored Nixon to be dramatic and sweep across the stage when she introduced him. Nixon demurred, telling her, "Oh Hortense, that's just too dramatic for me."[69] Donald Fantz was the master of ceremonies, and his son Donnie provided musical entertainment on the organ. A decade earlier, when Fantz and Nixon were in the 20-30 Club, young Donnie had come down with spinal meningitis and was not expected to survive. The first thing Dick did on taking the podium was to say to the audience, "Folks, didn't you enjoy that organ playing? I want to tell you something. Do you remember here about ten years ago, all of us in Whittier were saying our prayers and watching for reports and just hoping and praying for a young boy who was up at Murphy Memorial Hospital who wasn't expected to live at all? That was young Donnie Fantz, and he played the organ for you tonight."[70]

Unlike Nixon's first congressional campaign, this time he didn't get a chance to debate his opponent, as Douglas declined his invitations. The two candidates made just one joint appearance at the Beverly Hills High School auditorium.[71] Douglas agreed to attend the meeting, but only because Nixon was scheduled to be out of the area and unlikely to attend.[72] However, Nixon and Roy Day drove in and stayed at the Beverly Hilton Hotel, anticipating the opportunity, and when Nixon appeared, ready to debate, Douglas was so flustered that she left without taking any questions before Nixon had even finished speaking.[73]

Nixon's campaign continued building momentum, boosted by support from the minority community. Well-known African Americans supported Nixon, who spent the evening before Election Day at the home of UCLA standout and Rams football star Kenny Washington in Douglas's Fourteenth Congressional District, in the heart of inner-city Los Angeles. Nixon mingled with the guests, including Washington's teammates Deacon Dan Towler and Woody Strode; then everyone gathered around to sing as Nixon played the piano.[74] The *Los Angeles Sentinel*, a local African American newspaper, enthusiastically endorsed Nixon.[75] Prominent Hispanics such as Consuelo Castillo de Bonzo and Reyes Gutierrez also encouraged support for Nixon. Castillo de Bonzo announced, "Regardless of creed, origin or nationality, I sincerely hope and believe that a vote for Richard Nixon for United States Senator is our best guarantee for keeping our country free and strong."[76]

The highlight of Nixon's campaign was on November 2, when he held a massive old-fashioned torchlight parade and rally at the Hollywood American Legion Stadium. Many celebrities attended and made appearances on Nixon's behalf.[77] Then, the day before the election, the campaign held a rally across Southern California as Nixon caravanned to each of his Los Angeles headquarters.[78]

On Election Day, November 7, 1950, once Dick and Pat had voted, they went to the beach for a picnic. It was too cold, however, so they caught a movie in Long Beach.[79] The evening was spent at their Senate campaign headquarters in the Garland Building to follow the tallying of votes before joining Norman and Buff Chandler in the third-floor editorial department of the Los Angeles Times Building.[80] Buff, who met Dick and Pat for the first time that evening, immediately saw Nixon as a "selfless man" who had "the look of the Eagle," which she described as an "intensity and a drive and something that you cannot put your hands on."[81] Once Nixon knew he was going to win the election, the group moved the celebration to the Chandlers' sixth-floor apartment for a congratulatory libation before heading to the Ambassador for the first of many victory celebrations.[82] As they spent the night hopscotching from one victory party to another, whenever there was an available piano, Dick played "Happy Days Are Here Again."[83]

Whittier and Yorba Linda solidly supported their hometown son. Twice as many Whittier Democrats voted for Nixon in the primary as for Douglas, and in the general election he outpolled Douglas 9,187 to 2,198 in Whittier and 504 to 92 in Yorba Linda.[84] Statewide, he won by 680,000 votes, the largest margin of victory of any Republican candidate nationwide.[85] Overall, Nixon won by a whopping 59 to 41 percent margin of victory.[86] Shortly after the election, Senator Downey graciously resigned his seat, which allowed Governor Warren to appoint Nixon to fill Downey's final six weeks in office, providing Nixon an immediate advantage in the seniority-based Senate.[87]

Despite the subsequent accusations against Nixon regarding the Senate campaign, summed up with Douglas branding Nixon "Tricky Dick," it was Douglas who "waged a campaign that would not be equaled for stridency, ineptness, or self-righteousness until George McGovern's presidential bid twenty-two years later."[88] In total, nine of the eleven major papers in the state backed Nixon.[89] Douglas herself acknowledged, "I was defeated in 1950, and have no intention to carry a vendetta against Mr. Nixon for the rest of my life."[90] Nixon felt the same way, noting that campaigns were heated contests after which he did not hold "any personal grudges."[91]

Nixon spent several weeks making the rounds and thanking his supporters, for which one contributor was especially appreciative: Don Lycon, an executive of Standard Oil in Whittier, who earlier had provided Herman Perry with funds for what proved to be an unsuccessful campaign to unseat Voorhis in 1944. In 1946 Lycon directed Perry to use the remaining funds as he saw fit, and Perry spent the money in favor of Nixon. Once elected to the Senate, Lycon proudly introduced Senator-elect Dick Nixon to his associates in the dining room of the Standard Oil building.[92] Mineral rights to the surrounding areas were controlled by Standard Oil. However, the Nixon gas station sold only Richfield Oil Company gasoline because Frank was so taken with Ida M. Tarbell's *History of the Standard Oil Company*, which exposed Standard Oil for using unfair tactics to put smaller oil companies out of business, that he declared, "I hate Standard Oil and everybody who works for them."[93] Frank and Dick must have appreciated the irony.

Despite having an increasingly hectic schedule as a senator, Nixon's personal relationships remained strong. Whenever he returned to California, he'd tell friends and family, "Come over, we'll have a buffet lunch and sit around and chew the rag a little." That way, he'd see everyone at once instead of trying to see people individually, which was all but impossible given his busy agenda.[94] Tom Knudsen, a converted Voorhis supporter who had grown to know Nixon well, said, "He is a very warm-hearted man. When he is speaking politically he has to maintain a certain reserve, but among friends, he does not. He lets his hair down."[95]

Senator Nixon's "district" became the entire state of California, so his schedule usually required that he stay in centrally located downtown Los Angeles rather than in Whittier on his frequent trips home. His favorite hotels were the Ambassador and the Biltmore, where he often stayed, generally traveling without fanfare. In March 1951 Nixon returned to Los Angeles for a long weekend, culminating in Whittier College's fiftieth anniversary celebration. Arriving after an overnight flight, Nixon had what he considered a light meeting schedule because, as he put it, "I will want to spend all the time possible with my mother in Whittier."[96]

But there was always time for the party faithful, and the next evening Pat and Dick attended the Republican Congressional Dinner in the Biltmore Bowl.[97] Nixon addressed a Senate proposal to appoint a commission to investigate morality in the federal government in response to scandals within the Truman administration. He told the crowd, "When we have to have a commission to tell us what is right and what is wrong, God help America."[98]

Nixon served as master of ceremonies at the Whittier College Golden Anniversary Dinner, held at the Ambassador.[99] He had arranged for the immensely popular John Foster Dulles to be the keynote speaker, and the sold-out celebration was front-page news.[100] Profoundly grateful for his efforts, the Whittier College Board of Trustees passed a resolution of gratitude for their "most illustrious alumnus."[101]

The national political landscape was changing as 1952 approached. At a November 16 press conference in Los Angeles, Nixon remarked that Robert Taft and Dwight Eisenhower were frontrunners for the 1952 Republican presidential nomination but that California governor Warren was the "strongest dark horse." Many speculated there was a chill between Earl Warren, who had been governor since 1943, and Nixon. Yet Nixon, never one to attack a fellow Republican, later maintained that he and Warren were "not unfriendly," but rather, "we are two individuals going our own ways."[102]

As the year progressed, the Nixons sold their Honeysuckle property.[103] Within months of the sale, Pat and Dick purchased a modest tract home on Anaconda Street in East Whittier, into which Frank and Hannah moved, having relocated from the East Coast.[104] That December, before visiting with family for the traditional Christmas dinner at the Milhous residence, Dick met Bebe Rebozo through Sen. George Smathers, a Florida Democrat, who arranged for his friend Bebe to entertain Nixon during a vacation to his state.[105] Bebe eventually became Dick's confidant and lifelong friend; however, after their initial vacation together, a relationship seemed unlikely, as Bebe wrote to Smathers to lament that Nixon "doesn't drink whiskey; he doesn't chase women; he doesn't even play golf."[106]

In early 1952 Nixon rode the City of Los Angeles train from Chicago to Los Angeles, arriving Sunday morning, February 10, after a day and a half on the rails.[107] Rather than travel with staff, Nixon borrowed Evlyn Dorn to handle his dictation during his stay at the Biltmore.[108] Nixon's first stop was the Beverly Hilton Hotel to join *Los Angeles Times* political editor Kyle Palmer at a luncheon, followed by back-to-back Lincoln Day events at Elwood Robinson's West Los

Angeles residence and then Dana Smith's South Pasadena home.[109] Pat was unable to join him on all the trips because of the challenges of traveling with Tricia and Julie, but Dick always shared the details of his adventures. Later he wrote to Robinson, "When I got back Pat particularly enjoyed my description of everything, including the house, the grounds, what the ladies wore and the refreshments!"[110]

Nixon occasionally received perks because of his status, and he liked to pass these along with a personal note. He sent Hollywood Park Turf Club passes to distribute to party members with this proviso: "Incidentally, of course, the condition of your receiving these tickets is that I get a 25% cut any time you cash in on the Daily Double!"[111] When Pacific Theatres gave Nixon an annual pass, he forwarded it to Jack Drown with a handwritten note: "They tell me they do a lot of 'neckin' in these joints—maybe you and Helene had better go case the joints!"[112]

In April he returned to attend a luncheon for the Los Angeles County Bar Association in the Alexandria Hotel Ballroom.[113] While he was in town, the Los Angeles Republican Party held an unprecedented $100-a-plate dinner in his honor, and on April 16, 4,200 people dined with Nixon at the Shrine auditorium.[114] The following day Nixon, who attended services with his family whenever he could and was unfailingly loyal to his church, was the main attraction at a $25-a-plate fundraising dinner held by the East Whittier Friends Church.[115] Dick contributed $100, telling his hosts "to purchase tickets for people who might not be able to afford them" because he did not "believe there should be any 'free riders' at the dinner."[116] At the time friction between President Truman and Nixon, dating back to the Hiss case, was well known, as was Truman's talent as a pianist. When Nixon arrived at the dinner in the church basement, seeing the piano he used to play as a boy, Dick made light of tension between him and Missouri native Truman, telling the group, "You know I used to play the piano right in this basement" as he sat down and played "Missouri Waltz."[117] The most pressing issue was speculation as to who would be the Republican nominee for president. Gen. Dwight Eisenhower and Sen. Robert Taft were the frontrunners, and Nixon, confiding that Eisenhower had the best chance of winning the election, freely discussed Republican politics with his fellow parishioners.[118]

During this halcyon period, Nixon was happily married with two young daughters, and at thirty-nine years of age, he had seen his prominence rise a mere eighteen months into his six-year Senate term. After twenty years out of power, the Republican Party was ready to launch a dramatic comeback, with Richard Nixon positioned to lead the charge.

NINE

Vice-Presidential Campaign

1952

In July 1952 Richard Nixon attended the Republican National Convention in Chicago. Here he met Jackie Robinson, who had broken Major League Baseball's color barrier after playing football and baseball for UCLA. A fellow Republican and Nixon supporter, Robinson had hit a home run in the All-Star Game the day before. After congratulating him on his performance, Nixon then told Robinson about watching him play football for UCLA at the Coliseum thirteen years before. Nixon described how Robinson's teammate Kenny Washington, also a Nixon supporter, had thrown a sixty-yard touchdown pass to Robinson. Listening to him recount that particular play, Robinson was struck by the depth of Nixon's sports knowledge.[1] Nixon's former campaign manager Harrison McCall described the meeting: "While Robinson had undoubtedly met a lot of notables during his career, nevertheless I was sure there was one person he would never forget."[2]

Along with McCall, Nixon brought numerous California Committee friends and supporters, including Jack Drown and Roy Day, to the convention, where Gen. Dwight Eisenhower was nominated as their presidential candidate.[3] Herbert Brownell, Eisenhower's friend and confidant, noted that the thirty-nine-year-old Nixon was an "ideal candidate for vice president. He was young, geographically right, had experience both in the House and Senate with a good voting record, and was an excellent speaker."[4] Ever since the Hiss case, the GOP faithful recognized Nixon as an exciting stump speaker, but Nixon laughed off any rumors of his impending selection, telling reporters, "We have better men in California other than myself."[5] Likewise, when reporters attempted to question Pat on the subject, she deflected, stating that she and Dick did not take such speculation seriously. She jokingly described herself as "his man Friday" and "chief cook, bottle washer, chauffeur and what-not" for the family. She also revealed that she was a good cook, that Nixon's favorite cuisine was Mexican, and that he was especially "crazy about enchiladas."[6] The reality is that both Richard and Pat were very much interested in Nixon being selected as Eisenhower's running mate. The couple had worked consistently to advance Nixon's career in every endeavor.

Being chosen as Eisenhower's running mate was "the culmination of . . . a phenomenally fast rise to national prominence."[7] Only seven years earlier Pat and Dick, who was still a naval officer, had witnessed Eisenhower's New York ticker-tape parade, and now Nixon was on his ticket.[8] Pat was "thrilled, flabbergasted, amazed and speechless." She immediately began looking forward to campaigning in the fall, saying that she and Dick "always work as a team," and she enjoyed the variety of people she met on the campaign trail.[9] However, she admitted, "Leaving the girls is the only thing I won't like about campaigning."[10]

On Monday morning, July 28, the Nixon family flew to Los Angeles, gathering at their Anaconda Street residence before joining fellow Whittierites for a welcome home celebration.[11] The Nixons led a parade consisting of palomino riders, a Marine Corps color guard, the Monterey Park Band, veterans marching groups, various service groups, numerous dignitaries, and Don and Clara Jane Nixon, heading up Philadelphia Avenue from Whittier High School to Whittier College's Hadley Field.[12] Watching his former student drive through town, Professor Albert Upton observed that Nixon's face had the expression of one "greeting an old friend" as he and Pat saw familiar people and buildings along the parade route.[13]

Practically all of Whittier turned out for the celebration, described by the *Long Beach Press Telegram* as "tumultuous, friendly, joyous, the warm outpouring of happiness of a city mighty proud of two young people and mighty glad to have them home again."[14] Thousands packed the parade route, and a crowd of twenty thousand greeted Pat and Dick at Hadley Field, where Whittier College even rolled out the purple carpet.[15] Gov. Earl Warren introduced Nixon to the cheering crowd, saying, "All the people of California are rejoicing at your success, Dick."[16] In a nod to his football days, Nixon told his supporters, "You know it took me eighteen years to do it, but I finally made it. I've got off the bench and onto the playing field."[17] Once the official ceremony ended, the Nixons stayed and greeted everyone present before heading over to the Ambassador for the night.[18]

The following morning the Nixons launched an unofficial yet thoroughly exhaustive campaign. California appearances included San Francisco, Sacramento, and Santa Barbara, and Dick often ran into many childhood friends along the campaign trail.[19] When he saw Edward Breitkreutz in San Francisco, Nixon recognized his old college classmate immediately and joked to Breitkreutz's wife, "Oh, I could tell you a lot about Ed, but I don't think I better do it."[20]

As September neared, the Eisenhower-Nixon campaign established a strong foundation with offices throughout Southern California, including satellite offices in Whittier, downtown Los Angeles, and Pomona.[21] Nixon's friend John Reilly served as chairman of the Whittier Eisenhower-Nixon Campaign Committee, and Dana Smith, Nixon's Senate campaign finance chairman, served as chairman of the Southern California Committee of Eisenhower Volunteers.[22]

Once Nixon had been elected to the Senate, his California Committee had set up a fund to offset his political expenses. Dairyman Tom Knudsen and fellow supporters felt that Nixon had "advanced very quickly, and that it might be difficult for him to keep his feet on the ground. We decided that the best way would be to invite him to come back and speak to his constituents in the state of California from time to time. We realized that he had no opportunity to accumulate any funds, as a congressman, and for that reason it would be impossible for him to come out here at his own expense."[23] Smith agreed to serve as the fund's trustee.[24]

On September 14, 1952, following a taping of *Meet the Press*, political columnist Peter Edson took Nixon aside and asked, "Senator, what is this 'fund' we hear about? There is a rumor to the effect that you have a supplementary salary of $20,000 a year, contributed by a hundred California businessmen. What about it?"[25] Nixon immediately gave Edson Dana Smith's telephone number and told him to call Smith for a complete explanation of the fund. Impressed, Edson reflected that Nixon "didn't attempt to duck the question in any way," gave a straightforward description of the nature of the fund, and immediately provided Smith's telephone number as "the best source for further details."[26] Rather than $20,000 a year, the fund totaled $18,235, contributed by seventy-six supporters over two years (averaging $240 per donor).[27] Once Smith received inquiries regarding the fund, he even released the names of all the contributors and the amounts they had contributed.[28]

The official start of the fall vice-presidential campaign was a rally in Pomona three days later, followed by a campaign swing north through the western states.[29] Pomona was selected because Nixon believed in luck, and since his successful congressional and Senate races had started in Pomona, his vice-presidential campaign would too.[30] Herman Perry, Tom Bewley, and John Reilly arranged for a special Union Pacific streamline ten-car train to be brought in from Utah to make the round trip from Whittier to Pomona and back, filled with Nixon's family and friends.[31] Perry donned an engineer's uniform, and Frank, bursting with pride, dressed up as the motorman.[32] On Tuesday, September 16, the Nixons flew into Ontario to spend the night at the Mission Inn, where they were married twelve years before.[33] It was their last night together before they began Dick's first campaign for national office.

At noon on September 17 Nixon held a stag luncheon at the inn to exchange campaign ideas with close friends, while Pat spent the afternoon at a homecoming event in Artesia.[34] The campaign festivities started at 7:00 that bright, warm fall evening at the Pomona train station, with the Pomona Municipal Band playing "The Sunshine of Your Smile" and "There's a Great Day Coming, Mañana."[35] Before an audience of fifteen thousand, Nixon "launched the major assault phase of the Republican campaign" with a speech that had the excited air of a "religious revival," like those he had attended as a boy with his father.[36] As the crowd gathered around the Santa Fe El Capitan, nicknamed the Dick Nixon Special, Roy Day's daughters dressed up as cowgirls and sang "Ragtime Cowboy Joe" for the crowd.[37] Governor Warren introduced Nixon, accidentally stating, "I now present to you the next President of the United States," a promotion Nixon jokingly accepted before the delighted crowd.[38]

In his nationally televised speech, Nixon charged Truman with heading a "scandal-a-day administration" because of the numerous entanglements involving officials accepting gifts, including a

White House secretary who had been given a $9,000 fur coat.[39] Once Nixon concluded his remarks, he and Pat, along with their campaign team and members of the press, boarded the train at 9:00 p.m. as millions watched on live television.[40] Murray Chotiner, Patrick Hillings, William Rogers, and Jack Drown joined Nixon in his private Pullman car.[41] Jack, a self-employed businessman and not a typical campaign professional, had taken time off to serve as Nixon's train manager for the campaign.[42] He brought along a Helms Bakery whistle to signal the engineer from the caboose for the train to depart as Nixon concluded his remarks at each "whistle stop."[43]

As Nixon campaigned north along the West Coast, the "Nixon fund" story was spreading throughout the national media. The *New York Post* claimed that Nixon had a secret millionaires' fund devoted exclusively to his financial benefit.[44] As a media storm gathered, numerous papers across the country began to call for Nixon's removal from the vice-presidential ticket. Some members of the media clearly sought to cast Nixon in a false light, even going so far as to plant empty liquor bottles and glasses outside his room when he stayed in a Portland hotel in hopes of catching a compromising picture.[45] But Nixon's hometown friends, including Lyle Otterman, who handled the escrow on Nixon's home purchase and was familiar with his finances, knew the allegations were false.[46] So did Herman Perry, the town banker who had handled the Nixon family finances since Dick's infancy, was intimately involved in the fund's disbursements, and understood the current situation as one where "someone made political hay with no fault on Nixon's part."[47]

Nevertheless, the Democrats continued to attack Nixon over the fund, in part because he was an easier target than war hero General Eisenhower.[48] As the champion of the Hiss case who had defeated Helen Gahagan Douglas for the Senate seat, Nixon more than any other political figure represented the cultural changing of the guard from the New Deal policies of the Roosevelt and Truman administrations.[49] Plus the Republican Party, and Nixon in particular, had been campaigning on the slogan that there was "a scandal a day" in the Truman administration.[50] As media pressure mounted, Dick and Pat discussed whether he should withdraw from the ticket. Nixon was galvanized by his wife's vigor as she insisted, "You can't think of resigning."[51]

Rather than withdraw, Nixon turned to his roots for strength. Hannah sent a message saying, "I will be thinking of you," her euphemism for "I am praying for you."[52] Tom Bewley and John Reilly, who had once climbed the hills of Whittier to arrange whitewashed rocks into a large letter *N* for Nixon, flew to Portland to offer their support.[53] When they met in Nixon's hotel room, Bewley told Dick, "We just flew up to tell you . . . that all the folks back in Whittier are behind you 100 per cent." Moreover, the East Whittier Friends Church had held a special prayer session for him.[54] Helene Drown even arranged for the Sisters of the Light order of nuns in Long Beach to hold a special mass for Nixon.[55] Dick attended services at the First Friends Church in Portland, Oregon, and afterward reported to Bewley, "I'm not worried anymore."[56] As for those trying to drive him off the Republican ticket, Nixon's protégé Patrick Hillings urged him, "Don't get mad at them, just beat them."[57]

With most television and radio commentators predicting that Nixon would be removed from the ticket, Dick and Pat again discussed what to do. Pat advised, "We both know what you have to do, Dick. You have to fight it all the way to the end, no matter what happens!"[58] After several consultations involving the Republican National Committee, Eisenhower, and Nixon, it was agreed that Dick would explain his side of the Nixon fund on national television. Eisenhower's parting words to Nixon were "Good luck and keep your chin up."[59] The Republican Party purchased a thirty-minute block of primetime television starting at 6:30 p.m. on Tuesday, September 23, so Nixon could reveal the circumstances of the fund. Convinced this was do or die for his political career, Nixon explained, "If I considered the broadcast a success, I would stay on the ticket. If I thought it was a failure, I would get off. Now everything was up to me, the challenge was clear, and I must prepare to meet it."[60]

In spite of the mounting tension, Nixon maintained his sense of humor. After midnight, he called a press conference. "I have come down to announce that I am breaking off," he said, and then paused deliberately. The reporters gasped, expecting a statement of resignation from the ticket. Nixon smiled and continued, telling the newsmen that he was breaking off the campaign to make a nationwide broadcast.[61] The train schedule was canceled, and on Monday, September 22, the Nixon campaign party flew to Los Angeles to prepare a half-hour speech that he would give just over twenty-four hours later.[62]

On their arrival, Pat went to Jack and Helene Drown's new home in Rolling Hills, where she stayed until late the following day.[63] Nixon's campaign team occupied a thirty-two-room wing of the Ambassador. Typically, he would work for at least a week on a major speech, but now he had less than two days to prepare the most important speech of his life.[64] On the flight from Portland, Nixon tried to write notes on issues he wanted to cover in his speech.[65] At the Ambassador, he initially met with his advisors, listening to their suggestions.[66] Eventually, preferring an individual process when it came to making personal decisions, Nixon told them, "All right fellows, I am going into the bedroom and think about this."[67] He then worked through the afternoon and early evening, barely touching the hamburgers sent up by room service.[68] That evening Nixon and William Rogers spent an hour swimming in the hotel pool, then walked the residential streets behind the Ambassador, providing Nixon an opportunity to clear his mind and run through his thoughts with Rogers.[69]

Nixon knew he must accomplish three goals: explain and defend the fund, ward off any future attacks, and launch a counterattack.[70] He had to take his case to the American voters and convince them of his integrity.[71] For Nixon, "the broadcast must not be just good. It had to be a smash hit."[72] As part of his defense, fifty attorneys and accountants from Gibson, Dunn & Crutcher and Price Waterhouse performed a legal analysis and financial audit of the fund.[73]

When news of Nixon's fund broke, Stephen Mitchell, chairman of the Democratic National Committee, commented, "If a fellow can't afford to be a Senator, he shouldn't seek the office." That assertion reminded Nixon of Lincoln's quote "God must have loved the common people, he made so many of them," so he called Paul Smith and Albert Upton in the middle of the night to confirm that the quote was indeed Lincoln's.[74] Professors Smith, Upton, and Charles Cooper rifled through books at the Whittier College Library into the wee hours of the morning to verify the quote.[75]

No typed copy of Nixon's speech existed.[76] Shortly before the broadcast, Sherman Adams, Eisenhower's chief of staff, called Chotiner to find out what Nixon was going to say. After Chotiner replied that he really didn't know, Adams responded, "Oh come now, you must know. He has a script, doesn't he?" To which Chotiner replied, "No." "What about the press?" asked Adams. "We've set up television sets in the hotel room for them, and we have shorthand reporters to take it down, page by page," answered Chotiner. "Look, we have to know what is going to be said," Adams insisted. "Sherm," Chotiner replied, "if you want to know what's going to be said, you do what I'm going to do. You sit in front of the television and listen."[77]

Nixon declined the chance to rehearse because he felt he needed all the available time to prepare his remarks.[78] One hour before the speech, New York governor Tom Dewey, the 1948 presidential candidate, called to urge Nixon to resign from the ticket. Dewey advised that he had polled campaign leaders and they believed resignation was proper, implying that Eisenhower agreed with this assessment.[79] The call was a blow to Nixon, who asked his staff to leave him so that he could decide what to do in the final half hour before leaving for the broadcast.[80] Alone, Nixon deliberated for those thirty minutes. He later reflected, "The final decision in a crisis of this magnitude must not represent the lowest common denominator of a collective judgment; it must be made alone by the individual primarily involved."[81]

At this critical moment, Chotiner walked in, interrupting Nixon, and told him that if he was off the ticket, Chotiner was going to call a press conference, telling all and naming names. Nixon credited Chotiner's "cold, realistic logic" for breaking the tension and allowing Nixon to think "clearly and decisively."[82] At 5:30 on Tuesday evening Nixon knew he was out of time, so he collected his notes, stuffed them in his pocket, and went across the hall to pick up Pat. Together they walked down the hotel corridor to the elevator, with the entire campaign staff lining the hall in silent support.[83] To Nixon, "It seemed like the last mile." Then as he and Pat passed Rose Mary Woods, she provided simple encouragement: "Good luck, Senator."[84]

During the twenty-minute drive to the El Capitan studio, Dick rode in the front seat so he could make a final review of his notes, and no one spoke.[85] By the time they arrived at the studio, Nixon had decided not to follow the course of action suggested by Eisenhower's advisors, but rather to submit the case to the country and let the people decide.[86]

Arriving at the El Capitan at 6:05 p.m., twenty-five minutes before the broadcast, they found the 750-seat theater empty except for cameramen and electricians on stage.[87] Nixon went for a stage check and lighting adjustments ten minutes before the broadcast, but he refused to rehearse, stating, "I don't want this to be or look like an act."[88] The director asked him what movements he would be making during the speech, to which Nixon replied, "I don't have the slightest idea. Just keep the camera on me."[89] When asked if he had timed his speech, Nixon held up five sheets of paper and said, "I'm talking from notes, but don't worry about that," before returning to his dressing room to sit with Pat.[90]

Three minutes before the single most important event of the 1952 campaign, Dick confessed to Pat, "I just don't think I can go through with this one." Pat reassured him, "Of course you can," and they walked to the stage with producer Ted Rogers. Otherwise, the theater was empty except for those essential to the production.[91] Frank Jorgensen, who had been at the Ambassador with Nixon, went home to a dinner party he was hosting, and as he turned on the television, he told his guests, "Watch what happens. The American people will absolutely endorse this one-hundred percent."[92]

On cue, Nixon began: "My fellow Americans, I come before you tonight as a candidate for the vice presidency and as a man whose honesty and integrity has been questioned."[93] Nixon did not read his speech and he had no teleprompters. As he continued, the tension drained from his body, and he realized he felt calm and confident as he explained the nature of the fund, that none of it went to his personal use, and that all the money was used for political expenses.[94] He pointed out that attorneys and accountants from Gibson, Dunn & Crutcher and Price Waterhouse had found nothing wrong with the fund and accounted for all moneys.[95]

Nixon then listed all his and Pat's assets and liabilities, totaling $27,000 and $38,500, respectively.[96] He admitted that his family had received a gift, a dog they named Checkers, and that they were going to keep the dog no matter what. This memorable comment served a dual purpose: it tugged at the heartstrings of all dog-owning families and was also a jab at the Democratic Party. (Eight years earlier President Roosevelt had made a reference to his dog, Fala, in a speech.)[97] In response to DNC chairman Mitchell's declaration that "if a fellow can't afford to be a Senator, he shouldn't seek the office," Nixon commented, "I don't agree with Mr. Mitchell when he says that only a rich man should serve the Government, in the United States Senate, or in the Congress. I don't think that represents the thinking of the Democratic Party, and I know it doesn't represent the thinking of the Republican Party."[98]

The speech was broadcast over 64 NBC stations, 194 CBS radio stations, and almost the entire 560-station Mutual Broadcasting System radio network.[99] That night fifty-eight million Americans watched, the largest audience ever to view a political event.[100] Throughout the speech, Pat sat on the stage in rapt attention, and for those familiar with Pat and Dick, such a sight was no surprise. Ray Arbuthnot, a rancher from La Verne who first met Nixon in the 1946 congressional campaign and recognized Dick as a serious-minded man with a "fine sense of humor," described how he had seen Pat watch Dick's speeches in the past: "She looked at him, very tender, you could feel that she was just rooting that nothing should go wrong."[101]

The speech profoundly affected all those involved in its production. When William Rogers saw that the cameramen were crying, he realized "the broadcast had turned defeat into victory."[102] Studio director Ted Rogers explained that it was the toughest program he had ever directed, "not only because of the importance of the principle involved, but rather because Nixon ignored practically all established rules of TV production." Nixon told Rogers he wanted to be completely on his own; camera angles, posing, and timing meant nothing to him. He was just anxious to get before the cameras and tell his side of the story. But the drawback, since he wouldn't rehearse, was that he was still talking when the program went off the air.[103]

Thankful the experience was behind him, Nixon told Rogers, "Let's get out of here and get a fast one. I need it."[104] As they drove away from the El Capitan, Dick, seeing an Irish setter running alongside their car, wryly commented, "Well, at least we got the dog vote."[105] In the twenty minutes it took to drive back to the Ambassador, a crowd had gathered there to greet the Nixons.[106] Nixon described the scene: "The long lobby which had been so quiet when we left for the broadcast an hour and a half before was now filled with people. . . . They literally mobbed us, pounding Pat and me on the back shaking our hands, cheering, characterizing the broadcast as 'great,' 'magnificent,' and with other superlatives. It took us almost a half-hour to make our way through the crowds to our room."[107] Even more people jammed the telephone lines to the Ambassador with calls of support for Nixon.[108] By 10:30 p.m. the Nixons departed the Ambassador to resume their campaign.[109]

Nixon had successfully turned himself into an asset as the Republican campaign soared, securing him as a national figure. He was the best-known vice-presidential candidate in history, drawing the largest crowds.[110] All told, of the over four million letters and telegrams sent in response to his speech, they ran 350–1 in favor of Nixon.[111] Typical of the letters was a wire sent by Mr. and Mrs. Mold of Los Angeles: "You did make us cry a little. We love you, we trust you, and we are voting for you. We are asking our congregation to pray for you Sunday, Yom Kippur day, so that God gives you the strength to carry on."[112] General Eisenhower even received a unique telegram saying, "Dear General: I am trusting that the absolute truth may come out concerning this attack on Richard, and when it does I am sure you will be guided right in your decision, to place implicit faith in his integrity and honesty. Best wishes from one who has known Richard longer than anyone else. His Mother."[113]

Nixon wrote notes to all his friends, thanking them for their support, and postcards to his supporters.[114] Having reflected on the statement Eisenhower made early in the crisis that Nixon had to be "clean as a hound's tooth" to stay on the ticket, Nixon formed the Order of the Hound's Tooth with friends Jack and Helene Drown, his staff, and the press corps who had been with him from Pomona to Portland and back to Los Angeles as charter members, with his dog Checkers serving as mascot.[115]

Nevertheless, the experience left deep scars, and more than twenty years later Nixon admitted that the agony of the fund crisis had stripped the fun and excitement from campaigning.[116] The bias in media coverage was blatant: Democrat Adlai Stevenson controlled a fund worth $146,000 that the media ignored.[117] That this same media attacked Nixon for having a $20,000 fund that he did not control was a double standard not lost on Nixon.[118]

One month later Nixon returned to California for a four-day campaign swing. On October 29 he gave a nationally televised speech from the KNXT television studio in Los Angeles, directed to "the forgotten men and women of America," charging that "the average American family is caught in a squeeze of high prices on the one side and high taxes on the other."[119] Nixon implored the television audience to vote for General Eisenhower, who was the only candidate able to "clean up this mess," since "[he is] not tied to the big city bosses, he is not tied to Harry Truman and he is not tied to the big labor bosses."[120]

On the drive from Los Angeles to Yorba Linda, Pat and Dick stopped in East Whittier to see his parents, Don and Clara Jane, and their children, Lawrene, Donnie, and newborn Ricky, named after his famous uncle.[121] In Yorba Linda, George Kellogg, a family friend since before Dick's birth, was to introduce Nixon, but instead he asked Pat to do the honor. Afterward, Pat told him, "I want to thank you, Mr. Kellogg, because that was the first time in my life that I have been asked to introduce my husband, and I take that as quite a compliment."[122]

Nixon's campaign swing through his home turf was a big event, and during additional stops at the City Park in Brea, Barton's Corner in Yorba Linda, the Orange County Courthouse, and Laguna Beach City Hall, excited kids were let out of school early so they could see Nixon speak.[123] Throughout the tour, he took aim at Stevenson and President Truman. Before he finished the day at the Wilton Hotel in Long Beach, Nixon told the excited crowds that the previous summer, when Adlai Stevenson had admitted that he was not equipped physically or mentally to be president, Truman's response was "That's my man." Nixon added, "When it comes to picking men, Harry Truman is the champion lemon picker of our time."[124]

Nixon's final California campaign tour began in Long Beach with an appearance at the band shell on the beach before a crowd of three thousand.[125] He then zigzagged across Los Angeles: through Grevillea Park on La Brea Boulevard in Inglewood and past the beach at Palisades Park in Santa Monica, the Beverly Hills City Hall, Van Nuys–Sherman Oaks Memorial Park, Magnolia and Hollywood Way in Burbank, the Pasadena City Hall, and the Alhambra Public Library on Main Street before taking a brief rest back at the Ambassador.[126] The schedule was so full that the campaign team barely had time to stop and pick up box lunches to eat along the way.[127] Finally, Nixon concluded his swing with his fourteenth event of the day: a speech at the Hollywood Legion Stadium.[128] Three thousand wildly cheering supporters joined numerous Hollywood celebrities in a show of support for their hometown candidate.[129] Speaking at the boxing stadium, Nixon continued to "toss body blows" at Stevenson, linking him to Truman's secretary of state Dean Acheson, even joking that "Stevenson holds a Ph.D. degree from Acheson's college of cowardly Communist containment."[130]

On Election Day, November 4, the Nixons, who had decided to watch the election returns with his California Committee rather than with Eisenhower, flew to Ontario, landing at 11:15 a.m. From there they drove straight to Whittier, arriving to vote by noontime.[131] Nixon spent the day with Rogers in Laguna Beach, walking along the ocean at the old Hotel Riviera and even playing a pickup football game with some marines they had met. At one point during the game, Dick dropped a pass, causing one marine to joke, "You'll make a better vice president than football player," before quickly adding, "Sir."[132]

Nixon and Rogers returned to the Ambassador for a reception in the Gold Room. By 6:00 that evening the thirty-nine-year-old Richard Nixon knew that his victory would be by a landslide, and it was: the Eisenhower-Nixon ticket won by a decisive margin of 55.1 to 44.4 percent of the popular vote. The Electoral College was even more lopsided: 442 to 89 electoral votes, with Ike carrying thirty-nine of the forty-eight states.[133]

Frank, Hannah, and the entire Nixon family celebrated in a large suite on the second floor of the Ambassador. When word came that Stevenson was about to speak, the party moved downstairs into the hotel's main ballroom to watch the Democratic candidate concede the race on the television, then watch President-elect Eisenhower's victory speech, after which Nixon took the stage and spoke to his supporters.[134] The entire Nixon family was elated, and Frank was overheard boasting, "I'm the father of the vice president," to which Hannah responded, "I'm the mother of Richard Nixon."[135] Dick's success meant everything to his father, confirming that what Frank believed was true—"that in America, with hard work and determination, a man can achieve anything."[136] In pursuit of the vice presidency, Dick traveled forty-six thousand miles, spoke at 143 whistle-stops, and visited 214 cities. All the while, the campaign song "The Sunshine of Your Smile" played at his appearances.[137]

Southern California celebrated Dick Nixon's rise to national prominence. On Wednesday, December 31, the Nixons flew to Los Angeles, where they were greeted by his brother Don and an official from the Tournament of Roses, who escorted them to the Huntington Hotel in Pasadena.[138] The following day Nixon served as grand marshal of the Rose Parade and Rose Bowl game, where Pat's beloved USC defeated the University of Wisconsin.[139] Dick arranged for both his and Pat's families to have tickets to the parade and game.[140] Having flown in for the day's events, the Nixons left immediately after hosting a dinner at the Ambassador for key friends and supporters that made up the core of his California Committee.[141]

Hannah was immensely proud of her son's accomplishments, and just before his inauguration, she gave him a handwritten note:

To Richard:

You have gone far, and we are proud of you always—I know that you will keep your relationship with your Maker as it should be, for after all, that, as you must know, is the most important thing in this life.

With love,
Mother

Nixon kept this note in his wallet for the rest of his life.[142]

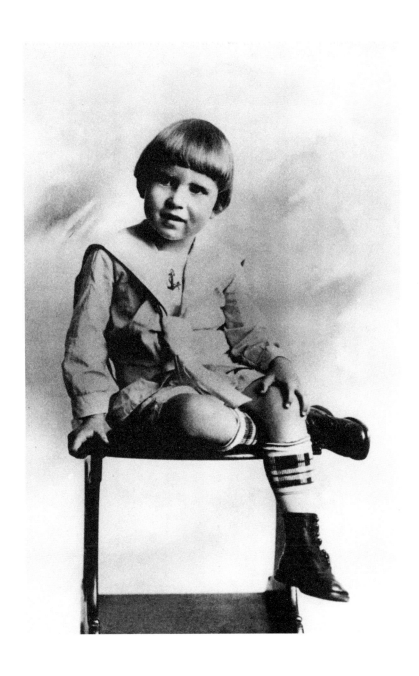

1. Four-year-old Richard Milhous Nixon in 1917. Richard Nixon Foundation.

2. Dick as a blind man, with girlfriend Ola Florence Welch, on Whittier High's Dress Up Day in 1930. Courtesy of Whittier College Special Collections and Archives, Wardman Library, Whittier, California.

3. Dick (#12) at Whittier College, always ready to play yet rarely sent to the field (1933). Courtesy of Whittier College Special Collections and Archives, Wardman Library, Whittier, California.

4. Dick (*left*) with girlfriend Ola Florence, her friend Roberta, and his brother Harold, suited up for a play date in the local snow-covered mountains (1930). Courtesy of Whittier College Special Collections and Archives, Wardman Library, Whittier, California.

5. Pat Ryan, a spirited young woman, with her roadster near her home in Artesia. Richard Nixon Foundation.

6. Dick snow skiing when the sport was still in its infancy. Richard Nixon Foundation.

7. Pat and Dick (*far right*) at the wedding of Virginia and Curtis Counts in 1940. Richard Nixon Foundation.

8. Nixon (*bottom left with helmet*) and his fellow servicemen in 1943. Home was never far from their minds. Richard Nixon Foundation.

9. Nixon with Democratic mascot. In 1948 Nixon cross-filed in the Democratic primary—and won—effectively reelected by the Democratic Party. Richard Nixon Foundation.

10. Dick campaigning from the tailgate of his customized Woody wagon in 1950. Pat and Dick frequently traveled the state in the Woody while campaigning. Richard Nixon Foundation.

11. The vice president elect and
Pat Nixon returning from Mexico
in December 1952, tan, rested,
and ready. AP Photo / BHR.

12. Nixon letting his hair down while traveling in 1953. He traveled more
extensively than any previous vice president. Richard Nixon Foundation.

13. Hollywood legends Zeppo Marx, Danny Kaye, and Danny Thomas, along with PGA pro Eric Monti (*third from left*), praying for Dick to win on the links. Richard Nixon Foundation.

14. Julie, Pat, and Dick enjoying a sundae along with Tricia (*not pictured*) on Main Street USA at Disneyland in 1959. Richard Nixon Foundation.

15. Nixon entertaining Tricia's birthday party guests with songs on the piano in 1953. Richard Nixon Foundation.

16. Dick gamely wearing a chef's cap and apron after being asked for his favorite recipe (1953). Richard Nixon Foundation.

17. Pat and Dick stepping out for a night at the Hollywood Bowl in 1955. Richard Nixon Foundation.

18. (*opposite bottom*) Ike and Dick enjoying a hearty laugh (1959). Richard Nixon Foundation.

19. Southern California celebrating its native son as the 1960 Rose Parade grand marshal. Richard Nixon Foundation.

20. Longtime friends Bob Hope and Dick Nixon, sizing up each other's noses (1963). Courtesy of Whittier College Special Collections and Archives, Wardman Library, Whittier, California.

21. President and Mrs. Nixon on what they called "one of their happiest days in the White House," the wedding of their daughter Tricia to Edward Cox in the Rose Garden on June 12, 1971. Richard Nixon Foundation.

22. President Nixon relaxing,
enjoying the serenity of La Casa
Pacifica. Richard Nixon Foundation.

23. The president enjoying a light moment as everyone scurries about at the La Casa Pacifica helipad (1973). Richard Nixon Foundation.

24. Nixon arriving at the El Toro Marine Air Station in California on August 9, 1974, the day of his resignation. The anguish was apparent on his face. Richard Nixon Foundation, courtesy of Patrick O'Donnell.

25. Dick cheering on his beloved Angels
baseball team (1979). As he recovered from
the depths of his resignation, Dick lived his
mantra displayed on this sign: "Never Give
Up!" Richard Nixon Foundation.

26. Dick playing the piano in 1975. At home with just each other, Dick often played for Pat. Richard Nixon Foundation.

27. Richard Milhous Nixon, with Julie and Melanie Eisenhower and Tricia (*standing*) and Christopher Cox, clearly enjoying life as a grandfather (1979). Richard Nixon Foundation.

TEN

Vice President

1953–56

O n January 20, 1953, a week and a half after his fortieth birthday, Richard Milhous Nixon was sworn in as vice president of the United States, the second youngest as of this writing. Many friends and family traveled east for the inauguration. Whittier College classmate Tolbert Moorhead was impressed at how Nixon expressed his appreciation on seeing him: "Dick has a way about him that is very beautiful. If you're his friend, you're his friend."[1] Since the cost was prohibitive for some, whenever Dick received any complimentary tickets, he passed them along to those who might otherwise be unable to attend.[2]

Knowing that many of his Whittier relatives had never been to Washington DC, Nixon arranged for them to tour the Capitol Building and join him for lunches in the Senate Dining Room. As vice president elect, Nixon was provided a car with a part-time driver, which he sent to chauffeur his cousin Lucille Parsons, her husband and parents, and Frank and Hannah on a tour of George Washington's estate. When the group stopped for lunch at Washington's old teahouse in Arlington, the driver planned to wait outside alone, but Lucille and the others insisted he join them for lunch. It was the first time the chauffeur, who had driven families of presidents, vice presidents, and senators, had ever been extended such a courtesy.[3]

The Nixon family's preference for simplicity was evident when the time came to dress for the inaugural ball, where formality reigns supreme.[4] Frank took one look at his tuxedo and declared, "I am not going to wear those blasted tails!" causing Hannah to lament, "I don't know what I'm going to do with him." Dick stepped in, telling his mother, "I'll handle Dad." Just before it was time to leave, he announced, "All right, Dad, we're getting into these clothes," and uncharacteristically, Frank did as told. Entering the ball and finding his table, Frank dramatically flipped his tails up as he sat down, telling his table guests, "They made me do it."[5]

In addition to his part-time driver, Nixon now had a staff of eleven and was assigned a Secret Service agent, Jack Sherwood, who had spent ten years on the White House detail. Nixon's Secret Service protection was part-time, with Sherwood only covering his office hours and when he attended events of more than three hundred guests. Sherwood recalled that Nixon "wasn't much interested" in protection but agreed to try it for a few months.[6] His home life did not measurably change; the vice president had no official residence, so Pat and Dick continued to live in their modest home, focusing on providing Tricia and Julie as normal an upbringing as possible.

One of Nixon's first acts as vice president was to stand for women's equality. The duties of the Office of the Vice President include delivering official proclamations and resolutions from the states to the Senate. Loie Gaunt, a staffer since Nixon's Senate years, was assigned the task, but the first time she tried to carry it out, she was told by the Senate sergeant at arms that the job had to be done by a man. Gaunt returned to the office and informed "the Boss," as the staff affectionately referred to Nixon. Incredulous, Nixon responded, "What? What is this?" He immediately went to the Senate chamber, where he advised the sergeant at arms that Gaunt was assigned the duty, was able to carry out the job, and was the person from his office who was going to perform the duties from that day forward, which she did.[7]

Hannah had arranged to save the red carpet on which Dick stood when he was sworn in as vice president.[8] When she showed the red carpet to Dick's Whittier College classmate Nathaniel George, he told her, "Well, he's going to send you another, because one day, he'll be president."[9] Yet as proud as she was of Dick, Hannah was careful to treat her sons equally.[10] Whenever asked how her son was, she replied, "Well, which son do you mean? I have three and I am proud of them all."[11] She never hesitated to tell Dick what was on her mind, and family friend Hoyt Corbit remembered Hannah calling Dick when an issue arose that she felt he should know about. "She talked to Richard without any question and told him quietly what she thought." Dick didn't interrupt her; he simply said, "Thank you, Mother."[12]

He was the first vice president ever to preside over a cabinet meeting and also the first sent on an official worldwide goodwill mission.[13] In January 1954 the Delta Sigma Chi journalism fraternity at USC, in conjunction with the *Daily Trojan*, unanimously voted Nixon "Man of the Year."[14] Announcing the award, the *Daily Trojan* explained, "Nixon has climbed . . . from political nothingness to a vice president who is really the number two man in national stature."[15] *Time* magazine proclaimed Nixon the "Eisenhower administration official most likely to succeed."[16] The *Hayward Daily Review* editorialized that Nixon was "more devoted to principles than politics; more to men and women and less to the votes they represent."[17]

Despite Dick's rapid political ascent, the Nixons remained unpretentious. When Pat was introduced to India prime minister Jawaharlal Nehru while on their first tour of Asia and the Far East, she calmed her nerves by telling herself, "You are just Pat Nixon from Artesia."[18] They had that same attitude, "humility without being obviously humble," wherever they went.[19] On his first trip home as vice president, Dick spent the night with the Boy Scouts at the Irvine Ranch, where he bartered with the kids, trading a signed business card for a "scalp" and a fountain pen for a rattlesnake skin.[20] When a local newspaper asked to write a story about his accomplishments as vice president, he gamely donned an apron and chef's hat and perused the family refrigerator for a photo, even sharing his favorite chili con carne recipe.[21]

Regardless of his political success, Pat and Dick were far from wealthy. Nixon's net take-home pay as vice president was just over $2,000 a month, so rather than maintain a residence in California, in May 1954 the Nixons sold the house on Anaconda Street, where Frank and Hannah had lived since moving back to California. Dick's parents wanted to buy the nearby Macy house, a large white frame structure on three-quarters of an acre, set back in an orange grove along Beach Boulevard at the county line, so Dick negotiated its purchase.[22] The nine-room home had an elevator, which was a convenience for Frank, who suffered from arthritis; for entertaining, it had a twenty-by-forty-foot living room, which Hannah loved.[23]

Nixon was "a loyal Whittier man every day of his life," and his hometown was close to his heart.[24] He frequently wrote to his friends, including Marshall Johnson Clow, whose family had helped take care of Nixon's ailing brother Harold over twenty years earlier, telling Marshall, "I shall never forget the kindness which you showed Harold and all the rest of the Nixons."[25] He gladly accepted an invitation to speak at the 1954 Whittier College commencement, where he was awarded an honorary doctorate of laws.[26] The vice president dedicated a three-day weekend to the event and planned to stay with his parents at their new house.[27]

He was greeted at Los Angeles International Airport by Tony Pierno, the Whittier College student body president; Clint Harris and William Soeberg, Nixon's teammates from Whittier College; and his former professor Charlie Cooper. They all returned via Florence Boulevard in a three-car motorcade, with Secret Service agents in the lead and following cars.[28] They were in the middle car, with Harris, who often provided vehicles for Nixon when he was in town, driving; Secret Service agent Rex Scouten and Soeberg sharing the front seat; and Pierno, Nixon, and Cooper in the back seat.[29] At the intersection of Broadway and Florence in South Central Los Angeles, a vehicle driven by a young man who'd had too much to drink, along with his female companion, careened around the corner. His vehicle hit the lead Secret Service car, sideswiped Nixon's car, and then hit the third car, thus disabling both Secret Service vehicles.[30] The vice president stood on the corner for over an hour at nightfall, waiting for the Secret Service to obtain two replacement cars. Soon a slight African American man approached and asked if he was Mr. Nixon, to which he replied, "I am, and who are you?" The man identified himself, and they shook hands. Then the man put his hand in his pocket and announced, "I ain't ever gonna wash that one again," as they both roared with laughter.[31]

At the commencement ceremony, he was warmly welcomed back to campus. Nixon accepted his honorary degree not for himself, but for his entire class of 1934, explaining that his classmates had become teachers, businessmen, bankers, farmers, and lawyers, and that it took far more courage for a teacher to face fifty students than for him to speak to fifty million people through a television broadcast.[32] He exhorted the graduates that both political parties needed their effort and commitment, pointing out that Christian colleges like Whittier were important to democracy, as they recognized "the fundamental truth that education which is not based soundly on philosophy and religion is no more than technological cleverness," and urged that each graduate be dedicated to public service in some way.[33]

Following the ceremony, Nixon met the graduating seniors and their families on the school tennis courts.[34] When Pierno, Nixon's host for the weekend festivities, came through the reception line with his fiancé and his and her families, Dick welcomed the couple by saying, "Hey, I hear you two are getting married?" to which Pierno replied, "Yes." Nixon asked, "When?" and then, before anyone could respond, announced, "Well, I am vice president, and I must be able to perform weddings," and with that he conducted an impromptu wedding ceremony.[35]

Professor Cooper, marveling at the number of hands Nixon shook, remarked that his hand must be tired. Dick replied, "That's not as great as the strain of looking in the eye of each person with whom you shake hands, so that he knows that you're greeting him as a person."[36]

Just before the Whittier commencement, Herman Perry had died of a heart attack, and while in town, Nixon met with Perry's son Hubert to express his condolences.[37] Herman had attended the 1952 inauguration, and Dick had given him the flag that was flown over the Capitol Building as Nixon was sworn in as vice president.[38] Nixon had also developed a friendship with Herbert Hoover, who was living at the Waldorf Astoria in New York City. He knew that Hoover happened to be Herman's favorite president, so he had arranged for Herman, Hubert, and Hubert's wife, Louise, to spend an evening with Hoover in his suite. Hubert later reflected, "That evening was the highlight of my father's life."[39]

Nixon welcomed all his friends and supporters to his home and office when they visited Washington DC. Whittier College classmate Harley McClure observed, "The vice president's door seemed to always be very accessible to people from Whittier."[40] When Mel Rich, Nixon's friend from the Whittier 20-30 Club, was in Washington and the hotel desk clerk told him, "I have a message here for you to call the vice president," Rich was so surprised that Nixon had tracked him down at his hotel that he replied, "The vice president of what?"[41]

Nixon often met friends, explaining the function of government to their children, giving tours to scout troops, and taking pictures on the steps of the Capitol.[42] When childhood friend and classmate Mary Pickering, her husband, and their three sons visited, he surprised the boys by telling them how he used to deliver groceries to their mother when they were youngsters.[43] Nixon, who enjoyed seeing friends and family from home, was known to take guests down to the Senate floor to sit in the vice president's chair.[44]

By 1954 Dick's younger brother Ed was working at the Santa Fe Drilling Company in Signal Hill, California, when a ladder crushed his left hand, seriously injuring the entry-level roughneck. He was hospitalized for two weeks at the Bixby Knolls Hospital, where Dick made a special trip to check on his brother's condition, bringing along Don and Hannah.[45] Ed described the excitement of his visit: "The hospital staff was all agog, scurrying around with excitement and seeking autographs."[46]

Nixon was Eisenhower's chief campaigner for the Republican Party, with *Newsweek* dubbing him "the sparkplug of the entire Republican campaign."[47] When Nixon returned to Long Beach on October 27 to speak at the band shell at Rainbow Pier just before the midterm elections, he was so popular that his entire motorcade route was published in advance to enable onlookers a chance to see Nixon as he drove by.[48]

Nixon traveled with minimal staff.[49] His former law office provided him with space to work, and his former secretary Evlyn Dorn worked for Nixon as well, even accompanying him on campaign swings throughout the state.[50] Evlyn had dedicated herself to Nixon's success since she first worked for him in the 1930s, and she now served as the functional equivalent of his field office representative, albeit unpaid and working out of her home.[51]

In the six weeks leading up to the November 2, 1954, midterm elections, Nixon traveled twenty-six thousand miles, visited ninety-five cities in thirty states, and made speeches on behalf of 186 House, Senate, and gubernatorial candidates.[52] During this process, Nixon realized that his heart wasn't in the battle, and for the first time, he acknowledged how much the agony of the fund crisis had stripped the fun and excitement of campaigning from him: "I resented being constantly vilified as a demagogue or a liar or as the sewer dwelling denizen of the Herblock cartoons. As the attacks became more personal, I sometimes wondered where party loyalty left off and masochism began."[53] Tricia and Julie were reaching an impressionable age, and neither Pat nor Dick wanted their father to be the bad guy of American politics.[54] Clearly, Nixon "loved the pressure of great events," but he also had a sensitive side, and following the November election, he noted in a personal memorandum, "Politicians must be able not to take issues to heart—fight and forget—twist and turn—I live each one—and hard ones."[55] Nixon was frank: "Politics is not for the weak of heart. Even grizzled types like me get bruised," before cautioning, "Never admit it, though."[56]

Nixon's sensitive side was no surprise to those close to him, who knew him as friendly and well liked, and several claimed they didn't know anyone who actually knew him and didn't like him.[57] Despite his tough exterior on the campaign trail, reporter Stewart Alsop and those who engaged with Nixon found him to be "interesting and likable," as well as a formidable politician.[58] When Alsop encouraged Nixon to take up a hobby to soften his image, Nixon demurred, "You've got to be what you are, and you can't pretend to be something different."[59] With this straightforward style, Nixon won over reporters once hostile toward him, such as Earl Mazo of the *New York Herald Tribune*, who concluded, "Mr. and Mrs. Nixon have been gracious, kind and friendly. Leaving politics aside, they are a couple of decent human beings."[60]

In March the Nixons were able to fly commercially direct from Washington DC to Los Angeles for the first time, and on arrival, they went straight to Frank and Hannah's before attending a dinner party at the La Verne home of Ray Arbuthnot, a charter member of Nixon's California Committee.[61] Afterward, Nixon, who appreciated hospitality and frequently corresponded with friends and supporters, complimented Ray: "The beautiful buffet, the refreshments, and the hospitality were tops in every respect and my only regret is that I couldn't have spent two or three days drinking in the beauty of the countryside!"[62]

Nixon attended services at the East Whittier Friends Church with his parents and brothers, staying after to mingle with fellow parishioners.[63] He maintained his membership and financially supported the church, sending contributions for new choir robes one year and new hymnals another, as he believed that "now more than ever, those of us in public life have need of spiritual guidance and direction in solving the problems which confront us daily."[64]

Dick and Pat then joined her brother Tom, a commander in the navy reserve, at the annual inspection of the naval and marine air reservists at the Los Alamitos Naval Air Station in Long Beach.[65] Nixon stressed the importance of the military as he addressed an audience of fifty thousand: "We have created great military strength in the United States because strength is the only way in which to deal with a potential enemy," adding that the United States pursued peace, but "peace without surrender." Following his remarks, the U.S. Navy's elite Blue Angels delighted the crowd with an aerial acrobatics show. Afterward, Brig. Gen. F. H. Lamson-Scribner complimented the vice president: "The prestige of the inspection was greatly enhanced by your presence."[66]

At the Ambassador, Nixon attended the Republican luncheon, where he demonstrated his loyalty in his usual low-key manner.[67] Dick arranged for Dana Smith, whose fund had nearly derailed his vice-presidential candidacy, to join him at the head table.[68] Rather than avoid the man who had indirectly caused him so much grief, Nixon openly spent time with Smith and never wavered in his friendship. In November 1952 Nixon even had President-elect Eisenhower write to Smith, thanking him for his support.[69] Over the years, Nixon and Smith often wrote to each other, and Nixon sent a personal letter to Smith on learning that his young son had died.[70] Eisenhower recognized Nixon's compassion, sending a telegram to the luncheon attendees: "With all of you in Los Angeles, I join in tribute to our vice president, a man who has demonstrated his dedication to our country. His warmth of heart, his sincerity and human touch have won the affection of many millions here and in distant countries. With you, who are his neighbors, I am happy that I can call Dick Nixon my friend."[71]

That evening at the Biltmore, Nixon addressed the World Affairs Council, on which several members of Nixon's California Committee served.[72] In a nationwide broadcast, Nixon, who had just completed a monthlong tour of Central America and the Caribbean, was introduced by Gen. Omar Bradley.[73] Addressing concerns about Communist expansion in the West, Nixon explained that it was important the United States demonstrate to its southern neighbors that "we have a continued interest in their welfare and not just think of them in time of crisis," telling the audience, "A consistent economic policy is the best hope for a bulwark against Communist encroachment in this hemisphere."[74]

When Disneyland opened on July 17, Pat and Dick made a special trip to be among the thousands to experience the new attraction. They took their daughters and Don's family to visit the theme park, where Walt Disney and Davy Crockett, portrayed by Fess Parker in his popular TV role, presented Nixon with a key to Main Street City Hall.[75] From Tomorrowland to Fantasyland and everything in between, including flying to the moon on Star of Polaris and piloting the Mark Twain riverboat, the Nixon families thoroughly enjoyed the new theme park.[76]

In August 1955 the Nixon family returned to Southern California for a nine-day vacation at Frank and Hannah's Beach Boulevard home.[77] Enjoying the warm Southern California summer, they relaxed with Pat's family at her childhood home in Artesia; drove down to San Diego for lunch with youngest brother Eddie Nixon, who was serving in the navy; and had Sunday dinner with Dick's California Committee at journalist Kyle Palmer's Beverly Hills home, always "superb in the great Palmer tradition."[78] They attended a family gathering at Don's home and joined the larger Milhous family reunion at the La Sierra Avenue home of Uncle Oscar and Aunt Olive Marshburn, pillars of the East Whittier Friends Church. Yet another evening Don gave Dick a tour of his restaurant, after which they dined on Nixonburgers at Don's drive-in.[79] Pat and Dick both loved Southern California's beaches and set aside two afternoons to introduce their daughters to the Pacific Ocean.[80] Whittier College classmate and local car dealer Clint Harris lent Dick a convertible so they could drive in Southern California style. He was greatly amused to find a stash of footballs and beach toys when Nixon returned the car.[81]

Nixon relaxed playing golf, albeit poorly. After spending the day at Los Angeles Country Club with California Committee member Asa Call, he complimented his host: "The company was tops, the refreshments and food could not be surpassed. The only weak part of the day as far as I was concerned was my golf game!"[82] Nixon squeezed in another round at Hillcrest Country Club with Harry Brand, publicity director for 20th Century Fox Studios.[83] His playing partners included entertainers Eddie Fisher, Danny Thomas, Milton Berle, Jack Benny, and George Burns.[84] Later Nixon joked with Brand about one of his errant golf shots: "I hope you will tell Eddie Fisher again how glad I am that he turned out to be such a good dodger—otherwise we might have had a casualty in our midst!"[85]

Friendship and loyalty were important to Nixon.[86] He and Pat joined Norm and Buff Chandler for a night out, beginning with dinner at the Chandlers' apartment in the Los Angeles Times Building. Buff, who was president of the Hollywood Bowl Association, was working with several of Nixon's California Committee members to save the bowl from financial collapse. After dinner, they all attended the celebration of the Festival of the Americas, conducted by Leonard Bernstein at the bowl, where Nixon served as honorary president.[87]

Pat and Dick were delighted to attend an after-party reception at the Sunset Boulevard home of Ed Pauley, a well-known Democrat, staying past two in the morning.[88] When famed *Los Angeles Times* columnist Hedda Hopper saw Pat and asked her who helped her with her beautiful makeup, Dick, standing nearby, smiled as he complimented his wife: "That's no make-up, that's just Pat."[89]

Some local supporters were opposed to his socializing with Pauley and expressed their dismay, but Nixon downplayed the criticism, reassuring prominent Los Angeles attorney J. Stanley Mullin, founding partner of Sheppard, Mullin, Richter & Hampton, "I wanted you to know that while the reception is being given in Mr. Pauley's home, it is being given by the civic committee which is sponsoring the Festival of the Americas. Otherwise, you may be sure I would not be attending it!"[90] Taking the protest in stride, he wryly told another, "I certainly hope no irreparable damage was done—at least to our side!"[91]

The reality was that Nixon and Pauley had a cordial relationship dating back to Nixon's Senate campaign, when Pauley silently endorsed Nixon. After the Festival of the Americas party, Nixon complimented Pauley: "Pat and I have attended receptions in many of the capitals of the world—as well as in Washington—and we both said on our way home from the Pauleys' that we had never seen a more beautiful home or a party that was more superb in every respect."[92] Pauley, in turn, was equally effusive: "The vice president could not have been more cordial, nor could he have assisted Mrs. Pauley and I in entertaining our guests more graciously."[93]

Shortly after this event, former president Truman and his wife stayed at Pauley's home for several days. Truman and Nixon had no relationship to speak of since the Alger Hiss case, and Truman asked Pauley if the stairs in his home were the same stairs shown in a photograph of Pauley with Nixon. When Pauley said they were, Truman commented, "Well, you know, I had a very peculiar feeling when I saw his picture with you on those stairs in your home. You know, he once called me a traitor." Pauley replied, "Well, I have heard that, but I had also heard that you were confused about it, that it didn't happen." Later, when Pauley met the vice president in Washington and mentioned the incident, Nixon assured him that this was not something he had actually said; he had been misquoted. To the contrary, Nixon told Pauley, he had "a very kindly feeling toward Mr. Truman" and was sorry Truman felt otherwise. Pauley reported this to Truman and came away believing he had helped mend fences between the former president and current vice president.[94]

Nixon corresponded with friends he could not see on his visits home, complimenting them for their accomplishments, keeping abreast of personal tragedies, and always writing when someone suffered a death in the family.[95] He also had a terrific network of local friends and relatives to look in on Frank and Hannah, and he frequently expressed his appreciation to those who cared for his parents as they grew older, writing notes to say, "I want you to know how deeply I appreciate your kindness."[96] In addition to visiting his parents whenever he was in town, Pat and Dick also frequently wrote to them, updating them on the family's activities and telling them of different political figures who had asked about them.[97]

A month after the Nixons returned to Washington, President Eisenhower suffered a heart attack while visiting his mother-in-law in Denver, and the news reached Dick at home in the early afternoon. When acting attorney general William Rogers joined Nixon, he could see the vice president was upset and had been crying at the news of Eisenhower's condition.[98] Hoping to avoid the media, the two went straight to Rogers's house, and Rogers was struck by Nixon's reaction to the crisis, noting that it was "contrary to his whole nature to say 'what will I do if the president dies.'"[99] Instead, trying to determine what the vice president's legal position was when the president was incapacitated, Nixon asked, "What does the Constitution say?" The attorney general replied, "I'm sorry, I don't have the vaguest idea."

Rogers immediately picked up the phone to have copy of the Constitution sent over. "For God's sake, don't do that!" exclaimed Nixon. "If it ever gets out that the Vice President and the Attorney General don't know what the Constitution says, we'd look like a couple of complete idiots." Rogers then found a copy of the Constitution in the front of his *Farmers' Almanac*, but the Constitution had no provision for such a circumstance.[100] Yet Nixon was confident both in himself and in the president's belief that he could stand in for him, as six months earlier, Eisenhower had commented at the White House Correspondents' Dinner that he was "gratified that Nixon was there to take his place should anything happen," adding that Nixon's "stock was very high in the White House."[101]

The Republican Party had been successful in California since 1946, when Nixon was first elected to the House of Representatives. The first signs of a fracture surfaced in late 1955, as Eisenhower's first term was coming to a close. Following the president's heart attack, California governor Goodwin Knight became a "shadow contender" should Eisenhower decide not to run for reelection in 1956.[102] Knight, who had been lieutenant governor, was elevated to governor once Eisenhower appointed Earl Warren as chief justice of the United States. Knight, who was then elected to the governorship in 1954 and considered Nixon a future rival for the White House, warned that Eisenhower would lose California with Nixon on the ticket in 1956.[103] In response, on the eve of the 1956 Republican National Convention, former Minnesota governor Harold Stassen started a "dump Nixon" campaign, supported by Governor Knight, the only other prominent Republican to do so.[104]

Stassen and Knight failed to realize how strongly Eisenhower supported Nixon, as demonstrated in this statement by the president: "Anyone who attempts to drive a wedge of any kind between Dick Nixon and me has just as much chance as if he tried to drive it between my brother and me."[105] While Eisenhower had earlier advised Nixon to take a cabinet post of his choosing, with the sole exception of secretary of state (reserved for John Foster Dulles), he did so because he believed Nixon would have difficulty being elected president after serving as vice president. Stassen and Knight misread Eisenhower's motives and mistakenly thought they could lead a "dump Nixon" charge, and after their move to replace Nixon on the ticket failed, they were excoriated by the press. The *Los Angeles Times* declared Stassen and Knight were the "biggest flops" of the Republican National Convention: "Ready for the mortuary of political ambition are two gentlemen who have made more headlines, done more talking and accomplished less than any politicians of our time."[106] The *Washington Evening Star* was especially pointed: "There's one thing about Harold Stassen—he likes to go down with his ship, and he doesn't care how many times it's sunk."[107]

On Saturday, August 18, Dick arrived at the Republican National Convention in San Francisco, the city chosen partly as a nod to Nixon's aspirations.[108] Frank was terribly upset that he was not well enough to attend the convention, and his condition worsened when he suffered a ruptured abdominal artery at 4:00 a.m. on Wednesday, August 22.[109] Refusing to be hospitalized, Frank remained at home under the care of Dr. I. N. Kraushaar, the Nixon family physician. Within four hours, Dick, Pat, and Don Nixon flew to Los Angeles on a charter, joining Hannah and Eddie at Frank's bedside.[110]

Up to sixty reporters camped out in front of the Nixon residence on Beach Boulevard, many suspecting that Frank's illness was really just a sympathy-gaining ruse for Dick in response to the tactics of Stassen and Knight.[111] The Nixons "were not people who were given to talking about their family problems," yet Dick told Dr. Kraushaar, "Well, you go out and ask them to pick out one of the reporters to come here in the house and to go through the house, to see my father, interview him, and see just exactly what the conditions are." The designated reporter was brought upstairs to see for himself that Frank Nixon lay in bed, his arthritis so bad that he had small pieces of sponge rubber between his fingers and toes because any movement was agonizing.

In spite of his suffering, Frank told his son, "You get back there, Dick, and don't let that Stassen pull anymore last-minute funny business on you." When Dick asked if he could do anything to lighten his father's spirit, Frank had only one request: to talk to Fulton Lewis Jr. As Dick arranged the call to Lewis, Frank perked up, beaming when he heard his favorite radio commentator on the telephone line. Later that afternoon brothers Dick, Don, and Ed watched the convention on the television in their parents' living room as Massachusetts governor Christian Herter placed Nixon's name in nomination for vice president.[112] The next morning, August 23, Pat and Dick returned to San Francisco so that Nixon could give his acceptance speech, proposing harmony and party unity despite the divisive conduct of Stassen and Knight.[113] Afterward, Nixon's staff wired him, "Congratulations to our wonderful Boss, not only on your re-nomination, but also for your magnificent acceptance speech. In our opinion, no one could ever top you!"[114]

A week later Dick rushed to his father's bedside, as Frank, barely clinging to life and knowing his condition was terminal, insisted on dying at home.[115] With the national campaign on the verge of kicking off, local businessmen came together to provide Nixon's staff, encamped at the nearby William Penn, with office materials, a typewriter, and a dictation machine so Dick could try to get some work done while keeping vigil with his father.[116]

On the evening of September 3 Frank asked his son to shave him because he was too weak to do it himself.[117] Dick then wanted his father to rest and offered him some warm milk. Frank was reluctant to drink it until Dick spiced it with a splash of Kahlúa, one of the few times Frank had ever tasted alcohol. "My, that was good, what was it?" he asked as he lay back on his pillow. "Just a tonic," replied Dick, adding, "Now get a good night's sleep and I'll see you in the morning." "Goodnight Dick, but I don't think I'll be here in the morning," whispered Frank. Those were the last words spoken between father and son, as Frank slipped into a coma and died the next day, September 4, 1956.[118] Dick, Don, and Ed were at his side, with Hannah gently holding his hand as he passed.[119] Although Dick had experienced the loss of several family members, this was the first time he had watched it take place, and cousin Frances Timberlake remembered later how Dick "stood on the patio by himself for a long time, just stood there quietly."[120]

A few years earlier Hannah had become quite ill, and Frank's eyes had filled with tears when he talked about her condition. Family friend Mildred Mendenhall explained, "They really were close. He would have been just heartbroken if anything had happened to her because he loved her dearly."[121] Dick succinctly summed up their relationship: "My father was a Methodist, my mother a Quaker, they got married, compromised, and my father became a Quaker, too. So that's the way it worked out, peace without surrender."[122] Ed explained, "For all his gruff ways, Dad usually went along with what Mom wanted."[123]

Frank's death left Dick the eldest male in the family, and his father's influence was tremendous. Journalist Kyle Palmer said a few years later, "He came from a family that had to do its own chores and his mother and father were the most unpretentious people, simple folk, and a great deal of the simplicity of his boyhood [and his] background show up in his own complexion. . . . He is a very simple man and yet without seeming to carry any particular profundity, he is a very subtle man."[124] The vice president was scheduled to be in Los Angeles for several days during the first week of September to attend a convention, political meetings, and dedications.[125] After his father's passing, Nixon canceled all appearances with the exception of the American Legion Convention and a ceremony honoring Peru, explaining that he would speak at the convention "because President Eisenhower asked me to do it and I feel I am his representative."[126]

After his appearance before the American Legion at the Shrine Auditorium, Nixon went to Santa Ana College, where he presented a helicopter to the government of Peru on behalf of the Wycliffe Bible Translators. The organization was working with the Amazonian Indians in the Peruvian jungle to condense the tribal language into writing, create a dictionary, and then translate the Bible into that language.[127] Though Nixon never explicitly said as much, the dedication must have provided a measure of comfort at such a spiritually challenging time. Only days earlier, as Frank lay dying, the Nixon family had turned to the Bible for comfort and guidance and sought solace from ministers who were longtime family friends. Dick drew an analogy to an incident when a customer once dropped a watermelon in their store and it burst when it hit the ground, splattering all over everything.[128] For Dick, when people read the Bible, there was no limit to how far the word of God spread, just as the watermelon had burst open everywhere.[129]

On September 7 Rev. George Jenkins officiated Frank Nixon's funeral at the East Whittier Friends Church, which overflowed with friends and family.[130] Manville Saxton, a Whittier College classmate, fellow Orthogonian, and member of the Glee Club, sang "Beyond the Sunset" and "Beautiful Isle of Somewhere," the latter a tribute to his father's love of politics.[131] As a young boy, Frank had ridden horseback in a parade with President William McKinley, who complimented Frank's horse. Thereafter, Frank was a lifelong Republican, so Dick selected "Beautiful Isle of Somewhere" because it was McKinley's favorite song.

Frank's longtime friends served as pallbearers, including Bill Ross, a liberal Democrat who sold bacon and ham to the Nixon store, and with whom Frank had loved to argue politics.[132] The church was filled with 150 flower arrangements, and among the many expressions of sympathy were condolences from Dwight and Mamie Eisenhower, as well as the president of Nicaragua.[133] Frank was buried at the Milhous plot in Rose Hills, and at the graveside service Dick and Pat discovered that Pat's parents' graves were adjacent to the Nixon family plot.[134] After the services, Dick personally wrote to each of the friends who had assisted him during his father's final days, thanking them for their thoughtfulness at such a difficult time.[135]

The Nixons departed from Southern California the morning following Frank's funeral. Less than two weeks later Dick returned to officially kick off the reelection campaign.[136] As a demonstration of party unity, Nixon accepted Governor Knight's offer to introduce him at the event, where supporters packed the Whittier High School auditorium, with another thousand cheering out front.[137] After spending the night at the nearby William Penn, Dick made an unannounced breakfast visit to the Campus Inn cafeteria at Whittier College to mingle with the students, as well as the waiters, waitresses, dishwashers, and fry cooks.[138] William Marumoto, the student body president, reflected, "He was a very warm, compassionate, sincere person. He really made an effort to talk to each of the students on an individual basis and spend some time with them. He really made an impression on all of us."[139]

With core California Committee members Pat Hillings, Bob Wilson, Joe Holt, Herb Klein, Murray Chotiner, and Bob Finch serving as the keys to Nixon's California political operation, the state was solidly in support of President Eisenhower and favorite son Dick Nixon, which allowed him to campaign across the nation for the next seven weeks.[140] As in 1952 Jack Drown accompanied Nixon as train manager. All the hard work of such an engaging campaign soon paid off, as the Eisenhower-Nixon ticket went on to win California by close to six hundred thousand votes.[141] Nationally, they received 57 percent of the vote, and the future looked bright for Richard Nixon and the Republican Party.[142]

··
Preparation

1957–60

C ivil rights came to the forefront in the United States when, in the mid-1950s, the Supreme Court issued its decision in *Brown v. Board of Education* desegregating southern schools. Yet even before this, Frank and Hannah had raised their boys to treat all people as equals, as Dick explained: "My Quaker background . . . is primarily responsible for my strong convictions in the field of civil rights. From the earliest days in our family there was never any discussion of prejudice, either racial or religious, and all through my early years and also in Whittier College, this whole problem of civil rights was not simply a legal issue to us but it was, above all, a great moral issue."[1] Whenever Dick's Whittier College classmate Nathaniel George and his wife visited the Nixon Restaurant, they were welcomed as members of the "family," where no one was ever excluded based on race or religious background.[2]

In February 1957 Nixon traveled to Africa, where he met Martin Luther King Jr. at the independence ceremony for Ghana.[3] Nixon asked King to spend some time with him, and they had a long talk, at the end of which the vice president invited the reverend to meet with him after they returned to the United States.[4] Before their initial meeting, King had no affinity toward Nixon, but after their time together in Africa, he viewed Nixon as "a superb diplomat."[5]

In April, with Nixon's encouragement, the Eisenhower administration proposed the 1957 Civil Rights Bill, the first legislation of its kind put forth since Reconstruction.[6] Nixon and King met for a second time, after which King wrote to Nixon, "Let me say how deeply grateful we are to you for your assiduous labor and dauntless courage in seeking to make the Civil Rights Bill a reality. This has impressed people all across the country, both Negro and white. This is certainly an expression of your devotion to the highest mandates of the moral law."[7] For Nixon, civil rights were not a question of being liberal or conservative, as he believed "human rights have nothing to do with ideological consideration."[8] Nor were his words hollow gestures; according to biographer Conrad Black, when Nixon purchased a new home in DC, he refused to sign a race-restrictive covenant on the resale of the home, which at the time was considered a standard restriction on every transaction.[9]

On Saturday, February 15, 1958, Pat and Dick returned to Los Angeles for the first time since his reelection.[10] Joined by a thousand well-wishers, Hannah and Don greeted the couple at the airport, where the Nixons enthusiastically shook hands and signed autographs before heading to the Statler Hotel downtown.[11] Preferring more intimate gatherings to catch up with those closest to him, Nixon enjoyed a leisurely lunch with his mother in his suite, after which he met with Adela Rogers St. Johns, a journalist and longtime friend to whom he had delivered groceries thirty years earlier. After Hannah and Pat, St. Johns was one of the most influential women in his life. Nixon later told her, "I hope you know how much I appreciate your friendship as well as your advice and continued loyal support."[12]

By 1958 the Cold War had heated up significantly, courtesy of the space race between the Soviet Union and the United States. Many believed the Soviet Union had gained the upper hand after launching Sputnik into space first. In anticipation of his trip to California, Nixon was confident in American ingenuity, admitting, "We sometimes are slow starters in a contest where new inventions are involved," but "we are fast finishers and put our unequalled natural resources and energies into the task of doing what needs to be done."[13]

At NASA's Jet Propulsion Laboratory in Pasadena and the California Institute of Technology, the academic home of the laboratory, Nixon dismissed the growing concern over the quality of a U.S. education: "I am more than ever convinced that we need have no fears along that line. These young men are thinking imaginatively, not for purely military purposes but for future peaceful uses," commending the university's research in developing multipurpose food to combat world hunger.[14] To Nixon, winning the space race meant little if the United States lost the battle for independence for the world's free nations. He believed that the "greatest enemy in so many areas is hunger, feeding on Communist propaganda which poisons minds if it does not fill stomachs."[15]

When the Los Angeles Press Club presented Nixon with a gold lifetime honorary membership, he held a televised "no holds barred" press conference before a panel of reporters. The vice president, "lean, alert and fast on his feet," grinned happily as he responded to inquiries.[16] Reflecting on the space race, Nixon enthusiastically admitted that he supported "exploring the unknown just for the sake of exploring the unknown," but he also cautioned that Americans should be well-rounded: "We must not ape the Soviets and become simply atheistic, materialistic scientists. There is more to life than science."[17]

Much of the emerging military defense industry was based in California, and the state enjoyed many economic gains during the post–World War II era. In keeping with the state's financial successes, California enjoyed a fine crop of Republican hopefuls, with Governor Knight and U.S. senator William Knowland both up for reelection in 1958. Gov. Earl Warren appointed Knowland to the U.S. Senate in 1945, after Hiram Johnson died in office. Knowland won a special election in 1946 and was reelected in 1952. He served as the Senate majority leader from mid-1953 through the end of 1954, but since the Republican Party lost its majority in the November 1954 election, Knowland became Senate minority leader. California was in the unique position of being home to three highly successful Republicans, Nixon, Knight, and Knowland, each of whom had presidential ambitions for 1960.

Rather than run for reelection for his Senate seat, Knowland challenged fellow Republican Knight for the governorship. A victory would put Knowland in charge of the Republican Party in California, thereby increasing his stock for 1960. The issue dividing Knowland and Knight was a ballot proposition enacting the "right to work," which Knowland endorsed but Knight opposed. Just a few days ahead of Nixon's arrival in Southern California, Governor Knight announced that he would run for Knowland's Senate seat rather than defend against fellow Republican Knowland's gubernatorial challenge.[18] Knowland made his decision to challenge Knight without any consultation with President Eisenhower or Vice President

Nixon, and the result undermined California's Republican foothold, as voters disapproved of this flip-flopping of offices.[19]

Nixon refused to stake a position on the right-to-work issue and instead worked with business leaders and union organizations to eliminate discrimination in employment.[20] He met with Crispus Attucks Wright, the son of a former slave, who was a Republican candidate for the assembly.[21] When Wright graduated from USC Law School in 1938, he was denied membership in the Los Angeles County Bar Association because he was an African American, and some Republicans, such as Goodwin Knight, quit the association in protest.[22] Not surprisingly, Nixon and Wright immediately hit it off. At the Ambassador, the vice president convened the President's Committee on Government Contracts, whose purpose was to eliminate discrimination in employment. Nixon took his role seriously, working with more than two hundred business leaders to achieve the committee's goal.[23] Administrative aide Bob King remembered how tears came to Nixon's eyes as he watched a film the committee produced on the difficulties of African Americans in finding employment.[24] Former First Lady Eleanor Roosevelt complimented Nixon, later writing that he "has done a very good job on elimination of discrimination in work done under government contracts."[25]

In the fall of 1958 Nixon campaigned tirelessly for the Republican Party and even asked Jack Drown to be Knowland's Southern California campaign chairman.[26] Although Senator Knowland and Governor Knight both won their primaries for each other's offices, Knowland complained that he was making a poor showing in his race because of a lack of funds. While Nixon did not enjoy asking for campaign contributions, he solved Knowland's problem with one swing through California in October, raising $750,000.[27]

Despite Nixon's best efforts, Senator Knowland and Governor Knight split the party, which enabled Pat Brown to win the California governorship and John Engle to win the Senate race. The "internecine warfare" among Republicans swept the Democrats to victory in six of seven statewide offices, causing Nixon to bemoan, "We might well have taken the whole state of California—everything—if we hadn't gotten into such a fight among ourselves there."[28]

In February 1959 Nixon returned to California to gauge the damage from the Knowland-Knight debacle.[29] Throughout his twelve-year political career, the presumptive leaders of the Republican Party were Nixon and fellow Californians Earl Warren, Bill Knowland, and Goodwin Knight. With Warren appointed chief justice by Eisenhower and Knight and Knowland's recent defeats, Nixon was now perfectly poised to take control of the California Republican Party and run for president in 1960.

Because the Los Angeles County Republican chairmanship was in some respects more powerful than the state party chairmanship, Nixon knew it was important for his political future to rebuild the Republican Party base there.[30] Nixon, unabashedly Republican, mended fences as he told the Los Angeles County Republican Party Central Committee, "I don't think that we could make a greater mistake than to say that because some people don't like being called conservatives the Republican Party should stop being conservative. We should be proud of what we believe."[31]

He solidified his base by meeting with the Federation of Republican Women, the Southern California County Republican chairmen, Young Republican leaders, state and county officials, and assembly leaders. Then he turned his attention to finances, meeting with California Committee members Ed Valentine and Henry Salvatori and the Los Angeles Republican finance group to evaluate the damage to the Republican Party's fundraising abilities.[32]

It was time for Nixon to stand as his own politician and develop his base of support, and his California Committee was an integral component. The Nixons returned to California in June 1959, staying in Jack Wrather's owner's suite at the Disneyland Hotel.[33] Once the family was settled in, Julie and Tricia were given the run of Disneyland, affording Pat and Dick the opportunity to spend the day at Whittier College.[34] At the Stauffer Patio, Nixon joked, "We have here what is known in present diplomatic parlance as a 'package deal,'" as he dedicated three new buildings—the Walter F. Dexter Student Center, Susan and Clifford Johnson Residence Hall for Women, and John Stauffer Lecture-Laboratory—and oversaw the groundbreaking ceremony for the construction of the new Whittier College Memorial Chapel, a music building, and another women's residence hall.[35]

Pleased to be back on campus, Nixon warmly told the crowd, "It is good to return to one's old home and find oneself among old friends." When he was a student, the school bookstore had been an oversize janitor's closet, and the student lounge the steps at the entrance of Founders Hall. The college had developed significantly in the quarter century since the vice president's graduation, due in part to Nixon's affiliation with the small college and the introductions he made on behalf of it during what he referred to as "an age of plenty."[36] He humorously contrasted the present campus to what he remembered from his years there: "The only architectural achievement I can recall in the four Depression-troubled years of my residence was the Orthogonian fountain there, which housed, from time to time, a few disconsolate gold fish."[37] He was proud of his alma mater and believed that the availability of a well-rounded education was in the best interest of American enterprise: "I can assure you that if the privately-endowed, church-related, independent college of liberal arts ever fades from the American scene, what you and I think of as private enterprise will be dead as the dodo."[38]

At the college commencement ceremony that followed, Nixon urged the graduates to fight prejudice: "On the Whittier Campus, what really counts is not a man's family, how much money he might have, the color of his skin, his racial or national background, but his character. From the day a man or woman enters Whittier College he learns to respect the God given dignity of his fellow students and his fellow man."[39] As a Quaker who had seen war firsthand, he reflected on his upbringing, pointing out that a student could not attend Whittier without sharing a common faith in human decency and coming away with a concern for peace and human rights: "As you leave this friendly campus, I do not need to tell you that you will be stepping into a world where men fear one another, hate one another, war with one another. It is in such a world that the quality of that faith is to be tested."[40]

However much he was a partisan politico on the campaign trail, known to put on toe-to-toe battles to win elections, Nixon fully appreciated the profound difference between campaigning for office and governing in office, particularly because governing is infinitely more complex and difficult.[41] As an elected representative, he encouraged the graduates to seek the best they had to offer their fellow man, their chosen political parties, and themselves:

Wherever you go and whatever you do, let your example help to make men see a little clearer the glory of justice, the beauty of friendliness. May you ever have as your goal not simply the aim of making a good living for yourself for which your Whittier education has admirably prepared you but the higher objective of making this nation and this world a better place for all to live in. Wherever you see prejudice and hatred—strike it down. Wherever you encounter ignorance and provincialism—speak up for intelligent community and world responsibility. Above all, remember that when you receive your degree your education has just begun. Resist the temptation to settle down, to become smug and complacent, to become oblivious to misery and disease and sadness of others around you. Never forget that a republic cannot long endure without self-discipline and self-educating leaders. I urge you to participate in the activities of the political party of your choice. Both our major parties need the new blood and the new leadership which the college graduates of 1959 can provide if America is to meet the challenge of world responsibility which is ours. May you go on learning the rest of your lives to the end that you may not only enjoy the fruits but unselfishly fulfill the promise of your Whittier and American heritage.[42]

The Whittier College Board of Trustees was so grateful to Nixon that one trustee, Victor York, a former client of Nixon's and president of York Oil Company, commissioned artist John Orth to paint Nixon's portrait. In thanking York, Nixon commented, "I must admit, however, that I have some doubts about what even so well and favorably known an artist as John Orth could do with the subject with which he has been confronted!"[43]

The following morning Dick joined Hannah for services at the East Whittier Friends Church. Seeing Nixon come in with his mother, Rev. Charles Ball observed, "It was a very gratifying experience on her part."[44] Nixon had always had a close relationship with his parents, and after his father died, Dick kept close tabs on Hannah and often sent for her to attend events in Washington.[45] The topic of the sermon was "Micah: What does the Lord require of thee but to do justly, love mercy, and walk humbly with thy God?" which was Nixon's favorite verse.[46] After the services, Dick stayed to talk with the fellow parishioners he'd known through the years, enjoying "an old homecoming on the church grounds."[47]

Then Nixon and his family joined Walt Disney, Hedda Hopper, and Art Linkletter for lunch in Disney's apartment over the Main Street, U.S.A., Firehouse at Disneyland.[48] On the eighty-six-degree August afternoon, twenty-two thousand people came out to watch the Nixons, in a 1908 Oldsmobile, lead a parade celebrating the park's expansion. The parade included popular Disney characters Mickey Mouse, Donald Duck, Pluto, Davy Crockett, and Zorro, as well as a band of seventy-six trombone players playing "Seventy-Six Trombones," and made its way down Main Street. Ten thousand multicolored balloons were released as Nixon waded through the crowd, shaking hands and signing autographs, promising he "had time for everyone."[49]

The following day the Nixon family visited Yorba Linda, where a school now stood on Frank's former lemon orchard., and Jesse Waldren, the groundskeeper, lived in Dick's birthplace home.[50] Nixon told the four hundred elementary students that the hope for peace lay with the children of the world, observing that while many things differ from country to country, the children are always the same: "The hates and prejudices are not among the children."[51]

Dick and his brother Don were close, and Don and Clara Jane frequently picked up the Nixons at the airport.[52] Don's kids enjoyed lengthy visits with their aunt Pat and uncle Dick, as Don's daughter Lawrene reflected: "He's always the same and he always will be the same. Uncle Dick had time to sit and talk. And oh, we had the most marvelous conversations at dinner."[53] Clara Jane's fondest memory of her brother-in-law was when Dick sent her a gold ring with diamonds following Frank's death. He enclosed a handwritten note on the vice president's stationery, saying, "Thank you for the loving care of Mother." The gift was significant to her for two reasons: Quakers did not normally wear jewelry, and Dick had personally shopped for the gift.[54]

Don, well liked and considered by friends "pretty savvy in the business sense," had succeeded in growing the family business over the years.[55] Like Frank before him, Don employed relatives and local kids and treated all his employees well.[56] Initially offering freezer lockers in which his customers kept their meats, he added a bakery and diner, even providing catering service.[57] A drive-in and a second restaurant were eventually opened in East Whittier, followed by a larger grocery store, and all did very well.[58]

With three locations in East Whittier, Don formed a corporation and branched out to Fullerton and Anaheim, near Disneyland, with yet another restaurant planned for Yorba Linda.[59] But he expanded too quickly and had to borrow money in an attempt to keep his business afloat, taking an unsecured loan of $200,000 from Howard Hughes.[60] When Dick found out, he tried to have the funds returned; when that was not possible, he insisted the loan be secured with real property, so Hannah pledged the original Nixon market corner lot.[61] Despite his efforts, Don was devastated when his businesses failed and Hannah lost her property.[62] Hannah remained stoic: "When I realized my son Donald was in financial difficulties, I offered to mortgage my property. I was most willing to do it for him, as any mother would be willing to help her son."[63]

Dick and Don maintained their relationship through these financially turbulent times, even bantering about each other with friends. When Dick ran into Irvin Chapman, he said, "You see Don. Can't you get him to lose some weight? He's going to kill himself carrying all that weight around." Chapman replied, "Well, the last time I saw Don, he told me, 'Next time you see Dick, can't you get him to slow down a bit? He's going to kill himself running all over the country and the world.'"[64]

Nixon was reenergized with each visit home. As the 1960 presidential contest grew near, he told a friend, "Nowhere can we find the same warmth and friendliness than in our home town! It will always be our home and we never fail to come away with an added sense of purpose and dedication."[65] The Nixons returned to Southern California to celebrate the Fourth of July, spending the morning with family at Hannah's home before Dick dedicated the new Los Angeles Memorial Sports Arena in honor of the men who had lost their lives in World War II and Korea.[66] At the time, this was the largest single-span arena in the world, designed to host basketball, ice hockey, and track events, and was to host the 1960 Democratic Convention.[67] At the dedication, Nixon astutely predicted to a crowd of twenty thousand that the upcoming presidential contest "may turn out to be the battle of the century."[68]

Afterward, Nixon took in the American Handicap race from the directors' lounge in the Turf Club at Hollywood Park and presented the trophy to jockey Tommy Barrow, who rode Hillsdale to victory before fifty thousand racing enthusiasts.[69] The Nixon and Drown families enjoyed a quiet dinner at the modest Hyatt House Hotel before returning to the Los Angeles Memorial Coliseum, adjacent to the sports arena. Here Dick and daughter Julie led the opening parade for the twenty-seventh annual American Legion fireworks show before seventy-six thousand people.[70] As part of the celebration, everyone lit a match as a "never to be forgotten birthday salute" in honor of Julie's eleventh birthday before the famed annual fireworks show, which Nixon described as "a truly great spectacle."[71]

Less than three weeks later, on July 23, 1959, Nixon landed in Moscow for a visit that resulted in the famous Kitchen Debate. When Nixon and Soviet premier Nikita Khrushchev met at the Kremlin, Khrushchev was abrasive because the U.S. Congress had passed the Captive Nations Resolution, an open attack on Communist imperialism.[72] "This resolution stinks," Khrushchev shouted at Nixon. "It stinks like horse shit, and nothing smells worse than that!" Nixon, knowing his own childhood experiences, retorted, "I am afraid that the chairman is mistaken. There is something that smells worse than horse shit—and that is pig shit." Caught off guard, Khrushchev laughed and exclaimed, "You are right, there!"[73]

Growing up in Yorba Linda, Nixon had dreamed of seeing the world. Now in Russia as vice president, he was so excited that he couldn't sleep that first night in Moscow. So early in the morning he woke his Secret Service agent Jack Sherwood, and together with a Russian escort, they drove to the Danilovsky Market, where Nixon compared the Soviet market with the one he "had known as a boy in the United States."[74] Later that day Nixon and Khrushchev engaged in their Kitchen Debate, a series of discussions they held while touring the American National Exhibition at Sokolniki Park in Moscow. There the vice president, a tough-minded advocate of capitalism, told Khrushchev as they passed a model American grocery store, "You may be interested to know that my father owned a small general store in California, and all the Nixon boys worked there while going to school." Nixon knew that an honest store needed only one scale, informing Khrushchev that at the Danilovsky Market that morning, he had observed people weighing their purchases on a second scale to verify they hadn't been cheated by the state, at which Khrushchev quickly changed the subject.[75]

The vice president had flown to the USSR on the new Boeing 707 presidential aircraft, and Nixon was rightly proud of the developing Southern California aerospace industry. When Khrushchev saw him off at the airport, Nixon could see he was impressed with the new jet. Upping the ante, the pilot, Maj. Bill Conine, having discussed the matter with Nixon's military aide Don Hughes, offered a "maximum performance takeoff" with a steep climb once airborne. Hughes described the maneuver to Nixon, telling him it would make a great show. Nixon asked, "Like a skyrocket?" When Hughes nodded in the affirmative, Nixon exclaimed, "By all means!"[76]

Shortly after the Soviet Union trip, on August 30 the vice president returned to California and was met by Don, who drove him straight to the Ambassador.[77] Nixon loved the Ambassador, and the feeling among the hotel staff was mutual. The hotel held a suite for him, along with at least six other rooms, whenever he came to town. Nixon preferred the Royal Suite, with two rooms and a seven-foot king-size bed. It was the same suite in which Khrushchev stayed when he visited Los Angeles a few weeks later.[78]

Nixon came to town to address cheering VFW conventioneers at the First Methodist Church auditorium, where he clashed with AFL-CIO president George Meany over how to deal with the Russians.[79] The controversy was Nixon's recent trip to the Soviet Union and Khrushchev's upcoming September visit, which Nixon supported in order for President Eisenhower to "mince no words" with the Soviet leader and because the vice president welcomed "a greater exchange of persons and ideas between the free world and the Communist world."[80] He further believed the visit would afford Khrushchev the opportunity to see firsthand the resolve of a United States that wanted "peace with justice, not the peace of surrender or appeasement." Meany insisted that "no good can come from such a visit," but Nixon explained, "We have been on the defensive long enough. It is time for us to take the offensive and help make the whole world realize that the Communist idea is not a super idea, that the Communist leaders are not supermen, and that the Soviet Union is not a super nation."[81]

The visit was the first opportunity for H. R. "Bob" Haldeman, a friend of Nixon's assistant Loie Gaunt from her days at UCLA, to be an advance man, handling all the legwork involved with the trip.[82] Afterward, James Hughes, Nixon's military aide, dryly wrote to Haldeman, "This is probably the last time I will do this so you can accept this note of thanks for all the future occasions when an expression of gratitude might be required."[83] Nixon's aides and close California Committee supporters viewed themselves as a family, of which Haldeman was now a member.[84]

Hoping to "enjoy a little California sunshine," the Nixons returned in early November, staying at the Beverly Hilton.[85] At a reunion of the original Committee of 100 at the Santa Anita Flamingo-Ramada, Nixon told his earliest supporters, most of whom were now good friends, "It was exactly fourteen years ago, although not as late as tonight, that we were over at the William Penn in Whittier. Little did any of us anticipate that we would meet here tonight under these circumstances. I know I didn't."[86] Relaxed among his most trusted friends, Nixon promised, "Whatever the future may bring, you can be sure that our longtime California friendships will always be the most meaningful."[87]

Nixon was developing as a politician in the age of television, and coverage of his trip included Dick shopping for ties and strolling through Beverly Hills with Pat. Far from the days of his first campaign in 1946, when Roy Day had to persuade Nixon to refrain from buying flashy ties, by 1959 Dick was advising Pat as to which ones were too flashy for television.[88] Reporters joined Nixon for his morning walk, and when he stopped for breakfast, they asked his waitress if she knew who he was. After she admitted that she didn't, Nixon smiled wryly and introduced himself by saying, "I'm Bob Hope."[89]

While Nixon was enjoying Southern California, his supporters on the East Coast announced their intent to place his name on the New Hampshire ballot as a candidate for president.[90] Nixon was now officially running for president, and he wanted to be in his home state when the announcement was made. California supported Nixon, naming him the grand marshal of the Pasadena Rose Parade on January 1, 1960.

Arriving in Los Angeles on December 31, 1959, the Nixon family attended all the pre-parade activities, including the noon kickoff luncheon. Nixon engaged the crowd, throwing out footballs and telling them, "When I played at Whittier College, I was no better than a third string end. But I consider myself an expert on the subject of football. When you sit on the bench for four years next to the coach, you can really learn a lot."[91] Refusing complimentary passes, Nixon insisted on paying for twenty tickets for both his and Pat's families to attend the Rose Parade and football game.[92] Whittier had entered a float in the parade, and later Nixon saluted the city: "I thoroughly enjoyed the privilege of taking part in the Rose Bowl festivities and the Whittier float made me proud indeed of my home town's part in making it a most memorable occasion for the Nixons."[93]

Barely a month later, at the request of Carroll Archer, Nixon joined a thousand guests, including 175 student members, at the California Newspaper Publishers Association convention at the Statler Hotel.[94] Archer, the incoming president of the association, had written the first editorial endorsing Nixon in 1946.[95] Nixon put the student editors at ease, explaining that he had tried unsuccessfully to write for his student newspapers and was in awe at being in their presence: "You know, the reason I never made it is because I could never meet the deadlines. Writing, to me, is a very difficult assignment . . . when it comes to sitting down and writing speedily and well, that requires a mental discipline of the very highest order."[96]

Nixon and Pat Brown attended an unlimited question-and-answer session, where Nixon reminded the governor that they had first met in 1949: "All I can say, neither of us expected to be where we are today."[97] He also lamented that he and his wife had not been able to spend as much time in California as they would have liked over the years, sharing his sentiments for his home state: "Governor Brown, I have been sitting here enjoying this program for a number of reasons and I thought I might share them with you right at the outset. I think that when you come into a room, there is nothing that really gives you a bigger lift than to hear 'California, Here I Come.' From the time that the organ was blasting out that favorite tune of ours, memories, naturally, have been going through my mind."[98]

At ease with the publishers, Nixon was introduced not as a presidential candidate but "a Californian . . . a man of whom we are all extremely proud."[99] He joked that in all the introductions of Pat over the years, one of the most surprising occurred in Utah: "Now I present to you the next wife of the vice president." He added, "Imagine what an impact it had in Utah, too." Nixon had recently delivered a campaign speech in Chicago in which he proposed that the United States must remain vigilant in fighting Communism all over the world, and he noted that when the *Los Angeles Times* reported his speech, the headline read, "Nixon Kicks Off Race by Refusing to Stand Pat," but the *Chicago Tribune* reduced the headline to "Can't Stand Pat—Nixon."[100]

In a wide-ranging discussion covering domestic policy, civil rights, and foreign policy, he interwove his Republican philosophy that the role of government was to "supplement rather that supplant what individuals and private enterprise can do in economic growth and economic development."[101] He pointed out that the Soviet Union had a disgraceful record of antisemitism, then told of visiting a concentration camp in Poland where over two hundred thousand Jews were killed by the Nazis. As he stood in one of the rooms, a reporter revealed to Nixon, "Thirty of my relatives were killed right there." Nixon saw firsthand "why it is very important that all of us who believe in freedom of religion and press and expression . . . must stand firmly against evidences of racial or religious or any other kind of prejudice and stand firmly for the equality of opportunity in every respect."[102]

At an appearance on the *Paul Coates Show* at the KTTV studio, Nixon expanded on his comments: "We've all got to look right into our own hearts. And we have to recognize that prejudice of some type exists virtually in everybody. And what we have to do is direct all of our efforts toward removing prejudice where we have it toward others—as well as seeing it in others. And we also have to put ourselves in the other fellow's place."[103] On a personal note, he described how some of Julie's classmates were discussing a fellow student who was an African American, and his daughter's only comment to her playmates was "Well, as far as I'm concerned, it isn't how you look but how you act that counts."[104] Nixon understood that racism could not be eliminated merely by passing a law, since a law was "only as good as the will of the people to keep it."[105] Rather, he was convinced that "if we're going to solve this problem, it must be solved in the hearts of our people."[106]

Southern Californians went out of their way to accommodate

Nixon, and Nixon did not take such hospitality for granted. He complimented the management of the Ambassador and Biltmore for making him feel "right at home," and he wrote letters to personally thank those involved in his trips, from Frank Valente, the maître d' at the Ambassador, to anyone else who extended a courtesy to the Nixons.[107] When writing to business owners and managers, he often thoughtfully mentioned their employees by name when expressing his appreciation.[108] Whether it was Tricia and Julie's escorts at Disneyland, the cake baker for the Yorba Linda visit, the boy who carried his blankets at the Rose Bowl game, or a stewardess on a flight, Nixon had kind words for everyone involved in his visits.[109] Even for those who routinely provided accommodations or services, such as Clint Harris lending automobiles, Nixon always remembered to say thank you.[110]

Nixon shared the benefits of his office in small personal ways with friends, inviting Whittier College classmate William Hornaday, now a minister, to Washington DC to serve as guest chaplain when Nixon presided over the U.S. Senate.[111] Nixon appeared on *This Is Your Life* with Whittier classmate Ralph Veady, who had lost both legs in an accident, praising Veady as an inspiration.[112] When Jack and Helene Drown visited Washington in April 1958, Pat and Dick hosted a party for the couple at their home, which included several Southern California congressmen and their wives, as well as Attorney General William Rogers and his wife, Adele.[113] Nixon and the Drowns had a special relationship. Helene wrote letters to Dick on political issues, acknowledging that she knew he was busy, but the matter was important and would take only a few minutes to review. Dick playfully responded, "I just spent five minutes reading a letter which you indicated could be read in three."[114]

Having traveled half a million miles "by airplane, automobile, oxcart and boat," Richard Nixon had visited fifty-five countries and met thirty-five presidents, fifteen prime ministers, and numerous kings, queens, and sultans.[115] He transformed the office of the vice president and was a hero to his hometown.[116] By 1960 the forty-seven-year-old Nixon had prepared himself for the presidency through sheer hard work and determination.[117] He preferred to write his own speeches, generally refusing to entirely rely on a speechwriter, as he felt he couldn't take somebody else's words and make them his own.[118] He once confided to an aide, "If I speak them, I've got to write them."[119]

He remained an affectionate family man. According to Kyle Palmer, "When there is time to steal away from Washington, he doesn't look to the nightspots and the nightclubs; he goes somewhere where he can rest with his family. He and his wife are exceedingly close in their understanding, their love of their two little girls; they have a very wonderful family life, an aspect of that life which is seldom understood or seen by the public."[120] Hannah said that Tricia and Julie were Richard's "biggest pleasure." Each morning the Nixons had breakfast together, and just as when Richard was growing up, they said a prayer and shared family worship.[121] Dr. Edward Elson, pastor at the National Presbyterian Church, also described the Nixons' family life: "It is a common practice for the busy Nixon family to find their way together to sporting events, a few days at the beach, a family picnic, or a holiday away from public gaze. The children keep friendship with boys and girls of all stations and religions. It is obvious that this spirit of love and tolerance was developed by careful training and teaching by their parents. Apparently their faith embraces all mankind."[122]

Early in their marriage, Dick told Pat "there was going to be no blustering" in their home, and there wasn't; he never raised his voice or spanked his daughters, preferring discussions as a form of discipline.[123] His parenting reflected his belief "that the home should be a place where you help each other and where there's real comfort."[124] So each night when he came home from work, he would ask his youngest daughter, "Well Julie, what did you do for your country today?" to which Julie always replied, "Well Daddy, I cheered you up and so I helped my country today."[125] Then he'd put on music to play in the background as the family sat down for dinner.[126]

His daughters saw him as the optimist of the family. "Whenever we had a family discussion," Julie explained, "Tricia and I would look over at each other, and we'll know in a minute that Dad, to end the conversation, will say, 'Oh, there's no problem. It's going to be fine. Everything has worked out well.'"[127] No doubt, as one of five boys, Nixon found having two daughters to be an eye-opening experience, and he was naturally protective of them.[128] Years before, on February 11, 1948, Nixon had been walking down ice-covered steps while carrying Tricia in his arms, when he slipped and landed on his back and elbows, clutching Tricia to protect her from injury. In the fall, Nixon suffered a triple fracture to the left elbow and a simple fracture to the right elbow, but Tricia was uninjured.[129]

Pat and Dick consulted each other on everything about their daughters and successfully shielded them from politics as long as possible.[130] When Dick became vice president, Jacqueline Lee Bouvier, then a photojournalist for the *Washington Times-Herald*, approached Julie and asked her, "Do you play with Democrats?" Julie responded, "What's a Democrat?"[131] But as the girls grew, they naturally understood more and more of their father's work, and while Nixon spent as much time as he could with them, like many fathers, he wished he could have spent more.[132] One day the vice president flew to San Francisco to give a speech, planning to leave early in the morning from Washington and fly back that night. When Nixon arrived at the San Francisco airport, to everyone's surprise, he had brought his daughters. Pat later explained that the girls had simply gotten up that morning, packed suitcases, and said, "Mommy, we want to go with Daddy."[133]

Equal parts family man and party man, Nixon knew he was the hatchet man of the Eisenhower administration, not because he enjoyed it but because he was effective.[134] At the same time, many held the opinion articulated by Southern Californian Lloyd Harnish, who had supported him since 1946, that Nixon's "sincerity and fortitude in trying to carry out his policies, irrespective of whether they're popular or not, has endeared him to a lot of conservative people in this country, irrespective of party."[135] Yet Nixon was very clear in separating his personal life from his political life, believing that "a politician has personal friends with whom he shares ideals and political friends with whom he shares interests."[136] Reserved in large groups, he was more informal among friends, as George Milias, who served in the California State Assembly, explained that Dick had a fine sense of humor and particularly enjoyed "telling jokes that are related to politics or are related to people that he knows or has met in Washington."[137]

Nixon's administrative assistant Bob Wilson described an incident that demonstrated Nixon's personality and so impressed Wilson that he instantly knew it was one he would never forget. A few years earlier Wilson had accompanied Nixon outside of Vienna, where they visited a group of refugees on a Saturday just before Christmas. They went into an auditorium to watch a Christmas program put on by the children. Nixon was seated in the front row, and the children who were in the program came down off the stage and clustered around him, although they didn't really know who he was "but inherently lik[ed] him." Wilson described how two little girls climbed up on Nixon's knee, "and one little girl, in particular, [was] patting his cheek with her hand and looking up with adoring eyes at him as the program continued on the stage." Wilson noted "the obvious emotional feeling that he had as a father of little girls himself for those two children who were undergoing a tremendous change in their lives and were looking to someone for a feeling of security and finding it in this stranger who was so kind to them."[138]

A few moments later Dick took to the stage and helped hand out Christmas presents that had been donated for the children. His innate shyness manifested in near embarrassment as the little boys stood on their tiptoes and try to kiss him on the cheek as they received their presents from him. Nixon then made "a very touching speech" to the families present, stating how much he hoped that they would find the security and happiness they were looking for when they ultimately arrived in their new home countries.[139] As he looked about the stage, Nixon saw a piano, so he gathered the American newsmen around him to sing as he played "Jingle Bells" for the children. For Bob King, the incident reflected Nixon's "ability to recognize simple things in putting over an important message that he felt he should deliver."[140] Don Nixon's daughter Lawrene recognized this same sentiment in her uncle Dick: "I don't care what color they are, what religion they are, or where they live. They could be in the darkest ghetto or the highest hilltop house, he really enjoys young people."[141]

One day while Nixon was presiding over the Senate, a young minister who had given the invocation asked Dick to sign an autograph for his nine-year-old daughter, who was being treated for leukemia. A few days before, Sophia Loren had visited the vice president and gave him two beautiful Italian walking dolls for Tricia and Julie. When Nixon learned that the minister's daughter was sharing a room with another nine-year-old girl who also had leukemia, he went home and spoke to his girls, who enthusiastically agreed that their father should take the dolls to the minister's daughter and her roommate. Nixon related the experience: "My half-hour visit with them was one of the most memorable experiences of my eight years as vice president. I shall never forget the delight in their eyes as they played with their new dolls. If they had looked closely, they might have seen the tears in mine as I thought of the tragic fact that these two beautiful children had only a little time left to live."[142] Having lost two brothers, he knew firsthand that "expressions of sympathy to people who are ill are always deeply appreciated."[143]

Although Nixon worked to separate his political life from his personal life, both were inextricably intertwined at his core, a quality his friends admired.[144] California Committee member Alphonzo Bell noted that Nixon "has a tremendous sincerity in purpose. He really knows the problems that face the nation. However, he has the warmth, the genuine friendliness in addition to the serious knowledge of world affairs."[145] More often than not, people were in awe at meeting the vice president, and he always tried to make them feel at ease.[146] George Milias described Nixon as a well-rounded politician prepared to be president: "The thing that impresses one about Dick Nixon is an aura of greatness that seems to pervade the atmosphere when you're talking to him. You have a feeling that his thoughts are so perceptive that they give you the feeling that this man is truly great. There was just something there that most politicians and most of our leaders don't have. That type of spark that gives you the feeling from the start that this individual is very likely going right straight to the top."[147]

TWELVE

Presidential Campaign

1960

S tanding alone on the national stage, Nixon swept the Republican primaries, receiving over 85 percent of the vote. Marking
his first event as national leader of the Republican Party, the
1960 GOP Convention clearly reflected his principles.[1] With racial
tensions running high, he could have promoted a platform that kept
silent on issues like support for Black sit-in strikes at "whites only"
lunch counters in the South and government intervention to secure
federal job equality for Black workers, which "almost certainly would
have carried the Southern states for the GOP" and won the election.
Nixon understood this, but instead he crafted the most liberal civil
rights platform ever accepted by the Republican Party.[2] His Quaker
upbringing "had instilled in him an unshakable moral conscience on
civil rights and racial equality," and honoring that heritage, Nixon
arranged for Reverend Ball of the East Whittier Friends Church to
give the invocation at the convention.[3]

Nixon's August 2, 1960, return to Southern California was carried
live on local television.[4] He was met at Los Angeles International
Airport by Walt Disney and other celebrities, along with thousands
of supporters singing "Richard Nixon, Here You Come" to the tune
of "California, Here I Come" as he exited the plane.[5]

Two weeks before his August arrival, the 1960 Democratic Convention was held at the Memorial Sports Arena in Los Angeles, a
venue Nixon had dedicated only a year earlier. Nixon quipped to
his supporters, "You know, after hearing some of the things they
were saying about me here, I was almost afraid to come home!"
Humor aside, believing the great strength of America was not in
its government, but rather in its people, Nixon related a campaign
theme based on personal conviction: "Every boy and girl in this
country must have an equal opportunity for an education. He must

have an equal opportunity to reach the top—or putting it in baseball language—you know, we all can't get home runs but every boy and girl in America is entitled to his time at bat. That's the way to build a great America."[6]

At the Hyatt House Hotel, Nixon held a press conference where he predicted, "This will probably be the closest election in this century in this country."[7] He knew that he and Sen. John F. Kennedy were in for a battle. Believing the "great power and prestige" of the office of the president required that "races for the presidency should give the voters something to be for instead of something to be against," Nixon promised a campaign based on important issues rather than personalities.[8] To Nixon, "Between issues and personalities, I think where you draw the line is where you question the motives of an individual, his honesty, his personal honesty, as did Senator Kennedy in his acceptance speech. As you will note, I did not reply in kind and I shall not reply in kind throughout this campaign."[9]

True to his word, Nixon refused to discuss Kennedy's medical issues, of which Nixon had firsthand knowledge because they had served together in Washington DC for fourteen years and sometimes traveled together. Kennedy had even delivered a $1,000 check to help Nixon defeat Democrat Helen Gahagan Douglas in the 1950 Senate race. What's more, when Kennedy had adrenal failure in 1954 following a spinal fusion surgery, Nixon had visited him in the hospital and knew of the senator's need for regular traction and daily cortisone injections.[10] Though his campaign team recommended making political capital out of Kennedy's poor health, especially since Kennedy had exploited fellow Democrat Lyndon Johnson's history of heart disease during the Democratic primaries, Nixon refused.[11]

Likewise, he handled religious differences with the sensitivity of a Whittier Quaker.[12] When questioned about Kennedy's possible conflict of loyalties between the pope and governing the United States, Nixon neutralized the issue: "I have no doubt whatever about Senator Kennedy's loyalty or about his ability to put the Constitution of the United States above any consideration." Further, Nixon welcomed the opportunity to repudiate anyone who used religion as an issue and ordered his supporters "not to discuss religion, not to raise it, not to allow anybody to participate in the campaign who does so."[13] Nevertheless, Kennedy continued making personal attacks, and when the media wrote of Don Nixon's borrowing $200,000 from Howard Hughes in a failed attempt to save his businesses, inferring that Hughes received tens of millions of dollars in benefits from the government as a result, Kennedy did nothing to discourage the reporting, although there was no evidence to support it.[14]

On the evening of August 2 Nixon received a hero's welcome at Whittier College's Hadley Field, with thousands of supporters lining the route to campus.[15] Pat and Dick arrived in an open convertible, slowly making their way through throngs of cheering admirers, before Nixon, joined on stage by his wife and mother, took to the podium at the ten-yard line.[16] Don arranged for 160 of their relatives to sit together, and Dick joked that there were so many Nixons and Milhouses that he was sure to win the White House if his entire family voted.[17] He thanked the local community for his success: "If it hadn't been for the people here, for what you've done, we wouldn't be in the position that we're in now, and we want you to know how deeply we appreciate what you've done through the years in our campaigns."[18]

Nixon complimented his Whittier teachers for shaping his political career by instilling three guiding principles: individual responsibility, concern for people less fortunate, and devotion to peace. "Not a static peace, meaning absence of war, but a creative, vital peace," he explained. Stating that America needed a president who would not "owe his election to captains of industry or captains of labor," Nixon pledged "to devote all that is in me, my whole life which comes from this community, to work for the kind of world you believe in."[19] Though he and Pat were leaving at 4:00 the next morning to fly to Hawaii, he promised to stay to shake the hand of everyone attending the event—and he did.[20] He followed up the homecoming rally by writing to local supporters, thanking them for attending and predicting, "With such effective shoulders to the wheel as yours, I am more encouraged than ever that we can see California on the winning Republican side of the ticket all the way this November."[21]

Having promised to visit all fifty states in his campaign, Nixon crisscrossed the nation, barnstorming one state after another. Several significant campaign events were planned in Southern California, and at 10:00 p.m. on October 11, Hannah welcomed Pat and Dick at the Burbank airport.[22] The rallying crowd of 15,000 included 1,500 teenage Nixonettes wearing pleated dresses, sashes, and Nixon boater hats. Many of his supporters had been waiting hours for his arrival, and Nixon told them, "This decision we make on November 8 could be the most important decision you'll ever make in your life. And in all humility, I deeply appreciate the tremendous responsibility that places upon me."[23] Taking genuine pleasure in his return to California, Nixon shared his reflections on the campaign, saying, "I suppose some of you wonder: What do you think about when you travel all over the country?" He told of the dreams of a child and the hopes of a centenarian he met on the campaign trail before answering, "We remember the people from whom we came."[24]

Nixon visited NBC's Burbank studios on October 12 to tape an interview with Chet Huntley and David Brinkley for *The Campaign and the Candidates.*[25] During the interview, the newsmen warned Nixon that they would try to annoy him, but he rose to the challenge: "I have been annoyed by experts, so go right ahead." Unfazed by their prodding, he succinctly described the difference between himself and John Kennedy: "I put my faith, as far as economic growth is concerned, not in expanding the public sector of the economy, what government does as such; but I put my faith in having the government do those things that will stimulate the private sector of the economy, stimulate what individuals will do. I put my faith in private and individual enterprise as the major engine of progress. I do not have confidence in turning to huge, massive government programs simply for the sake of stimulating economic growth."[26]

At the All States Society picnic at Recreation Park in Long Beach later that day, Nixon's cousin Sheldon Beeson sat talking with Pat. As Dick began to speak from the historic band shell, Pat tapped Sheldon on the knee, pointed to her husband, and whispered, "Let's listen to Dick." Sheldon was struck by Pat's devotion: "There she was, sitting, listening and paying such good attention to him, as if he was going to say something fresh this time."[27] Those who knew Nixon well long recognized this deep affection between Pat and Dick.[28] As Helene Drown put it, Pat felt "he is a great man, and entitled to the respect of being listened to, and therefore she would set the example of listening just as attentively as she would expect anyone in the audience to listen to him."[29] Their friends also knew that

Dick's feelings for his wife ran just as deep, and as one noted, "But for Pat, he wouldn't be where he is."[30] Even so, those closest to the couple knew that their perception of Dick was not universal. The public image was that Nixon "is supposed to be anti-something," said Jack Drown. "But I don't think Dick uses 'anti' in his vocabulary."[31] Rather, he said, Dick had a fundamental kindness "that never changed." Similarly, those close to Pat felt that she was a wonderful lady and a wonderful wife, warm and understanding.[32]

Nixon proposed ambitious ideas, including healthcare, which he had long supported. He reminded his audience that in 1948, as a congressman, he had "introduced one of the first bills providing that all of our older people would be able to obtain medical care insurance."[33] He explained how that commitment was rooted in his family's personal experiences: "The year that my father died, in 1956, when he was seventy-five, the doctor bills that he had were over two thousand dollars. My mother, the same year, had operations and doctor bills which cost fifteen hundred dollars. My mother and father were not rich people. I remember they dug into their savings, they're very proud, and they proceeded to pay the bills just as you would if you were able to do so."[34] However much of a proponent he may have been of widespread healthcare, Nixon was not a proponent of a single-payer government system: "We want to be sure that we don't put our doctors on the federal payroll. We want to be sure that they have the independence to provide the finest care."[35] Nor did Nixon support an individual mandate requiring the purchase of insurance, saying, "In America, I don't believe that anybody that doesn't want it should be forced to have it."[36]

Finishing the day with a picnic at Knott's Berry Farm, where he was greeted by torch lights, music, and skyrockets, Nixon spoke with gusto: "Certainly, I am sure all of you realize what a great thrill it is for Pat and me to come back to my own home county of Orange to find one of the largest, one of the most spectacular, one of the most enthusiastic campaign meetings of this entire election campaign, and we thank you for it."[37] He was nostalgic, recalling when Knott's Berry Farm "was just a roadside stand, a man and his wife selling very, very good boysenberry pie."[38]

Meanwhile, the first debates between major party presidential candidates in televised history were having a significant impact on the campaign. A month before the first debate, Nixon had banged his knee on the edge of a car door in Greensboro, North Carolina, and was admitted to Walter Reed Hospital two weeks later for a series of under-the-kneecap antibiotic injections.[39] The first debate, held on September 26, 1960, followed his discharge from the hospital, and though his health was generally good, he looked ill in contrast to Kennedy, who appeared healthy.[40] Even Hannah called Rose Mary Woods to ask if her son was "feeling all right."[41] Dick had loved milkshakes since the days when Evlyn Dorn picked them up for him at McNair's Drugstore in Whittier, so to regain his healthy appearance for the future debates, he added them to his diet.[42]

The candidates squared off four times, with the third debate a split-screen event held on October 13 during Nixon's swing through Southern California. Nixon appeared from the ABC Studio in Hollywood, while Kennedy was broadcast from New York.[43] Spending the day at the Ambassador preparing, Nixon drew strength when the *Los Angeles Times* officially endorsed him the morning of the debate.[44] Arriving at the studio, Nixon stopped in to see his friend Efrem Zimbalist Jr., an actor on the set of *77 Sunset Strip*. As they discussed camera angles and Zimbalist offered tips before the debate, Nixon confessed, "My trouble is my nose."[45]

Nixon wanted the campaign to be based on substantive discussion of issues rather than simply being a popularity contest. When asked if he would debate Kennedy, Nixon relied on his lifelong education and training: "I think what you need is a discussion of the issues without texts, without notes, where the candidates in depth go into specific issues so people can learn how they think and how they react to the questions that are raised by each other in the course of the debate." As a result, the candidates agreed to not use notes in the debates, but Senator Kennedy, taking advantage of their separate studios, breached their agreement.[46] Despite his frustration, Nixon, who only learned at airtime that Kennedy had a stack of notes, still dominated the debate.[47]

After spending the night at the Ambassador, Nixon awoke at 4:00 a.m., called his aide Don Hughes, and went to Ollie Hammond's for a morning hamburger and glass of milk.[48] A couple of hours later, at a breakfast meeting in the Cocoanut Grove, Nixon entertained celebrity supporters, including Jimmy Stewart, Donna

Reed, and Samuel Goldwyn's personal attorney, Mendel Silberberg. He described how he and Pat couldn't afford the Grove when they were dating: "We sat in the little bar outside, listening to the music emanating from inside."[49] Then he drew an analogy to his college football days, saying that he sat on the bench for four years without taking the field, but since becoming a politician, he often found himself on football fields to make speeches. And now here he was at the Grove.[50]

Turning to more serious matters, Nixon noted that anyone could claim to be in favor of civil rights, but more important than words was a person's life experiences. He had never forgotten the one and only time his grandfather Francis Milhous spoke crossly to him after the family had attended another church service that was not as restrained as a typical Quaker service. The preacher was rather flamboyant, and afterward the youngsters were mimicking him and saying, "My, he was a terrible preacher." Nixon's grandfather came to him and counseled, "Richard, thee must never say anything about a man of God unless it's something good. If thee doesn't have something good to say, say nothing."[51] This message resonated with Nixon in his belief that "civil rights is not a Southern problem, but a national problem It is not a legal problem; it is a moral problem."[52]

In a speech at the USC campus on October 14, Nixon promised the students that he was not there "to spoon-feed the audience with his pet ideas."[53] Instead, he connected with the students, telling them how Pat had worked her way through USC after her parents died and offering to answer all their questions, even jesting that it would give him practice for the final debate with Kennedy. Believing in the youth of America and their participation in the political process, he encouraged the students to go into politics, telling them that both parties needed new blood and that although the financial rewards of public service were limited, the nonmonetary rewards were tremendous. "It isn't enough today for a man or a woman just to be a good doctor, a competent lawyer, a successful business man. You have had the best educations in the world. Those who have had the experience that you have had simply have to raise the tone of the political life of your communities and see that the political organizations bring to the top the best men and the best women that we have."[54]

Following that speech, Nixon headed to an afternoon appearance at the Eastland Shopping Center in West Covina, near Whittier. During the drive, memories of his youth and early political career came flooding back. West Covina hadn't even existed when he first ran for office, and he waxed sentimental with the hometown crowd that had gathered at the shopping center: "My friends here in my home district, the 25th District of California, I want you to know that we'll have many crowds in this campaign in the next three and a half weeks, and we've had many in the last couple of months, but there are none that will touch us more than this one, and that will move us more because this is our home."[55] Recognizing faces in the crowd, Nixon called out the names of supporters from early campaigns, telling those assembled, "You can imagine that this is a special occasion for us, not only that you come out in such great numbers on such a beautiful day to spend time with us, but also because it is for us a homecoming and a reminder of how much has happened and how much we owe to you. And so, we thank you again today."[56] He wove his homegrown beliefs with America's guiding principles:

The real strength of America is in its ideals. It's in the homes, in the churches, in the schools in America. What do I mean? There is a great battle going on, a battle that is going to be decided in this last half of the twentieth century. Whoever is the next President has got to lead the United States and the free world in that battle. What's going to count? What we believe is going to count. Our ideals, our faith in God, our belief in the dignity of all men, our belief in the rights of all men, in equality of opportunity, our belief that every nation has the right to be independent and all people have the right to be free.[57]

He then underscored the basic difference between his and Kennedy's philosophies: "Every time there's a problem, they say start with Washington and work down to the people. And we have exactly the opposite philosophy."[58] Nixon believed, as he stated in his All States Society speech, that "the reason America got where it is in the world today is not what government has done, but what people have done. We must never forget that."[59]

Personal campaign appearances served him well. Nixon was able to have a "terrific emotional impact" on people meeting him "face to face," as he joked, reminisced, and revealed himself and his beliefs.[60] At each stop, he related how his father had influenced his vision for the future: "My father never used to say, 'I want to talk about the good old days.' He said, 'You know, I don't want to go back to the good old days. In this country we never want to go back and we're never satisfied with the present. We always want to go forward into a better future.' And that's what we want to do. We want a better future."[61] He often repeated his father's refrain: "I believe in the American dream because I have seen it in my own lifetime."[62]

That evening he delivered his first major foreign policy speech of the campaign at the World Newspaper Forum. Nixon, typically reserved, flashed his sense of humor when introduced by his friend Jerry Lewis.[63] Nixon related an earlier experience when he had tried to tell a joke after Lewis introduced him and the comedian had scolded him, saying, "Look, you stick to your business and I'll stick to mine."[64] The vice president also couldn't resist making light of his strong work ethic on the campaign trail: "They say 'What day do you sleep?' and I say 'Every Thursday is set out for sleeping as far as this campaign is concerned.'"[65]

Earlier that month, on October 3, he had met for lunch with President Eisenhower, who was scheduled to campaign with Nixon for a final push toward Election Day.[66] Ike had been exercising to build stamina, and the plan was to hold an event in Los Angeles at which the speakers would be Eisenhower; Nixon's running mate, Sen. Henry Cabot Lodge Jr. of Massachusetts; Gov. Nelson Rockefeller; and Nixon.[67] In referring to the Nixon-Lodge campaign, Ike declared, "We could have found no two better men to head the Republican ticket."[68] However, Mamie Eisenhower, who feared that Ike's heart could not survive the stress, called Pat the night before Dick's lunch with Ike, begging the Nixons not to allow Ike to campaign and swearing them to secrecy. Putting Eisenhower's health above his own political ambitions, Nixon did not allow Ike to campaign on his behalf in the last push of the election.[69]

As the campaign wound down, Nixon returned to Los Angeles on a rainy November 5. He was met at the Van Nuys Airport by Mayor Norris Poulson, Hollywood celebrities such as Johnny Grant, Nixonettes, and thousands of other supporters, some of whom brought dogs wearing "Nixon" sweaters.[70] Nixon knew his campaign was going well when drenching rain couldn't dampen the enthusiasm of the crowd, but he cut his remarks short because of the thunder and lightning, joking with the crowd, "I'm not so concerned about myself, but I don't want any Republican voter to have pneumonia on Election Day."[71]

With Election Day now just three days away, Nixon attended Sunday services at Immanuel Presbyterian Church, next door to the Ambassador, then departed for Alaska, completing his pledge to campaign in all fifty states.[72] From Anchorage, he traveled to Wisconsin and Michigan before returning to Southern California, landing at the Ontario Airport for the closing rally of the 1960 campaign at 2:00 a.m. on November 8, Election Day.[73]

Ronald Reagan led a busload of celebrity friends to greet Nixon, and more than fifteen thousand supporters waited at the airport.[74] The vice president received tremendous support from the Hollywood community, with Jack Warner, president of Warner Brothers, taking out full-page ads for Nixon in newspapers across the country, from the *New York Times* to the *Long Beach Press Telegram*.[75] Following the rally, Pat, Dick, and their daughters finally arrived at the Ambassador at 4:00 a.m., where they felt "it was good to be home."[76]

The grueling campaign was a race to the finish. Campaign manager Robert Finch summed it up: "We will never see a campaign like it again—two men, forty-seven and forty-three, fighting with every ounce of strength."[77] Nixon, who believed it was the greatest election of the century because both candidates were outstanding, later revealed, "Of the five presidential campaigns in which I was a direct participant, none affected me more than the campaign of 1960. It was a campaign of unusual intensity. Jack Kennedy and I were both in the peak years of our political energy, and we were contesting great issues in a watershed period of American life and history."[78]

Dick and Pat voted at 7:30 a.m. at Whittier precinct 33, in the living room of Roger and Mary McNey's home.[79] Mary served the Nixons coffee and introduced them to her children, who had voted for Nixon in a mock election at school. After the adults had cast their ballots, Mary told the Nixons, "This is one of the most exciting days of my life." Dick replied, "It is for us, too!"[80] Pat and Dick then split up, with Pat taking Julie and Tricia to spend the day with Jack and

Helene Drown.[81] Dick said to his aide, Don Hughes, "Come with me; Sherwood has a car."[82]

Nixon, Hughes, Secret Service agent Jack Sherwood, and Los Angeles police officer John Di Betta climbed into a white convertible, and as Hughes recalled, "We got in a 'cops and robbers' chase. Di Betta was driving; the press was following us, so we took off, turned a corner, saw an open garage, and drove into it in order to ditch the press. And it worked: the press just drove on by. So we backed out and continued on our way." Initially, Nixon guided the group on a tour through his hometown, and since he knew from experience that it was going to be a long day, he told them, "No politics. No radio." Hughes figured such a prohibition "should last about seventeen minutes" as they drove around Whittier, past homes where Nixon had lived and schools he'd attended.[83] Then they turned toward the coast and continued driving south, as Nixon suggested driving to Mexico for a final "good will visit" to a foreign country as vice president.[84]

Hughes drove through San Diego, with Nixon asleep in the front seat. When they reached the border, a Mexican border guard recommended lunch at the Old Heidelberg Restaurant. Recognizing Nixon, the owner opened his restaurant for them at 11:00 a.m. Soon the mayor of Tijuana joined them, and the group enjoyed margaritas and a hearty Mexican lunch, staying until about 1:30 p.m. When Hughes finally called Bob Finch, he asked incredulously, "You're where?" Hughes simply responded, "We're in T.J."[85]

On the drive back north, Hughes chuckled when they stopped at lights and people pulled up next to them, looked over, and then did a double take at seeing Nixon in the front seat. At one point they were even pulled over for speeding, although once the officer realized who the passenger was, they were allowed to continue on their journey without a citation.[86] Passing through San Juan Capistrano, Nixon told Hughes, "As one of the Catholics on my staff, I am going to show you a historic Catholic Mission." He guided them to Mission San Juan Capistrano, where he conducted an impromptu tour.[87] When Nixon opened one classroom door, the nun inside was quite startled to see the vice president but immediately held up her fingers in a "V for Victory" sign. Soon all the nuns came out as Nixon and Hughes entered the chapel, where they sat for fifteen minutes "for an interlude of complete escape" from the campaign.[88] Afterward, they returned to the Ambassador. Reflecting on the experience years later, Hughes surmised, "I had a feeling he had that planned."[89]

The election was a cliff-hanger, and although Kennedy initially led, the vote count narrowed the gap as the evening progressed.[90] Even so, Nixon could see it was not enough. At 11:30 p.m. Tricia came into his suite, greeting her father: "Hi, Daddy, how is the election coming?" Nixon replied, "I'm afraid we lost, honey," a moment that Tricia later described as "the saddest day of my life."[91] Pat, always a fighter, urged Nixon to hold out hope and not concede until they knew for sure that he had lost.[92]

Finally, at 12:15 a.m. Nixon took the stage as Johnny Grant was leading the crowd in a chorus of "We want Nixon, we want Nixon! We want Nixon to be President!" to the music of "Merrily We Roll Along."[93] Nixon conceded to his cheering supporters, "If the present trend continues, Senator Kennedy will be the next President of the United States."[94] He then went upstairs to rest, until Julie woke him up at 4:00 a.m., asking, "Daddy, how did the election finally come out?" His sad reply was "Julie, I'm afraid we lost."[95] Losing the presidential election was a "shattering defeat" for Nixon, but he put on his game face for his little girl, bringing Julie into the drawing room of the suite, calling room service, and ordering them breakfast.[96]

Between the August GOP Convention and Election Day, Nixon had traveled sixty-five thousand miles, visited all fifty states, and made 180 scheduled speeches.[97] On November 8 Kennedy received 34,226,731 votes to Nixon's 34,108,157, a difference of one-half vote per precinct.[98] But California came through for its native son, and although Democratic voter registration outnumbered the Republicans by 1,368,922 eligible voters, Nixon received a majority of the 6,506,578 votes cast, all because Nixon enjoyed vast Democratic support in his home state.[99]

Just before noon, as the Nixons prepared to leave the Ambassador for their return flight to Washington, members of the California Committee came in a steady stream to offer condolences and words of support.[100] When the Nixons were ready to depart, they walked down the hotel corridor to say goodbye to Hannah and Don, and Dick could see that Don was very upset, blaming the loss on news reports of his financial troubles.[101] Dick reflected, "The hardest thing about losing is not how it affects you personally but to see the terrible disappointment in the eyes of those who have been at your side through this and other battles. It was particularly hard for Don." Before leaving, Don said to Dick apologetically, his voice breaking, "I hope I haven't been responsible for your losing the election." Nixon reassured his brother, "The only place the charge meant anything was here in California, and we are going to carry California."[102]

The lobby of the Ambassador was packed with people cheering them as they departed, yet Pat Hillings described the trip to Los Angeles International Airport as "a sad funeral cortege."[103] Despite the tremendous letdown of losing the election, as he flew east, Nixon told his aide Peter Flanigan, "Here's one thing we can be satisfied about. This campaign has laid to rest forever the issue of the candidate's religion and presidential politics. Bad for me perhaps, but good for America."[104] Just as he had predicted throughout the campaign, the election was the closest of the century. As Tom Wicker of the *New York Times* wrote in 1968, "Nobody knows to this day whom the American people really elected president in 1960. Under the prevailing system John F. Kennedy was inaugurated, but it is not at all clear if this was really the will of the people, or, if so, by what means and margin that will was expressed."[105]

In the first week of December Nixon met with Earl Mazo, who had just published the first four in a planned series of twelve investigative articles on voter fraud in Texas and Chicago for the *New York Herald Tribune.* Mazo's investigation revealed that in Texas, which Kennedy carried by approximately 46,000 votes, at least 100,000 votes officially tallied for the Kennedy-Johnson ticket appeared to be "nonexistent," and in Chicago, "mountains of sworn affidavits by poll watchers and disgruntled voters" were testimony to the alleged cheating. Kennedy had carried Illinois by only 8,858 votes out of 4,757,409, but when Nixon and Mazo met, Nixon told him, "Earl, those are interesting articles you are writing—but no one steals the Presidency of the United States."[106] Mazo described his reaction: "I thought he was kidding, but he was serious. I looked at him and thought, 'He's a goddamn fool.'"[107]

They spoke for over an hour about the campaign and the odd vote patterns in various places. Then, continent by continent, Nixon "enumerated potential international crises that could be dealt with only by the President of a united nation, not one torn by the sort of partisan bitterness and chaos that inevitably would result from an official challenge of the election result."[108] Still, Nixon could not persuade Mazo to drop the story, so he called the reporter's bosses at the *Herald Tribune* and implored them to stop the series. In the end, Mazo's editors pulled him off the story.[109]

In mid-December, having flown to Florida to meet with Nixon, who was on vacation, Kennedy opened by saying, "Well, it's hard to tell who won the election at this point."[110] Yet through it all, Nixon put "decency before politics" and rejected a recount even though he knew there were good legal grounds.[111] Ike was willing to raise money to support a legal challenge, and Dick's heart told him to do it, but his head said no. He then explained his two fundamental reasons:

> One, it would have meant the United States would be without a president for almost a year before the challenges in Illinois and Texas could be taken. I felt that the country couldn't afford to have a vacuum in leadership for that period. Two, even if we were to win in the end, the cost in world opinion and the effect on democracy in the broadest sense would be detrimental. In my travels abroad, I had been to countries in Latin America, Africa and the Far East that were just starting down the democratic path. To them, the United States was the example of the democratic system. So if in the United States an election was found to be fraudulent, it would mean that every pipsqueak in every one of those countries would be tempted, if he lost the election, to bring a fraud charge and have a coup.[112]

The 1960 election was a great blow to Hannah, who simply stated, "It must be God's will. We will have to accept it." True to her nature, she never said anything derogatory about President Kennedy or his family.[113] Hannah received letters of support from around the world. When Rev. George Ball stopped in to see Hannah one day and found her responding to stacks of letters in longhand, he was shocked and offered to write a single generic response. Hannah refused, telling the reverend, "No, they took time, and they wrote to me, so I have to write to them."[114] Hannah had instilled this value of expressing personal gratitude in her son, and after his election loss, Nixon wrote to all his volunteers who had assisted him in various campaign events. A typical Nixon letter complimented his supporters: "Losing the closest election in history was naturally a keen disappointment to us. That part will fade into the background, however, as the months and years go by. But we shall never forget your important contribution to our success in carrying our home state."[115]

Vice President Nixon was in Washington DC through the inauguration but did not want to do anything seen as impeding Kennedy's limelight. Family friend Roger Johnson recognized that Dick and his family were "very, very disappointed," though he also saw that Nixon "handled himself beautifully" during the transition period.[116] The vice president was invited to the Annual Service of Intercession and Holy Communion on January 3, 1961, at the National Presbyterian Church. Minister Edward Elson offered to reserve his "usual pew," but Nixon initially responded in the negative, saying, "This should be Kennedy and Johnson's show," although ultimately he relented and attended.[117]

On January 6, addressing a joint session of Congress as vice president, Nixon had the nearly unprecedented duty of having to announce the result of an election in which he had been defeated and declare his opponent's victory, the first time this had been done in a hundred years. He told Congress, "I do not think we could have a more striking and eloquent example of the stability of our Constitutional system and of the proud tradition of the American people of developing, respecting and honoring institutions of self-government. In our campaigns, no matter how hard-fought they may be, no matter how close the election may turn out to be, those who lose accept the verdict, and support those who win."[118] He then stated that, having served in government for fourteen years, first in the House, then in the Senate, and finally as vice president, "It is indeed a very great honor for me to extend to my colleagues in the House and Senate on both sides of the aisle who have been elected, to extend to John F. Kennedy and Lyndon Johnson, who have been elected President and Vice President of the United States, my heartfelt best wishes, and to extend to you those best wishes as all of you work in a cause that is bigger than any man's ambition, greater than any Party. It is the cause of freedom, of justice, and peace for all mankind."[119]

Through it all, Pat held her head high. She had campaigned "day in and day out, week in and week out, month in and month out," and was poised, warm, and friendly, a tremendous asset to her husband's political ambition.[120] Journalist Roy Howard told Nixon that of all the wives of presidential candidates that he had covered over his fifty-year career, he had never seen one to surpass Pat Nixon "as a campaigner and a gracious lady throughout."[121] To Albert Mattei, a Nixon supporter since the 1940s, Pat was "loved by everyone, Democrats and Republicans, and is very, very proud of her husband."[122]

Finding himself without a job for the first time in his life, Nixon sought advice from California Committee member Earl Adams, who recommended that Nixon take a position with one of five Southern California law firms, which included Adams's own firm. Nixon accepted this proposal.[123] But before leaving Washington DC he had one piece of unfinished business.

Dorothy Cox Donnelly was Nixon's appointment secretary, and since he had lost the election, Nixon knew her position was being terminated. Likewise, since her husband's position as a lobbyist on the staff of the Civil Aeronautics Board was a political appointment, his job would also come to an end with the new administration. So Nixon called Kennedy to ask, as a personal favor, if one of the Donnellys could be found a job. "Oh, yes, sure, I remember Dorothy from your Senate office—the little one with the bun on the back of her head," Kennedy responded. Everyone at the Civil Aeronautics Board was astonished when its Republican appointee was confirmed in his new post a few days later at the direction of the White House. "When I found out afterwards about this act of mercy involving the Vice President and the President-elect which allowed our fragile family finances to survive, I was astounded," Dorothy recalled. "Mr. Nixon never said a word to me about it, and yet this little story is so characteristic of his sensitivity and his willingness to reach out to someone in trouble with a kindness."[124]

THIRTEEN

Welcome Home

1961

Following Kennedy's inauguration, the Nixons returned to Southern California on February 28, 1961. Wanting their daughters to have as smooth a transition as possible, the couple decided that Dick would move to Los Angeles first to begin working, while Pat would stay in Washington DC with the girls until their school year ended in June. To cheer up her father, Julie wrote him a tribute poem and sent it to Grandma Hannah so it would be in Southern California when he arrived: "My Dad—Handsome and kind / Always on time / Loving and good / Does things he should / Humorous, funny / Makes the day seem sunny / Helping others to live / Willing to give / His life for his beloved country / That's my DAD!"[1]

Pat initially accompanied Dick back to California.[2] Tanned and fit, with big smiles on their faces, the two walked off the plane hand in hand. They were greeted by Hannah, former governor Goodwin Knight, and 4,500 well-wishers as the Whittier High School marching band played "California, Here I Come."[3] Deeply moved at the outpouring of support, Nixon told the crowd, "We're glad to be back. Of course, we didn't expect to come back exactly this way, but if we had to come back anywhere, we're glad it's to California."[4] He then laid out his short-term goals. "We have three things to do: look for a house, look for a job and get a California driver's license."[5] The *Alhambra Post-Advocate* summed up the general feeling of the Golden State: "The Nixons are home. California wishes them well-deserved abundant rest and relaxation."[6]

The Los Angeles County Board of Supervisors proclaimed March 1 "Welcome Home Dick and Pat Nixon Day," and 1,600 guests joined the Nixons at the Los Angeles Press Club's sold out homecoming banquet at the Beverly Hilton Hotel.[7] Though out of public office,

Nixon intended to devote all his free time to leadership in public affairs.[8] Thus the question immediately arose as to whether he would run for governor in 1962, and Nixon took advantage of the curiosity: "I thought this might be an occasion to make an important announcement. . . . It has been a difficult decision to reach. . . . I like competition. I like contests. I like taking sides." The crowd fell silent as Nixon paused before he announced, "Since the Washington Senators have moved to Minnesota, I am going to cheer for the Los Angeles Angels."[9]

After first visiting Mamie and President Eisenhower in Palm Springs, the Nixons began shopping for a new home, touring houses from across the South Bay.[10] Their basic requirements were that it be large enough for their family "plus a modest amount of entertaining," with grounds sufficient to afford privacy and a location convenient to both Los Angeles International Airport and Dick's new law office in downtown Los Angeles.[11]

Having been in Washington DC for fourteen years, Pat and Dick now had total assets consisting of $48,000 from the sale of their home.[12] Once Pat returned east to be with Tricia and Julie, Richard took up residence at the Statler Hilton Hotel, staying there for the month of March.[13] Needing longer-term housing, but still on a tight budget, he then moved to apartment 602 in the Gaylord Hotel on Wilshire Boulevard, across from the Ambassador.[14] He often dined at the nearby Perino's or the Cocoanut Grove but was also just as likely to eat TV dinners while sitting on his couch.[15] Conrad Hilton had made sure that he was well cared for while at the Statler, and Nixon later thanked his friend: "For you to be so generous as to take care of me and my staff on my return to private life was an act of thoughtfulness which I shall always remember."[16]

Diving back into politics, Nixon made his first political speech to Republican members of the California State Assembly. The speech almost didn't happen, as Nixon arrived in the state capital in a "stolen" car. State Republican Party chairman John Krehbiel, a member of Nixon's California Committee since 1948, was at the El Mirador Hotel across from the capitol building, waiting to pick Nixon up at the airport, when State Senator Jack McCarthy offered the use of his Lincoln Continental, which he told Krehbiel "was in the basement." McCarthy meant the capitol parking garage, but Krehbiel thought he meant the El Mirador parking garage, where coincidentally a Lincoln with the keys in it was parked. When Krehbiel returned with Nixon, the car's irate owner was waiting with the police. Fortunately, the owner was a Republican and didn't file charges.[17]

Professionally, Nixon took an "of counsel" position at California Committee member Earl Adams's firm, Adams, Duque & Hazeltine, with an annual salary of $60,000.[18] Adams had initially offered Nixon a job in 1946 if he lost that first congressional race, and Nixon joked that it took him fourteen years to get the right qualifications to join the firm.[19] Launching into the private sector, he was assisted by Secret Service agent Jim Golden, who had developed such a strong relationship with and loyalty to Vice President Nixon that he resigned from the government to continue working with Nixon.[20] Rose Mary Woods also stayed on, as Nixon's personal secretary, as did Loie Gaunt and aides Don Hughes, Robert Finch, and Bob Haldeman.[21] Attorney Waller Taylor was second in command at Adams Duque. Waller and his father, Reese, who was president of Union Oil of California, had been friends with Nixon since the early 1950s, and Waller was assigned as Nixon's "point man" within the firm.[22]

Adams Duque was in the Pacific Mutual Building, a few blocks from the Statler Hilton, so Nixon initially could walk to the office. A tireless worker, Nixon arrived at 7:30 a.m. on his first day, only to discover the firm did not open its doors until 9:00. Woods remembered that Nixon "walked round and round outside those offices for the next hour and a half" until the firm opened.[23] Ironically, he wound up being ten minutes late, as he stopped to explain to a supporter how to get a job with the post office.[24]

When Nixon moved into his nicely appointed, dark wood–paneled suite on the eleventh floor, he brought a couch that was so large it had to be hoisted up the side of the building.[25] Nixon's office was appropriate for his position in the firm; the members of Adams Duque did not expect that he was there to practice law but to generate business.[26] But as Bill Henry of the *Los Angeles Times* knew, "The guiding purpose in Dick Nixon's life is to do just as good a job as it is possible for any human being to do."[27] Soon the associates in the firm realized that they'd find Nixon still working in the office until 10:00 or 11:00 p.m.[28]

Nixon returned to Whittier to buy a 1961 Oldsmobile 98 sedan from college classmate Clint Harris, his favorite car dealer.[29] Nixon described his new wheels as "a four-door job with all the gadgets." Pat and the girls picked the color, a light blue called azure mist. Before driving the car off the lot, Nixon had to take his driver's license exam at the Whittier branch of the Department of Motor Vehicles. He missed one question on the test, incorrectly marking that a signal must be given continuously for two hundred feet before making a turn, rather than one hundred feet. "At least I was on the precautionary side," he quipped.[30]

As he settled into his life in Southern California, Nixon realized that he was suffering the letdown of defeat.[31] Fortunately, California was the perfect place to transition from public to private life, since the climate was superb, and there were numerous recreational and cultural activities to help him adjust.[32] Exceedingly popular, Nixon received two hundred invitations to speak each week.[33] Pat, Tricia, and Julie joined Dick at the Miramar Hotel in Santa Monica for an Easter vacation arranged by friend and former congressman Donald Jackson, who was living at the Miramar. Nixon later joked to Jackson, "When I talked with Julie the other evening, she asked me if the pool at our new home would be as nice as the Jackson's."[34]

Pat and the kids soon returned east, and Nixon turned his attention to lawyering, bolstered by support from his California Committee and titans from both Hollywood and the Los Angeles business community who held "welcome home" dinner parties in his honor.[35] Justin Dart, president of the Rexall Drug Company, acknowledged, "I couldn't know how to rate a fellow any higher than I do Dick Nixon." He described Nixon as warm, friendly, and an interested conversationalist, a man who conducted himself in such a manner "that he'd won the respect of almost everyone who was interested in politics in this community."[36] Adams Duque also hosted parties at the California Club to celebrate Nixon's joining the firm, with guest lists including everybody who was anybody in Los Angeles.[37] Between his popularity and tremendous range of contacts, Nixon brought in an incredible amount of business for Adams Duque, and in just two years the firm tripled in size.[38]

Nixon was hands-on in his approach to the practice of law. He consulted with clients and assisted in the "ultimate decisions" made on their behalf.[39] Though successful, he was not guided by fees and turned down many important cases that had been brought to the firm simply because he was there. Earl Adams remembered one case that required a sizable staff and would have proceeded for years, likely generating fees in the millions. Yet Nixon decided against taking on the client because he felt "that somewhere along the way it might involve a government agency and he, as former vice president, could not in good conscience be a part of anything that might remotely appear to be a conflict of interest."[40]

Far from taking a break from politics, he met the board of the Republican Advisory Committee, consisting of top African American leaders, for breakfast at the Statler Hilton on April 14 and spoke on issues important to the Black community.[41] Nixon believed the GOP should promote African American participation, telling E. Frederic Morrow, appointed by Eisenhower as the first Black person to hold an executive position in the White House, "The project of improving our Party's appeal to Negroes—and to other groups for that matter—is not one which can be put off until the few months preceding the next election. Rather it is one which must be undertaken now."[42]

Nixon charmed and inspired fellow Republicans at speaking engagements across Southern California and motivated the party faithful.[43] "Unflinching, animated, and absolute in his opinions," Nixon gave this consistent message: "Now is the time to match the first words with deeds. And it won't be done by telling the American people they have to sacrifice, then on the other hand comforting them by telling what the government can do for the people." He believed that it was unnecessary and wrong "to turn to government for the solution of all problems," and his message was well received, with the managing editor of the *San Bernardino Daily Sun* later telling him, "I only wish you could have heard the comments from the scores of people after the event. They were all high in their praise."[44]

Nixon understood and appreciated the hard work of volunteers and always made time to visit with and thank the Republican faithful.[45] When he learned that FBI agent Carl Underhill had been ordered to refrain from promoting or attending his events, Nixon immediately wrote to his friend J. Edgar Hoover, director of the FBI, who had just visited Nixon's home and with whom he had pending dinner plans.[46] Dick assured Hoover that Underhill's assistance was nonpolitical and expressed his hope "that Mr. Underhill's career in the Bureau will in no way suffer because of his participation in a purely civic, as distinguished from a political, affair."[47]

His hometown remained close to his heart. Pat and Dick were honorary chairpersons of the Whittier-area Girl Scout Council cookie sale for 1961, and Dick celebrated Yorba Linda's annual Pioneer Days.[48] Nixon was also attentive to his extended family and friends. He went to see his niece Patricia Marshburn, a student at the California School for the Deaf, and when in Orange County, he often visited Hannah and Don's family.[49] Dick had remained very close to his brother, and Don's was the only telephone number Nixon carried on him other than those of his immediate office staff.[50]

Nixon received many honors on his return to Los Angeles. In May he was the closing speaker when the Boys Clubs of America held its first annual convention on the West Coast. At the Big Brothers annual dinner at the Beverly Hilton Hotel, Nixon was honored as "the American who has been the greatest inspiration to our youth in terms of honesty, integrity and patriotism."[51] Jack Warner joined Nixon at the head table, Ronald Reagan served as master of ceremonies, and Walt Disney presented Nixon with the inaugural award.[52] Afterward, Warren Woodall, executive director of the Big Brothers of Greater Los Angeles, told Nixon, "It goes without saying that one of the real highlights of the evening was your warm reception of our twenty-eight Little Brothers. These youngsters are our life's blood and, please believe me, the opportunity to shake hands with you was one of the greatest things ever to happen to them."[53] Rather than simply accept the award and make a speech, Nixon refused to be paid an honorarium and instead made a donation to the Big Brothers. In response, composer and playwright Meredith Willson of *The Music Man* fame, impressed with Nixon's "wisdom, understanding and patience," wrote, "Your Big Brothers check floored me. . . . I am utterly and completely at a loss for words. God bless you."[54]

On July 3 Nixon attended the National Biennial Convention of the City of Hope. He pointed out that the organization existed because Americans put their faith "in idealism and in moral and spiritual strength," then expanded on his belief in idealism:

Idealists, to be sure, are sometimes annoying people to have around—very hard to live with. And this is not because they are impractical day-dreamers; precisely the opposite, it is because they are hard task masters. It is because they will not let us forget that each one of us is endowed with something called a conscience. And it is because they keep on insisting that the run of human and material values—like comfort and abundance and worldly success—are of infinitely less worth than the moral and spiritual values—like service and obligation, and willing submission to goals and purposes that transcend our own lives and times. But hard as they may be to live with, always calling us to the duty we owe our consciences, we can literally thank God for idealists.[55]

The nearly one thousand attendees gave him a ten-minute standing ovation at the conclusion of his remarks.[56] Over his objection, Nixon was often sent monetary compensation for his appearances, and when the City of Hope sent him a $2,000 honorarium, he responded by advising, "I am following my usual practice of contributing the proceeds of your very generous honorarium to several charitable institutions listed below: City of Hope $1,000; American Cancer Society $500; Crippled Children's Society $500; Times Summer Camp Fund $250." Nixon actually donated more to these charities than he received from the City of Hope.[57]

Dick's social calendar was booked, including lunch with Sam Goldwyn, cocktails at Conrad Hilton's, dinners with Norm and Buff Chandler followed by evenings at the Hollywood Bowl, intimate dinners with Ronald and Nancy Reagan at their Pacific Palisades home, and Kyle Palmer's Sunday dinners.[58] When Nixon could not be with friends, he wrote to them, and when Jack Drown's father passed away, Dick's handwritten note touched the man so deeply that Drown later described it as "one of the most beautiful letters he ever wrote."[59]

Keeping the promise he'd made on returning to Los Angeles, Nixon became an Angels fan, even attending their home opener at the old Wrigley Field with team owner Gene Autry.[60] After the Angels lost, Nixon consoled Autry: "Since I can now qualify as an expert on losing the close one, I think I am in a pretty good position to give you and your colleagues some advice as to how to take it."[61]

Nixon enjoyed combining the camaraderie of friendship with a little wagering on the golf course.[62] Following a match at Irvine

Ranch, he wrote to his host, Charlie Thomas, "After playing the way I did in the first nine I couldn't imagine that I would have ended up with the low net among eight sterling golfers to whom you were serving that delicious gin concoction for lunch."[63] In his customary style, he sent letters to his playing partners, thanking them and promising to put his winnings "in escrow recognizing that next time I can't possibly be as lucky so that I can be prepared to pay my debts when they come due."[64]

As though he weren't busy enough, with prodding from old friend and journalist Adela Rogers St. Johns, Nixon agreed to write a book about his experiences, and he also signed on to write a regular column for the Times Mirror Company.[65] He even returned to Washington DC to meet President Kennedy at the White House, where Nixon had a seventy-five-minute visit with Kennedy regarding the Bay of Pigs fiasco—at Kennedy's request, because the president respected Nixon's insight.[66] Afterward, "composed and in full command" at a White House press conference, rather than disparage Kennedy, Nixon told the press there was "nothing more irresponsible" than for a citizen outside the government and not privy to the facts to "pop off" against the president, "and I don't intend to do that."[67]

In preparation for the June arrival of his wife and daughters, Dick rented director Walter Lang's Brentwood house.[68] Neighbors included popular actors Cesar Romero and Fred MacMurray, both friends of Nixon's.[69] Pat's warm welcome home included an honorary degree from her alma mater, the University of Southern California.[70] Once the family was together, Nixon bought a lot in Truesdale Estates, at 410 Martin Lane in Beverly Hills, on which to build a new house that would have seven bathrooms, five bedrooms, three fireplaces, a library, a thirty-foot-long living room, and a swimming pool. Harpo and Groucho Marx later became the Nixons' neighbors.[71]

By midsummer the Republican National Committee contacted Nixon, lamenting the complete lack of leadership in California and pointing out that the party would gladly follow his direction.[72] The state Republican Party had been decimated in the 1958 election mess between Knight and Knowland, and Nixon, who had carried the state in 1960, was the only Republican to win in California, making him the titular leader. Nixon embraced the thought of uniting the California Republican Party and held a working session at his house, followed by dinner with party leaders including Assemblyman Joe Shell and state Republican Party vice chairman Cap Weinberger.[73] Those working sessions turned into lunch meetings at the California Club, which then led to strategy meetings and consultations with California Committee members at both his Adams Duque office and the "Republican" Suite 10334 in the adjacent Biltmore Hotel.[74]

While Dick debated whether to run for governor, he and Pat invited Bebe Rebozo to spend Labor Day weekend with them, and Bebe accepted their invitation, telling Nixon, "The consequences of my having visited your household, if it gets out, may be the final chapter in your political life. If you are willing to take this chance I promise to do my best not to live up to my ill-gotten and undeserved reputation."[75] In response, Nixon assured Bebe, "All of us are looking forward to having you with us for the Labor Day weekend. You can't back out of it now—we are literally counting the days. Please let me know when you arrive so we can either meet you or arrange to have a wealthy widow who owns a liquor store and has a house (home that is!) be on hand to greet you."[76]

With Bebe in tow, Nixon joined Randolph Scott and Don Jackson for a round of golf at the Bel-Air Country Club on PGA National Hole in One Day.[77] They were a great foursome: Scott was a well-known, carefree actor; Rebozo was one of Nixon's closest friends; and Jackson, who had known Nixon since their 1946 congressional campaigns, was "a totally undisciplined spirit."[78] Feeling lucky on the third hole, a 155-yard par three, Nixon took out his trusted five iron and teed up his "Mr. Vice President" golf ball, hitting a hole in one. He said jubilantly, "It's the greatest thrill of my life, even better than being elected."[79] There could be no better metaphor for Richard Nixon's personal and professional success in Southern California at that point in time, one of the busiest periods he ever experienced.[80] The only question was whether he would run for governor.

FOURTEEN

Governor's Race

1961–62

onsidering a run for governor of California over the summer
of 1961, Nixon expressed mixed feelings: "I still lean strongly
against the idea, primarily because my entire experience is
national and international affairs, and the idea of concentrating
almost exclusively on state issues for four years simply has no appeal
to me."[1] Eisenhower, J. Edgar Hoover, and California Republican
Party chairman Cap Weinberger encouraged him to enter the race
for the good of the party, and Nixon, whom the *Los Angeles Times*
editorialized as "*the* Mr. Republican of the contemporary scene,"
knew no one else in California could unite the party after the Knight-
Knowland disaster of 1958.[2] But many close to him argued against
taking on popular incumbent Pat Brown, including his mother,
and she was hardly alone: Rose Marie Woods and Robert Finch
thought it was a mistake, as did Herb Klein and Roy Day.[3] Even
General MacArthur and former president Herbert Hoover advised
against the race.[4]

The Nixons held a family meeting over dinner on September 25 to
discuss the decision to run for governor, which Nixon described: "I
went over the pros and cons. Then Pat said, 'Well, I just want to say
one thing. If you decide to run, you are going to run on your own.
I'm not going to be there campaigning with you as I did when you
ran for the House, the Senate, for Vice President and for President.'
And so she left the room, and the girls were in tears."[5] Tricia jumped
up and hugged her father, crying, "Daddy, come on—let's show 'em!"[6]
A short time later Pat, although devoted to her husband's political
ambition, told Dick, her voice trembling with disappointment, "I
have thought about it some more, and I am more convinced than
ever that if you run it will be a terrible mistake. But if you weigh
everything and still decide to run, I will support your decision. I'll

be there campaigning just as I always have."[7] Ultimately, in deciding to run for an office in which he was not truly interested, Nixon ignored his own maxim: "What separates the men from the boys in politics is that the boys seek office to *be* something and the men seek office to *do* something."[8]

Two days later Nixon announced his candidacy at the Statler Hilton.[9] When asked why Teamster boss Jimmy Hoffa had a prior trust deed on Nixon's Truesdale Estates property, he was blunt: "I have been threatened and warned before this press conference tonight that every dead cat and every old story would be thrown up and used against me. Let me just say that nobody is going to frighten me. Nobody is going to drive me out of this contest, and that as far as this kind of smear is concerned . . . I intend to no longer take it lying down."[10] Believing that in 1960 he had been the subject of one of the worst smear campaigns launched against a candidate, this time Nixon laid down the gauntlet: "I serve warning, here and now, that anything of this sort, dealing with matters having nothing to do with my capabilities for governor of the state, that have nothing to do with my record in public office, that anybody who makes charges of this type will have to answer for them, and they will be in the fight of their lives."[11]

Nixon's only other purely statewide California race had been the 1950 Senate campaign. He was now a private citizen with an active social life, a full-time lawyer, and the writer of a syndicated column and also a book, *Six Crises*. Pat was enjoying the Southern California lifestyle, and Tricia and Julie were enrolled at the prestigious Marlborough School. As he launched his candidacy, Nixon continued to juggle family, leisure, lawyering, writing, and public appearances through the end of 1961. Activities ranged from joining Buff and Dorothy Chandler at the *Los Angeles Times* Woman of the Year presentation to enjoying dinners at the homes of California Committee friends.[12] When the Nixons were not out and about town, they frequently entertained at their home.[13]

Adela Rogers St. Johns, a friend since the days when Nixon had delivered groceries to her ranch, had talked Nixon into writing *Six Crises*.[14] She had supported every Nixon campaign since 1946 and was known to gush, "I do love Dick Nixon just like he was almost my own child."[15] Her favorite story of Nixon was when, after working all day on *Six Crises*, she had to leave to meet her son Dickie. Nixon offered to drive her, but she preferred to take a taxi, explaining, "I'd just as soon not ride with Mr. Nixon behind the wheel. He's a bad driver." But Nixon prevailed, and they immediately got lost. Finally finding their way, they arrived at Dickie's house, where, unbeknownst to Nixon and St. Johns, he was hosting a meeting with half a dozen television producers. As they walked in, St. Johns jokingly chided Nixon: "I knew you'd get lost." Nixon, oblivious to Dickie's guests, exasperatedly asked Dickie, "How do you put up with her? I've had her all day, and honestly . . ." "Well," Dickie interrupted, "that's up to you. I told you when you started." St. Johns again chided Nixon: "This is a fine thing. I have been working with you all day long, and what I have put up with, your nonsense!" Nixon, who suddenly became aware of all the other men present, warmly retorted, "Well, God bless you, we're going to get a good book, aren't we?" After he was introduced to the room, Nixon patted Dickie on the back, then kissed St. Johns before departing. The television producers sat in a moment of dead silence, before one of the men, impressed by Nixon's relaxed humor, blurted out, "*That* was *Dick Nixon*? Well, where the hell has HE been?"[16]

Nixon immediately went to work setting up his campaign. Adams Duque was located in the Pacific Mutual Building, adjacent to the Biltmore Hotel, with the Statler Hilton just a few blocks away. Between the Statler and the Biltmore were two private membership organizations, the Jonathan Club and the California Club. These five venues were the anchors of Nixon's campaign, which hosted intimate meetings, meals, and strategy sessions within that four-block radius.[17]

By October Nixon had met with numerous Republican leaders, including his extensive California Committee friends, who formed his core financial supporters.[18] Nixon hired Sandy Quinn as his publicist, then turned to organizing women supporters, meeting with various powerful California Committee women, including Margaret Brock, Athalie Clarke, Lucille Hosmer, and Pat Hitt.[19] The daughter of John Reilly of Whittier, Hitt had become an integral member of Nixon's inner circle since she initially helped him get his start in politics in 1946, and she had participated in each of his campaigns since.[20]

For the first time in Nixon's career, he had a serious Republican primary challenger when Joe Shell, a conservative assemblyman from Bakersfield, entered the governor's race. Knowing he must unify the fractured party to win the governorship, Nixon met with the California Republican Assembly, promising "a fighting campaign." Yet he would focus his energy against only Democrat Pat Brown, as Nixon explained that he planned to address the problems confronting California and the Brown administration's failure to solve those issues, and not his fellow Republican challenger: "I am proud that in my entire public life I have never attacked my fellow Republican candidates and I don't intend to begin now."[21]

The morning of November 6, 1961, Nixon was working on *Six Crises* at his Brentwood home when he called Sandy Quinn at the Adams Duque office: "Sandy, I wonder if you could come out here, because the canyon is on fire and there are fire trucks everywhere, and we are all going to have to evacuate."[22] Quinn jumped in his car and raced to Nixon's home, arriving to find residents frantically clearing out their homes. As he pulled up to Nixon's residence, Dick, wearing a tie and wingtips, was carrying a painting out to his car. Quinn was amazed by Nixon's calm while everyone else was scrambling.[23] Of the 484 homes that were destroyed and another 190 that were damaged, the Nixon home was spared.[24]

Nixon was equally unflustered behind the wheel of a car, even though his driving skills (or lack thereof) gave others pause. One day Nixon drove himself to the Adams Duque office on Sixth Street, a major artery through downtown Los Angeles. Walking into his office, he asked Quinn to join him, bringing his young publicity man to the window overlooking the City of Angels. Nixon pointed to the street below, asking Quinn, "Can you take care of that? I don't know what to do with it." Sandy was amazed to see Nixon's car abandoned in the middle of Sixth Street, with the keys in the ignition.[25]

As the year came to a close, the Nixons celebrated the Thanksgiving and Christmas holidays with Don and Clara Jane and Pat's family at her brother Tom Ryan's house.[26] Longtime California Committee friend Kyle Palmer was terminally ill with leukemia, putting a damper on the Christmas spirit.[27] After attending church services on Christmas Eve, the Nixon family spent the evening with Palmer and his family, and then on New Year's Day, Nixon again stopped in to visit his ailing friend.[28]

As 1962 commenced, so did Nixon's primary campaign against Joe Shell. Celebrating his January birthday with the Whittier Area Chamber of Commerce at the Whittier College Student Union, Nixon reminisced with his old friends, admitting to those gathered that although his mother had not wanted a life of politics for him, he had no regrets; he knew he could not sit on the sidelines, allowing the "crooks and crackpots" on the "political right and radical left" to dominate political action through bullying tactics. Rather, he believed, "We need participation by the great majority," which he felt he represented.[29]

On January 24, at an appearance before the Personnel and Industrial Relations Association at the Statler, Nixon, who felt that his "life can be best served—will be most useful—in public life," was frank about why he engaged in public service:

> I realize this isn't a political meeting. But I am a politician. To pretend I am anything else would be to mislead you. I hope that you are all politicians. Am I asking you to be partisan? No. Am I asking you join the skeleton organization of folks who make their living by being politicians? Hardly. You are successful at your own business or you wouldn't be here. But I contend that you've also got to be a politician. You can't afford not to be. You owe it to our country. A politician is one who is concerned with government and who has a philosophy of government. Yes, I'm a politician. I don't believe that free government can survive unless every citizen is a politician. Yes, I'm a politician. I think being a politician is the most important obligation of any man who believes in freedom. It isn't easy to let freedom reign. But it is the duty of every American patriot to work at it. Freedom takes thought and dedication. Freedom can't live in a vacuum. It demands dedicated servants who love it and will work for it. It demands politicians. They are the servants of freedom. It is our philosophy. It is the business of believing in freedom—not just for ourselves but for every living human being. It is not being afraid to be a politician.[30]

Nixon was known to give a "thumping good" speech, captivating "even the stoutest Democrats," and his attendance at the May 1 Junior Barristers of the Los Angeles County Bar Association luncheon drew the largest turnout in the group's history. There he told the young attorneys that a "lawyer must be a man of reason. He proves himself on unpopular causes." He then announced his opposition to the Francis Amendment, a ballot proposition banning Communists from holding public office.[31] No American political figure of his generation was more consistently attacked in the *Daily Worker* and the *People's Daily World* than Nixon, an avowed anti-Communist.[32] Yet he was not opposed to teaching Communism in school, believing that using education as a means to counter Communism was a more thoughtful and effective approach.[33] Nixon was no doomsday politician, telling his audiences, "I never engage in 'scare talk.' But I do believe in honest talk." Saying, "Communism is the major threat of our time," Nixon explained to his audiences, "We need intelligent, hard hitting discussion of it at the adult level and in our schools as well."[34]

A strong military was not enough to win the battle against Communism; rather, Nixon's Quaker upbringing guided his belief that "what we must do is turn our energies and our creative thought to the positive goal of building a true community of free nations and freedom loving people, everywhere in the world."[35] Nixon supported exchange programs as an important means of teaching foreign students what the United States represents: "Dollar for dollar there is no particular program that contributes more international good will, justice and peace than cultural exchange."[36]

Nixon visited college campuses throughout Southern California, with thousands welcoming him at each venue.[37] He took questions from the students, taking time to explain that conservatism was "a force for progress, not reaction." He delighted in engaging them, as he believed, "Young people have to know that America has gotten great not because of what government has done primarily but because of what individual and private enterprise has done. The trouble today with America is not too much patriotism or too little patriotism but too little knowledge."[38]

He also viewed education as an issue of states' rights. Nixon, whose wife was a former teacher and whose daughters were still in school, believed that local control over issues like schools and education was paramount.[39] He promoted bond issues to raise the necessary funds for construction of new schools and universities, rather than looking to the federal government to solve the problem:

"Whoever pays the bills calls the tune. If we turn to Washington for assistance, and sit back and wait for the federal government to assume the ever-mounting burden of education costs, then we are inviting control of our local schools by the federal bureaucracy."[40] Nixon firmly believed, "We should never turn to government where private individuals can do the job."[41] He and Pat joined in the opening ceremony of the nation's first self-supporting braille library on Pico Boulevard in Los Angeles, created to liberate blind children from dependence on government subsidies and grant them an equal opportunity with sighted children.[42] Nixon's belief in states' rights extended to business and regulatory matters, and he opposed federal regulation of the poultry market as undue intrusion on state farmers and the "corner food store." Nixon rejected what he considered "bureaucratic dictation" from the federal government, stating, "All we want is a fair shake for everyone—producer, processor, and consumer."[43]

It was in John Kennedy's best interest for Nixon to lose in November, with Democratic senator Hubert Humphrey promising, "California is the battleground for 1962. When you need help, press the button, place the order, and we will be out to finish the job we started on Dick Nixon in 1960."[44] Yet Nixon was undaunted: "They can send all the talent they want to out here—they can send Bobby and Teddy, and Joe with all his Jack; we're ready for them. We're out to beat them to a pulp."[45] Ultimately, both President Kennedy and Bobby Kennedy did in fact campaign throughout California against Nixon.[46] In a further attempt to defeat Nixon and eliminate him as a candidate in 1964, the Kennedys initiated a strategy that kept Nixon entangled in IRS audits, but despite these tactics, Nixon still went all out to win.[47]

Throughout the campaign, Nixon made every effort to reach out to minorities, saying, "Look at my record. Throughout my life I have fought against race hatred. I have fought for equality of opportunity for all people. Whenever we have racial bigotry or religious bigotry it weakens America. I never look upon Americans and try to break them down in terms of a race or a creed or a class."[48] Speaking from the pulpit at the Pasadena Westminster Presbyterian Church's twenty-fifth anniversary celebration for the Pasadena Association for the Study of Negro Life and History on February 11, Nixon argued that white men could not expect to have equal rights and opportunities so long as any minority was denied the same rights and opportunities.[49] Nixon worked to establish Republican community centers in traditionally Black and Hispanic areas that were open seven days a week, offering free polio shots, legal services, scholarships, and mock employment interviews.[50]

While visiting a Republican community center in the heart of South Central Los Angeles, Nixon discussed a recent letter in which a young man first expressed his fear that there were no jobs available to either himself or his community, then lamented the plight of his friends and relatives.[51] He understood that the young writer was "expressing more than dismay at the cruelty of blind discrimination; he was also expressing real concern for his future and wondering whether there was any hope."[52] Nixon opined, "It is little wonder we see the formation of organizations such as the Black Muslims—a group that has turned its back on hope and retreated to violence and racism as a solution."[53] Rejecting violence in any form and believing, "We cannot have progress if we are going to encourage class and racial distinctions," Nixon instead advocated for a more positive approach, promising that as governor, he would "use the moral and persuasive powers of the office to bring employers together for voluntary action in the field of equal job opportunities, and opportunities for promotion."[54]

Crispus Attucks Wright became the Southern California vice chairman of the Nixon for Governor campaign.[55] The son of a slave, Wright, along with other lawyers, founded the Blackstone Club in the 1920s after African Americans were denied membership in other bar associations. The name was changed to the Langston Law Club in 1943 and the John M. Langston Bar Association in 1968.[56] At the Rodger Young Auditorium in Los Angeles, Wright introduced Nixon to four hundred doctors, lawyers, and dentists from the Black community.[57] "It is simply not in the best interests of our state to deny jobs to any Californian because of race, color, religion or any other factor that has nothing to do with how well a man can do a job," Nixon assured the group. "It is a question of simple justice."[58]

Likewise, Nixon reached out to the Hispanic community, visiting the La Opinion newspaper offices and holding a Win with Nixon rally at East Los Angeles Junior College, where Nixon was blunt: "California needs the talents of the Mexican Americans."[59] Holding a Mexican American dinner at the Biltmore Hotel, billed as "An Evening with the Nixons," Dick implored the guests that Californians "must recognize and appreciate the value of diversity in our society."[60]

Nixon's approach to religion mirrored his approach to race. He met people of all faiths, from the Baptist Ministers Alliance at the McCoy Memorial Baptist Church in South Central to the Church of Jesus Christ of Latter Day Saints on South Manhattan Place in Los Angeles.[61] He was warmly received before the largest-ever crowd at the Guardians of the Jewish Home for the Aged dinner meeting at the Beverly Hilton.[62] Mendel Silberberg, Samuel Goldwyn's attorney and longtime California Committee member, lauded Nixon's "proven friendship for both the Jewish people and the State of Israel."[63] Addressing the group, Nixon compared his Quaker background to Judaism as he "praised the voluntary approach to charity in America which exemplified what the Quakers call 'concern' for their fellow man, and what the Jews call 'tzedakah.'"[64]

Since over a million more Democrats than Republicans registered to vote in California, Nixon had to have complete Republican support plus significant Democratic support to defeat Pat Brown. Although one of his goals was to solidify the California Republican Party after the debacle of 1958, Nixon held firm to his longtime beliefs about the John Birch Society, a group of anti-Communists led by Robert Welch, who had charged that Eisenhower was "aiding and abetting the Communist conspiracy."[65] Nixon felt strongly that "every American should have 'extreme' feelings about his religion, his country, his political beliefs and the threat of Communism" and has a right to express his viewpoint. But he opposed Welch's group as extremists, and early in the campaign, he called on the California Republican Assembly, "acting in the great tradition of our party for individual liberties and civil rights," to repudiate the John Birch Society and its leadership.[66] Campaigning in Long Beach, Nixon amplified his comments about the society, declaring it was "irrefutable that you could not be a Birch Society member and a member of the Republican Party."[67] With Joe Shell running to his right, this position split the California Republican Party, whose votes Nixon needed to win.[68]

Despite being in a tight campaign, with a split party and needing funds, Nixon was charitable. He raised money for his friend Gene Brito, a Rams football player diagnosed with amyotrophic lateral sclerosis (ALS, or Lou Gehrig's disease), and even made a substantial contribution himself.[69] After the Nixons attended a gathering of the Orange County chapter of the National Secretaries Association, the group was so impressed that they sent Nixon a campaign contribution, which he immediately donated back to their scholarship fund.[70] When Nixon spoke at a $100-a-plate dinner at the Beverly Hilton in honor of Father Patrick Peyton's twentieth year at Notre Dame, Nixon was so moved that he sent a contribution, explaining, "After meeting and hearing Father Peyton, I became more convinced than ever before that there should be no freeloaders at a dinner honoring him."[71]

Cousin Sheldon Beeson fondly remembered the day Nixon celebrated his aunt Jane and uncle Harold Beeson's fiftieth wedding anniversary reception at the Whittier First Friends Church: "I asked Dick if he would come and say a few words to Mother and Father. You should have heard the way he expressed himself. It was just a real tribute to them."[72] Sadly, not all pauses from the campaign were for joyous events, as in the midst of the primary, Nixon's longtime friend Kyle Palmer succumbed to leukemia, with Nixon serving as a pallbearer at the funeral.[73]

On March 4 Pat and Dick joined Ronald and Nancy Reagan for the Reagans' tenth wedding anniversary party at the Beverly Hilton Hotel's Star on the Roof bar.[74] Between 1948 and 1962 Reagan transitioned from a Democrat who campaigned for Harry Truman to a staunch Republican. Throughout those transitional years, Nixon was the preeminent Southern California Republican, and during that time, Dick and Ron developed a lasting friendship. Nixon believed in the Jeffersonian Republican principle "that the greatest guarantee of freedom is decentralization of power," declaring, "Our experience as a free people shows beyond a doubt that free men will sooner bring about the common good but regulated men always find ways to exploit society as a whole."[75] These beliefs resonated with Ronald Reagan.

Nixon was the first southwestern individualist to be a national candidate. In fact, this was his clarion call: "In this fall's election let our voice ring out from the West, saying 'We, the people of California, with a great tradition of seeking opportunity, with a true frontier spirit, cast our vote for free enterprise, self-reliance, local responsibility, and for the best State Government in America."[76] He was open about his philosophy regarding reliance on government in solving problems: "We look first to the individual citizen. If the task is too great for the individual or his family, we turn next to our private or non-governmental institutions. If private groups cannot do the job we turn to local government—to our cities and towns and special districts. Only if the level of government closest to the people fails in its task, or lacks the resources, do we turn to the higher level of government."[77]

Just over two months before the primary election, when *Six Crises* was released, Nixon commented wryly, "I am now a Republican egghead."[78] The book, detailing six seminal events in his political life, was an immediate bestseller. Whether at Whittier's Broadway department store or the May Company on Wilshire, Nixon was amazed as crowds stood in line for hours to meet him. He liked to joke that he couldn't understand the book's popularity until a woman came up and handed him her copy of *Six Crises* with her sales receipt, which stated *Sex Crises*.[79]

Nixon's Martin Lane home was finally completed in the midst of the campaign.[80] The large ranch-style house, with its expansive view of Los Angeles, was the first home Pat and Dick had ever been able to buy and build from scratch.[81] Nixon credited *Six Crises* with providing the funds necessary for the home, which he described as "the house the book built."[82]

The Nixons immediately set about entertaining at home, hosting festive events where they spent more on libations than food, at a rate of at least two to one.[83] Guests spanned the arc of Nixon's life, from Whittier friends to Hollywood celebrities to business leaders to politicians, many of whom were loyal members of his California Committee.[84] Nixon also used his home for business, holding a breakfast meeting with a group of young state assemblymen known as the Young Turks because they bucked the conventional leadership in the assembly.[85] Nixon reached out to this group to learn firsthand their insights and analysis of the political landscape from the perspective of their varying districts.[86] Gordon Cologne, one of the Young Turks, was impressed when Nixon welcomed him at the door, then showed him the expansive views of Los Angeles.[87] But Cologne was even more impressed with the manner in which Nixon met with the politicians and demonstrated his grasp of each issue affecting the state.[88]

On May 29, 1962, just before the primary election, Nixon hosted a statewide television and radio telethon, inviting inquiries from the broadcast audience: "Let the questions be rough and tough; fire in hard fast ones, sinkers, sliders, or low curves—knucklers or even splitters—I'll answer them."[89] He was frank about his earnings and financial status, explaining that he was able to buy his Truesdale Estates home with the equity from his Washington DC home plus the proceeds from his sales of *Six Crises*.[90] He addressed claims of smear tactics in previous campaigns: "I have always campaigned hard on the issues and I have never campaigned on personalities."[91] On difficult issues, such as the death penalty, Nixon was forthright: "I am a Quaker. . . . No one likes to be in a position of taking the life of another person. But the death penalty is part of the law of this state and I think it should remain a part of the law of this state. You must weigh the life of the guilty person against the lives of innocent people that might be taken if that deterrent were not used."[92] On a lighter note, he admitted that if he had not been a lawyer and politician, he "would have liked to have been a sportswriter."[93]

With the June 5 primary upon them, Pat and Dick spent the evening watching election returns at the Beverly Hilton. A victorious Nixon received a telegram from Eisenhower: "Dear Dick: Hearty congratulations to you and love to Pat as you head into the main battle all your friends will be pulling for your overwhelming victory in November."[94]

The primary battle with Joe Shell had left Nixon badly bruised, and he knew the only way he could win in November was to have 100 percent of the Republican vote and one million Democrats cross party lines to support him.[95] Yet Nixon chose principle over political expediency when he announced his bold stance toward the John Birch Society: "I recognize that as the leader of my party I have a responsibility to support all nominees selected by Republican voters in the primary election. But because of my belief that the totalitarian leadership of the John Birch Society by Robert Welch is diametrically opposed to the interests of the Republican Party and the nation I shall conduct my campaign independently of Republican nominees who continue to accept Welch's leadership." Nixon knew that by making such a statement, he would not receive 100 percent of the Republican vote, but he did it because it was the right thing to do.[96]

The Nixons kicked off the fall campaign the evening of September 11 with a party at their Martin Lane home for their entire staff, longtime California Committee supporters, and representatives of all the major media.[97] The following morning Nixon officially commenced his gubernatorial campaign at 9:00 a.m. at the Los Angeles County Fairgrounds in Pomona, with his original Committee of 100 attending in his honor.[98] Nixon believed there was an "atmosphere of victory in the air" in Pomona, as his first congressional race and his 1950 Senate and 1952 vice-presidential campaigns had all been launched there.[99] As he helicoptered to the small city on the eastern edge of Los Angeles County, Nixon saw how the landscape had changed over the years. The orange, lemon, and avocado groves were mostly gone, replaced by thousands of homes and shopping centers. That morning he related what he had seen to his political philosophy: "What created all this wealth? What created this progress? Government didn't create it. The instrument of progress for California and the nation is private individual enterprise and I'm for more of it rather than less of it."[100]

From Pomona, Nixon flew to San Diego for a noon rally, followed by an afternoon event in Sacramento before finishing the day in Oakland, where he directed the Oakland Municipal Band.[101] The day reflected the campaign, as Bill Bagley, a California assemblyman who campaigned daily with Nixon, fondly recalled: "We were always on a bus or in a car or a on plane."[102]

Nixon's campaign blanketed Southern California, from a meeting with workers slinging tuna at canneries in San Pedro to a predawn visit to the Los Angeles produce market where he had picked up goods every morning for the family store in his youth.[103] Embracing the cultures of Southern California, he campaigned at Tom's Burger Stand in East Los Angeles, then was off to Chinatown, where the consul general for the Republic of China held a reception for him at General Lee's Restaurant, honoring the fifty-first anniversary of the founding of Taiwan.[104]

For all of Nixon's foreign policy experience, his campaign was sidetracked by an international crisis. Some sixteen months earlier Nixon had forewarned that the Kennedy administration policies toward Cuba gave the Soviet Union a false impression as to America's resolve to resist any aggressive moves in Cuba.[105] At a September 18 press conference in the Los Angeles Room of the Statler Hotel, Nixon reiterated that the time had come for President Kennedy to take stronger action against Cuba.[106] Not believing Kennedy's announcement just two weeks earlier that there was no evidence of offensive weapons in Cuba, Nixon encouraged the president to take a firm stance and pledged unqualified support should President Kennedy decide to quarantine Cuba to stop the Soviets from arming the nation with missiles.[107] Yet the United States took no action. Then one month later, on October 15, 1962, the United States discovered that the Soviet Union was supplying Cuba with nuclear weapons. President Kennedy ordered a quarantine of Cuba, and the Soviet Union threatened that it would retaliate. The two countries were at the brink of war for thirteen days.

One of Nixon's greatest campaign challenges had been demonstrating that even with his foreign policy expertise, he was interested in domestic issues affecting California. Since early September he'd been making weekly radio broadcasts in which he detailed his robust domestic agenda and promised "dynamic leadership to preserve and improve the natural and man-made beauty of our state so that California will be an even better place to live and work."[108] He proposed achieving equal opportunity for all with new jobs; lowering taxes; cutting the cost of government; fighting crime; improving highway safety, education, agriculture, aid to senior citizens, and civil defense; and fighting Communism.[109] But as Bill Bagley noted, "At every campaign stop he was asked about the Cuban Missile Crisis. The media would portray Nixon as not concerned with state issues."[110]

Ultimately, on October 28 Soviet premier Khrushchev announced that the missiles would be dismantled. That evening Nixon held a press conference at ABC Television Center in Los Angeles and spoke to a statewide audience as an American citizen in support of President Kennedy: "It is of vital importance in times like this that America speak with one voice to the world."[111]

Nixon saw the criticism of his foreign policy expertise meaning a lack of concern over domestic issues as unfounded, as national and state issues were closely connected: "Education, highways, our urban problems, law enforcement, all are very closely related to what happens in Washington."[112] At the same time, Nixon believed a campaign was properly limited to issues rather than personalities, and he was hypersensitive to criticism of his family. The easiest way to upset Nixon was to attack him on personal subjects.[113] To his chagrin, the $200,000 loan that Howard Hughes had made to Don became a more significant issue in the governor's race than in the 1960 presidential contest.[114] When Nixon and Brown held their one and only debate at the Fairmont Hotel in San Francisco, this single issue continued to dog Nixon.[115]

Former president Eisenhower, the only Republican who was a bigger draw than Richard Nixon at the time, lent his support. In October Nixon and Eisenhower flew to San Francisco for a ticker-tape parade through downtown, followed by lunch at the St. Francis Hotel.[116] Nixon then returned to Los Angeles for a fundraising dinner at the Palladium, while Eisenhower hosted a companion dinner at the Cow Palace, with both appearances broadcast on closed circuit television.[117]

Hollywood certainly made every effort to elect Nixon as well. Dick Powell performed camera tests to determine his best side, and Ronald and Nancy Reagan led virtually all of Hollywood's royalty to come out in favor of Nixon.[118] Even rival gossip columnists Hedda Hopper and Louella Parsons were united in their support for Nixon.

To build momentum, Nixon ran an old-fashioned Victory Express Train from Santa Barbara south to Los Angeles, overnighting at the Union Pacific Station. The next morning the train rolled out of Union Station for the last whistle-stop campaign ever in Southern California, with trackside events peppering the rails from Pico Rivera to San Diego.[119]

Late in the evening on November 2 Nixon arrived at the Biltmore Hotel for a marathon preparation session for a campaign telethon broadcast from the KTTV Channel 11 studio.[120] The event, the final of seven telethons he held throughout the state, was an unprecedented five hours long.[121] Over 3,700 questions were submitted by viewers, with Nixon responding on 217 subjects.[122] The top ten topics across the state were education, law enforcement, labor, welfare, taxes and spending, civil rights, state employees, agriculture, Communism, and Cuba.[123]

The day before the election Nixon rallied the troops by visiting the various Los Angeles area campaign offices, from the Wilshire Boulevard headquarters south to Culver City, and east from Compton to his hometown of Whittier.[124] Wrapping up his tour, he joined Paul Keyes for Chinese takeout at his Adams Duque office.[125] Feeling pessimistic about his chances of victory, Nixon went home afterward to forewarn his daughters that he knew he would lose the election.[126]

Election Day, November 6, marked the culmination of a fourteen-month campaign, with over seventy-five thousand volunteers and a cadre of Nixonettes.[127] But it wasn't enough. Shortly before midnight the Nixons arrived in the Beverly Hilton ballroom and acknowledged that the voting trends were not encouraging. Pat and the girls eventually went home, while Nixon remained overnight with his campaign team.[128] When the final votes were counted, Richard Nixon lost by less than three hundred thousand out of nearly six million votes cast. With Pat Hillings, Murray Chotiner, Jack Drown, Herb Klein, Ray Arbuthnot, and Rose Mary Woods gathered with Nixon in the presidential suite, the evening was, according to Hillings, "like a wake for the Nixon faithful."[129]

In the morning press secretary Herb Klein read Nixon's concession to the press, while Nixon met with members of his staff to thank them for their help.[130] It was an emotional scene: secretaries were crying and everyone was embracing Nixon, who was visibly moved. During this poignant moment, Klein returned to inform Nixon that the reporters were insisting on a personal appearance, so he entered the pressroom, where a hundred newspeople were waiting. He began, "Good morning, gentlemen, I'd like to make a statement of my own."[131] He spoke freely to the reporters, concluding, "Just think how much you're going to be missing. You don't have Nixon to kick around anymore. Because, gentlemen, this is my last press conference, and I hope that what I have said today will at least make television, radio, the press recognize that they have a right and a responsibility, if they are against a candidate give him the shaft, but also recognize if they give him the shaft, put one lonely reporter on the campaign who will report what the candidate says now and then. Thank you, gentlemen, and good day."[132]

Nixon was angry but found satisfaction in taking on the press.[133] As California historian Kevin Starr noted, "The press had not been favorable to Nixon during the campaign, or even fair, reporting with glee his verbal gaffes about running for governor of the United States and, on another occasion, suggesting that he was running for president in 1964 rather than for governor in 1962."[134] Violating a sacred rule at a press conference, Hillings and other Nixon supporters in the back of the room stood and cheered in support.[135] Nixon then walked from the room, telling Herb Klein, "I gave it to them right in the ass. It had to be said, goddammit. It had to be said."[136] Sandy Quinn and campaign volunteer Pete Wilson walked with Nixon to his car, where Nixon turned to his young staffers and spoke his last words of the campaign: "I am sorry I let you down."[137]

The overwhelming media reaction to Nixon's loss and last press conference was that he was finished as a politician. *Time* magazine reported, "Barring a miracle, Richard Nixon can never hope to be elected to any political office again."[138] ABC went so far as to invite convicted felon Alger Hiss as a guest on a news special titled *The Political Obituary of Richard Nixon.*[139]

For all that was said about Nixon's "last press conference," his friends knew him to be thoughtful, sensitive, shy, and reserved. He had just completed an exhausting campaign with the odds stacked against him, and yet he gave the campaign his every ounce of energy. Since September 12 Nixon had traveled over twenty thousand miles throughout California and had met with over half a million people.[140] Many believed the final press conference revealed a flash of temper from a man known to control his emotions, but Jack Drown, who knew Nixon better than most, had a different view: "I've never seen him lose his temper publicly but once, and frankly, I'm not too certain but that he did that deliberately."[141]

Drown and Ray Arbuthnot were with Nixon before the press conference and prevailed on him to meet with reporters lest the media "hound him from then on."[142] Nixon agreed, and Drown described how, as they walked to the pressroom, "you could almost see the temperature starting to boil. . . . He was working himself up."[143] But for Drown, "it was one of the most beautiful elocutions on foreign policy" that he'd ever heard, although "the press never bothered to print any of that."[144] There were even reports that Nixon had been drinking before the press conference, which all those who spent the night with him deny. As Pat Hillings remembered, "We'd been up in that room all night and, contrary to a lot of reports, Nixon was not drunk. In fact, he never drank much. On this occasion, he had a Scotch or two; he was exhausted, bitter, unhappy, but he was not drunk."[145]

Pat Nixon was also quite angry, and Nixon's cousin Dorothy Beeson could see that she felt the voters didn't appreciate her husband.[146] Although she had initially been against the campaign, she had fully committed herself to the effort. Bill Bagley reflected, "She was the strength. She was loyal. She knew what we were doing. We were running for governor and by God, she was there. She was always there, a quiet stalwart."[147] Nixon dealt with the loss as his Whittier football coach Chief Newman had taught him years earlier, and when he arrived home from the Beverly Hilton after the press conference, he counseled his daughters: "In life, you don't always win and it's difficult to lose, but you just go on. You go on with your head high."[148] With that he took a well-deserved break from the public eye, staying at California Committee member Margaret Brock's Malibu beach house for a week.[149]

Richard Nixon had enjoyed meteoric success, never losing an election in his first fourteen years in office. But now he was a two-time loser, with his fall much more rapid than his rise. The decision to run for governor had been a huge mistake, which he now acknowledged.[150] Some of those close to him felt his heart just hadn't been in the campaign, although he still felt his greatest use was in the public arena.[151] Now at a crossroads, he sought the best direction in which to rehabilitate his political life as leader of the Republican Party.

FIFTEEN

Wilderness Years

1963–68

Having lost the 1962 gubernatorial election, Nixon was unsure of his future, but one lesson was clear, as he had written in *Six Crises*: "Reaction and response to a crisis is uniquely personal in the sense that it depends on what the individual brings to bear on the situation—his own character, his training, his moral and religious background, his strengths and weaknesses."[1]

Professionally, Nixon could continue practicing law at Adams Duque, but returning full-time was highly impractical, as Nixon believed his life was best spent and most useful in public service rather than solely in private practice. Earl Adams did not want him to leave, as Nixon was easy to work with and "never threw his weight around to assume a position of importance at all."[2] Long-time friends offered support. Tom Bewley, Nixon's first law partner, wrote, "I am very proud of you and it has been a great experience in my life to have been associated with you."[3] Knowing his public life was not over, Nixon told Bewley, "To the extent my obligation to provide for my family will permit, I should continue to devote as much of my time as possible to participation in public affairs."[4] Nixon recognized that any individual judging the quality of life in terms of lack of stress, leisure time, or absence of criticism should stay out of politics, but he also felt that "not to be involved in conflict would be an unsatisfactory way to live," and yet the issue was how to stay in politics.[5]

Before he needed to make any decisions, the Nixons had some entertaining to do. On January 7, 1963, while the American Football Coaches Association held its conference in Los Angeles, the Nixons hosted a reception for the sporting community.[6] Friends, sportswriters, and celebrities joined coaches and players from various sports at the Nixon home. The guest list included tennis great Jack Kramer,

U.S. Open golf champion Billy Casper, Triple Crown winner Johnny Longden, boxing champion Jimmy McLarnin, legendary football coaches Woody Hayes and John McKay, along with actors Johnny Weissmuller and Chuck Connors.[7] The following evening the Nixons held an intimate reception for local sportswriters and their spouses.[8] The Nixons spent more time with the Eisenhowers, and when Dick turned fifty on January 9, the former president expressed his well wishes: "Felicitations on your birthday and may the years ahead be filled with only good things for you, Pat and for the girls."[9]

In late April Dick held a luncheon in the Fireside Room at the California Club, where he announced his decision to move to New York.[10] In doing so, Nixon had turned down several lucrative business offers, including positions as the chairman of Chrysler, chairman of Pepsi-Cola International, chief executive officer of the Dreyfus Corporation, president of a midwestern university, and commissioner of Major League Baseball.[11] Instead, he arranged for Elmer H. Bobst, a businessman and friend whom Nixon had known since 1953, to introduce him to the Wall Street firm of Mudge, Stern, Baldwin & Todd, which became Nixon, Mudge, Rose, Guthrie & Alexander.[12] Close friend Ronald Reagan understood why Nixon was moving east, and his only advice was that it was time for Dick and Pat to enjoy the good life that they "so richly deserved."[13]

The city and county of Los Angeles brought together business leaders to organize an honorary luncheon for Richard Nixon at the Biltmore Bowl. The event was a bipartisan affair at which Nixon was honored by business and professional groups, municipal and county governments, and both the Republican and Democratic Parties. In preparation, Democrats Kenneth Hahn and Frank Bonelli of the Los Angeles County Board of Supervisors introduced a motion to award an honorary scroll to Nixon. Hahn explained his support of the idea: "He is a great American. We might have disagreed with his political statements, but he lived in Whittier, he represented California and he deserves recognition for his services."[14]

The celebration was held on June 7, and Dr. Ezra Ellis, who had been a cheerleader at Whittier College during Nixon's high school years, gave the benediction.[15] With Art Linkletter serving as master of ceremonies, the packed event, which included the entire Los Angeles Board of Supervisors and Mayor Sam Yorty, was a smashing success.[16] Lighthearted moments included when Nixon was presented with several telegrams, the first of which was from Joe Kennedy: "Sorry Dick. Just heard from our lawyers. No chance of adopting you legally."[17] Another was from actor Peter Lawford, President Kennedy's brother-in-law: "Best wishes. Thought you'd like to know I've just signed to star in film version of your book *Six Crises*."[18] The last, from the Caracas, Venezuela, Chamber of Commerce, simply stated, "When planning your vacation trip, don't forget the fun available south of the border."[19] Pat and Dick loved the event, with Nixon calling the celebration "one of the highlights of our years in public life."[20]

Although the Nixons moved to New York immediately after the luncheon, Dick missed Southern California and returned for a visit before the end of summer.[21] He often made trips west, always visiting his mother, who was back living in her modest home across from the East Whittier Friends Church, as well as his wide spectrum of California Committee friends and supporters. He also spent time working out of the Adams Duque office and golfing at Los Angeles Country Club.[22] Often when the management of favorite hotels learned Nixon was coming to town, they invited him to stay there; these included the Bel Air Hotel, Biltmore Hotel, Statler Hotel, Holiday Inn, and even the International Hotel near the airport.[23]

Always willing to support his alma mater, in June 1965 Nixon returned to spend a weekend at Whittier College.[24] He broke ground for the new women's dormitory and dedicated the Bonnie Bell Wardman Library, joking with the crowd, "It is hard to believe that I was graduated from Whittier College in the year 1934—thirty years ago. After that, I graduated in law at Duke, and in 1960 I almost graduated from the Electoral College—except I flunked debating."[25] Reminiscing, he pointed out that when he attended Whittier College, students lived in Wardman Hall, worked out in Wardman Gymnasium, made phone calls on Wardman telephone lines, and went to movies at Wardman Theatre, and with that he dedicated the library: "Not to the common man, but to the uncommon men and women who made an institution like this possible. I dedicate it to uncommon men and women like Aubrey and Bonnie Bell Wardman."[26] As longtime members of Nixon's California Committee, as well as the most significant contributors to Whittier College,

Aubrey and Bonnie were "delighted beyond words" to have Nixon oversee the dedication.[27]

While on campus, Nixon ran into professor Charlie Cooper, with whom he had maintained a relationship since college. Nixon later wrote to Cooper, "I want you to know how much I have appreciated your friendship and support through the years. I realize that some of the positions I have taken on public issues may not have been in accord with your own views, not to mention some of the opinions of some of your colleagues in the intellectual community. You may be sure your Quaker tolerance of the dissenting opinion where I am concerned is most appreciated."[28] The next afternoon, on seeing Bob Hope before the commencement ceremony, Nixon boomed, "Congratulations, Doctor!"[29] Nixon hooded his good friends Hope and Sen. Margaret Chase Smith as they were awarded honorary degrees, after which Hope quipped that Nixon was the "assistant pro at the White House."[30] On a serious note, Hope later told Dick, "We were discussing the event on the way back home from Whittier; however, the main topic was how great you look. So something is agreeing with you and whatever it is—if you can find out—don't stop!"[31]

Nixon enjoyed promoting Whittier College. On his trip to the USSR in 1959, he met Don Kendall, then in charge of Pepsi-Cola's International Division. They became fast friends, with Kendall offering Nixon the position of chairman of the board of Pepsi-Cola International and special counsel, but Nixon declined.[32] Nixon was often a dinner guest at Kendall's house on the East Coast, where he enjoyed engaging Don's daughter Donna in conversations concerning education, America's youth, and the issues of the day.[33] When Donna was considering which university to attend, Nixon advised, "Broaden your horizons, study international relations at Whittier College." So she applied, Nixon wrote her a letter of recommendation, and she was admitted.[34] For his part, Nixon modestly credited Donna's admission to Dr. Paul Smith's love of Pepsi rather than his own influence.[35] Smith, Nixon's former history professor, was now president of Whittier College. But the reality was that a letter from Nixon opened doors, and Nixon wrote such letters whenever he could, such as to help his former Secret Service agent Jim Golden secure employment with Lockheed and aid numerous children of his friends seeking admission to schools and universities.[36]

Nixon, a serious man not prone to small talk, was known to members of his California Committee as sincere, warm, and engaging, with a sense of humor, and someone who enjoyed good conversation.[37] Nixon's cousin Jessamyn West, the well-known novelist, who had been a self-described Socialist in her youth, commented, "I'm a Democrat, I'm not ... politically pushing Richard, but I feel in what I've seen of him and when I've talked to him, I feel a real warmth in the man."[38] As with politics, he viewed conversation as an art, not a science, although not "as unstructured as modern art," and he considered it an invaluable tool for which he should be prepared. He preferred talking one on one, eschewed taking notes, and did not violate confidences.[39]

Stuart Spencer, who was running a local candidate's U.S. Senate campaign, encountered Nixon in 1966 in Casper, Wyoming. The two had first met in Spencer's parents' living room during Nixon's 1946 congressional campaign. He was surprised to run into Pat Hillings, who was in town with Nixon for a speaking engagement. Spencer explained that he had an early morning meeting and retired to his room.

As the campaign's Steering Committee convened the next morning, the door opened at 8:00 a.m., and in walked Dick and Hillings. Spencer described the scene, his fondest memory: "Nixon walked around the room—he knew everyone there—and greeted each person. When he got to me, he just said, 'Hello, young man.' Then he worked himself around the room and back to the door. He stood and looked at everyone, nodded toward me, and said, 'That's one smart young pol. I'd listen to him. He knows what he is doing.' Everyone was so taken in and enthralled that I could have told them that we need to go jump off a bridge to win the race and they would have followed without question."[40]

Nixon supported his extended family in many ways, as when he had Don and Clara Jane's children stay with them in New York.[41] When cousin Merle West was president of the National Institute of Rug Cleaners, Nixon rearranged his schedule to speak at the institute's Washington DC convention.[42] When another cousin was having marital trouble, Nixon met and counseled him during a trip to Whittier.[43] And when the son of a distant cousin committed suicide, Nixon consoled the family and provided financial assistance.[44]

Nixon was busy, yet throughout the 1960s he continued working toward a future bid for the White House. He firmly believed that a person must always pursue a new goal: "As long as you're driving forward to something else, you will remain alive; you'll be vibrant; and you'll have something to live for. But once you feel that you've got it made and are going to retire and have nothing more to live for, then you tend, I think, to wither away."[45] So Nixon decided to pass on the presidential race, having determined that his best chance of eventually being elected to the White House was through vigorous campaigning on behalf of other Republicans in 1964. Even before Kennedy's assassination, Nixon had predicted that Goldwater would be the next Republican presidential candidate. As for a possible Nixon-Goldwater ticket, he demurred, saying, "That will certainly stir up the animals!"[46] Privately, Nixon confided to Billy Graham that he did not believe Goldwater could win but promised, "I'm going to do everything I can to help him."[47]

As part of a twenty-five-thousand-mile campaign trip covering thirty-six states in the thirty-one days leading up to the election, Nixon made a swing through California, supported by his California Committee.[48] After landing at the Ontario airport, Nixon headed straight to Bridges Auditorium for the Claremont Colleges convocation before crisscrossing throughout the Los Angeles Basin on his way to joining Pat Hitt as the main speaker at a Women for George Murphy for Senate event.[49] Nixon's philosophy was that he was "willing to do everything necessary to see that the Republicans nominate and elect their most popular and qualified man in 1964," so he refused "to be on the sidelines," instead preferring to be "in the thick of the battle."[50]

The hard work of campaigning seemed to be in vain; the Republicans were beaten badly in 1964. Yet even after the GOP suffered devastating losses, Nixon continued to work hard for Republicans. Foreseeing victory, he predicted, "Our defeat was a shattering one, but history tells us that, out of the ashes of such setbacks, the greatest victories are eventually forged."[51] Between the 1964 election and the beginning of the 1966 campaign season, Nixon logged more than 127,000 miles and visited all fifty states to speak before four hundred groups.[52]

Following Goldwater's defeat in 1964, while many debated the direction of the party, Nixon's advice was simple: "It's not a time to divide Republicans."[53] Furthermore, on the national level, he felt it was "imperative to work out a solution to prevent driving Goldwater and his supporters out of the party."[54] GOP moderates and liberals spoke of backing a moderate candidate to derail support for Ronald Reagan's bid to unseat Gov. Pat Brown, but Nixon told the party faithful they were mistaken in "ganging up on Ronald Reagan."[55] Instead, Nixon launched an all-out attack on Democrats in general, and Governor Brown and President Lyndon Johnson in particular.[56]

In 1965 Nixon traveled to Los Angeles for a series of events in support of Robert Finch, candidate for lieutenant governor.[57] Nixon was loyal to those who worked for him, and Finch had been his administrative assistant when he was vice president, as well as manager of Nixon's 1960 presidential campaign.[58] Speaking to Finch supporters at a dinner at the Hollywood Palladium, organized by Nixon's California Committee, Nixon told the crowd, "Unless we Republicans can make one party of ourselves, there is going to be one party in the nation and it won't be ours."[59]

Rather than getting caught up in Republican infighting, Nixon proposed that voters adopt a "standard of action" policy where, before making a decision on any political proposal or action, two questions were answered: "(1) Is it fair and good for me? (2) Is it fair and good for the other two hundred million people in our country?" Nixon believed that in making such an analysis, voters would find that the Republican Party was the party of the people.[60] His one caveat was that he continued to advocate that members of the John Birch Society either quit the group or leave the Republican Party.[61] Nixon used his national platform to attack racist policies, and seeing an opportunity for the GOP to be the party of the future in the South, he advised in a national editorial, "The Republican opportunity in the South is a golden one, but Republicans must not go prospecting for the fool's gold of racist votes. Southern Republicans must not climb aboard the sinking ship of racial injustice. They should let Southern Democrats sink with it, as they have sailed with it. Any Republican victory that would come from courting racists, black or white, would be a defeat for our future in the South and our party in the nation. It would be a battle won in a lost cause."[62]

Strategically, Nixon knew he had to slowly build momentum for

1968, so he routinely sent copies of his remarks to reporters, political leaders, and his California Committee, along with an explanation of his reasoning.[63] After his campaign swing through California, Nixon wrote to Albert Cole, general manager of *Reader's Digest*, enclosing a copy of his remarks and telling Cole that while the Republican Party had been attacked for four years because of the far right, the Democratic Party had even greater problems with the far left.[64] Likewise, he frequently corresponded with journalists on pressing issues such as Vietnam.[65]

As the 1960s progressed, Richard Nixon kept pace with the changing times and was known to joke, "There is only one thing that I want to keep the record straight on: I was stoned in Caracas. I was stoned by rocks."[66] In May 1966, tanned and fit, he returned for a four-day swing through California on Finch's behalf and brought along Jack Kemp, a Los Angeles native and star quarterback for the Buffalo Bills, who was also active in politics.[67] The first order of business was filming an appearance on *Newsmakers* at KNXT Studios, where Nixon predicted Ronald Reagan would defeat Pat Brown in the governor's race.[68] While in Los Angeles, Nixon honed his analysis by meeting with former CIA director John McCone, who had served both Presidents Kennedy and Johnson, for a healthy discussion on U.S. foreign policy.[69]

Nixon's campaign swing for Finch culminated in a $50-a-plate dinner at the Newporter Inn in Newport Beach, where Nixon anticipated Republicans would do well in 1966, in part because President Johnson was having a difficult time with the press.[70] "I'm an expert on that, too," he deadpanned.[71] A month later, when Ronald Reagan won the Republican primary to challenge incumbent Pat Brown for the governorship, Nixon complimented his friend on his good judgment in a race that "was conducted with great ability, dignity and effectiveness."[72] Nodding to their similar upbringings as country boys, Nixon advised that while there would be a media onslaught against him in the coming months, Reagan would do well to "just sit tight in the buggy!"[73]

Within a few weeks Nixon was back in California on behalf of Reagan's bid to unseat Brown.[74] Dick was the keynote speaker at a dinner to raise money and symbolize party unity, originally planned to be held at the Hollywood Palladium but moved to the Los Angeles Sports Arena to accommodate the overwhelming demand for tickets.[75] Art Linkletter served as master of ceremonies, and a capacity crowd packed the arena to see Nixon speak against Johnson's promised Great Society, proposing that the G O P counter with the "Free Society."[76] Organized by longtime California Committee member Margaret Brock, the dinner raised over $300,000. The following morning, after breakfasting with Finch, Nixon attended a candidate forum at the Hacienda Hotel in San Pedro, where he predicted Reagan would beat Brown by eight hundred thousand votes.[77] Dick and Pat then finished the day at with an intimate dinner at Ronnie and Nancy Reagan's San Onofre residence.[78]

During these years Hannah remained active in her local community, and she was one of the beloved members of the La Habra Republican Women Federated.[79] But as she aged well into her seventies, she slowed down.[80] Nixon took care of his mother as she grew older, frequently calling to help her make any important decisions and to let her know where he was going and what he was doing.[81] In 1965, while visiting Hannah after she had undergone a major operation, with little hope of recovery, Nixon told her, "Mother, don't give up." In turn, Hannah sat upright and replied, "Richard, don't you give up. Don't let anybody tell you you are through."[82] This was their last conversation; although she survived surgery, Hannah's condition deteriorated as she suffered a stroke that left her completely disabled, requiring full-time care. She was moved to the nearby Whitmar Nursing Complex, where her sister Jane Beeson, who had given Dick piano lessons as a boy, enjoyed taking Hannah into the reception area and playing the piano for her.[83] In 1966 Nixon made special arrangements to spend Mother's Day with Hannah and his brother Don, and he returned in September to spend the weekend visiting her.[84]

Janet Goeske, who had grown close to Hannah since Democratic senator Sheridan Downey recommended that she work for Nixon's 1950 Senate campaign, was present and saw the pain on Dick's face as his mother, suffering the "total darkness of dementia," could no longer recognize her own family.[85] When Hannah died three weeks later, on Saturday, September 30, 1967, condolences poured in from around the world. Gen. Douglas MacArthur wrote from Vienna, Austria, and former president Eisenhower telegrammed from Gettysburg. President Johnson sent a telegram from the White House, telling Dick, "I hope you can find some consolation in the memories of your lives together, and the splendid example she leaves for the fine family for which she was so rightly proud." The Los Angeles County Board of Supervisors adjourned in memory of Hannah Nixon on October 3.[86]

Banks of flowers filled East Whittier Friends Church, and so many members of the press were in attendance that many locals had to stand outside, where there were almost as many people as inside.[87] Rev. George Jenkins, pastor at the time Frank had passed away, opened the service with a scripture lesson and prayer. Billy Graham spoke next, and then Charles Ball delivered a message as Hannah's pastor.[88] During the service, Nixon openly wept; he later observed that this was only the second time in his life that he had cried in public, the first being when he met General Eisenhower in Wheeling, West Virginia, following the fund crisis.[89] At the end of the service, after everyone had filed past the coffin and exited the church, the Nixon family gathered around the open casket so that Dick, with tears streaming down his face, could make a final tribute to his mother and privately express his sense of loss.[90]

Hannah Nixon was buried alongside Frank, Arthur, and Harold in the Milhous plot at Rose Hills, which Dick considered "one of the most beautiful cemeteries in the world."[91] Following the services, he insisted that the entire Nixon-Milhous clan meet at the original Milhous home for dinner, and as he walked through the family home, talking with relatives, memories of life in Whittier flooded back.[92] Afterward, Dick responded to condolence letters and also wrote to thank everyone involved with Hannah's service.[93] Reflecting on his life in Whittier, Nixon told Pastor Charles Ball, "All of us have been richly blessed because Mother left us with a storehouse full of warm and loving memories that will be the source of many happy thoughts in all the days to come."[94]

Nixon maintained his strong connection with his California Committee through personal letters, and whenever someone suffered an accident, malady, or demise, Nixon was swift to provide words of support.[95] When Mendel Silberberg died, Nixon sent $100 to the National Jewish Children's Hospital in his honor.[96] Though his relationship with Norm and Buff Chandler had been strained because of his ill-fated gubernatorial campaign, when Nixon learned that Norman had undergone surgery, he immediately wrote to express his best wishes for a speedy recovery.[97] Buff responded by telling Nixon, "I like to think on those happy occasions" enjoyed with Dick, Pat, and Norman through the years.[98] In reply, Nixon admitted, "The association I have been privileged to enjoy with Norman and you through the years has been a treasured one for me, and I particularly regret that my ill-fated gubernatorial effort created some rough edges for everyone concerned."[99] In addition, Nixon offered to help raise funds for the construction of the Dorothy Chandler Pavilion in downtown Los Angeles, named in Buff's honor.[100] On its completion, Buff was named Man of the Year by the Beverly Hills B'nai B'rith, with Nixon serving on the Honorary Committee.[101] Nixon said regarding this award, "I think the greatest tribute I can pay to Mrs. Chandler is that no man could have accomplished what she did in providing the superb leadership which created the magnificent Los Angeles Music Center."[102]

With the 1968 presidential election on the horizon, Nixon was ready for the race. Eisenhower had previously commented on Nixon's experience, "There is no man in the history of America who has had such careful preparation for carrying out the duties of the Presidency."[103] Gov. Tom Dewey estimated that Nixon had gained twenty years of experience in his first five years as vice president.[104] Nixon's years out of office provided him with important perspective as well, which he summed up as follows: "Defeat is never fatal unless you give up. When you go through defeat, you are able to put your weaknesses in perspective and to develop an immune system to deal with them in the future. You never know how strong you are when things go smoothly. You tap strength you didn't know you had when you have to cope with adversity."[105]

When he returned to Los Angeles in December, Abner and Marie England, who had provided Nixon with cars in his earliest campaigns, held a white-tie party at the Beverly Hilton in Pat and Dick's honor.[106] The guests, many of whom were California Committee members, were entertained by the Hawaiian Orchestra, accompanied by authentic Polynesian dancers, and Dick was introduced as the next president of the United States.[107] While in town, Nixon appeared on friend Sam Yorty's Sunday television show, where he predicted that the great issue of 1968 would be racial injustice.[108] Expressing why he felt African Americans had every reason to feel that promises had not been fulfilled, he said that the Black person "has been encouraged to believe that his historic injustices would be righted, his burdens lifted and the obstacles to progress removed— immediately," and then added, "Worse than not keeping a promise is making a promise that cannot be kept."[109]

Nixon characterized the 1960s as his "wilderness years," and during this period he reflected on how politics and government had changed under the Kennedy and Johnson administrations. Nixon came from a family that didn't believe in taking anything from the government, and his perspective was that the government should not be used against an individual.[110] But in the 1960s the White House was much different than it had been in the Eisenhower years.[111] For three straight years the Kennedys directed the IRS to audit Nixon, and then Bobby Kennedy personally audited the Hughes loan to Don Nixon, ultimately finding no wrongdoing on Dick's part.[112] Nixon's old friend William Rogers noted:

> The Dick Nixon I knew was one of the most kindhearted, straightforward and ethical individuals you could ever hope to meet. In business and money matters, he was always that way. Yet I think that around this time he began to make a difference between personal ethics and political ethics. He was affected by watching what went on in the White House, first with the Kennedys who stopped at nothing—womanizing, abusing the IRS and the Justice Department and so on—and then with Lyndon Johnson, who was just totally unscrupulous. I believe Nixon saw what happened with those presidents and said to himself, "That's the way the game's to be played."[113]

As 1967 drew to a close, race riots ignited across the United States, and the antiwar movement erupted on college campuses nationwide.[114] On March 31, 1968, Lyndon Johnson announced that he would not run for reelection; four days later, on April 4, Rev. Martin Luther King Jr. was assassinated. As rioting broke out in over a hundred cities in twenty-nine states, Nixon was particularly upset by King's death, calling it "a great personal tragedy for everyone who knew him, and a great tragedy for the nation."[115] Nixon attended King's funeral but chose to sit by himself toward the back for the service rather than jockey for a seat in the front.[116] Afterward, he marched with future Los Angeles Laker Wilt Chamberlain, who endorsed Nixon's candidacy because Chamberlain knew he championed civil rights and equality of opportunity for everyone, having supported Billy Graham's mid-1960s efforts to fully integrate religious crusades in the South.[117]

Two months later, on June 5, after Robert Kennedy was assassinated as he walked through the kitchen of the Ambassador, Nixon issued a statement describing the senator as "one of the great popular leaders in American History" and declaring his death "a terrible tragedy for both the family and for a nation that has known too many tragedies in recent times."[118] He declared a moratorium on his personal campaigning and attended Kennedy's funeral mass at St. Patrick's Cathedral in New York.[119] Despite ongoing violence across the nation, the primary campaign eventually continued, and Nixon was ultimately selected as the Republican nominee for president at the GOP Convention in Miami. Nixon told the audience, "I see the face of a child," and concluded his acceptance speech with reference to his California upbringing:

He hears a train go by at night and he dreams of faraway places where he'd like to go. It seems like an impossible dream. But he is helped on his journey through life. A father who had to go to work before he finished the sixth grade, sacrificed everything he had so that his sons could go to college. A gentle, Quaker mother, with a passionate concern for peace, quietly wept when he went to war but she understood why he had to go. A great teacher, a remarkable football coach, an inspirational minister encouraged him on his way. A courageous wife and loyal children stood by him in victory and also defeat. And in his chosen profession of politics, first there were scores, then hundreds, then thousands, and finally millions who worked for his success. And tonight he stands before you—nominated for President of the United States.[120]

Gov. Ronald Reagan welcomed the Nixon family home to California.[121] Campaign headquarters were opened, with Lt. Gov. Robert Finch serving as chairman of the California campaign.[122] Nixon was upbeat, visiting Knott's Berry Farm and Disneyland, riding the Mark Twain paddleboat, and even injecting a touch of humor into the campaign when Paul Keyes arranged for him to appear on the popular television show *Laugh-In*, for which Nixon was paid a $2.10 appearance fee for delivering one line: "Sock it to me."[123]

As the campaign continued into the fall, one concern among those closest to Nixon was his 1962 "You don't have Nixon to kick around anymore" statement. Murray Chotiner and Pat Hillings reviewed the press conference, trying to anticipate how the Democrats would use it to their advantage. Hillings described their reaction: "Nixon was in total control. . . . Chotiner and I looked at each other and said, 'Let them use it.' And they never did, because they obviously came to the same conclusion, that he looked good."[124]

By 1968 Eisenhower's heart condition had deteriorated to the point that he could not campaign for Nixon. During the 1960s Eisenhower's grandson David began dating Julie Nixon, and they planned to marry in December. Julie described how, when she and David visited Ike during the campaign, "He showed the electrodes attached to his chest. Each one had a circle saying Nixon. They were campaign decals he had pasted on by himself."[125]

Nixon barnstormed across the country with this campaign theme: "America can't be a good place for any of us unless it is a good place for all of us."[126] In mid-September he returned to Southern California, where more than three thousand supporters greeted him at his birthplace and the adjacent Richard Nixon School in Yorba Linda.[127] There he told the crowd, "This used to be the site of my father's nine-acre lemon grove, but it didn't grow very good lemons. I'm glad to see now that it's growing a better crop—children."[128] After a brief rest at the Disneyland Hotel, Nixon held a rally for over ten thousand at the Anaheim Convention Center.[129] Pat Boone, Edgar Bergen, a chorus of singers, and a marching band performed for the crowd in a rally "so laced with showmanship that it was one of the high points of the Nixon campaign."[130] Many leading Hollywood celebrities supported Nixon's candidacy, and celebrity politicians including Ronald Reagan and George Murphy hosted $1,000-a-plate fundraiser dinners in Cincinnati and Detroit, which were connected via closed-circuit television, with Art Linkletter, as usual, acting as master of ceremonies.[131]

In October Nixon returned yet again, greeted at the Los Angeles International Airport by Mayor Sam Yorty.[132] From there he commenced a whirlwind tour of Southern California, starting at the Santa Monica Civic Auditorium, where he was presented a key to the city before a standing-room-only crowd.[133] As he was heading to Southern California, Nixon learned that Whittier had named a high school for John F. Kennedy, so when reporters asked if he was upset that his hometown had only recently named a grammar school after him, Nixon quipped, "I want to tell you, this year I want a college named after me, the electoral college."[134]

After a Panorama City rally, Nixon met at the Holiday Inn with Democrats Celso Marino and Martin Castillo, who were with a group called Mexican Americans for Nixon. Following their meeting, Nixon commended the Mexican American community for "initiating a new era of self help and self pride" that made them "a vital part of the action of America."[135] In Burbank, Nixon mentioned how Hubert Humphrey had recently compared the 1968 race to Harry Truman's "Give 'em hell!" comeback of 1948. The crowd roared as Nixon told them, "It's one thing to give 'em hell; it's another thing to give them Humphrey!"[136]

Concluding his campaign on Monday, November 4, Nixon rallied the troops with a final visit to campaign headquarters on Wilshire Boulevard in Los Angeles.[137] That evening Nixon and Humphrey both held nationally televised telethons. During Nixon's four-hour broadcast, questions were called in by the public at the rate of 130,000 an hour, and the general consensus was that Nixon pulled ahead of Humphrey with his substantive responses.[138] Finally, at 2:00 a.m., Nixon arrived at his suite at the Century Plaza Hotel, having delivered 178 speeches in person and on the radio and television in the eight weeks since Labor Day.[139] The next morning, November 5, 1968, was Election Day. Nixon called Norm Chandler and thanked him for all the support he, Buff, and the Los Angeles Times had provided through the years.[140] Pat and Dick then headed to the Los Angeles International Airport for a late morning flight to New York on their campaign plane, named for his daughter Tricia.[141] As he crossed the country, Nixon looked out the window at the landscape below and wondered, "How many of these people did I reach?"[142]

Votes were tallied throughout the night. In the end, with 43.42 percent of the popular vote and 301 electoral votes, Nixon was elected president. Nixon's California Committee friends and hometown supporters had always been confident that he would reach the presidency.[143] Raymond Fleischman of the Whittier 20-30 Club reflected, "After his defeat for Governor . . . a lot of people had written him off. Well, I hadn't, because I knew that Dick had a lot more in him than to accept any defeat like that."[144] Family friend Roberta Dorn, the daughter of Nixon's first legal secretary, Evlyn Dorn, worked on the campaign and joined Don and Clara Jane Nixon in Dick's suite at the Waldorf Astoria on election night. She excitedly called her mom, gushing, "I was just with the president-elect!"[145] Nixon reflected on his long journey to the White House: "There is no question that running for governor was a bad risk. But the road to victory is sometimes paved with defeat. By running and losing, I stayed on the sidelines in 1964 and was able to regroup and run again."[146] The first order of business for Nixon, who loved the ocean from his childhood, was a postelection vacation at the beach in Florida.

Paying tribute to his Southern California upbringing, on December 5 the president-elect was the honored guest for an event organized by California Committee friends, A Salute to the Mexican-American Community of Los Angeles, held at the Century Plaza Hotel in Century City.[147] He then headed to Palm Springs for the Republican Governors' Conference, staying with Ronald Reagan at the estate of Walter Annenberg.[148] Annenberg, who was Jewish, built a golf course on his property because many Palm Springs country clubs would not allow Jews to play.[149] After hosting a luncheon for Nixon and his guests, Annenberg was approached by Nixon, who casually asked if he would accept an appointment as ambassador to the Court of St. James's. The appointment was significant, as Annenberg would be the first Jewish ambassador to England. Annenberg excused himself and went outside by the pool, where he shared the news with his wife, as Nixon enjoyed the heartwarming experience of watching Walter and Leonore both laugh and cry at the same time.[150]

On January 1 Nixon joined Ronald Reagan at the Rose Bowl to cheer on Pat's USC Trojans, ranked number two in the country, as they took on Woody Hayes's top-ranked Ohio State Buckeyes.[151] For Nixon, the Rose Bowl was "the prize game of all bowl games," but unfortunately for USC, Ohio State won the national championship.[152] The following day President-elect Richard Milhous Nixon helicoptered to Long Beach Memorial Hospital for his preinauguration physical, performed by his longtime doctor, John Lungren.[153] Once cleared for office, he headed to a nationally televised welcome home celebration held in his honor by his California Committee before a capacity crowd at the Anaheim Convention Center.[154] There team-mates from the Whittier College football squad presented Nixon with a symbolic bench from his playing days.[155]

In Whittier, Evlyn Dorn worked feverishly long-distance with her daughter Roberta, back in DC, to finalize all the arrangements for Whittierites to attend the inaugural festivities. Justifiably proud, the local community felt "it was like an American dream" to see their native son become the U.S. president.[156] Three days before the inauguration, 203 passengers—Nixon and Milhous family members, former classmates, and friends—flew on Trans World Airlines Flight 18 from Southern California to Washington DC to witness the first Californian sworn in as president of the United States.[157]

SIXTEEN

President

1968–74

The celebratory inaugural ceremonies were tempered by Nixon family humility. Attending a performance by pianist André Watts, Nixon sat with his aunt Jane Beeson, who had first taught him to play the piano. Nixon was delighted when Aunt Jane pointed to the stage, leaned over, and told him, "Now, Richard. If thee had practiced more on the piano, thee could have been down there instead of up here!"[1] Rev. Charles Ball of the East Whittier Friends Church conducted a preinaugural prayer service, and afterward, in a tribute to the quiet services of his youth, Nixon complimented his friend: "Well, we had a good period of Quaker silence, didn't we?"[2] President Nixon and the First Lady attended six inaugural balls, and as they were leaving the last, Richard, smiling broadly, announced, "They gave me the key to the White House. I have to go there now to see if it fits."[3]

Nixon's first official act was to host a reception for family and friends in the White House. No members of the press, staff, or other administration officials were invited. For cousin Lucille Parsons, "It was such a thrill to hear the Marine Band play 'Hail to the Chief,' and then announce 'Mr. President and Mrs. Nixon.'"[4] As Virginia Counts approached Nixon in the receiving line, she reminded herself, "Now, you mustn't say, 'Dick'; you have to say, 'Mr. President.'" On reaching Nixon, she told him, "It's really great to call you 'Mr. President' after all these years, Dick." In turn, Nixon simply reached out and gave Virginia a kiss.[5] When he saw Pat Hillings, he was lighthearted: "Hillings, I know you're going to be unhappy about this, we don't have any Scotch. Johnson took the whole liquor cabinet with him when he left."[6]

President Nixon kept in touch with California Committee friends, especially Ronald Reagan, Bob Hope, and Paul Keyes, as well as his brother Don and other family members.[7] Nixon was seen as "relaxed and friendly," the same "very warm, human individual" he was always known to be.[8] He reached out on special occasions, including both times of celebration and of sorrow.[9] Even if traveling, he'd interrupt a state visit, as he did on learning his friend Ray Arbuthnot's wife had died.[10] After the death of Gene McGovern, with whom he had served in the South Pacific, Nixon called Gene's widow, Mary, on Christmas Day to let her know he was thinking of her.[11] For Curtis Counts, the most heartwarming characteristic about Nixon was that he never changed in his relationships with his friends: "One of the things that he does today that he did twenty-five, thirty years ago, is that he is appreciative of performance and he would write individuals such as myself, if there was an accomplishment that came to his attention, and congratulate them. If you got promoted, he would write and tell you how pleased he was. If somebody died in the family, like the mother or father of any of the group that we were running around with, he would write a letter that was really tremendous."[12]

Bob Hope was the most frequent guest and entertainer Nixon invited to the White House; others celebrities who visited included Sammy Davis Jr., Fred Astaire, John Wayne, Frank Sinatra, the Carpenters, and Jackie Robinson.[13] Shortly after Robinson's untimely death, Nixon welcomed his widow, Rachel, to the White House for the state dinner in honor of New Zealand prime minister Norman Kirk.[14] Visits by California Committee members were social, political, and official, including "off the record" meetings, dinners in the private residence, Oval Office visits, and state dinners.[15] Rather than have a White House social secretary arrange invitation lists, Nixon requested that Rose Mary Woods handle these duties to ensure that his closest friends, family, and colleagues would be invited to White House events.[16]

The Nixon family revered the White House, but Richard enjoyed it the most.[17] According to his daughter Julie, until their "last day in the White House, they had a 'pinch me' attitude about the house and its history."[18] As Nixon, who always wore a tie at dinner, stepped off the elevator leading to the second-story residence, "the family could expect to hear a jaunty two-note whistle."[19] The Nixons did their best to ensure that all their guests would feel perfectly at ease, while at the same time wanting to share a sense of the extraordinariness of their experience. When friends and family brought their children to visit, Nixon gave them the run of the house and commonly escorted his guests to the front door when they departed.[20]

Bipartisan in his socializing, Nixon arranged events with Lyndon Johnson and Harry Truman and also hosted prominent California Democrats Ed Pauley and Jimmy Roosevelt at the White House.[21] Nixon was rumored to have had a feud with Supreme Court chief justice Earl Warren dating back to Warren's days as governor of California, and if true, he must have delighted in having Warren swear him in as president.[22] Regardless of their history, once in office, Nixon hosted a White House dinner in honor of Warren, even including former California governor Pat Brown.[23]

Nixon hosted his Whittier College thirty-fifth-year reunion at the White House, welcoming everyone and making sure they were treated as VIPs.[24] Dolores Ball was impressed that even though there was an aide to announce each guest, Nixon needed no assistance as he addressed his classmates by name—and in some instances by nickname.[25]

But the biggest event was Tricia Nixon's Rose Garden wedding.[26] The wedding was private, rather than political, and virtually the entire guest list of 398 consisted of relatives and friends.[27] Although it rained most of the day, the skies cleared at the appointed hour, and Tricia Nixon and Edward Cox exchanged their vows. As the wedding ceremony ended, rain began falling again, causing a friend to mention to the president that he was sorry about the rain. "Oh no," Nixon replied. "Soft rain caresses a marriage."[28]

Bestowed with the honor of the presidency, Nixon chose in turn to honor those whose works and service he most admired. Nixon hosted the Disney family at the White House for the Walt Disney Commemorative Medal Ceremony, authorized by a joint resolution of Congress.[29] In a White House ceremony, he awarded his longtime friends Adela Rogers St. Johns and Bill Henry with the Presidential Medal of Freedom, along with six other journalists.[30] Nixon even paid a special visit to Samuel Goldwyn's Beverly Hills home to present him with the Medal of Freedom. Thanking Nixon, Goldwyn effused, "Everything he does is wonderful. You are my favorite President. That is saying enough."[31]

Nixon brought many California Committee members to work in his White House, including Robert Finch, Pat Hitt, former congressman Donald Jackson, Curtis Counts, Murray Chotiner, and Roger Johnson.[32] Leonard Firestone, Walter Annenberg, and John Krehbiel were appointed as ambassadors, as was Kenneth Rush, one of Nixon's law school professors.[33] Hollis Mathews Dole, who served with Nixon in the South Pacific, became assistant secretary for the Department of Interior, and Los Angeles businessman Roy Ash was tapped to help Nixon reorganize the government.[34] Rose Mary Woods, Marje Acker, and Loie Gaunt, each with nearly twenty years' service with Nixon, joined the White House staff. When Loie's father died and she had to return to Southern California to care for her mother early in Nixon's administration, the new president arranged for her to work for his old friend Leonard Firestone.[35]

Members of Nixon's California Committee also influenced progressive decisions. In 1970 the Comprehensive Alcohol Abuse and Alcoholism Prevention, Treatment, and Rehabilitation Act was passed, the first legislation of its kind to provide federal support for treatment of alcoholism as a public health concern.[36] Members of Nixon's cabinet recommended he veto the legislation. Then California Committee member Tom Pike, a recovering alcoholic since the 1940s, wrote to Nixon arguing in favor of the legislation. Pike enlisted the support of Nixon friend Don Kendall, and ultimately the legislation became law.[37]

In his youth, Nixon saw his mother take time out each day for meditation on pressing concerns, and he engaged in this practice to reflect on and analyze issues, selecting an office away from the West Wing in the Old Executive Office Building where he could be alone.[38] "Good ideas seldom popped into my head in the commotion of a meeting," he explained; rather, he preferred to make decisions in solitude.[39] He also maintained a list of a hundred questions on issues from U.S. domestic policy to foreign affairs throughout the world, which he updated every day, as he believed he should know every answer.[40]

Nixon's religious faith was, in his own words, "intensely personal and intensely private," and to those who knew him, while he did not wear his spiritual beliefs on his sleeve or quote scripture in any political speech, it was clear that Nixon was "a deeply religious man."[41] Beginning the first Sunday after his inauguration, President Nixon held church and prayer services in the White House.[42] Nixon preferred a private service to the disruption caused by descending on a church with teams of Secret Service agents and the White House press corps.[43] Rev. Billy Graham delivered the first sermon in the East Room; before the service began, Nixon played hymns on the piano upstairs as Billy's wife, Bev, sang.[44] Paul Smith, Nixon's Whittier College history professor, led a sermon as well. Smith was not an ordained minister, but he was a Quaker, and Nixon believed all Quakers to be "ministers by their belief." Smith was moved at how the Nixons played host to his grandchildren on this special day.[45] While in office, Nixon invited religious leaders of many faiths to preach, including several Californians: Pastor Eugene Coffin of the East Whittier Friends Church, Rabbi Edgar F. Magnin of the Wilshire Boulevard Temple, and Minister Edward V. Hill of the Mount Zion Missionary Baptist Church in Los Angeles, one of several African American ministers to deliver a White House sermon.[46]

Nixon extended invitations to administration officials, senators and representatives, and government employees, including chauffeurs and mechanics, to attend services. For the first services, Nixon invited the White House telephone operators, who were stunned, as they had never been invited to a White House event despite years, in some cases decades, of service.[47] Ted Kennedy and California Democratic senator Alan Cranston attended services with Nixon, as did former president Lyndon Johnson and future presidents George H. W. Bush and George W. Bush.[48] So did Earl Warren, even after his retirement from the U.S. Supreme Court.[49] After each service, Nixon had a social hour with fellow parishioners for coffee, doughnuts, and photographs.[50]

Raised to believe in equality of opportunity, Nixon created the Office of Minority Business Enterprise to foster minority businesses.[51] Having grown up with Hispanics, he was familiar with their struggles, and shortly after becoming president, Nixon promoted the Cabinet Committee on Opportunities for Spanish-Speaking Peoples.[52] Its goal was economic empowerment for Hispanics, and Nixon appointed Henry Ramirez to head the committee.[53] When Ramirez mentioned to Nixon that he had worked closely with the boys and girls from "Jim Town," adjacent to Whittier, Nixon threw his arms into the air, laughed, and said to Ramirez, "Jim Town, Jim Town. It's been twenty years since I heard that word. Oh, I had so many friends, people I went to school with, that are from Jim Town. My, how I would like to see them again."[54] Nixon later invited Ramirez to the White House Sunday services when Archbishop Humberto Sousa Medeiros of Boston delivered the sermon. Seeing Ramirez with his wife and children, Nixon took Ramirez by the arm and introduced him to the archbishop, telling Medeiros, "One of the reasons I like Henry so much is that he and I were both poor and both picked oranges in the same groves, and that's the kind of people I like to have in my administration, people who came from the bottom and know what it is to be poor. We have that understanding."[55]

Determined to desegregate southern schools, Nixon advised his staff to accomplish their goal in a quiet way: "We don't poke our fingers in their eyes. We don't rub their noses in it. We don't get our name in the newspapers—but we do it."[56] When civil rights leader Whitney Young, executive director of the National Urban League, died of a heart attack in Nigeria, Nixon sent a plane to retrieve his body and eulogized him at his funeral.[57] Nixon later explained his rationale for his actions regarding minority economic opportunity and desegregation: "The existence of an urban underclass is a blight on our record and a challenge to our beliefs. It is not a question of trying to achieve equality in outcomes but one of ensuring equality of opportunity."[58]

Within two months of taking office, Nixon made his first trip to Southern California, to view the damage from nearly one hundred thousand barrels of oil spilled off the coast of Santa Barbara.[59] Having personally witnessed the Los Angeles Basin's transformation into an enormous sprawling suburban community with smog clouding the sky, Nixon knew government action was necessary to preserve open spaces and restore clean air, water, and land.[60] Less than a year later his 1970 State of the Union address set out the most far-reaching environmental agenda ever put forth by a U.S. president, stating, "Clean air, clean water, open spaces—these should once again be the birthright of every American."[61] Nixon established the U.S. Environmental Protection Agency, and over the next few years his proposals became the National Environmental Policy Act; Clean Air Act; Oil Pollution Act; Noise Control Act; Clean Water Act; Marine

Protection, Research and Sanctuaries Act (Ocean Dumping Act); and Coastal Zone Management Act.[62]

Dick and Pat's favorite beaches were in San Clemente and nearby Dana Point. After surveying the oil spill cleanup efforts, Nixon took advantage of the opportunity to spend two nights at the Cotton estate in San Clemente in search of a new home for working vacations.[63] Fortunately, the adjacent Loran Coast Guard Station allowed the president's helicopter to land almost in the property's backyard. The home was built in 1927 for Hamilton H. Cotton, an early Democratic Party supporter, and only a set of train tracks separated the estate from the beach. Franklin Roosevelt once visited, arriving by train for an overnight card game. The setting was perfect: a large, Spanish-style California Mission Revival home modeled after a country estate, surrounding a central courtyard, with a second-story study where Nixon could work, plus a guest house. The Nixons loved the property, bought it, and renamed it La Casa Pacifica.[64]

The home was relatively isolated in the sleepy town of San Clemente. The twenty-nine-acre estate was perfectly situated: the Coast Guard station was to the southeast, the Pacific Ocean lay to the west, and John Severson, the laid-back founder of Surfing magazine, lived in the house to the north. One lone road led in from the northeast.[65] Nixon could enjoy walks on the sand and swim in the ocean.[66] Camp Pendleton, with a golf course and private beach, was minutes to the south, and El Toro Marine Air Station, with runways sufficient for Air Force One, was a short helicopter ride away. Residents welcomed the First Family to the area and frequently gathered along the fence at the San Clemente helipad when the president traveled, with Nixon often greeting the well-wishers.[67] Modest executive offices were established at the Coast Guard station, to which Nixon could either walk or ride a golf cart from the residence.[68]

While in town on their first visit, the Nixons went to nearby San Juan Capistrano, where Cardinal James Francis McIntyre of the Los Angeles Archdiocese gave them a tour of the San Juan Capistrano Mission—the same mission Nixon had toured on Election Day in 1960.[69] Afterward, Richard and Pat hosted a luncheon for the traveling press corps at the nearby El Adobe restaurant.[70] Nixon had loved Mexican food since the days of his youth, and his sister-in-law Clara Jane often sent her homemade enchiladas to him at the White House.[71] Naturally, El Adobe became a favorite venue for the Nixons.[72]

President Nixon ultimately spent 270 days at La Casa Pacifica—nearly nine months. The Nixons were a very close family, with Tricia living at the White House before her marriage, traveling with her parents, and staying at La Casa Pacifica. Having taken up official residence in Orange County, the Nixons eventually had to register to vote. Landing the president's helicopter at the original Orange County Courthouse, where Nixon had tried cases as a young attorney, the Nixon family registered as Orange County voters.[73] They voted at Concordia Elementary School, down the road from La Casa Pacifica. The students were excited at having the president nearby and sent Nixon numerous birthday cards, and in response, Nixon dropped in on their classes to personally thank them.[74]

La Casa Pacifica was an ideal place for Nixon to enjoy extended working vacations, balancing presidential responsibilities with walks, swimming, and golf.[75] Gavin Herbert, president and CEO of Allergan, also owned Roger's Gardens, a local nursery, and he volunteered to oversee the grounds, even organizing a gardening club to help maintain the beautiful property.[76] The estate had a large patio from which to watch spectacular sunsets or enjoy casual meals and a pool that Nixon especially loved.[77]

Nixon installed a three-hole, nine-tee practice course at La Casa Pacifica, where he and his friends could work on their golf game.[78] For more competitive rounds, there was the solitude of the Camp Pendleton golf course.[79] Rev. Billy Graham's summer home at Pauma Valley golf course and Walter Annenberg's private golf estate in Palm Springs were short helicopter rides inland.[80] Nixon even landed the presidential helicopter at Bob Hope's Toluca Lake residence to golf with Hope, Jimmy Stewart, and Fred MacMurray at Lakeside Country Club.[81] Whenever he played, Nixon enjoyed giving out monogrammed golf balls, but he also cautioned the recipients, "Use it only for putting. I wouldn't want someone to find it all cut up lying in the rough. He might think I hit it there."[82]

Aside from golf, Nixon's greatest love was the ocean. In addition to the beach at La Casa Pacifica, Camp Pendleton's Red Beach was a secluded part of an eighteen-mile stretch of coastline held by the marine base since World War II.[83] Nixon was partial to Red Beach, where he could enjoy the rolling, breaking waves of the Pacific Ocean in solitude, and as he walked its sands in 1969, he thought of Santa Monica, Long Beach, and the other great Southern California beaches he had frequented as a boy.[84] Realizing that millions of people wanted to enjoy beaches, but many were too crowded, Nixon worked with the Marine Corps at Camp Pendleton to secure six miles of coastline to be declared excess and opened to the public, including San Onofre, one of the most popular surf breaks in the United States.[85]

The act was typical of Nixon, who did not believe that an Environmental Protection Agency regulatory scheme was the only method by which to reach his goals of clean air, water, and land for all Americans. Knowing from personal experience that not everyone could afford a trip to Yellowstone or Yosemite, Nixon also sought to bring the parks to the people. His instruction in dealing with excess federal land was "When in doubt, make a park out of it."[86] In total, 642 new parks were created during Nixon's presidency, and he acknowledged that this initiative "wouldn't have happened unless I had taken a walk on the beach two years ago at San Clemente and walked an extra mile and saw the great possibilities and decided that the time had come for Presidential initiative," noting that it had faced "very deep . . . bureaucratic opposition."[87]

Nixon enjoyed leaving the solitude of La Casa Pacifica to savor the local surroundings. Often accompanied by Bebe Rebozo, he took off on golf cart rides through the adjacent neighborhood of Cypress Shores.[88] Other days, Nixon explored San Clemente and surrounding communities.[89] For trips to San Clemente, Nixon preferred a Lincoln Continental over the presidential limousine. He and Rebozo frequently drove alone, with the Secret Service following in a chase car.[90] Adventures into town included stops at Bob Kutcher's Bay Cities Ace Hardware to buy beach balls, Walgreens, and William Taylor's Pharmacy to buy Russell Stover candy for Pat.[91] Occasionally, he ventured for drives through the neighborhoods of his youth, even visiting his birthplace, before heading to McDonald's for a Big Mac and chocolate milk.[92]

Southern California offered many recreational activities for Nixon, from cheering on the Angels baseball and Rams football teams to sailing the famed *Columbia*, winner of the 1958 America's Cup.[93] From the patio of La Casa Pacifica, the Nixons had an inviting view of Catalina Island. Richard and Tricia decided to visit the island on the spur of the moment, greeting the surprised townspeople and local students as they walked through the beach resort of Avalon, even letting local residents explore the president's helicopter.[94]

Six months into Nixon's presidency, *Apollo 11* landed on the moon, and the Nixons held a state dinner in honor of the iconic mission. By hosting the official dinner at the Century Plaza Hotel in Los Angeles, Nixon honored his brother Harold, who had earned an aviation certification before his untimely death, and took the opportunity to deliver the ultimate thank-you to the California Committee members who were unable to attend his inauguration.[95] That night President and Mrs. Nixon, joined by their family and friends, as well as the entire House of Representatives, the Senate, governors, ambassadors, and other dignitaries, celebrated the *Apollo 11* astronauts and all those who had helped achieve the epic goal of a moon landing.[96]

Although La Casa Pacifica was remote, the Nixons frequently entertained there, with events such as dinner parties or watching football on New Year's Day with Jack Drown and Bebe Rebozo.[97] Nixon often assembled diverse and interesting gatherings, from small dinners with notables like Bob Hope, Arnold Palmer, Gerald Ford, or Henry Kissinger to large affairs with guest lists filled with Hollywood luminaries.[98]

In addition to Franklin Roosevelt, Nixon hosted Lyndon and Lady Bird Johnson at La Casa Pacifica.[99] Ronald Reagan was a frequent guest for official and intimate events.[100] Both George H. W. Bush and Gerald Ford visited, as did astronaut Neil Armstrong, an American hero.[101] Nixon welcomed Japanese prime minister Eisaku Satō to the comfortable setting of his home overlooking the Pacific, and he hosted Republic of Vietnam president Nguyen Van Thieu to discuss U.S. support to the war-torn country.[102]

During the height of the Cold War, the United States and Soviet Union held a summit in Washington DC. Nixon wanted Soviet leader Leonid Brezhnev to see how developed the United States was so he might understand "the possibilities that were open to him in the field of economic cooperation."[103] On June 22, 1973, Nixon and Brezhnev flew to Southern California to continue the summit in the sunshine, and as they choppered from El Toro to San Clemente, Nixon had Brezhnev occupy the president's window seat so he could see the beauty of Nixon's home state.[104] Once at La Casa Pacifica, Nixon and Brezhnev held meetings throughout the day and into the evening in the president's study.[105] Across the driveway from the main residence was a guesthouse where Brezhnev was to stay, with a wine cellar below. But when his security detail entered the cellar, they startled a skunk, which promptly sprayed the area, so Brezhnev moved into Tricia Nixon's room in the main house.[106] Her bedroom, which was beautifully decorated in feminine colors, was not large, so for Nixon, having "this big bear of a man" staying in such a room "was really something to see."[107]

During dinner that first evening, there was a sudden knock at the door, and a young Russian stewardess from Brezhnev's plane arrived with Russian security, under the pretense of "taking dictation." The Secret Service refused to let her stay until Nixon and Brezhnev conferred, and ultimately Nixon consented, not surprised by the fact that Brezhnev was "a ladies' man."[108] During their summit, considering giving his guest a Dictaphone as a minor state gift, Nixon asked Brezhnev if he used one and later explained Brezhnev's response: "He says 'Oh, no, no, no. I never want to use a Dictaphone machine. I don't like to dictate to an impersonal machine,' and then with a little sort of wink, he said, 'I'd much rather dictate to a pretty girl. You know, when you wake up in the middle of the night and want to make a note, it's very useful to have somebody there in the room to give it to.'"[109]

Having the world's two most powerful men together in Southern California was a momentous occasion that Nixon shared with his California Committee. Knowing his guest of honor loved western movies and Hollywood stars, Nixon hosted a pool party for Brezhnev.[110] The Soviet leader delighted in meeting Ronald Reagan, Chuck Connors, and Clint Eastwood.[111] Later, during dinner, Nixon proposed a toast to Brezhnev, hoping "that we could bring peace for our children, for [Brezhnev's] children, and for our grandchildren and the children of the world."[112] Teary, Brezhnev stood and hugged Nixon, then requested to see the Nixons alone, at which time he presented the president with a scarf, telling him, "Every stitch in this scarf represents affection from the people of Russia to the people of the United States and from Mrs. Brezhnev and me to you and Mrs. Nixon."[113]

Some of the Nixon administration's most significant achievements had their roots in Southern California, including ending both the Vietnam War and the draft. On July 13, 1971, when Henry Kissinger arrived at the La Casa Pacifica helipad, Nixon was excited to greet his national security advisor on his return from the Far East, which had included secret negotiations with China.[114] Two days later the presidential helicopter unit was on thirty-minute standby when it received a call to fly President Nixon and his entourage to NBC Studios in Burbank to announce the opening of relations with China.[115] Arrangements were completed on such short notice that as Nixon's five-helicopter squadron flew north, a much faster Huey had to be dispatched to scout out a landing site. Once a parking lot was selected, NBC crews worked feverishly to disconnect electrical power, then unbolt and remove light poles to make an impromptu helipad.[116] The trip was shrouded in secrecy, but as Nixon exited the helicopter, he leaned into the cockpit and told his pilot, Col. Gene Boyer, "I want you and your crew to come in and witness what is going to be announced. This is historic."[117] Since there was no ground crew aside from his mechanic and the NBC guards, Boyer had to lock up the helicopter.[118]

Following the nationwide speech, Nixon, Haldeman, and Kissinger dined at Perino's before being picked up at a nearby FBI helipad.[119] As Colonel Boyer watched Nixon return to the helicopter, he could see the president was walking on air. On boarding, Nixon asked Boyer, "Did you see it? What did you think?" Boyer replied, "I think it's absolutely great," to which Nixon responded, "Good," as he settled into his seat.[120]

Deeply committed to the U.S. troops, Nixon welcomed home the First Marine Division from Vietnam at Camp Pendleton, awarding its members the Presidential Unit Citation. He was equally committed to ending the conflict with honor and securing the release of the 591 Americans held as prisoners of war by the North Vietnamese.[121] Having visited wounded World War I soldiers at the Barry Veterans Hospital in West Los Angeles with his grandmother Almira, Nixon considered himself a devoted pacifist who understood that "war compromises principles. War is evil. All war is wrong. All killing is wrong." He later admitted, "A day did not pass during my years in the White House that I did not hate the war in Vietnam."[122]

The Paris Peace Accords were signed on January 27, 1973, bringing an end to the Vietnam War. A few weeks later, on February 12, while in San Clemente, Nixon spoke over the phone to Col. Robinson Risner, the first U.S. prisoner of war released by North Vietnam.[123] Since being elected, President Nixon had been determined to end conscription in favor of an all-volunteer military, and at La Casa Pacifica, he met with the Selective Service Youth Advisory Committee to discuss this possibility.[124] Despite initial opposition, Nixon successfully ended the draft.

Personal relationships remained strong through the Nixon presidency. The *Los Angeles Times*, still under the management of Dorothy and Norm Chandler's son Otis, endorsed Nixon in 1968 and 1972, just as it had in every one of his campaigns dating back to 1946.[125] During his second year in office, Nixon attended the reception and performance of *Musical Theatre Cavalcade* in honor of Dorothy Chandler at the pavilion named in her honor.[126]

On December 26, 1973, the Nixons took United Airlines Flight 55 from Dulles to Los Angeles International Airport, the one and only time a U.S. president has flown on a commercial airline.[127] They were en route to the La Jolla wedding of Gen. Walter Tkach, the president's White House physician, which Nixon had no intention of missing.[128] But considering the high fuel prices of the OPEC embargo, Nixon wanted to avoid any criticism of extravagant fuel usage for a presidential vacation.[129] Weddings were special occasions for the Nixons, and they arranged to be in California for the nuptials of nephew Richard Ryan, at the Four Square Church in Van Nuys, and Maureen Finch, at the La Canada Presbyterian Church.[130]

But the biggest wedding event in Southern California for the Nixons was that of Don's daughter Lawrene at St. Andrews Presbyterian Church, with the reception at the Newporter Inn.[131] Knowing that some might be intimidated by the president's presence, Nixon was very informal, insisting that no special arrangements be made for him; he requested instead that he be seated with his extended family so he could talk to everyone.[132] Before he left, Nixon's aunts, uncles, nieces, nephews, and cousins gathered around as he complimented the women, telling them that they hadn't changed a bit over the years before joking, "Neither has Bill Milhous, because he was always bald. Just as bald as he is now."[133] That evening Nixon called his sister-in-law Clara Jane, congratulating her on her daughter's wedding.[134]

By 1972 President Nixon was ready for his next campaign.[135] Following the GOP Convention in Miami, Nixon was welcomed home to California by Ronald Reagan, Pete Wilson, and Art Linkletter.[136] Over ten thousand celebrants surrounded the grounds of the Western White House, with traffic backed up for fifteen miles on the interstate.[137]

In September the Nixons attended a packed Victory '72 dinner at the Century Plaza Hotel with numerous California Committee members. Bob Hope provided the entertainment, and Ronald Reagan toasted the couple.[138] Nixon spoke in low, wistful tones, reminiscing about his political career—"You know how long that road has been"—and then acknowledged his California Committee, noting that his journey had included his oldest friends.[139] After an overnight stay at the Century Plaza, Nixon, in typical fashion, had the hotel staff assemble so he could personally thank each of them for their hard work.[140]

Nixon's final campaign speech was on Saturday, November 4. Governor Reagan met the president at the Ontario airport for the final rally, alongside a diverse group of entertainers, including Jimmy Stewart, Jack Benny, Danny Thomas, the Carpenters, Glenn Ford, Johnny Grant, and Red Skelton, while Les Brown and his band entertained the audience.[141]

The morning of November 7, at Concordia Elementary School, the Nixons voted for the last time with Richard's name on the ballot, and afterward, the couple stayed to greet supporters.[142] That evening Richard Nixon received an overwhelming 60.7 percent of the popular vote and 520 electoral votes, losing only Massachusetts and Washington DC, for a total of 17 electoral votes, to George McGovern. With that he became the first Republican ever to win a majority among blue-collar workers, Catholics, members of labor union families, and voters with only grade school education.[143] Furthermore, Nixon's margin of victory of 17,999,528 votes is the largest ever, and only Franklin Roosevelt received more electoral votes (523 in 1936).[144]

The second inaugural celebration mirrored the first, but shortly after the festivities concluded, Richard Nixon's second term became consumed with the Watergate scandal, the result of a break-in at the Democratic National Headquarters that had taken place at 2:30 a.m. on June 17, 1972, at the Watergate Hotel in Washington DC.[145] When Nixon first heard about the break-in, he thought "it sounded preposterous: Cubans in surgical gloves bugging the DNC!" He later explained, "I dismissed it as some sort of a prank."[146] It was a reasonable reaction, certainly, given that there was no logical reason for the break-in: by May 1972 Nixon's reelection was near certain. Inflation was less than 3 percent, the U.S. GNP was growing at the rate of over 6 percent per year, real incomes were rising at 4 percent, federal taxes were down by 20 percent since 1969 for the average family, and the stock market was rising steadily.[147]

Far from a prank, the Watergate break-in had been authorized by members of Nixon's administration, and Nixon attempted to cover up any White House involvement to protect those close to him.[148] Nixon, believing "that in any organization loyalty must run down as well as up," requested that the CIA be instructed to ask the FBI to cease its investigation.[149] In taking this action, Nixon ignored his own forewarning made ten years earlier in Six Crises: "We often hear it said that truly 'big' men are at their best in handling big affairs, and that they falter and fail when confronted with petty irritations—with crises which are, in other words, essentially personal."[150]

Watergate had connections to Southern California. Nearly a year before the break-in, on July 17, 1971, Nixon had met with Egil "Bud" Krogh on the patio at La Casa Pacifica to discuss an investigation into the theft and subsequent leaking of the Report of the Office of the Secretary of Defense Vietnam Task Force, commonly referred to as the Pentagon Papers, to the media. Krogh recalled, "I came away knowing that I was being asked to deal with a national security crisis of the utmost importance. My mission was simply to find out why these documents had been stolen and what lay behind the theft."[151]

Ultimately, Krogh managed the "Plumbers" unit, created to stop White House leaks and responsible for the Watergate break-in. In the months after the break-in, the unit's link to the White House was revealed, triggering congressional scrutiny and investigations. By February 1973 the Senate formed the Select Committee on Presidential Campaign Activities. This became known as the Watergate Committee, empowered to "conduct an investigation and study of the extent, if any, to which illegal, improper or unethical activities were engaged in by any persons . . . in the presidential election of 1972."[152]

In July 1973 Nixon aide Alex Butterfield revealed to the Watergate Committee the existence of the taping system the president had installed in certain areas of the White House to document his conversations. Since the tapes were not subject to subpoena at the time, Nixon could have destroyed them but chose not to. The Watergate Committee and special prosecutor then subpoenaed certain tapes to determine the level of White House involvement in Watergate and the attempted cover-up. Nixon challenged the subpoena in court but still did not destroy the tapes, and on October 12 the U.S. Court of Appeals made a 5–2 ruling that the president must obey the special prosecutor's subpoena to hand over nine of the White House tapes related to Watergate.[153] Over the next ten months the Nixon administration fought over the extent of the tapes to be released, and it was during this period that Nixon asked Rose Mary Woods to transcribe the subpoenaed tapes. However, when it was later discovered that there was an 18.5-minute gap that Woods might have caused in the transcription process, she became subject of investigation by the special prosecutor.

When it came to protecting those close to him, Nixon provided them with better counsel than he provided himself. He asked Duke Law School classmate Charles S. Rhyne to represent Woods. Rhyne, a Democrat, was a frequent White House guest, attending intimate get-togethers such as Pat Nixon's surprise birthday party and the Duke Law School class of 1937 reunion, Oval Office meetings, religious services, official state dinners, and ceremonies.[154] In 1971 Nixon had called Rhyne when he was having difficulty selecting a U.S. Supreme Court nominee, and Rhyne suggested Lewis F. Powell Jr., who was eventually nominated and confirmed by the Senate.[155] By July 1974 Special Prosecutor Leon Jaworski knew that no case had been developed against Woods, who was represented pro bono by Rhyne, so he took her lawyer to lunch and offered not to press any charges in return for a promise of silence from Woods and Rhyne.[156] His deal was a success, and the media virtually ignored the agreement and lack of any charges against Woods.[157]

In the spring of 1974 Nixon released edited transcripts of some of the subpoenaed tapes. Whenever an offensive word appeared in the transcripts, it was replaced with the words "expletive delet-ed." The deleted expletives mainly consisted of "goddamn," "hell," "damn," "Christ," "for Chrissake," "what in the name of Christ," and "oh, God."[158] The saltiest language used by the president was "crap," "shit," and "asshole."[159] As it turned out, Nixon, a navy man, spoke like a sailor.[160] He explained his refusal to allow publication of these words: "If my mother ever heard me use words like that, she would turn over in her grave."[161] Nixon's hometown friends understood his feelings, but where the transcripts said "expletive deleted," everyone's imagination ran wild.[162] In the introduction to the paperback edition of the tapes, R. W. Apple Jr. claimed that "'s-h-i-t' was the mildest of the deleted expletives"; however, this claim was false.[163]

Julie Nixon remembered the impact: "The American myth that presidents are always presidential, that they sit in the Oval Office talking in lofty and quotable phrases was shaken by the transcripts."[164] Part of the problem was the manner in which Nixon analyzed issues, tending to surround himself with advisors who disagreed with his proposals and using conversation as a means of thinking aloud. As Nixon biographer Jonathan Aitken explained, "His technique was to review a situation or an item of information from every conceivable angle. He would consider all the options from the hair-raising to the statesmanlike."[165] The habit was partly attributable to Nixon's Quaker roots; at the East Whittier Friends Church, issues concern-ing church members were discussed until there was consensus as to what action to take.[166]

The Watergate Committee and special prosecutor insisted on the release of the actual tapes, but Nixon refused on constitutional grounds and appealed to the U.S. Supreme Court. Pat's opposition was more practical: "How can any individual survive a public reading of private conversations?"[167] As 1974 progressed and the pressure of Watergate intensified, Murray Chotiner, Nixon's trusted political consultant since his first campaign in 1946, died from injuries he suffered in a car accident.[168] The loss devastated Nixon, who released the following statement: "I am profoundly saddened by the death of Murray Chotiner. For more than a quarter of a century he has been an ally in political battles, a valued counselor and a trusted friend. His friendship never wavered; in periods of adversity it grew stronger. . . . In life he had my respect and deep friendship; he will forever have my gratitude. I shall miss him."[169]

As the pressure continued to mount against his presidency, Nixon, who had two foreign trips planned, remained mindful of those working for him. He told Rose Mary Woods, "Marje Acker has not been on any foreign trips—she should go on one. I have two planned this spring, one to Egypt and one to Russia. Let her pick which one she wants to go on."[170] Acker selected Russia, thinking she'd never have another chance to go to a Communist country. Later Nixon complimented her, saying, "You picked the right trip."[171]

In July Nixon returned to La Casa Pacifica for the final stay of his presidency.[172] Describing the pressure of Watergate, Nixon recorded in his diary, "I intend to live the next week without dying the death of a thousand cuts. This has been my philosophy throughout my political life. Cowards die a thousand deaths, brave men only die once."[173] Through it all, friends and family supported him, and the *Los Angeles Times*, which had endorsed Nixon in every campaign since 1946, was one of the few major daily newspapers that never called on him to resign.[174] On July 21, as articles of impeachment were being considered, Roy Ash welcomed the Nixons to his Bel Air home for a reception in Richard's honor. Virtually the entire California Committee attended to show support for their friend and president.[175]

Nixon's last public appearance in Southern California as president was at the Century Plaza Hotel, where he spoke about the economy.[176] Two days later, on July 27, while Nixon swam at his beloved Red Beach, the House Judiciary Committee approved the first article of impeachment against Nixon, charging that the president obstructed the investigation into the Watergate case.[177] Demands to release the tapes continued to intensify; Pat thought they should be destroyed, as did Roy Day and other supporters, who actually recommended burning the tapes on the White House lawn.[178] Instead, on August 5 Nixon released the "smoking gun" tape from the June 23, 1972, meeting where he had requested that the CIA instruct the FBI to cease its investigation into the Watergate break-in. In the resulting uproar, as Nixon lost the majority support of his fellow Republicans in the House and Senate, he knew he had to resign.[179]

Through it all, Pat was the one holding everything together. To

Helen Thomas, a White House correspondent through ten administrations, it was clear that Pat loved Richard very much.[180] Similarly, close friend Helene Drown observed to Julie Nixon Eisenhower, "Your father never had a better admirer. At times she would tell me she was 'angry' or 'furious' about a decision, but always, overriding it all, was a tremendous respect for him about the little things and the big. She said so many times that I can almost repeat it verbatim, 'He always knows the right thing to say,' because she herself found public speaking difficult. Most of all, she had respect for the enormous problems he was dealing with."[181]

Pat was adamantly opposed to Richard's resigning, and yet in those final days, she began packing their belongings in anticipation of his resignation.[182] Later Richard observed, "Very perceptive of her. With us sometimes, as it is between people who are very close, the unspoken things go deeper than the spoken. She knew what I was going to do."[183] Julie and Tricia were also against resignation and urged their father to fight all the way through an impeachment trial.[184] While Nixon was trying to decide what to do, he asked Tricia to walk with him in the White House Rose Garden, where she had been married only three years earlier.

On the evening of August 8, Nixon invited thirty friends from the House and Senate to the White House, where they met in the Cabinet Room, adjacent to the Oval Office. Standing at the center of the room, on the west side of the large conference table, Nixon began to speak earnestly and calmly, explaining that he had never felt that he was a quitter. He then recalled that while at Whittier College, he had been the only man Whittier entered in a mile race at an intercollegiate track meet. He was running as fast as he could but led only one man. Determined not to come in last, he kept running until he finally made it, finishing next to last. Most of those present in the room that night were crying, and Nixon's voice rose higher as he, too, started to cry, telling his friends, "I hope you don't think I let you down!" before leaving the room. Congressman Bob Wilson, a member of Nixon's California Committee, recalled, "I confess it was one of the most emotional things I've ever been through."[185]

Nixon then walked into the Oval Office and announced his resignation to the nation, effective the following day at noon.[186] His primary reason for resigning was to avoid having a president "in the dock for alleged illegal activities," feeling strongly that the nation needed to move forward with a new administration. That evening Nixon asked Henry Kissinger to kneel with him in silent prayer in the Lincoln Bedroom. The next morning, August 9, 1974, Nixon met with three hundred members of his administration in the East Room to say goodbye.[187] He thanked each person one by one and gave an impromptu speech saying he was proud of every one of them and the fact that no one in his administration had "ever profited at the public expense or the public till. . . . Mistakes, yes. But for personal gain, never."[188]

He then turned to his life and moving forward:

We think that when someone dear to us dies, we think that when we lose an election, we think that when we suffer a defeat that all is ended. We think, as T.R. [Theodore Roosevelt] said, that the light had left his life forever.

Not true. It is only a beginning, always. The young must know it; the old must know it. It must always sustain us, because the greatness comes not when things go always good for you, but the greatness comes and you are really tested, when you take some knocks, some disappointments, when sadness comes, because only if you have been in the deepest valley can you ever know how magnificent it is to be on the highest mountain.[189]

Finally, he concluded: "And so, we leave with high hopes, in good spirit, and with deep humility, and with very much gratefulness in our hearts. . . . Not only will we always remember you, not only will we always be grateful to you, but always you will be in our hearts and you will be in our prayers."[190]

At 10:06 a.m. Nixon departed the White House on Army One for Andrews Air Force Base, from which he would make his way back to California.[191] Colonel Boyer had watched Nixon stand on the steps of the helicopter hundreds of times, but he recalled that he had never before seen the president gesture with such spirit and purpose: "I had the undeniable feeling that he wanted us to know it wasn't because he was a quitter."[192] Once in the helicopter, Pat said, "It's so sad, it's so sad." Nixon reflected on his family, Pat, Tricia and Ed, Julie and David, and thought how "no one could have been a more supportive, loving, kind family" and "how lucky" he was to have them. As the helicopter continued on to Andrews Air Force Base, Nixon found himself thinking not of the past but of the future, and in that moment the ballad of Sir Andrew Barton came to mind: "I am hurt but I am not slain / I'll lay me down and bleed a while / Then I'll rise and fight again."[193]

Colonel Boyer and his copilot, Carl Burhanan, knew Nixon to be a considerate man since the first time they had flown him, landing on the beach in Santa Barbara five years earlier. Both pilots were impressed that first day, when Nixon leaned into the cockpit and told them, "Thanks for a nice flight."[194] They had flown President Johnson and his family, from whom neither of the pilots had ever received any acknowledgment, nor did they expect any. During Nixon's tenure, Burhanan was promoted to White House pilot, serving as the first African American to fly a president. As the Nixons prepared to depart the helicopter this last time, Pat stepped to the cockpit with tears in her eyes and told the pilots, "Oh, thank you so much for the many trips."[195] Nixon followed suit, and when he looked at Boyer, he saw tears welling up in the colonel's eyes. Nixon, fighting back his emotions, told him, "Stop that. Stop those tears. I have to walk over there," pointing across the tarmac to Air Force One, "and it would be better for me if I did not see your tears as the last thing I saw as I left this helicopter."[196]

At 10:17 a.m. Air Force One lifted off. With an average flight speed of six hundred miles per hour, Nixon would be in California by noon.[197] Sgt. Lee Simmons, the first and only African American steward when he was assigned to Air Force One in 1970, was also the first promoted to chief steward, and he was Nixon's favorite.[198] Approximately fifteen stewards were assigned to fly with the president, but Nixon always requested Simmons. In fact, he asked Simmons to travel with the First Lady as a military aide whenever she traveled without the president. Simmons accompanied the First Lady to Monrovia, Liberia, when William Tolbert, the grandson of an American slave, was inaugurated as the nation's president, and he stayed in the guesthouse with Mrs. Nixon during their visit. Later, when Tolbert visited the White House, Nixon made sure that Simmons and his wife were on the guest list for the state dinner. As they came through the receiving line, Nixon explained to Tolbert, "Lee and his wife are very special guests here tonight," adding how long they had flown together. Simmons recalled that Nixon "was very pleasant and nice to be around. He was very comfortable. I thoroughly enjoyed being with him, and he seemed to enjoy being with me."[199]

Simmons told Nixon how sorry he was that he and Mrs. Nixon were leaving the presidency, adding, "I want to thank you for all you have done for me and my family." Nixon replied, "Now Lee, I've been wanting to tell you how much I appreciate all the good care and all the nice things you've done for me and Pat. Just remember, tomorrow is a new day. You can't let things get you down. You can't stay down. You have to pick yourself up and keep going. Life goes on." Nixon, paused, then looked directly at Simmons and told him, "Lee, I am going to miss you, and I hope the best for you and your family." Sergeant Simmons and the president hugged, as an emotional Nixon whispered to him, "We had a lot of great trips together, Lee." Regaining his composure, Nixon asked, "Lee, what time is it?" Simmons responded, "Noon." Nixon said, "Well, have Ron Zeigler come in. I think we'll have a couple martinis."[200] Zeigler was Nixon's press secretary. Nixon then lunched on shrimp cocktail, prime rib, baked potato, green beans, tossed salad, coffee, and cheesecake.[201]

In addition to family, members of his administration accompanied Nixon on the flight home, and after lunch, Nixon walked the length of the plane, stopping at every seat to say a few words to each person.[202] As the plane reached Southern California and circled El Toro Marine Base, Nixon could see hundreds of cars waiting to get into the already overflowing parking area on the base.[203] A crowd of five thousand stood waiting to welcome Pat and Richard home.[204] The temperature was eighty-two degrees, a perfect Southern California day.[205] As Nixon departed the plane, he heard a voice in the crowd say, "Whittier is still for you, Dick."[206]

Nixon spoke briefly to those assembled: "Many statements have been made and this is not the time to bore you with another one. It is perhaps appropriate for me to say very simply this: having completed one task does not mean that we will just sit back and enjoy this marvelous California climate and do nothing."[207] Lois Lundberg, chairperson of the Orange County Republican Party, listened as Nixon told the crowd, "We are going to continue to be proud that we, like you, are Californians and are back home again."[208]

As Nixon concluded his remarks, everyone began to sing "God Bless America," first softly and then louder.[209]

From El Toro, the Nixons took a helicopter to the Loran Coast Guard Station, where they were greeted by Paul Presley, owner of the San Clemente Inn, and Johnny Grant, mayor of Hollywood.[210] From the helipad, the family headed to the house alone. Gavin Herbert, who had received a call the day before instructing him to "get the house ready," was the sole person to meet Nixon at the house. "I met Nixon at the back door of the house," he recalled. It had been "a very traumatic experience—he looked very haggard and crushed. He looked terrible."[211] Nixon was grateful to Herbert for "providing a place of peace" when he arrived.[212] Surrounded only by his family, Richard Nixon was now alone at La Casa Pacifica, his presidency having ended with no celebration, no fanfare. That evening he stood on the bluff overlooking the Pacific, watching the waves crash on the beach.[213]

SEVENTEEN

Exile and Rehabilitation

1974–80

For exactly five years and six months from the day of his resignation, Richard and Pat Nixon lived in self-imposed exile
at La Casa Pacifica.[1] Nixon spent the first weekend with Bebe
Rebozo, taking him to Dana Park, where Dick and Pat had enjoyed
their first dates, and then down to Nixon's beloved Red Beach.[2] By
Tuesday Nixon commenced a routine of being in his executive offices
by 7:00 a.m., dressed in a business suit, ready for work.[3]

During the official six-month transition period, several of Nixon's
White House staff joined him in San Clemente. The team included
former press secretary Ron Ziegler, Jack Brennan, Steve Bull, and
Ken Khachigian, all of whom tried to maintain their sense of humor,
referring to themselves as the "government in exile."[4] Ziegler and
Nixon met every day for hours on end, but as time went on, Richard became depressed, often speaking for hours about what he had
endured. Occasionally, Nixon and Ziegler drowned their sorrows
in alcohol, but for the most part, the former president poured out
his thoughts while Ziegler dutifully listened.[5]

There were extensive negotiations with the Ford administration
regarding a pardon, with Nixon sometimes expressing his desire
to go to trial. In the unlikely event he was actually convicted of a
crime, Nixon believed that he could adjust to a prison sentence:
"All I'd need would be a good supply of books and a hard table to
write on. Some of the best literature in history has been written in
jail—look at Gandhi and Lenin."[6] Fortunately, his resolve was never
put to the test, and on Sunday, September 8, 1974, President Ford
pardoned him. Knowing the pardon was imminent, Nixon retreated
to Walter Annenberg's Palm Desert estate for a long weekend to
avoid the media camped out at the gates of La Casa Pacifica when
the announcement was made. Nixon explained his acceptance of

the pardon: "It was the most painful decision of my political career, and one in which I had no other choice. To accept a pardon is to, in effect, admit guilt of a crime. I would have preferred to have fought that issue out in the impeachment proceedings before the resignation or in a trial after the resignation. But as [attorney Jack] Miller made abundantly clear to me, I did not have the financial resources or the physical strength to go through not only one but several trials which would have undoubtedly resulted had there been no pardon."[7]

Nixon's initial intention was to issue a simple statement: "In accordance with the law I accept this pardon." But after negotiations with the Ford administration, he released a statement summarizing his feelings on Watergate—feelings he held for the rest of his life:

No words can describe the depth of my regret and pain at the anguish my mistakes over Watergate have caused the nation and the Presidency—a nation I so deeply love and an institution I so greatly respect. I know that many fair-minded people believe that my motivations and actions in the Watergate affair were intentionally self-serving and illegal. I now understand how my own mistakes and misjudgments have contributed to that belief and seem to support it. This burden is the heaviest of all to bear. That the way I tried to deal with Watergate was the wrong way is a burden I shall bear for every day of the life that is left to me.[8]

Rather than feeling relief, Nixon became despondent after the pardon. Annenberg could see his friend was discouraged and tried to bolster him, explaining, "Whether you have been knocked down or are on the ropes, always remember that life is ninety-nine rounds."[9] But as Nixon sank deeper into depression, his physical condition declined. Ken Khachigian was struck by how stoop-shouldered and worn he appeared.[10] Compounding matters, Nixon had suffered from phlebitis in his left leg, with swelling of veins caused by blood clots, since June. On September 11 longtime California Committee friend and family doctor John Lungren visited him to examine his phlebitis. Lungren could see that Nixon needed to be hospitalized, yet Nixon resisted, telling him, "If I go to the hospital, I'll never get out of there alive."[11]

Lungren recognized that Nixon's resignation, combined with the isolation of La Casa Pacifica, was causing him to suffer emotionally, which manifested in physical trauma. "Nixon's fear of dying was great," Lungren said, "and yet it was completely uncharacteristic."[12] Five days later Lungren found that Nixon's condition had worsened, so he prevailed on him to go to the hospital, explaining that if a blood clot were to break free and enter the lungs, it would be fatal.[13] Finally, on Monday, September 23, Nixon was admitted to Long Beach Memorial Hospital, where he remained until October 4.[14] During those two weeks he received some two thousand get-well cards and telegrams.[15]

At one point during his hospital stay, Nixon vomited all over one of the hospital staff. This reminded him of a similar incident years before, while helping law school classmate Charles Rhyne with his studies when Rhyne was in the hospital. Now, while convalescing, Nixon kept calling Rhyne, causing his phone to ring incessantly. Rhyne was home alone, not wanting to talk to anyone following the recent death of his wife. When he finally picked up, Nixon asked, "Why don't you answer your phone? I bribed a hospital orderly to bring me this telephone and could not remember any telephone number except yours and then you haven't answered. This is the first telephone number I have personally dialed in years."[16] Nixon asked if Rhyne remembered "spew[ing] all you had eaten for the past week onto the distinguished father of the hospital manager." Then he added, "Well, the same thing just happened to me."[17] Reminiscing, the two cheered each other up, laughing loudly, until Nixon's laughter drew the attention of the hospital attendants, who promptly took away the telephone.[18]

Pat visited Dick every day, and most evenings they enjoyed McDonald's hamburgers while watching *Bonanza*.[19] After a few weeks of antibiotics, Nixon was ready to be discharged. As he left the hospital, Nixon rose from his wheelchair, announcing, "I feel great. Just great."[20] Nixon's condition did not improve at home, however, and he was readmitted to Long Beach Memorial less than three weeks later, on October 24.[21] When Nixon arrived in his white Cadillac, Ray Mackey, a sanitation man, was compacting cardboard boxes in the parking lot. To Mackey's surprise, Nixon, in typical style, looked over and greeted him: "Hi there."[22]

Lungren called in Dr. Wiley Barker from UCLA Medical Center, who explained the need for surgery: "If you look at this clot cross-eyed, it will kill you." Nixon replied, "I've got too many things to do to go on being sick. Let's just get it out of the way." Emergency surgery was performed at 5:30 a.m. on Tuesday, October 30, during which an eighteen-inch clot large enough to kill Nixon and "three other men as well" was removed from his leg.[23]

Following surgery, the president was the sole patient on the seventh floor of the hospital.[24] Nixon's valet, Manolo Sanchez, was with him when his eyes closed, and he whispered, "Is that you Manolo? Manolo, I don't think I'm going to get out of here alive." Nixon then slumped into unconsciousness, and his eyes rolled back into his head as he went into cardiovascular shock. At least four pints of blood had seeped into his abdomen; his blood pressure fell to fifty-five over twenty, then sixty over zero. His nurse called out, "Condition blue holding!"[25] Nixon's only recollection was his nurse slapping his face and shouting, "Richard, wake up! Richard!"[26] Knowing that Nixon could die within the hour, Lungren and his team worked frantically to reverse the vascular shock as Nixon held on.[27] When Dick woke, he admitted to Pat, "I don't think I'm going to make it," to which Pat responded, "Don't talk that way. You have got to make it. You must not give up."[28] For two days Nixon was in critical condition, receiving a total of eight pints of blood.[29]

To Frank Gannon, a White House assistant who was part of Nixon's transition team to San Clemente, "Nixon looked utterly helpless."[30] He had an embolism that could move at any time, and his doctors explained that it would be at least twelve hours before the anticoagulant drugs might start to dissolve it. Nixon's voice sounded "surprisingly strong" as he told Gannon he knew he might not live through the night but wanted to use what could be his last hours to talk for posterity—mainly about what he had achieved and what he hoped to do. So Gannon sat with Nixon through the night, which he described as "a moving and terrifying experience."[31]

President Ford was in Los Angeles and wanted to visit, but his advisors recommended against it. Ford responded, "If there's no place in politics for human compassion, there's something wrong with politics. I'm going to leave it to Pat."[32] President Ford called Pat: "Hello, Pat? This is Jerry Ford. How's the President? I don't want to push it, but would it help if I came down there?" And Pat replied,

"I can't think of anything that would do him more good."[33] The next morning the doors to Nixon's room were accidentally locked when Ford arrived with his chief of staff, Dick Cheney. Nixon awoke to hammering and hacksawing, as a carpenter had to be called to remove the doors to his suite.[34] For twenty minutes, Nixon and Ford looked at each other through the glass until the doors were removed and they could visit in person. At the end of their visit, Ford told his friend and colleague of twenty-five years, "I just want to thank you for all you did for me." Nixon replied, "I'm not feeling too well, but I am going to make it. . . . Your visit has meant a lot to me. Mr. President, I am deeply grateful." President Ford grasped Nixon's hand, whispering, "Be well."[35]

Cardinal Henry Manning visited from Los Angeles, and Chairman Mao called from China, telling Nixon that he considered him "one of the greatest statesmen in history."[36] Billy Graham and his wife arranged for a plane to fly outside Nixon's hospital room window towing a banner that read, "NIXON—GOD LOVES YOU AND SO DO WE."[37] When Ronald Reagan, whose loyalty to Nixon remained steadfast, heard that the former president had slipped into shock, he snapped, "Maybe that will satisfy the lynch mob."[38] Through it all, Pat stayed at his side, holding his hand. With her support, Nixon gradually improved and was discharged on November 14, 1974.[39]

For the first time in nearly thirty years, Nixon did not believe he needed the national press, so he excluded the media from his recovery, and on his release from Long Beach Memorial, he retreated to the solitude of La Casa Pacifica. Not caring for the effects of codeine, he found he could manage the physical pain but soon became disconsolate in his solitude, reflecting in his diary, "I have a rather depressed feeling again. I have simply got to get over this because we just can't continue to exist with nothing but depression or bad news coming in."[40]

Lungren regularly made house calls, and though Nixon tried his best to work through this difficult period, his doctor observed that he was descending into despair.[41] Nixon described his depression as "a disintegration of the will to live," by which his purpose in life was lost and his "enthusiasm for achievement exhausted." His doctor recommended golf and more social interaction.[42] While he was depressed, Marje Acker was amazed that Nixon never gave any impression that he was feeling sorry for himself.[43] Instead, he held out hope, recording in his diary, "Some way there must be a way to come back. To come back from this vale of tears through which we have passed. Not just a vale of tears, buckets of them have been shed."[44] Yet as Nixon tried to follow Lungren's advice, neither he nor Pat wanted to leave the safe confines of La Casa Pacifica, which in many ways was an ideal place for him to recover because he loved the Pacific and believed "the ocean was his stress reliever."[45]

Nixon preferred not to venture out into public, wanting to avoid both sympathy from supporters and heckles from detractors.[46] At the same time, he knew he would survive the postresignation depression: "We will see it through. We've had tough times before and we can take the tougher ones that we will have to go through now. That is perhaps what we were made for—to be able to take punishment beyond what anyone in this office has ever had before particularly after leaving office. This is a test of character and we must not fail the test."[47] Gradually, he began to leave La Casa Pacifica, beginning with simple outings like picking up Julie at the airport, dining out, and visiting Don and Clara Jane at their Newport Beach home, where they enjoyed dinners on the patio overlooking the bay.[48]

One day Gavin Herbert was caring for the La Casa Pacifica grounds when a Secret Service agent asked if Herbert could come in and talk to Nixon. As Herbert sat down with the president, Nixon, who believed that "after a man is President, there is nothing he can do," looked at him and asked, "Gavin, what am I going to do with the rest of my life?" Herbert was stunned at the question, but just then there was a knock at the door and a navy corpsman came in to check Nixon's blood pressure, giving Herbert a moment to collect his thoughts. Once the corpsman had left, Herbert suggested he write a book, to which Nixon replied, "I can't write."[49] But he knew he had to do something.

On December 7 Nixon recorded in his diary:

I simply have to pull myself together and start the long journey back—live through the agony of the balance of the tapes whatever they are; fight over the papers, whatever comes at the trial, and do the only creative thing that perhaps I have left to do which is to write a book—maybe one, maybe more—and to follow it with speeches, television of course where possible, which will maybe put some of these things in perspective. I think that Ron [Ziegler] and Frank [Gannon], both in a kind way are trying to tell me that there is a hell of a lot of hatred out there and mistrust and that we cannot underestimate it. . . . I do not want to feel depressed today. I rather feel it however, and yet maybe such a day is the day to start coming back—maybe this afternoon—to make the first outline on the book and during the next week try to continue along this process.[50]

And thus Nixon slowly began working to regain his health.

Despite his illness, the Watergate-related investigations continued, and Nixon was subpoenaed to testify in Washington DC.[51] On November 25 he was examined by a panel of three doctors at La Casa Pacifica for Judge John Sirica to confirm that Nixon was not able to sit for a deposition.[52] Ultimately, in June 1975 the president appeared before the Washington DC grand jury for eleven hours at the Loran Coast Guard Station regarding the federal investigation into Bebe Rebozo.[53] Nixon viewed the investigation of Rebozo as a disgraceful abuse of power by U.S. attorneys, but he knew his best friend was a strong man who could withstand the scrutiny, and in fact, no charges were ever filed against Rebozo.[54] But the continuing investigation took its toll, and Nixon later described his condition at the time: "For the first time in my life, I was a physical wreck; I was emotionally drained; I was mentally burned out. . . . I could see no reason to live, no cause to fight for. Unless a person has a reason to live for other than himself, he will die—first mentally, then emotionally, then physically."[55]

As Christmas approached, Nixon tried to lift his spirits. Although his physical health was improving, his spiritual health concerned him, as "a healthy vegetable is still a vegetable." He invited Frank Sinatra and Paul Keyes to La Casa Pacifica for lunch, and the interaction must have helped, because two days later, the Sunday before Christmas, Nixon called Earl Adams to wish him a Merry Christmas.[56] "I'm weak, but I think I'm improving," Nixon told Adams. "After the first of the year, Pat and I are going to begin seeing people. If you're down this way, drop in to see us."[57] Still, Julie Nixon Eisenhower reflected, "Christmas 1974 was the lowest point in my father's life."[58] She described her parents' first year in

San Clemente: "The small triumphs of the day were discussed at dinnertime. Mother reporting her progress of weeding the circle in front of the house, my father with news of an exchange of letters with one of his favorite sports figures."[59] One morning Pat said, "Dick, I don't know how you keep going." He replied, "I just get up in the morning to confound my enemies."[60]

Yet the couple slowly began to return to life. On January 9, 1975, Pat threw Dick a surprise party for his sixty-second birthday.[61] Foreign governments sent gifts, including a two-pound jar of caviar from the shah of Iran.[62] Nixon told his guests, "Never dwell on the past. Always look to the future."[63] His "biggest laugh of the evening" was when he saw Bob Abplanalp's gift, an apron that proclaimed, "I got my job through The New York Times."[64] In celebration of his birthday, Nixon devised a strategy for his recovery. To regain his physical health, he planned long walks with his Irish setter, King Timahoe, in addition to golf and regularly swimming in his pool.[65]

From August 9, 1974, through February 9, 1975, there was an official "transition" period between the Nixon and Ford administrations, and on the last day, a Saturday, Pat and Richard held a small party for a few friends and the departing transition staff.[66] Former military aide Jack Brennan became Nixon's chief of staff, assisted by Frank Gannon, Diane Sawyer, Ken Khachigian, and Loie Gaunt.

On February 22 the Nixons enjoyed their first public outing, attending a dinner party hosted by Walter and Lenore Annenberg at their estate in Palm Desert, joining friends Ronald and Nancy Reagan, Bob Hope, Frank Sinatra, Barbara Marx, and other guests. After dinner, Nixon spoke to the group for ten minutes, during which he reflected on his current isolation compared with when he lived in the large and spacious White House as president: "When you are on top, it is filled with all your friends." He "paused and smiled self-consciously," as though reflecting on his current circumstances, then continued, "Afterward, you don't need a house so large," as guests wiped away tears. Although down, he assured his friends, "I am not out."[67] As Nixon had promised Earl Adams at Christmas, by February 1975 he was seeing guests up to three times a week and knew that these relationships were important to his recovery:

No one can recover spiritually from a major loss without the help of others. Politics is not a team sport. While a political figure depends on others in many ways, he ultimately rises and falls as a result of his own decisions and actions. A personal defeat therefore is an isolating experience. In an unsuccessful campaign, staff members share in the loss, but only the candidate suffers a personal defeat. Spiritual recovery is hastened by overcoming the sense of isolation, by recognizing the fact that your family, friends and supporters still stand with you, and by putting the defeat in perspective.[68]

Nixon's visitors included family, California Committee members, politicians and former administration officials, and spiritual leaders Billy Graham, Rabbi Baruch Korff, and Norman Vincent Peale.[69] One day James Cagney and Paul Keyes stopped by for lunch, and as they were leaving, Cagney vigorously shook Nixon's hand, telling him, "Well, Mr. President, thanks to you there are no American boys dying anywhere in the world. There are no American boys fighting anywhere. Thanks to you, we are talking to China and we have an understanding with Russia."[70] Nixon responded, "Yes Jimmy, we did all the big things right and we screwed up the goddamned little things."[71]

As former administration officials who had been entangled in Watergate were released from prison, Nixon met with them.[72] Visibly moved when he met Bud Krogh, Nixon asked his guest, "Tell me about what prison is like." Krogh explained, "You have to choose between making it a positive or negative experience," then added that he relied on his spiritual faith to cope with confinement. Nixon and Krogh also discussed the burglary of Daniel Ellsberg's psychiatrist that Krogh had orchestrated. Ellsberg had released the Pentagon Papers, and Krogh authorized the break-in hoping to obtain evidence to discredit Ellsberg. Nixon questioned whether he had somehow known about it. Krogh was astonished and categorically denied that Nixon had ordered the break-in or had any advance knowledge of it. Yet Nixon agonized over the issue. "Do you think I should plead guilty?" he inquired. "Do you feel guilty Mr. President?" asked Krogh. "No I don't. I just don't" was Nixon's response, prompting Krogh to advise, "Then you can't, you can't do that."[73]

Former assistant Dwight Chapin visited La Casa Pacifica after his incarceration. Chapin had worked for Nixon since the 1962 governor's race, and as his assistant, he had introduced Nixon to hundreds of people over the years. "Usually Nixon was very smooth, compassionate. He put people at ease because he knew they were nervous meeting him," explained Chapin. "But on this occasion, Nixon was nervous. It was very difficult for him. He told my daughters Kimberly and Tracy . . . he fumbled around with his words trying to say that I had been faithful and loyal." Overall, Nixon "wanted to apologize and explain to my daughters and wife that I was a good man."[74]

Another visitor was Bruce Herschensohn, who had been a speech writer and advisor to Nixon in the White House. Herschensohn had argued against Nixon's resigning, and he left government service when the president did. He had always been impressed that Nixon had traveled to eighty countries, and he became determined to do the same. When he visited La Casa Pacifica, he told Nixon, "I've always admired that you had been to eighty countries, and on my last trip I hit eighty countries." Nixon just looked at Herschensohn without visual approval or disapproval. Herschensohn thought he had made a mistake in comparing his visits to Nixon's, so he admitted, "I guess I am exaggerating because I count Vatican City and Guam." Nixon's eyes narrowed, and with a slight smile, he replied, "So do I."[75]

Having kept in touch with his former chief of staff, Bob Haldeman, Nixon asked him one day whom he was voting for in the upcoming California primary election.[76] Haldeman replied, "In case you've forgotten, in California convicted felons can't vote." After a moment of silence, Nixon laughed and said, "Well, in that case, I'll vote twice," at which Haldeman laughed as well.[77] Nixon also reached out to members of his California Committee.[78] When Kenneth Ball returned home after open heart surgery and the phone rang, his wife, Dolores, "almost dropped the phone" when she realized Nixon was calling to check up on his old Whittier classmate. There was no fanfare, just Nixon and Kenneth enjoying a nice conversation between old friends.[79]

Nixon took Watergate and its impact on the elections very seriously. In 1976, when Robert Finch ran for U.S. Senate from California, many were concerned about his electability, given his close association with and propensity to defend Nixon.[80] Nixon knew that if Finch continued to defend him, it would hurt Finch's chances in the election. Nixon instructed Lois Lundberg, chairperson of the Orange County Republican Party, "Tell Bob to say anything bad about me that he needs to."[81] Eventually, Nixon, who was assigned the White House code name Wizard, even began secretly advising President Ford on his 1976 election bid.[82]

As Nixon gradually recovered his physical strength and mental stamina, he still faced challenges related to Watergate. Congress had reduced his $100,000 per year office expense allowance to $60,000. Ken Khachigian described how Nixon reacted to the budget issues: "He would sit there figuring away on his yellow pads, and even when the sums just couldn't be made to add up, he would end up saying, 'Oh, well, it will work out.'"[83] A ready solution would have been to accept speaking fees, but despite the monetary pressures, Nixon maintained his lifelong refusal of paid speaking engagements.[84]

Pat was devastated by Watergate, believing in her heart that her husband had done more for his country than any other president.[85] The post-Watergate healing process was slow for her, as she had no staff support, not even a secretary.[86] In May 1975 Pat made her first solo public appearance when she traveled to Cerritos for the dedication of the Patricia Nixon Elementary School.[87] Two months later Pat asked daughter Julie, who had been married for over six years, to come for a visit. When Julie explained that she couldn't leave home while her husband, David, was preparing for his second-year law school exams, Pat protested, "You only have one person to take care of there, but two broken people here."[88]

However slow their recovery, the overall plan was to just try to relax. Dick enjoyed Don Diego cigars, and on Sunday evenings he and Pat watched *Kojak* by the fire.[89] Occasionally, they invited the staff over for impromptu parties, where Dick played show tunes on the piano or led them in renditions of the USC football cheer.[90] The Drowns often visited so that Jack and Dick could play gin or watch football, while their wives spent hours entertaining each other. Once Pat and Helene were even so bold as to spend a day in Tijuana together incognito.[91]

Golf became an increasingly important facet of Nixon's exercise regimen. Typically playing at Camp Pendleton and other nearby courses, Nixon enlisted Jack Brennan, his chief of staff, as his golfing partner.[92] Brennan was a perfect playing partner because the two men "knew and understood each other, and Nixon could just be himself."[93] Brennan described those early times: "Almost every day I said to myself, 'Don't make mistakes; the guy is still fragile; don't let him get hurt.' So on that basis my priority was to take him to places where he'd be sure to get a good welcome. I remember the first time we played golf how terrified he was that someone on the course would shout abuse at him. When the opposite happened and people kept coming over to him to shake his hand, he was boosted right up. That taught me something and set a pattern."[94]

His first time back on the links, Nixon shot a 125 and almost quit on the spot, but he enjoyed the "warm companionship" with Brennan.[95] Golf became his "lifesaver," and the year after his resignation, he made his first public appearance playing golf with the International Brotherhood of Teamsters at La Costa Country Club of Carlsbad.[96] Shore Cliffs in San Clemente became his favorite local course, where he often played three times a week, up to twenty-seven holes per outing.[97] By November 14, 1975, Nixon reported, "I was shooting a few pars on the course and was back to par physically."[98] When he finally broke 80, "it was like climbing Mount Everest."[99]

After retaining renowned agent Irving "Swifty" Lazar, Nixon signed a book deal in 1975 for which he received a $2.5 million advance.[100] He began working on his memoirs by telling his staff, "We won't grovel; we won't confess; we won't do a mea culpa act; but we will be one hundred per cent accurate."[101] He quickly developed a schedule in which he would arrive at his office between 6:00 and 7:00 in the morning; work all day dictating, reviewing, and correcting the dictation until late in the afternoon; then go for a swim with Pat or play golf. This routine remained constant seven days a week, 365 days a year for three years.[102] Frank Gannon described Nixon as "a demanding taskmaster, but at the same time kind, considerate and always fascinating to work with."[103]

Frequently, Pat and Dick dined on their poolside terrace or enjoyed watching the first-run film prints sent by their Hollywood friends.[104] Loie Gaunt, Nixon's office manager, saw that "they definitely had a strong and loving marriage. They couldn't have been closer."[105] Family friends Louise and Roger Johnson recognized genuine closeness, "a camaraderie" between them.[106] For their thirty-fifth wedding anniversary in June 1975, the Nixons went for a drive around Dana Point, visiting Golden Lantern Street, where Dick had proposed to Pat on the bluffs overlooking the beach.[107] For dinners out, their local favorites were Olamendi's in Dana Point, Mille Fleurs in Rancho Santa Fe, and El Adobe in San Juan Capistrano, which featured a dish named for Nixon called the President's Choice, a combination of chile rellenos, Spanish rice, refried beans, and a beef enchilada.[108]

Quiet time alone with Pat offered Richard his only respite from the traumas of his dark days, and throughout his recovery, he continued his media blackout. Then a unique opportunity arose when David Frost, a British interviewer, approached Nixon, proposing a series of television interviews. A deal was struck, and beginning on August 9, 1975, Frost and Nixon had a series of meetings at La Casa Pacifica to get to know one another.[109] The resulting Frost-Nixon interviews were filmed at the Dana Point split-level residence of H. L. Smith, in twelve sessions, lasting three and a half hours each, spanning the five weeks from March 23 through April 20, 1977.[110] The Smith residence was selected because it was large, close to La Casa Pacifica, and in a gated community.[111]

The Secret Service thoroughly vetted the Smiths and their residence before agreeing to the location. When the property was initially searched, the agents supposedly looked everywhere, including inside the washer and dryer, yet somehow missed all the munitions in various drawers and the hundreds of guns in the house—mainly in one wall-length cabinet in a bedroom and also under the house. On the first day of filming, the Secret Service agents were mortified when they discovered the guns during a final once-over, but it was too late to change locations, so two agents were then posted at the door of the bedroom during the filming.[112]

Different topics were covered on different days, and the day before the Watergate session commenced, Nixon asked his barber, Ken Allan, how he should handle the issue. Allan's advice was simple: "Don't be a Philadelphia lawyer about it, Mr. President. Just say you screwed up."[113] On May 4, 1977, when the Frost-Nixon interviews aired, the nation watched as Nixon admitted guilt, expressed remorse, and apologized: "I let down my friends. I let down the country. I let down our system of government and the dreams of all those young people that ought to get into government but think it's all too corrupt. . . . I let the American people down. And I have to carry that burden with me for the rest of my life."[114] Nixon did not watch the interviews, citing the Old Testament advice to Lot's wife, "Never look back." But fifty-five million Americans watched the Frost-Nixon interviews, and afterward, polls showed that 44 percent felt more sympathetic toward Nixon.[115]

The Nixons' personal life included several memorable events during this period. The family had an enjoyable July 4, 1976, bicentennial weekend, including Friday evening at El Adobe, followed by a Saturday dinner hosted by Ken Allan in the Grand Ballroom of the Newport Beach Marriott. On Monday they drove to Jack and Helene Drown's home for daughter Julie's twenty-eighth birthday party.[116] Nixon had fun, mimicking Henry Kissinger and discussing politics, and later joked about Julie's birth in Washington: "It was hot as hell. There was no air conditioning then." Pat was at Columbia Hospital, where "most of the doctors were Communists or incompetents or worse, but we had gotten Pat a good Republican doctor. So I went up to the hospital room . . . and the doctor said, 'Dick, you've got a great big beautiful baby girl.'" Then he winked at Julie, saying, "And she's still my great big beautiful baby girl."[117]

Two days later, in the afternoon of July 7, Pat had been reading *The Final Days* by Bob Woodward and Carl Bernstein, then joined Dick for a swim, during which she suffered a mild stroke. The next morning Dick, recognizing there was a problem, immediately arranged for her to be taken to Long Beach Memorial Hospital.[118] Dick spent every day with Pat and was always upbeat, kissing her on the cheek, slipping his hand into her left hand, and asking, "Well, let me feel your grip."[119]

In the months that followed, Pat diligently undertook a physical therapy regimen, working daily to recover from the effects of the stroke. During this time, Southern California's local communities came together for Pat, and the following spring, on March 25, 1977, Whittier dedicated and named a fountain in her honor. One evening the Nixons drove to Whittier to view the fountain, which they thought was beautiful.[120] Later that summer the Nixons dedicated a wishing well made of hand-painted tiles to the Patricia Nixon Elementary School, with a plaque that reads, "May all your good wishes come true."[121]

Meanwhile, Nixon continued working on his memoirs. Not surprisingly, the most difficult part for him was Watergate, which Nixon hated thinking and writing about. There were many facts he didn't know, a sentiment reflected in his initial description of Watergate: "It was like a gnat buzzing in front of my eyes. I kept saying, 'Bob, take care of it.' But the gnat kept getting bigger, and one day, the gnat swallowed me."[122] However, Nixon was diligent and sat working with assistants for hours. Diane Sawyer set the record with a six-and-a-half-hour session with no break, not even to use the restroom.[123] Later Nixon reflected that writing the book "provided the therapy that was needed for a full spiritual recovery by enabling me to put Watergate behind me."[124] For the final editing, he worked with Robert Markel, vice president of Grosset & Dunlap, and even had him over for dinner one night. Markel recalled that Nixon was in high spirits: "Over Alaskan king crab and two bottles of '55 Chateau Margaux, Nixon held forth on foreign affairs, pausing now and again to swap mildly dirty cracks about Barbara Walters with Manolo in Spanish."[125]

In late 1978 Ken Allan helped arrange a Republican Party fund-raiser at California Committee member Athalie Clarke's house in nearby Corona Del Mar.[126] The party was limited to fifty couples, who paid $1,000 per person.[127] John Wayne greeted Nixon with a bear hug and later presented him with a Boehm sculpture of a horse, saying, "You know, Mr. President, it's kinda ironic giving this horse to you after the rough ride you been having in Washington." Nixon laughed, held up the horse, and replied, "You never know, one day this horse may gallop again."[128] Nixon enjoyed the event so much that he even suggested he host a party at La Casa Pacifica, and shortly thereafter Pat and Richard began entertaining at their home.[129]

In celebration of San Clemente's fiftieth anniversary, the Nixons opened La Casa Pacifica to the public on February 26, 1978, during which time 7,800 visitors toured the grounds.[130] On May 21 they hosted a release party for Nixon's *Memoirs*, which sold 365,000 hardback copies in six months, making it the best-selling presidential autobiography of the twentieth century.[131] The following weekend Pat and Richard welcomed all the Vietnam POWs to their home.[132] Initially, the POWs had been planning a reunion in Los Angeles and wanted Nixon to join them, but once he heard their plans, Nixon insisted he host the event at La Casa Pacifica, giving the POWs the run of the property.[133]

Nixon loved baseball, especially the Angels, and its owner, Gene Autry, was a longtime California Committee friend. Nixon's chief of staff, Jack Brennan, was a member of the Angels' advisory board, and one night after a game, Brennan approached Autry in the parking lot on the way to his car and asked if he would invite Nixon to a game. Autry replied that President Nixon "was always welcome at Angel Stadium," so in June 1978 Brennan arranged for Nixon to take in a game from Autry's private box.[134] Nixon cheered on the home team and sang "Take Me Out to the Ball Game" during the seventh-inning stretch, but more important to Brennan, "President Nixon was welcomed very warmly by everyone from the elevator operator to the ushers and especially by the fans in attendance. This gave Nixon much needed confidence."[135] Nixon attended several more games that season, sitting behind the Angels' dugout with the crowd.[136]

John Moynihan, Gene Autry's personal assistant, saw Nixon simply as "a real pleasant guy who was always a gentleman."[137] Whenever the team invited Nixon to visit the locker room, Moynihan was impressed at how Nixon "never walked with an aide. No one feeding him information. He was really good."[138] Nixon could engage any team member in a discussion of his statistics as a player. More than one astonished player commented to Moynihan, "How the hell does he know me?"[139]

In 1979 Nixon bought season tickets and attended twenty games, of which the Angels won fourteen. Nixon explained his dedication: "Donny Baylor [an Angels outfielder] tells me he needs me here to get those hits. So if it takes me to be here, I'll drop whatever I'm doing to come out."[140] The team reciprocated, and when they won the Western Division, the players invited Nixon into the clubhouse to celebrate, even pouring champagne over his head.[141]

On August 15, 1978, the Nixon family reached a milestone in Southern California when Jennie Elizabeth Eisenhower was born to Julie and David at San Clemente General Hospital. Nixon wrote to his first granddaughter:

> In the years ahead you will have many happy moments. But in life you must expect some disappointments and sadness. At such times

you will always be sustained by the fact that so many people love you so much. We all look forward to the excitement of watching you grow into a lovely young lady. Your Great Grandfather, President Eisenhower, had the great gift of being able to light up a room with his smile. My fondest wish, which I know will come true, is that you have that same gift. Whatever you do, where ever you go, and whatever you become, we shall always be proud of you. RN.[142]

Richard showed off his new granddaughter at every opportunity, and three more grandchildren soon followed. Being a grandfather added a new dimension to Nixon's life. Ken Khachigian was touched by "how sweet Nixon was with his grandchildren [and] how he talked to them—his voice." He recalled, "When his grandson Christopher was born, he had an otherworldly look on his face when he saw Christopher."[143] Nixon was fond of quoting former Bulgarian president Todor Zhivkov: "You are a very rich man. Having grandchildren is the greatest wealth a man can have." He also reflected on how he hoped he could be an influence, just as his grandmother Almira Milhous had been for him: "She was an inspiration to me and I hope that years later my four grandchildren will conclude that Mrs. Nixon, who is an excellent grandmother, and I have been an inspiration to them."[144]

Nixon knew his greatest accomplishments were in foreign affairs and refused to let his resignation impair the progress made with China. In February 1976 he and Pat had visited China and met with its leadership, and on his return, Nixon had briefed Brent Scowcroft, national security advisor to President Ford.[145] Later he had encouraged China's minister of culture to allow his friend Frank Sinatra to appear in concerts in China.[146] Now, on November 29, 1978, Nixon traveled to England, where he addressed the Oxford Union. Ken Khachigian, who accompanied Nixon, described the setting: "Oxford was crazy—it was wild. There was no sound system. It was a dank sort of old place. There is a building behind the Oxford Union, and there were students in that building shouting and yelling throughout Nixon's talk. But he just worked his way through his speech."[147] Nixon declared to the audience, "My political life is over, but so long as I have breath in my body I am going to talk about the great issues that affect the world. I'm not going to keep my mouth shut. I am going to speak out for peace and freedom." Regarding Watergate, Nixon said, "Some people say I didn't handle it properly and they're right. I screwed it up. And I paid the price. Mea culpa. But let's get on to my achievements. You'll be here in the year 2000 and will see how I'm regarded then."[148] Khachigian thought "it was the most extraordinary thing" he'd ever seen.[149]

While in London, as Nixon dined with former Labor prime minister Harold Wilson, he observed, "Well, Harold, you and I are two surviving members of a small club. We have held real power but now we're out." Nixon then asked, "But what I really want to know from my fellow club member is how do you fill your days? Do you read? Do you write? Are you preparing some great testament?" Wilson replied: "As a matter of fact, Dick, I'm spending a lot of time on Gilbert and Sullivan." In return, Nixon commented, "I'm quite a Gilbert and Sullivan buff myself. In my college days I was one of the stage managers for a couple of productions—*Pinafore* and the *Pirates of Penzance*." Wilson rose to the challenge: "When I was a lad I served a term / As office boy to an Attorney's firm." Nixon joined in: "I cleaned the windows and I swept the floor / And I polished up the handle of the big front door." The former leaders continued together, "I polished up that handle so carefullee / that now I am the ruler of the Queen's Navee." They continued, concluding after four verses, "Stick close to your desks and never go to sea / And you all may be rulers of the Queen's Navee."[150]

At the conclusion of his trip to England, Nixon summed up his thoughts on staying in the political arena:

> Two things really sort out the men from the boys. Belief in the cause, and determination to fight for it. You have to be ready to fight through all life's ups and downs. There is really no such thing as a down because the only thing that finishes a politician is quitting. I've been down a few times so I know. Disappointment doesn't finish you. Being in what your enemies call disgrace doesn't finish you. Only quitting does that. You have to stay in the arena. . . . Even when you're down and bleeding and being kicked in the nuts, you have to get up and fight back. You can always do it. And when you feel you can't go on, you must do it. If the cause is great enough, it's worth fighting back . . . that's what makes a politician.[151]

In December 1978 Nixon started to exchange private correspondence with President Jimmy Carter, and six months later, less than five years after his resignation, Carter, a Democrat, invited him to attend a White House dinner.[152] Having returned to public life, in mid-1979 the Nixons realized that it was time to move from their beloved Southern California. Their daughters lived on the East Coast, and the Nixons wanted to be close to them.[153] Still, they intended to leave on their terms and in their style.

In May 1979 Nixon made his last visit to Whittier College, attending his forty-fifth reunion at the home of classmate Roy Newsom, now president of the college.[154] Nixon presented Newsom with a watch and also brought each class member six highball glasses embossed with the presidential seal. Afterward, Nixon wrote a personal letter to Alice Newsom, thanking her for arranging the party.[155] That July Pat and Dick hosted a poolside reception for fifteen astronauts and three hundred guests to commemorate the tenth anniversary of the Apollo moon landing.[156] The event was attended by many Hollywood friends, but unfortunately, John Wayne was not present, having succumbed to cancer a few days earlier.[157]

A month after Wayne's death the Nixons made a $100,000 donation to the American Cancer Society in honor of John Wayne and several others.[158] Such generosity was not limited to friends. John Tunney, a Democrat, was the junior senator from California when, on October 31, 1973, he called for Nixon to resign the presidency, one of the first senators to make such a public declaration. When Tunney's father, legendary boxer Gene Tunney, died in 1978, Nixon wrote to Tunney, expressing sympathy and including a significant contribution to his father's favorite charity. The letter brought John to tears.[159]

One of Nixon's favorite restaurants was Perino's, where he had celebrated with Haldeman and Kissinger following the July 1971 announcement of the breakthrough with China, and now, in August 1979, Pat Hillings hosted a final dinner party for Nixon there.[160] The celebrations continued over Labor Day weekend, when Pat and Richard hosted several parties at La Casa Pacifica. The first was for soon-to-be-departing staff, and another was in celebration of John Mitchell's birthday, with 250 guests, where Nixon toasted, "John Mitchell has friends, and he stands by them."[161] The next day the couple hosted the Angels and five hundred California Committee friends, neighbors, and community members whom the Nixons simply wanted to thank for their hospitality.[162]

On November 25 Pat and Dick opened La Casa Pacifica to the Republican Party for a final fundraising party.[163] At $1,000 per couple, the event was an immediate sellout as four hundred revelers joined the Nixons for one last farewell.[164] During the party, Nixon told his guests that his heart would always be in California, where "it all began."[165]

The Nixons' last weeks in Southern California before moving to New York were a whirlwind of activity. For Dick's sixty-seventh birthday, on January 9, 1980, his staff gave him a traditional gift of a bouquet of red roses, one for each year of his life. The Nixons had small get-togethers, meeting with Richard's aunts Jane Beeson and Olive Marshburn, classmates Nate George and Bill Brock from Whittier College, and even his first-grade teacher from Yorba Linda.[166] As a boy, Richard had made the drive to Arizona many times to visit Hannah and his ailing brother, Harold. He had also toured the Southwest during his college days when competing in debate, back when the roads were not paved and traveling by car was arduous. Now, knowing these were his last days living in Southern California, Nixon borrowed George Argyros's motor home and hit the open road with Bebe Rebozo. The initial plan was to tour Nevada and Arizona, although the trip had to be cut short because of bad weather.[167]

Southern California had cocooned Richard Nixon, allowing him time to heal. The county of his birth provided the perfect setting for his rebirth. Nixon loved La Casa Pacifica and was known to ask, "Isn't this marvelous?" while standing on the bluffs overlooking the sea. Then he would comment, "This is a wonderful, wonderful place."[168] The post–White House years at La Casa Pacifica provided him with the time and space to recover, which ultimately allowed Nixon to reenter public life on his own terms.

Most of those who knew him well were not disillusioned with Nixon, the man. Saddened, yes, but they still knew him to be a fundamentally decent person. As Roy Newsom stated, "I feel that Nixon is as honest as I am."[169] And as he ventured out, the community welcomed him. But Orange County was not the power center that New York City was, and Nixon never intended to stay at La Casa Pacifica permanently. He knew he would inevitably return to New York, because the very qualities that allowed Nixon to heal also began to strangle him. Pat told Julie their reason for leaving Southern California: "We are just dying here slowly."[170]

As a former world leader and the most significant U.S. politician in the second half of the twentieth century, Nixon prepared to return to the world stage, having rehabilitated himself. His plan was simple and straightforward: "I shall continue to speak up for the policies that will lead to peace and freedom as long as I live. If people are interested in what I have to say, they can tune in. If they aren't, they do not have to. I intend to continue to speak out on the important issues for those who do want to hear my views."[171] With that the Nixons departed California on February 9, 1980, five years to the day from the end of his transition from the presidency.[172]

EIGHTEEN

Evening

1980–94

Immediately after moving to the East Coast, Nixon began planning a permanent presence in Southern California with the development of the Richard Nixon Library and Museum. Whittier had long assumed that the library would be built on land above the college. San Clemente proposed a site as well, which made sense given its proximity to La Casa Pacifica.[1] Then Yorba Linda submitted a proposal for a library site built around Nixon's birthplace.

Nixon made it a point to return to Southern California often. In 1982 he was the guest of honor at an Orange County Republican dinner at the Disneyland Hotel ballroom.[2] Continuing his personal choice of refusing honoraria, Nixon paid for his own airfare and hotel lodging, and he even purchased a $1,500 table for the Whittier College Young Republicans.[3] Sitting at the head table with former Orange County Republican chairperson Lois Lundberg, he was about to get up to speak when he suddenly leaned over and told Lois, "I have decided to not give the speech I intended. This wonderful group of young people have so moved and inspired me that I intend to talk about youth and the future." He then made a few notes on his dinner program outlining the new speech, which he handed to Lois, saying, "This might be something you might like to have."[4] Following "a dynamic and inspiring speech," he stayed an extra hour and a half to sign autographs for the crowd.[5]

In 1984 Nixon made his last journey through Whittier to speak at the funeral of his aunt Olive Marshburn, attending her services at the First Friends Church, where his parents had met on Valentine's Day some eighty years earlier.[6] While he was in Southern California, Franklin Roosevelt's eldest son, Jimmy, a longtime friend, arranged for Nixon to speak at Chapman College before the largest crowd gathered since his resignation ten years earlier.[7] The Hutton Sports

Center could accommodate less than half the 6,500 seats requested, so screens had to be set up on campus for the enthusiastic overflow crowds to view the speech.[8] Although Nixon was relaxed as he discussed the outline of his approach to world peace, the day had not begun this way. Seventy-one-year-old Richard Nixon had to descend seventeen flights of stairs at the Irvine Marriott after a dryer malfunctioned and caught fire, and the fire department ordered the hotel evacuated.[9]

Time magazine White House correspondent Hugh Sidey, who had written Nixon off in 1974 for "charting himself a course straight into the sloughs of history," now proclaimed the man a "strategic genius" after reading Nixon's books *The Real War* and *Real Peace*.[10] For the ten-year anniversary of Nixon's resignation, John Gruber of the *New York Times* wrote, "A decade later he has emerged at seventy-one years of age as an elder statesman, commentator on foreign and domestic affairs, adviser to world leaders, a multimillionaire and a successful author and lecturer honored by audiences at home and abroad."[11]

Even when unable to attend special events, Nixon's presence was felt from a distance. In 1986, as the Orange County Republican Party planned to roast Chairman Tom Fuentes, Nixon wrote a consoling letter to Fuentes. Nixon understood he was to be "raked over the coals" by his so-called friends, concluding, "As one who knows a little about being on the receiving end, I wanted to let you know that my sympathies will be with you. But if they get too rough, let me know. I'll send [G. Gordon] Liddy to take care of them."[12]

California Committee member Gavin Herbert and his wife, Ninetta, joined Richard for dinner one evening. Nixon sensed that Ninetta was nervous in his presence, so he started the conversation by asking her what she thought of women's fashion. Nixon maintained that he could tell where a woman was from based on her fashion. Herbert later reflected fondly, "Can you imagine talking twenty minutes about women's fashion with Richard Nixon?"[13] Nixon's knowledge of women's fashion was no surprise to Donna Kendall, the daughter of Nixon longtime friend Don Kendall. After Whittier College, Donna acquired a Halston fashion shop on Madison Avenue and Sixty-Eighth Street, which happened to be along Nixon's favorite walking route. Nixon occasionally stopped in, and Donna recognized that "Nixon liked women and was interested in women. If something interested him then he took the time to learn about it. He had intellectual curiosity."[14]

When Bruce Herschensohn, a commentator with ABC TV in Los Angeles, and his good friend, television anchor Jerry Dunphy, were in New York, Nixon took them to lunch at 21. According to Herschensohn, "Nixon was great in restaurants. He'd go up to a table, point at a drink, and tell the patron, 'You better be careful; those things creep up on you.'"[15] After lunch, when they exited 21, a large crowd gathered around Nixon. The police soon came for crowd control, and Herschensohn did exactly what he had when Nixon was in office, telling him, "Mr. President, you are going to be late for your next meeting," providing Nixon a graceful exit. But this time Nixon looked at Herschensohn and said, "Cancel it." Herschensohn walked back into 21, waited a sufficient amount of time to cancel the fictitious meeting, then rejoined Nixon on the street. Nixon asked, "Did you cancel the meeting?" "Yes," replied Herschensohn, to which Nixon responded, "Good, thank you."

By the 1980s George Argyros had acquired the Seattle Mariners baseball team. When Nixon visited his younger brother Ed in Seattle, Argyros arranged to take him to a game. Sitting together in the owner's box in the front row, Argyros worried about how the fans might react to his guest, but when the cameras showed Nixon on the big screen in the Kingdome, the crowd gave him a standing ovation. "He waved to all the fans, and it was just terrific," said Argyros. After the game, Argyros took Nixon into the player's clubhouse, where he spoke to every player, the manager, and the coaches and actually knew the names and statistics of the twenty-five players. "They were all thrilled to have the president in the locker room," said Argyros. "They loved it, and so did he. He was a big hit!"[16]

Of Nixon's California Committee friends and supporters, Ronald Reagan achieved the greatest political success. In Nixon's eyes, Reagan was "one of the most decent men" he had known, and when Reagan was elected president, Nixon called his old friend and addressed him as Mr. President, to which Reagan humbly replied, "Now, Dick, we've known each other a long time."[17] When Reagan was running for reelection, Nixon advised him on his campaign team:

You need at least two or three nut cutters who will take on the op-position so that you can take the high road. I know that because of your innate decency and loyalty to your friends that you are repelled at the thought of dropping people who are loyal to you but who are not effective on the stump or on TV. But I urge you to bite the bullet and do what is necessary to field a tough, intelligent, hard-hitting team for the 1984 campaign. . . . I speak from experience. Some charge me with being too tough on subordinates. In retrospect had I been tougher I might have avoided some of the problems which plagued me at the last.[18]

In February 1987, after Ronald Reagan's former national security advisor, Robert McFarlane, attempted suicide by drug overdose, his first visitor at Bethesda Naval Hospital was Richard Nixon, who had flown down from New Jersey just to see him. For McFarlane, Nixon "was just unbelievably sympathetic. He urged me to remember that Churchill and de Gaulle had suffered their 'black dogs' and said that even though I would be portrayed by the media as a weak figure, I would overcome the setback of my suicide attempt." They talked about prayer and the Bible, to which McFarlane had turned for support. Nixon told him, "That's good. You need an anchor. Your strong faith will take you through this." Nixon asked a number of questions that got McFarlane thinking about what he was going to do when he got out of the hospital. "I recall the warmth in his voice when he said, 'From now on, don't look back. Get busy, go earn yourself some money. You've done the right things in the past, now look to your future. You can do it.' Coming from him, I can't tell you what a tonic the encouragement was."[19]

Sadly, in June 1987, after a four-year battle, Richard's brother Don succumbed to cancer.[20] However much he would miss his brother, Nixon was thankful that Don's suffering was over and reflected, "I was fortunate to have been raised in a close and loving family and will always cherish the memories of those years when we were growing up together in Yorba Linda and Whittier."[21]

While certain chapters of his life drew to a close, intellectually Nixon felt the 1980s were the most vital, creative period of his life.[22] He received over 6,400 speaking invitations from all over the United States and 1,200 from abroad, and he wrote five books.[23] John Taylor, who assisted Nixon on several books and served as his chief of staff, noted, "The more time I spent with him, the more I realized that here was an extraordinarily powerful and unorthodox intellect which simply had to exercise itself."[24]

Ultimately, Yorba Linda was selected as the site for the Richard Nixon Library and Museum, which was to be built by the Nixon Foundation entirely from $25 million in private funding.[25] When Nixon established the foundation back in August 1983, he had relied on both of his brothers and his California Committee friends, among others, as original members of the board.[26] Now Nixon tapped Hugh Hewitt to oversee the construction and grand opening, and on December 2, 1988, Julie Nixon Eisenhower hosted the groundbreaking celebration with Henry Kissinger and 1,500 guests.[27] There was an air of excitement as Yorba Linda even declared Nixon's birthday a holiday.[28]

On July 19, 1990, the Richard Nixon Library and Museum was dedicated. Joining Nixon and his family for the grand opening ceremonies were former administration officials; California governor George Deukmejian; Presidents Ford, Reagan, and Bush; California Committee friends and supporters; and fifty thousand well-wishers.[29] Vicki Carr sang the national anthem, followed by Billy Graham giving the invocation.[30] Each president spoke of Nixon with equal parts humor and praise. President Ford began: "Mr. President, Mr. President, Mr. President, if I overlooked any President, please stand up."[31] He then looked at Nixon, with a nod to his beautifully restored birthplace, and told his longtime friend, "You can come home again."[32] Next, Ronald Reagan quipped, "Much has been written about Richard Nixon, some of it has even been true," before complimenting him: "Richard Nixon is a patriot who believes in American people. Richard Nixon is a man who understands the world, a man whose accomplishments of his foreign policy will go down in history. His foreign policy is universally acknowledged as brilliant. I don't think it is an exaggeration to say the world is a better place—a safer place because of Richard Nixon."[33] Sitting president George Bush amplified Reagan's words: "His actions not only changed the course of America, but the entire world. He signed the first agreement to limit arms. His trip to China ended two decades of isolation. He was a true architect of peace. Richard Nixon came from the heart of America."[34]

An ebullient Nixon told the crowd, "We have been to Versailles, we've been to Westminster, to the Kremlin, to the Great Wall of China . . . but nothing, nothing we have ever seen matches this moment to be welcomed home again so warmly on this day by our friends." Pointing to the house in which he was born, Nixon continued: "Let me tell you, it's a long way from Yorba Linda to the White House. I believe in the American Dream because I've seen it come true in my own life. I want your dreams to come true as well. You will suffer disappointments in life and sometimes you will be very discouraged. But the greatest sadness is to travel through life without knowing either victory or defeat."[35]

That evening there was a dinner in honor of Pat and Richard's fiftieth wedding anniversary at the Century Plaza Hotel in Los Angeles.[36] Over the postpresidency years, Pat was known to comment to friends that she never expected to live long enough to see her husband's reputation restored, but as the day drew to a close, she joyfully told Loie Gaunt, "I'm tired but I'm happy tired."[37] In full agreement, Nixon complimented his longtime advance man, Ron Walker, saying, "This is one of the happiest days of my life."[38]

Nixon hosted events whenever he was in town, including dinners and other gatherings with California Committee members such as Bob Hope. One such evening, Lois Lundberg presented Nixon with some expensive crystal. He opened the gift, then looked at his guests with a smile on his face and said, "Oh my. This is so beautiful. Do you think I could wrap it up and give it to Pat so she'll think I gave it to her?" His friends roared with laughter.[39]

In November 1991 the Nixons attended the star-studded opening of the Ronald Reagan Presidential Library, where Nixon saw many old friends and invited them to a reception he was having that evening for the docents at his own library. Many, including Bob Hope, Buddy Ebsen, and Arnold Schwarzenegger, joined Nixon to thank the volunteers at his library. In the summer of 1992 Nixon and his son-in-law David Eisenhower, both dedicated baseball fans, hosted an All-Time Baseball Greats luncheon that included many Hall of Fame players, from Johnny Bench and Rollie Fingers to Bob Feller and Ted Williams.

Richard Nixon, one of the most important political figures of the twentieth century, was aging gracefully.[40] Reflecting on his life in his 1990 book, *In the Arena*, he quoted Sophocles, "One must wait until the evening to see how splendid the day has been," adding:

I can look back and say that the day has indeed been splendid. In view of the ordeals I have endured, this may strike some as being an incredible conclusion. I believe, however, that the richness of life is not measured by its length but by its breath, its height, and its depth. . . . I have never lost sight of my destination—a world in which peace and freedom can live together. I have won some great victories and suffered some devastating defeats. But win or lose, I feel fortunate to come to that time in life when I can finally enjoy what my Quaker grandmother would have called "peace at the center."[41]

Now that he could "finally enjoy . . . peace at the center," Nixon expressed his humor more frequently. One of his favorite holidays was Halloween, and each year he opened his yard to hundreds of children and their parents as he passed out candy.[42] When one of the trick-or-treaters approached him wearing a Nixon mask, the former president joyfully shook his hand, telling the man, "Well, Mr. President, it's a pleasure to meet you."[43] In his late seventies, Nixon liked to tell the story about how, when he developed a heart fibrillation problem, his doctor recommended he quit drinking alcohol. When he shared the suggestion with Bebe Rebozo, his friend quipped, "My God, get a second opinion *at once!*"[44]

When Nixon was invited to address Congress in early 1993, making a play on MacArthur's famous words, he declared from the House floor, "Old politicians sometimes die, but they never fade away!"[45] Nevertheless, the reality was that both Nixons, now in their ninth decade, were indeed fading. Pat, a lifelong smoker, was diagnosed with emphysema in the early 1990s. Her last public appearance was at the dedication of the Ronald Reagan Presidential Library in November 1991, where she collapsed in the unusual heat.[46] By December 1992 she was very weak, and in March 1993 Pat entered the first of several hospitalizations as her condition worsened.[47]

For years Pat had always rebounded, fighting to regain her strength, but that March she was diagnosed with lung cancer. Pat told Dick, "I'm going to make it," but he was inconsolable. Monica Crowley, his foreign policy assistant at the time, described his reaction: "Nixon made no attempt to conceal his despair. Sadness crept into everything he did and every word he spoke. He often left sentences unfinished and walked aimlessly down the hallways of his office and home. He neither ate nor slept well. He stared out of windows, and he paced."[48]

Nixon, who did not believe in funerals, knew he had to begin planning for Pat's service.[49] As her condition worsened, she fought even harder to live. Despite many trips to the hospital, Richard always brought her home, where he enjoyed taking her out onto their patio so she could enjoy the sunshine.[50] All the family could do was to make Pat comfortable as she slowly slipped away before their eyes, although she was coherent virtually to the end, even remembering their fifty-third wedding anniversary on June 21.[51] Early the following morning, Pat was sitting in a chair with her eyes closed, but she perked up on hearing Richard's voice. His last words to his wife were: "Your family loves you, the country loves you and people all over the world love you." Pat smiled at her husband's tribute, as he leaned over and kissed her forehead.[52] She then slipped into a coma, and at 5:45 a.m. on June 22, 1993, Pat Nixon passed away.

Married for fifty-three years and one day, Pat and Dick had a marriage described by friends as "a very incredible relationship."[53] John Taylor expressed Dick's devotion to his wife: "Without question, the person whose company and opinion President Nixon valued most while I was his chief of staff was Mrs. Nixon's. His latter years have been characterized by the extreme attentiveness of his feelings toward her."[54] Billy Graham officiated at a private funeral service for Pat at the Nixon Library on June 26, with 350 in attendance, including Presidents Reagan and Ford.[55] As Graham escorted him to his seat before the ceremony, Nixon broke down, devastated at losing the love of his life.[56] California governor Pete Wilson and Sen. Robert Dole eulogized Pat. Following the service, Nixon approached the Reagans, and overcome with grief, he cried on Nancy's shoulder as Ron put his arm around his old friend.[57]

Just as they always had, the Nixon family greeted all their guests, and then Dick spoke lovingly of Pat, telling the guests how it was Pat's strength that carried him through the fund broadcast in 1952 and the dark days following his resignation: "Had it not been for Pat, I would not have made it politically or physically. She never gave up." He described her incredible willpower, working every day with a spinning wheel in the courtyard of La Casa Pacifica to rehabilitate herself after she suffered a stroke. He also told of their relationship with their children and grandchildren and how they "were their close friends, not distant grandparents."[58] Nixon then concluded:

How would Pat like to be remembered? Seventy-five years ago in that little house here in which I was born in 1913, I used to hear the train whistle in the night and dream of places far away I hoped to visit someday. 1952 was my favorite campaign. It was the last whistle stop campaign. As the train pulled into the station, Jack Drown would put a recording of the campaign song on the public address system. Some of you may remember the lyrics: "I like the sunshine of your smile." I hope you will remember this day, the spectacular beauty of the flowers, the superb music, the eloquence of the eulogies. But above all, when you think of Pat, I hope you will always remember the sunshine of her smile. She would like that.[59]

In the months following Pat's death, Richard's pain turned to loneliness. When Monica Crowley visited him at home, he told her, "There's no one here. Can you hear how quiet it is? Listen to that silence. My God!"[60] He had a housekeeper to help cook his meals, but otherwise he was completely alone. On January 20, 1994, President Nixon celebrated the twenty-fifth anniversary of his inauguration with a luncheon at the Nixon Library. He was joined by numerous California Committee members, including Roy Newsom, who was ill and had to be helped to the podium so that he could have his picture taken with Nixon. As the two old friends reminisced, they had tears in their eyes.[61]

George Argyros related how, in the months that followed, Nixon knew the end was near: "Nixon called and asked if I would meet with him. He wanted to discuss some things that were very personal to him. He said 'George, I have to see you.' I said 'Sure. When?' He replied 'As soon as you can.'"[62] Yet Nixon still maintained a heavy workload, completing his tenth book, *Beyond Peace*, and traveling to Russia in March. Even in his final years, Nixon kept up with his California Committee friends and supporters, calling or writing personal notes when any of his intimates experienced a significant life event. As old friends passed away, he contacted their families to tell them how much their loved ones meant to him.[63] Julie Schlesinger worked for the Nixons in their home, and when her husband, Edward, suffered a stroke ten months after Pat's death, Dick sat down and penned him a note of encouragement.[64] That very afternoon, on April 18, Nixon suffered a massive stroke, and for two days he was unable to see or speak before lapsing into a coma on April 20.

As a man who always thought to write to others, Nixon was repaid for his many years of kindness with an outpouring of letters, beginning with Ronald Reagan, who told his friend, "There's no doubt you have the tenacity and stubbornness to recover from this setback, Dick. You're the feistiest one of us all and you've got a huge cheering section rooting for you."[65] Two days later Richard Nixon died at 9:08 p.m. on Friday, April 22, 1994.[66]

From his Quaker youth, Nixon rarely displayed his emotions and maintained a lifelong humility that did not require fanfare.[67] Not wanting a state funeral, Nixon had prepared what he believed would be a simple service beside his birthplace, yet a grateful nation held a state funeral for him in Yorba Linda.[68] Presidents Clinton, Bush, Reagan, Carter, and Ford attended, as did numerous politicians, foreign dignitaries, and California Committee friends and supporters. For Whittier classmate Roy Newsom, whose health continued to decline, the decision to attend was easy. He told his wife, Alice, "I *have* to go to the service."[69]

Bringing his life full circle, Nixon's remains arrived in Southern California on Tuesday, April 26, 1994, at the El Toro Marine Corps Air Station, on the very same plane in which he had flown to California after resigning the presidency two decades before. As he lay in state at the Nixon Library, more than seventy-five thousand people waited in line throughout the day, into the night, and through the next morning to pay their respects, despite intermittent rain.[70]

As with Pat's service, Billy Graham officiated. He told those assembled, "The world has lost a great citizen, America has lost a great statesman, and those of us who knew him have lost a personal friend."[71] Along with President Clinton, Henry Kissinger and Sen. Bob Dole eulogized President Nixon. Dole was a fellow veteran whose right hand had been permanently injured in World War II. He had to offer his left hand in greeting, so invariably there were awkward moments when the recipient realized Dole couldn't shake with his right hand. Dole's fondest memories of Nixon were from the early days of their relationship, when he was a junior senator from Kansas. Whenever Dole entered the Oval Office, he recalled, Nixon always jumped up, walked around his desk, and put out his left hand to greet his friend. "It's those little things in life that count," Dole reflected.[72]

Empathy and attention to detail were lessons Nixon learned early in life. While he was attending Whittier College, chemistry professor Gus Ostrom gave a chapel lecture titled "Polish the Heel of Your Shoe," in which he explained that it was the little things in life that truly mattered.[73] Nixon learned empathy firsthand at an early age, having an uncle who had lost his right hand in a brush cutter. Then at college, Nixon was in student government along with classmate Ralph Veady, who had lost both legs in an accident.[74] From these and other experiences, Nixon knew to accept all people as respected equals, treating them in a manner that made them feel comfortable.[75]

In honor of his upbringing, the Nixon Library sits on the nine acres originally purchased by Frank and Hannah. The architecture has its roots in Quaker simplicity, with Nixon's birthplace, on a hill above the library, serving as the emotional anchor of the design. A long reflecting pool serves as the axis, leading the eye straight from Nixon's boyhood home to his library. Architect Richard Poulos described his vision: "Nixon's journey from humble obscurity to national leadership is a central symbol in the way the library is laid out."[76] According to Poulos, Nixon had two demands regarding the architectural character of the library: "He wanted a traditional, not a modernist building, and he insisted that the library create a welcoming atmosphere that would encourage people to visit and often return."[77]

The grounds are beautifully landscaped, with a rose garden, an amphitheater, and the reflecting pool, and throughout the campus are subtle reminders of Nixon's numerous relationships. The rose garden, outside the Pat Nixon Gallery and adjacent to Pat and Richard's final resting place, is named for Gavin Herbert, who faithfully maintained the grounds at La Casa Pacifica. Col. Gene Boyer, who flew the Nixons from the White House South Lawn on August 9, 1974, tracked down that same helicopter and painstakingly restored it to its original condition, then arranged for its permanent display on the grounds. Several California Committee members have designated areas that bear their names. The Loker Center was named for Katherine Loker, a member of Nixon's California Committee for over forty years, who donated the funds for a forty-seven-thousand-square-foot exact re-creation of the East Room of the White House. The center also includes conference rooms and a gallery for traveling exhibits.[78] The Annenberg Court, named for Walter and Leonore Annenberg, serves as the entrance pavilion to the Loker Center.

The Nixons' graves are marked with simple headstones, and just beyond where they are buried is Nixon's birthplace. Inside, the furnishings are original, thanks in large part to the painstaking work of Don and Clara Jane Nixon. In the front bedroom, where Nixon was born, the bed has the original wrought iron frame. Back when Dick was first running for Congress, Clara Jane had cut the legs off the headboard and put it in her garden to grow sweet peas, since Dick liked them so much. Once the birthplace was being restored, she located the headboard in a barn at the Milhous home, took it to an antique dealer friend, found a match, and had legs welded back on. After Hannah died, Dick had told Clara Jane that he wanted only one item from their parents: the clock that Franklin and Almira Milhous had given Frank and Hannah on their wedding day. That clock now sits on the fireplace mantle.[79]

Frank and Hannah Nixon had taught their children their love and commitment to family and friends through their actions. They welcomed nephew Russell Harrison Jr., then a teenager, into their home after Hannah's sister Elizabeth died and her husband remarried, causing friction with the young man.[80] Likewise, they opened their home to young Herman Brannon when his family fell on hard economic times. When a nephew was killed in an accident, they stepped in to arrange the burial and ensured that the party at fault underwrote the expenses.[81] When niece Lucille Parsons was to be married, her father disapproved, so Frank and Hannah baked the wedding cake for Lucille's special day.[82] And when neighborhood friend Ralph Palmer was wed, the Nixons gave him a wedding shower.[83]

Hannah and Frank's courtship of four months resulted in a forty-eight-year marriage, ending with Frank's death on September 4, 1956. In that time, they had five boys, three of whom, Dick, Don, and Ed, grew into adulthood and each married the love of his life. Married for fifty-three years, until her death in 1993, Dick and Pat had two children, Tricia and Julie, who both married as young adults, had children, and are still married to their original spouses. Don and Clara Jane wed in 1942 and were together forty-five years, until Don's death in 1987, and Ed and Gay were married nearly fifty-seven years, from 1957 until Gay's death in 2014. Tricia and Julie had each been married only a short while when the scandal of Watergate ravaged the nation. Despite public turmoil, the fact that the Nixon family has not suffered the problems of divorce or alcohol or drug abuse, which have afflicted so many other prominent families, is a genuine testament to the strength and character of their family.

Through the years, particularly after the 1952 fund crisis and the election losses of 1960 and 1962, Pat longed for a life outside of politics, but despite her misgivings, she loved Dick, devoted her life to him, and was his perfect partner.[84] Nixon compared politics to a fast-moving river: "Once you get into this great stream of history, you can't get out. You can drown. Or you can be pulled ashore by the tide. But it is awfully hard to get out when you are in the middle of the stream—if it is intended that you stay there."[85] He viewed politics as "a necessary evil to get the position you need to affect the course of events."[86] Nixon understood that he had the ability to lead and influence our nation's history. Rather than being apprehensive and insecure, he was supremely confident in his abilities.[87]

Because of the way he treated them and others equally, Nixon's staff was incredibly loyal. Evlyn Dorn, who was Nixon's legal secretary in 1939, and Rose Mary Woods, Nixon's assistant since 1951, were dedicated to Nixon for the rest of their lives. Marje Acker and Loie Gaunt were both with Nixon for over forty years, and for Acker, Nixon was "a kind and thoughtful man with incredible self-discipline, a deep inner faith and keen intellect."[88] More than fifteen years after his death, Loie reflected, "It was a wonderful relationship. It meant everything to me. I thought he was the person who could do more for our country than anyone else, and he needed help and I wanted to be a part of that. I did very ordinary things with people in an atmosphere that was very thrilling to be a part of. As a family, I admired them both. They were really wonderful people, and I still feel close to them."[89]

Monica Crowley, who joined his staff in the last years of his life, found Nixon to be "kind, trusting, magnanimous, warm, and witty, willing to share his wisdom, experience, joys, and regrets openly and freely. He was a brilliant teacher and a fine man."[90] This is exactly the person Nixon's friends knew him to be.[91] At the same time, as Richard Spaulding, who had played football with Dick Nixon at Whittier College, reflected, he "wasn't easy to get to know and was easy to misunderstand if you didn't know him fairly well."[92] According to Democrat Charles Rhyne, who knew Nixon as a warmhearted man since their law school days, the majority of the American public did not appreciate Nixon's human nature and compassion.[93] But for those who did know him, as Spaulding pointed out, he "had a flashing smile that suddenly seemed to show you a whole personality."[94] California Committee friend George Argyros, who served as ambassador to Spain in the Reagan administration, succinctly described how Nixon's friends and supporters felt: "He was like an encyclopedia to be with. He was very engaging. He had a great perspective on the world. I really enjoyed our friendship. He was an amazing man. He was sensitive, accomplished, well versed, with a very realistic view of the world."[95]

Although the Watergate scandal destroyed Nixon's second term, his first term was wholly successful and led to an astounding re-election. Coincidentally, in his 1960 biography on Nixon, Bela Kornitzer, who died years before Nixon became president, relayed a story told by celebrated English painter Philip de László: "An art student once produced a portrait which was praised as a great work of art. Shortly, however, the genius of the young artist declined; his works showed signs of mediocrity and, in his later years, he was a failure." When Laszlo was asked for an explanation, he replied, "This young man once produced a masterpiece. Even if all of his subsequent works failed, one must never forget that once in his life he reached perfection."[96]

Over the course of his life, Richard Nixon knew twelve U.S. presidents, and in many ways, he was the Republican response to the Democratic Party's control of the White House over the five terms of Franklin Roosevelt and Harry Truman. In fact, Roosevelt and Nixon were the only U.S. politicians to have their names appear on national ballots five times; Nixon was the only man in history elected twice as both vice president and president; and more people voted for Richard Nixon than for any other U.S. politician.[97] Following his resignation, Richard Nixon never became bitter and never gave up on himself or his beloved country. After a period of time spent healing, he continued to work and speak out, eventually becoming America's respected elder statesman. Over sixty years earlier, when Nixon was graduating from high school, he spoke at his prom as president of the Scholastic Society. In his speech, titled "Leaves and Thorns," Nixon explained to his classmates that life would have its up and downs, and that as "we go for berries we must not mind the thorns."[98] This was how he lived his life.

After seeing Nixon "at the bottom after he almost died," Gavin Herbert could not "imagine anyone being able to come back and gain so much respect," and yet Herbert witnessed Nixon's incredible comeback firsthand.[99] For lifelong friend Hubert Perry, "The very fact that Nixon was able to bounce back from Watergate shows you the extent of his character."[100] As Billy Graham declared at Nixon's funeral, "His public service kept him at the center of events that shaped our destiny."[101] President Bill Clinton echoed this sentiment when, at Nixon's funeral, he said to the world, "May the day of judging President Nixon on anything less than his entire life and career come to a close."

Richard Milhous Nixon was shaped by a pioneer spirit, family-instilled tenacity, loyalty to friends and family, and a tireless work ethic, all founded on his devout faith.[102] He steadfastly rode out his life's adventure to the very end; at the moment he succumbed to a massive stroke, he was reviewing the last round of edits to his eleventh and final book.

Marje Acker, who spent her adult life working with Dick Nixon, summed up her feelings: "I wouldn't trade my life for anything, even if I knew how his term was going to end."[103] Reflecting on the perilous voyage of politics, Nixon liked to quote St. Thomas Aquinas: "If the highest aim of the captain were to preserve his ship, he would keep it in port forever."[104] There were high peaks and deep valleys, times of great personal triumph and dark times that tested his soul, but in these extremes, Richard Nixon was forged. Ultimately, Nixon's legacy was not one of defeat but of perseverance, and California can be proud of its native son, who dedicated his life not merely to leading the country but to changing it for the better.

Richard Milhous Nixon: his name is synonymous with Watergate, the political scandal that continues to loom over Nixon's presidency and tarnish his legacy. As a result, we too often focus on the scandal rather than his achievements, on the controversy surrounding him and not on the man himself. Although many Americans regard this man as a scoundrel, a cheat, and a liar, those who knew him knew that he was none of these. Noting the disparity between the public perception and the private person, Nixon's cousin Jessamyn West, the novelist, observed, "We want the facts to fit the preconceptions. When they don't, it is easier to ignore the facts than to change the preconceptions."[105] To do so is not only historically inaccurate but also an injustice to this man from humble beginnings who rose to our nation's highest office, propelled by his intelligence, sensitivity, and desire to serve the common good.

Notes

Note: All dates are month/day/year.

1. New Beginnings

1. Morris, *Richard Milhous Nixon*, 30; Nixon, *Memoirs*, 8.
2. CSUF, Myra Barton, 6; CSUF, Jane Beeson, 4; WC, Mabel Smith Roberts, 16–17.
3. CSUF, Myra Barton, 4.
4. WC, Elsie Haigler, 6, 17; CSUF, Edith Timberlake, 22.
5. CSUF, Charles Bell, 10; CSUF, Edith Brannon, 5; CSUF, Richard Gauldin, 6.
6. Gen. 3:19 (King James Version); Aitken, *Nixon*, 8.
7. Aitken, *Nixon*, 8.
8. CSUF, Sheldon Beeson, 6; Ambrose, *Nixon*, 1:14; Donald Jackson, "The Young Richard Nixon: His Friends, Teachers, Classmates and Rivals Talk about Him, from the Early Days in Yorba Linda to the Moment He Entered Politics," *Life*, 11/6/1970.
9. WC, Charles E. Cooper, 4.
10. Aitken, *Nixon*, 9.
11. WC, Claren Morris, Richie Morris, Loretta Cook, and Bewley Allen, 7; BK, #2 Hannah Nixon, 9–10; CSUF, Edith Timberlake, 22; WC, Edith Timberlake, Olive Marshburn, and Oscar Marshburn, 1–2.
12. WC, Russell Harrison Sr., 15; WC, #1 Olive and Oscar Marshburn, 2; WC, #3 Olive and Oscar Marshburn, 2; BK, #2 Hannah Nixon, 9–10.
13. CSUF, Ralph Shook, 3–4; WC, Ralph Shook, 15–16; CSUF, Merle West, 6.
14. CSUF, Ralph Shook, 12, 15; CSUF, Edith Timberlake, 27; CSUF, Merle West, 6–7.
15. CSUF, Myra Barton, 11; BK, #2 Hannah Nixon, 10; Kornitzer, *Real Nixon*, 33; "Milhous-Nixon Wedding Solemnized," *Register*, 6/27/1908.
16. WC, Claren Morris, Richie Morris, Loretta Cook, and Bewley Allen, 7.
17. CSUF, Paul Smith, 9; Jackson, "Young Richard Nixon."
18. CSUF, Edith Timberlake, 31.
19. CSUF, Hadley Marshburn, 5; WC, #1 Olive and Oscar Marshburn, 2.
20. CSUF, Edith Timberlake, 31, 35; Nixon Family Collection, box 1:19, Frank to Hannah, n.d., corr.
21. WC, Myra Barton, 9; *Orange County Directory*, 1919, 1922.
22. WC, #1 Gailerd Page and Viola Page, 2; CSUF, Paul Ryan, 2; CSUF, Felix Stein, 3–4; Kornitzer, *Real Nixon*, 36.

23. CSUF, Cecil Pickering, 1; Jackson, "Young Richard Nixon"; Gellman, *Contender*, 10; Nixon, *Memoirs*, 1.

24. CSUF, George Kellogg and R. Fay Young, 25; Gellman, *Contender*, 10.

25. CSUF, Ralph Navarro, 6–7.

26. CSUF, Richard Gauldin, 16, 20; Jackson, "Young Richard Nixon."

27. CSUF, Ralph Navarro, 6–7.

28. WC, Hurless Barton, Hoyt Corbit, Edward Nixon, 7; CSUF, Fred Johnson, 18.

29. CSUF, Fred Johnson, 18.

30. BK, #2 Hannah Nixon, 10; Gellman, *Contender*, 10.

31. CSUF, Virginia Shaw Critchfield, 11, 15, 19; CSUF, Richard Gauldin, 4–5; CSUF, Fred Johnson, 1; CSUF, George Kellogg, 5; CSUF, Mary Rez, 8; CSUF, Paul Ryan, 8, 11; CSUF, Mary Skidmore, 3.

32. BK, #2 Hannah Nixon, 10, 11.

33. Gellman, *Contender*, 10.

34. CSUF, #1 Hoyt Corbit, 47; CSUF, #2 Hoyt Corbit, 9, 13.

35. CSUF, #2 Hoyt Corbit, 10–11, 18.

36. CSUF, Ollie Burdg, 12; Nixon and Olson, *Nixons*, 26–27.

37. CSUF, Ralph Navarro, 16–17; Jackson, "Young Richard Nixon."

38. Nixon and Olson, *Nixons*, 27.

39. WC, Homer Bemis, 22; WC, #1 Gailerd Page and Viola Page, 2.

40. WC, Temperance R. Bailey, 2; WC, Hurless Barton, Hoyt Corbit, Edward Nixon, 3; Brodie, *Richard Nixon*, 67.

41. CSUF, George Kellogg, 10.

42. CSUF, Ella Furnas and Blanche McClure, 1, 4, 9.

43. CSUF, Ella Furnas and Blanche McClure, 10.

44. CSUF, Ella Furnas and Blanche McClure, 2; Aitken, *Nixon*, 10; Kornitzer, *Real Nixon*, 24, 34; Nixon and Olson, *Nixons*, 30; Nixon, *Memoirs*, 1.

45. WC, Homer Bemis, 22; WC, #1 Gailerd Page and Viola Page, 2; Brodie, *Richard Nixon*, 67.

46. CSUF, #2 Hoyt Corbit, 9; WC, W. Hurless Barton, G. Hoyt Corbit, Edward Nixon, 2, 3.

47. Dmohowski, "From a Common Ground," 219.

48. CSUF, Gerald Shaw, 19–20.

49. CSUF, #2 Hoyt Corbit, 19–20; WC, W. Hurless Barton, G. Hoyt Corbit, Edward Nixon, 14; WC, Austin Marshburn, 21; CSUF, Paul Ryan, 15.

50. Aitken, *Nixon*, 11; Nixon and Olson, *Nixons*, 27.

51. BK, #4 Hannah Nixon, 1.

52. JA, Nixon Video Transcript A4, n.d.; Nixon and Olson, *Nixons*, 27.

53. CSUF, Floyd Wildermuth, 24; Nixon and Olson, *Nixons*, 110–11.

54. WC, #2 Oscar and Olive Marshburn, 15; BK, #2 Hannah Nixon, 14; Morris, *Richard Milhous Nixon*, 43; Nixon, *Memoirs*, 1.

55. Otto Friedrich, "Richard Nixon: I Have Never Been a Quitter," *Time*, 5/2/1994, 43.

56. WC, Austin Marshburn, 21–23, with attached Austin Marshburn to Nixon, 7/9/1971, corr., and Nixon to Austin Marshburn, 10/7/1971, corr.; JA, Nixon Video Transcript A2, n.d.

57. WC, Austin Marshburn, 21–22; JA, Nixon Video Transcript A2, n.d.

58. CSUF, #2 Hoyt Corbit, 15; Kornitzer, *Real Nixon*, 35.

59. JA, Nixon Video Transcript A2, n.d.

60. WC, Hurless Barton, 5.

61. WC, Russell Harrison Jr., 7.

62. CSUF, Virginia Shaw Critchfield, 1, 9; CSUF, Richard Gauldin, 16; WC, #1 Gailerd Page and Viola Page, 4; CSUF, Gerald Shaw, 1–3.

63. CSUF, Gerald Shaw, 58.

64. CSUF, Virginia Shaw Critchfield, 1, 8; CSUF, Ralph Navarro, 16; WC, #1 Jessamyn West, 8; *Orange County Directory*, 1919.

65. WC, #1 Jessamyn West, 9, 23; CSUF, Floyd Wildermuth, 13.

66. WC, #1 Jessamyn West, 9.

67. WC, Hoyt and Julia Corbit, 13; WC, Richard Gauldin, 18; CSUF, Ralph Navarro, 15–17; CSUF, Floyd Wildermuth, 13.

68. Aitken, *Nixon*, 12.

69. CSUF, Gauldin, 16; CSUF, Gerald Shaw, 1–3.

70. CSUF, Hoyt Corbit, 5; Yorba Linda Map, Sanborn Map Company, 3/22/1920.

71. CSUF, David Cromwell, 2; CSUF, Paul Ryan, 2; CSUF, Mary Skidmore, 7; CSUF, Felix Stein, 3–4; CSUF, Catherine Travaglia, 8–9; CSUF, Herb Warren, 7; Butz, *Yorba Linda*, 47–48.

72. Butz, *Yorba Linda*, 47–48.

73. CSUF, William Barton, 5; CSUF, Felix Stein, 2.

74. WC, Richard Gauldin, 12–13, 15.

75. CSUF, Richard Gauldin, 1, 15, 17–18; WC, Richard Gauldin, 15.

76. CSUF, David Cromwell, 2, 13.

77. WC, Hurless Barton, Hoyt Corbit, Edward Nixon, 10, 13; CSUF, Johnson, 13; CSUF, Mary Rez, 7, 10–11.

78. Butz, *Yorba Linda*, 48.

79. CSUF, Virginia Shaw Critchfield, 40; CSUF, Mary Skidmore, 3.

80. CSUF, Virginia Shaw Critchfield, 39.

81. CSUF, Hoyt Corbit, 13.

82. Elliott, *Whittier College*, 14.

83. CSUF, Fred Johnson, 8; CSUF, Glenn Shaffer, 4–5.

84. CSUF, Hoyt Corbit, 12; CSUF, #2 Hoyt Corbit, 9; WC, Joe Johnson, 14; CSUF, Fred Johnson, 34–35; CSUF, George Kellogg and R. Fay Young, 40; CSUF, Glen Shaffer, 4–5; Nixon and Olson, *Nixons*, 28.

85. CSUF, Hoyt Corbit, 12; CSUF, Ella Furnas and Blanche McClure, 8; CSUF, Fred Johnson, 8; CSUF, Mary Skidmore, 2; Aitken, *Nixon*, 18.

86. CSUF, William Barton, 4–5; CSUF, Jane Beeson, 18; WC, Hoyt and Julia Corbit, 11, 14–15; CSUF, Furnas, 7–8; CSUF, Gauldin, 10; WC, Joe Johnson, 15; CSUF, Jessamyn West, 6; WC, #1 Jessamyn West, 22; Kornitzer, *Real Nixon*, 76.

87. WC, #1 Jessamyn West, 22.

88. CSUF, Ella Furnas and Blanche McClure, 7; CSUF, Jessamyn West, 6; Kornitzer, *Real Nixon*, 77.

89. WC, Mary Rez, 15.

90. Kornitzer, *Real Nixon*, 39.

91. WC, Mary Rez, 27.

92. CSUF, Mary Rez, 9; WC, Mary Rez, 27.

93. JA, Nixon Video Transcript A7–8, n.d.

94. WC, Floyd Wildermuth and Ruby Wildermuth, 1.

95. WC, Joe Johnson, 9.

96. WC, Joe Johnson, 12.

97. WC, Floyd Wildermuth and Ruby Wildermuth, 6.

98. CSUF, Ellen Cochran, 2–3; CSUF, Hoyt Corbit, 11–12; CSUF, Yoneko Dobashi Iwatsuru, 2; CSUF, Mary Skidmore, 3; WC, Mary Skidmore, 2; CSUF, Catherine Travaglia, 15.

99. CSUF, Paul Ryan, 13.

100. CSUF, Mary Skidmore, 1.

101. CSUF, Paul Ryan, 13; CSUF, Mary Skidmore, 2; WC, Mary Skidmore, 14; CSUF, Herb Warren, 8.

102. CSUF, Ella Furnas and Blanche McClure, 1, 2, 8, 9.

103. CSUF, Mary Skidmore, 1–2, 4.

104. "Skipped Grade," *Daily News/East Whittier Review*, 1/19/1969; CSUF, Ellen Cochran, 5–6; WC, Ellen Cochran, 13.

105. CSUF, Ellen Cochran, 3–4; WC, Ellen Cochran, 13–14; CSUF, #2 Hoyt Corbit, 16; CSUF, Yoneko Dobashi Iwatsuru, 3–4, 6; CSUF, Cecil Pickering, 24–25; CSUF, Mary Elizabeth Rez, 16; CSUF, Gerald Shaw, 4; CSUF, Mary Skidmore, 2–4, 10.

106. CSUF, Ralph Shook, 9; CSUF, Virginia Shaw Critchfield, 8, 12; CSUF, Yoneko Dobashi Iwatsuru, 6; CSUF, Mary Rez, 15; CSUF, Gerald Shaw, 3; CSUF, Richard Gauldin, 2; CSUF, Merle West, 26.

107. Aitken, *Nixon*, 17; CSUF, William Barton, 8.

108. CSUF, Gerald Shaw, 4–5; Butz, *Yorba Linda*, 78.

109. CSUF, William Barton, 8.

110. CSUF, Ellen Cochran, 3–4; CSUF, Cecil Pickering, 24–25; Jackson, "Young Richard Nixon"; Mazo, *Richard Nixon*, 14.

111. Aitken, *Nixon*, 11; Nixon, *In the Arena*, 88.

112. Nixon, *In the Arena*, 126.

113. Aitken, *Nixon*, 11–12.

114. CSUF, Gerald Shaw, 24; Aitken, *Nixon*, 11.

115. CSUF, Merle West, 25–26; WC, #1 Merle West, 2.

116. WC, Hurless Barton, Hoyt Corbit, Edward Nixon, 15.

117. CSUF, Ollie Burdg, 9; WC, Hoyt and Julia Corbit, 7; CSUF, Virginia Shaw Critchfield, 11; CSUF, George Kellogg and R. Fay Young, 40–41; CSUF, Cecil Pickering, 6; CSUF, Ryan, 11; WC, #1 Gailerd Page and Viola Page, 12; Clyde Snyder, "Yorba

Linda Club Recalls Founding," *Los Angeles Times*, 2/25/1962; Nixon, *Nixons*, 32; Butz, *Yorba Linda*, 35.

118. CSUF, William Barton, 8; CSUF, Richard Gauldin, 7–8; CSUF, Cecil Pickering, 9; WC, Mary Rez, 24.

119. CSUF, Virginia Shaw Critchfield, 40.

120. Schulte, *Young Nixon*, 15.

121. CSUF, Ollie Burdg, 3.

2. Early Success

1. CSUF, Myra Barton, 8; CSUF, Blanche Burum, 14; Whittier Area Chamber of Commerce bulletin, n.d.

2. WC, #1 Jane Beeson, 7; CSUF, Hadley Marshburn, 4; CSUF, Oscar Marshburn and Olive Marshburn, 5; CSUF, Elizabeth Paldanius, 6; WC, Edith Timberlake, Olive Marshburn, and Oscar Marshburn, 3; *Whittier City Directory*, 1922–23.

3. WC, Ralph Howe, 3; CSUF, Oscar Marshburn and Olive Marshburn (Olive Marshburn), 5.

4. WC, Edward Flutot, 3; WC, Russell Harrison Sr., 12; WC, Robert Sillivan and Mary Sillivan, 7–8; Kornitzer, *Real Nixon*, 38.

5. CSUF, Edith Brannon, 2–3; CSUF, Blanche Burum, 15; CSUF, Elizabeth Cloes, 5; CSUF, Regina Kemp, 11; WC, #2 Cecil Sperring, 13; Jackson, "Young Richard Nixon."

6. CSUF, Charlotte Craig, 1; WC, Edward Flutot, 3; CSUF, Elizabeth Glover, 1; CSUF, Fred Johnson, 31; CSUF, William Milhous, 10–11; CSUF, H. Esther Williams, 4.

7. CSUF, Ball, 5; CSUF, Blanche Burum, 15; CSUF, Edith Brannon, 2–3; CSUF, H. Esther Williams, 10; WC, H. Esther Williams, 13.

8. WC, #1 Anne Gilmore, 2; WC, Russell Harrison Sr., 12; CSUF, Oscar Marshburn and Olive Marshburn, 5; CSUF, Harry Schuyler, 3; *Whittier City Directory*, 1932, 1942; Morris, *Richard Milhous Nixon*, 71; Nixon, *Memoirs*, 2; Nixon and Olson, *Nixons*, 34; "He Was a Serious and Shy Young Man," *Daily News/East Whittier Review*, 1/19/1969.

9. CSUF, Herman Brannon and Agnes Brannon, 12; CSUF, J. Douglas Brannon, 2; CSUF, #1 Hoyt Corbit, 67; WC, #1 Harry Schuyler, 10.

10. CSUF, Edith Brannon, 9–10; CSUF, J. Douglas Brannon, 5, 11; CSUF, Raymond Burbank, 1, 7; CSUF, Martha Cato and Wilma Funk, 3; CSUF, Lucille Parsons, 13.

11. CSUF, Gerald Kepple, 10.

12. CSUF, Herman Brannon, 10; WC, Louise Williams, 2.

13. CSUF, Charlotte Craig, 6; WC, #1 Anne Gilmore, 2; CSUF, Oscar Marshburn and Olive Marshburn, 5.

14. CSUF, Martha Cato and Wilma Funk, 4–5; WC, Lyman Dietrick, 6; WC, Harriett Hudspeth, 26; WC, #1 Charles William Milhous, 2; WC, Cecil Sperring, 2, 7, 11; WC, #1 Merle West, 14–15; Nixon and Olson, *Nixons*, 65.

15. CSUF, Martha Cato and Wilma Funk, 5, 11–12.

16. CSUF, Martha Cato and Wilma Funk, 4–5.

17. CSUF, Sheldon Beeson, 3–4; CSUF, Herman Brannon, 22–23; CSUF, Martha Cato and Wilma Funk, 11–12; WC, Harriett Hudspeth, 26; WC, #2 Edward Nixon, 5; Nixon and Olson, *Nixons*, 65.

18. WC, John Arrambide, 9, 13; WC, Charles E. Cooper, 10; CSUF, Guy Dixon, 7; CSUF, Ralph Palmer, 17–18; WC, Mel Rich, 5; CSUF, Harry Schuyler, 1–2; CSUF, H. Esther Williams, 1.

19. CSUF, Herman Brannon and Agnes Brannon, 11; CSUF, Lyle Sutton, 10; Ambrose, *Nixon*, 1:14; Jackson, "Young Richard Nixon."

20. WC, Cecil Sperring, 9–10.

21. WC, #1 Harry Schuyler, 9; CSUF, Robert Sillivan and Mary Sillivan, 5; WC, Robert Sillivan and Mary Sillivan, 19; Nixon and Olson, *Nixons*, 65.

22. CSUF, Charlotte Craig, 5; CSUF, Oscar Marshburn and Olive Marshburn, 5.

23. WC, Russell Harrison Sr., 15; CSUF, Oscar Marshburn and Olive Marshburn, 5; WC, Cecil Sperring, 3, 12.

24. WC, Dorothy Bishop, 2–3, 5–6; WC, #1 Anne Gilmore, 5; WC, Mabel Schuyler and Roger Schuyler, 10; WC, Raymond Wheatley, 5; WC, Lola Williams, 5.

25. Mathony, *Whittier Revisited*, 67, 141.

26. WC, Russell Harrison Sr., 17.

27. CSUF, Hadley Marshburn, 4; CSUF, Paul Smith, 17–18.

28. BK, #4 Hannah Nixon, 4; Nixon, *In the Arena*, 92–93.

29. WC, Charles Eric Milhous, 11; BK, #4 Hannah Nixon, 4; Kornitzer, *Real Nixon*, 47–49.

30. CSUF, Edith Brannon, 16.

31. CSUF, Helen Letts, 3.

32. CSUF, Herman Brannon and Agnes Brannon, 23–24; WC, Herman Brannon, 3–4.

33. CSUF, Herman Brannon and Agnes Brannon, 23–24.

34. WC, Herman Brannon, 10.

35. CSUF, Myra Barton, 9; CSUF, Edith Brannon, 7; CSUF, Charlotte Craig, 1, 4; CSUF, Ralph Palmer, 4; WC, Robert Sillivan and Mary Sillivan, 35.

36. CSUF, J. Douglas Brannon, 6.

37. WC, Raymond Burbank, 23–24; CSUF, Charlotte Craig, 4.

38. CSUF, Charles Ball, 2; CSUF, Herman Brannon and Agnes Brannon, 4; CSUF, J. Douglas Brannon, 6; CSUF, Martha Cato and Wilma Funk, 13; CSUF, Charlotte Craig, 7; WC, Mabel Schuyler and Roger Schuyler, 16; Aitken, *Nixon*, 46; Morris, *Richard Milhous Nixon*, 72, 86; Nixon, *Memoirs*, 13–14; Nixon and Olson, *Nixons*, 60, 62.

39. CSUF, Edith Brannon, 3, 7, 14; CSUF, Herman Brannon and Agnes Brannon, 14; CSUF, J. Douglas Brannon, 3, 5–6, 12; WC, Raymond Burbank, 9; CSUF, Martha Cato and Wilma Funk, 14; CSUF, Charlotte Craig, 4; CSUF, Oscar and Olive Marshburn, 2; CSUF, Ralph Palmer, 16; WC, #2 Gladys Starbuck, 2.

40. CSUF, Eugene Coffin, 10–11; CSUF, Ralph Palmer, 4–5.

41. CSUF, Edith Brannon, 10, 13; WC, Harriett Hudspeth, 22; CSUF, Helen Letts, 6.

42. CSUF, Raymond Burbank, 4; WC, Raymond Burbank, 18–19.

43. CSUF, Jane Beeson, 16; CSUF, Edith Brannon, 3; CSUF, J. Douglas Brannon, 6; WC, Raymond Burbank, 18–19; CSUF, Charlotte Craig, 8; WC, Harriett Hudspeth, 17, 23; Charles William Milhous, 2; WC, Forest Palmer, 16; CSUF, Ralph Palmer, 1; WC, Ralph Palmer, 16.

44. WC, Raymond Burbank, 17.

45. CSUF, Robert Sillivan and Mary Sillivan, 14, 21; WC, Robert Sillivan and Mary Sillivan, 12; CSUF, Robert Sillivan, 21.

46. Nixon and Olson, *Nixons*, 62; CSUF, Raymond Burbank, 4; CSUF, Lucille Parsons, 8; CSUF, Herman Brannon and Agnes Brannon, 14, 25.

47. CSUF, Raymond Burbank, 5.

48. CSUF, Lucille Parsons, 15.

49. CSUF, Edwin Sanders, 4–5.

50. CSUF, Herman Brannon and Agnes Brannon, 14; CSUF, J. Douglas Brannon, 6; CSUF, Martha Cato and Wilma Funk, 13; CSUF, L. Parsons, 8, 11–12.

51. CSUF, Edith Brannon, 3; CSUF, Herman Brannon and Agnes Brannon, 8, 14; CSUF, Martha Cato and Wilma Funk, 14; CSUF, Helen Letts, 13; WC, Forest Palmer, 16; WC, Robert Sillivan and Mary Sillivan, 12, 14.

52. CSUF, Martha Cato and Wilma Funk, 14; CSUF, Helen Letts, 13.

53. CSUF, Raymond Burbank, 12; CSUF, Charlotte Craig, 16.

54. WC, Lawrene Anfinson, 15; CSUF, Elizabeth Paldanius, 30–31; CSUF, Floyd Wildermuth, 26; Nixon, *In the Arena*, 95.

55. WC, Raymond Burbank, 14.

56. CSUF, Lyall Sutton, 5–6.

57. CSUF, Herman Brannon, 2; CSUF, Herman Brannon and Agnes Brannon, 2, 22–23, 34; WC, Herman Brannon, 2; CSUF, J. Douglas Brannon, 3, 5; CSUF, Raymond Burbank, 4, 6, 11; WC, Raymond Burbank, 14; CSUF, Jane Beeson, 9; CSUF, Sheldon Beeson, 3; WC, Sheldon Beeson, 10–11; WC, Lyman Dietrich, 10–11; WC, Russell Harrison Jr., 19; WC, Harriett Hudspeth, 12; CSUF, Oscar Marshburn and Olive Marshburn, 10; WC, Oscar Marshburn and Olive Marshburn, 7; WC, #2 Charles E. Milhous, 8; BK, Don Nixon, 7; BK, #3 Hannah Nixon, 3; CSUF, Harry Schuyler, 5; WC, #2 Mabel Schuyler and Roger Schuyler, 24; CSUF, Robert Sillivan, 17–18; CSUF, Lyall Sutton, 5–6; Gellman, *Contender*, 11.

58. CSUF, Ray Burbank, 11.

59. WC, Russell Harrison Jr., 19.

60. CSUF, Ralph Palmer, 10.

61. CSUF, Jane Beeson, 16; WC, #2 Jane Beeson, 5; WC, Earnest Lamb, Ashton Otis, and Myra Barton, 6; CSUF, Mildred Mendenhall, 4–5; BK, #2 Hannah Nixon, 14; WC, #2 Mabel Schuyler and Roger Schuyler, 20; WC, Robert Sillivan and Mary Sillivan (Mary Sillivan), 31–32; Nixon, *Memoirs*, 14.

62. CSUF, Raymond Burbank, 17; Aitken, *Nixon*, 47; Romans 8:31 (King James Version).

63. CSUF, Herman Brannon, 3, 17; WC, #2 Harry Schuyler, 4; WC, Robert Sillivan and Mary Sillivan, 13.

64. CSUF, Herman Brannon, 28.

65. CSUF, Herman Brannon, 28; WC, Herman Brannon, 8.

66. CSUF, Raymond Burbank, 6–7; CSUF, J. Douglas Brannon, 13; CSUF, Robert Sillivan, 5–6; WC, Robert Sillivan and Mary Sillivan, 20.

67. CSUF, Herman Brannon, 14; CSUF, Raymond Burbank, 6; CSUF, Lucille Parsons, 11, 13; CSUF, Merle West, 6; WC, #2 Jessamyn West, 16; WC, #1 Merle West, 7; WC, #1 Jessamyn West, 17; JA, Richard Nixon Post-Presidency Memo A17, n.d.; Nixon, *In the Arena*, 85–86.

68. CSUF, Raymond Burbank, 12.

69. CSUF, Herman Brannon and Agnes Brannon, 28.

70. CSUF, Helen Letts, 6; CSUF, Lucile Parsons, 11–12; CSUF, Herman Brannon, 8.

71. JA, Richard Nixon Historic Video Transcript, 5/3/1975, 40.

72. WC, Raymond Burbank, 4.

73. WC, Mildred Fink, 17; WC, Edith Nunes, 11; CSUF, Lucille Parsons, 12–13.

74. WC, Russell Harrison Jr., 18–19; WC, Russell Harrison Sr., 8; CSUF, Lucille Parsons, 3.

75. CSUF, Lucille Parsons, 20.

76. CSUF, Mildred Beard, 3; CSUF, J. Douglas Brannon, 15; CSUF, Edith Brannon, 2–3; CSUF, Helen Letts, 23; CSUF, H. Esther Williams, 4–5; Morris, *Richard Milhous Nixon*, 72.

77. CSUF, Lucille Parsons, 12.

78. WC, #1 Harry Schuyler, 9; CSUF, H. Esther Williams, 9; JA, Richard Nixon Post-Presidency Memo A22, n.d.

79. CSUF, Jane Beeson, 11; WC, Edith Comfort, 11; CSUF, Elizabeth Glover, 10–11; CSUF, Harry Schuyler, 3–4; CSUF, H. Esther Williams, 4–5; WC, #2 H. Esther Williams, 10; Nixon Family Collection, Perfect Attendance Certificate, 11/9/1923.

80. WC, Kathryn Bewley, 3; CSUF, Blanche Burum, 3.

81. CSUF, Sheldon Beeson, 3–4.

82. CSUF, Blanche Burum, 17.

83. CSUF, Elizabeth Glover, 2; JA, Richard Nixon, Historic Video Transcript, 5/3/1975, 7.

84. JA, Richard Nixon, Historic Video Transcript, 5/3/1975, 7; WC, Linniel Taylor, 8; "Biography of Richard Nixon," *Daily News/East Whittier Review*, 1/19/1969; Aitken, *Nixon*, 27; Kornitzer, *Real Nixon*, 52.

85. Nixon, *In the Arena*, 86–87.

86. WC, Harriett Hudspeth, 32; WC, Linniel Taylor, 8–9; JA, Richard Nixon Historic Video Transcript, 5/3/1975, 8–9; Nixon, *In the Arena*, 86–87.

87. CSUF, Elizabeth Glover, 14; Jackson, "Young Richard Nixon"; Nixon, *In the Arena*, 105–6.

88. JA, Richard Nixon Historic Video Transcript, 5/3/1975, 9–10.

89. Nixon, *In the Arena*, 86–87.

90. JA, Richard Nixon Historic Video Transcript, 5/3/1975, 10–11.

91. WC, Jack Drown, 7; CSUF, Fred Johnson, 16; BK, Richard Nixon, 20–21; Nixon and Olson, *Nixons*, 190.

92. WC, #2 Jane Beeson, 22; CSUF, Ralph Palmer, 14; CSUF, Lucille Parsons, 7; WC, #1 Merle West, 13.

93. Nixon and Olson, *Nixons*, 109.

94. CSUF, Sheldon Beeson, 9.

95. CSUF, Mildred Beard, 5; CSUF, Sheldon Beeson, 3–4; WC, Linniel Taylor, 15.

96. WC, John Arrambide, 11, 14, 24; CSUF, Blanche Burum, 3–5; CSUF, George Chisler, 5; WC, Linniel Taylor, 13; CSUF, H. Esther Williams, 3.

97. WC, #2 Jane Beeson, 2; Nixon, *Memoirs*, 9; Nixon and Olson, *Nixons*, 85.

98. CSUF, Virginia Critchfield, 6.

99. CSUF, Sheldon Beeson, 15.

100. CSUF, Jane Beeson, 19; WC, Harriett Hudspeth, 11; BK, #2 Hannah Nixon, 15; BK, #4 Hannah Nixon, 2; BK, Hubert Perry House (Harriett Hudspeth), 4; CSUF, Paul Smith, 6; Eisenhower, *Pat Nixon*, 254; Nixon, *Memoirs*, 178.

101. WC, Forest Palmer, 15; CSUF, Paul Smith, 6.

102. WC, #2 Jane Beeson, 9–10; WC, Winifred Todd, Helen Cameron, and Harold Cameron (Winifred Todd), 14.

103. CSUF, Jane Beeson, 12; Nixon Family Collection, Richard Nixon, "Autobiography," 10/20/1925; Aitken, *Nixon*, 26–27.

104. WC, William Alan Milhous, 8; JA, Richard Nixon Historic Video Transcript, 5/3/1975, 37; WC, Edith Timberlake and Philip Timberlake (Edith Timberlake), 16; WC, #2 H. Esther Williams, 1; "Pages from a President's History . . . ," *Daily News/East Whittier Review*, 1/19/1969; Nixon Family Collection, East Whittier Graduating Exercises Program, 6/2/1926.

105. CSUF, Louis Jones, 8; WC, Hadley Marshburn, 12, 14.

106. CSUF, Myra Barton, 4–5; CSUF, Hadley Marshburn, 5; WC, Mabel Roberts, 8.

107. CSUF, Dorothy Beeson, 1–2; CSUF, Sheldon Beeson, 3, 25–26; CSUF, Martha Cato and Wilma Funk, 3; CSUF, Hadley Marshburn, 5; WC, Howard Marshburn, 2, 17; CSUF, Oscar Marshburn and Olive Marshburn, 10; JA, Richard Nixon Historic Video Transcript, 5/3/1975, 29; WC, Edith Nunes, 6; Aitken, *Nixon*, 19; Nixon, *Memoirs*, 9, 13.

108. Nixon and Olson, *Nixons*, 55.

109. WC, #2 Jane Beeson, 6; WC, Mildred Fink, 12; WC, Josephine Harrison, 7; WC, William Harrison, 13; WC, #2 William Harrison, 1–2; WC, Priscilla Timberlake MacLeod and Patricia Jane MacLeod, 12; WC, Howard Marshburn, 5; WC, #3 Oscar Marshburn and Olive Marshburn, 8; WC, #2 Charles E. Milhous, 8; WC, Philip Timberlake and Elizabeth Paldanius, 14–15; Nixon and Olson, *Nixons*, 57–58.

110. WC, Mildred Fink, 13.

111. CSUF, Herman Brannon and Agnes Brannon, 7; CSUF, Sheldon Beeson, 4–5.

112. Aitken, *Nixon*, 19; Nixon, *In the Arena*, 91.

113. CSUF, Jane Beeson, 14; CSUF, Oscar Marshburn and Olive Marshburn, 2; WC, Winford Nixon, 8; WC, #2 Harry Schuyler, 3; CSUF, Robert Sillivan and Mary Sillivan, 4; Nixon, *In the Arena*, 192.

114. Aitken, *Nixon*, 25–26.

115. Nixon and Olsson, *Nixons*, 34.
116. Kornitzer, *Real Nixon*, 65–66.
117. Aitken, *Nixon*, 26; Nixon, *Memoirs*, 10.
118. Nixon and Olson, *Nixons*, 34.
119. CSUF, Jane Beeson, 17; JA, Richard Nixon Historic Video Transcript, 5/3/1975, 38; WC, Harry Schuyler, 9; CSUF, Paul Smith, 21; Aitken, *Nixon*, 48; Gellman, *Contender*, 10.
120. CSUF, Charles Ball, 3. Wheaton University has it that Rader conducted services at Angelus Temple during January–March 1926. "Jazz Age Evangelism," https://www2.wheaton.edu/bgc/archives/exhibits/cgt/rader23textonly.html.
121. Aitken, *Nixon*, 48.
122. Aitken, *Nixon*, 26, 48; Gardner, "Richard Nixon," 8, 23.

3. Nixonville

1. CSUF, Albert Haendiges, 28; CSUF, Oscar Marshburn and Olive Marshburn, 7; CSUF, Lyall Sutton, 4; CSUF, Winifred Winget, 2–3.
2. CSUF, Rowe Boyer, 4; CSUF, Dean Burney, 5; CSUF, Regina Kemp, 1–2; CSUF, Oscar Marshburn and Olive Marshburn, 6; CSUF, Lyall Sutton, 1–2.
3. WC, Homer Bemis, 5; WC, Edward Fluton, 6.
4. CSUF, Dean Burney, 1.
5. CSUF, Helen Dryer, 2.
6. CSUF, Helen Dryer, 3.
7. CSUF, Rowe Boyer, 11–12; CSUF, Richard Heffern, 2; CSUF, C. Robert McCormick, 4.
8. CSUF, Rowe Boyer, 4; CSUF, Dean Burney, 3; CSUF, Irvin Chapman, 10, 13; CSUF, James Grieves, 7; CSUF, Heber Holloway, 2; CSUF, C. Robert McCormick, 4; CSUF, Merle West, 27.
9. CSUF, Dean Burney, 1.
10. *Whittier City Directory*, 1928.
11. CSUF, Bert Harris, 2.
12. CSUF, Bert Harris, 5; CSUF, Virginia Critchfield, 11; CSUF, Gerald Shaw, 12, 36, 40; *Whittier City Directory*, 1928.
13. Nixon and Olson, *Nixons*, 113; *Whittier City Directory*, 1928; CSUF, Bert Harris, 2; CSUF, James Grieves, 7.
14. Nixon and Olson, *Nixons*, 52; Nixon, *In the Arena*, 104.
15. WC, Herman Brannon, 12; CSUF, Virginia Critchfield, 51; BK, #2 Hannah Nixon, 15; WC, Charles Rothaermel, 9; CSUF, Gerald Shaw, 47.
16. CSUF, Rowe Boyer, 2, 4–5, 10; CSUF, Richard Heffern, 4.
17. CSUF, Richard Heffern, 4–5.
18. WC, Helen Letts, 3, 11; CSUF, C. Robert McCormick, 3; JA, Richard Nixon Historic Video Transcript, 5/3/1975, 18–19; Aitken, *Nixon*, 28.
19. "Lowell and Vicinity," *Whittier News*, 2/15/1928; CSUF, Merle West, 27.
20. Nixon Family Collection, box 11:6, Richard Nixon, "The Ever-Increasing Strength of the Constitution"; CSUF, C. Robert McCormick, 3.

21. JA, Richard Nixon Historic Video Transcript, 5/3/1975, 11–13; Fullerton High School, *The Pleiades*, 1928.

22. CSUF, Dean Burney, 10–11.

23. CSUF, Rowe Boyer, 3; CSUF, James Grieves, 13; WC, Charles Rothaermel, 7–8; WC, #2 Charles Rothaermel, 2–3; CSUF, Gerald Shaw, 42; Jim McCurdie, "Arky Vaughn," *Los Angeles Times*, 1/13/1986.

24. CSUF, James Grieves, 3–4, 11; CSUF, Gerald Shaw, 42.

25. CSUF, Irvin Chapman, 11; CSUF, James Grieves, 4; CSUF, C. Robert McCormick, 3; WC, Charles Rothaermel, 9; McCurdie, "Arky Vaughn."

26. CSUF, Irvin Chapman, 4; CSUF, Forest Randall, 26.

27. CSUF, Elizabeth Cloes, 5; CSUF, Helen Dryer, 7–8.

28. CSUF, Marcelina Arroues, 7–9, 17–18, 20; CSUF, Rowe Boyer, 6–7; CSUF, James Grieves, 9; WC, Ralph Howe, 20; CSUF, Gerald Shaw, 50.

29. CSUF, Rowe Boyer, 6–7.

30. CSUF, Marcelina Arroues, 8–9, 17–18, 20; CSUF, James Grieves, 9; WC, Ralph Howe, 20.

31. BK, Hubert Perry House (Harriet Hudspeth), 4; WC, Harriett Hudspeth, 29–31.

32. CSUF, Rowe Boyer, 3, 12; CSUF, Irvin Chapman, 10–11; CSUF, James Grieves, 7; CSUF, Bert Harris, 3; CSUF, Richard Heffern, 6–7; CSUF, Helen Letts, 3; CSUF, C. Robert McCormick, 4; WC, Charles Rothaermel, 7; CSUF, Gerald Shaw, 28, 39; CSUF, Merle West, 27; CSUF, Merton Wray, 12.

33. CSUF, Jane Beeson, 15; CSUF, Gerald Shaw, 39.

34. CSUF, Charlotte Craig, 6; CSUF, Sheldon Beeson, 6; WC, Russell Harrison Sr., 12; WC, Mabel Schuyler and Roger Schuyler (Roger Schuyler), 6; Mathony, *Whittier*, 64; Nixon and Olson, *Nixons*, 34.

35. CSUF, Sheldon Beeson, 6; WC, #1 Anne Gilmore, 22–23; WC, Forest Palmer, 9; WC, Mabel Schuyler and Roger Schuyler (Roger Schuyler), 7; CSUF, Lyall Sutton, 10; Kornitzer, *Real Nixon*, 38.

36. CSUF, Herman Brannon, 2; CSUF, Herman Brannon and Agnes Brannon (Agnes Brannon), 29; CSUF, Martha Cato, 10; CSUF, Irvin Chapman, 18–19; CSUF, Elizabeth Cloes, 4; CSUF, Joanne Dale, 4; WC, Leonidas Dodson, 13; CSUF, Elizabeth Glover, 4–5; CSUF, Albert Haendiges, 11; WC, George Irving Sr., 4–6; CSUF, Louis Jones, 7; CSUF, I. N. Kraushaar, 2–3; CSUF, William A. Milhous, 3; WC, William Alan Milhous, 2; CSUF, Marion Nichols, 16; CSUF, Lyle Otterman; WC, Ralph Palmer, 8; WC, Charles Post, 7; CSUF, Forest Randall, 7; CSUF, Arthur Remley, 14; WC, Mel Rich, 9–10; WC, Cecil Sperring, 4; WC, #2 Cecil Sperring, 15; WC, William Starkey, 16; WC, Arthur Sucksdorf, Florence Sucksdorf, and Ethel Garliepp, 20; CSUF, Lyall Sutton, 10.

37. CSUF, Arthur Remley, 14.

38. CSUF, Martha Cato, 15; CSUF, Arlene Randall, 2–3; CSUF, Forest Randall, 4.

39. CSUF, Charlotte Craig, 2; WC, Charles E. Cooper, 10; CSUF, Emmett Ingrum, 17; CSUF, Mildred Mendenhall, 1; CSUF, William A. Milhous, 2; WC, Lola Williams, 2; Kornitzer, *Real Nixon*, 38.

40. CSUF, Herman Brannon and Agnes Brannon (Agnes Brannon), 29; WC, Charles E. Cooper, 10; CSUF, Charlotte Craig, 6; WC, Leonidas Dodson, 13; WC, #1 Charles L. Milhous, 13; CSUF, William A. Milhous, 2–3; WC, William Alan Milhous, 2; CSUF, Marion Nichols, 16; WC, Ralph Palmer, 8; WC, Charles Post, 7; WC, Mel Rich, 9–10; WC, Cecil Sperring, 4; WC, #2 Cecil Sperring, 15; WC, William Starkey, 16; WC, Arthur Sucksdorf, Florence Sucksdorf, and Ethel Garliepp, 20; CSUF, H. Esther Williams, 1, 4; WC, Lola Williams, 2; Kornitzer, *Real Nixon*, 38.

41. Aitken, *Nixon*, 21.

42. CSUF, Martha Cato, 10–11.

43. CSUF, H. Brannon, 20; CSUF, Martha Cato, 10–11; BK, Hubert Perry House (Ralph Palmer), 6.

44. CSUF, Edith Brannon, 3; CSUF, Charlotte Craig, 9; CSUF, Martha Cato and Wilma Funk, 5, 9; CSUF, Helen Letts, 3; CSUF, Floyd Wildermuth, 21.

45. WC, Lawrene Anfinson, 14; CSUF, Martha Cato and Wilma Funk, 9; WC, Wanda Meeker, 20.

46. WC, Herman Brannon, 9; WC, Claren Morris, Richie Morris, Loretta Cook, and Bewley Allen, 16; CSUF, Lucille Parsons, 3–4; BK, Hubert Perry House (Ralph Palmer), 2; WC, Mabel Schuyler and Roger Schuyler, 10–11; WC, Robert Sillivan and Mary Sillivan, 20; WC, #2 Merle West, 1; JA, Richard Nixon Post-Presidency Memo A19–20, n.d.; Nixon, *In the Arena*, 92–93.

47. CSUF, Barbara Mashburn, 2; WC, #1 Merle West, 16–17; WC, #2 Merle West, 1.

48. CSUF, Ella Furnas, 5; WC, Merle Lally, 1–2.

49. CSUF, Martha Cato and Wilma Funk, 5, 9.

50. CSUF, Martha Cato and Wilma Funk, 5.

51. CSUF, Martha Cato and Wilma Funk, 4, 12.

52. CSUF, Martha Cato and Wilma Funk, 4, 12, 17.

53. WC, Merritt Burdg, 12; CSUF, Charlotte Craig, 10; CSUF, Mildred Mendenhall, 1; WC, #2 Charles L. Milhous, 2; WC, Mary (Moffett) Pickering, 9; WC, Charles Post, 13; WC, Adela Rogers St. Johns, 7; WC, Arthur Sucksdorf, Florence Sucksdorf, and Ethel Garliepp, 3; CSUF, Lyall Sutton, 10; WC, Herbert Tebbets, 11.

54. WC, Jane Barr, 15; WC, Merritt Burdg, 12; CSUF, Charlotte Craig, 10; WC, Lyman Dietrick, 4; WC, Mary (Moffett) Pickering, 9; WC, Charles Post, 3; CSUF, Arlene Randall, 4; WC, Adela Rogers St. Johns, 7; WC, Arthur Sucksdorf, Florence Sucksdorf, and Ethel Garliepp, 3; CSUF, Lyall Sutton, 9–10; WC, Herbert Tebbets, 11; WC, Floyd Wildermuth, 4–5; Kornitzer, *Real Nixon*, 47; Schulte, *Young Nixon*, 196.

55. CSUF, Floyd Wildermuth, 5–7; WC, Floyd Wildermuth, 7.

56. CSUF, Floyd Wildermuth, 5–7; WC, Floyd Wildermuth, 7.

57. WC, Robert E. Downey, 15; BK, Don Nixon, 9.

58. WC, George Irving Jr., 5; WC, Forest Palmer, 18; CSUF, Arlene Randall, 9; CSUF, Harry Schuyler, 3–4; WC, #2 Gladys Starbuck, 8–10; Nixon and Olson, *Nixons*, 74, 174.

59. CSUF, Sheldon Beeson, 6; Nixon, *In the Arena*, 88.

60. Nixon, *In the Arena*, 93.

61. WC, #1 Merle West, 12.

62. CSUF, Floyd Wildermuth, 7.

63. CSUF, Myra Barton, 6; CSUF, Dorothy Beeson, 5; CSUF, Jane Beeson, 6; CSUF, Herman Brannon (Agnes Brannon), 19; CSUF, Charlotte Craig, 9; CSUF, Ella Furnas, 5–6; WC, Russell Harrison Jr., 6; CSUF, Helen Letts, 23–25; CSUF, William A. Milhous, 9; CSUF, Lucille Parsons, 4; WC, Charles Post, 8; WC, Stephen Schatz, 2; WC, Mabel Schuyler and Roger Schuyler, 9; WC, #2 Thomas Seulke, 15; CSUF, Floyd Wildermuth, 24.

64. WC, George Irving Sr., 4.

65. CSUF, William A. Milhous, 9; WC, Mabel Schuyler and Roger Schuyler, 12, 18.

66. WC, Mabel Schuyler and Roger Schuyler, 12.

67. CSUF, Ella Furnas, 5–6; CSUF, William A. Milhous, 15; WC, Charles Post, 8.

68. CSUF, Ella Furnas, 6; CSUF, Marion Nichols, 11–12; WC, Stephen Schatz, 3.

69. Aitken, *Nixon*, 49.

70. CSUF, Ralph Palmer, 13; Nixon Family Collection, box 10:6, 4/5/1928, corr.

71. Aitken, *Nixon*, 50; Nixon, *In the Arena*, 93–94.

72. Aitken, *Nixon*, 50.

73. Aitken, *Nixon*, 51.

74. WC, Priscilla Timberlake MacLeod and Patricia MacLeod, 36; Mazo, *Richard Nixon*, 20.

75. CSUF, Bert Harris, 3; Mazo, *Richard Nixon*, 20.

76. WC, Marshall Clow, 25; WC, Julie Nixon Eisenhower, 3–4; WC, Verna Hough, 3; WC, William Carleton Milhous, 23.

77. Aitken, *Nixon*, 51.

78. CSUF, Edith Brannon, 4–5.

79. CSUF, Edith Brannon, 4.

80. CSUF, Barbara Mashburn, 9; CSUF, Marion Nichols, 4; CSUF, Lyall Sutton, 4; Kornitzer, *Real Nixon*, 59; Morris, *Richard Milhous Nixon*, 89.

81. CSUF, Beard, 6; WC, Harriett Hudspeth, 19; CSUF, Arlene Randall, 12; CSUF, Forest Randall, 5; Schulte, *Young Nixon*, 127.

82. CSUF, Agnes Brennan, 1; CSUF, Earl Chapman, 12; CSUF, Albert Haendiges, 6–7; WC, #1 Mel Rich, 9.

83. CSUF, Mildred Beard, 4.

84. CSUF, Arlene Randall, 9; CSUF, Arthur Remley, 10.

85. JA, Richard Nixon Historic Video Transcript, 5/3/1975, 33–34.

86. CSUF, Dolores Ball, 10–11; CSUF, Mildred Beard, 3; CSUF, Earl Chapman, 5; WC, Donald Fantz, 2; CSUF, Albert Haendiges, 4; WC, Harriet Haisman, 9; BK, Huber Perry House (Alice Walker), 1; WC, #2 Mel Rich, 2.

87. WC, George Buehler, 5; WC, Robert Downey, 6; CSUF, Heber Holloway, 3; WC, Tolbert Moorhead, 2; CSUF, Forrest Randall, 15.

88. CSUF, Doug Ferguson, 6; Kornitzer, *Real Nixon*, 56.

89. CSUF, Edith Brannon, 6, 15; CSUF, Herman Brannon, 6; CSUF, Earl Chapman, 14; CSUF, Raymond Burbank, 22; CSUF, Martha Cato, 7; WC, Harriett Hudspeth, 10; CSUF, Knighton, 16; CSUF, Helen Letts, 3; WC, Alice Rosenberger, 5–6.

90. CSUF, Harold Stone, 1; WC, Harold Stone, 1, 5–6.

91. WC, George Buehler, 3–4; WC, Ola Florence Jobe, 24; CSUF, Alice Newsom, 32; WC, Roy Newsom, 7; Aitken, *Nixon*, 59; Gellman, *Contender*, 13–14; Morris, *Richard Milhous Nixon*, 98.

92. WC, Jack Mele, 1, 4; "He Won the Presidency," *Daily News/East Whittier Review*, 1/19/1969.

93. JA, Richard Nixon Historic Video Transcript, 5/3/1975, 37.

94. WC, George Buehler, 2; WC, Frances King, 5; CSUF, Marion Nichols, 1–2; JA, Richard Nixon Historic Video Transcript, 5/3/1975, 37–38; WC, Tom Phelan, 3, 5–6; Morris, *Richard Milhous Nixon*, 98; Gellman, *Contender*, 13–14; Nixon, *Memoirs*, 14.

95. CSUF, Albert Haendiges, 4–5; WC, Orton Keith Wood, 4; CSUF, Douglas Ferguson, 6.

96. CSUF, Albert Haendiges, 4–5.

97. WC, Dorothy Bishop, 16; CSUF, Merton Wray, 1–3.

98. WC, Charles Post, 5; CSUF, Merton Wray, 3–5; WC, Merton Wray, 4–6.

99. CSUF, Wayne Long, 7; Schulte, *Young Nixon*, 204.

100. CSUF, Marion Nichols, 9–10.

101. CSUF, Albert Haendiges, 9; WC, Beatrice Hawkins, 5; CSUF, Marion Nichols, 1–2, 8; "District Finals at Monrovia on Friday," *Whittier News*, 4/9/1930; Nixon, *In the Arena*, 89.

102. WC, Charles E. Cooper, 23; WC, Ruth Garrett, 26; CSUF, Elizabeth Glover, 4; CSUF, Long, 7; CSUF, Forest Randall, 16; WC, #1 Mel Rich, 21.

103. WC, Clyde Irwin, 12.

104. WC, #1 Charles William Milhous, 2; JA, Richard Nixon Historic Video Transcript, 5/3/1975, 10–11; Nixon, *In the Arena*, 87–88.

105. WC, Raymond Burbank, 18–19; CSUF, Dolores Ball, 10; WC, George Buehler, 2; CSUF, George Chisler, 5; WC, Robert Downey, 5; CSUF, Douglas Ferguson, 6–7; CSUF, Albert Haendiges, 5; WC, Harriett Hudspeth, 5; WC, Clyde Irwin, 12; WC, Frances King, 2; CSUF, Wayne Long, 5; CSUF, Barbara Mashburn, 7–8; WC, Helen Netzley and Byron Netzley (Helen Netzley), 11; CSUF, Lyle Otterman, 6–7; WC, Alice Snedecor, 1–2, 4–5.

106. CSUF, Dolores Ball, 10; CSUF, Dean Burney, 2, 9; WC, Robert Downey, 7; WC, Donald Fantz, 13; CSUF, James Grieves, 6, 25–26; WC, Russell Harrison Jr., 25; WC, Beatrice Hawkins, 9; CSUF, C. Robert McCormick, 4; CSUF, Merton Wray, 5; Kornitzer, *Real Nixon*, 56; Schulte, *Young Nixon*, 127.

107. WC, Harriet Haisman, 9; JA, Richard Nixon Historic Video Transcript, 5/3/1975, 34; WC, June Steck, 3, 22.

108. WC, Ola Florence Jobe, 4, 16; JA, Richard Nixon Historic Video Transcript, 5/3/1975, 34.

109. WC, Ola Florence Jobe, 16–18; JA, Richard Nixon Historic Video Transcript, 5/3/1975, 34–36.

110. David, *Lonely Lady*, 49.

111. JA, Richard Nixon Historic Video Transcript, 5/3/1975, 34–36; Aitken, *Nixon*, 59.

112. JA, Richard Nixon Historic Video Transcript, 5/3/1975, 34–36; Aitken, *Nixon*, 59.

113. WC, Ola Florence Jobe, 17–18.

114. CSUF, Doug Ferguson, 4.

115. WC, Ola Florence Jobe, 23; WC, Tolbert Moorhead, 2–3; Hubert Perry, interviews by author, 12/8/2009, 12/9/2009, 1/5/2010, 1/6/2010, 2/22/2010, 9/8/2010, 11/10/2010, 11/18/2010; Aitken, *Nixon*, 60; Kornitzer, *Real Nixon*, 54.

116. "Friendly Cousins," *Daily News/East Whittier Review*, 1/19/1969; CSUF, Merle West, 22.

117. David, *Lonely Lady*, 50.

118. CSUF, Albert Haendiges, 9.

119. WC, Oscar Marshburn and Olive Marshburn (Olive Marshburn), 10; Kornitzer, *Real Nixon*, 46.

120. WC, Paul Gardner, 5–6; Eisenhower, *Pat Nixon*, 57; Mazo, *Richard Nixon*, 13.

121. CSUF, Earl Chapman, 4.

122. CSUF, Herman Brannon, 18–20.

123. WC, Frances King, 2.

124. CSUF, Marion Nichols, 3; JA, Richard Nixon Historic Video Transcript, 5/3/1975, 39; Aitken, *Nixon*, 29.

125. Gellman, *Contender*, 12.

4. Depression-Era Education

1. JA, Richard Nixon Historic Video Transcript, 5/3/1975, 39–40; Aitken, *Nixon*, 30; Nixon, *Memoirs*, 15.

2. Aitken, *Nixon*, 31.

3. CSUF, Marion Nichols, 15; CSUF, Lyle Otterman, 1.

4. CSUF, Joe Gaudio, 20; CSUF, Albert Haendiges, 7, 14; CSUF, Lyle Otterman, 23; Mathony, *Whittier*, 67, 141.

5. CSUF, Robert Farnham, 16; CSUF, Joe Gaudio, 20; CSUF, William Hornaday, 4.

6. BK, #1 Hubert Perry, 7; Elliott, *Whittier College*, 87; Morris, *Richard Milhous Nixon*, 115; Jackson, "Young Richard Nixon."

7. CSUF, C. Richard Harris, 6; CSUF, Newt Robinson, 7; "Frosh Enter College Life as Rock Battle with Sophs Ensues," *Quaker Campus*, 9/19/1930.

8. CSUF, C. Richard Harris, 6; CSUF, Byron Netzley, 12.

9. CSUF, Byron Netzley, 12; "Frosh Outpush Sophs to Win Annual Scrap," *Quaker Campus*, 9/26/1930.

10. CSUF, Bruce Burchell, 5; CSUF, Joanne Dale, 10, 12, 16; CSUF, Ezra Ellis, 2; CSUF, William Hornaday, 13.

11. CSUF, Bruce Burchell, 11–12.

12. CSUF, Bruce Burchell, 7; CSUF, Joanne Dale, 23.

13. CSUF, Bruce Burchell, 7, 15; Schulte, *Young Nixon*, 192.

14. CSUF, Regina Kemp, 4; CSUF, Joanne Dale, 10; CSUF, Wood Glover, 7; CSUF, William Duncan, 5; Elliott, *Whittier College*, 25, 47.

15. WC, #1 Tom Bewley, 13; CSUF, Herman Fink, 10; WC, Paul Gardner, 5–6; WC, Ola Jobe, 23; CSUF, Regina Kemp, 9; CSUF, Marjorie Knighton, 5–6; CSUF, Dean Triggs, 71; CSUF, Edwin Wunder, 11; "Office Will Check Chapel Attendance," *Quaker Campus*, 10/13/1933; Jackson, "Young Richard Nixon."

16. CSUF, Bruce Burchell, 4; CSUF, William Hornaday, 30.

17. CSUF, George Chisler, 1; CSUF, Herman Fink, 10.

18. CSUF, Raymond Burbank, 2; CSUF, Bruce Burchell, 7; CSUF, Wood Glover, 7; Morris, *Richard Milhous Nixon*, 118, 133; Nixon, *Memoirs*, 19.

19. CSUF, George Jenkins, 8; CSUF, Robert Halliday, 5; CSUF, Dolores Ball, 5.

20. CSUF, Wood Glover, 3; Nixon, *Memoirs*, 19.

21. WC, #1 Clint Harris, 7; CSUF, Dean Triggs, 62; Aitken, *Nixon*, 33; Elliott, *Whittier College*, 151; Jackson, "Young Richard Nixon."

22. CSUF, John Chapin, 11; CSUF, Herman Fink, 6–8; CSUF, Joe Gaudio, 7, 23; CSUF, Nathaniel George, 2; WC, #4 Wallace Newman, 1, 3; Kornitzer, *Real Nixon*, 110.

23. Kornitzer, *Real Nixon*, 109.

24. WC, #2 Clint Harris, 9–10; CSUF, Byron Netzley, 4; Nixon, *In the Arena*, 115; Nixon, *Memoirs*, 19.

25. CSUF, Robert Halliday, 7; CSUF, John Chapin, 13.

26. CSUF, John Chapin, 13.

27. Nixon Family Collection, box 11:17, *Pigskin Review Oxy–Whittier*, n.d.; CSUF, John Chapin, 12; Aitken, *Nixon*, 34.

28. CSUF, Wood Glover, 3; WC, Murle Mashburn, 8; CSUF, Byron Netzley, 3–4; CSUF, Howard Rupard, 9; CSUF, William Soeberg, 8–9.

29. WC, #2 Kenneth Ball, 20; BK, Hubert Perry, 1; "Nixon Is House Hunting," *Los Angeles Herald-Express*, 3/23/1961; Kay Waymire, "Nixon Gets His Driver's License," *Los Angeles Examiner*, 3/23/1961; "Nixon Buys New Auto, Gets Driver's License," *Los Angeles Times*, 3/23/1961; Kornitzer, *Real Nixon*, 109.

30. CSUF, Robert Halliday, 2.

31. WC, Keith Wood, 20.

32. WC, #4 Wallace Newman, 1; Kornitzer, *Real Nixon*, 110.

33. CSUF, Joe Gaudio, 12.

34. CSUF, Dean Triggs, 39, 61; CSUF, Lucille Parsons, 7; Nixon and Olson, *Nixons*, 78.

35. CSUF, William Duncan, 6, 8; CSUF, Joe Gaudio, 18–19; CSUF, Nathaniel George, 7, 11; CSUF, Byron Netzley, 11.

36. CSUF, Nathaniel George, 11; CSUF, Setsuko Tani, 5; CSUF, Sandy Triggs, 10.

37. Schulte, *Young Nixon*, 192.

38. CSUF, William Duncan, 7; CSUF, Joe Gaudio, 18.

39. JA, #2 Richard Nixon Historic Video Transcript, 5/4/1975, 11–12; Mazo, *Richard Nixon*, 23; Aitken, *Nixon*, 37–38.

40. CSUF, Robert Halliday, 15; CSUF, William Hornaday, 4.

41. CSUF, Joe Gaudio, 4; CSUF, William Hornaday, 18–19; CSUF, William Soeberg, 14; Elliott, *Whittier College*, 155.

42. CSUF, Joe Gaudio, 4; CSUF, William Hornaday, 4, 18–19.
43. CSUF, Joe Gaudio, 4; CSUF, Wood Glover, 9; CSUF, William Krueger, 7; CSUF, Byron Netzley, 2.
44. CSUF, Wood Glover, 9; CSUF, Dean Triggs, 11; Elliott, *Whittier College*, 155.
45. CSUF, Robert Halliday, 15.
46. CSUF, Ezra Ellis, 6–7; CSUF, Robert Halliday, 15–16; WC, Mary Pickering, 14.
47. CSUF, Robert Halliday, 15–16; Schulte, *Young Nixon*, 219.
48. CSUF, Robert Halliday, 15–16; CSUF, Wood Glover, 4–5; BK, Paul Smith and Albert Upton, 22; WC, Frank Swain, 2; Elliott, *Whittier College*, 157–58.
49. JA, *#2* Richard Nixon Historic Video Transcript, 5/4/1975, 9; CSUF, Manville Saxton, 11; Nixon Family Collection, box 11:13, Glee Club Program, *Ambassadors of Song*; Aitken, *Nixon*, 35.
50. WC, Joseph Cosand, 4; JA, Richard Nixon Historic Video Transcript, 5/3/1975, 42.
51. WC, Harley McClure, 18.
52. WC, Gerald Bruce, 9–11; CSUF, Joe Gaudio, 7; WC, Harley McClure, 10; CSUF, Manville Saxton, 5; CSUF, Edwin Wunder, 2–3; "Whittier Glee Clubs Complete Northern Tour," *Quaker Campus*, 4/13/1934; Nixon Family Collection, box 11:13, Glee Club Program, *Ambassadors of Song*.
53. "Council Seeks Solution to Fraternity Question as New Society Formed," *Quaker Campus*, 10/31/1930.
54. Elliott, *Whittier College*, 48.
55. Elliott, *Whittier College*, 92.
56. Elliott, *Whittier College*, 126.
57. Elliott, *Whittier College*, 126.
58. Elliott, *Whittier College*, 138.
59. WC, #1 Kenneth Ball, 26; WC, #1 Tom Bewley, 20; CSUF, Bruce Burchell, 10; CSUF, Joanne Dale, 13, 20; CSUF, Marjorie Knighton, 3; CSUF, Barbara Mashburn, 15; Elliott, *Whittier College*, 138.
60. CSUF, William Duncan, 1; CSUF, John Chapin, 4–5; CSUF, William Krueger, 6; CSUF, Byron Netzley, 3; CSUF, Hubert Perry, 5; CSUF, Dean Triggs, 2; JA, Richard Nixon Historic Video Transcript, 5/3/1975, 41.
61. WC, #2 Kenneth Ball, 20; WC, #1 Clint Harris, 1; WC, #2 Clint Harris, 9–10, 16; CSUF, Murle Mashburn, 1; WC, Murle Mashburn, 6–7, 12–13; CSUF, Byron Netzley, 3; WC, #2 Wallace Newman, 1; WC, #4 Wallace Newman, 5; CSUF, Newt Robinson, 1; WC, Alice Snedecor, 9; CSUF, Edward Sowers, 8; CSUF, Dean Triggs, 36; CSUF, Edward Warner, 5.
62. CSUF, Robert Halliday, 14; WC, Murle Mashburn, 12–13; CSUF, Byron Netzley, 1; JA, Richard Nixon Historic Video Transcript, 5/3/1975, 41; WC, #2 Newt Robinson, 9; CSUF, Dean Triggs, 18; CSUF, Sandy Triggs, 7; WC, #2 Albert Upton, 1–2; Elliott, *Whittier College*, 150.
63. CSUF, C. Richard Harris, 7; CSUF, Regina Kemp, 2, 7–8; CSUF, Hubert Perry, 5; WC, Keith Wood, 12.
64. CSUF, Bruce Burchell, 4, 9–10; CSUF, George Chisler, 4; CSUF, William Duncan, 10; CSUF, Robert Farnham, 3; CSUF, Herman Fink, 1, 4; CSUF, Robert Halliday,

8; CSUF, William Hornaday, 8; CSUF, Emmet Ingrum, 11, 26; CSUF, Regina Kemp, 7; CSUF, William Krueger, 8–9; CSUF, E. V. and Patricia Lindstrom, 2; CSUF, Barbara Mashburn, 16; WC, Byron Netzley and Helen Netzley, 13; CSUF, Lyle Otterman, 10; BK, Paul Smith and Albert Upton, 4–5; CSUF, Dean Triggs, 17–18, 21, 23, 26; CSUF, Edward Warner, 3–4; Elliott, *Whittier College*, 147.

65. CSUF, John Chapin, 7, 15; CSUF, Herman Fink, 3; CSUF, Emmet Ingrum, 26; CSUF, William Krueger, 8–9; WC, Murle Mashburn, 12–13; CSUF, Byron Netzley, 2, 4–5; WC, Byron Netzley and Helen Netzley, 13; BK, Paul Smith and Albert Upton, 8–9; WC, Keith Wood, 113; Gellman, *Contender*, 14.

66. CSUF, William Krueger, 8–9; CSUF, William Duncan, 3; CSUF, Byron Netzley, 1, 5; "Old Orthogonian Officers Retained," *Quaker Campus*, 2/13/1931.

67. CSUF, William Duncan, 1–2; CSUF, William Krueger, 8–9; JA, Richard Nixon Historic Video Transcript, 5/3/1975, 41.

68. CSUF, Newt Robinson, 11; Aitken, *Nixon*, 33; Nixon, *Memoirs*, 17.

69. CSUF, Herman Fink, 1; CSUF, William Duncan, 2; Gellman, *Contender*, 15.

70. CSUF, Wood Glover, 4.

71. CSUF, John Chapin, 14; CSUF, Joe Gaudio, 8; CSUF, William Hornaday, 27.

72. WC, Murle Mashburn, 12–13; CSUF, Dean Triggs, 13, 17–18.

73. CSUF, John Chapin, 5.

74. CSUF, Marjorie Knighton, 6; CSUF, Byron Netzley, 12; CSUF, Newt Robinson, 11; CSUF, Dean Triggs, 69; CSUF, Sandy Triggs, 9.

75. CSUF, Mildred Beard, 9; CSUF, Barbara Mashburn, 16; Hubert Perry, interviews by author, 12/8/2009, 12/9/2009, 1/5/2010, 1/6/2010, 2/22/2010, 9/8/2010, 11/10/2010, 11/18/2010.

76. CSUF, Bruce Burchell, 13; CSUF, Joe Gaudio, 11; CSUF, Newt Robinson, 10; WC, #2 Newt Robinson, 17; CSUF, Dean Triggs, 12; Kornitzer, *Real Nixon*, 109; Jackson, "Young Richard Nixon."

77. CSUF, George Chisler, 4; CSUF, Robert Farnham, 3; CSUF, Albert Haendiges, 11; CSUF, Regina Kemp, 8; CSUF, Dean Triggs, 13, 21.

78. WC, #2 Kenneth Ball, 9; CSUF, William Duncan, 1–2; CSUF, Herman Fink, 116; CSUF, Joe Gaudio, 9; CSUF, Elizabeth Glover, 6–7; CSUF, Albert Haendiges, 11; CSUF, William Hornaday, 26; CSUF, Barbara Mashburn, 16; CSUF, Harold Space, 4; CSUF, William Soeberg, 11; CSUF, Edward Sowers, 13–14.

79. CSUF, Arlene Randall, 18–19.

80. CSUF, Joanne Dale, 8–9, 11.

81. WC, Ola Jobe, 8–9.

82. WC, William Brock, 12–13; CSUF, Murle Mashburn, 1; CSUF, Dean Triggs, 7, 84.

83. CSUF, Herman Fink, 13–14; WC, #1 Tom Bewley, 17, 142; Joseph Dmohoski, interview by author, 10/13/2011; Nixon, *In the Arena*, 105; Elliott, *Whittier College*, 142; "Honors for President Paul Smith," *Daily News/East Whittier Review*, 1/19/1969.

84. CSUF, Wood Glover, 6; CSUF, Newt Robinson, 3; CSUF, Dean Triggs, 40.

85. CSUF, Wood Glover, 6; WC, Tolbert Moorhead, 19.

86. CSUF, Herman Fink, 1; CSUF, William Hornaday, 27; CSUF, Wood Glover, 6; Schulte, *Young Nixon*, 233.

87. Kornitzer, *Real Nixon*, 113–14.

88. CSUF, Elizabeth Paldanius, 33.

89. Kornitzer, *Real Nixon*, 113; Jackson, "Young Richard Nixon."

90. WC, Horace McConnell, 6–7; CSUF, Merle West, 3–4; WC, #1 Merle West, 22; WC, #3 Merle West, 2; Jackson, "Young Richard Nixon"; "Friendly Cousins," *Daily News/East Whittier Review*, 1/19/1969; Elliott, *Whittier College*, 149.

91. CSUF, Byron Netzley, 5–6.

92. CSUF, Kenneth Ball, 7; CSUF, William Hornaday, 26; CSUF, Richard Spaulding, 6; CSUF, Dean Triggs, 92–93.

93. Elliott, *Whittier College*, 151; Aitken, *Nixon*, 247.

94. Nixon, *In the Arena*, 117–18.

95. CSUF, John Chapin, 6; CSUF, E. V. and Patricia Lindstrom, 8; CSUF, Joe Gaudio, 16; CSUF, William Krueger, 10; WC, Murle Mashburn, 14; CSUF, William Soeberg, 1; CSUF, Edward Sowers, 6–7; CSUF, Dean Triggs, 6–7; *Whittier City Directory*, 1931.

96. CSUF, Joe Gaudio, 15; JA, Richard Nixon Historic Video Transcript, 5/3/1975, 43.

97. JA, Richard Nixon Historic Video Transcript, 5/3/1975, 43.

98. CSUF, Marjorie Knighton, 22–23; CSUF, George Jenkins, 9; CSUF, Regina Kemp, 7; CSUF, Newt Robinson, 10; CSUF, Dean Triggs, 17–18.

99. CSUF, Joe Gaudio, 11–12; CSUF, C. Richard Harris, 10.

100. WC, Edward Breitkreutz, 14; CSUF, John Chapin, 4–5, 9; CSUF, Edward Sowers, 10; "Daugherty Elected by 2–1 Vote; Nixon Wins," *Quaker Campus*, 5/6/1932.

101. CSUF, John Chapin, 5, 9; CSUF, Krueger, 6; CSUF, Dean Triggs, 64–65; Joseph Dmohowski, interview by author, 10/13/2011.

102. CSUF, Kenneth Ball, 3; WC, #2 Kenneth Ball, 13–14; CSUF, Manville Saxton, 4; "Freshman Team Wins Interclass Debates," *Quaker Campus*, 12/12/1930.

103. CSUF, Kenneth Ball, 1, 6; WC, #2 Kenneth Ball, 15; CSUF, Bruce Burchell, 3; WC, Lotus Gartin, 24; CSUF, Albert Haendiges, 9; WC, #3 Clint Harris, 18; WC, Murle Mashburn, 16; CSUF, Byron Netzley, 5; WC, Camilla Simmons and William Simmons (Camilla Simmons), 7; WC, Helen Smith, 6; Aitken, *Nixon*, 45.

104. CSUF, Newt Robinson, 14; Kornitzer, *Real Nixon*, 112.

105. JA, #2 Richard Nixon Historic Video Transcript, 5/4/1975, 4; CSUF, Lyle Otterman, 15; WC, Sheppard Watson, 4; Elliott, *Whittier College*, 156; Kornitzer, *Real Nixon*, 52–53.

106. CSUF, C. Richard Harris, 18; CSUF, Smith, 3; Nixon, *Memoirs*, 17–19; "Poet Debaters Are Snowbound on Speaking Trip," *Quaker Campus*, 2/10/33; "Richard Nixon Places First in Men's Extempore Contest," *Quaker Campus*, 11/24/1933; Schulte, *Young Nixon*, 194.

107. CSUF, Robert Farnham, 19.

108. CSUF, Kenneth Ball, 9; CSUF, Albert Haendiges, 9; CSUF, Marjorie Knighton, 14–15; WC, Marjorie Knighton, 10; WC, Barbara Mashburn, 10; WC, Murle Mashburn, 16; BK, Paul Smith and Albert Upton, 11–13; WC, #1 Albert Upton, 20; WC, #2 Albert Upton, 7; CSUF, Edwin Wunder, 9.

109. CSUF, Robert Farnham, 25; CSUF, William Hornaday, 13.

110. CSUF, Albert Haendiges, 10; CSUF, Joe Gaudio, 14; Hubert Perry, interviews by author, 12/8/2009, 12/9/2009, 1/5/2010, 1/6/2010, 2/22/2010, 9/8/2010, 11/10/2010, 11/18/2010; Elliott, *Whittier College*, 66.

111. CSUF, John Chapin, 5; CSUF, Dean Triggs, Jewel Triggs, and Robert Gibbs (Dean Triggs), 11–12.

112. BK, Paul Smith and Albert Upton (Albert Upton), 21; Kornitzer, *Real Nixon*, 106.

113. CSUF, Smith, 3; CSUF, Barbara Mashburn, 13; Nixon Family Collection, box 11:13, *Pirates of Penzance* Program; Aitken, *Nixon*, 38; Nixon, *Memoirs*, 17–19; Schulte, *Young Nixon*, 194.

114. CSUF, Robert Farnham, 15–16.

115. WC, Barbara Mashburn, 15; Kornitzer, *Real Nixon*, 108.

116. Elliott, *Whittier College*, 150; Nixon Family Collection, box 11:13, *Bird in Hand* and *Philip Goes Forth* Whittier College Programs; "'Trysting Place' Is Freshman Choice for Chapel Period," *Quaker Campus*, 3/20/1931; Kornitzer, *Real Nixon*, 106.

117. BK, Paul Smith and Albert Upton, 11–13; WC, #2 Albert Upton, 10; CSUF, Dean Triggs, 73; "First Offering in New Poet Theater Is a Distinct Success," *Quaker Campus*, 11/18/1932; Whittier College, *Acropolis*, 1933.

118. CSUF, Marjorie Knighton, 16; WC, William Brock, 17–18; CSUF, Lyle Otternan, 18.

119. Aitken, *Nixon*, 24.

120. WC, Margaretha Lohmann, 4, 9.

121. CSUF, Kenneth Ball, 1; CSUF, Nathaniel George, 2; CSUF, Richard Philippi, 12; WC, Setsuko Tani, 5; "Richard Nixon Named to Lead Frosh Class," *Quaker Campus*, 9/19/1930; "Nixon Reelected Freshman Leader," *Quaker Campus*, 2/27/1931; Elliott, *Whittier College*, 155.

122. WC, Tolbert Moorhead, 3–4; "Exhaust Valve," *Quaker Campus*, 5/15/1931; "He Was Nixon's Protégé," *Daily News/East Whittier Review*, 1/19/1969.

123. "Bosio Winner in Student Body Finals," *Quaker Campus*, 5/22/1931; Elliott, *Whittier College*, 155.

124. JA, #2 Richard Nixon Historic Video Transcript, 5/4/1975, 12–13; WC, Richard Thomson, 7; "Daugherty Elected"; Aitken, *Nixon*, 36; Elliott, *Whittier College*, 157.

125. CSUF, Bruce Burchell, 14; CSUF, Robert Farnham, 11; CSUF, Herman Fink, 16; CSUF, William Hornaday, 6, 24; WC, John Arrambide, 24.

126. JA, #2 Richard Nixon Historic Video Transcript, 5/4/1975, 12–13; "He Lost to Nixon," *Daily News/East Whittier Review*, 1/19/1969; Aitken, *Nixon*, 36–37.

127. CSUF, Joe Gaudio, 8; CSUF, Byron Netzley, 4.

128. CSUF, Bruce Burchell, 2, 6; CSUF, Robert Farnham, 6–7; CSUF, Richard Spaulding, 9; WC, Richard Spaulding, 5–6; WC, Edwin Wunder, 4.

129. CSUF, William Duncan, 5; CSUF, Joe Gaudio, 6–7; CSUF, William Hornaday, 23–24; Elliott, *Whittier College*, 155.

130. CSUF, William Hornaday, 24.

131. CSUF, William Hornaday, 3; Joseph Dmohowski, interview by author, 10/13/2011.

132. Elliott, *Whittier College*, 69.

133. CSUF, Kenneth Ball, 7; WC, #1 Tom Bewley, 28; CSUF, Wood Glover, 4; CSUF, Albert Haendiges, 3; CSUF, Emmett Ingrum, 8; CSUF, Helen Letts, 7; JA, #2 Richard Nixon Historic Video Transcript, 5/4/1975, 13; BK, Hubert Perry, 1; WC, Helen Smith, 9; CSUF, Sandy Triggs, 9, 21; WC, #2 Jessamyn West, 16; CSUF, Merton Wray, 13; "Nixon Thomson Nominated for Student Prexy," *Quaker Campus*, 5/5/1933; Kornitzer, *Real Nixon*, 102; Schulte, *Young Nixon*, 192, 210.

134. CSUF, Raymond Burbank, 22; CSUF, William Hornaday, 34; CSUF, Dean Triggs, 101; Schulte, *Young Nixon*, 211.

135. CSUF, Elizabeth Glover, 9; JA, #2 Richard Nixon Historic Video Transcript, 5/4/1975, 13–14.

136. WC, #1 Grant Garman, 20; CSUF, George Jenkins, 8; JA, #2 Richard Nixon Historic Video Transcript, 5/4/1975, 14–15; BK, Paul Smith and Albert Upton, 5; CSUF, Dean Triggs, 70, 73; Aitken, *Nixon*, 37; Eisenhower, *Pat Nixon*, 50–52.

137. CSUF, C. Richard Harris, 19; Whittier College, *Acropolis*, 1934.

138. WC, #2 Cecil Sperring, 1, 4; Nixon and Olson, *Nixons*, 44.

139. Aitken, *Nixon*, 52; Mazo, *Richard Nixon*, 20; Nixon, *Memoirs*, 12; Nixon and Olson, *Nixons*, 45; Jackson, "Young Richard Nixon."

140. Aitken, *Nixon*, 52; Mazo, *Richard Nixon*, 20; Nixon, *Memoirs*, 12; Nixon and Olson, *Nixons*, 45; Jackson, "Young Richard Nixon."

141. Aitken, *Nixon*, 53.

142. CSUF, Emmett Ingrum, 18; Obituary, *Santa Ana Register*, 3/9/1933; Phil White, White Emmerson, email message to author, 12/7/2009.

143. JA, Richard Nixon Historic Video Transcript, 5/3/1975, 44; WC, #1 Merle West, 16; Nixon and Olson, *Nixons*, 47.

144. CSUF, J. D. Brannon, 16; CSUF, Joe Gaudio, 6; CSUF, Hubert Perry, 5; CSUF, Smith, 25; Kornitzer, *Real Nixon*, 46.

145. Kornitzer, *Real Nixon*, 36.

146. CSUF, Smith, 6; Mazo, *Richard Nixon*, 15; Kornitzer, *Real Nixon*, 46; Nixon and Olson, *Nixons*, 75.

147. CSUF, Martha Cato, 5–6; CSUF, Ralph Palmer, 7; WC, #2 Merle West, 3; WC, #3 Merle West, 1, 3; Nixon, *Memoirs*, 5; Nixon and Olson, *Nixons*, 69.

148. CSUF, Lyle Otterman, 37; Elliott, *Whittier College*, 18.

149. WC, Jane Barr, 3, 7; WC, Sheldon Beeson, 12; CSUF, Hadley Marshburn, 5–6; WC, Howard Marshburn, 16; WC, Wanda Meeker, 5; CSUF, Mildred Mendenhall, 1–2; WC, Calvin Burdg Milhous, Phillip Milhous, and Oliver Milhous, 18–19; WC, Charles Eric Milhous, 4–5; WC, #1 Charles William Milhous, 24; WC, Claude Theodore Milhous, 3; WC, Forrest Palmer, 19; CSUF, Robert Sillivan and Mary Sillivan, 26; WC, Robert Sillivan and Mary Sillivan, 24; WC, Arthur Sucksdorf, Florence Sucksdorf, and Ethel Garliepp, 24.

150. WC, Jane Barr, 29; CSUF, Elizabeth Cloes, 2, 6; WC, Elizabeth Cloes, 5; WC, Forrest Easley, 8; CSUF, Helen Letts, 3; CSUF, Harold Stone, 11; WC, Arthur Sucksdorf, Florence Sucksdorf, and Ethel Garliepp, 21; BK, #2 Hannah Nixon, 26.

151. WC, Jane Barr, 10; CSUF, Sheldon Beeson, 6–7; WC, Forrest Easley, 8; CSUF, Lyle Otterman, 37; CSUF, Lucille Parsons, 4; WC, Camillia Simmons and William Simmons, 15; WC, Arthur Sucksdorf, Florence Sucksdorf, and Ethel Garliepp, 9.

152. WC, Russell Harrison Jr., 7, 15–16.

153. WC, Jane Barr, 10; CSUF, Mildred Mendenhall, 11–12; BK, Hubert Perry House (Alice Walker), 4; CSUF, Robert Sillivan, 11; WC, #1 Gladys Starbuck, 10; WC, #2 Gladys Starbuck, 2; CSUF, Harold Stone, 11; WC, #3 Merle West, 4; CSUF, Floyd Wildermuth, 13–14.

154. CSUF, I. N. Kraushaar, 5; WC, I. N. Kraushaar, 9; WC, #2 Charles Eric Milhous, 16.

155. WC, Jane Barr, 15–16; WC, Theodore Marshburn, 17; WC, Charles Eric Milhous, 4–5; CSUF, Elizabeth Paldanius, 35; WC, #3 Merle West, 5.

156. WC, #1 Jessamyn West, 12; WC, #2 Jessamyn West, 14.

157. CSUF, Kenneth Ball, 8; CSUF, Smith, 2, 161; Mazo, *Richard Nixon*, 21–23.

158. CSUF, William Hornaday, 9, 33; CSUF, Bruce Burchell, 9.

159. WC, Kenneth Ball, 13; CSUF, George Jenkins, 8.

160. CSUF, Ellis, 13; CSUF, Wood Glover, 8; CSUF, William Hornaday, 33; CSUF, Lyle Otterman, 16–17; WC, Merton Wray, 17.

161. WC, #1 Kenneth Ball, 12–13; CSUF, William Hornaday, 9–10; JA, Richard Nixon Historic Video Transcript, 5/3/1975, 11–13; CSUF, Arlene Randall, 22; BK, Paul Smith and Albert Upton, 2–3; WC, Paul Smith, 13; Nixon, *In the Arena*, 105; Schulte, *Young Nixon*, 216.

162. BK, Richard Nixon, 6; Mazo, *Richard Nixon*, 26.

163. CSUF, Louis Jones, 1; BK, Paul Smith and Albert Upton, 20–21, 27; CSUF, Smith, 2; WC, #2 Paul Smith, 13–14.

164. CSUF, John Chapin, 14; BK, Perry House (Harriet Hudspeth), 2; Kornitzer, *Real Nixon*, 113.

165. CSUF, Robert Halliday, 10; CSUF, Regina Kemp, 4; CSUF, Byron Netzley, 12; CSUF, Lyle Otterman, 17; BK, Hubert Perry, 1; Hubert Perry, interviews by author, 12/8/2009, 12/9/2009, 1/5/2010, 1/6/2010, 2/22/2010, 9/8/2010, 11/10/2010, 11/18/2010.

166. CSUF, Robert Halliday, 11; CSUF, Emmett Ingrum, 9–10; CSUF, Richard Philippi, 13.

167. CSUF, Dean Triggs, 102.

168. WC, #2 Kenneth Ball, 2; WC, #3 Clint Harris, 21–22; CSUF, Knighton, 7; CSUF, Setsuko Tani, 3–4; CSUF, Dean Triggs, 74; WC, Keith Wood, 17; CSUF, Edwin Wunder, 2–3.

169. CSUF, Dolores Ball, 5; WC, #3 Clint Harris, 14–15; BK, Hubert Perry, 2.

170. CSUF, Mildred Beard, 4; CSUF, John Chapin, 8; CSUF, Herman Fink, 3; CSUF, Joe Gaudio, 17; CSUF, Regina Kemp, 3; WC, Marjorie Knighton, 12; CSUF, Barbara Mashburn, 19–20; CSUF, Lyle Otterman, 11; CSUF, Hubert Perry, 3; CSUF, Newt Robinson, 11; CSUF, Harold Space, 9; CSUF, Dean Triggs, 21, 75, 80–81; "Sophomores to Give Dinner Dance Soon," *Quaker Campus*, 11/20/1931.

171. WC, Helen Hampson, 10–11.

172. WC, Richard Spaulding, 4–5; Kornitzer, *Real Nixon*, 113.

173. CSUF, Oscar and Olive Marshburn, 10; CSUF, Wood Glover, 5; WC, Harley McClure, 4–5, 7; Nixon Family Collection: Harley McClure, Wood Glover, Don Shindy, John Chapin, Lincoln Dietrick, Charles Kendle, Carl Siegmund, Gail Jobe, Clint Harris, Dick Harris, Dick Spaulding, Joe Gaudio, 6/10/1934, corr. to Frank, Hannah, and Richard Nixon; "Meeting Celebrates Third Anniversary of Orthogonian Society," *Quaker Campus*, 11/18/1932.

174. WC, Edith Nunes, 19, 26, 29; WC, Marygene Wright, 5–6.

175. WC, Edith Nunes, 19, 26, 29.

176. WC, Edith Nunes, 32.

177. WC, Jane Barr, 13; WC, Edward Breitkreutz, 10; WC, Gerald Bruce, 13; CSUF, John Chapin, 10, 14; WC, Eleanor Comroe, 8; WC, Pauline Cook, 11, 16, 18–19; CSUF, Joanne Dale, 25; WC, Lyman Dietrick, 10; CSUF, Robert Farnham, 17; CSUF, Herman Fink, 7; CSUF, William Hornaday, 6; CSUF, Emmet Ingrum, 8, 13; WC, Jo Marcelle, 6; CSUF, Barbara Mashburn, 17; WC, Murle Mashburn, 12–13; WC, Harley McClure, 11; CSUF, Byron Netzley, 1–2, 6, 10; WC, Byron Netzley and Helen Netzley, 14; WC, Edith Nunes, 20, 23; CSUF, Lyle Otterman, 25, 36; CSUF, Ralph Palmer, 27; BK, Hubert Perry, 2–3; CSUF, Newt Robinson, 14, 29–30; CSUF, Howard Rupard, 4–6, 14; WC, Vince Sinatra, 9; WC, Helen Smith, 7; BK, Paul Smith and Albert Upton, 5; WC, Alice Snedecor, 1–2, 7, 12; CSUF, Edward Sowers, 4; CSUF, Harold Space, 3; WC, Richard Spaulding, 4, 8–9; WC, Setsuko Tani, 4; CSUF, Dean Triggs, 107; WC, #2 Albert Upton, 11, 18; CSUF, Ralph Veady, 3; WC, Ralph Veady, 8; CSUF, Edward Warner, 10; WC, Gustav White, 9; CSUF, Edwin Wunder, 2–3; Kornitzer, *Real Nixon*, 108–9; Schulte, *Young Nixon*, 193.

178. WC, Edward Breitkreutz, 6; CSUF, Bruce Burchell, 7, 15; CSUF, Nathaniel George, 4; CSUF, Elizabeth Glover, 11; WC, Helen Hampson, 8; CSUF, Emmett Ingrum, 20; BK, Hubert Perry, 2; CSUF, Newt Robinson, 8; WC, Alice Rosenberger, 8; CSUF, Manville Saxton, 10; CSUF, William Soeberg, 10 ("should be president someday"); WC, Richard Spaulding, 8–9; WC, Herbert Tebbetts, 11; CSUF, Dean Triggs, 88; WC, Keith Wood, 14; Schulte, *Young Nixon*, 192.

179. WC, #2 Kenneth Ball, 18; CSUF, Herman Fink, 19–20; CSUF, Nathaniel George, 2; CSUF, Emmett Ingrum, 25; CSUF, Byron Netzley, 10; BK, Paul Smith and Albert Upton, 10; BK, Annabelle Tupper, 2; WC, #1 Albert Upton, 21; Schulte, *Young Nixon*, 193.

180. CSUF, Joe Gaudio, 2.

181. WC, Edith Nunes, 21.

182. Aitken, *Nixon*, 62; CSUF, Emmett Ingrum, 19.

183. WC, Ola Jobe, 26.

184. Mazo, *Richard Nixon*, 24.

185. CSUF, William Duncan, 11; CSUF, William Soeberg, 10; Aitken, *Nixon*, 44.

186. Nixon Family Collection: Harley McClure, Wood Glover, Don Shindy, John Chapin, Lincoln Dietrick, Charles Kendle, Carl Siegmund, Gail Jobe, Clint Harris, Dick Harris, Dick Spaulding, Joe Gaudio, 6/10/1934, corr. to Frank, Hannah, and Richard Nixon.

187. Elliott, *Whittier College*, 146; Kornitzer, *Real Nixon*, 101, 115.

188. BK, Paul Smith and Albert Upton, 10.

189. WC, #1 Olive Marshburn and Oscar Marshburn, 6; WC, Edward Rubin, 6; Nixon, *In the Arena*, 428.

190. WC, M. William Adelson, 5; WC, Fredrick Albrink, 35; WC, Arthur Brooks, 13; Aitken, *Nixon*, 68.

191. Kornitzer, *Real Nixon*, 111.

192. Aitken, *Nixon*, 73; Kornitzer, *Real Nixon*, 124.

193. WC, Joseph Hiatt Jr., 10; WC, Hale McCown and Helen McCown, 14; Aitken, *Nixon*, 73.

194. WC, Charles Rhyne, 4; Aitken, *Nixon*, 73.

195. WC, Fredrick Albrink, 16; Aitken, *Nixon*, 72; Nixon, *In the Arena*, 96.

196. Aitken, *Nixon*, 72.

197. Aitken, *Nixon*, 72; Ambrose, *Nixon*, 1:9; Black, *Life in Full*, 4.

198. Aitken, *Nixon*, 72; Ambrose, *Nixon*, 1:9; Black, *Life in Full*, 4.

199. WC, Lyman Brownfield, 9; Jackson, "Young Richard Nixon."

200. WC, Lyman Brownfield, 9.

201. WC, Lyman Brownfield, 9; Jackson, "Young Richard Nixon."

202. WC, David Cavers, 3–5; JA, Richard Nixon Historic Video Transcript, 5/3/1975, 5.

203. WC, Arthur Brooks, 15; WC, Lyman Brownfield, 16–17; WC, Lon Fuller, 3; WC, John Holland, 3; WC, Ethel Hunter, 5, 13; WC, Richard Kiefer, 19; WC, Harland Leathers, 2; WC, Hale McCown and Helen McCown, 3, 6, 13; WC, Sigrid Pedersen, 5–6; WC, Kenneth Rush, 6, 11; WC, Caroline Stoel, 6; WC, Thomas Stoel, 7–8.

204. Aitken, *Nixon*, 77.

205. WC, John Holland, 8; WC, William Roalfe, 7.

206. WC, Frederick Albrink, 5; WC, Arthur Brooks, 14; WC, William Roalfe, 8.

207. WC, Marie Actis, 2–4; WC, Edward Rubin, 7–8.

208. WC, Marie Actis, 6, 9; WC, Phebe Linney, 8.

209. WC, Marie Actis, 5; WC, Phebe Linney, 3–4, 6–7.

210. Aitken, *Nixon*, 76; Gellman, *Contender*, 7.

211. JA, Richard Nixon Historic Video Transcript, 5/4/1975, 1; WC, Benjamin Horack, 30; CSUF, Smith, 10; Aitken, *Nixon*, 76.

212. WC, Marie Actis, 6; WC, Sigrid Pedersen, 7, 12; WC, Thomas Stoel, 1.

213. WC, Fredrick Albrink, 20; JA, #2 Richard Nixon Historic Video Transcript, 5/4/1975, 40–42; CSUF, Marygene Wright, 10; Aitken, *Nixon*, 77.

214. CSUF, Kenneth Ball, 20.

5. Service to Community and Country

1. WC, Marshall Clow, 16, 35, 37; WC, Harriett Haisman, 10, 13.

2. WC, #1 Dorn, 6; CSUF, Judith Loubet, 7–8; Aitken, *Nixon*, has Wingert & Bewley on "lower floors" (85), and Eisenhower, *Pat Nixon*, has it on the second floor (61); Gellman, *Contender*, 17–18; Mazo, *Richard Nixon*, 28; Morris, *Richard Milhous Nixon*, 184, 632; Nixon and Olson, *Nixons*, 101; Schulte, *Young Nixon*, 241.

3. WC, #2 Tom Bewley, 1; CSUF, Paul Smith, 2; JA, #1 Richard Nixon Historic Video Transcript, 5/4/1975, 2.

4. wc, #1 Tom Bewley, 1–2.

5. bk, Tom Bewley, 1; wc, #1 Tom Bewley, 3; wc, #2 Tom Bewley, 5.

6. wc, #1 Tom Bewley, 3; csuf, Edith Timberlake, 31.

7. wc, #2 Tom Bewley, 1.

8. wc, William Hughes, 4; csuf, Paul Smith, 2.

9. csuf, Paul Smith, 2.

10. bk, Tom Bewley, 1–2.

11. Aitken, *Nixon*, 80.

12. wc, #2 Tom Bewley, 1–2.

13. wc, #2 Tom Bewley, 1–2, 5; csuf, Judith Loubet, 9.

14. bk, Tom Bewley, 2; wc, #2 Tom Bewley, 3.

15. Aitken, *Nixon*, 79.

16. wc, #2 Tom Bewley, 4.

17. bk, Tom Bewley, 2; wc, #2 Tom Bewley, 4, 10; csuf, Judith Loubet, 12.

18. wc, #2 Tom Bewley, 10; Gellman, *Contender*, 17–18.

19. bk, Tom Bewley, 2; Aitken, *Nixon*, 81; Gellman, *Contender*, 17–18.

20. wc, #2 Tom Bewley, 11; bk, Tom Bewley, 2; wc, Frank Chandler, 2; wc, Guy Dixon, 17, 20–21; ucb, Frank Jorgenson, 7; Schulte, *Young Nixon*, 212; "His Law Partner: Interested in Issues," *Daily News/East Whittier Review*, 1/19/1969; Mazo, *Richard Nixon*, 28–29; Schulte, *Young Nixon*, 212.

21. wc, Guy Dixon, 18.

22. David, *Lonely Lady*, 37–38.

23. wc, #2 Tom Bewley, 18; wc, #3 Evlyn Dorn, 9; Eisenhower, *Pat Nixon*, 51.

24. wc, #2 Tom Bewley, 14.

25. Kornitzer, *Real Nixon*, 128.

26. Brodie, *Richard Nixon*, 137.

27. Schee v. Holt, 56 Cal. App. 2d 364 (1942); Aitken, *Nixon*, 81–82; Brodie, *Richard Nixon*, 137–38.

28. Nixon Family Collection, 1938 Nixon Datebook.

29. wc, #2 Tom Bewley, 23; wc, #4 Evlyn Dorn, 2; wc, Jack Drown (Evlyn Dorn), 23; wc, Roger Johnson, 12; Mazo, *Richard Nixon*, 28; "Her Prediction: The Presidency," *Daily News/East Whittier Review*, 1/19/1969; *Whittier City Directory*, 1939.

30. wc, #1 Tom Bewley, 24–25.

31. wc, #2 Tom Bewley, 21; Nixon, *In the Arena*, 142.

32. wc, Jack Drown, 8–9, 20; Nixon, *Memoirs*, 22.

33. wc, Jack Drown, 8–9; Kornitzer, *Real Nixon*, 129–30.

34. Aitken, *Nixon*, 82.

35. wc, #2 Tom Bewley, 11; Mazo, *Richard Nixon*, 28.

36. Nixon Family Collection, Nixon Notebook, n.d.

37. bk, Tom Bewley, 5.

38. bk, Tom Bewley, 5; Brodie, *Richard Nixon*, 134; David, *Lonely Lady*, 42.

39. bk, Tom Bewley, 6; wc, #2 Tom Bewley, 18; Jackson, "Young Richard Nixon."

40. wc, #1 Tom Bewley, 20–21.

41. WC, #2 Tom Bewley, 23.

42. WC, #2 Tom Bewley, 23; WC, George Buehler, 5; WC, #1 Evlyn Dorn, 6; WC, #3 Evlyn Dorn, 7; WC, #4 Evlyn Dorn, 1; WC, Jack Drown (Evlyn Dorn), 21; CSUF, Judith Loubet, 8.

43. WC, #2 Tom Bewley, 25.

44. WC, Raymond Black, 5–6.

45. WC, Raymond Black, 19.

46. WC, Frank Chandler, 2.

47. WC, Henry Akerd, 18; WC, Temperance Bailey, 9–10; WC, Raymond Black, 7; CSUF, Jasper Burch, 6; CSUF, Bruce Burchell, 3, 15–16; WC, Earl Daniels, 5–6; WC, Alyce Koch, 6, 12; CSUF, Lyle Otterman, 25; WC, Herbert Jay Perry, 4; CSUF, Mrs. Benjamin Roberts and Bill Roberts, 17.

48. WC, #2 Tom Bewley, 15–16.

49. WC, #2 Tom Bewley, 4, 15; WC, #2 William Harrison, 2.

50. Nixon Family Collection, Notebook and 1940 Nixon Datebook; Mazo, *Richard Nixon*, 28–29.

51. JA, Richard Nixon Historic Video Transcript, 5/4/1975, 4; Jackson, "Young Richard Nixon"; Aitken, *Nixon*, 80, 82.

52. WC, Temperance Bailey, 9–10; Nixon Family Collection, Notebook.

53. WC, Jane Beeson, 2; CSUF, Guy Dixon, 22; WC, Roger Johnson, 6; CSUF, Harold Stone and Alberta Stone, 18; Kornitzer, *Real Nixon*, 128–29.

54. CSUF, Sheldon Beeson, 12; CSUF, Judith Loubet, 28; WC, Arthur Sucksdorf, Florence Sucksdorf, and Ethel Garliepp, 13.

55. CSUF, Lucille Parson, 6; Gellman, *Contender*, 7; Nixon and Olson, *Nixons*, 91–92; Schulte, *Young Nixon*, 226.

56. CSUF, Martha Cato and Wilma Funk, 11.

57. CSUF, Wallace Black, 1.

58. CSUF, Wallace Black, 4, 9; WC, Wallace Black, 3.

59. WC, Wallace Black, 4–6.

60. CSUF, Wallace Black, 12–13.

61. CSUF, Elizabeth Cloes, 8; WC, Elizabeth Cloes, 8; CSUF, Garman, 7; JA, Richard Nixon Historic Video Transcript, 5/4/1975, 11–12; "Mr. President, First Lady," *Daily News/East Whittier Review*, 1/19/1969; Schulte, *Young Nixon*, 244.

62. WC, Wallace Black, 4–6; WC, #2 Grant Garman, 8, Nixon Family Collection, *Night of January 16th* Program.

63. WC, Wallace Black, 4–6.

64. CSUF, Elizabeth Cloes, 8; WC, Raymond Fleischman, 10; Schulte, *Young Nixon*, 224, 230, 239.

65. JA, Richard Nixon Historic Video Transcript, 5/4/1975, 11–12; Eisenhower, *Pat Nixon*, 54–55; Morris, *Richard Milhous Nixon*, 204.

66. CSUF, Elizabeth Cloes, 2; WC, Elizabeth Cloes, 6–7; Morris, *Richard Milhous Nixon*, 204.

67. CSUF, Elizabeth Cloes, 2; Aitken, *Nixon*, 86; Kornitzer, *Real Nixon*, 134; Mazo, *Richard Nixon*, 30–31; Schulte, *Young Nixon*, 230.

68. CSUF, Elizabeth Cloes, 2; WC, Elizabeth Cloes, 7; Eisenhower, *Pat Nixon*, 54–55; Morris, *Richard Milhous Nixon*, 204.

69. CSUF, Grant Garman, 5; WC, #2 Grant Garman, 5–6.

70. CSUF, Elizabeth Cloes, 3; CSUF, Grant Garman, 4.

71. Aitken, *Nixon*, 86–87.

72. CSUF, Elizabeth Cloes, 2–3; WC, Elizabeth Cloes, 7; Schulte, *Young Nixon*, 224.

73. WC, Elizabeth Cloes, 7.

74. Mazo, *Richard Nixon*, 31.

75. CSUF, Elizabeth Cloes, 7; CSUF, Grant Garman, 6; Nixon Family Collection, 1938, 1939, and 1940 Nixon Datebooks; BK, #2 Hannah Nixon, 27; David, *Lonely Lady*, 51.

76. Nixon and Olson, *Nixons*, 241; David, *Lonely Lady*, 22; Schulte, *Young Nixon*, 229.

77. CSUF, Marian Conde, 2; CSUF, Frampton, 7; CSUF, Charles Gallaher, 1, 114; Aitken, *Nixon*, 87; Brodie, *Richard Nixon*, 150. Beet dumps are huge mounds of beets piled high for the trucks to come get them.

78. CSUF, Marian Conde, 3; CSUF, Lura Waldrip, 20; Eisenhower, *Pat Nixon*, 18.

79. CSUF, Myrtle Raine Borden, 3; CSUF, Louise Raine Gwinn, 8.

80. CSUF, Myrtle Raine Borden, 3; CSUF, Louise Raine Gwinn, 7–8.

81. CSUF, Myrtle Raine Borden, 2; David, *Lonely Lady*, 28.

82. CSUF, Myrtle Raine Borden, 12; CSUF, Carmen Griffin, 3; CSUF, Louise Raine Gwinn, 4.

83. CSUF, Myrtle Raine Borden, 8; WC, George Corcoran, 2–3; Mazo, *Richard Nixon*, 31.

84. CSUF, Myrtle Raine Borden, 7, 14; CSUF, Louise Raine Gwinn, 4; Mazo, *Richard Nixon*, 32.

85. CSUF, Myrtle Raine Borden, 8; CSUF, Iona McHatton, 4.

86. CSUF, Myrtle Raine Borden, 8–9, 16; CSUF, Marian Conde, 8; CSUF, Howard Frampton, 4; CSUF, Charles Gallaher, 2–4; CSUF, Louise Raine Gwinn, 7; CSUF, Saragrace Philippi, 2; Eisenhower, *Pat Nixon*, 22.

87. CSUF, Louise Raine Gwinn, 3; CSUF, Marcia Wray, 5; Nixon, *In the Arena*, 270.

88. CSUF, Myrtle Raine Borden, 3, 9, 20; CSUF, Carmen Griffin, 2; CSUF, Louise Raine Gwinn, 4, 17; CSUF, Gordon McHatton, 10; CSUF, Vivian Montgomery, 5; CSUF, Lura Waldrip, 19; David, *Lonely Lady*, 28.

89. CSUF, Marietta Baron, 1, 7; CSUF, Lois Findly, 1–2; CSUF, Marcia Wray, 8, 16–17.

90. CSUF, Baron, 2; CSUF, Marian Conde, 7; CSUF, Lois Findly, 1–2, 6; CSUF, George Gortikov, 1–2.

91. CSUF, Adams, 1, 3; CSUF, Marietta Baron, 2, 8, 12; CSUF, Ralph Burnight, 2, 8; CSUF, Marian Conde, 4; CSUF, Lois Findley, 2; CSUF, George Gortikov, 2; CSUF, Louise Raine Gwinn, 9; CSUF, Blanche Holmes, 6; CSUF, Vivian Montgomery, 2, 6; CSUF, Leona Myler, 3; CSUF, George Shoals, 3; CSUF, Madeline Thomas, 2, 6.

92. CSUF, Marietta Baron, 8; CSUF, Myrtle Raine Borden, 9; CSUF, Louise Raine Gwinn, 9.

93. CSUF, Myrtle Raine Borden, 2, 12; CSUF, Charles Gallaher, 10; CSUF, George Gortikov, 10; CSUF, Louise Raine Gwinn, 2, 22–23; CSUF, Ira Holmes, 5.

94. CSUF, Louise Raine Gwinn, 22.

95. CSUF, Myrtle Raine Borden, 2, 13–14; CSUF, Louise Raine Gwinn, 2.

96. CSUF, Louise Raine Gwinn, 10; "Novel Surf Board and Canoes Made," *Long Beach Press*, 2/26/1921.

97. CSUF, Marian Conde, 3; CSUF, George Gortikov, 10; CSUF, Blanche Holmes, 11; Eisenhower, *Pat Nixon*, 29.

98. CSUF, Myrtle Raine Borden, 3, 18–19; CSUF, Howard Frampton, 10, 12; CSUF, Louise Raine Gwinn, 1, 14; CSUF, Blanche Holmes, 2; Eisenhower, *Pat Nixon*, 33.

99. CSUF, Howard Frampton, 11.

100. Eisenhower, *Pat Nixon*, 33; Woodbury College, email message to author, 8/19/2009.

101. David, *Lonely Lady*, 32; Nixon, *In the Arena*, 270.

102. David, *Lonely Lady*, 32.

103. CSUF, William Boyce, 12; CSUF, Mary Gardiner, 2–3; CSUF, C. Robert McCormick, 5–6; CSUF, Mabel Myers, 3–4, 11–12; Aitken, *Nixon*, 87–88; Eisenhower, *Pat Nixon*, 34–35.

104. CSUF, Blanche Holmes, 1–3; CSUF, Marcia Wray, 13.

105. CSUF, Mary Gardiner, 6; CSUF, Blanche Holmes, 1–3; David, *Lonely Lady*, 31.

106. WC, Virginia Counts, 3; CSUF, Mary Gardiner, 13; Eisenhower, *Pat Nixon*, 42, 45.

107. Eisenhower, *Pat Nixon*, 42; David, *Lonely Lady*, 35; Mazo, *Richard Nixon*, 32.

108. Aitken, *Nixon*, 88; Morris, *Richard Milhous Nixon*, 653.

109. Brodie, *Richard Nixon*, 153; Eisenhower, *Pat Nixon*, 44, 48; David, *Lonely Lady*, 36–37; Mazo, *Richard Nixon*, 33.

110. WC, Edna Collins, Bewley Allen, and Katherine Sorensen (Edna Collins), 1–2; WC, Margaret Theriault, 4–5; Eisenhower, *Pat Nixon*, 52.

111. WC, Robert Blake, 6; CSUF, Joyce Ernstberger, 3; CSUF, Eloise Hilberg, 4; CSUF, Marian Hodge, 4; CSUF, Heber Holloway, 6; CSUF, Edith Holt, 6; WC, Betty Kenworthy, 5–6, 9; WC, Frances King, 6; WC, Jennie Lavin, 9; WC, Freida Skinner, 2; CSUF, Frances Timberlake, 8; CSUF, Ellen Waer, 1–2; CSUF, Samuel Warren, 2; Nixon, *In the Arena*, 103.

112. CSUF, Martha Cato and Wilma Funk, 21; CSUF, Marian Hodge, 4; WC, Frances King, 7; CSUF, Marion Nichols, 13.

113. Aitken, *Nixon*, 89.

114. WC, Robert Blake, 7.

115. Eisenhower, *Pat Nixon*, 58.

116. CSUF, Marion Nichols, 12.

117. Eisenhower, *Pat Nixon*, 145 (citing *Collier's Magazine*).

118. Gellman, *Contender*, 19.

119. WC, Harriet Hudspeth, 4; CSUF, Judith Loubet, 9; WC, Judith Loubet, 2; Morris, *Richard Milhous Nixon*, 195.

120. JA, Richard Nixon Historic Video Transcript, 5/4/1975, 31–33.

121. WC, William Ryan, 6.

122. WC, Lawrene Anfinson (Evlyn Dorn), 20; WC, Virginia Buckman, 3; WC, Virginia Counts, 9; WC, #1 Evlyn Dorn, 4; WC, Jack Drown, 13; WC, Alyce Geiger

Koch, 7–8; WC, Eugene Koch, 3; Nixon Family Collection, box 17:13, 1940 Nixon Datebook; Nixon, *Memoirs*, 24; "Her Prediction."

123. WC, #2 Kenneth Ball, 4, 5, 19; Aitken, *Nixon*, 91.

124. WC, Alyce Koch, 8, 19; Nixon Family Collection, box 17:13, 1940 Nixon Datebook; Aitken, *Nixon*, 91; Nixon, *Memoirs*, 24–25.

125. WC, Elizabeth Cloes, 20; JA, Richard Nixon Historic Video Transcript, 5/4/1975, 13, 17–18; Nixon Family Collection, box 17:13, 1940 Nixon Datebook; Aitken, *Nixon*, 91; Nixon, *Memoirs*, 24–25; Schulte, *Young Nixon*, 227.

126. CSUF, Adams, 4; WC, John Arrambide, 26; CSUF, Dorothy Beeson, 10; WC, Matthew Bender, 2; CSUF, Brakensiek, 3; WC, Thomas Ryan, 2; Eisenhower, *Pat Nixon*, 67; Nixon, *Memoirs*, 25.

127. CSUF, Muriel Adams, 4; WC, John Arrambide, 26; CSUF, Dorothy Beeson, 10; WC, Matthew Bender, 2; CSUF, Brakensiek, 3; WC, Thomas Ryan, 2; Nixon Family Collection, 1941 Nixon Datebook; Eisenhower, *Pat Nixon*, 67; Nixon, *Memoirs*, 25.

128. Aitken, *Nixon*, 90.

129. WC, Virginia Counts, 9–10; Aitken, *Nixon*, 91; Eisenhower, *Pat Nixon*, 61.

130. JA, Richard Nixon Historic Video Transcript, 5/4/1975, 13, 17–18; Aitken, *Nixon*, 90–91; Eisenhower, *Pat Nixon*, 61, 65; Kornitzer, *Real Nixon*, 139; Nixon, *Memoirs*, 24.

131. Kornitzer, *Real Nixon*, 139.

132. WC, #2 Tom Bewley, 7–8; WC, #3 Tom Bewley, 1; JA, Richard Nixon Historic Video Transcript, 5/4/1975, 7–8; *Directory of Attorneys*; Nixon Family Collection, box 17:13, 1940 and 1941 Nixon Datebooks.

133. WC, #2 Tom Bewley, 7–8.

134. WC, #3 Tom Bewley, 1, 4; Nixon Family Collection, Citri-Frost Stock Certificate, 6/15/1940; Nixon Family Collection, box 18, K. D. Miller to Citrifrost Stockholders, n.d., corr.

135. Nixon Family Collection, box 18, K. D. Miller to Citrifrost Stockholders, n.d., corr.; Nixon Family Collection, box 18, Application for Building Permit, 3/8/1939.

136. WC, #2 Tom Bewley, 8; WC, #3 Tom Bewley, 4; Nixon Family Collection, box 18, K. D. Miller to Citrifrost Stockholders, n.d., corr.; Nixon Family Collection, box 18, Los Angeles County Department of Building and Planning.

137. Nixon Family Collection, box 18, K. D. Miller to Citrifrost Stockholders, n.d., corr.

138. Nixon Family Collection, box 18, K. D. Miller to Citrifrost Stockholders, n.d., corr.

139. WC, #2 Tom Bewley, 8; WC, #3 Tom Bewley, 4, 7.

140. BK, Tom Bewley, 5; WC, #2 Tom Bewley, 8; WC, #3 Tom Bewley, 6; WC, #3 Edith Holt, 3; Aitken, *Nixon*, 84; Kornitzer, *Real Nixon*, 130; Mazo, *Richard Nixon*, 29–30.

141. WC, #3 Tom Bewley, 6.

142. CSUF, William Seale, 2.

143. WC, #2 Tom Bewley, 24.

144. Nixon, *In the Arena*, 135.

145. WC, Henry Akard, 19; CSUF, Arthur Remley, 4.

146. CSUF, Donald Fantz, 9–10; WC, Donald Fantz, 3.

147. WC, Henry Akard, 19; CSUF, Wallace Black, 6; CSUF, Donald Fantz, 24; WC, Donald Fantz, 3; CSUF, Ferguson, 11, 14; WC, Raymond Fleischman, 2.

148. CSUF, Donald Fantz, 9–10, 23.

149. WC, Henry Akard, 4; CSUF, Wallace Black, 6; CSUF, Doug Ferguson, 10; WC, #3 Clint Harris, 3; WC, #1 Mel Rich, 21; "Richard Nixon Elected Head of 20-30 Club," *Whittier News*, 6/7/1939; Jackson, "Young Richard Nixon."

150. WC, Henry Akard, 15–17; CSUF, Wallace Black, 6; CSUF, Donald Fantz, 10–11; WC, Donald Fantz, 13; CSUF, Doug Ferguson, 10–11; Nixon Family Collection, box 11:19, 1940 and 1941 Nixon Datebooks; "Lions Hear Governor of 20-30 Clubs," *Whittier News*, 4/28/1938.

151. CSUF, Donald Fantz, 12, 22; WC, Donald Fantz, 3, 13; CSUF, Doug Ferguson, 12; WC, Raymond Fleischman, 6; WC, H. Ferris Gregory, 3; WC, #3 Clint Harris, 3; JA, Richard Nixon Historic Video Transcript, 5/4/1975, 28–29.

152. CSUF, Donald Fantz, 22; CSUF, Doug Ferguson, 12; WC, Raymond Fleischman, 6; WC, H. Ferris Gregory, 6; CSUF, Arthur Remley, 12; "20-30 Club To Install New Leader," *Whittier News*, 1/13/1940.

153. "To Discuss Propositions at Meeting Tuesday Night at the Bailey Auditorium," *Whittier News*, 10/24/1938; "Propositions on Ballot Explained to Audience at Bailey Auditorium," *Whittier News*, 10/26/1938.

154. "Expect 300 at Inter-Service Club Banquet," *Whittier News*, 11/5/1938.

155. CSUF, Irvin Chapman, 16; JA, Richard Nixon Historic Video Transcript, 5/4/1975, 6; WC, Orin Nowlin, 2–3, 5, 7; "Short News Items of Local Interest," *Whittier News*, 6/2/1941; "Richard Nixon to Head Orange Co. Cities Group," *Whittier News*, 6/5/1941; Aitken, *Nixon*, 84–85; Brodie, *Richard Nixon*, 154; Eisenhower, *Pat Nixon*, 56; Gellman, *Contender*, 18; Mazo, *Richard Nixon*, 30–31; Nixon, *Memoirs*, 22–23.

156. "Richard Nixon Is Only Candidate for Alumni President," *Whittier News*, 11/10/1938; Jackson, "Young Richard Nixon"; Elliott, *Whittier College*, 161.

157. CSUF, Glenn Kelly, 3–4; CSUF, Harry Schuyler, 7.

158. CSUF, Muriel Kelly, 13–14; JA, Richard Nixon Historic Video Transcript, 5/4/1975, 6–7; Aitken, *Nixon*, 84–85; Elliott, *Whittier College*, 161; Gellman, *Contender*, 18; Nixon, *In the Arena*, 268; "His Law Partner," *Daily News/East Whittier Review*, 1/19/1969; Jackson, "Young Richard Nixon."

159. WC, Alice Linton, 19; WC, Thomas Seulke, 5; WC, Robert Sillivan and Mary Sillivan, 32; WC, Arthur Sucksdorf, Florence Sucksdorf, and Ethel Garliepp, 4–5, 13.

160. WC, Raymond Burbank, 5; WC, Hadley Marshburn, 21; CSUF, Mildred Mendenhall, 2, 14–15; JA, Richard Nixon Historic Video Transcript, 5/4/1975, 28–29; WC, #2 Gladys Starbuck, 15, 19; WC, Arthur Sucksdorf, Florence Sucksdorf, and Ethel Garliepp, 16; Mrs. Geo. McWhirter, "East Whittier and Lowell," *Whittier News*, 7/20/1938.

161. WC, George Irving Jr., 11.

162. wc, Julie Nixon Eisenhower, 9; wc, #2 Anne Gilmore, 25, 33; wc, George Irving Jr., 3; wc, #2 Charles Eric Milhous, 4; wc, Charles Post, 8; wc, Lola Williams, 11; David, *Lonely Lady*, 52.

163. wc, Jane Barr, 7; wc, George Irving Jr., 3, 6; bk, #2 Hannah Nixon, 28.

164. Nixon and Olson, *Nixons*, 102–3.

165. wc, #4 Clint Harris, 8; ja, Richard Nixon Historic Video Transcript, 5/4/1975, 29; Nixon and Olson, *Nixons*, 103.

166. Nixon and Olson, *Nixons*, 105.

167. csuf, Floyd Wildermuth, 11; Ed Nixon, interviews by author, 1/9/2010, 5/7/2010; Ed Nixon, email message to author, 1/29/2010; *Whittier City Directory*, 1942; Los Angeles County Recorder, Deed, 7/18/1939; Morris, *Richard Milhous Nixon*, 194–95; Nixon and Olson, *Nixons*, 88.

168. csuf, Floyd Wildermuth, 11.

169. wc, Hannah Reeves and Truman Reeves, 5–6; wc, Marygene Wright, 4; Nixon and Olson, *Nixons*, 116–17.

170. csuf, Judith Loubet, 14; ja, Richard Nixon Historic Video Transcript, 5/4/1975, 10–11.

171. csuf, Mrs. Benjamin Roberts and Bill Roberts, 2, 11, 14; David Margolick, "Town Debates Its Decaying Sliver of Nixon's Life," *New York Times*, 6/26/1992.

172. csuf, Harold Stone, 4; wc, Harold Stone, 10.

173. csuf, Mrs. Benjamin Roberts and Bill Roberts, 2–3.

174. wc, I. N. Kraushaar, 1; wc, Harold Stone, 12.

175. csuf, Jasper Burch, 2–3.

176. ja, Richard Nixon Historic Video Transcript, 5/4/1975, 10–11; csuf, Mrs. Benjamin Roberts and Bill Roberts, 15; wc, Harold Stone, 9–10; Nixon Family Collection, box 17:13, 1940 Nixon Datebook.

177. wc, Joseph Seppi, 2–3; csuf, Harold Stone, 2; wc, Harold Stone, 9–10.

178. csuf, Jasper Burch, 4; "High Court Made Topic of Club Address," *Whittier News*, 11/29/1940.

179. csuf, Harold Stone, 2; wc, Harold Stone, 6, 14; Nixon Family Collection, box 17:13, 1940 Nixon Datebook; Aitken, *Nixon*, 85; "Kiwanians of Whittier Host to La Habrans," *Whittier News*, 2/20/1940.

180. wc, Harold Stone, 10.

181. ja, Richard Nixon Historic Video Transcript, 5/4/1975, 13–15; csuf, Harold Stone, 22–23.

182. wc, Freida Skinner, 3; Nixon Family Collection, box 17:13, 1940 and 1941 Nixon Datebooks.

183. Aitken, *Nixon*, 92–93; Eisenhower, *Pat Nixon*, 61, 65; David, *Lonely Lady*, 8–9.

184. wc, Eugene Koch, 13; Aitken, *Nixon*, 92–93; David, *Lonely Lady*, 54.

185. wc, Thomas Seulke, 6.

186. csuf, Judith Loubet, 21, 38; wc, Judith Loubet, 2.

187. wc, Virginia Buckman, 2; wc, George Irving Jr. (Evlyn Dorn), 13; wc, Judith Loubet (and Evlyn Dorn), 5; ja, Richard Nixon Historic Video Transcript, 5/4/1975, 11–12.

188. CSUF, Edith Holt, 6; WC, #2 Edith Holt, 5; WC, #2 Alyce Koch, 2–4; Marygene Wright, interviews by author, 9/7/2011, 3/11/2014.

189. WC, Edna Collins, Bewley Allen and Katherine Sorensen, 3; WC, Virginia Counts, 5; CSUF, Edith Holt, 5; WC, #1 Alyce Koch, 21; JA, Richard Nixon Historic Video Transcript, 5/4/1975, 18–19; JA, Richard Nixon Historic Video Transcript, 5/6/1975, 9; Aitken, *Nixon*, 93; Eisenhower, *Pat Nixon*, 69; David, *Lonely Lady*, 8; Morris, *Richard Milhous Nixon*, 227; "Miss Patricia Ryan, Mr. Nixon Plight Marriage Vows," *Whittier News*, 6/22/1940.

190. Nixon and Olson, *Nixons*, 118–19.

191. CSUF, Edith Timberlake, 49; Eisenhower, *Pat Nixon*, 69; Nixon and Olson, *Nixons*, 118–19.

192. WC, Kathryn Bewley, 5; CSUF, Ella Furnas and Blanche McClure, 6; WC, Josephine Harrison, 11; Nixon and Olson, *Nixons*, 118–19; "Miss Patricia Ryan, Mr. Nixon."

193. JA, Richard Nixon Historic Video Transcript, 5/4/1975, 21–22, 27–28; Eisenhower, *Pat Nixon*, 70; Morris, *Richard Milhous Nixon*, 229; Cramer, "La Habra."

194. WC, Jack Drown, 11; WC, #1 Alyce Koch, 22; JA, Richard Nixon Historic Video Transcript, 5/4/1975, 21–22, 27–28; CSUF, Phil Studebaker, 8–9; Nixon Family Collection, box 17:8, canceled envelope addressed to Pat Nixon (no return sender or address), 12/28/1940; Aitken, *Nixon*, 94; Gellman, *Contender*, 20; Morris, *Richard Milhous Nixon*, 229.

195. BK, Jack and Helene Drown, 12; WC, Jack Drown, 11; JA, Richard Nixon Historic Video Transcript, 5/4/1975, 21–22; WC, Alice Snedecor, 1–2, 16–18; Nixon Family Collection, D. A. Stouffer to Pat Nixon, 7/6/1941, corr.; Aitken, *Nixon*, 94.

196. CSUF, Hadley Marshburn, 3; Nixon Family Collection, Western Union Telegram, Office of Price Administration to Richard Nixon, n.d.; *Whittier City Directory*, 1942; Aitken, *Nixon*, 94; Eisenhower, *Pat Nixon*, 70; Morris, *Richard Milhous Nixon*, 229.

197. BK, Jack and Helene Drown, 1; WC, #1 Alyce Koch, 22; Eisenhower, *Pat Nixon*, 71.

198. WC, Virginia Buckman, 1; CSUF, Samuel Warren, 9; Kornitzer, *Real Nixon*, 136.

199. BK, Jack and Helene Drown, 1; Maureen Nunn, interview by author, 9/6/2010; Kornitzer, *Real Nixon*, 136.

200. BK, Jack Drown, 2, 5.

201. WC, Jack Drown, 14; Nixon Family Collection, box 17:13, 1941 Nixon Datebook.

202. CSUF, Martha Cato, 21–22.

203. WC, Jack Drown, 10–11; WC, Harold Smith (and Evlyn Dorn), 1–2; Eisenhower, *Pat Nixon*, 71.

204. WC, Jack Drown, 10–11; Eisenhower, *Pat Nixon*, 71; David, *Lonely Lady*, 194.

205. WC, Kathryn Bewley, 5; WC, Wallace Black, 8; WC, Curtis Counts, 3–4; WC, Virginia Counts, 4, 8, 10; WC, #1 Evlyn Dorn, 4; WC, #3 Dorn, 7; BK, Jack and Helene Drown, 12; WC, Jack Drown, 2, 11; WC, Josephine Harrison, 11–13; CSUF, Edith Holt, 15; WC, #1 Alyce Koch, 2, 7–8, 23; WC, Eugene Koch, 3; CSUF, Marion Nichols, 13; JA, Richard Nixon Historic Video Transcript, 5/4/1975, 21–22; CSUF, Harold Stone, 5; WC, Harold Stone, 21–22; WC, Floyd Wildermuth, 12.

206. CSUF, Doug Ferguson, 13; CSUF, Muriel Kelly, 6, 10; WC, Alyce Koch, 6, 12; WC, Eugene Koch, 4; CSUF, Judith Loubet, 29; WC, Judith Loubet (and Evlyn Dorn), 8; WC, James Stewart, 7; WC, Virginia Counts, 4.

207. WC, Eugene Koch, 3, 7, 10; WC, Jack Drown, 10–11; WC, #1 Alyce Koch, 12; WC, #2 Jessamyn West, 16; William Wright, interview by author, 3/11/2014.

208. Aitken, *Nixon*, 94.

209. WC, Virginia Counts, 5; WC, Lyman Dietrick, 3–4.

210. WC, #3 Tom Bewley, 7.

211. Nixon Family Collection, box 18, Nixon to T. Brewster, 6/17/1941, corr.

212. Nixon Family Collection, box 17:13, 1940 Nixon Datebook, 12/12/1940, 12/17/1940; 1941 Nixon Calendar; Kornitzer, *Real Nixon*, 130.

213. WC, #2 Tom Bewley, 9; Aitken, *Nixon*, 83, 221.

214. JA, Richard Nixon Historic Video Transcript, 5/4/1975, 7–8; Aitken, *Nixon*, 83.

215. JA, Richard Nixon Historic Video Transcript, 5/4/1975, 26–27; Nixon Family Collection, box 18, OPA to Nixon, 11/19/1941, telegram.

216. JA, Richard Nixon Historic Video Transcript, 5/4/1975, 26–27.

217. JA, Richard Nixon Historic Video Transcript, 5/4/1975, 25–26; Eisenhower, *Pat Nixon*, 75; Nixon, *Memoirs*, 26.

218. CSUF, Muriel Kelly, 8.

219. "Nixon to Washington," *Whittier News*, 1/2/1942.

220. WC, Harland Leathers, 2, 6; WC, William Roalfe, 1–2; Kornitzer, *Real Nixon*, 143.

221. Kornitzer, *Real Nixon*, 143.

222. CSUF, Paul Smith, 22.

223. WC, Edwin Bronner, 5–6; CSUF, Paul Smith, 22.

224. WC, Edwin Bronner, 5–6.

225. WC, Raymond Burbank, 28; WC, Sheldon Jackson, 5–6; CSUF, Harold Walker, 2–4.

226. WC, Kathryn Bewley, 7.

227. WC, Homer Bemis, 16; WC, Robert Blake, 5; WC, Joseph Cosand, 2–3; WC, Robert Downey, 16; WC, Grant Garman, 1; WC, #3 Clint Harris, 12; WC, Hadley Marshburn, 26; WC, Howard Marshburn, 19; CSUF, Theodore Marshburn, 9; WC, Calvin Milhous, Phillip Milhous, and Oliver Milhous, 2–3; WC, Charles Leonard Milhous, 15–16; WC, #2 Charles Leonard Milhous, 1–2; WC, Claude Milhous, 2; WC, William Alan Milhous, 1; CSUF, William A. Milhous, 7–8; CSUF, A. C. Newsom, 5; CSUF, Marion Nichols, 19–20; JA, Richard Nixon Historic Video Transcript, 5/3/1975, 22–23; WC, Gailerd Page and Viola Page, 4–5; WC, #1 Mel Rich, 10–11; WC, #2 Harry Schuyler, 5; WC, #1 Gladys Starbuck, 3–4; Brodie, *Richard Nixon*, 163.

228. CSUF, Kenneth Ball, 21–22; WC, Charles Leonard Milhous, 16.

229. WC, Merton Wray, 14.

230. WC, #1 Tom Bewley, 30.

231. CSUF, Wallace Black, 10.

232. JA, Richard Nixon Historic Video Transcript, 5/4/1975, 38–39; Aitken, *Nixon*, 99.

233. CSUF, Mildred Beard, 10–11; CSUF, Martha Cato and Wilma Funk, 6–7; WC, Dorris Gurley, 7; JA, Richard Nixon Historic Video Transcript, 5/6/197511; CSUF, Lucille Parsons, 9; CSUF, Floyd Wildermuth, 11.

234. WC, #1 Evlyn Dorn, 5.

235. Aitken, *Nixon*, 100; Morris, *Richard Milhous Nixon*, 246; Nixon and Olson, *Nixons*, 120; Nixon, *Memoirs*, 27–28.

236. WC, #1 Evlyn Dorn, 5; Aitken, *Nixon*, 100; Morris, *Richard Milhous Nixon*, 246; Nixon and Olson, *Nixons*, 120; Nixon, *Memoirs*, 27–28.

237. Aitken, *Nixon*, 100.

238. JA, Richard Nixon Historic Video Transcript, 5/4/1975, 44–45.

239. WC, Carl Fleps, 5–6.

240. WC, Carl Fleps, 5–6, 14; JA, Richard Nixon Historic Video Transcript, 5/6/1975, 11–12.

241. WC, Carl Fleps, 5–6.

242. WC, Hollis Dole, 2–3; WC, Carl Fleps, 5–6.

243. WC, Hollis Dole, 3; WC, Jonathan Dyer, 14–15.

244. WC, Hollis Dole, 3.

245. WC, Hollis Dole, 3–4, 13; JA, Richard Nixon Historic Video Transcript, 5/6/1975, 16–18.

246. WC, Hollis Dole, 4; WC, Jonathan Dyer, 14–15, 17.

247. WC, Hollis Dole, 4; WC, Jonathan Dyer, 16–18; JA, Richard Nixon Historic Video Transcript, 5/4/1975, 45–46.

248. WC, Hollis Dole, 4; WC, Jonathan Dyer, 14–15, 17–18.

249. WC, Jonathan Dyer, 14–15; JA, Richard Nixon Historic Video Transcript, 5/4/1975, 45–46.

250. WC, Jonathan Dyer, 17–18.

251. WC, Hollis Dole, 4–6; WC, Carl Fleps, 5–6; JA, Richard Nixon Historic Video Transcript, 5/4/1975, 47–48.

252. BK, James Stewart, 1, 3, 6; WC, James Stewart, 5.

253. BK, James Stewart, 5.

254. BK, James Stewart, 5.

255. BK, James Stewart, 8.

256. WC, Hollis Dole, 6–7; BK, James Stewart, 8; WC, James Stewart.

257. WC, James Stewart, 6, 9; Aitken, *Nixon*, 104.

258. WC, James Stewart, 6; JA, Richard Nixon Historic Video Transcript, 5/4/1975, 46; Aitken, *Nixon*, 104.

259. Aitken, *Nixon*, 108–9.

260. WC, #4 Evlyn Dorn, 4–5; CSUF, Mrs. Benjamin Roberts and Bill Roberts, 11; CSUF, Harold Walker, 3–4.

261. CSUF, Raymond Burbank, 2; WC, Raymond Burbank, 12; WC, #1 Albert Upton, 29.

262. WC, Lawrene Anfinson, 22, 24.

263. WC, Hollis Dole, 5–6; WC, Carl Fleps, 15.

264. JA, Richard Nixon Historic Video Transcript, 5/6/1975, 21; Aitken, *Nixon*, 110; Nixon, *Memoirs*, 30.

265. WC, Edith Nunes, 17; Aitken, *Nixon*, 107.

266. Marygene Wright, interviews by author, 9/7/2011, 3/11/2014.

267. WC, Hollis Dole, 11; WC, Jonathan Dyer, 23; WC, Charles Gronert, 4; WC, Stanton Haight, 9; BK, James Stewart, 3.

268. BK, James Stewart, 12; WC, James Stewart, 6.

269. WC, Hollis Dole, 3–6; JA, Richard Nixon Historic Video Transcript, 5/4/1975, 51; Nixon and Olson, *Nixons*, 121.

270. CSUF, William A. Milhous, 7; WC, William Alan Milhous, 1; JA, Richard Nixon Historic Video Transcript, 5/6/1975, 23–24; WC, James Stewart, 7; Aitken, *Nixon*, 111; Kornitzer, *Real Nixon*, 147.

271. BK, Paul Smith and Albert Upton, 14; Nixon and Olson, *Nixons*, 121.

6. Congressional Race

1. UCB, Frank Jorgensen, 1, 23; Aitken, *Nixon*, 114; Gellman, *Contender*, 41.

2. Aitken, *Nixon*, 115; Worthen, *Young Nixon and His Rivals*, 43.

3. CSUF, Linda Baker, 29; WC, Roy Day, 3–5; WC, Charles E. Cooper, 5.

4. PB, #1 Roy Day, 6–7; PB, Roy Crocker, 2; Aitken, *Nixon*, 130; Mazo, *Richard Nixon*, 43.

5. CSUF, Wallace Black, 14; CSUF, Donald Fantz, 20; BK, Hubert Perry, 1; BK, #1 Hubert Perry, 2, 7; Hubert Perry, interviews by author, 12/8/2009, 12/9/2009, 1/5/2010, 1/6/2010, 2/22/2010, 9/8/2010, 11/10/2010, 11/18/2010; Aitken, *Nixon*, 85; Nixon and Olson, *Nixons*, 1233.

6. WC, Frank Jorgensen, 2.

7. CSUF, Wallace Black, 19; BK, Hubert Perry, 13.

8. Eisenhower, *Pat Nixon*, 85.

9. PB, #2 Roy Day, 5; UCB, Frank Jorgensen, iii.

10. WC, John Buckley, 6; WC, Roy Day, 15; WC, Frank Jorgensen, 2.

11. BK, Tom Bewley, 3; WC, Charles E. Cooper, 5, 28–29; WC, Harold Lutz, 10–11; CSUF, Lyle Otterman, 26; BK, Annabelle Tupper, 5–6.

12. WC, Roy Day, 3–4; UCB, Frank Jorgensen, 7.

13. JA, Richard Nixon Historic Video Transcript, 5/4/1975, 50; Nixon, *In the Arena*, 212.

14. Nixon, *In the Arena*, 213.

15. Aitken, *Nixon*, 114; Eisenhower, *Pat Nixon*, 85; Mazo, *Richard Nixon*, 43.

16. Mazo, *Richard Nixon*, 44.

17. UCB, Roy Day, 17; CSUF, Donald Fantz, 13–15; WC, Donald Fantz, 5–6.

18. Eisenhower, *Pat Nixon*, 233; Nixon, *Memoirs*, 291; Toledano, *Nixon*, 41.

19. WC, John Rennenburg, 5–6; BK, James Stewart, 9, 15.

20. Kornitzer, *Real Nixon*, 144–45.

21. Nixon, *In the Arena*, 211.

22. WC, Matthew Bender, 4; CSUF, Carmen Griffin, 9; David, *Lonely Lady*, 64; Nixon, *Memoirs*, 34.

23. BK, Jack Drown, 15.

24. David, *Lonely Lady*, 64.

25. David, *Lonely Lady*, 63.

26. PB, #1 Roy Day, 7; WC, Roy Day, 4.

27. Nixon and Olson, *Nixons*, 123.

28. Nixon and Olson, *Nixons*, 123.

29. Rex Kennedy, Heard in the Barbershop, *Whittier News*, 10/29/1945; Mathony, *Whittier*, 83.

30. Aitken, *Nixon*, 115; "Road to the White House," *Daily News/East Whittier Review*, 1/19/1969.

31. Aitken, *Nixon*, 115; "Road to the White House."

32. UCB, Frank Jorgensen, 8; WC, Harrison McCall, 2–3, 10–11; Aitken, *Nixon*, 115; McIntyre, *Rememb'ring*, 203; Gellman, *Contender*, 32–33; Morris, *Richard Milhous Nixon*, 276, 279.

33. PB, Earl Adams, 4; UCB, McIntyre Faries, 103–4; WC, Harrison McCall, 10–11; Aitken, *Nixon*, 115.

34. UCB, Roy Day, 18; Eisenhower, *Pat Nixon*, 86; Morris, *Richard Milhous Nixon*, 276; Nixon, *Memoirs*, 35.

35. Eisenhower, *Pat Nixon*, 86; Kornitzer, *Real Nixon*, 154–55; Nixon, *Memoirs*, 35.

36. PB, Roy Crocker, 4–5; WC, Harold Lutz, 11; WC, Harrison McCall, 12; Nixon and Olson, *Nixons*, 123; Toledano, *Nixon*, 41.

37. PB, #1 Roy Day, 8; WC, Roy Day, 4; Aitken, *Nixon*, 116; Kornitzer, *Real Nixon*, 154.

38. UCB, Frank Jorgensen, 9; WC, Adela Rogers St. Johns, 3, 13; Eisenhower, *Pat Nixon*, 86; Morris, *Richard Milhous Nixon*, 282.

39. CSUF, Linda Baker, 39.

40. Eisenhower, *Pat Nixon*, 86; Gellman, *Contender*, 41.

41. CSUF, Linda Baker, 2–4; WC, Roy Day, 22; CSUF, Newt Robinson, 22.

42. CSUF, Linda Baker, 30–31, 57; Campaign 1946, box 1, Evans to Nixon, 11/8/1946, corr., and Nixon to Nixon, 11/13/1946, corr.; Gellman, *Contender*, 42.

43. CSUF, Wallace Black, 2, 14–15, 19; WC, #1 Albert Upton, 29–30; WC, #2 Albert Upton, 4–5; Gellman, *Contender*, 90.

44. Campaign 1946, box 1, Roy Day to Nixon, 3/14/1946, corr., and Nixon to Day, 3/17/1946, corr.; Aitken, *Nixon*, 119–21.

45. JA, Richard Nixon Historic Video Transcript, 5/6/1975, 15–18; Nixon, *In the Arena*, 213.

46. JA, Richard Nixon Historic Video Transcript, 5/6/1975, 16–19.

47. UCB, Frank Jorgenson, iv; Gellman, *Contender*, 43; Morris, *Richard Milhous Nixon*, 313.

48. Campaign 1946, box 1, C. C. Phillips to Nixon, 2/7/1946, corr.

49. UCB, Frank Jorgensen, iv; UCB, Day, 7–8; Gellman, *Contender*, 43.

50. UCB, Roy Crocker, 26; PB, #1 Roy Day, 6; UCB, Roy Day, 31; Gellman, *Contender*, 42, 90.

51. UCB, Roy Crocker, 23–24, 26–27; PB, Roy Crocker, 6; Gellman, *Contender*, 42.

52. UCB, Roy Crocker, 24.

53. WC, Frank Jorgensen, 4.

54. UCB, Earl Adams, 4; CSUF, Guy Dixon, 25; WC, Robert Downey, 10–11; Mazo, *Richard Nixon*, 43.

55. CSUF, Hadley Marshburn, 7.

56. Mazo, *Richard Nixon*, 43.

57. David, *Lonely Lady*, 67.

58. Eisenhower, *Pat Nixon*, 87; Gellman, *Contender*, 44.

59. Maureen Nunn, interview by author, 9/6/2010.

60. CSUF, Linda Baker, 2–4, 30–31, 64.

61. CSUF, Myra Barton, 11.

62. WC, Waymeth Garrett, 6–8; Los Angeles County Recorder, Deed, 3/23/1939.

63. WC, Waymeth Garret, 9; Clara Jane Nixon, interviews by author, 7/8/2010, 9/17/2010, 1/17/2011, 9/21/2011; Los Angeles County Recorder, Deed, 3/30/1939; Aitken, *Nixon*, 121; Gellman, *Contender*, 44; Nixon and Olson, *Nixons*, 119; *Whittier City Directory*, 1947.

64. WC, Roy Day, 8.

65. WC, Wallace Black, 9–10; WC, Waymeth Garrett, 11; Eisenhower, *Pat Nixon*, 87–88; Nixon, *In the Arena*, 213.

66. Nixon, *In the Arena*, 213.

67. Aitken, *Nixon*, 124.

68. CSUF, Linda Baker, 32–34; PB, #1 Roy Day, 9; UCB, Roy Day, 9, 48; Eisenhower, *Pat Nixon*, 89; David, *Lonely Lady*, 66; Mazo, *Richard Nixon*, 204; Nixon, *Memoirs*, 36.

69. CSUF, Linda Baker, 32–34; "Her Prediction: 'The Presidency,'" *Daily News/East Whittier Review*, 1/19/1969.

70. CSUF, Donald Fantz, 17.

71. WC, Roy Day, 7–8; Gellman, *Contender*, 44.

72. David, *Lonely Lady*, 67.

73. WC, Hannah Weeger, 2, 6.

74. CSUF, Wallace Black, 18–19; WC, Roy Day, 12; WC, Jack Drown, 5–6; CSUF, Lyle Otterman, 28; WC, Hannah Weeger, 4–5.

75. CSUF, Harold Stone, 23.

76. Crowley, *Nixon off the Record*, 123.

77. Campaign 1946, box 1: Hector Powell to Nixon, 2/27/1945, corr.; Ray Smith to Nixon, 3/12/1946, corr.; Roy Day to Clifford Ostler, 3/14/1946, corr.; Morris, *Richard Milhous Nixon*, 294.

78. WC, Marion Hodge, 10.

79. WC, Kathryn Bewley, 8; WC, #3 Clint Harris, 6; WC, Marion Hodge, 2; CSUF, Gerald Kepple, 9; CSUF, Harry Schuyler, 6; BK, James Udell, 5; WC, Lola Williams, 9.

80. WC, #4 Evlyn Dorn, 3–4.

81. Roberta Dorn, interviews by author, 10/22/2013, 11/15/2013.

82. WC, #4 Evlyn Dorn, 3–4; WC, Jack Drown (Evlyn Dorn), 21; "Her Prediction," 49; *Whittier City Directory*, 1946. In 1939 Dorn resided at 545 Bailey. *Whittier City Directory*, 1939.

83. Roberta Dorn, interviews by author, 10/22/2013, 11/15/2013.

84. Morris, *Richard Milhous Nixon*, 298.

85. BK, Kyle Palmer, 1–2.

86. Kornitzer, *Real Nixon*, 158–59.

87. BK, Norman Chandler, 1; Kornitzer, *Real Nixon*, 160–61.

88. BK, Norman Chandler, 6–7.

89. BK, Norman Candler, 1; Halberstam, *Powers*, 256; Kornitzer, *Real Nixon*, 160–61.

90. Nixon, *In the Arena*, 169.

91. Nixon, *In the Arena*, 250.

92. UCB, Earl Adams, 5; UCB, Roy Crocker, 27.

93. UCB, Frank Jorgensen, 10; WC, Tolbert Moorhead, 4–5; Eisenhower, *Pat Nixon*, 88; Gellman, *Contender*, 62; "Elect Richard Nixon Your Congressman," *Covina Argus Citizen*, 8/30/1946.

94. WC, Adela Rogers St. Johns, 3, 6; Gellman, *Contender*, 62.

95. Aitken, *Nixon*, 121; David, *Lonely Lady*, 64–66.

96. PB, Harrison McCall, 19.

97. PB, Harrison McCall, 10.

98. CSUF, Donald Fantz, 16–17; David, *Lonely Lady*, 65, 67.

99. Clara Jane Nixon, interviews by author, 7/8/2010, 9/17/2010, 1/17/2011, 9/21/2011.

100. Clara Jane Nixon, interviews by author, 7/8/2010, 9/17/2010, 1/17/2011, 9/21/2011.

101. CSUF, Harry Schuyler, 7; WC, Adela Rogers St. Johns, 15.

102. PB, Earl Adams, 18–19; UCB, Earl Adams, 6; *Thurston's Pasadena*; California Secretary of State, 1946 Nomination Papers.

103. WC, Patricia Hitt, 10; CSUF, Lucille Parsons, 18–19; WC, Charles Post, 14; WC, #1 Newt Robinson, 19–20; "Nixon Will Aid Farmers If Elected," *Whittier News*, 9/26/1946.

104. WC, Roy Day, 8–9.

105. WC, Roy Day, 9; CSUF, Donald Fantz, 16; Toledano, *Nixon*, 42–43.

106. Aitken, *Nixon*, 125; McDougal, *Privileged Son*, 177.

107. Mazo, *Richard Nixon*, 46.

108. UCB, Frank Jorgensen, 12; Morris, *Richard Milhous Nixon*, 317.

109. CSUF, Gerald Kepple, 8.

110. PB, Earl Adams, 13; PB, Roy Crocker, 2; Gellman, *Contender*, 69.

111. CSUF, Lucille Parsons, 23; Mazo, *Richard Nixon*, 48.

112. CSUF, Lyle Otterman, 26–27.

113. Hubert Perry, interviews by author, 12/8/2009, 12/9/2009, 1/5/2010, 1/6/2010, 2/22/2010, 9/8/2010, 11/10/2010, 11/18/2010.

114. Morris, *Richard Milhous Nixon*, 318–19.

115. Gellman, *Contender*, 72; Morris, *Richard Milhous Nixon*, 315.

116. WC, Ormond Flood, 2–3.

117. Kyle Palmer, "November Fifth: National House-Cleaning Day," *Los Angeles Times*, 9/22/1946.

118. Gellman, *Contender*, 77.

119. "Men's Glee Scores in Recent Concerts," *Quaker Campus*, 3/2/1934.

120. WC, Roy Day, 9–10; Gellman, *Contender*, 78; Kornitzer, *Real Nixon*, 189; Morris, *Richard Milhous Nixon*, 328; Nixon, *Memoirs*, 40.

121. WC, Roy Day, 9–10.

122. PB, #1 Roy Day, 12; CSUF, Gerald Kepple, 8; PB, Harrison McCall, 21; Gellman, *Contender*, 80; Nixon, *Memoirs*, 40.

123. WC, Robert Downey, 12; CSUF, Donald Fantz, 16; BK, Perry House (Alice Walker), 7; Nixon, *Memoirs*, 41.

124. WC, Charles E. Cooper, 26; CSUF, Guy Dixon, 23, 25.

125. PB, Earl Adams, 16; WC, Harold Lutz, 12.

126. "Hear Richard M. Nixon, Candidate for Congress," *Covina Argus Citizen*, 10/25/1946; Gellman, *Contender*, 74.

127. WC, Merritt Burdg, 9.

128. CSUF, Wallace Black, 13; "Nixon Rally Here Tonight," *Whittier News*, 11/4/1946.

129. Morris, *Richard Milhous Nixon*, 334.

130. Aitken, *Nixon*, 129; Lundberg, *Big Orange*, 2; Nixon and Olson, *Nixons*, 126; Graf, *Statistics*.

131. Aitken, *Nixon*, 129.

132. PB, #1 Roy Day, 16; PB, Harrison McCall, 14, 20.

133. Aitken, *Nixon*, 129.

134. Kornitzer, *Real Nixon*, 156.

135. Crowley, *Nixon off the Record*, 146.

7. National Prominence

1. WC, #2 Charles L. Milhous, 5–6; WC, Camilla Simmons and William Simmons (William Simmons), 26; WC, Clayton Votaw, 4–5.

2. CSUF, J. Douglas Brannon, 11; CSUF, Doug Ferguson, 16; WC, Merle Lally, 4; CSUF, Charles Milhous, 2–3; WC, Charles L. Milhous, 27; WC, #2 Charles L. Milhous, 8; CSUF, William Alan Milhous, 4–5; WC, William Alan Milhous, 2–3; BK, Don Nixon, 1–3; CSUF, Arlene Randall, 4; WC, Mabel Schuyler and Roger Schuyler (Roger Schuyler), 13; WC, #1 Thomas Seulke, 6; WC, #2 Thomas Seulke, 10; CSUF, Geri Studebaker, 7; Clara Jane Nixon, interviews by author, 7/8/2010, 9/17/2010, 1/17/2011, 9/21/2011; Aitken, *Nixon*, 286.

3. CSUF, Doug Ferguson, 17; WC, #2 Charles L. Milhous, 9; Aitken, *Nixon*, 21.

4. CSUF, William Alan Milhous, 5–6.

5. WC, Roger Johnson, 1–2, 7–8.

6. BK, Robert Finch, 1–2.

7. Brodie, *Richard Nixon*, 190.

8. Nixon, *In the Arena*, 216.

9. Mazo, *Richard Nixon*, 49.

10. Aitken, *Nixon*, 142; Eisenhower, *Pat Nixon*, 96; Gellman, *Contender*, 126; Morris, *Richard Milhous Nixon*, 363; Nixon, *Memoirs*, 49.

11. PPS 206, Herter Committee, box 1, HMS Queen Mary, List of Passengers, 10/4/1947.

12. Gellman, *Contender*, 138.

13. Kornitzer, *Real Nixon*, 164.

14. JA, Richard Nixon Historic Video Transcript, 5/3/1975, 16–17; Nixon, *In the Arena*, 216–17.

15. Nixon, *In the Arena*, 216.

16. Nixon, *In the Arena*, 216–17.

17. WC, John Reilly, 11; PPS 212, 1947 Nixon Datebook; Gellman, *Contender*, 139; Nixon, *In the Arena*, 216–17.

18. WC, Newt Robinson, 16–17; PPS 212, 1947 Nixon Datebook; Gellman, *Contender*, 139.

19. Herbert G. Klein, "Address Warns of Red Peril," *Alhambra Post-Advocate*, 10/20/1947; "Aid Europe Soon, Rep. Nixon Urges," *Bakersfield Californian*, 11/5/1947; "Legislator Fears Red Rule in Europe," *Long Beach Press Telegram*, 11/5/1947; "Congressman Nixon Will Discuss Need for Food in Europe at Meeting Monday," *Covina Argus Citizen*, 10/31/1947.

20. Klein, "Address Warns of Red Peril."

21. Klein, "Address Warns of Red Peril."

22. Nixon, *In the Arena*, 216–17.

23. PPS 212, 1947 Nixon Datebook.

24. BK, Bob DiGiorgio, 1–2.

25. "GOP Solons Disagree with Truman on Need for Quick Europe Aid," *San Mateo Times*, 10/24/1947; Nixon, *In the Arena*, 216–17; Nixon, *Six Crises*, 65.

26. Nixon, *Memoirs*, 52.

27. Kornitzer, *Real Nixon*, 165.

28. Kornitzer, *Real Nixon*, 166.

29. Gellman, *Contender*, 168.

30. Nixon, *In the Arena*, 217; Worthen, *Young Nixon*, 60–61.

31. Gellman, *Contender*, 169.

32. Gellman, *Contender*, 169.

33. Nixon, *Six Crises*, 45.

34. "California Solon Grounded Twice on 'Jinx' Flight," *Oakland Tribune*, 5/22/1948.

35. WC, Donald Fantz, 19; Gellman, *Contender*, 176–77.

36. Morris, *Richard Milhous Nixon*, 372–73.

37. Gellman, *Contender*, 178; Morris, *Richard Milhous Nixon*, 281, 373.

38. Gellman, *Contender*, 171.

39. Eisenhower, *Pat Nixon*, 98.

40. Halberstam, *Powers*, 256.

41. CSUF, William Price, 13–14.

42. CSUF, William Price, 13–14, 66.

43. Eisenhower, *Pat Nixon*, 98; Nixon, *Six Crises*, 45.

44. CSUF, Linda Baker, 59.

45. Eisenhower, *Pat Nixon*, 98; Nixon, *In the Arena*, 215; Nixon, *Memoirs*, 67.

46. Toledano, *Nixon*, 53.

47. Aitken, *Nixon*, 151–52.

48. Nixon, *Six Crises*, 2–3.

49. Nixon, *Six Crises*, 5.

50. Nixon, *Six Crises*, 5–6.

51. Nixon, *In the Arena*, 218–19.

52. Nixon, *Six Crises*, 10.

53. Nixon, *Six Crises*, 9–10.

54. CSUF, Kenneth Ball, 21–22; BK, Bob DiGiorgio, 4; WC, John Reilly, 11; WC, Floyd Wildermuth, 7–8.

55. Nixon, *Six Crises*, 68.

56. BK, Bob King, 9; BK, William Rogers, 1, 18.

57. BK, Bob King, 9; "Today in Washington," *Bakersfield Californian*, 9/7/1948; Nixon, *Six Crises*, 10.

58. BK, William Rogers, 1; Nixon, *Six Crises*, 12, 15.

59. BK, William Rogers, 2; Nixon, *Six Crises*, 55.

60. Nixon, *Six Crises*, 8.

61. Nixon, *Six Crises*, 23.

62. Nixon, *Six Crises*, 24.

63. Nixon, *Six Crises*, 37; Toledano, *Nixon*, 70.

64. Nixon, *Six Crises*, 39.

65. "Today in Washington," *Bakersfield Californian*, 9/3/1948; Black, *Life in Full*, 106.

66. WC, William Sparling, 6; Black, *Life in Full*, 121; Worthen, *Young Nixon*, 62.

67. Quoted in Nixon, *Six Crises*, 54.

68. Nixon, *Six Crises*, 66.

69. Starr, *Golden Dreams*, 204; Worthen, *Young Nixon*, 62.

70. Gellman, *Contender*, 257, 260.

71. Clara Jane Nixon, interviews by author, 7/8/2010, 9/17/2010, 1/17/2011, 9/21/2011.

72. WC, Lawrene Anfinson, 9; HMC, box 1, Nixon to Harrison McCall, 8/16/1948, corr.

73. CSUF, Charles Milhous, 7; CSUF, William Milhous, 14; WC, Arthur Sucksdorf, Florence Sucksdorf, and Ethel Garliepp, 6.

74. WC, Judith Loubet (Evlyn Dorn), 8; Joseph Vinatieri, interview by author, 3/21/2011; Bewley, Knoop & Nixon, negotiated checks to Nixon, 2/14/1946, 6/22/1946, 9/27/1946, 12/9/1946, 2/27/1947, 10/24/1947, 5/21/1948; PPS 207, box 1: Harry Schuyler to Nixon, 8/17/1948, corr.; Nixon to Harry Schuyler, 8/26/1948, corr.

75. PPS 207, box 1, Bewley, Knoop & Nixon invoice, 11/7/1949.

76. "Legion to Hear Spy Probe Chief," *Oakland Tribune*, 9/20/1948; Nixon, *Six Crises*, 45, 69.

77. PPS 207, box 1: Nixon to James Dyer, 7/16/1948, corr.; James Dyer to Nixon, 9/10/1948, corr.; Nixon to James Dyer, 2/8/1949, corr.; Speaking Engagements in District: September 1948, Inter-Office Memo; "Spy Probe Is Defended by Rep. Nixon," *Whittier News*, 9/9/1948; Gellman, *Contender*, 258.

78. PPS 207, box 1: Ted Johnson to Nixon, 9/16/1948, corr.; Speaking Engagements in District: September–November 1948, Inter-Office Memos.

79. PPS 207, box 1: Glenn Vaniman to Nixon, 11/9/1948, corr.; Speaking Engagements: September–November 1948; "Final Narrows Flood Control Ready," *Long*

Beach Press Telegram, 9/12/1948; "I Rise to Remark," *Corona Daily Independent,* 10/21/1948; Nixon, *Six Crises,* 45.

80. "Speedy Prosecutions Advised in Spy Probe," *Long Beach Press Telegram,* 10/6/1948.

81. "Chamber to Hear Rep. Nixon Speak," *Long Beach Independent,* 10/3/1948; Gellman, *Contender,* 260.

82. Nixon, *Six Crises,* 62–63.

83. CSUF, William Price, 9; PPS 207, box 1, Speaking Engagements: September–November 1948; Hillings, *Irrepressible Irishman,* 24.

84. CSUF, William Price, 9; Hillings, *Irrepressible Irishman,* 25.

85. CSUF, William Price, 22–23.

86. PPS 207, box 1, Speaking Engagements: September–November 1948.

87. "Nixon Urges Espionage Law," *Long Beach Press Telegram,* 9/16/1948.

88. "Red Prober Assails Clark; Called Back to Capital," *Oakland Tribune,* 9/22/1948; Nixon, *In the Arena,* 364.

89. Nixon, *Six Crises,* 65.

90. CSUF, Dean Triggs, Jewel Triggs and Robert Gibbs (Dean Triggs), 99–100.

91. Nixon, *In the Arena,* 353.

92. PPS 207, box 1, Speaking Engagements: September–November 1948.

93. Kornitzer, *Real Nixon,* 179.

94. WC, Jack Drown, 12–13.

95. "Radio: Art & Tires," *Time,* 3/13/1939, 59–61.

96. BK, Jack Drown, 22.

97. BK, Jack Drown, 23; Kornitzer, *Real Nixon,* 179–80.

98. CSUF, Donald Fantz, 18; WC, Donald Fantz, 14–15.

99. Clara Jane Nixon, interviews by author, 7/8/2010, 9/17/2010, 1/17/2011, 9/21/2011.

100. Editorial, "Random Notes," *Bakersfield Californian,* 4/22/1949; "Rep. Nixon Warns G.O.P. Policy of Action Needed," *Long Beach Press Telegram,* 4/20/1949; Editorial, *Long Beach Press Telegram,* 4/27/1949.

101. WC, William Hughes, 16; Los Angeles County Recorder, Deed, 4/11/1949; Morris, *Richard Milhous Nixon,* 635.

102. "Nixon's Leadership Qualities," *Daily News/East Whittier Review,* 1/19/1969, 28.

103. Worthen, *Young Nixon,* 60.

8. Senator

1. Nixon, *In the Arena,* 219–20; Nixon, *Memoirs,* 72.

2. Gellman, *Contender,* 279.

3. Eisenhower, *Pat Nixon,* 104.

4. WC, W. B. Camp, 5–6.

5. "Arcadia Young GOP Will Draft Nixon," *Long Beach Press Telegram,* 10/7/1949.

6. Gellman, *Contender,* 285–86.

7. Kornitzer, *Real Nixon,* 181.

8. PB, #1 Roy Day, 21; UCB, Roy Day, 35; WC, Roy Day, 5; Mazo, *Richard Nixon,* 72.

9. Nixon, *In the Arena,* 219; Nixon, *Memoirs,* 72.

10. Nixon, *In the Arena*, 219.

11. Aitken, *Nixon*, 179.

12. Quoted in Gellman, *Contender*, 272.

13. Nixon, *In the Arena*, 220.

14. Aitken, *Nixon*, 180; Nixon, *In the Arena*, 221.

15. Brodie, *Richard Nixon*, 177.

16. BK, Robert Finch, 16.

17. Kornitzer, *Real Nixon*, 180.

18. Gellman, *Contender*, 300.

19. BK, Bob DiGiorgio, 12; CSUF John Dinkelspiel, 6, 8–11, 17–18.

20. BK, Joseph Moore, 2–3.

21. Morris, *Richard Milhous Nixon*, 534.

22. UCB, Frank Jorgensen, 11, 18; Hillings, *Irrepressible Irishman*, 25–26.

23. Hillings, *Irrepressible Irishman*, 28.

24. UCB, Frank Jorgensen, 39–40; UCB, Roy Day, 27; Mazo, *Richard Nixon*, 74.

25. UCB, Earl Adams, 10.

26. BK, Aylett Cotton, 11; Gellman, *Contender*, 279; Worthen, *Young Nixon*, 72.

27. Aitken, *Nixon*, 181; Gellman, *Contender*, 287; Nixon, *Memoirs*, 73.

28. CSUF, William Price, 64–65; Campaign 1946, box 1, Garland to Nixon, 3/25/1946, corr.

29. UCB, Frank Jorgensen, 40–42, 67; PPS 207, box 1, Bernard Brennan to Roy Day, 11/23/1949, corr.

30. CSUF, William Price, 26–27.

31. Toledano, *Nixon*, 98.

32. UCB, McIntyre Faries, 15; Morris, *Richard Milhous Nixon*, 556; Nixon, *In the Arena*, 221.

33. Gellman, *Contender*, 296; Nixon, *In the Arena*, 221.

34. Nixon, *In the Arena*, 215, 221.

35. BK, Aylett Cotton, 18–19; WC, Adela Rogers St. Johns (and Evlyn Dorn), 12.

36. WC, Pat Hitt, 10.

37. Worthen, *Young Nixon*, 68.

38. Aitken, *Nixon*, 181; Nixon, *In the Arena*, 222.

39. Aitken, *Nixon*, 181.

40. Aitken, *Nixon*, 182; Nixon, *In the Arena*, 222.

41. Gellman, *Contender*, 299; Nixon, *In the Arena*, 222; Worthen, *Young Nixon*, 69.

42. Aitken, *Nixon*, 182.

43. Aitken, *Nixon*, 182; Worthen, *Young Nixon*, 70.

44. Gellman, *Contender*, 275.

45. Mazo, *Richard Nixon*, 78–79; Morris, *Richard Milhous Nixon*, 586–87.

46. Marilyn Forsha, "Reaching Out to the Sea . . . ," *Long Beach Heritage* 2, no. 2 (May 1982); "U.S. Senatorial Candidate Talks at Spit & Argue Club," *Long Beach Independent*, 4/26/1950; Schipske, *Early Long Beach*, 47.

47. "U.S. Senatorial Candidate Talks."

48. UCB, Frank Jorgensen, 53; BK, Jack Drown, 22; "Nixon Raps Truman Attitude on Reds," *Long Beach Press Telegram*, 4/26/1950; "Nixon Speech Picketed, but Peacefully," *Long Beach Independent*, 4/26/1950; Eisenhower, *Pat Nixon*, 71, 108; Morris, *Richard Milhous Nixon*, 558; Nixon, *In the Arena*, 222; Nixon, *Memoirs*, 73–74.

49. "Nixon Raps Truman Attitude"; "Nixon Speech Picketed"; Gellman, *Contender*, 275.

50. Gellman, *Contender*, 302.

51. Gellman, *Contender*, 303; "Nixon to Make Another U. by Sea Appearance," *Long Beach Independent*, 6/2/1950.

52. Gellman, *Contender*, 304.

53. BK, Ed Pauley, 2–3; Kornitzer, *Real Nixon*, 183.

54. "Hosmer Eyes 15,000-Odd Republican Votes Taken by Doyle in Primary Poll," *Long Beach Press Telegram*, 6/11/1950.

55. Worthen, *Young Nixon*, 68.

56. CSUF, Janet Goeske, 1–2, 30.

57. CSUF, Janet Goeske, 2, 10.

58. BK, Aylett Cotton, 7.

59. Eisenhower, *Pat Nixon*, 106–7.

60. Gellman, *Contender*, 319.

61. BK, James Udall, 1.

62. BK, James Udall, 1–2.

63. BK, James Udall, 3.

64. BK, James Udall, 6–7.

65. BK, James Udall, 11.

66. Gellman, *Contender*, 307.

67. BK, Alphonzo Bell, 1; Gellman, *Contender*, 231.

68. BK, Alphonzo Bell, 3.

69. Schulte, *Young Nixon*, 253.

70. WC, Donald Fantz, 16–18.

71. Gellman, *Contender*, 305.

72. WC, Roy Day, 13–14.

73. UCB, Roy Day, 23–24; WC, Roy Day, 13–14.

74. UCB, Roy Day, 34; WC, Roy Day, 17; WC, Adela Rogers St. Johns, 24; PPS 207, box 79, Nixon to Kenny Washington, 3/7/1958, corr.; Morris, *Richard Milhous Nixon*, 611.

75. Toledano, *Nixon*, 96.

76. Gellman, *Contender*, 324.

77. Gellman, *Contender*, 333; Nixon, *Memoirs*, 77.

78. Gellman, *Contender*, 332.

79. Aitken, *Nixon*, 191; Morris, *Richard Milhous Nixon*, 611.

80. BK, Dorothy Chandler, 1, 12; Morris, *Richard Milhous Nixon*, 611.

81. BK, Dorothy Chandler, 13.

82. BK, Dorothy Chandler, 18; BK, Norman Chandler, 9.

83. Aitken, *Nixon*, 192; Brodie, *Richard Nixon*, 244.

84. Mazo, *Richard Nixon*, 40.

85. Eisenhower, *Pat Nixon*, 110; Toledano, *Nixon*, 100–101; Worthen, *Young Nixon*, 74–75.

86. Aitken, *Nixon*, 192.

87. Toledano, *Nixon*, 102–3.

88. Gellman, *Contender*, 342; Nixon, *Memoirs*, 72–78.

89. Toledano, *Nixon*, 70.

90. Kornitzer, *Real Nixon*, 186.

91. BK, Richard Nixon, 21.

92. Hubert Perry, interviews by author, 12/8/2009, 12/9/2009, 1/5/2010, 1/6/2010, 2/22/2010, 9/8/2010, 11/10/2010, 11/18/2010.

93. WC, Forrest Palmer, 11–12; CSUF, Paul Smith, 23–24; Nixon, *Memoirs*, 6.

94. CSUF, Merle West, 23.

95. BK, Tom Knudsen and Val Knudsen (Tom Knudsen), 1, 4, 8; Kornitzer, *Real Nixon*, 189.

96. PPS 207, box 2, Nixon to Bernard Brennan, 3/28/1951, telegram.

97. PPS 207, box 2, Tom Pike to Nixon, 3/22/1951, corr.

98. "California Solons Demand Thorough House-cleaning of Demo Administration," *Long Beach Press Telegram*, 3/30/1951.

99. Gellman, *Contender*, 360.

100. "Read Sketch on John Dulles in This Issue," *Van Nuys News*, 3/19/1951.

101. PPS 207, box 2: William Jones to Nixon, 4/9/1951, corr.; Paul Smith to Nixon, 4/2/1951, corr.; Whittier College Resolution, 4/17/1951.

102. Mazo, *Richard Nixon*, 82–83, 87–88.

103. Los Angeles County Recorder, Deed, 5/29/1952.

104. CSUF, Doug Ferguson, 10; Los Angeles County Recorder, Deed, 3/27/1952; Ed Nixon, interviews by author, 1/9/2010, 5/7/2010; Morris, *Richard Milhous Nixon*, 653; Nixon and Olson, *Nixons*, 162.

105. WC, Priscilla Timberlake MacLeod and Patricia Jane MacLeod, 27–28; CSUF, Oscar Marshburn and Olive Marshburn, 16.

106. Aitken, *Nixon*, 198.

107. PPS 207, box 5: Nixon to Elwood Robinson, 1/26/1952, corr.; Rose Mary Woods to Bernard Brennan, 2/3/1952, corr.; Gellman, *Contender*, 419.

108. PPS 207, box 5, Rose Mary Woods to Tom Bewley, 2/4/1952, corr.

109. PPS 207, box 5: Bernard Brennan to Nixon, 2/6/1952, telegram; Elwood Robinson to Nixon, 1/22/1952, corr., Nixon to Elwood Robinson, 1/26/1952, corr., Nixon to Elwood Robinson, 2/20/1952, corr., Nixon to Dana Smith, 2/20/1952, corr.

110. PPS 207, box 5, Nixon to Elwood Robinson, 2/20/1952, corr.

111. HJD, Nixon to Jack Drown, 5/1/1952, corr.

112. HJD, Nixon to Jack Drown, 1/18/1952, corr.

113. PPS 207, box 6, Stevens Fargo to Nixon, 4/4/1952, corr.

114. PPS 207, box 6: Hal Ramser to Assemblymembers, 4/4/1952, corr.; Tom Pike to Nixon, 4/7/1952, corr.; Nixon to John Fowler, 5/7/1952, corr.; UCB, Frank Jorgensen, 31.

115. WC, #2 Mabel Schuyler and Roger Schuyler, 4; WC, Camilla Simmons and William Simmons, 12; PPS 207, box 6, J. D. Brannon to Nixon, 2/21/1952, corr.

116. PPS 207, box 6, Nixon to Emmor Ware, 3/20/1952, corr.

117. WC, #2 Mabel Schuyler and Roger Schuyler, 4; WC, Camilla Simmons and William Simmons, 12.

118. WC, Camilla Simmons and William Simmons, 12.

9. Vice-Presidential Campaign

1. Gellman, *Contender*, 434; "Bruin Touchdown Twins Score Win," *Press Democrat*, 10/29/1939.

2. Gellman, *Contender*, 434.

3. DSC, Dana Smith to Jack Drown, 6/13/1952, corr.

4. Mazo, *Richard Nixon*, 89.

5. WC, Harry McLaughlin, 2; Aitken, *Nixon*, 209.

6. Gellman, *Contender*, 435.

7. Nixon, *Six Crises*, 75.

8. JA, Richard Nixon Historic Video Transcript, 5/4/1975, 49.

9. Martha Kearney, "Candidates' Wives Seen as Assets in GOP Campaign," *Lebanon Daily News*, 7/12/1952.

10. Betty Pryor, "Mrs. Nixon Will Campaign with Husband," *Lowell Sun*, 7/12/1952; Gellman, *Contender*, 444.

11. PPS 207, box 7: "Come Join the Parade!" press release, n.d.; Itinerary for Senator Nixon, 7/26–8/13/1952, 1.

12. PPS 207, box 7: Inter-Office Communication re Tentative Parade Line-up, 7/22/1952; "Come Join the Parade!"; Nixon, *Six Crises*, 76.

13. WC, George Corcoran, 1; BK, Paul Smith and Albert Upton, 29–30.

14. Harry Karns, "20,000 in Whittier Cheer Richard Nixon," *Long Beach Press Telegram*, 7/29/1952.

15. "20,000 in Whittier Cheer."

16. Mazo, *Richard Nixon*, 99.

17. "I've Got Off the Bench . . . ," *Daily News/East Whittier Review*, 1/19/1969; Morris, *Richard Milhous Nixon*, 743.

18. PPS 207, box 7, Itinerary for Senator Richard Nixon, 7/29/1952.

19. CSUF, Mary Gardiner, 10; WC, Dorris Gurley, 12; PPS 207, box 7: Julian Dickenson to Nixon, 7/21/1952, corr.; 1952 Speaking Engagements Memorandum; Itinerary, 7/26–8/13/1952, 5.

20. WC, Edward Breitkreutz, 24.

21. UCB, Frank Jorgensen, 76.

22. ED, C. H. Saltmarsh John Reilly, 9/23/1952, corr.; ED, John Reilly to Moomaw Furniture, 11/13/1952, corr.; DSC, Dana Smith to Jack Drown, 1/13/1952, corr.

23. Nixon, *Six Crises*, 74.

24. BK, Tom and Val Knudsen, 5; Nixon, *Six Crises*, 74.

25. Nixon, *Six Crises*, 73.

26. Aitken, *Nixon*, 210.

27. Nixon, *Six Crises*, 90.

28. "List of Donors to Nixon Expense Fund," *Los Angeles Herald-Express*, 9/20/1952.

29. Campaign 1952 Vice Presidential, box 5, Senator Richard Nixon Itinerary Commencing 9/15/1952.

30. Mazo, *Richard Nixon*, 108; Nixon, *Six Crises*, 77.

31. WC, Forest Palmer, 12; WC, Alice Rosenberger, 3–4; ED: Tom Bewley to Rose Mary Woods, 9/9/1952, memo; C. H. Saltmarsh to John Reilly, 9/23/1952, corr.

32. WC, Forest Palmer, 12; ED, Tom Bewley to Rose Mary Woods, 9/9/1952, corr.

33. Eisenhower, *Pat Nixon*, 117; Morris, *Richard Milhous Nixon*, 754; Nixon, *Six Crises*, 78.

34. CSUF, Joyce Brakensiek and Nellamena Roach (Nellamena Roach), 6–7; CSUF, Carmen Griffin, 8; CSUF, Blanche Potter Holmes, 16; CSUF, Leona Myler, 15; Campaign 1952 Vice Presidential, box 5, Draft Telegram Invitation for Stag Luncheon from Nixon to Close Supporters, 9/15/1952 (handwritten); "Artesia Turns Out Today for Nixon's Pretty Wife," *Long Beach Independent*, 9/17/1952.

35. UCB, Frank Jorgensen, 65; UCB, Roy Day, 38a; HJD, Service Guide for the Dick Nixon National Campaign Tour, 9/17–11/4/1952, 16; Mazo, *Richard Nixon*, 99; Morris, *Richard Milhous Nixon*, 754–55.

36. HJD, Service Guide, 7; Mazo, *Richard Nixon*, 102, 107–8.

37. CSUF, Linda Baker, 45–46; HJD, Service Guide, 18; Lungren and Lungren, *Healing Richard Nixon*, 4; Nixon, *Memoirs*, 91.

38. Nixon, *In the Arena*, 244.

39. HJD, Service Guide, 17; Nixon, *Memoirs*, 79; Nixon, *Six Crises*, 88.

40. HJD, Service Guide, 18; Nixon, *Six Crises*, 78.

41. Lungren and Lungren, *Healing*, 4; Nixon, *Memoirs*, 91; Nixon, *Six Crises*, 79.

42. WC, Jack Drown, 2–3.

43. Marje Acker, interview by author, 7/7/2010.

44. Nixon, *Six Crises*, 81.

45. BK, Aylett Cotton, 22–23.

46. CSUF, Doug Ferguson, 10, 16; CSUF, Lyle Otterman, 30.

47. BK, Hubert Perry, 3, 5.

48. Nixon, *Six Crises*, 95.

49. CSUF, Irwin Gellman, 46.

50. Nixon, *Six Crises*, 88.

51. Aitken, *Nixon*, 212.

52. Nixon, *Six Crises*, 92.

53. CSUF, A. C. Newsom, 12–13.

54. Aitken, *Nixon*, 213; Nixon, *Six Crises*, 98.

55. HJD, Nixon to Helene Drown, n.d., corr.; Aitken, *Nixon*, 213.

56. Aitken, *Nixon*, 213.

57. Nixon, *In the Arena*, 288.

58. Aitken, *Nixon*, 213; Nixon, *Six Crises*, 94.

59. Nixon, *Six Crises*, 100.

60. Nixon, *Six Crises*, 101.

61. Nixon, *Six Crises*, 101.

62. Eisenhower, *Pat Nixon*, 121; Nixon, *Six Crises*, 104–5.

63. Maureen Nunn, interview by author, 9/6/2010; Eisenhower, *Pat Nixon*, 121; Morris, *Richard Milhous Nixon*, 814.

64. Mazo, *Richard Nixon*, 124.

65. Nixon, *Six Crises*, 103.

66. UCB, Frank Jorgensen, 66.

67. UCB, Frank Jorgensen, 66; BK, Robert Finch, 16.

68. Nixon, *Memoirs*, 101.

69. Lungren and Lungren, *Healing*, 48; Morris, *Richard Milhous Nixon*, 814; Nixon, *In the Arena*, 200; Nixon, *Six Crises*, 105–6.

70. Nixon, *Six Crises*, 102–3.

71. Nixon, *Six Crises*, 102–3.

72. Nixon, *Six Crises*, 102–3, 108.

73. Eisenhower, *Pat Nixon*, 121; Mazo, *Richard Nixon*, 115.

74. BK, Paul Smith and Albert Upton, 15; Nixon, *Six Crises*, 103, 108.

75. WC, Charles W. Cooper, 20; BK, Paul Smith and Albert Upton, 15.

76. Marje Acker, interview by author, 7/7/2010.

77. Mazo, *Richard Nixon*, 124–25.

78. Mazo, *Richard Nixon*, 126.

79. Aitken, *Nixon*, 214; Mazo, *Richard Nixon*, 127; Nixon, *Six Crises*, 110–11.

80. Mazo, *Richard Nixon*, 127.

81. Nixon, *Six Crises*, 96.

82. Mazo, *Richard Nixon*, 127–28.

83. Marje Acker, interview by author, 7/7/2010; Nixon, *Six Crises*, 112.

84. Marje Acker, interview by author, 7/7/2010; Nixon, *Six Crises*, 112.

85. Nixon, *Six Crises*, 112; Nixon, *In the Arena*, 201.

86. Mazo, *Richard Nixon*, 127–28.

87. Kornitzer, *Real Nixon*, 188; Morris, *Richard Milhous Nixon*, 825; Nixon, *In the Arena*, 201; Nixon, *Memoirs*, 99; Nixon, *Six Crises*, 112.

88. Toledano, *Nixon*, 138.

89. Nixon, *In the Arena*, 201.

90. Toledano, *Nixon*, 138.

91. Nixon, *Six Crises*, 112–13.

92. UCB, Frank Jorgensen, 66.

93. Nixon, *Six Crises*, 113.

94. Nixon, *Six Crises*, 113–14.

95. Nixon, *Six Crises*, 114.

96. Nixon, *Six Crises*, 114–15.

97. Nixon, *Six Crises*, 115.

98. Nixon, *Six Crises*, 115.

99. Mazo, *Richard Nixon*, 122.

100. Aitken, *Nixon*, 218.

101. BK, Ray Arbuthnot, 1, 3–4, 6.

102. Aitken, *Nixon*, 218.

103. Kornitzer, *Real Nixon*, 194.

104. Aitken, *Nixon*, 218.

105. Eisenhower, *Pat Nixon*, 124; Nixon, *Six Crises*, 118.

106. Aitken, *Nixon*, 218.

107. Nixon, *Six Crises*, 118.

108. Marje Acker, interview by author, 7/7/2010.

109. Mazo, *Richard Nixon*, 133.

110. Mazo, *Richard Nixon*, 135.

111. Aitken, *Nixon*, 218, 220; Morris, *Richard Milhous Nixon*, 844.

112. Campaign 1952 Vice Presidential, box 6, Memorandum re Wire Received at Ambassador Hotel from Mr. and Mrs. Mold, n.d.

113. Nixon, *Six Crises*, 124.

114. HJD, Nixon to Helene Drown, n.d., corr.; Campaign 1952 Vice Presidential, Postcard to Supporters, n.d.

115. HJD, Nixon to Jack Drown, 2/20/1953, corr.; Nixon, *Six Crises*, 93, 125.

116. BK, James Bassett, 1; Nixon, *In the Arena*; Nixon, *Memoirs*, 159.

117. David, *Lonely Lady*, 92.

118. Aitken, *Nixon*, 211.

119. Campaign 1952 Vice Presidential, box 5, Senator Nixon Itinerary, 10/29–11/4/1952; "Makes Plea to Elect Ike, Save Nation," *Long Beach Independent*, 10/30/1952.

120. "Makes Plea to Elect Ike."

121. WC, Frieda Skinner, 5; Clara Jane Nixon, interviews by author, 7/8/2010, 9/17/2010, 1/17/2011, 9/21/2011; "Dick Visits Family, Meets Nephew," *Long Beach Independent*, 10/31/1952; "Baby Nephew Stops Nixon Motorcade," *Los Angeles Times*, 10/31/1952.

122. CSUF, George Kellogg, 11.

123. CSUF, Helen Dryer, 5–6; Campaign 1952 Vice Presidential, box 5, Senator Nixon Itineraries, 10/22–28/1952, 10/29–11/4/1952; "Nixon Makes Major Talk in L.B. Today," *Long Beach Independent*, 10/31/1952.

124. Campaign 1952 Vice Presidential, box 5, Senator Nixon Itinerary, 10/29–11/4/1952; "Nixon Speaks Here Friday at 8:45 a.m.," *Long Beach Press Telegram*, 10/30/1952; "Nixon Vows Ike's Never Surrendered," *Long Beach Press Telegram*, 10/31/1952; Harry Fulton, "Good Demo Vote Asked by Nominee," *Long Beach Independent*, 11/1/1952; James Bacon, "Senator Says Adlai Ill-Suited for Job," *Oakland Tribune*, 11/1/1952.

125. "Ike's Never Surrendered, Nixon Asserts, 3000 in L.B. Hear Senator's High Tribute," *Long Beach Press Telegram*, 10/31/1952.

126. Campaign 1952 Vice Presidential, box 5, Nixon Itinerary, 10/29–11/4/1952; "Nixon Vows Ike's Never Surrendered," *Long Beach Press Telegram*, 10/31/1952; Morris, *Richard Milhous Nixon*, 833.

127. Campaign 1952 Vice Presidential, box 5, Nixon Itinerary, 10/29–11/4/1952.
128. Campaign 1952 Vice Presidential, box 5, Nixon Itinerary, 10/29–11/4/1952; "Senator Says Adlai Ill-Suited"; Aitken, *Nixon*, 223; Morris, *Richard Milhous Nixon*, 833.
129. "Senator Says Adlai Ill-Suited"; Mazo, *Richard Nixon*, 262; Morris, *Richard Milhous Nixon*, 863.
130. "Nixon Rips Adlai, Moves Northwest," *Long Beach Press Telegram*, 11/1/1952; "Senator Says Adlai Ill-Suited."
131. Campaign 1952 Vice Presidential, box 6, Senator Nixon Itinerary, 10/29–11/4/1952.
132. Nixon, *Memoirs*, 112–13; ED, Dorn to Woods, 6/9/1953, corr.
133. Morris, *Richard Milhous Nixon*, 863; Nixon and Olson, *Nixons*, 164; Nixon, *Memoirs*, 112–13.
134. BK, Aylett Cotton, 14–15, 23.
135. Eisenhower, *Pat Nixon*, 129.
136. Nixon, *Memoirs*, 7.
137. Eisenhower, *Pat Nixon*, 128, 134.
138. PPS 207, box 8, Tournament of Roses Trip Itinerary.
139. PPS 207, box 8: Tournament of Roses Trip Itinerary; Nixon to W. H. Nicholas, 12/4/1952, corr.
140. PPS 207, box 8: Rose Mary Woods to W. H. Nicholas, 12/13/1952, corr.; W. H. Nicholas to Rose Mary Woods, 12/19/1952, corr.
141. PPS 207, box 8: Bernard Brennan to Jack Drown, 12/29/1952, corr.; Tournament of Roses Trip Itinerary.
142. Aitken, *Nixon*, 224; Nixon, *Memoirs*, 117.

10. Vice President

1. WC, Tolbert Moorhead, 13.
2. CSUF, Lucille Parsons, 16–18.
3. CSUF, Lucille Parsons, 16–18.
4. Crowley, *Nixon off the Record*, 147.
5. CSUF, Lucille Parsons, 9; Crowley, *Nixon off the Record*, 147.
6. Eisenhower, *Pat Nixon*, 131.
7. Loie Gaunt, interviews by author, 12/28/2010, 2/7/2012.
8. CSUF, Nathaniel George, 4; CSUF, Dorothy Milhous, 5–6; WC, William Ryan, 6.
9. CSUF, Nathaniel George, 4; WC, Nathaniel George, 7.
10. CSUF, George Jenkins, 4.
11. CSUF, Charles Ball, 1; CSUF, Dorothy Beeson, 3; BK, Bob Wilson, 12.
12. WC, Hoyt and Julia Corbit, 19.
13. Mildred K. Flanary, "Vice President Joins Culinary Experts," *Long Beach Press Telegram*, 10/25/1953.
14. "U.S. Vice-President Nixon Named, 'Southern California Man of Year,'" *Daily Trojan*, 1/11/1954.
15. "U.S. Vice-President Nixon Named."

16. "The Vice-Presidency: From Teeming Shores," *Time*, 12/28/1953, 9.

17. Floyd Sparks, "Richard Nixon Has Grown a Lot," *Hayward Daily Review*, 2/15/1954.

18. CSUF, Elizabeth Cloes, 3.

19. BK, Dorothy Chandler, 4; CSUF, A. C. Newsom, 11; BK, #3 Hannah Nixon, 7.

20. PPS 207, box 12, Vice President's Schedule, 7/18–20/1953; "Nixon Addresses Scout Jamboree, Swaps for 'Scalp' and Snake Skin," *Long Beach Press Telegram*, 7/20/1953.

21. "Vice President Joins Culinary Experts."

22. WC, I. N. Kraushaar, 4; WC, Edward Nixon, 1; BK, #2 Hannah Nixon, 18; Anthony Pierno, interviews by author, 9/11/2009, 9/25/2009; ED, Hannah Nixon to Evlyn Dorn, 9/28/1953, corr.; Cramer, "La Habra"; Eisenhower, *Pat Nixon*, 159; Kornitzer, *Real Nixon*, 88.

23. CSUF, Edith Holt, 1; WC, Charles L. Milhous, 22; CSUF, Dorothy Milhous, 6; BK, #2 Hannah Nixon, 18; EDC, Evlyn Dorn to Nixon, 7/6/1954, corr.

24. WC, Edward Breitkreutz, 2, 9.

25. WC, Marshall Clow, 34–35.

26. "Vice President Returns after Two-Day Stay Here," *Whittier News*, 6/14/1954; Joseph Dmohowski, interview by author, 10/13/2011.

27. WC, Charles W. Cooper, 15–16; Anthony Pierno, interviews by author, 9/11/2009, 9/25/2009; PPS 207, box 22, Vice President's Schedule for California Trip, 6/11–14/1954.

28. WC, Charles W. Cooper, 15–17; CSUF, William Soeberg, 13; Anthony Pierno, interviews by author, 9/11/2009, 9/25/2009.

29. WC, Charles W. Cooper, 15–17; WC, Clint Harris, 5–6; Anthony Pierno, interviews by author, 9/11/2009, 9/25/2009.

30. WC, Charles W. Cooper, 15–17; CSUF, William Soeberg, 13; Anthony Pierno, interviews by author, 9/11/2009, 9/25/2009.

31. WC, Charles W. Cooper, 15–17; Anthony Pierno, interviews by author, 9/11/2009, 9/25/2009.

32. PPS 207, box 22, Berta Hamman Lee, "What the Home Folks Think of Dick Nixon," n.d.

33. Lee, "What the Home Folks Think"; BK, Paul Smith and Albert Upton, 26.

34. WC, Charles W. Cooper, 15–17; Anthony Pierno, interviews by author, 9/11/2009, 9/25/2009; PPS 207, box 22, Vice President's Schedule for California Trip, 6/11–14/1954; Mazo, *Richard Nixon*, 139.

35. Anthony Pierno, interviews by author, 9/11/2009, 9/25/2009.

36. WC, Charles W. Cooper, 15–17.

37. "Man Who Started Nixon in Politics Dies at 70," *Los Angeles Times*, 6/12/1954.

38. BK, Hubert Perry #1, 4.

39. BK, Hubert Perry #1, 4; Hubert Perry, interview by author, 12/8/2009, 12/9/2009, 1/5/2010, 1/6/2010, 2/22/2010, 9/8/2010, 11/10/2010, 11/18/2010.

40. CSUF, Irwin Chapman, 14; CSUF, Joe Gaudio, 27; WC, #2 Alyce Koch, 6–9; WC, Harley McClure, 20; CSUF, William A. Milhous, 14; CSUF, Lucille Parsons, 16–18;

csuf, Edith Timberlake, 54; csuf, Floyd Wildermuth, 24–26; Anthony Pierno, interviews by author, 9/11/2009, 9/25/2009.

41. wc, Melville Rich, 2.

42. csuf, Arthur Remley, 17; wc, Melville Rich, 2; wc, Charles Rothaermel, 6.

43. wc, Mary Pickering, 9.

44. wc, Earl Daniels, 5–6; csuf, Floyd Wildermuth, 24–26.

45. edc, Pat Nixon to Frank and Hannah Nixon, 9/30/1954, corr.; "Long Beach Paid Surprise Visit by Vice President," *Long Beach Press Telegram*, 10/11/1954; Nixon and Olson, *Nixons*, 174–75.

46. Nixon and Olson, *Nixons*, 174–75.

47. Quoted in Worthen, *Young Nixon*, 127. See also Mazo, *Richard Nixon*, 140; Toledano, *Nixon*, 178.

48. "Nixon Caravan Routes Wednesday," *Long Beach Press Telegram*, 10/26/1954.

49. Marje Acker, interview by author, 7/7/2010.

50. wc, Virginia Buckman, 3; ed, Evlyn Dorn to Nixon, 7/24/1955, corr.

51. ed: Rose Mary Woods to Evlyn Dorn, n.d., corr.; Rose Mary Woods to Evlyn Dorn, 5/14/1953, corr.; Rose Mary Woods to Evlyn Dorn, 8/5/1953, corr.; Rose Mary Woods to Evlyn Dorn, 7/28/1953, corr., Rose Mary Woods to Evlyn Dorn, 1/28/1954, corr.; Rose Mary Woods to Evlyn Dorn, 2/2/1954, corr.; Rose Mary Woods to Evlyn Dorn, 5/8/1954, corr.; Rose Mary Woods to Evlyn Dorn, 6/17/1954, corr.; Rose Mary Woods to Evlyn Dorn, 7/23/1954, corr.; Evlyn Dorn to Rose Mary Woods, 9/3/1954, corr.; Rose Mary Woods to Evlyn Dorn, 2/15/1955, corr.; Rose Mary Woods to Evlyn Dorn, 4/21/1955, corr.; John Krehbiel to Evlyn Dorn, 8/19/1955, telegram.

52. Aitken, *Nixon*, 232; Toledano, *Nixon*, 178.

53. Aitken, *Nixon*, 233.

54. Aitken, *Nixon*, 233.

55. Aitken, *Nixon*, 235, 237.

56. Crowley, *Nixon off the Record*, 141.

57. bk, Hubert Perry, 3; bk, William Rogers, 5; Hubert Perry, interviews by author, 12/8/2009, 12/9/2009, 1/5/2010, 1/6/2010, 2/22/2010, 9/8/2010, 11/10/2010, 11/18/2010.

58. Worthen, *Young Nixon*, 128.

59. Worthen, *Young Nixon*, 129.

60. Toledano, *Nixon*, 196–97.

61. pps 207, box 27, Schedule for California Trip, 3/12–15/1955.

62. csuf, A. C. Newsom, 10; pps 207, box 27, Nixon to Ray Arbuthnot, 3/21/1955, corr.

63. wc, Robert Sillivan and Mary Sillivan, 44; pps 207, box 27, Schedule for California Trip, 3/12–15/1955.

64. wc, Harriett Hudspeth, 28; wc, Arthur Sucksdorf, Florence Sucksdorf, and Ethel Garliepp, 16; pps 207, box 27, Nixon to Earl Reynolds, 4/29/1955, corr.

65. pps 207, box 27, Schedule for California Trip, 3/12–15/1955.

66. PPS 207, box 27, Brig. Gen. F. H. Lamson-Scribner to Nixon, 3/18/1955, corr.; "Nixon Talk to Precede Air Display," *Long Beach Independent*, 3/12/1955; "100,000 See Air Show at Navy Station," *Long Beach Independent*, 3/14/1955.

67. PPS 207, box 27, Schedule for California Trip, 3/12–15/1955.

68. PPS 207, box 27, Republican Workers' Luncheon Meeting Seating Chart, 3/14/1955.

69. DSC: Dwight Eisenhower to Dana Smith, 11/28/1952, corr.; Nixon to Dana Smith, 2/2/1953, corr.

70. DSC, Nixon to Dana Smith, 12/17/1953, 1/15/1954, 3/2/1954, 5/28/1954, 8/3/1954, 10/11/1955, 10/8/1956, corr.

71. PPS 207, box 27, Eisenhower to John Krehbiel, Chairman, Republican Central Committee of Los Angeles, 3/14/1955, telegram.

72. PPS 207, box 27: Schedule for California Trip, 3/12–15/1955; Walter Coombs to Rose Mary Woods, 3/28/1955, corr.

73. PPS 207, box 27, Schedule for California Trip, 3/12–15/1955.

74. "Nixon Chooses Southland for His Report on Tour of Latin-America," *Long Beach Independent-Press Telegram*, 3/13/1955; "Nixon Warns GOP It Must Build Party," *Long Beach Press Telegram*, 3/15/1955.

75. PPS 207, box 34: Vice President's Schedule, 8/9–18/1955; California Schedule, 8/5/1955; Itinerary of Vice President, 8/9–18/1955.

76. PPS 207, box 34, Star of Polaris Certificate, 8/11/1955.

77. PPS 207, box 34: Vice President's Schedule for California Trip, 8/9–18/1955; California Schedule, 8/5/1955; Itinerary of Visit of Vice President to Los Angeles Area, 8/9–18/1955; United States Secret Service, Protective Survey Report, 8/19/1955.

78. PPS 207, box 27: Schedule for California Trip, 3/12–15/1955; Nixon to Kyle Palmer, 3/25/1955, corr.; Murray Chotiner to Nixon, 2/28/1955, corr.; Bernard Brennan to Rose Mary Woods, 3/30/1955, corr.; Vice President's Schedule for California Trip, 8/9–18/1955; California Schedule, 8/5/1955; Itinerary of Vice President, 8/9–18/1955.

79. WC, Jeannette Cox, 14; CSUF, Oscar Marshburn and Olive Marshburn, 16; Marygene Wright, interviews by author, 9/7/2011, 3/11/2014; PPS 207, box 34: Vice President's Schedule, 8/9–18/1955; California Schedule, 8/5/1955; Itinerary of Vice President, 8/9–18/1955; Secret Service, Report, 8/19/1955.

80. PPS 207, box 34, Itinerary of Vice President, 8/9–18/1955.

81. WC, #4 Clint Harris, 5–6.

82. PPS 207, box 34: Vice President's Schedule, 8/9–18/1955; California Schedule, 8/5/1955; Itinerary of Vice President, 8/9–18/1955; Nixon to Asa Call, 8/25/1955, corr.

83. PPS 207, box 34: Vice President's Schedule, 8/9–18/1955; California Schedule, 8/5/1955; Itinerary of Vice President, 8/9–18/1955.

84. PPS 207, box 34, Itinerary of Vice President, 8/9–18/1955.

85. PPS 207, box 34, Nixon to Harry Brand, 8/24/1955, corr.

86. PPS 207, box 34: Vice President's Schedule, 8/9–18/1955; California Schedule, 8/5/1955; Robert Groves to Nixon, 8/18/1955, corr.; Itinerary of Vice President, 8/9–18/1955.

87. PPS 207, box 34: Schedule for California Trip, 8/9–18/1955; California Schedule, 8/5/1955; Itinerary of Vice President, 8/9–18/1955; Nixon to Buff Chandler, 8/23/1955, corr.; Secret Service, Report, 8/19/1955.

88. BK, Dorothy Chandler, 4; Kornitzer, *Real Nixon*, 231; PPS 207, box 34: Vice President's Schedule, 8/9–18/1955; Itinerary of Vice President, 8/9–18/1955; Secret Service, Report, 8/19/1955.

89. Hedda Hopper, "Civil War Spy Story to Star Fess Parker," *Los Angeles Times*, 8/19/1955.

90. PPS 207, box 34, Nixon to Stanley Mullin, 8/8/1955, corr.

91. PPS 207, box 34, Nixon to Charles Ducommun, 9/6/1955, corr.

92. PPS 207, box 34, Nixon to Ed Pauley, 8/27/1955, corr.

93. BK, Ed Pauley, 5.

94. BK, Ed Pauley, 5–6.

95. WC, Virginia Counts, 7–8; WC, Marshall Clow, 39; CSUF, Joanne Dale, 27; WC, Benjamin Horack, 23–24; BK, Hubert Perry, Alice Walker, Harriet Hudspeth, Mrs. Ralph Palmer, Jane MacMurray Troutner, Ralph Palmer, and Lionel Buck Taylor, 7; HMC, Nixon to Harrisson McCall, n.d., corr., and Nixon to Harrison McCall, 2/11/1958, corr.; EDC, Nixon to Tom Bewley, 5/8/1954, corr., and Nixon to Evlyn Dorn, 5/8/1954, corr.; PPS 207, box 79: Nixon to Hoyt Corbit, 2/26/1958, corr.; Nixon to J. Bennet Olson, 2/24/1958, corr.; Nixon to Kenny Washington, 3/7/1958, corr.; PPS 207, box 80: Nixon to Marilyn Davis, 2/26/1958, corr.; Nixon to Ray Arbuthnot, 3/6/1958, corr.; PPS 207, box 107, Nixon to Clint Harris, 7/8/1959, corr.; PPS 207, box 120: Nixon to Mabel Boardman, 12/18/1959, corr.; Nixon to John Garland, 11/11/1959, corr.; Nixon to Conrad Hilton, 11/10/1959, corr.; Nixon to T. Stanley Warburton, 12/2/1959, corr.; PPS 207, box 124: Nixon to Esther Barker, 2/19/1960, corr.; J. S. Brattain to Nixon, 2/5/1960, corr.; Nixon to J. S. Brattain, 2/10/1960, corr.; Nixon to Don Loker, 3/4/1960, corr.

96. EDC: Evlyn Dorn to Rose Mary Woods, n.d., corr.; Hannah Nixon to Evlyn Dorn, n.d., corr.; Evlyn Dorn to Rose Mary Woods, 6/9/1953, corr.; Rose Mary Woods to Evlyn Dorn, 1/28/1954, corr.; Tom Bewley to Rose Mary Woods, 1/29/1954, corr.; Evlyn Dorn to Rose Mary Woods, 2/12/1954, corr.; Evlyn Dorn to Rose Mary Woods, 2/15/1954, corr.; Evlyn Dorn to Rose Mary Woods, 3/10/1954, corr.; Evlyn Dorn to Nixon, 7/6/1954, corr.; Nixon to Evlyn Dorn, 6/17/1954, corr.; Nixon to Frank Urich, 8/25/1955, corr.; Tom Bewley to First National Bank, 9/21/1955, corr.; Rose Mary Woods to Don Nixon, 10/3/1955, corr.; Nixon to I. N. Kraushaar, 12/31/1955, corr.; Dottie Donnelly to Evlyn Dorn, 1/25/1956, corr.; Nixon to Evlyn Dorn, 6/13/1956, corr.; Evlyn Dorn to Nixon, 7/18/1956, corr.; Clara Jane Nixon, interviews by author, 7/8/2010, 9/17/2010, 1/17/2011, 9/21/2011; Marygene Wright, interviews by author, 9/7/2011, 3/11/2014.

97. ED, Richard Nixon to Frank Nixon, 2/2/1954, corr., and Pat Nixon to Frank and Hannah Nixon, 9/30/1954, corr.

98. BK, William Rogers, 14.

99. BK, William Rogers, 13.

100. Aitken, *Nixon*, 235–36.

101. "Eisenhower Praise Seen as Buildup for Nixon," *Bakersfield Californian*, 3/15/1955.

102. Mazo, *Richard Nixon*, 191; Starr, *Golden Dreams*, 191.

103. Mazo, *Richard Nixon*, 180.

104. Mazo, *Richard Nixon*, 180.

105. Mazo, *Richard Nixon*, 195.

106. L. D. Hotckiss, "It Was Day in Which Dumpers Got Dumped," *Los Angeles Times*, 8/23/1956; "Convention Had Its High Spots and Flops," *Los Angeles Times*, 8/24/1956.

107. Quoted in Mazo, *Richard Nixon*, 187.

108. UCB, Frank Jorgensen, 100; Republican National Committee, press release, 8/18/56; Eisenhower, *Pat Nixon*, 109.

109. JA, Nixon Video Transcript A15, n.d.; Eisenhower, *Pat Nixon*, 109; Nixon, *Memoirs*, 175.

110. WC, I. N. Kraushaar, 4; PPS 207, box 58: Office Memorandum, 8/23/1956; Vice President's Schedule, 8/22/1956.

111. CSUF, I. N. Kraushaar, 3–5; WC, I. N. Kraushaar, 5.

112. Nixon, *Memoirs*, 176; Nixon and Olson, *Nixons*, 186; Aitken, *Nixon*, has Frank at Whittier Hospital during the convention (243).

113. UCB, Frank Jorgensen, 102; PPS 207, box 57, Office Memorandum re Draft of Acceptance Speech, 8/10/1956; Eisenhower, *Pat Nixon*, 109; Nixon, *Memoirs*, 175–76.

114. PPS 207, box 57, Nixon's "Proud Staff in Washington, D.C. to Nixon," 8/24/1956, telegram.

115. "Nixon Father Loses Brave Fight to Live," *Los Angeles Times*, 9/5/1956; "Condolence Messages Come in Flood to Nixon," *Los Angeles Times*, 9/6/1956.

116. PPS 207, box 58: Evlyn Dorn to Rose Mary Woods, 9/10/1956, corr.; Jay-ness Delivery Order, 9/1/1956; Marje Acker, interview by author, 7/7/2010.

117. Nixon, *In the Arena*, 90–91.

118. WC, Edward Nixon, 1; "Nixon Father Loses Brave Fight"; Aitken, *Nixon*, 243.

119. "Nixon Father Loses Brave Fight"; Eisenhower, *Pat Nixon*, 109; Lungren and Lungren, *Healing*, 58; Nixon, *Memoirs*, 176.

120. CSUF, Frances Timberlake, 5–6; CSUF, Marygene Wright, 19; Nixon, *In the Arena*, 85–86.

121. CSUF, Mildred Mendenhall, 13.

122. Nixon and Olson, *Nixons*, 131.

123. PPS 207, box 147, Ambassador Hotel speech, 10/13/1960.

124. BK, Kyle Palmer, 12.

125. PPS 207, box 58, Vice President's Schedule, 9/5-7/1956.

126. "Condolence Messages Come in Flood."

127. PPS 207, box 58, Vice President's Schedule, 9/5-7/1956; PPS 207, box 59, Robert Finch to Nixon, 9/4/1956, Office Memorandum re "Helio Courier" Airplane.

128. csuf, George Jenkins, 3; csuf, Frances Timberlake, 5; wc, Elva Urich, 6.

129. csuf, Frances Timberlake, 5.

130. csuf, George Jenkins, 3; "Nixon Father Loses Brave Fight"; Nixon and Olson, *Nixons*, 186–87.

131. Nixon Family Collection, box 5, Frank Nixon Memorial Service Book; csuf, Manville Saxton, 11.

132. wc, Russell Harrison Jr., 13; csuf, Fred Johnson, 14; Nixon, *In the Arena*, 85–86.

133. Nixon Family Collection, box 5, Frank Nixon Memorial Service Book.

134. Clara Jane Nixon, interviews by author, 7/8/2010, 9/17/2010, 1/17/2011, 9/21/2011.

135. pps 207, box 58: Nixon to Clint Harris, 10/20/1956, corr.; Nixon to C. R. Kirkpatrick, 9/17/1956, corr.; Nixon to Ness, 10/20/1956, corr.; Office Memoranda re Thank-You Letters, 9/6/1956, 9/10/1956.

136. csuf, A. C. Newsom, 8; "Nixon Assails Truman for Attack on President," *Long Beach Independent*, 9/19/1956.

137. "Governor's Offer Closes Party Feud," *Long Beach Independent*, 9/19/1956.

138. wc, William Marumoto, 3–4; "His Teachers: They Were Magnificent," *Daily News/East Whittier Review*, 1/19/1969; Marje Acker, interview by author, 7/7/2010.

139. wc, William Marumoto, 3–4.

140. Stuart Spencer, interviews by author, 12/29/2010, 1/21/2011.

141. Mazo, *Richard Nixon*, 168.

142. Mazo, *Richard Nixon*, 182.

11. Preparation

1. wc, Lon Fuller, 10; bk, Richard Nixon, 2.

2. wc, Forrest Easely Jr., 12; csuf, Nathaniel George, 15; wc, Nathaniel George, 7; wc, Lloyd Harnish, 13.

3. Aitken, *Nixon*, 247.

4. Black, *Life in Full*, 350.

5. Mazo, *Richard Nixon*, 251.

6. Aitken, *Nixon*, 247; Black, *Life in Full*, 350–51.

7. Aitken, *Nixon*, 248.

8. Toledano, *Nixon*, 237.

9. Black, *Life in Full*, 351.

10. pps 207, box 100, Press Memorandum re Nixon Southern California Visit, 2/14/1958; "Nixon in Southland Plans Caltech Tour," *Independent Star News*, 2/16/1958.

11. pps 207, box 79, Itinerary for Vice President, 2/15–19/1958; "Nixon in Southland."

12. wc, Adela Rogers St. Johns, 3; St. Johns, *Honeycomb*, 366; pps 207, box 79: Nixon to Adela Rogers St. Johns, 3/31/1958, corr.; Itinerary for Vice President, 2/15–19/1958; Vice President's Schedule, 2/19/1958.

13. "Nixon Says U.S. Needs 'Confidence,'" *Whittier News*, 2/15/1958.

14. pps 207, box 79: Itinerary for Vice President, 2/15–19/1958; Vice President's Schedule, 2/17/1958; "Nixon Visits cit's Jet Laboratory," *Pasadena Independent Star News*, 2/17/1958.

15. "Visits Caltech's Jet Lab, LAUDS Science Projects," *Pasadena Independent Star News*, 2/17/1958.

16. PPS 207, box 79, Itinerary for Vice President, 2/15–19/1958; PPS 207, box 80, Vice President's Schedule, 2/18/1958; "Nixon Backs Tax Cut over U.S. Works," *Los Angeles Times*, 2/19/1958; "Nixon Out-Talks Persistent Newsmen," *Pasadena Star News*, 2/19/1958.

17. "Nixon Out-Talks Persistent Newsmen."

18. "Knight Decided Early Not to Run, Nixon Says," *Oakland Tribune*, 2/15/1958.

19. Worthen, *Young Nixon*, 170.

20. PPS 207, box 79, Itinerary for Vice President, 2/15–19/1958; "Nixon Out-Talks Persistent Newsmen."

21. PPS 207, box 80, Standard Bearers' Luncheon Roster, Statler Hotel, 2/18/1958.

22. Myrna Oliver, "Crispus A. Wright, 87; Son of Ex-Slave Became Lawyer and USC Benefactor," *Los Angeles Times*, 12/11/2001.

23. PPS 207, box 79, Itinerary for Vice President, 2/15–19/1958; PPS 207, box 80, Vice President's Schedule, 2/19/1958; "Federal Contracts Committee Meets," *Pasadena Star News*, 2/17/1958.

24. BK, Bob King, 6.

25. Eleanor Roosevelt, "My Day, August 11, 1960," *Eleanor Roosevelt Papers Digital Edition* (2017), accessed 11/2/2022, https://www2.gwu.edu/~erpapers/myday /displaydoc.cfm?_y=1960&_f=md004821.

26. WC, Jack Drown, 2–3.

27. "Nixon Pulls Party Out of a Bind," *Long Beach Press Telegram*, 10/17/1958.

28. CSUF, William Price, 48–49; Mazo, *Richard Nixon*, 207; Nixon, *Six Crises*, 233.

29. "The Greater Los Angeles Press Club Honors Richard M. Nixon, Vice President of the United States," *Hollywood Pictorial*, March 1959.

30. Shawn Steel, interview by author, 1/9/2013.

31. PPS 207, box 100, Itinerary for Vice President, 2/15–18/1959; Toledano, *Nixon*, 236.

32. PPS 207, box 100, Itinerary for Vice President, 2/15–18/1959.

33. PPS 207, box 108: Walt Disney to Nixon, 5/8/1959, corr.; Itinerary for Vice President, 6/13–17/1959; Vice President's Schedule, 6/13/1959.

34. PPS 207, box 108: Itinerary for Vice President, 6/12/1959; Schedule for Disneyland, 6/14/1959.

35. PPS 207, box 107: Vice President's Schedule, 6/13/1959; Commencement Week Program, Whittier College, 1959; Dedication and Ground-Breaking Ceremonies Program, Whittier College, 6/13/1959; Whittier College Dedication Ceremonies speech, 6/13/1959.

36. PPS 207, box 107, Whittier Dedication Ceremonies speech, 6/13/1959.

37. PPS 207, box 107, Whittier Dedication Ceremonies speech, 6/13/1959.

38. PPS 207, box 107, Whittier Dedication Ceremonies speech, 6/13/1959; "His Teachers: They Were Magnificent," *Daily News/East Whittier Review*, 1/19/1969.

39. PPS 207, box 107, Charge to the Graduating Class of Whittier College by the Vice President of the United States, 6/13/1959; "Nixon Helps Dedication at Whittier," *Los Angeles Times*, 6/14/1959.

40. PPS 207, box 107, Charge to the Graduating Class; "Nixon Returns for Birthday Celebration," *Redlands Daily Facts*, 6/15/1959.

41. Nixon, *In the Arena*, 323.

42. PPS 207, box 107, Charge to the Graduating Class.

43. PPS 207, box 107: Nixon to Victor York, 4/27/1959, corr.; Nixon to Tom Bewley, 7/18/1959, corr.; Toledano, *Nixon*, 153.

44. CSUF, Charles Ball, 1–2, 10; PPS 207, box 108, Vice President's Schedule, 6/14/1959; "From the Pastor's Study," *Friendly Visitor*, June–July 1959.

45. CSUF, Janet Goeske, 15; BK, Bob Wilson, 12.

46. CSUF, Charles Ball, 11–12.

47. CSUF, Charles Ball, 11.

48. PPS 207, box 108: Vice President's Schedule, 6/14/1959; Vice President and Mrs. Nixon's Schedule, 6/14/1959; Vice President's Disneyland Itinerary, 6/12/1959; Hedda Hopper, "Nixon Impressive in Whittier Speech," *Los Angeles Times*, 6/17/1959.

49. "Nixons Take Part in Disneyland Fun," *Long Beach Press Telegram*, 6/15/1959; "Nixon to Visit Birthplace, Head East," *Pasadena Star News*, 6/15/1959.

50. PPS 207, box 108: Schedule for Vice President and Mrs. Nixon, 6/15/1959; Vice President's Schedule, 6/15/1959.

51. "Nixon Says Children Hold Hope of Peace," *Long Beach Press Telegram*, 6/16/1959.

52. Clara Jane Nixon, interviews by author, 7/8/2010, 9/17/2010, 1/17/2011, 9/21/2011.

53. WC, Lawrene Anfinson, 21; PPS 207, box 122, Office Memoranda re Baltimore Colts Game with Nephew Don Nixon Jr., n.d., 12/13/1959, 12/22/1959; Don Nixon Jr., email correspondence with author, 7/9/2014, 7/14/2014.

54. Clara Jane Nixon, interviews by author, 7/8/2010, 9/17/2010, 1/17/2011, 9/21/2011.

55. CSUF, Doug Ferguson, 16; WC, Clyde Irwin, 6; CSUF, John Neyer, 7; CSUF, Elizabeth Paldanius, 36; WC, Lewis Pollard, 6; CSUF, William Seale, 31.

56. WC, Mary Biddle, 10–11, 14; WC, George Irving Sr., 8; WC, Theodore Marshburn, 14; CSUF, Charles Milhous, 2; WC, #2 Charles Milhous, 5.

57. WC, Mary Irving Biddle, 4; CSUF, Elizabeth Paldanius, 24.

58. CSUF, Douglas Brannon, 11; CSUF, Doug Ferguson, 17; WC, #2 Josephine Harrison, 14; WC, Clyde Irwin, 6; CSUF, A. C. Newsom, 6–7; WC, Lewis Pollard, 5; CSUF, Mrs. Benjamin Roberts and Bill Roberts (Bill Roberts), 6; WC, Mabel Schuyler and Roger Schuyler (Roger Schuyler), 14.

59. WC, Merle Lally, 4; CSUF, Charles Milhous, 2; WC, #2 Charles Milhous, 11; CSUF, William A. Milhous, 6; CSUF, A. C. Newsom, 7; BK, Don Nixon, 3–4.

60. WC, Lewis Pollard, 5.

61. Aitken, *Nixon*, 286–87, 300–301.

62. CSUF, William A. Milhous, 17–18; CSUF, John Neyer, 7; CSUF, William Seale, 29; WC, Glen Shay, 16.

63. EDC, Statement of Hannah M. Nixon, n.d.

64. CSUF, Irvin Chapman, 20.

65. PPS 207, box 110, Nixon to Milton MacLean, 7/9/1959, corr.

66. PPS 207, Vice President's Schedule, 7/4/1959.

67. PPS 207, box 110, Supervisor Warren Dorn, "Vice President Nixon to Dedicate Memorial Sports in the Arena," press release, 5/6/1959.

68. "New Arena Dedicated by Nixon," *Los Angeles Times*, 7/5/1959.

69. "To the Victor," *Los Angeles Times*, 7/5/1959; PPS 207, box 110, Vice President's Schedule at Hollywood Park, 7/4/1959.

70. PPS 207, box 111: Supervisor Warren Dorn, "Vice President Nixon to Dedicate"; Vice President's Schedule, 7/4/1959.

71. PPS 207, box 111: Nixon to Allen Daily Jr., 7/16/1959, corr.; Nixon to Warren Dorn, 7/16/1959, corr.

72. Nixon, *Six Crises*, 247, 250–51.

73. JA, Richard Nixon 1983-5-12 and 13, 22–25; Aitken, *Nixon*, 260.

74. JA, Richard Nixon 1983-5-12 and 13, 25, 27–28; Nixon, *Six Crises*, 248.

75. William Safire, "The Cold War's Hot Kitchen," *New York Times*, 7/24/2009; Nixon, *Six Crises*, 255.

76. James D. Hughes, interviews by author, 1/9/2010, 2/9/2011, 2/10/2011.

77. PPS 207, box 114, Vice President's Schedule, 8/30–31/1959.

78. PPS 207, box 114, Elliot Mizelle to J. D. Hughes, 11/16/1959, corr.; Black, *Life in Full*, 419.

79. PPS 207, box 114: Official Program, 60th VFW National Convention, 8/30–9/4/1959; Vice President's Schedule, 8/30–31/1959; "VFW Chief Unhappy over Visit," *Oxnard Press Courier*, 9/1/1959.

80. PPS 207, box 114, Office Memorandum re VFW and George Meany, 8/22/1959; "VFW Chief Unhappy."

81. "VFW Chief Unhappy"; "Meany, Nixon Clash on K," *Los Angeles Examiner*, 9/1/1959.

82. PPS 207, box 114, Vice President's Schedule, 8/30–31/1959; Loie Gaunt, interviews by author, 12/28/2010, 2/7/2012.

83. PPS 207, box 114, James D. Hughes to H. R. Haldeman, 9/8/1959, corr.

84. Loie Gaunt, interviews by author, 12/28/2010, 2/7/2012; James D. Hughes, interviews by author, 1/9/2010, 2/9/2011, 2/10/2011.

85. "GOP Morale Gaining, Says Nixon on Southland Arrival," *Beverly Citizen*, 11/3/1959.

86. "Nixon Reviews Years at Flamingo, Santa Anita," *Ramada Inn Bugler*, 12/15/1959; "Nixon Visits in Southland," *Whittier News*, 11/3/1959.

87. PPS 207, box 120, Nixon to Mabel Boardman, 12/18/1959, corr.

88. "Nixon Buys Neckies; Plays Round of Golf," *Los Angeles Times*, 11/5/1959.

89. "Nixon Jokes with Waitress, He's Bob Hope," *Redlands Daily Facts*, 11/4/1959.

90. "Nixon to Be Candidate in N.H. Primary," *Long Beach Press Telegram*, 11/6/1959.

91. PPS 207, box 122, Vice President's Schedule, 12/31/1959; "Nixon on Hand," *Pasadena Independent*, 1/1/1960; "Political Convention in Pasadena," *Long Beach Press Telegram*, 1/1/1960.

92. PPS 207, box 122, Office Memoranda re Rose Bowl Game, 12/1/1959, 12/28/1959.

93. PPS 207, box 122: Vice President's Schedule, 1/1/1960; Nixon to Karl Schwab, 1/14/1960, corr.; "Record Crowd Predicted for Annual Rose Parade," *Van Nuys News*, 1/1/1960.

94. PPS 207, box 124, Vice President's Schedule, 2/5/1960.

95. PPS 207, box 124: Vice President's Schedule, 2/5/1960; Bernard Brennan to Nixon, 8/19/1959, corr.; Carroll Parcher to Nixon, 1/29/1960, corr.; Richard Nixon California Newspaper Pubishers Association (CNPA) Q&A interview transcript, 2/6/1960, 1:45 p.m.

96. PPS 207, box 124: Vice President's Schedule, 2/6/1960; Nixon, CNPA Q&A interview, 11:45 a.m.

97. PPS 207, box 124: Vice President's Schedule, 2/6/1960; Nixon, CNPA Q&A interview, 1:45 p.m.

98. PPS 207, box 124, Nixon, CNPA Q&A interview, 1:45 p.m.

99. PPS 207, box 124, Nixon, CNPA Q&A interview, 1:45 p.m.

100. PPS 207, box 124, Nixon, CNPA Q&A interview, 1:45 p.m.

101. PPS 207, box 124, Nixon, CNPA Q&A interview, 1:45 p.m.

102. PPS 207, box 124, Nixon, CNPA Q&A interview, 1:45 p.m.

103. PPS 207, box 124: Vice President's Schedule, 2/6/1960; *Paul Coates Show* transcript, KTTV, 2/6/1960.

104. PPS 207, box 124, *Paul Coates Show* transcript.

105. PPS 207, box 124, *Paul Coates Show* transcript.

106. PPS 207, box 124, *Paul Coates Show* transcript.

107. PPS 207, box 22: Nixon to Kenneth Ball, 6/17/1954, corr.; Nixon to Clint Harris, 6/17/1954, corr.; Nixon to Kyle Palmer, 6/16/1954, corr.; Nixon to Aubrey Wardman, 6/17/1954, corr.; PPS 207, box 27: Nixon to J. P. Hoenig, 3/19/1955, corr.; Nixon to Frank Valente, 4/7/1955, corr.; PPS 207, box 34: Nixon to Edward Bernard, 8/23/1955, corr.; Nixon to W. M. Bishop, 8/24/1955, corr.; Nixon to Major E. F. Bush Hanson, 8/26/1955, corr.; Nixon to James Sinclair, 8/23/1955, corr.; Loie Gaunt, interviews by author, 12/28/2010, 2/7/2012.

108. PPS 207, box 108: Nixon to Walt Disney, 6/22/1959, corr.; Nixon to Walter Knott, 6/26/1959, corr.; PPS 207, box 111: Nixon to Supervisor Warren Dorn, 7/16/1959, corr.; Nixon to LAPD chief William Parker, 7/21/1959, corr.

109. PPS 207, box 107: Nixon to Ola Florence Jobe, 7/8/1959, corr.; Nixon to Paul Johnson, 7/2/1959, corr.; PPS 207, box 108: Nixon to Walt Disney, 6/22/1959 and 3/18/1960, corr.; Nixon to Sally Fallansbee and Nettie Stone, 10/12/1959, corr.; Nixon to Donna Jackson, 7/2/1959, corr.; Nixon to Lee Meyers, 7/21/1959, corr.; Nixon to C. J. Noell, 7/2/1959, corr.; Nixon to Jesse Waldren, 7/21/1959, corr.; PPS 207, box 110: Nixon to Fred Mitchell, 7/16/1959, corr.; PPS 207, box 110, Nixon to James Stewart, 7/16/1959, corr.; PPS 207, box 111: Nixon to Allen Daily Jr., 7/16/1959, corr.; Nixon to Frode Kilstofte, 7/21/1959, corr.; PPS 207, box 120, Nixon to Terry Boris, 12/17/1959, corr.; Nixon to Townsend Tucker, 11/10/1959, corr.; PPS 207, box 122: Nixon to Shirley Cross, 1/15/1960, corr.; Office Memorandum re Thank-You Letter, 1/8/1960; Office Memoranda, California Thank-You Letters, n.d.; PPS 207, box 124, Office Memoranda, Los Angeles Trip Thank-You

Letters, n.d.; PPS 207, box 159, Office Memoranda re CRA Convention Thank-You Letters, n.d.

110. PPS 207, box 34: Nixon to Frank Urich, 8/23/1955, corr.; Nixon to Tom Childs, 8/25/1955, corr.; Nixon to Clint Harris, 8/26/1955, corr.; PPS 207, box 58, Nixon to Clint Harris, 10/20/1956, corr.; PPS 207, box 79, Nixon to J. C. Meacham, 2/25/1958, corr.; PPS 207, box 80, Nixon to Philip Weber, 2/26/1958, corr.; PPS 207, box 100: Nixon to Don Daley, 6/25/1959, corr.; Nixon to William Greenhut, 2/29/1960, corr.; PPS 207, box 107, Nixon to Jane Randolph, 7/21/1959, corr.; PPS 207, box 114: Nixon to Elliot Mizelle, 9/30/1959, corr.; Nixon to Philip Weber, 9/27/1959, corr.; Vice President's Schedule for California Trip, 8/9–18/1955; HJD, Nixon to Jack Drown, 8/24/1955, corr.; PPS 207, box 120, Nixon to Robert Groves, 11/10/1959, corr.; PPS 207, box 122: Nixon to Vince Burns, 1/8/1960, corr.; Nixon to Stephen Royce, 1/8/1960, corr.; PPS 207, box 124, Nixon to J. C. Meacham, 2/29/1960, corr.

111. CSUF, William Hornaday, 11; 105 Cong. Rec., 10,359 (1959).

112. WC, Ralph Veady, 7–8.

113. PPS 207, box 84, Office Memorandum re Dinner Party Guest List, 4/19/1958.

114. HJD, Nixon to Helene Drown, 5/6/1959, corr.

115. PPS 207, box 124, Nixon, CNPA Q&A interview, 1:45 p.m.; "Nixon Returns 'Home,'" *Pasadena Independent*, 11/3/1959.

116. Lou Jobst, "Disneyland Crowd Cheers Dick Nixon," *Long Beach Independent*, 6/15/1959; Aitken, *Nixon*, 272.

117. BK, Bob King, 6; BK, Kyle Palmer, 17.

118. Loie Gaunt, interviews by author, 12/28/2010, 2/7/2012.

119. BK, Bob King, 17.

120. CSUF, Linda Baker, 34, 41; BK, Kyle Palmer, 11; Kornitzer, *Real Nixon*, 81.

121. CSUF, Edith Timberlake, 54; Kornitzer, *Real Nixon*, 272–73.

122. BK, #3 Hannah Nixon, 3; Kornitzer, *Real Nixon*, 241–42, 273.

123. WC, Julie Nixon Eisenhower, 9; WC, #2 Jessamyn West, 16.

124. WC, Julie Nixon Eisenhower, 10.

125. WC, Julie Nixon Eisenhower, 10.

126. WC, Julie Nixon Eisenhower, 10.

127. WC, Julie Nixon Eisenhower, 3.

128. CSUF, Lucille Parsons, 20.

129. Gellman, *Contender*, 156.

130. Loie Gaunt, interviews by author, 12/28/2010, 2/7/2012.

131. Aitken, *Nixon*, 208.

132. Nixon, *In the Arena*, 430.

133. BK, Aylett Cotton, 24.

134. WC, Jack Drown, 6.

135. WC, Lloyd Harnish, 11.

136. Nixon, *In the Arena*, 277.

137. BK, Norm Chandler, 3; WC, John Holland, 15, 17; BK, George Milias, 4–5.

138. BK, Bob Wilson, 8–9.

139. BK, Bob Wilson, 8–9.

140. BK, Bob Wilson, 8–9.

141. WC, Lawrene Anfinson, 22.

142. Nixon, *In the Arena*, 194.

143. Nixon, *In the Arena*, 197.

144. CSUF, Byron Netzley, 13.

145. BK, Alphonzo Bell, 2.

146. WC, Matthew Bender, 5; CSUF, William A. Milhous, 14.

147. BK, George Milias, 2–3.

12. Presidential Campaign

1. Aitken, *Nixon*, 270–71; Eisenhower, *Pat Nixon*, 188.

2. JA, Richard Nixon Historic Video Transcript, 5/3/1975, 19–20; Aitken, *Nixon*, 271.

3. CSUF, Charles Ball, 16; Aitken, *Nixon*, 271.

4. PPS 207, box 141, Vice President's Schedule, 8/2/1960; "Plan Big Nixon Welcome," *Pasadena Star News*, 8/2/1960; Nixon, *Six Crises*, 321.

5. PPS 207, box 141, Thank-You Letter List, n.d.; Jack Smith, "Nixon Gets Roaring Southland Greeting," *Los Angeles Times*, 8/3/1960; "Plan Big Nixon Welcome."

6. PPS 207, box 141, Whittier College speech transcript, 8/2/1960.

7. PPS 207, box 141: Hyatt House Memoranda, n.d.; Hyatt House Press Conference transcript, 8/2/1960.

8. PPS 207, box 141, Hyatt House Press Conference transcript; Crowley, *Nixon off the Record*, 41.

9. PPS 207, box 141, Hyatt House Press Conference transcript; *Long Beach Press Telegram*, 8/3/1960.

10. Aitken, *Nixon*, 136–37.

11. Aitken, *Nixon*, 276–77.

12. Aitken, *Nixon*, 279.

13. "A Not So Great Debate," *Pasadena Independent*, 10/14/1960; Nixon, *Six Crises*, 307, 329.

14. Aitken, *Nixon*, 286–87; Brodie, *Richard Nixon*, 436–37.

15. PPS 207, box 141, Vice President's Schedule, 8/2/1960; "15,000 at a Homecoming Celebration," *Daily News/East Whittier Review*, 1/19/1969; "Nixon Opens Campaign in Whittier," *Pasadena Independent*, 8/3/1960; Smith, "Nixon Gets Roaring Southland Greeting."

16. PPS 207, box 141, Office Memorandum re Whittier College Homecoming, n.d.

17. "20,000 Welcome Nixons," *Star News*, 8/3/1960.

18. PPS 207, box 141, Whittier College speech, 8/2/1960.

19. "Nixons Fly to Hawaii in History-Making Trip," *Long Beach Press Telegram*, 8/3/1960.

20. CSUF, E. V. Lindstrom and Patricia Lindstrom (E. V. Lindstrom), 10; Smith, "Nixon Gets Roaring Southland Greeting."

21. PPS 207, box 141: Thank-You Letter List; Nixon to Suzanne Lewis, 9/6/1960, corr.

22. PPS 207, box 147, Vice President's Schedule, 10/11/1960.

23. PPS 207, box 147: Vice President's Schedule, 10/11/1960; Burbank Airport speech transcript, 10/11/1960; "Nixon Drives for Home State Vote," *Pasadena Star News*, 10/12/1960; Nixon, *Six Crises*, 375.

24. PPS 207, box 147, Burbank Airport speech transcript.

25. PPS 207, box 147, Vice President's Schedule, 10/12/1960.

26. PPS 207, box 147, Richard Nixon, interview by Chet Huntley and David Brinkley, *The Campaign and the Candidates*, NBC, 10/15/1960.

27. CSUF, S. Beeson, 11–12; "Nixon Talks at L.B. Picnic Wednesday," *Long Beach Press Telegram*, 10/11/1960; "Throng Welcomes Nixon, Pat to L.B.," *Long Beach Press Telegram*, 10/13/1960.

28. BK, Ray Arbuthnot, 1, 6; BK, Jack Drown, 6; WC, Jack Drown, 2–3; PPS 207, box 147, Hotel Information Memoranda, 10/11–12/1960.

29. BK, Jack Drown, 11.

30. BK, Norm Chandler, 22; BK, Jack Drown, 6, 9–10, 16.

31. BK, Jack Drown, 17.

32. BK, Ray Arbuthnot, 1, 6; BK, Alphonzo Bell, 8; BK, Norm Chandler, 22; BK, Jack Drown, 19.

33. PPS 207, box 147, All States Society Long Beach speech transcript, 10/12/1960.

34. PPS 207, box 147, All States Society speech.

35. PPS 207, box 147, All States Society speech.

36. PPS 207, box 147, All States Society speech.

37. PPS 207, box 147: Vice President's Schedule, 10/12/1960; Knott's Berry Farm speech transcript, 10/12/1960; "V.P. Arrives in Southland," *Pasadena Independent*, 10/13/1960; "Aim L.B. Speech at Pensioners," *Long Beach Press Telegram*, 10/13/1960.

38. PPS 207, box 147, Knott's Berry Farm speech transcript.

39. Aitken, *Nixon*, 276.

40. Aitken, *Nixon*, 276–77.

41. Nixon, *Six Crises*, 341.

42. Nixon, *Six Crises*, 341.

43. PPS 207, box 147, Vice President's Schedule, 10/13/1960; "V.P. Arrives in Southland"; Lungren and Lungren, *Healing*, 69; Nixon, *Memoirs*, 220; Nixon, *Six Crises*, 346.

44. PPS 207, box 147, Vice President's Schedule, 10/13/1960; "Yes! Nixon for President," *Los Angeles Times*, 10/13/1960.

45. "Makeup Discussion," *Pasadena Independent*, 10/13/1960.

46. Walter T. Ridder, "GOP Camp Claims Foul over Note Use," *Long Beach Press Telegram*, 10/14/1960; Nixon, *Six Crises*, 347.

47. Ridder, "GOP Camp Claims Foul."

48. James D. Hughes, interviews by author, 1/9/2010, 2/9/2011, 2/10/2011.

49. PPS 207, box 147, Ambassador Hotel speech transcript, 10/13/1960.

50. PPS 207, box 147, Ambassador Hotel speech, 10/13/1960.

51. PPS 207, box 147, Ambassador Hotel speech, 10/13/1960.

52. PPS 207, box 147, Ambassador Hotel speech, 10/13/1960; Smith, "Nixon Gets Roaring Southland Greeting"; Joseph Alsop, "What Really Happened," *Pasadena Independent*, 8/3/1960.

53. PPS 207, box 147: James Bassett to Norman Topping, 9/30/1960, telegram; Vice President's Schedule, 10/14/1960; USC speech transcript, 10/13/1960.

54. PPS 207, box 147, USC speech, 10/13/1960.

55. WC, Dorothy Bishop, 15; PPS 207, box 147, Shopping Center speech transcript, 10/13/1960.

56. PPS 207, box 147, Shopping Center speech, 10/13/1960.

57. PPS 207, box 147, Shopping Center speech, 10/13/1960.

58. PPS 207, box 147, Shopping Center speech, 10/13/1960.

59. PPS 207, box 147, All State Society speech.

60. CSUF, Merle West, 17; PPS 207, box 147, Vice President's Schedule, 10/14/1960.

61. PPS 207, box 147, Beverly Hills City Hall speech transcript, 10/14/1960.

62. Eisenhower, *Pat Nixon*, 189.

63. PPS 207, box 147: Vice President's Schedule, 10/13/1960; Beverly Hilton Hotel speech, 10/13/1960; "World News Forum to Hear Nixon Tomorrow," *Pasadena Independent*, 10/13/1960; Nixon, *Six Crises*, 346.

64. PPS 207, box 147, Beverly Hilton Hotel speech.

65. CSUF, Merle West, 17; PPS 207, box 147, Beverly Hilton Hotel speech.

66. Aitken, *Nixon*, 284–85.

67. PPS 207, box 147: Tom Pike and John Krehbiel to Bob Wilson, 8/27/1960, corr.; Earl Adams to James Bassett, 9/12/1960, corr.; "Ike Hints Heavy Role in Campaign," *Pasadena Star News*, 8/2/1960.

68. "Nixon Talks at L.B. Pinic Wednesday," *Long Beach Press Telegram*, 10/11/1960.

69. Aitken, *Nixon*, 284–85.

70. PPS 207, box 149: Arrival Data Memorandum, 11/5/1960; Vice President's Schedule, 11/5/1960; Bill Broom, "Nixon Denounces Kennedy Remedy," *Independent Star News*, 11/6/1960; Tom Rreilly, "7000 Wait in Rain to Greet Richard Nixon," *Valley News*, 11/6/1960; Dee Hazen, "Rain-Soaked Crowd Happy—Nixon Arrives," *Valley News*, 11/6/1960.

71. Reilly, "7000 Wait in Rain"; Nixon, *Six Crises*, 370.

72. PPS 207, box 149, Vice President's Schedule, 11/6/1960; Nixon, *Six Crises*, 371.

73. Eisenhower, *Pat Nixon*, 195; *Long Beach Press Telegram*, 11/7/1960.

74. James D. Hughes, interviews by author, 1/9/2010, 2/9/2011, 2/10/2011; Bob Houser, "Dick Finale at Ontario Tonight," *Long Beach Press Telegram*, 11/7/1960; Nixon, *Six Crises*, 376.

75. Jack L. Warner, "An Open Letter," *Long Beach Press Telegram*, 11/7/1960.

76. Eisenhower, *Pat Nixon*, 196; Nixon, *Six Crises*, 376.

77. Crowley, *Nixon off the Record*, 127; Eisenhower, *Pat Nixon*, 192.

78. Crowley, *Nixon off the Record*, 29; Nixon, *Memoirs*, 214.

79. Bob Houser, "Dick Finale at Ontario Tonight," *Long Beach Press Telegram*, 11/7/1960; Nixon, *Six Crises*, 376–77.

80. Nixon, *Six Crises*, 376–77.

81. Eisenhower, *Pat Nixon*, 196.

82. James D. Hughes, interviews by author, 1/9/2010, 2/9/2011, 2/10/2011; M. I. Arrowsmith, "Nixon Votes, Takes Drive along Ocean," *Long Beach Press Telegram*, 11/8/1960.

83. James D. Hughes, interviews by author, 1/9/2010, 2/9/2011, 2/10/2011; Nixon, *Six Crises*, 377.

84. James D. Hughes, interviews by author, 1/9/2010, 2/9/2011, 2/10/2011; Nixon, *Six Crises*, 377–78.

85. James, D. Hughes, interviews by author, 1/9/2010, 2/9/2011, 2/10/2011; Nixon, *Six Crises*, 377–79.

86. James D. Hughes, interviews by author, 1/9/2010, 2/9/2011, 2/10/2011.

87. James D. Hughes, interviews by author, 1/9/2010, 2/9/2011, 2/10/2011.

88. James D. Hughes, interviews by author, 1/9/2010, 2/9/2011, 2/10/2011; Aitken, *Nixon*, 287–89; Eisenhower, *Pat Nixon*, 195; Nixon, *Memoirs*, 223; Nixon, *Six Crises*, 378–79.

89. James D. Hughes, interviews by author, 1/9/2010, 2/9/2011, 2/10/2011.

90. Hillings, *Irrepressible Irishman*, 87; Nixon, *Six Crises*, 384.

91. Nixon, *Six Crises*, 386.

92. David, *Lonely Lady*, 119.

93. Nixon, *Six Crises*, 388.

94. Eisenhower, *Pat Nixon*, 197; Nixon, *Memoirs*, 223.

95. Eisenhower, *Pat Nixon*, 196; Nixon, *Six Crises*, 392–93.

96. Nixon, *In the Arena*, 23; Nixon, *Six Crises*, 392–93.

97. Nixon, *Memoirs*, 223; Nixon, *Six Crises*, 375.

98. Nixon, *Memoirs*, 224; "1960 Presidential Election Results," John F. Kennedy Library, accessed 10/5/2022, https://www.jfklibrary.org/learn/about-jfk/life-of-john-f-kennedy/fast-facts-john-f-kennedy/1960-presidential-election-results.

99. "Will State Democrats Vote So?" *Pasadena Star News*, 10/12/1960; James C. Anderson, "California Election Still Question Mark," *Long Beach Press Telegram*, 11/7/1960.

100. Nixon, *Six Crises*, 393.

101. Eisenhower, *Pat Nixon*, 198; Nixon, *Six Crises*, 398.

102. Nixon, *Six Crises*, 398.

103. Hillings, *Irrepressible Irishman*, 88; Nixon, *Six Crises*, 398–99.

104. Aitken, *Nixon*, 280.

105. Wicker, foreword to *People's President*, 9.

106. Patricia Sullivan, "Earl Mazo, 87," *Washington Post*, 2/18/2007; Eisenhower, *Pat Nixon*, 200.

107. Sullivan, "Earl Mazo."

108. Sullivan, "Earl Mazo"; Eisenhower, *Pat Nixon*, 200.

109. Sullivan, "Earl Mazo"; Eisenhower, *Pat Nixon*, 200.

110. Aitken, *Nixon*, 291.

111. Aitken, *Nixon*, 275.

112. Aitken, *Nixon*, 291.

113. CSUF, Charles Ball, 13, 15, 21.

114. CSUF, Charles Ball, 8; WC, Elva Urich, 8.

115. PPS 207, box 141, Thank-You Letter List, 8/2/1960; PPS 207, box 149, Nixon to Herm Link, 12/29/1960, corr.; CSUF, Janet Goeske, 42 (reading Nixon to Janet Goeske, 12/9/1960, corr.)

116. WC, Roger Johnson, 9.

117. PPS 207, box 150: Rev. Edward Elson to Nixon, 12/13/1960, corr.; Nixon Memorandum, n.d. (handwritten).

118. PPS 207, box 150, Remarks by Vice President Richard Nixon before Joint Session of Congress, 1/6/1960 (handwritten).

119. PPS 207, box 150, Remarks by Vice President Nixon.

120. BK, Ray Arbuthnot, 6; BK, Alphonzo Bell, 8; CSUF, Edith Holt, 14; BK, Mrs. Bob King, 6; BK, Alice Longworth, 41.

121. Nixon, *Six Crises*, 374.

122. BK, Albert Mattei, 6.

123. UCB, Earl Adams, 19–20.

124. Aitken, *Nixon*, 292–93.

13. Welcome Home

1. Nixon Family Collection, box 8, Julie Nixon to Hannah Nixon, 1/30/1961, corr.

2. "Plan Reception at Airport for Nixons Tonight," *Inglewood Daily News*, 2/28/1961; "Nixon Returns to Home State Tonight," *Inglewood Daily News*, 2/28/1961; "Nixon Returns Home Tonight," *Inglewood Daily News*, 2/28/1961; "Dick Nixon Family Return Home Tonight," *Inglewood Daily News*, 2/28/1961.

3. "Nixon Hides Future Plans in Politics," *Barstow Desert Dispatch*, 3/1/1961; "Noisy Welcome Greets Nixons," *Ventura Star Free Press*, 3/1/1961.

4. "Nixon Hides Future Plans"; "Nixons Get Hearty Welcome to L.A.," *Press Telegram*, 3/1/1961; "Nixons to Be Honored at Banquet Tonight," *Santa Monica Evening Outlook*, 3/1/1961; "Noisy Welcome Greets Nixons," *Ventura Star Free Press*, 3/1/1961.

5. "Nixon Hides Future Plans"; "Nixons Get Hearty Welcome"; "Big Welcome Readied for Dick Nixons," *San Gabriel Valley Daily Tribune*, 2/27/1961; "Hundreds Greet Nixon in L.A.," *San Pedro News Pilot*, 3/1/1961; "Nixons to Be Honored"; "Noisy Welcome Greets Nixons."

6. "The Nixons Back Home," *Alhambra Post-Advocate*, 3/3/1961.

7. "Nixon Says He Plans to Stay in Public Life," *Los Angeles Times*, 3/2/1961; "Big Welcome Readied"; "Nixons to Be Honored."

8. "Nixon Says He Plans."

9. "Nixon Says He Plans."

10. "Nixons Will Lunch with Ike and Mamie Tomorrow," *Los Angeles Herald-Express*, 3/3/1961.

11. "Says Nixon: Would Like Home Here," *Whittier Daily News*, 3/3/1961; "Richard M. Nixon Family Hunts Home in Palsades," *Pacific Palisadian*, 3/3/1961.

12. PPS 207, box 164, Nixon Telethon Questions & Answers (Q&A) transcript, 5/29/1962; Nixon, *In the Arena*, 122.

13. "Richard Nixon Goes Back to Work at Law," *Los Angeles Times*, 3/15/1961.

14. PPS 207, box 150, J. C. Meacham to Nixon, 4/14/1961, corr.; Aitken, *Nixon*, 294; Nixon, *Memoirs*, 231.

15. PPS 212, 3/1961–6/1961 Nixon Calendars; Aitken, *Nixon*, 294.

16. PPS 207, box 151, Nixon to Conrad Hilton, 4/14/1961, corr.

17. Herb Caen, "Richard Nixon in a 'Stolen' Car," *Los Angeles Times*, 3/19/1961.

18. UCB, Earl Adams, 19; Aitken, *Nixon*, 294.

19. Nixon, *Memoirs*, 231.

20. James Golden, interview by author, 7/2/2010.

21. Loie Gaunt, interviews by author, 12/28/2010, 2/7/2012.

22. Anthony Pierno, interviews by author, 9/11/2009, 9/25/2009; James Powers, interview by author, 12/3/2009; Lane Tilson, interview by author, 4/27/2009; Alan Wayte, interview by author, 9/14/2009; PPS 207, Nixon to Reese Taylor, 8/23/1955, corr.

23. Aitken, *Nixon*, 294.

24. "Richard Nixon Goes Back to Work at Law," *Los Angeles Times*, 3/15/1961.

25. Anthony Pierno, interviews by author, 9/11/2009, 9/25/2009; Lane Tilson, interview by author, 4/27/2009.

26. Lane Tilson, interview by author, 4/27/2009.

27. BK, Bill Henry, 5.

28. Lane Tilson, interview by author, 4/27/2009; BK, Richard Nixon, 10.

29. WC, #4 Clint Harris, 10–11; "Nixon Is House Hunting," *Los Angeles Herald-Express*, 3/23/1961.

30. "Nixon Buys New Auto, Get's Driver's License," *Los Angeles Times*, 3/23/1961.

31. Nixon, *Memoirs*, 232.

32. Nixon, *Six Crises*, 424.

33. PPS 207, boxes 151–58, 3/1961–9/1961 Nixon Calendars; James Bassett, "Some Mistaken Ideas about Richard Nixon," *Los Angeles Times*, 3/19/1961.

34. PPS207, box 151: Office Memorandum to Nixon, 3/20/1961; Nixon to Joseph Massaglia Jr., 4/16/1961, corr.; Nixon to Don Jackson, 4/16/1961, corr.; Nixon, *Memoirs*, 232.

35. PPS 207, box 151, Office Memorandum Guest List, n.d.; PPS 212, box 10, 3/1961 Nixon Calendars.

36. BK, Justin Dart, 1–2, 5; PPS 207, box 151, Justin Dart Memorandum, n.d.; PPS 212, box 10, 3/1961–4/1961 Nixon Calendars.

37. PPS 207, box 154: Office Memoranda and Guest Lists for Law Firm Reception, n.d.; 6/1961 Nixon Calendars.

38. *Martindale-Hubbell Law Directory*, 1961–63.

39. UCB, Earl Adams, 21–22.

40. UCB, Earl Adams, 21–22.

41. PPS 207, box 151: Valley Knudsen to Nixon, 4/16/1961, corr.; Office Memorandum re Breakfast Meeting, 4/12/1961.

42. PPS 207, box 154: Road to Victory Dinner Remarks, 6/1/1961; Nixon to Frederic Morrow, 4/29/1961, corr.

43. PPS 207, box 154, Dick Nixon Trip to Orange, Riverside, and San Bernardino Office Memorandum.

44. PPS 207, box 154: Dick Nixon Trip Memorandum; David Ackley to Nixon, 6/19/1961, corr.; "'New' Nixon Here," *Barley Loaf*, 6/11/1961.

45. PPS 207, box 154: Ann Gallagher to Nixon, 6/8/1961, corr.; Nixon to Ann Gallagher, 9/11/1961, corr.; Dick Nixon Trip Memorandum.

46. PPS 207, box 154: Office Dinner Memorandum, 6/7/1961; 6/1961–8/1961 Nixon Calendars; Dick Darling to Nixon, 6/12/1961, corr.

47. PPS 207, box 154, Nixon to J. Edgar Hoover, 6/19/1961, corr.; Eisenhower, *Pat Nixon*, 205.

48. PPS 207, box 151, Barbara Mashburn to Pat and Richard Nixon, 3/14/1961, corr.; PPS 207, box 154: 5/19–21/1961 Schedule; Yorba Linda Chamber of Commerce to Nixon, 5/2/1961, corr.

49. PPS 207, box 154: Rose Mary Woods to H. R. Haldeman, 4/3/1961, corr.; Office Memorandum re Family Visit, n.d.; 3/1961–9/1961 Nixon Calendars; 5/19/1961 Schedule; Dick Nixon Trip Memorandum.

50. PPS 207, box 154, Office Memorandum, n.d.

51. PPS 207, box 154: John Gleason to Nixon, 4/21/1961 and 5/25/1961, corr.; Nixon Boys Club Remarks, 5/15/1961 (handwritten); 5/15/1961 Schedule; "Nixon Lauds Volunteer Help on Delinquency," *Los Angeles Times*, 5/16/1961.

52. PPS 207, box 154, Office Memoranda re Boys Club, 4/26/1961, 5/15/1961; "Nixon Lauds Volunteer Help."

53. PPS 207, box 154, Warren Woodall to Nixon, 5/17/1961, corr.

54. PPS 207, box 154: Meredith Willson to Nixon, 5/16/1961, corr.; Meredith Willson to Nixon, 6/5/1961, telegram.

55. PPS 207, box 156: Office Memorandum re City of Hope, n.d.; Ben Horowitz to Nixon, 5/22/1961, corr.; City of Hope Remarks, 7/3/1961.

56. PPS 207, box 156, Murray Webber to Nixon, 7/7/1961, corr.

57. PPS 207, box 155: Nixon to Ben Horowitz, 7/3/1961, corr.; Murray Webber to Nixon, 7/7/1961, corr.

58. PPS 207, box 154: Memorandum re Dinner with Reagans, n.d. (handwritten); Rose Mary Woods to Pat Nixon, 6/13/1961, corr.; Memorandum re Dinner Party; Office Memorandum, 6/7/1961; PPS 207, box 156, 7/12/1961 Schedule; PPS 212, box 10, 3/1961–9/1961 Nixon Calendars.

59. WC, Jack Drown, 4–5; HJD, Nixon to Jack Drown, n.d., corr.

60. PPS 207, box 151, Nixon to Gene Autry, 3/30/1961, corr.

61. PPS 207, box 151, Nixon to Bob Reynolds and Gene Autry, 4/29/1961, corr.

62. PPS 207, box 154, 5/19–21/1961 Schedule.

63. PPS 207, box 154, Nixon to Charles Thomas, 5/22/1961 and 6/8/1961, corr.

64. PPS 207, box 154: Nixon to Robert Barnes, 6/8/1961, corr.; Nixon to O. W. Richard, 6/8/1961, corr.

65. WC, Adela Rogers St. Johns, 3.

66. PPS 207, box 151, 4/10/1961 and 4/20/1961 Schedules.

67. Don Shannon, "U.S. Won't Abandon Cuba to Communists," *Los Angeles Times*, 4/21/1961; Rowland Evans Jr., "Kennedy and Nixon Talk on Cuba for 75 Minutes," *New York Herald Tribune*, 4/20/1961.

68. Eisenhower, *Pat Nixon*, 204; David, *Lonely Lady*, 122.

69. David, *Lonely Lady*, 122.

70. PPS 207, box 159, 1961 Appearances Memo, n.d.

71. Los Angeles County Recorder, Grant Deed for 410 Martin Lane, 6/16/1961; Aitken, *Nixon*, 297; Eisenhower, *Pat Nixon*, 204; David, *Lonely Lady*, 122.

72. PPS 207, box 156: Joseph Martin Jr. to Nixon, 5/25/1961, corr.; Nixon to Martin, 6/7/1961, corr.

73. PPS 207, box 156: Guest List for Republican Leader Meeting at Nixon Home, 7/11/1961; John Krehbiel Invitation to Republican Leaders for Meeting, 6/30/1961, corr.

74. PPS 207, box 156, Betty Williams to Rose Mary Woods, 8/6/1961, Office Memorandum.

75. PPS 212, box 10, 9/1961 Nixon Calendar; PPS 207, box 156, Bebe Rebozo to Nixon, 7/20/1961, corr.

76. PPS 207, box 156, Nixon to Bebe Rebozo, 8/17/1961, corr.

77. United Press International (UPI), "Hole-in-One," *Los Angeles Times*, 9/5/1961; Van Natta, *First off the Tee*, 236; Campbell and Landau, *Presidential Lies*, 158–59.

78. Hillings, *Irrepressible Irishman*, 188.

79. UPI, "Hole-in-One."

80. Nixon, *Memoirs*, 236.

14. Governor's Race

1. Aitken, *Nixon*, 297.

2. CSUF, Howard Rupard, 4–6; "Mr. Nixon's Announcement," *Los Angeles Times*, 9/29/1961; Eisenhower, *Pat Nixon*, 205; Mazo, *Richard Nixon*, 139; Nixon, *In the Arena*, 224.

3. CSUF, Rev. Charles Ball, 13; PB, Roy Day, 22; Eisenhower, *Pat Nixon*, 205.

4. Eisenhower, *Pat Nixon*, 205; Nixon, *In the Arena*, 224.

5. Aitken, *Nixon*, 298; Nixon, *Memoirs*, 239–40.

6. David, *Lonely Lady*, 123.

7. CSUF, Dorothy Beeson, 14; Aitken, *Nixon*, 298; Nixon, *Memoirs*, 248.

8. Aitken, *Nixon*, 297.

9. PPS 207, box 156, 9/27/1961 Nixon Calendar; Eisenhower, *Pat Nixon*, 207; Nixon, *Memoirs*, 240.

10. PPS 207, box 170, Statler Hilton Press Conference transcript, 9/27/1961.

11. PPS 207, box 170, Statler Hilton Press Conference transcript, 9/27/1961.

12. PPS 207, box 159: Herb Hazeltine to Nixon, 9/25/1961, corr.; Otis Chandler to Nixon, 11/24/1961, corr.; 12/1961, 10/1962, 11/1962, 11/19/1961 Nixon Calendars; 10/1/1962, 11/19/91 Schedules.

13. PPS 207, box 158, 10/24/1961 Nixon Calendar; PPS 207, box 159, 11/17/1961 Schedule.

14. WC, Adela Rogers St. Johns, 3; PPS 207, box 158, 11/8/1961 Nixon Calendar; PPS 207, box 159, 12/30/1961 Nixon Calendar.

15. PPS 207, box 164, Nixon Telethon Q&A transcript, 5/29/1962.

16. WC, Adela Rogers St. Johns, 14.

17. PPS 207, boxes 157, 160, 162, 170: 1961 Appearances Memo, n.d.; 10/12/1961, 11/5/1961, 1/1962, 3/12/1962, 4/20/1962, 7/13/1962, 7/19/1962, 9/26/1962 Nixon Calendars; 11/12/1961, 3/5/1962, 3/12/1962, 5/16/1962, 4/23/1962, 4/27/1962, 3/15/1962, 4/20/1962, 4/24/1962, 5/23/1962, 7/13/1962, 7/18/1962, 7/19/1962, 9/12–10/20/1962 Schedules; PPS 207, box 160: William Stover Memo, 1/22/62; California Club Dinner Guest List, 1/10/1962; PPS 207, box 161: California Club Guest List, 2/13/1962; 1/15/1962 Memo re 1/15/1962 California Club Luncheon; PPS 207, box 162: Bob Finch to Rose File Memo, 2/20/1962; 3/2/1962 Memorandum re 3/5/1962 California Club Luncheon; Background Memo re California Trucking Assn. Meeting at Jonathan Club, 4/18/1962; PPS 207, box 165, Nixon for Governor Memo, 6/4/1962, 7/13/1962; PPS 207, box 168, Southern California Nixon Campaign Leadershp Memos, 8/28/1962; PPS 207, box 170, Campaign Schedule Third Week.

18. PPS 207, box 157: 1961 Appearances Memo; 10/11/1961 Nixon Calendar.

19. PPS 207, box 157, 1961 Appearances Memo.

20. PPS 207, boxes 157, 168–69: 10/13/1961, 9/6/1962 Schedules; 8/20/1962 Nixon Calendar.

21. PPS 207, box 159, Calfornia Republican Assembly Remarks, 12/2/1961.

22. Sandy Quinn, interview by author, 7/18/2012.

23. Sandy Quinn, interview by author, 7/18/2012.

24. Sandy Quinn, interview by author, 7/18/2012.

25. Sandy Quinn, interview by author, 7/18/2012.

26. PPS 207, boxes 158–59, 11/1961, 12/1961, 12/19/1961 Nixon Calendars.

27. PPS 207, boxes 158–59, 12/28/1961 Nixon Calendar; "Nixon Says His Former Boss Kept Secret under Pressure," *Chico (CA) Enterprise-Record*, 9/21/1961.

28. PPS 207, boxes 159–50, 12/24/1961, 1/1962 Nixon Calendars.

29. PPS 207, box 160: Nixon Whittier Visit Remarks, 1/9/1962 (handwritten); Robert Bell to Nixon, 12/6/1961, corr.; Robert Bell to Nixon, 1/10/1962, corr.; Nixon to Robert Bell, 1/17/1962, corr.; Nixon to John Reilly, 1/17/1962, corr.; Nixon to Earl Myer, 1/17/1962, corr.

30. PPS 207, box 160: 1/24/1962 Schedule; Personnel and Industrial Relations Association Remarks, 1/24/1962; W. A. Stamper to Robert Haldeman, 12/21/1961, corr.; PPS 207, box 164, Nixon Telethon Q&A transcript, 5/29/1962.

31. PPS 207, box 162: F. W. Vickrey to Nixon, 3/23/1962, corr.; Glenn Carlson to Nixon, 5/3/1962, corr.; PPS 207, box 163, 5/1/1962, 5/3/1962 Schedules; David Massey, "Barrister's Inn," *Los Angeles Bar Bulletin*, 6/1962.

32. PPS 207, box 162, Tom Duggan Television Show Interview of Nixon transcript, 3/27/1962.

33. PPS 207, box 163: Junior Barrister's Luncheon Remarks, 5/3/1962; Notes re Barrister Remarks, 5/3/1962 (handwritten).
34. PPS 207, box 162: Duggan Interview of Nixon; Orange County Nixon Dinner Committee Remarks, 4/27/62.
35. PPS 207, box 162, Rotary Visa Program Remarks, 3/3/1962.
36. PPS 207, box 162, Rotary Remarks, 3/3/1962; Lee Belser, "Cultural Exchange Best Bid for Pease, Says Nixon," *Angeles Mirror*, 11/21/1961; "Culture's Influence Reaches Far," *Angeles Mirror*, 11/22/1961.
37. WC, Ralph Burnight, 3; PPS 207, boxes 162–63, 169–70, 4/27/1962, 5/11/1962, 5/25/1962, 9/12/1962–10/20/1962, 10/10/1962, 11/1/1962 Schedules; PPS 207, box 162: 3/19/1962, 3/20/1962, 3/31/1962, 5/25/1962, 10/10/1962, 10/16/1962 Nixon Calendars; Memo re L.A. State College Student Assembly, 4/27/1962; Tom Weinberg to Nixon, 3/9/1962, corr.; C. A. Oliphant to Nixon, 3/22/1962, corr.; National Forensic League Student Congress Remarks, 3/31/1962; Remarks re National Forensic League, 3/31/1962 (handwritten); PPS 207, box 163: Alvah Hall to Nixon, 5/14/1962, corr.; Nixon to Alvah Hall, 5/17/1962, corr.; PPS 207, box 171, Campaign Schedule Fifth Week; PPS 207, box 172: Campaign Schedule Seventh Week; Memo re Woodbury College Student Body, 10/23/1962; "Honors for President Paul Smith" and "The Nixon Books," *Daily News/East Whittier Review*, 1/19/1969; Bob Houser, "Nixon Backs 'True Frontier' in Four-Speech Tour of L.B.," *Long Beach Independent*, 3/24/1962.
38. PPS 207, box 162, Memo re L.A. State College Student Assembly, 4/27/1962; PPS 207, box 164, Nixon Telethon Q&A transcript, 5/29/1962; PPS 207, box 171, Office Memo re CalTech Visit, 10/10/1962; "Nixon Foresees Most Intensive Campaign in California History," *Newport Beach Daily Pilot*, 3/19/1962.
39. PPS 207, box 162: California Teachers Association Remarks, 4/28/1962; Junior Chamber of Commerce 31st Annual Youth Banquet Remarks, 4/24/1962.
40. PPS 207, box 162: Campaign Schedule, 4/2–8/1962; California Teachers Association Remarks; Santa Clara County School Board Remarks, 4/4/1962; Junior Chamber of Commerce Remarks, 4/24/1962.
41. PPS 207, box 169, Lancaster Rally Remarks, 9/14/1962.
42. PPS 207, box 169: David Hunter to Nixon Memo re Visit to Braille Library, 9/21/1962; 9/23/1962 Schedule.
43. PPS 207, box 162, Pacific Dairy and Poultry Association 38th Annual Convention Remarks; "Nixon Slated to Address 38th Annual PDPA Meet," *Western Milk and Ice Cream News*, 3/2/1962.
44. PPS 207, box 162, Duggan Interview of Nixon. Also noted in Nixon Telethon Q&A transcript, 5/29/1962; "Nixon Foresees Most Intensive Campaign in California History," *Newport Beach Daily Pilot*, 3/19/1962.
45. PPS 207, box 156, CBS Television with Walter Cronkite, *Eyewitness: The Decision of Richard Nixon*, transcript, 9/29/1961.
46. Whitney Shoemaker, "Democracy Winning, Kennedy Tells 88,000," *Long Beach Independent*, 3/24/1962; "Centers Criticism on Brown," *Long Beach Independent*, 3/24/1962.

47. Aitken, *Nixon*, 294.

48. PPS 207, box 164, Nixon Telethon Q&A transcript, 5/29/1962.

49. PPS 207, box 161: 25th Aniversary Celebration of the Pasadena Association for the Study of Negro Life and History Remarks, 2/11/1962; 2/11/1962 Schedule; "Nixon Urges Equality for All in U.S.," *Los Angeles Times*, 2/12/1960; "Nixon to Address Group in Pasadena," *Los Angeles Times*, 2/10/1962.

50. Stuart Spencer, interviews by author, 12/29/2010, 1/21/2011.

51. PPS 207, box 165: 6/1/1962 Schedule; Community Center Remarks, 6/1/1962.

52. PPS 207, box 165, Community Center Remarks.

53. PPS 207, box 165, Community Center Remarks.

54. PPS 207, box 165, Community Center Remarks.

55. PPS 207, box 168: Charles Williams to Nixon, 8/27/1962, corr.; Nixon to Paul Williams, 9/11/1962, corr.; Inter-Office Memo, 8/27/1962.

56. Myrna Oliver, "Crispus A. Wright, 87; Son of Ex-Slave Became Lawyer and USC Benefactor," *Los Angeles Times*, 12/11/2001; "History and Legacy of John M. Langston," John M. Langston Bar Association of Los Angeles, accessed 10/6/2022, https://www.langstonbar.org/history.

57. PPS 207, box 170: 9/12–10/20/1962 Schedule; Campaign Schedule Second Week; Office Memorandum re Medical, Dental and Pharmaceutical Association of Southern California and John Langston Law Club, 9/21/1962.

58. PPS 207, box 170, Medical, Dental and Pharmaceutical Association of Southern California and John Langston Law Club Remarks, 9/21/1962.

59. PPS 207, box 168: 8/21/1962 Schedule; 8/21/1962 Nixon Calendar; PPS 207, box 173: Campaign Schedule Eighth Week; Memo re East Los Angeles J.C. Rally, 10/27/1962; East Los Angeles Rally Remarks, 10/30/1962.

60. PPS 207, box 168: Memo re Clint Harris, n.d.; Rose Mary Woods to Herb Kalmbach, 8/22/1962, Memo; Office Memo re Mexican-American Committee for R.N., 8/24/1962; 8/29/1962 Nixon Calendar; Seventh Day Adventist Dinner, Biltmore Bowl Remarks, 8/29/1962; Herb Kalmbach to Nixon Inter-Office Memo re 8/29, "An Evening with the Nixons"; Arthur Sutton to Nixon, 9/5/1962, Inter-Office Memo re Mexican-American Independence Day Ceremonies; "An Evening with the Nixons" Invitation, 8/29/1962.

61. PPS 207, box 163, 5/8/1962 Schedule; PPS 207, box 173: Campaign Schedule Eighth Week; Memo re Baptist Ministers Alliance, 10/27/1962.

62. PPS 207, box 163, Guardians of the Jewish Home for the Aged Dinner Remarks, 5/1/1962; "Richard Nixon Helps Guardians Write New Dinner Meeting Attendance Record," *Guardian*, 5/1962.

63. "Richard Nixon Helps Guardians."

64. PPS 207, box 163, Lee Bishop to Nixon, 5/9/1962, corr.; "Richard Nixon Helps Guardians."

65. PPS 207, box 162, California Republican Assembly Remarks, 3/1/1962; Jack Kenny, "Benson Letter Backed Welch against Ike," *New American*, 11/16/2010.

66. PPS 207, box 162, California Republican Assembly Remarks, 3/1/1962.

67. "Centers Criticism on Brown," *Long Beach Independent*, 3/24/1962.

68. Jack Steele, "Nixon's Bircher Stand Splits GOP," Scripps-Howard, 2/26/1962.

69. PPS 207, box 161: 2/13/1962 Schedule; R. M. Woods to Charles Benedict, 3/9/1962, corr.; George Jensen, "Big Crowd Backs Brito in Illness," *Pasadena Independent*, 2/14/1962.

70. PPS 207, box 162: 4/27/1962 Schedule; Mary Clyde to Nixon, 4/28/1962, corr.; Nixon to Joyce Dell, 5/22/1962, corr.

71. PPS 207, box 168: 9/6/1962 Nixon Calendar; 9/8/1962 Schedule; Jack Haley to "Friend," n.d., corr.; Nixon to Raymond Burr, 9/10/1962, corr.; Nixon to Irene Dunne, 9/10/1962, corr.

72. CSUF, Sheldon Beeson, 27; WC, Sheldon Beeson, 8–9; PPS 207, box 163, 4/28/1962 Schedule.

73. PPS 207, box 162, 4/6/1962 Schedule.

74. PPS 207, box 162: Memo, 1/30/1962; 3/4/1962 Schedule.

75. PPS 207, box 164: Nixon Telethon Q&A transcript, 5/29/1962.

76. PPS 207, box 167: 8/5/1962 Schedule; Republican Central Committee Meeting Remarks, 8/5/1962.

77. PPS 207, box 159, Calfornia Republican Assembly Remarks, 12/2/1961.

78. PPS 207, box 162, Duggan Interview of Nixon.

79. PPS 207, box 162: 3/31/1962, 4/2/1962 Nixon Calendars; Irrigation Districts Association of California Remarks, 4/26/1962.

80. PPS 207, box 162, 4/9/1962 Schedule.

81. PPS 207, box 164, Nixon Telethon Q&A transcript, 5/29/1962; David, *Lonely Lady*, 122.

82. PPS 207, box 162, Duggan Interview of Nixon; PPS 207, box 164, Nixon Telethon Q&A transcript, 5/29/1962.

83. WC, Charles Rhyne, 8; PPS 207, box 163: Edmonde Haddad to Nixon, 5/8/1962, corr.; Mary Barber to Nixon, 5/9/1962, corr.; Leonards Liquors Statement, 5/10/1962; R. M. Woods to Carl Jud, 5/21/1962, corr.; Reception Guest List, 5/7/1962; PPS 207, box 164, Cocktails Guest Lists, 7/12–13/1962; PPS 207, boxes 165–66: 7/12/1962, 7/13/1962, 7/27–29/1962, 8/20/1962 Nixon Calendars; 7/12/1962, 7/13/1962, 8/6/1962, 8/20/1962 Schedules; PPS 207, box 166: Nixon House Party Invitation, 7/27/1962; Leonards Liquors Invoice, 7/27/1962; Abbey Rents Invoice, 7/31/1962; Manny Hammond Music Invoice, 7/31/1962; Jack and Leon Parking Service Invoice, 7/31/1962; Minnie Schotch Statement, 8/1/1962; Accounting of Expenses for 7/27–29/1962 Nixon House Parties, n.d.

84. CSUF, Nathaniel George, 16; PPS 207, boxes 162–65: 4/13/1962, 4/14/1962, 6/3/1962, 6/7/1962, 6/27/1962, 7/12/1962, 7/13/1962, 7/23/1962, 7/30/1962, 8/20/1962, 9/4/1962 Nixon Calendars; 4/14/1962, 4/15/1962, 5/5/1962, 6/3/1962, 6/7/1962, 6/21/1962, 7/12/1962, 7/13/1962, 7/23/1962, 7/25/1962, 7/26/1962, 7/30/1962, 8/6/1962, 8/20/1962 Schedules; PPS 207, box 165, Cocktails Guest List, 7/13/1962; PPS 207, box 166: Mary Pickford to Pat and Richard Nixon, 7/17/1962, corr.; Ed Johnson to Pat and Richard Nixon, 7/31/1962, corr.; Conrad Hilton to Pat and Richard Nixon, 7/31/1962, corr.

85. PPS 207, box 163, 5/14/1962 Schedule.

86. PPS 207, box 160: 1/29/1962 Schedule; Memo re Guest List, 1/31/1962.

87. Gordon Cologne, interview by author, 7/6/2012.

88. Gordon Cologne, interview by author, 7/6/2012.

89. PPS 207, box 164: Win with Nixon Telethon Memorandum, 5/22/1962; 5/29/1962 Schedule; 5/29/1962 Nixon Calendar; Memorandum re 5/29/1962 Telethon, n.d.; Nixon Telethon Q&A transcript, 5/29/1962; Pasadena Reception Huntington Sheraton Remarks, 5/31/1962.

90. PPS 207, box 164: Telethon transcript, 5/29/1962; Memo, 5/31/1962; Roger Kent Questions and [Nixon] Answers transcript, n.d.; PPS 207, box 162, Duggan Interview of Nixon.

91. PPS 207, box 164: Telethon transcript, 5/29/1962; Kent-Nixon Q&A transcript.

92. PPS 207, box 164, Telethon transcript, 5/29/1962.

93. PPS 207, box 164: Telethon transcript, 5/29/1962; Memo, 5/31/1962.

94. PPS 207, box 165: 6/5/1962 Nixon Calendar; 6/5/1962 Schedule; Eisenhower to Nixon, 6/6/1962, telegram; Nixon to Eisenhower, n.d., corr.

95. PPS 207, box 165, Nixon to G. A. Schaap, 9/11/1962, corr.; Hillings, *Irrepressible Irishman*, 93.

96. PPS 207, box 165: John Birch Society Statement, n.d.; Memo re San Bernardino Win with Nixon Rally, 10/18/1962.

97. PPS 207, box 168, Nixon Media and Staff Party Guest Lists, 9/11/1962.

98. PPS 207, box 169: Inter-Office Memorandum re Pomona Rally, 9/10/1962; Campaign Schedule First Week.

99. PPS 207, box 169, Pomona Campaign speech, 9/12/1962.

100. PPS 207, box 169, Pomona Campaign speech.

101. PPS 207, box 169: 9/12/1962 Nixon Calendar; Memo re Municipal Band, 9/12/1962.

102. Bagley, *California's Golden Years*, 19.

103. PPS 207, boxes 163, 169: 5/17/1962 and 9/6/1962 Schedules; Memo re Produce Market Visit, 9/6/1962; Bagley, *California's Golden Years*, 18.

104. PPS 207, box 169: 10/10/1962 Schedule; Campaign Schedule Fifth Week.

105. PPS 207, box 154, Road to Victory Dinner Remarks, 6/1/1961.

106. PPS 207, box 169: 9/18/1962 Schedule; Press Conference at Statler Hilton transcript, 9/18/1962.

107. PPS 207, box 169, Press Conference at Statler Hilton.

108. PPS 207, box 169, Campaign speech, 9/12/1962; PPS 207, box 170, Crime Broadcast Remarks, 9/23/1962; PPS 207, box 171, Senior Citizens Broadcast, 10/7/1962; PPS 207, box 172: Programs for a Greater California Remarks, 10/14/1962 and 10/21/1962; Crime Prevention Remarks, 9/25/1962.

109. PPS 207, box 173: Campaign Schedule Seventh Week; Programs for a Greater California Statewide Radio Address transcript, 10/28/1962.

110. Bagley, *California's Golden Years*, 17.

111. PPS 207, box 173: Campaign Schedule Seventh Week; Statewide Television speech transcript, 10/27/1962.

112. PPS 207, box 162, Duggan Interview of Nixon.

113. PPS 207, box 164, Kent-Nixon Q&A transcript; Aitken, *Nixon*, 301.

114. Aitken, *Nixon*, 301.
115. PPS 207, box 164: Glendale Rally Remarks, 5/25/1962; Memo, 10/1/1962.
116. PPS 207, box 169: 10/8/1962 Schedule; Campaign Schedule Fifth Week; "General Eisenhower's Political Itinerary as of October 5, 1962," press release, 10/5/1962.
117. PPS 207, box 169: 9/12–10/20/1962, 10/8/1962 Schedules; Campaign Schedule Fifth Week.
118. PPS 207, box 170: Paul Keyes to Nixon, 8/11/1962, Memo re Camera Tests; 9/26/1962 Schedule; Memo re *Meet the Press*, 10/7/1962; Guest List for Celebrities Luncheon at Romanoff's, 9/26/1962; Louelle Parsons to Nixon, 9/25/1962, telegram; Barbara Stanwyck to Nixon, 9/26/1962, telegram.
119. PPS 207, box 169: 10/18–19/1962 Nixon Calendar; 10/19/1962 Schedule.
120. PPS 207, box 173: Campaign Schedule Eighth Week; 11/3/1962 Schedule.
121. PPS 207, box 170, KTTV Telethon Card, 9/28/1962; PPS 207, box 171, Campaign Schedule Fifth Week; PPS 207, boxes 171–72: 10/5/1962, 10/16/1962, 10/22/1962, 11/3/1962 Nixon Calendars; 10/12/1962, 9/12–10/20/1962, 11/2/1962 Schedules; PPS 207, box 172, East Los Angeles Rally Remarks, 10/20/1962; PPS 207, box 173: Press Releases re Telethon, 10/28–29/1962; Win with Nixon Telethon Fact Sheet, 11/3/1962.
122. PPS 207, box 173, Campaign Analysis of Los Angeles Telethon, 11/3/1962.
123. PPS 207, box 173, Campaign Combined Analysis of Questions in First Six Telethons, 10/30/1962.
124. PPS 207, box 173, 11/5/1962 Schedule.
125. Eisenhower, *Pat Nixon*, 212.
126. Eisenhower, *Pat Nixon*, 212.
127. PPS 207, box 173, Memo re Seventy-Five Thousand Volunteers, n.d.
128. Lundberg, *Big Orange*, 10–11.
129. Brodie, *Richard Nixon*, 461; Hillings, *Irrepressible Irishman*, 93.
130. Marje Acker, interview by author, 7/7/2010.
131. Aitken, *Nixon*, 304; David, *Lonely Lady*, 123.
132. Nixon, *Memoirs*, 245; Eisenhower, *Pat Nixon*, 213.
133. Brodie, *Richard Nixon*, 463; Nixon, *In the Arena*, 225.
134. Starr, *Golden Dreams*, 216.
135. Hillings, *Irrepressible Irishman*, 94.
136. David, *Lonely Lady*, 124.
137. Sandy Quinn, interview by author, 7/18/2012.
138. Aitken, *Nixon*, 306.
139. "55 Years Ago: 'The Last Press Conference,'" Nixon Foundation, 11/14/2017, https://www.nixonfoundation.org/2017/11/55-years-ago-last-press-conference/.
140. PPS 207, box 172, *Meet the Candidate*, KRON TV, transcript, 10/23/1962.
141. BK, Ray Arbuthnot, 1, 3–4, 11; WC, Jack Drown, 2–3, 7–8; BK, Bob Finch, 11; BK, Bob Wilson, 2.
142. WC, Jack Drown, 7–8.
143. WC, Jack Drown, 7–8.
144. WC, Jack Drown, 7–8.

145. Hillings, *Irrepressible Irishman*, 93.

146. CSUF, Dorothy Beeson, 16.

147. Bagley, *California's Golden Years*, 19.

148. Eisenhower, *Pat Nixon*, 214.

149. Loie Gaunt, interviews by author, 12/28/2010, 2/7/2012; Sandy Quinn, interview by author, 7/18/2012.

150. WC, Roy Day, 11.

151. CSUF, William Price, 78.

15. Wilderness Years

1. Nixon, *Six Crises*, xvii.

2. PB, Adams, 23–24.

3. PPS 238, box 3, Tom Bewley to Nixon, 1/31/1963, corr.

4. PPS 238, box 3, Nixon to Tom Bewley, 3/11/1963, corr.

5. PPS 214, box 13, *Survey '65—Success*, KNBC TV, transcript, 6/12/1965.

6. PPS 214, box 1, Paul Dietzel to Nixon, 1/17/1963, corr.

7. PPS 214, box 1, Guest List, 1/7/1963; George Beahon, "In This Corner . . . ," *Rochester Democrat and Chronicle*, 1/14/1963.

8. PPS 214, box 1, Guest List, 1/8/1963.

9. PPS 214, box 1: Dwight Eisenhower to Nixon, 1/7/1963, corr.; Inter-Office Memo for Storage, 4/19/1966.

10. PPS 214, box 3: Guest List, 4/30/1963; Inter-Office Memo for Storage, 4/19/1966.

11. Aitken, *Nixon*, 308.

12. Aitken, *Nixon*, 308–9.

13. PPS 214, box 3: Ronald Reagan to Nixon, 6/4/1963, corr.; Nixon to Ronald Reagan, 6/9/1966, corr.; Nixon to Ronald Reagan, 7/18/1966, corr.

14. PPS 214, box 3, Nixon to Kenneth Hahn, 5/14/1963, corr.; "Nixon Scroll Award Voted by Supervisors," *Pasadena Independent*, 5/8/1963.

15. PPS 214, box 3: Inter-Office Memo for Storage; Benediction for the Dick and Pat Luncheon, 6/7/1963.

16. PPS 214, box 3, Nixon to Art Linkletter, 6/10/1963, 7/23/1963, corr.

17. PPS 214, box 3, Joe Kennedy to Nixon, 6/7/1963, telegram.

18. PPS 214, box 3, Peter Lawford to Nixon, 6/7/1963, telegram.

19. PPS 214, box 3, Caracas, Venezuela, Chamber of Commerce to Nixon, 6/7/1963, telegram.

20. PPS 214, box 3, Nixon to John H. Williams, 6/10/1963, corr.

21. PPS 214, box 3: Herb Hazeltine to Nixon, 9/10/1963, corr.; Nixon to Hazeltine, 9/12/1963, corr.; Pat Hillings to Nixon, 9/9/1963, corr.; Nixon to George Todt, 9/12/1966, corr.

22. WC, I. N. Kraushaar, 6; PPS 214, box 3: Guest List, 9/6/1963; Office Memo, 2/21/1965; Memo, n.d.; Nixon to John Lungren, 4/29/1965, corr.; Guest List, 6/9/1965; 6/11/1965, 6/12/1965, 7/10/1965, 9/25/1965, 6/23/1966, 6/24/1966 Schedules; Inter-Office Memo for Storage; Guest List, 6/24/1966; Nixon to Asa Call, 7/18/1966, corr.

23. PPS 214, box 13: Office Memo, 2/21/1965; 6/12/1965, 6/13/1965, 7/9/1965, 9/25/1965, 5/7–10/1966 Schedules; Memo, n.d.; Hernando Courtright to Nixon, 6/28/1965, telegram.

24. PPS 214, box 13: 6/11/1965 Schedule; Whittier Board of Trustees Minutes, 3/8/1965, 6/11/1965; Paul Smith to Nixon, 6/4/1965, corr.; Nixon to Mrs. Michael A. Gallucci, 6/7/1965, corr.; Mrs. Michael A. Gallucci, n.d., corr.

25. PPS 214, box 13: 6/11/1965 Schedule; Dedication of Bonnie Bell Wardman Library Remarks, 6/11/1965; Nixon to Paul Smith, 3/16/1965 and 6/4/1965, corr.; "A Library Grows," *Daily News/East Whittier Review*, 1/19/1969.

26. PPS 214, box 13, Dedication of Wardman Library.

27. PPS 214, box 13, Paul Smith to Nixon, 3/16/1965, corr.

28. PPS 214, box 13, Nixon to Charles Cooper, 8/2/1965, corr.

29. PPS 214, box 13: Paul Smith to Nixon, 6/4/1965, corr.; Tom Pasqua, "What Is Important to Men?"

30. PPS 214, box 13: 6/12/1965 Schedule; Pasqua, "What Is Important to Men?"

31. PPS 214, box 13, Bob Hope to Nixon, 6/21/1965, corr.

32. PPS 238, box 19, Don Kendall to Nixon, 4/26/1961, corr.

33. Donna Kendall, interview by author, 4/13/2011.

34. PPS 238, box 19: Kendall to Nixon, 12/11/1964, corr.; Nixon to Kendall, 12/28/1964, corr.; PPS 238, box 34: Nixon to Paul Smith, 12/28/1964, corr.; Paul Smith to Nixon, 2/4/1965, corr.; Donna Kendall, interview by author, 4/13/2011.

35. PPS 238, box 19, Nixon to Kendall, 2/2/1965, corr.

36. PPS 238, box 10: Douglas Knight (Duke University) to Nixon, 11/11/1965, corr.; Nixon to St. Paul's School, 12/16/1964, corr.; PPS 238, box 13: Nixon to Lockheed, 4/7/1965, corr.; Jim Golden (Lockheed) to Nixon, 7/30/1965, corr.; William Rhyne to Nixon, n.d., corr.; PPS 238, box 24, John Lungren to Nixon, 11/26/1965, corr.; PPS 238, box 35, Richard Trutanic to Nixon, 4/24/1965, corr.

37. WC, Jack Drown, 7; BK, Robert Finch, 11; WC, Waymeth Garrett, 30; BK, Bill Henry, 12; CSUF, Hugh Hewitt, 3; BK, John Krehbiel, 4; BK, Mary Alice Longworth, 33, 36; WC, Theodore Marshburn, 9; BK, Albert Mattei, 5; BK, Richard Nixon, 6; BK, #1 Hubert Perry, 7; WC, Adela Rogers St. Johns, 14; WC, Arthur Sucksdorf, Florence Sucksdorf, and Ethel Garliepp, 29; EDC, Statement by Wilt Chamberlain, 8/1/1968; Roberta Dorn, interviews by author, 10/22/2013, 11/15/2013; Donna Kendall, interview by author, 4/13/2011.

38. WC, #1 Jessamyn West, 14–15.

39. Nixon, *In the Arena*, 161–62.

40. Stuart Spencer, interviews by author, 12/29/2010, 1/21/2011.

41. CSUF, Frances Timberlake, 7; WC, Lola Williams, 14.

42. PPS 214, box 19: Inter-Office Memo, n.d.; Nixon to Merle West, 8/25/1965, corr.; West to Nixon, n.d., corr.; West to Nixon, 12/27/1965, corr.

43. PPS 238, box 15: Russell Harrison to Nixon, 6/22/1965, corr.; Nixon to Harrison, 8/24/1965, corr.

44. CSUF, Frances Timberlake, 6–7.

45. PPS 214, box 13, *Survey '65—Success*.

46. PPS 238, box 13, Nixon to Billy Graham, 11/7/1963, corr.; PPS 238, box 30, Nixon to Bebe Rebozo, 11/20/1963, corr.

47. Graham, *Just as I Am*, 525.

48. PPS 214, box 11: Office of Richard M. Nixon Press Release re 1964 Campaign Support, 9/29/1964; Memorandum re Nixon's 10/1964 Campaign Calendar; 10/1964 Itineraries of Richard M. Nixon; Memorandum re Participants in Mr. Nixon's 1964 Campaign Tour; Murray Chotiner to Nixon, 10/21/1964, corr.; PPS 214, box 10, Murray Chotiner to Nixon, 8/28/1964, corr.

49. PPS 214, box 11, 10/12/1964 Schedule.

50. PPS 214, box 5, Recent Statements by Richard M. Nixon in Response to Questions Concerning 1964 Campaign, 1/1964; Loie Gaunt, interviews by author, 12/28/2010, 2/7/2012.

51. PPS 238, box 25, Nixon to Robert McClure, 12/1/1964, corr.

52. Nixon, *Memoirs*, 272.

53. Dave Hope, "Coalition May Try to 'Stop Reagan,'" *Oakland Tribune*, 9/26/1965.

54. PPS 238, box 16, Nixon to Hillings, 12/22/1964, corr.

55. "GOP Fight: Nixon Neutral," *Los Angeles Herald Examiner*, 9/26/1965; Jack S. McDowell, "Nixon's Warning to GOP," *San Francisco Examiner and Chronicle*, 9/26/1965.

56. Carl Greenberg, "Nixon Calls 1966 Vote 'Battle for America,'" *Los Angeles Times*, 5/11/1966.

57. PPS 214, box 15, 9/23/1965 Schedule; Peter Kaye, "Party Unity Vital, Nixon Warns GOP," *San Diego Union*, 9/24/1965.

58. Greenberg, "Nixon Calls 1966 Vote."

59. PPS 214, box 15: An Evening for Robert Finch Dinner Program, 9/23/1965; 9/23/1965 Schedule; "Nixon Predicts Demo Battle to Gubernatorial Nomination," *San Diego Union*, 9/24/1965; Kaye, "Party Unity Vital."

60. PPS 214, box 15, 9/23/1965 California Trip Remarks, n.d.

61. Carl Greenberg, "Keep Differences Private, GOP Candidates Warned," *Los Angeles Times*, 9/26/1965.

62. PPS 214, box 21, Richard Nixon, North American Newspaper Alliance Column, 5/8/1966.

63. PPS 214, box 16: Nixon to James Copley, 9/29/1965, corr.; Nixon to Ralph de Toledano, 9/29/1965, corr.; Nixon to Dwight Eisenhower, 9/29/1965, corr.; Nixon to *Human Events* editor, 9/29/1965, corr.; Nixon to Walter Knott, 9/29/1965, corr.; Nixon to Hobart Lewis, 9/29/1965, corr.; Nixon to Robert McClure, 9/29/1965, corr.; Nixon to Raymond Moley, 9/29/1965, corr.

64. PPS 214, box 16, Nixon to Albert Cole, 9/29/1965, corr.

65. PPS 238, box 1, Nixon to Joseph Alsop, 12/23/1964, corr.; PPS 238, box 6, Murray Chotiner, 10/21/1964, corr.

66. PPS 214, box 22, "Pillars of American Freedom" Remarks, 5/10/1966.

67. PPS 214, box 22, 5/7–10/1966 Schedule; Memo to the Press, n.d.; "GOP Unity Enchances Chances, Nixon Says," *Los Angeles Times*, 5/8/1966.

68. PPS 214, box 22, 5/7–10/1966 Schedule; "Christopher or Reagan Can Beat Brown—Nixon," *Los Angeles Times*, 5/9/1966.

69. PPS 214, box 22: John McCone to Nixon, 4/6/1966, corr.; Nixon to John McCone, 5/25/1966, corr.

70. PPS 214, box 22, 5/7–10/1966 Schedule; Memo to the Press, n.d.; Greenberg, "Nixon Calls 1966 Vote."

71. Greenberg, "Nixon Calls 1966 Vote."

72. PPS 214, box 25, Nixon to Ronald Reagan, 6/9/1966, corr.

73. PPS 214, box 25, Nixon to Reagan, 6/9/1966, corr.

74. PPS 214, box 25, 6/23/1966 Schedule.

75. PPS 214, box 25, Republican State Central Committee Press Release, n.d.; Gladwin Hill, "Rival's Financial Backers Publicly Vow Support," *New York Times*, 6/14/1966.

76. PPS 214, box 25: 6/23/1966 Schedule; Fred Arnold to Nixon, 6/24/1966, corr.; Nixon to Arnold, 7/7/1966, corr.; Nixon to Linkletter, 7/23/1966, corr.; Sal Perrotta, "GOP Gala Attracts 11,500," *Los Angeles Herald Examiner*, 6/24/1966.

77. PPS 214, box 25: Margaret Brock to Nixon, 4/16/1966, corr.; Nixon to Margaret Brock, 7/19/1966, corr.; 6/24/1966 Schedule; John Green, "Nixon Injects Fighting Spirit into GOP," *San Pedro News Pilot*, 6/25/1966.

78. PPS 214, box 25: Inter-Office Memo, n.d.; 6/24/1966 Schedule; Nixon to Ronald Reagan, 7/18/1966, corr.

79. Lundberg, *Big Orange*, 35; Aitken, *Nixon*, 338.

80. WC, I. N. Kraushaar, 6.

81. PB, Earl Adams, 32–33; CSUF, Charles Ball, 16–17, 25; CSUF, Oscar and Olive Marshburn, 23; PPS 214, box 22: 5/7–10/1966 Schedule; Memo to the Press, n.d.; PPS 214, box 27, Inter-Office Memo, 12/7/1966; PP S238, box 37, Nixon to Victor York, 9/16/1965, corr.; Nixon, *Memoirs*, 287; "Nixon to Arrive Here Saturday," *Los Angeles Times*, 5/6/1966.

82. Aitken, *Nixon*, 340; Nixon, *In the Arena*, 94; Nixon, *Memoirs*, 289.

83. WC, #2 Jane Beeson, 6; CSUF, Muriel Kelly, 11; WC, I. N. Kraushaar, 6; WC, #2 Ed Nixon, 2; PPS 214, box 22, Nixon to Tom Duggan, 5/20/1966, corr.; "Service Set Tuesday for Mrs. Nixon," *Whittier Daily News*, 10/2/1967; *Whittier City Directory*, 1965; Nixon and Olson, *Nixons*, 221; Ed Nixon, interviews by author, 1/9/2010, 5/7/2010.

84. WC, I. N. Kraushaar, 6; CSUF, Oscar and Olive Marshburn, 23; WC, Lola Williams, 14; PPS 214, box 22: 5/7–10/1966 Schedule; Memo to the Press, n.d.; PPS 214, box 27, Inter-Office Memo, 12/7/1966; Eisenhower, *Pat Nixon*, 232; Nixon, *Memoirs*, 287; Harry Trimborn, "Mother of Nixon Succumbs at 82 in Whittier Hospital," *Los Angeles Times*, 10/1/1967; "Richard Nixon's Mother, Hannah, Dies Here Today," *Whittier Daily News*, 9/30/1967.

85. CSUF, Janet Goeske, 23; Ed Nixon, interviews by author, 1/9/2010, 5/7/2010.

86. PPS 424, box 3: Douglas MacArthur to Nixon, 10/3/1967, corr.; Dwight Eisenhower to Nixon, 10/1/1967, telegram; Lyndon Johnson to Nixon, n.d., telegram; James Mize to Donald Nixon, 10/6/1967, corr.; "Richard Nixon's Mother, Hannah,

Dies Here Today," *Whittier Daily News*, 9/30/1967; Harry Trimborn, "Mother of Nixon Succumbs at 82 in Whittier Hospital," *Los Angeles Times*, 10/1/1967; Eisenhower, *Pat Nixon*, 232; Nixon, *Memoirs*, 287.

87. CSUF, Charles Ball, 24; WC, #2 Mabel Schuyler and Roger Schuyler, 9; "Service Set Tuesday for Mrs. Nixon," *Whittier Daily News*, 10/2/1967; Aitken, *Nixon*, 339.

88. CSUF, Charles Ball, 24.

89. Aitken, *Nixon*, 339.

90. Graham, *Just as I Am*, 521–22.

91. PPS 424, box 3, Nixon to R. L. McNitt, 10/16/1967, corr.; "Richard Nixon's Mother"; Aitken, *Nixon*, 339–440; Nixon, *Memoirs*, 288.

92. CSUF, Janet Beeson, 19; CSUF, Lucille Parsons, 18–19; PPS 424, box 3, Nixon to Oscar Marshburn, 10/12/1967, corr.

93. PPS 424, box 3: Nixon to Ray Arbuthnot, 10/20/1967, corr.; Nixon to Charles Bell, 10/12/1967, corr.; Nixon to Evlyn Dorn, 10/24/1967, corr.; Nixon to Billy Graham, 10/12/1967, corr.; Nixon to George Jenkins, 10/13/1967, corr.; Nixon to I. N. Kraushaar, 10/19/1967, corr.; Nixon to Robert Walker, 10/12/1967, corr.; Nixon to David White, 10/12/1967, corr.; Nixon to Dorothy Yardley, 10/12/1967, corr.; Nixon to Jack Wrather, 10/12/1967, corr.

94. PPS 424, box 3, Nixon to Charles Bell, 10/25/1967, corr.

95. For example, PPS 214, box 20, Nixon to J. S. Fluor, 3/24/1966, corr.; PPS 214, box 22: Margaret Brock to Nixon, 4/2/1966, corr.; Margaret Brock to Pat Nixon, 5/30/1966, corr.; PPS 238, box 1, Nixon to Ray Arbuthnot, 6/23/1964, corr.; PPS 238, box 3: Nixon to Murray Chotiner, 5/28/1963, corr.; Rose Mary Woods to Tom Bewley, 9/71/1963, corr.; Tom Bewley to Rose Mary Woods, 9/25/1963, corr.; Tom Bewley to Nixon, 4/20/1965, corr.; Nixon to Tom Bewley, 5/3/1965, corr.; PPS 238, box 4: Nixon to Earl Adams, 11/20/1963, corr.; Earl Adams to Nixon, 11/29/1963, corr.; PPS 238, box 5: Murray Chotiner to Nixon, 1/7/1964, corr.; Nixon to Russell Harrison, 2/22/1964, corr.; PPS 238, box 8, Murray Chotiner to Nixon, 8/28/1964, corr.; PPS 238, box 13, Nixon to Herb Klein, 7/7/1966, corr.; PPS 238, box 19, Nixon to Mrs. Estes Kefauver, 8/19/1963, corr.; PPS 238, box 20, Nixon to Edward Kennedy, 6/23/1964, corr.; PPS 238, box 21: Henry Knoop to Nixon, 1/17/1964, corr.; Nixon to Knoop, 1/28/1964, corr.; Nixon to Tom Knudsen, 3/16/1963, corr.; Valley Knudsen to Pat and Richard Nixon, 10/22/1963, corr.; Nixon to Valley Knudsen, 11/7/1963, corr.; Tom and Valley Knudsen to Nixon, 3/15/1964, corr.; Nixon to Knudsen, 3/21/1964, corr.; Valley Knudsen to Pat and Richard Nixon, 7/8/1964, corr.; Valley Knudsen to Pat and Richard, 7/11/1964, corr.; Nixon to Valley Knudsen, 8/3/1964, corr.; Nixon to Tom Knudsen, 9/20/1965, corr.; Nixon to Valley Knudsen, 12/22/1965, corr.; Nixon to John Krehbiel, 6/26/1964, corr.; Nixon to John Krehbiel, 7/30/1964, corr.; Krehbiel to Nixon, 3/9/1965, corr.; PPS 238, box 24: John Lungren to Nixon, 9/28/1965, corr.; Lungren to Nixon, 11/2/1965, corr.; PPS 238, box 25: Chad and Katie McClellan to Nixon, 6/21/1963, corr.; Robert McClure to Nixon, 9/10/1963, corr.; McClure to Nixon, 6/16/1965, corr.; PPS 238, box 26: Nixon to Patricia Marshburn, 6/29/1964, corr.; Nixon to Oscar Marshburn, 8/17/1965, corr.; Nixon to Earl Mazo, 12/30/1963, corr.; PPS

238, box 28: Nixon to Lawrene Nixon, 11/4/1963, corr.; Lloyd Nolan to Nixon, n.d., corr.; Nixon to Nolan, 3/14/1964, corr.; PPS 238, box 29: Nixon to Ed Pauley, 7/28/1964, corr.; Hubert Perry to Nixon, 10/16/1963, corr.; Nixon to Hubert Perry, 11/5/1963, corr.; Hubert Perry to Nixon, 6/15/1965, corr.; Nixon to Perry, 8/20/1965, corr.; Nixon to Perry, 12/14/1965, corr.; PPS 238, box 30: Nixon to Peter Pitchess, 7/28/1964, corr.; Nixon to Pitchess, 8/16/1965, corr.; Pitchess to Nixon, 8/19/1965, corr.; George Putnam to Nixon, 12/30/1963, corr.; Nixon to George Putnam, 1/15/1964, corr.; Nixon to Putnam, 2/6/1964, corr.; Nixon to Putnam, 12/23/1965, corr.; Nixon to Bebe Rebozo, 9/3/1964, telegram; PPS 238, box 35: Nixon to Arthur Summerfield, 3/27/1961, corr.; Waller Taylor to Nixon, 12/16/1964, corr.; PPS 238, box 37: Bob Wilson to Nixon, 12/1/1964, corr.; Nixon to Mrs. Victor York, 12/20/1963, corr.; Nixon to Victor York, 9/16/1965, corr.; DSC: Nixon to Dana Smith, 5/17/1963, corr.; Nixon to Dana Smith, 6/29/1964, corr.; Nixon to Dana Smith, 5/12/1966, corr.; Nixon to Dana Smith, 12/6/1966, corr.; Nixon to Dana Smith, 3/4/1967, corr.; Nixon to Dana Smith, 11/10/1967, corr.

96. PPS 238, box 28: Nixon to National Jewish Children's Hospital, 8/6/1965, corr.; Nixon to Mrs. Mendel Silberberg, 7/6/1965, corr.

97. PPS 238, box 6: Nixon to Norman Chandler, 4/12/1963, corr.; Norman Chandler to Nixon, 5/16/1963, corr.

98. PPS 238, box 6, Dorothy Chandler to Nixon, 7/20/1964, corr.

99. PPS 238, box 6, Nixon to Dorothy Chandler, 7/27/1964, corr.

100. PPS 238, box 6, Nixon to Dorothy Chandler, 7/27/1964, corr.

101. PPS 238, box 6, Jack Spitzer to Nixon, 2/4/1965, corr.

102. PPS 238, box 6, Nixon to Jack Spitzer, 3/3/1965, corr.

103. Mazo, *Richard Nixon*, 188.

104. Mazo, *Richard Nixon*, 194.

105. Nixon, *In the Arena*, 25–26.

106. PPS 214, box 32: Robert A. Groves Card with Handwritten Note, n.d.; A. E. England to Nixon, 10/21/1967, corr.; Nixon to Robert A. Groves, 1/8/1968, corr.; Nixon to A. E. England, 1/12/1968, corr.

107. PPS 214, box 32, Handwritten Note, n.d.; Maggie Savoy, "Englands Honor Nixons at Ingathering of Friends," *Los Angeles Times*, 12/15/1967.

108. PPS 214, box 32: John Whittaker to Jack Rourke, 11/30/1967, corr.; Nixon to Jack Rourke, 1/8/1968, corr.; Richard Bergholz, "Nixon Leaves Door Open to Fight with Reagan in Primary," *Los Angeles Times*, 12/15/1967.

109. Bergholz, "Nixon Leaves Door Open."

110. PPS 214, box 13, *Survey '65—Success*.

111. Aitken, *Nixon*, 334–35; Black, *Life in Full*, 445.

112. Aitken, *Nixon*, 294; Black, *Life in Full*, 445.

113. Aitken, *Nixon*, 335.

114. Aitken, *Nixon*, 334.

115. PPS 214, box 35, Nixon to Coretta Scott King, 4/4/1968, telegram.

116. Bagley, *California's Golden Years*, 28–29; Bill Bagley, interviews by author, 1/6/2012, 3/5/2012.

117. PPS 214, box 35, Nixon to R. H. Williams, 4/16/1968, corr.; PPS 238, box 13, Billy Graham to Nixon, 6/9/1965, corr.; EDC, Statement by Wilt Chamberlain, 8/1/1968.

118. Richard Dougherty, "Kennedy Tributes: Body Lies in State in New York," *Los Angeles Times*, 6/7/1968; Aitken, *Nixon*, 350–51; Klein, *Making It Perfectly Clear*, 15.

119. Black, *Life in Full*, 526; Klein, *Making It Perfectly Clear*, 15.

120. Eisenhower, *Pat Nixon*, 242; Nixon, *Memoirs*, 315.

121. Don Irwin, "Reagan to Help Nixon Campaign in California," *Los Angeles Times*, 8/17/1968; Nixon, *Memoirs*, 316.

122. PB, Frank Jorgensen, 58, 109, 111.

123. Irwin, "Reagan to Help Nixon"; Wayne Warga, "How Network Censors Put Laugh-In to Taste Test," *Los Angeles Times*, 9/15/1968; "Dread Charisma," *Los Angeles Times*, 10/10/1968; PPS 214, box 36, Loie Grace Gaunt Memo, 3/15/2000.

124. Hillings, *Irrepressible Irishman*, 94.

125. Brodie, *Richard Nixon*, 361.

126. Don Irwin and Richard Bergholz, "Nixon Brings His Campaign Back to California," *Los Angeles Times*, 9/15/1968.

127. PPS 140, box 1: Nixon to Mr. and Mrs. Vince Ellingson, 9/27/1968, corr.; Nixon to Sterling Fox, 9/27/1968, corr.; Howard Seelye, "More Than 3,000 Greet Nixon on His Return to Birthplace," *Los Angeles Times*, 9/17/1968.

128. Seelye, "More Than 3,000 Greet Nixon."

129. PPS 140, box 1, Nixon to Jose Arias, 10/6/1968, corr.; "Police Coordinate Protection for Nixon at Rally in Anaheim," *Los Angeles Times*, 9/15/1968; Seelye, "More Than 3,000 Greet Nixon"; Howard Seelye, "Nixon, Humphrey Camps a Contrast," *Los Angeles Times*, 9/20/1968.

130. "Police Coordinate Protection"; Richard Bergolz, "Nixon Will Not Curb Issue of Law and Order," *Los Angeles Times*, 9/17/1968.

131. PPS 140, box 1, Nixon Reception, Beverly Hilton Guest List, 9/17/1968; Richard Bergholz, "Dinners in 20 Cities to Aid Nixon Campaign," *Los Angeles Times*, 9/16/1968; Joyce Haber, "John Wayne Eye Patched for Role," *Los Angeles Times*, 10/8/1968.

132. PPS 140, box 3, Inter-Office Memo re Los Angeles Visit, 10/9/1968; "Nixon to Campaign in L.A. Area Today," *Los Angeles Times*, 10/9/1968.

133. "Nixon to Campaign"; Don Irwin, "Nixon, 5,000 Fans Override Hecklers at L.A.-Area Rally," *Los Angeles Times*, 10/10/1968.

134. Stuart Loory, "Nixon Drive Functions Smoothly, Efficiently," *Los Angeles Times*, 10/10/1968.

135. Irwin, "Nixon, 5,000 Fans."

136. Irwin, "Nixon, 5,000 Fans."

137. Richard Bergholz, "It's Even-Steven: Close Vote Predicted Today," *Los Angeles Times*, 11/5/1968.

138. Aitken, *Nixon*, 367.

139. Don Irwin, "Nixon Awaits Results in N.Y Hotel Suite," *Los Angeles Times*, 11/6/1968; Nixon, *Memoirs*, 309.

140. Halberstam, *Powers*, 403.

141. Nixon, *Memoirs*, 306, 330; Eisenhower, *Pat Nixon*, 246.

142. Crowley, *Nixon off the Record*, 127.

143. WC, Raymond Fleischman, 12; CSUF, Barbara Mashburn, 28.

144. WC, Raymond Fleischman, 12.

145. Roberta Dorn, interviews by author, 10/22/2013, 11/15/2013.

146. Nixon, *In the Arena*, 225.

147. PPS 214, box 36, A Salute to the Mexican-American Community of Los Angeles Dinner Program, 12/5/1968.

148. Lynn Lilliston, "Mrs. Reagan Will Host First Ladies," *Los Angeles Times*, 12/2/1968.

149. Wilson, *Confessions*, 151.

150. Wilson, *Confessions*, 152–53.

151. "Winning Floats in Rose Parade," *Los Angeles Times*, 1/2/1969.

152. "The President-Elect: Welcome Home," *Time*, 1/10/1969, 20.

153. Lungren and Lungren, *Healing*, 22–23.

154. CSUF, #2 Hoyt Corbit, 14; Butz, *Yorba Linda*, 163.

155. CSUF, #2 Hoyt Corbit, 17; CSUF, Cecil Pickering, 30; Hubert Perry, interviews by author, 12/8/2009, 12/9/2009, 1/5/2010, 1/6/2010, 2/22/2010, 9/8/2010, 11/10/2010, 11/18/2010.

156. CSUF, C. Robert McCormick, 7; CSUF, Marion Nichols, 24–25; CSUF, Elizabeth Paldanius, 55–56; CSUF, Forrest Randall, 32; WC, William Sparling, 7; CSUF, Sandy Triggs, 21.

157. WC, #2 Evlyn Dorn, 4; Lundberg, *Big Orange*, 45.

16. President

1. CSUF, Sheldon Beeson, 23; CSUF, Jane Beeson, 20; CSUF, Lucille Parsons, 8.

2. CSUF, Charles Ball, 25.

3. David, *Lonely Lady*, 131–32.

4. CSUF, Helen Letts, 29; CSUF, Marion Nichols, 24–25; CSUF, Elizabeth Paldanius, 59–60; CSUF, Lucille Parsons, 18–19.

5. WC, Virginia Counts, 11.

6. Hillings, *Irrepressible Irishman*, 116.

7. President Richard Nixon's Daily Diary, 1/27/1969, 2/6/1969, 2/12/1969, 2/20/1969, 2/22/1969, 3/4/1969, 3/14/1969, 3/15/1969, 3/16/1969, 3/23/1969, 4/19/1969, 4/28/1969, 5/15/1969, 6/20/1969, 6/22/1969, 6/23/1969, 7/15/1969, 8/24/1969 9/23/1969, 10/15/1969, 11/4/1969, 11/18/1969, 11/26/1969, 12/6/1969, 12/9/1969, 12/30/1969, 1/2/1970, 1/9/1970, 3/6/1970, 3/16/1970, 3/30/1970, 4/12/1970, 4/16/1970, 4/17/1970, 4/19/1970, 4/28/1970, 4/30/1970, 5/1/1970, 5/3/1970, 5/6/1970, 5/7/1970, 5/9/1970, 5/12/1970, 5/26/1970, 5/31/1970, 6/1/1970, 6/11/1970, 6/16/1970, 6/27/1970, 6/30/1970, 7/2/1970, 7/5/1970, 7/7/1970, 7/8/1970, 7/17/1970, 8/2/1970, 8/16/1970, 8/28/1970, 10/7/1970, 11/3/1970, 12/10/1970, 1/1/1971, 1/5/1971, 1/7/1971, 1/8/1971,

1/9/1971, 1/12/1971, 1/14/1971, 1/23/1971, 2/9/1971, 2/14/1971, 2/20/1971, 2/28/1971, 3/1/1971, 3/31971, 3/5/1971, 3/6/1971, 3/18/1971, 3/20/1971, 3/29/1971, 4/7/1971, 4/18/1971, 4/23/1971, 4/24/1971, 4/25/1971, 5/3/1971, 6/9/1971, 8/1/1971, 8/11/1971, 8/23/1971, 8/27/1971, 9/14/1971, 10/5/1971, 10/19/1971, 10/22/1971, 10/26/1971, 11/14/1971, 11/15/1971, 11/16/1971, 11/25/1971, 11/28/1971, 12/22/1971, 12/31/1971, 1/3/1972, 1/4/1972, 1/7/1972, 1/9/1972, 1/10/1972, 1/21/1972, 1/25/1972, 1/26/1972, 1/30/1972, 2/5/1972, 2/9/1972, 3/9/1972, 6/10/1972, 6/21/1972, 6/29/1972, 7/1/1972, 7/7/1972, 7/8/1972, 7/19/1972, 7/22/1972, 8/16/1972, 8/22/1972, 9/28/1972, 9/29/1972, 10/8/1972, 10/18/1972, 10/22/1972, 11/7/1972, 11/9/1972, 11/10/1972, 11/16/1972, 11/17/1972, 11/26/1972, 12/10/1972, 12/18/1972, 12/21/1972, 12/26/1972, 12/31/1972, 1/9/1973, 1/23/1973, 1/24/1973, 2/13/1973, 2/15/1973, 3/39/1973, 4/2/1973, 4/30/1973, 5/25/1973, 5/28/1973, 6/13/1973, 7/3/1973, 7/14/1973, 8/6/1973, 8/22/1973, 8/23/1973, 8/29/1973, 9/5/1973, 9/29/1973, 10/8/1973, 10/20/1973, 11/17/1973, 12/23/1973, 1/9/1974, 1/10/1974, 1/15/1974, 1/30/1974, 2/25/1974, 3/18/1974, 4/10/1974, 5/13/1974, 6/24/1974, 7/16/1974. Daily Diaries may be found online at https://www.nixonlibrary.gov /president/presidential-daily-diary.

8. WC, #2 Tom Bewley, 16; CSUF, Rowe Boyer, 4; CSUF, J. D. Brannon, 16; WC, Curtis Counts, 5–6; WC, #1 Josephine Harrison, 15; CSUF, Regina Kemp, 15; CSUF, Lucille Parsons, 18, 20, 24; WC, Sigrid Pederson, 12.

9. WC, Virginia Buckman, 4; WC, Basil Nixon (Dorn), 5; Elizabeth Cloes Collection, Nixon to Elizabeth Cloes, 5/4/1971, corr.; ED, Nixon to Evlyn Dorn, 11/23/1970, corr.; HMC, Nixon to Harrison McCall, 6/7/1972, 6/28/1972, corr.; HMC, Nixon to Mrs. Robert Stifel, 10/3/1972, corr.; Nixon's Daily Diary, 12/25/1969, 12/25/1970, 8/21/1971, 12/24–25/1971, 4/18/1972, 12/25/1972, 12/25/1973; CSUF, Robert Sillivan, 26; Faries, *Rememb'ring*, 200–201.

10. Nixon's Daily Diary, 4/15/1972.

11. WC, Mary McGovern, 8; CSUF, Robert Sillivan, 26.

12. WC, Curtis Counts, 5.

13. Nixon's Daily Diary, 3/16/1969, 3/24/1969, 10/14/1969, 11/4/1969, 12/14/1969, 4/4/1970, 5/11/1970, 7/23/1970, 8/4/1970, 12/17/1970, 2/18/1971, 2/23/1971, 2/27/1971, 4/5/1971, 4/12/1971, 4/19/1971, 4/26/1971, 11/2/1971, 11/17/1971, 12/7/1971, 1/28/1972, 1/30/1972, 4/20/1972, 6/15/1972, 11/21/1972, 12/18/1972, 1/19/1973, 2/1/1973, 2/18/1973, 3/1/1973, 3/3–4/1973, 3/6–8/1973, 4/8/1973, 4/10/1973, 4/17/1973, 5/1/1973, 5/15/1973, 5/24/1973, 6/5/1973, 6/18/1973, 12/4/1973, 3/7/1974.

14. Nixon's Daily Diary, 9/27/1973.

15. Nixon's Daily Diary, 3/7/1969, 3/11/1969, 3/16/1969, 7/1/1969, 8/8/1969, 9/25/1969, 10/10/1969, 10/14/1969, 10/20/1969, 11/4/1969, 11/6/1969, 2/7/1970, 3/15–21/1970, 4/4/1970, 5/26/1970, 7/23/1970, 9/23/1970, 10/13/1970, 2/18/1971, 2/27/1971, 3/2/1971, 3/5/1971, 3/17–18/1971, 4/5/1971, 4/16/1971, 6/22/1971, 10/8/1971, 10/12/1971, 10/28/1971, 3/9–18/1972, 4/17/1972, 4/20/1972, 9/15/1972, 9/30/1972, 10/13/1972, 11/8/1972, 12/9–12/1972, 12/19/1972, 12/20/1972, 2/1/1973, 3/1/1973, 3/6–7/1973, 6/11/1973, 6/18/1973, 9/13/1973, 9/27/1973, 10/9/1973, 12/15/1973, 3/15/1974.

16. Marje Acker, interview by author, 7/7/2010.

17. Eisenhower, *Pat Nixon*, 296.

18. Eisenhower, *Pat Nixon*, 297.

19. Eisenhower, *Pat Nixon*, 296–97.

20. WC, Raymond Henle, 6–7; CSUF, Lucille Parsons, 20; WC, Carl and Martha Stambaugh (Ed Nixon), 10; Eisenhower, *Pat Nixon*, 284.

21. Nixon's Daily Diary, 3/21/1969, 12/11/1969, 4/5/1970, 5/26/1970, 2/1/1973.

22. Worthen, *Young Nixon*, 195.

23. Nixon's Daily Diary, 4/23/1969.

24. CSUF, Dolores Ball, 22–24; CSUF, Regina Kemp, 12–13; WC, Murle Mashburn, 17; CSUF, Setsuko Tani, 7–8; WC, Setsuko Tani, 15–16; Nixon's Daily Diary, 7/13/1970.

25. CSUF, Dolores Ball, 22–24.

26. Nixon's Daily Diary, 6/11–12/1969.

27. WC, Virginia Counts, 9; WC, Mary McGovern, 10; Nixon's Daily Diary, 6/12/1971.

28. David, *Lonely Lady*, 142.

29. Nixon's Daily Diary, 3/25/1969.

30. Nixon's Daily Diary, 4/22/1970; Richard Nixon, "Remarks on Presenting the Presidential Medal of Freedom to Eight Journalists," 4/22/1970, Gerhard Peters and John T. Woolley, American Presidency Project, https://www.presidency .ucsb.edu/node/239681.

31. Nixon's Daily Diary, 3/27/1970; Richard Nixon, "Remarks on Presenting the Presidential Medal of Freedom to Samuel Goldwyn," 3/27/1971, Gerhard Peters and John T. Woolley, American Presidency Project, https://www.presidency .ucsb.edu/node/241143.

32. WC, Roger Johnson, 2; Nixon's Daily Diary, 3/20/1969, 2/7/1970, 8/13/1971.

33. WC, Kenneth Rush, 3.

34. WC, Hollis Dole, 1.

35. Loie Gaunt, interviews by author, 12/28/2010, 2/7/2012.

36. Brown and Brown, *Biography of Mrs. Marty Mann*, 281.

37. Brown and Brown, *Biography of Mrs. Marty Mann*, 282.

38. CSUF, Raymond Burbank, 22; CSUF, Charlotte Otis Craig, 6; CSUF, William Hornaday, 16; CSUF, Hadley Marshburn, 10; Haldeman, *Haldeman Diaries*, 19.

39. Nixon, *In the Arena*, 342.

40. Ron Walker, interview by author, 12/6/2013.

41. CSUF, Charles Ball, 19; CSUF, Raymond Burbank, 22; CSUF, Charlotte Otis Craig, 6; BK, Robert Finch, 14; CSUF, William Hornaday, 15–16; BK, Bob King, 2; BK, Kyle Palmer, 12; CSUF, Ralph Palmer, 22; WC, Sheppard Watson, 15; Nixon, *In the Arena*, 96.

42. CSUF, Raymond Burbank, 3; Nixon's Daily Diary, 1/26/1969, 3/16/1969, 4/27/1969, 6/29/1969, 9/28/1969, 11/16/1969, 12/14/1969, 1/11/1970, 2/1/1970, 2/8/1970, 3/15/1970, 2/1/1970, 4/26/1970, 9/13/1970, 12/20/1970, 3/3/1971, 5/9/1971, 10/10/1971, 3/19/1972, 2/25/1973, 4/15/1973, 10/14/1973, 12/16/1973, 3/17/1974.

43. Nixon, *In the Arena*, 97–98.

44. Nixon's Daily Diary, 1/26/1969, 5/3/1970; Graham, *Just as I Am*, 533–34.

45. Nixon's Daily Diary, 7/20/1969; CSUF, William Hornaday, 34; WC, Paul Smith, 22; Elliott, *Whittier College*, 161.

46. WC, Harriet Hudspeth, 28–29; PPS 207, box 120, Glenard Lipscomb to Donald Hughes, 11/4/1959, corr.; Nixon's Daily Diary, 1/24/1971, 3/7/1971, 4/18/1971, 5/9/1971, 10/10/1971, 11/14/1971, 3/19/1972, 12/17/1972, 1/21/1973, 3/11/1973, 4/15/1973; Graham, *Just as I Am*, 533–34.

47. Marje Acker, interview by author, 7/7/2010; CSUF, Raymond Burbank, 3.

48. Nixon's Daily Diary, 7/13/1969, 4/5/1970.

49. Nixon's Daily Diary, 4/5/1970, 1/24/1971, 3/7/1971.

50. CSUF, Raymond Burbank, 3; Nixon's Daily Diary, 4/27/1969, 6/29/1969, 9/28/1969, 11/16/1969, 12/14/1969, 1/11/1970, 2/1/1970, 2/8/1970, 3/15/1970, 2/1/1970, 4/26/1970, 9/13/1970, 12/20/1970, 3/3/1971, 5/9/1971, 10/10/1971, 3/19/1972, 2/25/1973, 4/15/1973, 10/14/1973, 12/16/1973, 3/17/1974.

51. Nixon's Daily Diary, 3/5/1969.

52. Ramirez, *Chicano*, 25–26, 51.

53. Ramirez, *Chicano*, 36–38, 49–50.

54. WC, Henry Ramirez, 6–7.

55. WC, Henry Ramirez, 6–7.

56. Aitken, *Nixon*, 394.

57. WC, Lon Fuller, 12.

58. Nixon, *In the Arena*, 356.

59. BK, Robert Finch, 12–13; Nixon's Daily Diary, 3/21/1969; Lundberg, *Big Orange*, 77; Gene Boyer, interviews by author, 6/10/2010, 6/14/2010, 12/7/2010, 12/15/2010; Aitken, *Nixon*, 342; Nixon and Olson, *Nixons*, 352.

60. Nixon and Olson, *Nixons*, 352.

61. Richard Nixon, "Annual Message to the Congress on the State of the Union," 1/22/1970, Gerhard Peters and John T. Woolley, American Presidency Project, https://www.presidency.ucsb.edu/node/241063.

62. Aitken, *Nixon*, 397–98.

63. BK, Robert Finch, 12–13; Nixon's Daily Diary, 3/21/1969; Gene Boyer, interviews by author, 6/10/2010, 6/14/2010, 12/7/2010, 12/15/2010; Aitken, *Nixon*, 342; Nixon and Olson, *Nixons*, 352.

64. Eisenhower, *Pat Nixon*, 271.

65. *Time*, 9/7/1970.

66. Nixon's Daily Diary, 3/22/1969.

67. Nixon's Daily Diary, 8/19/1971, 2/12/1973, 3/30/1973; *Time*, 9/7/1970.

68. Eisenhower, *Pat Nixon*, 272.

69. Nixon's Daily Diary, 3/22/1969.

70. Nixon's Daily Diary, 3/22/1969.

71. Clara Jane Nixon, interviews by author, 7/8/2010, 9/17/2010, 1/17/2011, 9/21/2011.

72. Nixon's Daily Diary, 6/4/1969.

73. Nixon's Daily Diary, 1/8/1970; Gene Boyer, interviews by author, 6/10/2010, 6/14/2010, 12/7/2010, 12/15/2010; GB, Flight Logs, 1402–50.

74. Nixon's Daily Diary, 11/3/1970, 1/13/1971.

75. Nixon's Daily Diary, 5/30/1970, 6/28–29/1970, 7/1–2/1970, 7/4–5/1970, 7/26–27/1970, 7/30/1970, 8/1–2/1970, 9/5/1970, 7/9/1972, 8/26/1972, 8/29/1972, 4/6/1973.

76. WC, Virginia Counts, 7; Gavin Herbert, interview by author, 1/5/2011.

77. Nixon's Daily Diary, 8/10–11/1969, 12/30/1969, 5/29–30/1970, 6/27–28/1970, 7/2–5/1970, 7/25–28/1970, 7/31/1970, 8/2/1970, 8/21–24/1970, 8/26–30/1970, 9/2/1970, 9/4–6/1970, 11/1/1970, 11/4/1970, 3/27/1971, 7/7/1971, 8/23–25/1971, 8/27/1971, 8/29/1971, 8/30–31/1971, 8/30–31/1971, 9/1–2/1971, 11/24–26/1971, 11/28/1971, 1/5/1972, 1/7–8/1972, 7/1–10/1972, 7/12–18/1972, 8/24–30/1972, 9/1–5/1972, 11/5–7/1972, 2/9–12/1973, 4/2–4/1973, 4/6–7/1973, 6/24–28/1973, 8/20/1973, 7/12/1974.

78. Nixon's Daily Diary, 5/30/1970, 7/28/1970, 8/22/1970, 8/23/1970, 8/26/1970, 8/30/1970, 8/23/1971, 8/27/1971, 8/29/1971, 8/30/1971, 9/1/1971, 9/2/1971, 11/25–26/1971, 7/2/1972, 7/3/1972, 7/7/1972, 7/8/1972, 7/13/1972, 7/17/1972, 8/28/1972, 11/5/1972, 4/1/1973, 4/3/1973, 4/6/1973; Campbell and Landau, *Presidential Lies*, 163.

79. Nixon's Daily Diary, 8/15/1969, 8/19/1969, 8/25/1969, 9/5/1969, 9/6/1969, 1/2/1970, 8/26/1970, 7/17/1974; Gene Boyer, interviews by author, 6/10/2010, 6/14/2010, 12/7/2010, 12/15/2010; GB, Flight Logs, 1406–620.

80. Nixon's Daily Diary, Graham: 8/16/1969, 8/19/1969; Annenberg: 8/17/1969, 1/4–6/1970, 5/1–2/1971, 11/27/1971, 1/9–12/1974, 7/15–16/1974.

81. Gene Boyer, interviews by author, 6/10/2010, 6/14/2010, 12/7/2010, 12/15/2010; GB, Flight Logs, 1235–730; Nixon's Daily Diary, 1/3/1970.

82. Campbell and Landau, *Presidential Lies*, 160.

83. Nixon's Daily Diary, 5/30/1970, 6/27/1970, 7/3/1970, 7/25/1970, 1/9/1971, 7/14/1971, 8/30/1971, 2/9/1973, 4/3/1973, 4/4/1973, 6/26/1973, 6/28/1973, 6/30/1973, 7/1/1973, 7/2/1973, 7/3/1973, 7/4/1973, 7/6/1973, 8/25/1973, 7/23/1974.

84. Nixon's Daily Diary, 8/22/1969, 8/24/1969, 8/29/1969, 8/30/1969, 8/31/1969, 7/4/1970, 7/5/1970, 7/31/1970, 8/2/1970, 8/23/1970, 8/29/1970, 8/30/1970/ 9/2/1970, 9/4/1970, 9/5/1970, 9/6/1970, 4/4/1971, 7/8/1971, 7/10/1971, 7/11/1971, 7/12/1971, 7/13/1971, 7/17/1971, 8/20/1971, 8/21/1971, 8/22/1971, 8/23/1971, 8/25/1971, 8/27/1971, 9/1/1971, 9/2/1971, 7/2/1972, 7/3/1972, 7/4/1972, 7/5/1972, 7/6/1972, 7/7/1972, 7/8/1972, 7/9/1972, 7/10/1972, 7/11/1972, 7/12/1972, 7/13/1972, 7/14/1972, 7/15/1972, 7/16/1972, 8/25/1972, 8/26/1972, 8/28/1972, 9/2/1972, 9/3/1972, 9/4/1972, 11/6/1972, 7/4/1973, 7/8/1973, 8/22/1973, 8/23/1973, 8/24/1973, 8/27/1973, 8/28/1973, 8/30/1973, 8/31/1973, 7/13/1974, 7/14/1974, 7/16/1974, 7/71/1974, 7/18/1974, 7/19/1974, 7/20/1974, 7/21/1974, 7/22/1974, 7/26/1974, 7/27/1974.

85. "Remarks Announcing Plans to Make Land in Camp Pendleton, California, Available for Public Recreational Use," 3/31/1971, Gerhard Peters and John T. Woolley, American Presidency Project, https://www.presidency.ucsb.edu/node /241179; Nixon's Daily Diary, 3/31/1971.

86. Aitken, *Nixon*, 398.

87. "Remarks Announcing Plans"; Nixon's Daily Diary, 3/31/1971; Aitken, *Nixon*, 398–99.

88. Nixon's Daily Diary, 5/29/1970, 8/28/1972.

89. Nixon's Daily Diary, 8/15/1969, 1/7/1970, 5/29/1970, 11/3/1970 2 hrs., 7/12/1972, 8/29/1972, 9/4/1972, 4/4/1973 2.5 hrs., 4/6/1972 1.5 hrs., 7/4/1972, 4/7/1973 3.5 hrs., 6/27/1973 2 hrs., 6/29/1973 1.5 hrs., 7/1/1973 2 hrs., 8/28/1973 1 hr.

90. Nixon's Daily Diary, 9/6/1969; Stephen Bull, interview by author, 12/31/2014.

91. Nixon's Daily Diary, 5/29/1970; "Nation: Richard Nixon Slept Here," *Time*, 9/7/1970, 13; "Nixon Visits Downtown San Clemente," *Long Beach Press Telegram*, 9/7/1969.

92. Nixon's Daily Diary, 8/1/1970, 2/11/1973 2 hrs., 1/9/1974; Helen Thomas, "Nixon Stops at McDonald's in Banning, Gets 'Big Mac,'" *Redlands Daily Facts*, 1/10/1974.

93. Nixon's Daily Diary, 8/23/1969, 9/6/1969, 7/26/1970; Douglas B. Cornell, "Nixon Delays Trop Decision," *Long Beach Press Telegram*, 9/7/1969.

94. Gene Boyer, interviews by author, 6/10/2010, 6/14/2010, 12/7/2010, 12/15/2010; GB, Flight Logs, 1455–519, 1634–55; Jack Brennan, interview by author 11/11/2010; Nixon's Daily Diary, 1/8/1971; "President Nixon and Tricia Vsit Catalina," *Catalina Islander*, 1/14/1971.

95. Nixon Family Collection, Student's Certificate issued to Harold Nixon from Aviation Institute of U.S.A., 10/9/1930.

96. Nixon's Daily Diary, 8/13/1969; Nixon and Olson, *Nixons*, 254; Eisenhower, *Pat Nixon*, 272.

97. WC, Lawrene Anfinson, 23; Nixon's Daily Diary, 8/29/1969, 1/1/1970, 1/6/1970, 9/4/1970, 3/31/1971, 4/5/1971, 7/1/1971, 7/12/1971, 1/8/1972, 1/5/1974, 11/27/1971.

98. Nixon's Daily Diary, 6/26/1970, 7/2/1970, 1/6/1971, 8/27/1972, 2/12/1973, 8/22/1973. At a reception for his celebrity supporters, guests included June Allyson, Desi Arnaz, Frankie Avalon, Rona Barrett, Jack Benny, George Burns, Glen Campbell, Dick Clark, Chuck Connors, Scatman Crothers, Mike Curb, Vic Damone, Sammy Davis Jr., Roy Disney, Jimmy Durante, Clint Eastwood, Buddy Ebsen, Barbara Eden, Ralph Edwards, Chad Everett, Douglas Fairbanks Jr., Eddie Fisher, Connie Francis, Eva and Zsa Zsa Gabor, George Hamilton, Susan Hayward, Charlton Heston, Paul and Miriam Keyes, Cheryl Ladd, Michael Landon, Art Linkletter, Rich Little, Dick Martin, Jayne Meadows, Mary Tyler Moore, Agnes Moorehead, Wayne Newton, Lloyd Nolan, Buck Owens, Gene Raymond, Ronald Reagan, Tex Ritter, Buddy Rogers, Dan Rowan, Kurt Russell, Cybill Shepherd, Frank Sinatra, Red Skelton, Jill St. John, Jimmy Stewart, Rudy Vallee, Abigail Van Buren, Jack Warner, John Wayne, Lawrence Welk, Meredith Willson, Jack Wrather, and Richard Zanuck.

99. Nixon's Daily Diary, 8/27/1969; Dwight Chapin, interview by author, 6/10/2010.

100. Nixon's Daily Diary, 7/27/1970, 4/2/1971, 8/20 and 25/1971, 2/12/1973.

101. Nixon's Daily Diary, 8/28/1969, 1/6/1971, 7/19/1974.

102. Nixon's Daily Diary, 1/6–7/1972, 4/3/1973.

103. JA, Richard Nixon, Historic Video Transcript, 5/12–13/1983, 104–5.

104. Nixon's Daily Diary, 6/22/1973; JA, Richard Nixon, Historic Video Transcript, 5/12–13/1983, 104–5.

105. Nixon's Daily Diary, 6/22/1973.

106. Dwight Chapin, interview by author, 6/10/2010; Gavin Herbert, interview by author, 1/5/2011.

107. JA, Richard Nixon, Historic Video Transcript, 5/12–13/1983, 105–6.

108. JA, Richard Nixon, Historic Video Transcript, 5/12–13/1983, 106; Dwight Chapin, interview by author, 6/10/2010.

109. JA, Richard Nixon, Historic Video Transcript, 5/12–13/1983, 88.

110. Nixon's Daily Diary, 6/23/1973; JA, Richard Nixon, Historic Video Transcript, 5/12–13/1983, 104–6. The guests included Earl Adams, Gene Autry, Edgar Bergen, Pat Boone, Foster Brooks, Ed Carter, Chuck Connors, Roy Crocker, Mike Curb, Justin Dart, Clint Eastwood, Buddy Ebsen, Chad Everett, Bob Finch, Leonard Firestone, Glenn Ford, Herb Hazeltine, Gavin Herbert, Bob Hope, Burl Ives, Paul Keyes, Art Linkletter, Tony Martin, Barbara Marx, Ed Pauley, Tom Pike, Paul Presley, Ronald Reagan, Cesar Romero, Dan Rowan, Rosalind Russell, Henry Salvatori, Frank Sinatra, Red Skelton, Barbara Stanwyck, Jill St. John, Waller Taylor, Paul Truesdale, Meredith Willson, and Jack Wrather.

111. JA, Richard Nixon, Historic Video Transcript, 5/12–13/1983, 105–6.

112. JA, Richard Nixon, Historic Video Transcript, 5/12–13/1983, 108–9.

113. Nixon's Daily Diary, 6/24/1973; JA, Richard Nixon, Historic Video Transcript, 5/12–13/1983, 108–9, 114; Eisenhower, *Pat Nixon*, 373–74.

114. Dwight Chapin, interview by author, 6/10/2010; Nixon's Daily Diary, 7/13/1971.

115. Nixon's Daily Diary, 7/15/1971; Gene Boyer, interviews by author, 6/10/2010, 6/14/2010, 12/7/2010, 12/15/2010; GB, Flight Logs, 1745–823; Aitken, *Nixon*, 429.

116. Gene Boyer, interviews by author, 6/10/2010, 6/14/2010, 12/7/2010, 12/15/2010; Boyer, *Inside*, 270–71.

117. Gene Boyer, interviews by author, 6/10/2010, 6/14/2010, 12/7/2010, 12/15/2010; Boyer, *Inside*, 270–72.

118. Gene Boyer, interviews by author, 6/10/2010, 6/14/2010, 12/7/2010, 12/15/2010; Boyer, *Inside*, 270–72.

119. Nixon's Daily Diary, 7/15/1971; Boyer, *Inside*, 272.

120. Boyer, *Inside*, 272.

121. Nixon's Daily Diary, 4/30/1971.

122. CSUF, Mildred Mendenhall, 16; CSUF, Gerald Shaw, 24; JA, Richard Nixon, Historic Video Transcript, 5/12–13/1983, 197; Aitken, *Nixon*, 11; Brodie, *Richard Nixon*, 162; Nixon, *In the Arena*, 396.

123. Nixon's Daily Diary, 2/12/1973.

124. CSUF, Eugene Coffin, 14; Nixon's Daily Diary, 8/28/1972; Martin Anderson, interviews by author, 10/26/2010, 12/8/2010; Aitken, *Nixon*, 331, 396–97.

125. Halberstam, *Powers*, 561.

126. Nixon's Daily Diary, 8/27/1970.

127. Nixon's Daily Diary, 12/26/1973.

128. Nixon's Daily Diary, 12/26–27/1973.

129. Eisenhower, *Pat Nixon*, 396.

130. Nixon's Daily Diary, 8/20/1971, 3/31/1973.

131. CSUF, Charles Ball, 26; CSUF, Dorothy Beeson, 7–8; Clara Jane Nixon, interviews by author, 7/8/2010, 9/17/2010, 1/17/2011, 9/21/2011; Nixon's Daily Diary, 6/27/1970.

132. CSUF, Dorothy Beeson, 7; WC, #2 Evlyn Dorn, 7–8; WC, #2 Josephine Harrison, 7; WC, Ernest Lamb, 7–8.

133. WC, Charles William Milhous, 30.

134. Nixon's Daily Diary, 6/27/1970; Clara Jane Nixon, interviews by author, 7/8/2010, 9/17/2010, 1/17/2011, 9/21/2011.

135. PB, Roy Day, 37.

136. Nixon's Daily Diary, 8/24/1972.

137. Lundberg, *Big Orange*, 77.

138. Nixon's Daily Diary, 9/27/1972; "Nixon Picks Up $2 Million in 1-Day Calif. Campaign," *Long Beach Press Telegram*, 9/28/1972.

139. "Nixon Picks Up $2 Million."

140. Nixon's Daily Diary, 9/28/1972.

141. Nixon's Daily Diary, 11/4/1972; Gene Boyer, interviews by author, 6/10/2010, 6/14/2010, 12/7/2010, 12/15/2010; GB, Flight Logs; Eisenhower, *Pat Nixon*, 351.

142. Nixon's Daily Diary, 11/7/1972; Boyer, *Inside*, 302; Eisenhower, *Pat Nixon*, 351.

143. Nixon and Olson, *Nixons*, 315–16; Aitken, *Nixon*, 448.

144. "Presidential Elections, 1789–2020," Infoplease, accessed 12/27/2010, http://www.infoplease.com/ipa/A0781450.html.

145. Nixon's Daily Diary, 1/19/1973, 1/21/1973.

146. Aitken, *Nixon*, 445.

147. Aitken, *Nixon*, 441.

148. Crowley, *Nixon off the Record*, 149–50.

149. Aitken, *Nixon*, 473–78; Nixon, *In the Arena*, 40.

150. Nixon, *Six Crises*, xvii.

151. Aitken, *Nixon*, 421.

152. Aitken, *Nixon*, 482, 498–99.

153. Aitken, *Nixon*, 506–7.

154. Nixon's Daily Diary, 3/16/1969, 8/8/1969, 12/14/1969, 4/26/1971, 10/28/1971, 5/9/1972, 2/22/1973, 6/5/1973, 6/18/1973, 12/3/1973; Rhyne, *Working for Justice*, 161, 578.

155. Rhyne, *Working for Justice*, 158–59.

156. Rhyne, *Working for Justice*, 170, 409.

157. Aitken, *Nixon*, 511–12; Eisenhower, *Pat Nixon*, 388, 390.

158. Luke Nichter, coauthor of *Nixon Tapes*, email correspondence with author, 10/11/2014; Aitken, *Nixon*, 515.

159. Aitken, *Nixon*, 515.

160. Nichter email, 10/11/2014.

161. Ambrose, *Nixon*, 3:329.

162. CSUF, Guy Dixon, 29–20.

163. Nichter email, 10/11/2014; Apple, Introduction, 2; Aitken, *Nixon*, 515–16; Ambrose, *Nixon*, 3:329; Eisenhower, *Pat Nixon*, 409.

164. Eisenhower, *Pat Nixon*, 409.

165. Aitken, *Nixon*, 383.

166. CSUF, Raymond Burbank, 8.

167. Eisenhower, *Pat Nixon*, 410.

168. Brodie, *Richard Nixon*, 176.

169. Hillings, *Irrepressible Irishman*, 124–25.

170. Marje Acker, interview by author, 7/7/2010.

171. Marje Acker, interview by author, 7/7/2010.

172. Nixon's Daily Diary, 7/12/1974.

173. Eisenhower, *Pat Nixon*, 415.

174. McDougal, *Privileged Son*, 314.

175. Nixon's Daily Diary, 7/21/1974.

176. Nixon's Daily Diary, 7/25/1974.

177. Eisenhower, *Pat Nixon*, 415; Nixon's Daily Diary, 7/27/1974.

178. CSUF, Linda Baker, 18–19; David, *Lonely Lady*, 163.

179. Black, *Life in Full*, 972–76.

180. David, *Lonely Lady*, 191.

181. Eisenhower, *Pat Nixon*, 417.

182. Nixon, *Memoirs*, 1063; Nixon-Gannon Interviews, Walter J. Brown Media Archives and Peabody Awards Collection, University of Georgia Libraries, Athens, 6/10/1983, day 7, tape 3, 13:27, 23:24.

183. Eisenhower, *Pat Nixon*, 417; Nixon-Gannon Interviews, 23:24.

184. David, *Lonely Lady*, 182.

185. Wilson, *Confessions*, 205–6.

186. Nixon's Daily Diary, 8/8/1974.

187. Nixon, *In the Arena*, 14, 97.

188. Aitken, *Nixon*, 522–23.

189. Aitken, *Nixon*, 524.

190. Aitken, *Nixon*, 524.

191. Anson, *Exile*, 15. Boyer has liftoff recorded at 9:58 a.m. for an eight-minute flight to Andrews. Gene Boyer, interviews by author, 6/10/2010, 6/14/2010, 12/7/2010, 12/15/2010; GB, Flight Logs.

192. Boyer, *Inside*, 361.

193. Aitken, *Nixon*, 524.

194. Boyer, *Inside*, 179, 359; Gene Boyer, interviews by author, 6/10/2010, 6/14/2010, 12/7/2010, 12/15/2010; Carl Burhanan, interviews by author, 1/5/2011, 1/6/2011, 1/12/2011.

195. Gene Boyer, interviews by author, 6/10/2010, 6/14/2010, 12/7/2010, 12/15/2010.

196. Boyer, *Inside*, 363; Gene Boyer, interviews by author, 6/10/2010, 6/14/2010, 12/7/2010, 12/15/2010; Carl Burhanan, interviews by author, 1/5/2011, 1/6/2011, 1/12/2011.

197. Anson, *Exile*, 15–16.

198. Lee Simmons, interviews by author, 1/16/2012, 1/19/2012, 7/19/2012.

199. Lee Simmons, interviews by author, 1/16/2012, 1/19/2012, 7/19/2012.

200. Lee Simmons, interviews by author, 1/16/2012, 1/19/2012, 7/19/2012; Anson, *Exile*, 19.

201. Lee Simmons, interviews by author, 1/16/2012, 1/19/2012, 7/19/2012; Anson, *Exile*, 19.

202. Lee Simmons, interviews by author, 1/16/2012, 1/19/2012, 7/19/2012; Jason Schultz, supervising archivist at Nixon Library, email correspondence with author, 10/27–28/2014.

203. Nixon, *In the Arena*, 12.
204. Eisenhower, *Pat Nixon*, 429.
205. Anson, *Exile*, 21.
206. Eisenhower, *Pat Nixon*, 429; Nixon, *In the Arena*, 12.
207. Anson, *Exile*, 23; David, *Lonely Lady*, 198–99.
208. Anson, *Exile*, 23; Lundberg, *Big Orange*, 78.
209. Lundberg, *Big Orange*, 78.
210. Eisenhower, *Pat Nixon*, 430; Anson, *Exile*, 24.
211. Gavin Herbert, interview by author, 1/5/2011.
212. Nixon, *In the Arena*, 13.
213. Anson, *Exile*, 25.

17. Exile and Rehabilitation

1. David, *Lonely Lady*, 8.
2. Anson, *Exile*, 26.
3. Aitken, *Nixon*, 529; Anson, *Exile*, 30.
4. JVB, Jack Brennan to Kathy Emory, 8/20/1974, corr.; JVB, Memorandum from the Great State of La Casa Pacifica, 8/22/1974; JVB, Bill Brennan, Memorandum re Procedures to be Utilized Temporarily under the Presidential Transition Act of 1963, 9/11/1974; Ken Khachigian, interview by author, 12/17/2010.
5. Aitken, *Nixon*, 530.
6. Aitken, *Nixon*, 531.
7. Aitken, *Nixon*, 531.
8. Aitken, *Nixon*, 531–32.
9. Nixon, *In the Arena*, 82.
10. Ken Khachigian, interview by author, 12/17/2010.
11. Lungren and Lungren, *Healing*, 17.
12. Lungren and Lungren, *Healing*, 17.
13. Lungren and Lungren, *Healing*, 2, 12, 17, 19, 21; Nixon, *In the Arena*, 16–17.
14. Anson, *Exile*, 69; Eisenhower, *Pat Nixon*, 433; Lungren and Lungren, *Healing*, 22, 34.
15. Anson, *Exile*, 70.
16. Rhyne, *Working for Justice*, 240–42.
17. Rhyne, *Working for Justice*, 240–42.
18. Rhyne, *Working for Justice*, 240–42.
19. Eisenhower, *Pat Nixon*, 433–34.
20. Anson, *Exile*, 71.
21. Nixon, *In the Arena*, 17
22. Anson, *Exile*, 75.
23. Anson, *Exile*, 76–77.
24. Eisenhower, *Pat Nixon*, 435.
25. Aitken, *Nixon*, 533; Anson, *Exile*, 79; Nixon, *In the Arena*, 17.
26. Aitken, *Nixon*, 533.
27. Lungren and Lungren, *Healing*, 87.

28. Aitken, *Nixon*, 533; Nixon, *In the Arena*, 17.

29. Anson, *Exile*, 79–80.

30. Aitken, *Nixon*, 533.

31. Aitken, *Nixon*, 533.

32. Anson, *Exile*, 81.

33. Anson, *Exile*, 81–82.

34. Aitken, *Nixon*, 533–34.

35. Aitken, *Nixon*, 534; Lungren and Lungren, *Healing*, 91.

36. Aitken, *Nixon*, 534; Anson, *Exile*, 122, 145; Lungren and Lungren, *Healing*, 89–91.

37. Graham, *Just as I Am*, 553–54.

38. Anson, *Exile*, 145.

39. Anson, *Exile*, 82; Eisenhower, *Pat Nixon*, 435–37; David, *Lonely Lady*, 204; Lungren and Lungren, *Healing*, 99.

40. Aitken, *Nixon*, 534.

41. JVB, List of the President's Appointments from 2/9/1975.

42. Lungren and Lungren, *Healing*, 131–32, 137.

43. Marje Acker, interview by author, 7/7/2010.

44. Aitken, *Nixon*, 535.

45. Marje Acker, interview by author, 7/7/2010; Judy Johnson, interviews by author, 5/28/2010, 6/7/2010.

46. Aitken, *Nixon*, 534–35.

47. Aitken, *Nixon*, 534–35.

48. JVB, President's Appointments from 2/9/1975; Clara Jane Nixon, interviews by author, 7/8/2010, 9/17/2010, 1/17/2011, 9/21/2011.

49. Gavin Herbert, interview by author, 1/5/2011; Anson, *Exile*, 273.

50. Aitken, *Nixon*, 535.

51. Nixon, *In the Arena*, 19.

52. Lungren and Lungren, *Healing*, 105–6; Nixon, *In the Arena*, 19.

53. Aitken, *Nixon*, 539; Anson, *Exile*, 111.

54. Aitken, *Nixon*, 539; Anson, *Exile*, 111.

55. Nixon, *In the Arena*, 19.

56. Lungren and Lungren, *Healing*, 113; Nixon, *In the Arena*, 28.

57. UCB, Earl Adams, 34.

58. Eisenhower, *Pat Nixon*, 437.

59. Eisenhower, *Pat Nixon*, 439.

60. Eisenhower, *Pat Nixon*, 439.

61. David, *Lonely Lady*, 200.

62. David, *Lonely Lady*, 201.

63. Anson, *Exile*, 89.

64. David, *Lonely Lady*, 201.

65. Aitken, *Nixon*, 537; Anson, *Exile*, 177.

66. Anson, *Exile*, 97.

67. "Nixon Talk at Dinner Brings Tears to Friends," *Bakersfield Californian*, 2/24/1975; Anson, *Exile*, 99–100.

68. J V B, President's Appointments from 2/9/1975; J V B, President's Appointments, 1977; J V B, President's Schedule of Appointments, 1979; Nixon, *In the Arena*, 28.

69. C S U F, Dolores Ball, 21, 24; C S U F, Alice Newsom, 41–43; E D, Evlyn Dorn to Nixon, 10/5/1974, corr.; J V B, President's Appointments from 2/9/1975; J V B, President's Appointments, 1977; J V B, President's Schedule of Appointments, 1979; Anson, *Exile*, 72.

70. J V B, President's Appointments from 2/9/1975.

71. Eisenhower, *Pat Nixon*, 440.

72. Loie Gaunt, interviews by author, 12/28/2010, 2/7/2012.

73. Aitken, *Nixon*, 530.

74. Dwight Chapin, interview by author, 6/10/2010.

75. Anson, *Exile*, 203.

76. Anson, *Exile*, 147.

77. Bruce Herschensohn, interviews by author, 11/20/2012, 12/5/2012.

78. C S U F, Linda Baker, 49–50; C S U F, Dolores Ball, 24; C S U F, Joanne Dale, 26.

79. C S U F, Dolores Ball, 22–24; Jeffrey Ball, email correspondence with author, 10/31/2013.

80. Lois Lundberg, interviews by author, 12/10/2010, 1/4/2011, 3/29/2011.

81. Lundberg, *Big Orange*, 86.

82. Anson, *Exile*, 144.

83. Aitken, *Nixon*, 540.

84. Aitken, *Nixon*, 540; Nixon, *In the Arena*, 123.

85. David, *Lonely Lady*, 199.

86. David, *Lonely Lady*, 2.

87. Eisenhower, *Pat Nixon*, 441.

88. Eisenhower, *Pat Nixon*, 443.

89. Anson, *Exile*, 252.

90. Judy Johnson, interviews by author, 5/28/2010, 6/7/2010; Anson, *Exile*, 116–17, 177, 244.

91. Eisenhower, *Pat Nixon*, 441; David, *Lonely Lady*, 10.

92. Anson, *Exile*, 177.

93. Jack Brennan, interview by author, 11/11/2010.

94. Aitken, *Nixon*, 536.

95. Campbell and Landau, *Presidential Lies*, 152–53; Nixon, *In the Arena*, 27.

96. Anson, *Exile*, 117–18; Campbell and Landau, *Presidential Lies*, 152.

97. J V B, Scorecards from 8/16/1976, 9/2/1976, 7/20/1977, 7/21/1977; Jack Brennan, interview by author, 11/11/2010; Campbell and Landau, *Presidential Lies*, 164.

98. Campbell and Landau, *Presidential Lies*, 164; Lungren and Lungren, *Healing*, 141.

99. Nixon, *In the Arena*, 187–88.

100. Aitken, *Nixon*, 538; Anson, *Exile*, 73.

101. Aitken, *Nixon*, 538.

102. Aitken, *Nixon*, 537.

103. Aitken, *Nixon*, 538.

104. David, *Lonely Lady*, 3–5.

105. Loie Gaunt, interviews by author, 12/28/2010, 2/7/2012.

106. Eisenhower, *Pat Nixon*, 440.

107. David, *Lonely Lady*, 8–9.

108. Loie Gaunt, interviews by author, 12/28/2010, 2/7/2012; Judy Johnson, interviews by author, 5/28/2010, 6/7/2010; Ken Khachigian, interview by author, 12/17/2010.

109. JVB, President's Appointments, 1977; Anson, *Exile*, 114, 135, 151.

110. Martha Smith, interviews by author, 2/1/2010, 2/3/2010; JVB, President's Appointments, 1977; Anson, *Exile*, 155.

111. Martha Smith, interviews by author, 2/1/2010, 2/3/2010.

112. Martha Smith, interviews by author, 2/1/2010, 2/3/2010.

113. JVB, President's Appointments, 1977; Anson, *Exile*, 155, 161.

114. Aitken, *Nixon*, 541; Lungren and Lungren, *Healing*, 147, 168.

115. Aitken, *Nixon*, 542.

116. Ken Khachigian, interview by author, 12/17/2010; Anson, *Exile*, 119, 138–39; Eisenhower, *Pat Nixon*, 447.

117. Anson, *Exile*, 139–41.

118. Anson, *Exile*, 141; Eisenhower, *Pat Nixon*, 449; David, *Lonely Lady*, 176, 204; Lungren and Lungren, *Healing*, 159.

119. Eisenhower, *Pat Nixon*, 450; David, *Lonely Lady*, 2; Lungren and Lungren, *Healing*, 161.

120. Mathony, *Whittier*, 77.

121. Eisenhower, *Pat Nixon*, 455.

122. Aitken, *Nixon*, 538; Anson, *Exile*, 179.

123. Aitken, *Nixon*, 538.

124. Nixon, *In the Arena*, 28–29.

125. Anson, *Exile*, 183.

126. "Richard M. Nixon in Orange County," *Orange County Register*, 4/24/1994.

127. Lundberg, *Big Orange*, 97–98.

128. Aitken, *Nixon*, 537; Anson, *Exile*, 117.

129. Lundberg, *Big Orange*, 97–98; Lois Lundberg, interview by author, 12/10/2010, 1/4/2011, 3/29/2011.

130. David, *Lonely Lady*, 11.

131. Aitken, *Nixon*, 538; Eisenhower, *Pat Nixon*, 456; RNFC, 1978 Photo Index.

132. RNFC, 1978 Photo Index.

133. Rodney Knutson, interview by author, 10/8/2009; Orson Swindle, interview by author, 3/16/2010.

134. Jack Brennan, interview by author, 11/11/2010.

135. Anson, *Exile*, 188–89; Jack Brennan, interview by author, 11/11/2010; John Moynihan, interview by author, 4/21/2010.

136. John Moynihan, interview by author, 4/21/2010.

137. John Moynihan, interview by author, 4/21/2010.

138. John Moynihan, interview by author, 4/21/2010.

139. John Moynihan, interview by author, 4/21/2010.

140. Anson, *Exile*, 189.

141. Anson, *Exile*, 189.

142. Eisenhower, *Pat Nixon*, 456–57.

143. Ken Khachigian, interview by author, 12/17/2010.

144. Aitken, *Nixon*, 565.

145. Anson, *Exile*, 127, 133.

146. JVB, Nixon to Huang Zen, 5/3/1979, corr.

147. Ken Khachigian, interview by author, 12/17/2010.

148. Aitken, *Nixon*, 547.

149. Ken Khachigian, interview by author, 12/17/2010.

150. Aitken, *Nixon*, 549–50.

151. Aitken, *Nixon*, 551–52.

152. Aitken, *Nixon*, 553.

153. "Nixons to Make Home in New York, Friend Says," *Los Angeles Times*, 7/17/1979.

154. JVB, President's Schedule of Appointments, 1979.

155. CSUF, Alice Newsom, 40.

156. "Nixon Pays Tribute to Astronauts," *Ukiah Daily Journal*, 7/16/1979; Anson, *Exile*, 212.

157. "Wayne Estate Put at $6.8 Million," *New York Times*, 6/21/1979; "Nixon Pays Tribute to Astronauts"; Anson, *Exile*, 212.

158. United Press International, "Nixons Give Memorial Gift," 8/6/1979; Clyde Haberman and Albin Krebs, "Notes on People: More Gift Giving by the Richard M. Nixons," *New York Times*, 7/7/1979.

159. Bruce Herschensohn, interviews by author, 11/20/2012, 12/5/2012.

160. Anson, *Exile*, 212; Jack Brennan, interview by author, 11/11/2010.

161. Anson, *Exile*, 212–14.

162. "Last Party Over, Nixons Heading for Peking," *Orange County Register*, 9/5/1979.

163. "Nixon's Last Party at La Casa Pacifica," *Santa Cruz Sentinel*, 11/26/1979.

164. "Nixon's Last Party."

165. "Nixon's Last Party."

166. RNFC, 1980 Photograph Index; JVB, President's Schedule of Appointments, 1979.

167. RNFC, 1980 Photograph Index; George Argyros, interview by author, 11/1/2011.

168. Anson, *Exile*, 209.

169. CSUF, Linda Baker, 49–50, 60; CSUF, Dolores Ball, 21; CSUF, Alice Newsom, 42–43; CSUF, William Price, 95–96; ED, Evlyn Dorn to Nixon, n.d. [1978], corr.; Tom Bewley to Nixon, 1/4/1980, corr.; JVB, President's Appointments from 2/9/1975; JVB, President's Appointments, 1977; JVB, President's Schedule of Appointments, 1979; RNFC, 1979 Photograph Index; Boyer, *Inside*, 270, 385–86; Brodie, *Richard Nixon*, 19; Nixon, *In the Arena*, 279–82; interviews by author with: Marje Acker, 7/7/2010; George Argyros, 11/1/2011; Gene Boyer, 6/10/2010, 6/14/2010, 12/7/2010, 12/15/2010; Tom Fuentes, 10/28/2011; Loie Gaunt, 12/28/2010, 2/7/2012; Gavin Herbert, 1/5/2011; Bruce Herschensohn, 11/20/2012, 12/5/2012; Don Kendall, 3/29/2011; Ken Khachigian, 12/17/2010; Lois Lundberg, 12/10/2010, 1/4/2011, 3/29/2011; Hubert Perry, 12/9/2009, 12/8/2009, 1/5/2010,

1/6/2010, 2/22/2010, 9/8/2010, 11/10/2010, 11/18/2010; Sandy Quinn, 7/18/2012; Stuart Spencer, 12/29/2010, 1/21/2011; and Ron Walker, 12/6/2013.

170. Eisenhower, *Pat Nixon*, 458.

171. Nixon, *In the Arena*, 81.

172. Aitken, *Nixon*, 553; Anson, *Exile*, 208–9.

18. Evening

1. Lois Lundberg, interviews by author, 12/10/2010, 1/4/2011, 3/29/2011.

2. Anson, *Exile*, 262.

3. Jeffrey Perlman, "Nixon Visit—Just like Old Times," *Los Angeles Times*, 4/23/1982.

4. Lundberg, *Big Orange*, 109.

5. Lois Lundberg, "Richard M. Nixon in Orange County," *Orange County Register*, 4/24/1994; Lundberg, *Big Orange*, 107, 109; Lois Lundberg, interviews by author, 12/10/2010, 1/4/2011, 3/29/2011.

6. Marygene Wright, interviews by author, 9/7/2011, 3/11/2014.

7. G. M. Bush, "Central County: 4,000 Expected for Nixon Foreign Policy Address at Chapman," *Los Angeles Times*, 5/9/1984; Maura Dolan, "The Return of Richard Nixon," *Los Angeles Times*, 5/16/1984; Mary Lou Hopkins, "More Than 1,000 Guests in Schweitzer Mall," *Los Angeles Times*, 5/17/1984.

8. Dolan, "Return of Richard Nixon."

9. Dolan, "Return of Richard Nixon."

10. Aitken, *Nixon*, 559.

11. Quoted in Aitken, *Nixon*, 560.

12. TF, Nixon to Tom Fuentes, 9/3/1986, corr.; Tom Fuentes, interview by author, 10/28/2011.

13. Gavin Herbert, interview by author, 1/5/2010.

14. Donna Kendall, interview by author, 4/13/2011.

15. Bruce Herschensohn, interviews by author, 11/20/2012, 12/5/2012.

16. George Argyros, interview by author, 1/20/2011.

17. Crowley, *Nixon off the Record*, 24, 216.

18. Aitken, *Nixon*, 557.

19. Aitken, *Nixon*, 556.

20. TF, Nixon to Tom Fuentes, 7/20/1987, corr.; Tom Fuentes, interview by author, 10/28/2011; Kenneth Reich, "Brother of Ex-President Nixon Dies," *Los Angeles Times*, 6/30/1987.

21. TF, Nixon to Tom Fuentes, 7/20/1987, corr.; Tom Fuentes, interview by author, 10/28/2011.

22. Nixon, *In the Arena*, 48.

23. Nixon, *In the Arena*, 78–79.

24. Aitken, *Nixon*, 563.

25. CSUF, Hugh Hewitt, 5; Richard Breene and Lonn Johnston, "Ground Broken for Nixon Library in Orange County," *Los Angeles Times*, 12/3/1988.

26. Nixon's Daily Diary, 9/3/1969, 8/28/1970.

27. CSUF, Hugh Hewitt, 2, 7; Richard Breene and Lonn Johnston, "Ground Broken for Nixon Library in Orange County," *Los Angeles Times*, 12/3/1988.

28. Mary Lou Fulton, "Yorba Linda Moves to Declare Nixon Holiday," *Los Angeles Times*, 9/6/1989.

29. CSUF, Dolores Ball, 3; CSUF, Hugh Hewitt, 6.

30. Graham, *Just as I Am*, 547; Lundberg, *Big Orange*, 153.

31. Lundberg, *Big Orange*, 153–54.

32. Lundberg, *Big Orange*, 153–54.

33. Lundberg, *Big Orange*, 154.

34. Lundberg, *Big Orange*, 155–56.

35. Sandy Quinn, interview by author, 7/18/2012; Aitken, *Nixon*, 567–68.

36. Graham, *Just as I Am*, 547.

37. Aitken, *Nixon*, 569.

38. Aitken, *Nixon*, 569.

39. Lois Lundberg, interviews by author, 12/10/2010, 1/4/2011, 3/29/2011.

40. John F. Stacks, "Victory in Defeat," *Time*, 5/2/1994, 29.

41. Nixon, *In the Arena*, 432–33.

42. Crowley, *Nixon in Winter*, 364–65.

43. Crowley, *Nixon in Winter*, 365.

44. Aitken, *Nixon*, 571.

45. Crowley, *Nixon off the Record*, 172.

46. Crowley, *Nixon in Winter*, 381.

47. Crowley, *Nixon in Winter*, 381.

48. Crowley, *Nixon in Winter*, 382.

49. Crowley, *Nixon in Winter*, 383.

50. Crowley, *Nixon in Winter*, 385.

51. Crowley, *Nixon in Winter*, 387.

52. Crowley, *Nixon in Winter*, 393.

53. Lundberg, *Big Orange*, 203.

54. Aitken, *Nixon*, 564–65.

55. Crowley, *Nixon in Winter*, 393; Graham, *Just as I Am*, 547.

56. Graham, *Just as I Am*, 547; Lundberg, *Big Orange*, 203; Marje Acker, interview by author, 7/7/2010.

57. Crowley, *Nixon in Winter*, 393.

58. Lundberg, *Big Orange*, 205–7.

59. Lundberg, *Big Orange*, 207–8.

60. Crowley, *Nixon in Winter*, 394.

61. CSUF, Alice Newsom, 44; Marje Acker, interview by author, 7/7/2010.

62. George Argyros, interview by author, 1/20/2011.

63. CSUF, Linda Baker, 52; Marje Acker, interview by author, 7/7/2010; CSUF, Linda Baker, 52; EDC, Nixon to Evlyn Dorn, 11/28/1980, corr.; EDC, Evlyn Dorn to Pat Nixon, 7/19/1984, corr.; EDC, Nixon to Evlyn Dorn, 3/12/1985, corr.; EDC, Evlyn Dorn to Pat Nixon, 1/20/1989, corr.; Hillings, *Irrepressible Irishman*, 171.

64. RNFC, Nixon to Edward Schlesinger, 4/18/1994, corr.

65. RNFC, Ronald Reagan to Richard Nixon, 4/19/1994, corr.

66. Stacks, "Victory in Defeat," 28; Crowley, *Nixon in Winter*, 401.

67. BK, Ray Arbuthnot, 3–4; WC, #1 Tom Bewley, 23; CSUF, Joanne Dale, 27; CSUF, Doug Ferguson, 18; WC, Russell Harrison Sr., 21; BK, Hubert Perry, Harriett Hudspeth, Ralph Palmer, Mrs. Ralph Palmer, Lionel Buck Taylor, Jane Troutner, Alice Walker, 7; BK, James Stewart, 13–14; WC, Thomas Stoel, 10; BK, Bob Wilson, 3.

68. Trent Lott, interview by author, 12/12/2013.

69. CSUF, Linda Baker, 52; CSUF, Alice Newsom, 44.

70. Lundberg, *Big Orange*, 221.

71. Graham, *Just as I Am*, 549–50.

72. Robert Dole, interview by author, 12/23/2010.

73. WC, #1 Tom Bewley, 15.

74. WC, Charles Leonard Milhous, 1, 19; WC, Ralph Veady, 2.

75. WC, Ralph Veady, 7.

76. Leon Whiteson, "Nixon Library Hits Close to Home," *Los Angeles Times*, 7/19/1990.

77. Whiteson, "Nixon Library."

78. "Katherine B. Loker, 1915–2008," *Los Angeles Times*, 6/29/2008.

79. Clara Jane Nixon, interviews by author, 7/8/2010, 9/17/2010, 1/17/2011, 9/21/2011.

80. WC, Russell Harrison Jr., 15–16.

81. WC, Calvin Burdg Milhous, Phillip Milhous, and Oliver Milhous (Phillip Milhous), 28–29.

82. CSUF, Lucille Parsons, 14.

83. WC, Harriett Hudspeth, 24; WC, Ralph Palmer, 7.

84. David, *Lonely Lady*, 211.

85. Mazo, *Richard Nixon*, 157.

86. Crowley, *Nixon off the Record*, 5.

87. Crowley, *Nixon off the Record*, 5.

88. Marje Acker, interview by author, 7/7/2010.

89. Loie Gaunt, interviews by author, 12/28/2010, 2/7/2012.

90. Crowley, *Nixon off the Record*, vii.

91. WC, Richard Spaulding, 8; WC, Adela Rogers St. Johns, 22; WC, Ada Sutton, 28.

92. WC, Richard Spaulding, 8.

93. WC, Charles Rhyne, 14.

94. WC, Richard Spaulding, 8.

95. George Argyros, interview by author, 1/20/2011.

96. Kornitzer, *Real Nixon*, 343.

97. Otto Friedrich, "I Have Never Been a Quitter," *Time*, 5/2/1994, 43.

98. CSUF, Marion Nichols, 1–3; WC, Ola Florence Jobe, 18.

99. Gavin Herbert, interview by author, 1/5/2011.

100. Brett Sporich, "A Nixon Not Seen by Many: Old Friends Reflect on Determined Man," *Whittier News*, 4/21/1994.

101. Graham, *Just as I Am*, 550.
102. BK, Richard Nixon, 1.
103. Marje Acker, interview by author, 7/7/2010.
104. Nixon, *In the Arena*, 226.
105. West, *Quaker Reader*, 2.

Bibliography

Archives and Manuscript Materials

Bewley, Knoop & Nixon, negotiated checks to Nixon. Bewley, Lassleben & Miller, LLP, Papers. Private collection of Bewley, Lassleben & Miller, LLP.

BK. Bela Kornitzer Papers. Interviews. Drew University, Madison NJ.

Bronson, Leisa G. Oral History Interview. Conducted 1989 by Enid H. Douglass, Oral History Program, Claremont Graduate School, for the California State Archives State Government Oral History Program.

Cramer, Esther R. "La Habra and the President." Unpublished manuscript, 1971. White House Special Files Collection. Richard Nixon Presidential Library, Yorba Linda CA.

CSUF. Oral History Program. California State University, Fullerton.

ED. Evlyn Dorn Papers. Private collection of Roberta Dorn.

Gardner, Richard. "Richard Nixon: The Story of a Fighting Quaker." Unpublished manuscript. Richard M. Nixon Collection. Whittier College Library, Whittier College, Whittier CA.

GB. Gene Boyer Papers. Private collection of Gene Boyer.

JVB. John V. Brennan Papers. Providence College, Providence RI.

Los Angeles County Archives. Los Angeles County Recorder.

Los Angeles Examiner Collection. University of Southern California, Los Angeles.

Maureen Nunn Papers. Private collection of Maureen Nunn.

National Archives, Richard Nixon Presidential Library, Yorba Linda CA.

    Campaign 1946.

    Campaign 1952 Vice Presidential.

    Nixon Family Collection.

    PPS. Pre-Presidential Series.

    Richard Nixon Foundation.

        DSC. Dana Smith Collection.

        EDC. Evlyn Dorn Collection.

        Elizabeth Cloes Collection.

        HJD. Helene and Jack Drown Collection.

        HMC. Harrison McCall Collection.

        JA. Jonathan Aitken Collection.

        Judy Johnson Collection.

RNFC. Richard Nixon Foundation Collection.

Roy Day Collection.

Orange County Archives. Orange County Recorder, Santa Ana CA.

PB. Paul Bullock Papers. Interviews. UCLA Charles E. Young Research Library, Special Collections, Los Angeles.

Richard Nixon Room. Permanent exhibit at Whittier Museum, Whittier Historical Society, Whittier CA.

TF. Tom Fuentes Papers. Private collection of Tom Fuentes.

UCB. Richard M. Nixon in the Warren Era Collection. Earl Warren Oral History Project. Bancroft Library, University of California, Berkeley.

WC. Richard Nixon Oral History Project. Whittier College, Whittier CA.

Published Works

Aitken, Jonathan. *Nixon: A Life*. Washington DC: Regnery, 1994.

Ambrose, Stephen E. *Nixon*. Vol. 1, *The Education of a Politician, 1913–1962*. New York: Simon & Schuster, 1987.

———. *Nixon*. Vol. 2, *The Triumph of a Politician, 1962–1972*. New York: Simon & Schuster, 1989.

———. *Nixon*. Vol. 3, *Ruin and Recovery, 1973–1990*. New York: Simon & Schuster, 1991.

Anson, Robert Sam. *Exile: The Unquiet Oblivion of Richard M. Nixon*. New York: Simon & Schuster, 1984.

Apple, R. W., Jr. Introduction to *The White House Transcripts*, by Richard M. Nixon. New York: Bantam, 1974.

Babcock, Gwendolyn Garland. *The Ancestry of John Jewett Garland*. San Marino CA: Self-published, 1992.

Bagley, William. *California's Golden Years: When Government Worked and Why*. Berkeley CA: Berkeley Public Policy Press, 2009.

Black, Conrad. *A Life in Full: Richard M. Nixon*. New York: PublicAffairs, 2007.

Boyer, Gene. *Inside the President's Helicopter*. With Jackie Boor. Brule WI: Cable, 2011.

Brinkley, Douglas, and Luke Nichter. *The Nixon Tapes*. Boston: Houghton Mifflin Harcourt, 2014.

Brodie, Fawn. *Richard Nixon: The Shaping of His Character*. New York: Norton, 1981.

Brown, Sally, and David R. Brown. *A Biography of Mrs. Marty Mann: The First Lady of Alcoholics Anonymous*. Center City MN: Hazelden, 2001.

Burke, Margret Tante. *Are the Stars Out Tonight? The Story of the Famous Ambassador and Cocoanut Grove*. Los Angeles: Forum, 1980.

Butz, March. *Yorba Linda: Its History*. Santa Ana CA: Pioneer, 1970.

Campbell, Shepherd, and Peter Landau. *Presidential Lies*. New York: Macmillan. 1998.

Costello, William. *The Facts about Nixon: An Unauthorized Biography*. New York: Viking, 1960.

Crowley, Monica. *Nixon in Winter*. New York: Random House, 1998.

———. *Nixon off the Record: His Candid Commentary on People and Politics*. New York: Random House, 1996.

David, Lester. *The Lonely Lady of San Clemente: The Story of Pat Nixon*. New York: Harper Collins, 1978.

Dean, John. *Blind Ambition*. New York: Simon & Schuster, 1976.

Directory of Attorneys. Los Angeles: Parker & Baird Co., 1938.

Dmohowski, Joseph. "From a Common Ground: The Quaker Heritage of Jessamyn West and Richard Nixon." *California History* 73, no. 3 (Fall 1994): 216–39.

Dobbs, Michael. *King Richard: Nixon and Watergate; An American Tragedy*. New York: Knopf, 2021.

Ehrlichman, John. *Witness to Power: The Nixon Years*. New York: Simon & Schuster, 1982.

Eisenhower, Julie Nixon, ed. *Eye on Nixon: A Photographic Study of the President and the Man*. New York: Hawthorn Books, 1972.

———. *Pat Nixon: The Untold Story*. New York: Simon & Schuster, 1986.

Elliot, Charles, Jr. *Whittier College: The First Century on the Poet Campus*. Redondo Beach CA: Legends, 1986.

Faries, McIntyre. *Rememb'ring: One Man's Journey*. Glendale CA: Griffin, 1993.

Farrell, John. *Richard Nixon: The Life*. New York: Doubleday, 2017.

Ford, Gerald. *A Time to Heal: The Autobiography of Gerald R. Ford*. New York: Harper & Row, 1979.

Gellman, Irwin. *Campaign of the Century: Kennedy, Nixon, and the Election of 1960*. New Haven CT: Yale University Press, 2022.

———. *The Contender*. New Haven CT: Yale University Press, 1999.

———. *The President and the Apprentice: Eisenhower and Nixon, 1952–1961*. New Haven CT: Yale University Press, 2015.

Graf, William. *Statistics of the Congressional Election of November 5, 1946*. Washington DC: Government Printing Office, 1947. https://history.house.gov/Institution/Election-Statistics/1946election/.

Graham, Billy. *Just as I Am: The Autobiography of Billy Graham*. New York: HarperOne, 1997.

Greenberg, David. "Nixon in American Memory." In *Institutions of Public Memory: The Legacies of German and American Politicians*, edited by Astrid M. Eckert, 98–114. Washington DC: German Historical Institute, 2007.

Halberstam, David. *The Powers That Be*. New York: Alfred A. Knopf, 1979.

Haldeman, H. R. *The Ends of Power*. New York: Crown, 1978.

———. *The Haldeman Diaries*. New York: G. P. Putnam's Sons, 1994.

Hall, Perry D., ed. *The Quotable Richard M. Nixon*. Anderson SC: Droke House, 1967.

Herschensohn, Bruce. *The Gods of Antenna*. New Rochelle NY: Arlington House, 1976.

Hillings, Pat. *The Irrepressible Irishman: A Republican Insider; The Story of a Political Life*. Harold D. Dean, 1993.

Hope, Bob. *Have Tux, Will Travel: Bob Hope's Own Story*. New York: Simon & Schuster, 2003.

Klein, Herbert. *Making It Perfectly Clear: An Inside Account of Nixon's Love-Hate Relationship with the Media*. Garden City NY: Doubleday, 1980.

Kornitzer, Bela. *The Real Nixon: An Intimate Biography.* New York: Rand McNally, 1960.

Laird, Mel. *With Honor: Melvin Laird in War, Peace, and Politics.* Madison: University of Wisconsin Press, 2008.

The Legacy of Richard Nixon: A 30th Anniversary Conference. Richard Nixon Library and Birthplace, August 5, 2004.

Liddy, G. Gordon. *Will: The Autobiography of G. Gordon Liddy.* New York: St. Martin's Press, 1980.

Lundberg, Lois. *The Big Orange: The History of Republican Politics in Orange County, 1950–2000.* La Habra CA: Lundberg, 2001.

Lungren, John C., and John C. Lungren Jr. *Healing Richard Nixon: A Doctor's Memoir.* Lexington: University Press of Kentucky, 2003.

Mankiewicz, Frank. *Perfectly Clear: Nixon from Whittier to Watergate.* New York: Quadrangle, 1973.

Martindale-Hubbell Law Directory. New Providence NJ: Martindale-Hubbell, 1961–63.

Mathony, Virginia. *Whittier Revisited: The First 100 Years.* Whittier CA: Self-published, 1991.

Mazo, Earl. *Richard Nixon: A Political and Personal Portrait.* New York: Harper & Brothers, 1959.

McDougal, Dennis. *Privileged Son: Otis Chandler and the Rise and Fall of the L.A. Times Dynasty.* Cambridge MA: Perseus, 2001.

Morris, Roger. *Richard Milhous Nixon: The Rise of an American Politician.* New York: Henry Holt, 1989.

Nixon, Ed, and Karen Olson. *The Nixons: A Family Portrait.* Bothell WA: Book Publishers Network, 2009.

Nixon, Richard. *Beyond Peace.* New York: Random House, 1994.

——— . *In the Arena.* New York: Simon & Schuster, 1990.

——— . *Leaders.* New York: Warner Books, 1982.

——— . *The Memoirs of Richard Nixon.* New York: Grosset & Dunlap, 1978.

——— . *1999: Victory without War.* New York: Simon & Schuster, 1988.

——— . *No More Vietnams.* New York: Arbor House, 1985.

——— . *Real Peace.* Boston: Little, Brown, 1984.

——— . *The Real War.* New York: Warner Books, 1980.

——— . *Seize the Moment: America's Challenge in a One Superpower World.* New York: Simon & Schuster, 1992.

——— . *Six Crises.* Garden City NY: Doubleday, 1962.

Orange County Directory. Long Beach CA: Western Directory Company, 1919, 1922.

Ramirez, Henry. *A Chicano in the White House: The Nixon No One Knew.* Self-published, 2013.

Rhyne, Charles S. *Working for Justice in America and Justice in the World.* McLean VA: Friends of Legal Profession Public Services, 1995.

Rosen, James. *The Strong Man: John Mitchell and the Secrets of Watergate.* New York: Doubleday, 2008.

Schipske, Gerrie. *Early Long Beach.* Charleston SC: Arcadia, 2011.

Schulte, Renee K. *The Young Nixon: An Oral Inquiry*. California State University, Fullerton, Oral History Program, 1978.

Starr, Kevin. *Golden Dreams: California in an Age of Abundance, 1950–1963*. Oxford University Press, 2009.

Stern, Joan Irvine Smith. *Reflections of California: The Athalie Richardson Irvine Clarke Memorial Exhibition*. Irvine CA: Irvine Museum, 1994.

St. Johns, Adela Rogers. *The Final Verdict*. Garden City NY: Doubleday, 1962.

———. *The Honeycomb*. Garden City NY: Doubleday, 1969.

Stone, Roger. *Tricky Dick: The Rise and Fall and Rise of Richard M. Nixon*. New York: MFJ Books, 2017.

Swift, Will. *Pat and Dick: The Nixons, an Intimate Portrait of a Marriage*. New York: Threshold Editions, 2014.

Thomas, Evan. *Being Nixon: A Man Divided*. New York: Random House, 2015.

Thurston's Pasadena. Los Angeles: Los Angeles Directory Company, 1949.

Toledano, Ralph de. *Nixon*. 1956. Rev. ed., New York: Duell, Sloan and Pearce, 1960.

———. *One Man Alone: Richard Nixon*. New York: Funk and Wagnalls, 1969.

Van Natta, Don, Jr. *First off the Tee: Presidential Hackers, Duffers, and Cheaters from Taft to Bush*. New York: PublicAffairs, 2003.

West, Jessamyn. *The Quaker Reader*. New York: Viking, 1962.

Whittier, California, President Nixon's Hometown. Encino CA: Windsor, 1971.

Whittier City Directory. Los Angeles: Los Angeles Directory Company, 1922–23, 1928, 1931, 1932, 1939, 1942, 1947.

Wicker, Tom. Foreword to *The People's President: The Electoral College in American History and the Direct-Vote Alternative*, by Neil R. Peirce, 9–14. New York: Simon & Schuster, 1968.

———. *One of Us: Richard Nixon and the American Dream*. New York: Random House, 1991.

Wills, Garry. *Nixon Agonistes: The Crisis of the Self-Made Man*. Boston: New American Library, 1969.

Wilson, Bob. *Confessions of a Kinetic Congressman*. San Diego State University Foundation, 1996.

Woodstone, Arthur. *Nixon's Head*. New York: St. Martin's, 1972.

Worthen, James. *The Young Nixon and His Rivals: Four California Republicans Eye the White House*. Jefferson NC: McFarland, 2010.

Youngs, Bill. *The House That Brock Built*. N.p., 197–.

Index

Krehbiel, John, 186–87, 234
Krogh, Egil "Bud," 245, 263
Krueger, William, 40
Kruse, Arthur, 81
KTTV studio, 162, 209

La Casa Pacifica, 237–43, 248, 253, 255–75
La Costa Country Club (Carlsbad), 266
La Habra CA, 66
La Habra Heights, 63, 68
La Habra Kiwanis, 66
Lamson-Scribner, F. H., 138
Lancers, 40–41
Landreth, Verne, 36, 39–40
Lang, Walter, 192
La Opinion, 202–3
Latin Club, 31, 33
Laugh-In, 226
Lawford, Peter, 215
Lazar, Irving "Swifty," 266
League of Women Voters, 88
Leffingwell Ranch, 13, 28, 47
Lewis, Jerry, 177
Lincoln Day events, 81, 114–15
Lincoln-Douglas debates, 87
Linkletter, Art, 156, 214–15, 221, 226, 244
literary societies, 39
Lodge, Henry Cabot, Jr., 177
Logue, Bob, 31
Lohmann, Margaretha, 44
Loker, Katherine, 288
Loker Center, 288
Long, Wayne, 32
Long Beach CA: earthquake in (1933), 46; as gubernatorial campaign stop, 203; and midterms speech (1954), 136; Nixon's gambling winnings at, 52; and Nixon's life at law school, 54; and Nixon's speech at Rainbow Pier, 108; as Pat and Dick's first home after marriage, 68; as Pat's favorite beach,

60; as a vice-presidential campaign stop, 128
Long Beach Memorial Hospital, 229, 257–59, 268
Long Beach Pike, 25–26, 33, 61, 107
Long Beach Press Telegram, 118, 178
Loran Coast Guard Station, 237, 253, 261
Loren, Sophia, 166
Los Alamitos Naval Air Station, 138
Los Angeles Basin, 218, 236
Los Angeles CA: and the American Football Coaches Association conference, 213; and Barry Veterans Hospital, 242; and the Biltmore Hotel, 138, 163, 203, 209, 215; campaign headquarters in, 227; Democratic Convention in, 169–70; gubernatorial campaign in, 201–10; as mecca for youth (1920s), 25–27; and Nixon's fundraising for Dorothy Chandler Pavilion, 223; Nixons' move back to, 185–93; and the Paris Inn, 53; Pat's youth in and near, 60; presidential campaign in (1960), 177–78; and the return visit after vice-presidential reelection, 150; and the Rose Parade, 160–61; senatorial campaign in, 106, 111–15; and the Stoody estate, 66; and support of Robert Finch, 219, 220, 258; vice-presidential campaign in, 127–30; and Woodbury College, 61. See also Ambassador Hotel (Los Angeles); Beverly Hilton Hotel (Los Angeles)
Los Angeles Country Club, 139, 215
Los Angeles County Bar Association, 115, 152, 199–200
Los Angeles County Board of Supervisors, 185, 214, 222
Los Angeles County Fairgrounds (Pomona), 207
Los Angeles County Republican Party Central Committee, 153

childhood of, 5–6, 15; and close relationship with siblings, 29; death of, 280; on election night, 228; and family activities, 139; and Frank's last illness and death, 143–44; Howard Hughes's loan to, 157, 171, 209, 224; marriage of, 288–89; move of, into Frank and Hannah's home, 98; and Nixon, 69, 74, 190, 232; as Nixon market owner, 91; and Nixon's birthplace, 288; and Nixon's support of extended family, 217; and presidential campaign (1960), 180–81; and vice-presidential campaign, 128; at welcome home celebration (1952), 118; and working at father's store, 26, 27–28; and World War II send-off for Nixon, 71

Nixon, Frank (father): and Arthur's illness and death, 21–22; and Beach Boulevard, 133; character and personality of, 1–5, 15, 29; and Citri-Frost Company, 63; and civil rights, 149; courtship and marriage of, 2–3; and dedication to family, 37, 52; and dedication to Quaker community, 8; and Dick and Pat's marriage, 67–68; on Don's business personality, 91; and Edward's birth, 30; and farming, 9, 12; and Hannah, 30; illness and death of, 143–46, 156; at inauguration (1953), 131–32; and love of debate, 8, 33; and move back to Whittier, 114; and move east, 98; and move to Whittier, 13–15; and Nixon market startup, 26–28; and Nixon's birth, 4–5; and Nixon's childhood, 5–10, 12; and the Richard Nixon Library and Museum, 287; at Rose Hills, 222; settling of, in Yorba Linda, 3–5, 6; social network of, 141; and Standard Oil, 113; and the Stoody estate, 66; and support for local community, 47; and support for Nixon's political career, 86; and Tom

Bewley, 53; and tour car, 25; and vice-presidential campaign, 120, 129; work ethic of, 1–2, 34; and World War II send-off for Nixon, 71, 74

Nixon, Gay (sister-in-law), 289

Nixon, Hannah (née Milhous) (mother): and Arthur's illness and death, 21–22; and Beach Boulevard, 133; as caregiver for daughters, 86; and caring for TB patients in Arizona, 29; character and personality of, 15, 29, 34; and civil rights, 149; courtship and marriage of, 2–3; death of, 221–22; and dedication to Nixon's career, 53; and Dick and Pat's marriage, 67–68; and Don, 157; and Frank, 30; at inauguration (1953), 131–32; and move back to Whittier, 114; and move east, 98; and move to Whittier, 13; and Nixon market startup, 26–28; and Nixon's childhood, 5–10, 12; Nixon's devotion to, 155; on Nixon's religious faith, 22; and plain speech, 97; and presidential campaign (1960), 182–83; religious faith of, 17; and the Richard Nixon Library and Museum, 287; social network of, 141; and the Stoody estate, 66; and support for local community, 47; and vice-presidential campaign, 122, 129–30; as Whittier College graduate, 42; and World War II send-off for Nixon, 71, 74

Nixon, Harold (brother): birth of, 3; death of, 46; illness of, 29–31, 35; Nixon's honoring of, at state dinner, 240; and relationship to Nixon, 5, 9–10; and working at the gas station, 14

Nixon, Julie (daughter): and American Legion fireworks show, 158; birth of, 95; and birth of daughter, 270–71; and David Eisenhower, 226; and Disneyland, 153; at Marlborough School, 196; marriage of, 289; and Nixon's